Contents

KU-632-435

OPPOSITE ST PAUL'S CATHEDRAL **PREVIOUS PAGE** TRAFALGAR SQUARE

Introduction to
London

For the visitor, London is a thrilling place. Monuments from the capital's glorious past are everywhere, from medieval banqueting halls and the great churches of Christopher Wren to the eclectic Victorian architecture of the triumphalist British Empire. You can relax in the city's quiet Georgian squares, explore the narrow alleyways of the City of London, wander along the riverside walkways, and uncover the quirks of what is still identifiably a collection of villages. London is also incredibly diverse, ethnically and linguistically, offering cultural and culinary delights from right across the globe. And, of course, it's also very big. In fact, it's the largest capital in the European Union, stretching for more than thirty miles from east to west, and with a population of just under eight million. In other words, it really is the archetypal buzzing metropolis.

The capital's traditional landmarks – Big Ben, Westminster Abbey, Buckingham Palace, St Paul's Cathedral, the Tower of London and so on – continue to draw in millions of tourists every year. Things change fast, though, and regular emergence of new attractions ensures that there's plenty to do even for those who've visited before. In the last decade, all of London's world-class **museums**, **galleries** and institutions have been reinvented, from the Royal Opera House to the British Museum. With Tate Modern and the London Eye, the city now boasts the world's largest modern art museum and Europe's largest Ferris wheel. And thanks to the 2012 Olympics, the East End has had a boost and the tourist and transport infrastructure has had a major overhaul.

The biggest problem for newcomers is that the city is bewilderingly amorphous. Londoners cope with this by compartmentalizing their city, identifying strongly with the neighbourhoods in which they work or live, just making occasional forays into the West End, London's busy shopping and entertainment heartland. As a visitor, the key to enjoying London, then, is not to try and do everything in a single trip – concentrate on one or two areas and you'll get a lot more out of the place. And remember to take some

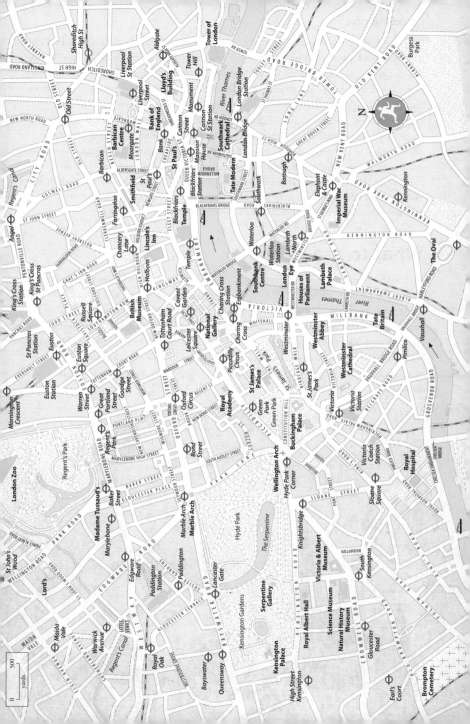

time out in the city's surprisingly large expanses of greenery: Hyde Park, Green Park and St James's Park are all within a few minutes' walk of the West End, while, further afield, you can enjoy the more expansive parklands of Hampstead Heath and Richmond Park.

You could spend days just **shopping** in London, too, mixing with the upper classes in the "tiara triangle" around Harrods, or sampling the offbeat weekend markets of Portobello Road, Brick Lane and Camden. The **music**, **clubbing** and **gay and lesbian** scenes are second to none, with an ever-growing selection of clubs and bars around Shoreditch and Dalston and new music festivals cropping up every summer. Mainstream **arts** are no less exciting, with regular opportunities to catch outstanding theatre companies, dance troupes, exhibitions and opera. The city's pubs have always had heaps of atmosphere, but food is a major attraction too, with over fifty Michelin-starred **restaurants** and the widest choice of cuisines on the planet.

What to see

Although the majority of the city's sights are situated north of the **River Thames**, which loops through the centre of the city from west to east, there is no single focus of interest. That's because London hasn't grown through centralized planning but by a process of agglomeration. Villages and urban developments that once surrounded the core are now lost within the vast mass of Greater London, leaving London's highlights widely spread, and meaning that visitors should make mastering the public transport system, particularly the Underground (tube), a top priority, or, failing that, jump on a Boris Bike.

THE ROUGH GUIDE TO

London

written and researched by

Rob Humphreys

with additional contributions by

Samantha Cook, Nicholas Jones, Andrew Mickel and James Smart

roughguides.com

Author picks

An expert on London, Rob Humphreys has lived in the city since 1988. Here are some of his tips and recommendations for getting off the beaten track.

Best small museum Try Sir John Soane's Museum (p.145), part art gallery, part museum, part period piece, or for something more contemporary, head for the strangely compelling Museum of Brands, Advertising & Packaging (p.278).

Best bus ride Ride on an old double-decker Routemaster (p.33) on the no. 9 and no. 15 routes, past the Albert Hall, Trafalgar Square and St Paul's Cathedral.

Leafiest hideaway Check out the secret College Garden in Westminster Abbey (p.58), the secluded benches in the gardens of Chiswick House (p.332), or the elevated pergola in Hill Garden on the Heath (p.303).

Hidden history Find out who Giro was (p.72), who's buried in the Cross Bones Cemetery (p.231), or which corner of London is forever Swiss (p.98).

A night at the museum Sip some wine and watch a fashion show at the V&A's monthly Friday Lates (p.249) or party with the animals at the summer-only Zoo Lates (p.286).

Eat all over the globe Start your day with a cinnamon bun and strong coffee at the *Nordic Bakery* (p.369), head to *Clark & Sons* (p.374) for a traditional British eel and pie lunch, then top it all off with some excellent Cantonese at *Mr Kong* (p.372).

Riverside pubs In the east, head for the *Town of Ramsgate* (p.392) or *The Gun* (p.392) in Docklands; in the west, try Richmond's *White Cross* (p.398) or Twickenham's *White Swan* (p.398).

> Our author recommendations don't end here. We've flagged up our favourite places – a perfectly sited hotel, an atmospheric café, a special restaurant – throughout the guide, highlighted with the ★ symbol.

OPPOSITE LONDON EYE AND HOUSES OF PARLIAMENT
FROM TOP SIR JOHN SOANE'S MUSEUM; THE NO.15 BUS

MULTIETHNIC LONDON

With around three hundred languages spoken and all the major religions represented, London is Europe's most ethnically **diverse** city. First-, second- and third-generation immigrants make up over thirty percent of the population, with the rest descended from French Huguenot refugees. The first immigrants were invaders like the Romans, Anglo-Saxons, Vikings and Normans, while over the last four centuries, the city has absorbed wave after wave of foreigners fleeing persecution or simply looking for a better life. In the postwar period thousands came here from the Caribbean and the Indian subcontinent; today's arrivals are more likely to come from the world's trouble spots (Somalia, Afghanistan, Iraq) or from new EU member states like Poland.

London doesn't have the sort of ghettoization that's widespread in the US, but certain areas have become **home from home** for the more established communities. Brixton and Dalston are the most prominent Afro-Caribbean and African districts; Dalston, along with Haringey, is also home to the largest Turkish and Kurdish communities; Southall is predominantly Punjabi; Wembley is a Gujarati stronghold; Acton has a sizeable Polish community; Hoxton is a Vietnamese neighbourhood. The East End, London's top immigrant ghetto, has absorbed several communities over the centuries, and is currently the heart of Bengali London, while the Jewish community has more or less abandoned the East End, and now has its largest Orthodox communities in Stamford Hill and Golders Green.

If London has a centre, it's **Trafalgar Square**, home to Nelson's Column and the National Gallery. It's also as good a place as any to start exploring the city, especially as the area to the south of here, **Whitehall and Westminster**, is one of the easiest bits to discover on foot. This was the city's royal, political and ecclesiastical power-base for centuries, and you'll find some of London's most famous landmarks here: Downing Street, Big Ben, the Houses of Parliament and **Westminster Abbey**. The grand streets and squares of **St James's**, **Mayfair** and **Marylebone**, to the north of Westminster, have been the playground of the rich since the Restoration, and now contain some of the city's busiest shopping zones: Piccadilly, **Bond Street**, **Regent Street** and, most frenetic of the lot, **Oxford Street**.

East of Piccadilly Circus, **Soho**, **Chinatown** and **Covent Garden** are also easy to walk around and form the heart of the West End entertainment district, where you'll find the largest concentration of theatres, cinemas, clubs, shops, cafés and restaurants. Adjoining Covent Garden to the north, the university quarter of **Bloomsbury** is the location of the ever-popular **British Museum**, a stupendous treasure house that boasts a wonderful central, covered courtyard. To the north of Bloomsbury lies the area around King's Cross and St Pancras stations, home to the **British Library** and now at the centre of a massive redevelopment project.

Welding the West End to the financial district, **Holborn** is a little-visited area, but offers some of central London's most surprising treats, among them the eccentric Sir John Soane's Museum and the secluded quadrangles of the Inns of Court, where the country's lawyers learn and ply their trade. Fashionable **Clerkenwell**, to the east of Holborn on the northern edge of the City, is visited mostly for its many popular bars and restaurants, but also has vestiges of London's monastic past and a radical history to be proud of.

A couple of miles downstream from Westminster, **The City** – or the City of London, to give it its full title – is the original heart of London, simultaneously the most ancient and

the most modern part of the metropolis. Settled since Roman times, the area became the commercial and residential heart of medieval London, with its own Lord Mayor and its own peculiar form of local government, both of which survive (with considerable pageantry) to this day. The Great Fire of 1666 obliterated most of the City, and although it was rebuilt the resident population has now dwindled to insignificance. Yet this remains one of the great financial centres of the world, with the most prominent landmarks these days being the hi-tech skyscrapers of banks and insurance companies. However, the Square Mile, as it's known, boasts its fair share of historic sights too, notably the **Tower of London** and a fine cache of Wren churches that includes the mighty St Paul's Cathedral.

The **East End** and **Docklands**, located to the east of the City, are equally notorious, but in entirely different ways. Impoverished and working-class, the East End is not conventional tourist territory, but its long history of immigration is as fascinating as is its recent emergence as a bolthole for artists and a destination for clubbers. With its converted warehouse apartments and hubristic tower blocks, Docklands is the converse of the down-at-heel East End, with the **Canary Wharf** tower – for three decades the country's tallest building – epitomizing the pretensions of the 1980s' Thatcherite dream.

The **South Bank**, **Bankside** and **Southwark** together make up the small slice of central London that lies south of the Thames. The Southbank Centre itself, London's little-loved concrete culture bunker, is enjoying a new lease of life – thanks, in part, to the tourist magnet of the London Eye, which spins gracefully over the Thames. Bankside, the city's low-life district from Roman times to the eighteenth century, is also enjoying a renaissance, with the Millennium Bridge linking St Paul's Cathedral with the former power station that is home to **Tate Modern**, London's popular museum of modern art.

In **Hyde Park** and **Kensington Gardens** you'll find the largest park in central London, a segment of greenery which separates wealthy west London from the city centre. The museums of **South Kensington** – the Victoria and Albert Museum, the Science Museum and the Natural History Museum – are a must, and if you have shopping on your agenda you may well want to investigate the hive of plush stores in the vicinity of Harrods, superstore to the upper echelons.

Some of the most appealing parts of north London are clustered around the Regent's Canal, which skirts the northern edge of **Regent's Park** and serves as the focus for the capital's busiest weekend market, held around **Camden Lock**. Further out, in the chic literary suburbs of Hampstead and Highgate, there are unbeatable views across the city from half-wild **Hampstead Heath**, the favourite parkland of thousands of Londoners.

The glory of south London is **Greenwich**, with its nautical associations, royal park and observatory (not to mention its Dome). Finally, there are plenty of rewarding day-trips up the Thames, southwest of the city centre from **Chiswick** to **Hampton Court**, an area that is liberally peppered with the stately homes and grounds of the country's royalty and former aristocracy, from Syon and **Kew**, to **Richmond** and Ham.

When to go

Considering how temperate the London **climate** is (see p.27), it's amazing how much mileage the locals get out of the subject. The truth is that summers rarely get really hot and the winters aren't very cold. In fact, it's impossible to say with any certainty what the weather will be like in any given month. May might be wet and grey one year and gloriously sunny the next; November stands an equal chance of being crisp and clear or foggy and grim. So, whatever time of year you come, be prepared for all eventualities, and bring a pair of comfortable shoes, as, inevitably, you'll be doing a lot of walking.

FREE LONDON

London can be an expensive place for locals and tourists alike. However, there are lots of things to enjoy in the capital that are one hundred percent free. Many of the leading museums and galleries, from the British Museum to Tate Modern, are free, and also offer a wide range of specialist talks, free tours, talks, films and activities. Public art galleries are mostly free to enter, as are all the **commercial galleries**, selling contemporary art, and the **auction houses** where you can catch a glimpse of anything from heirlooms to the work of established modern artists.

For high-quality **buskers** and entertainers head for Covent Garden and the South Bank. Free **lunchtime concerts** of classical music take place at various city centre churches, and at St Paul's Cathedral or Westminster Abbey, you can listen to choral **evensong**. Lastly, you'll find **free gigs** of every persuasion, rock, pop, folk, blues and jazz, flagged up every night of the week in *Time Out*.

The Queen puts on her free bit of pageantry each day with the Changing of the Guard on Whitehall, and gets out and about in her golden coach at least once a year to officially open Parliament. Finally, you might as well take advantage of London's wonderful green spaces, from the **royal parks** and the magnificent Heath to the tiny inner-city churchyards and splendidly overgrown cemeteries of the Victorian era. All – except Highgate Cemetery – are free of charge and often stage free events.

17

things not to miss

It's not possible to see everything that London has to offer in one visit – and we don't suggest you try. What follows, in no particular order, is a selective taste of the city's highlights; from outstanding art collections and historic architecture to vibrant markets and picturesque parks. Each highlight has a page reference to take you straight into the Guide, where you can find out more.

1 BRITISH MUSEUM
Page 106
The spectacular Great Court and the renovated Round Reading Room have brought new life to the world's oldest and greatest public museum.

2 TOWER OF LONDON
Page 180
Bloody royal history, Beefeaters, lots of armour, the Crown Jewels and ravens – and a great medieval castle.

3 HIGHGATE CEMETERY
Page 305
The city's most atmospheric Victorian necropolis, thick with trees and crowded with famous corpses, with Karl Marx topping the bill.

4 SHOPPING AT LIBERTY
Page 78
Just down the road from the scrum of Oxford Circus, this beautiful department store, housed in a grand, mock-Tudor building, is heaven for label aficionados and window-shoppers alike.

5 HAMPSTEAD HEATH
Page 301
Fly kites, look across London and walk over to Kenwood, for fine art, tea and cakes.

6

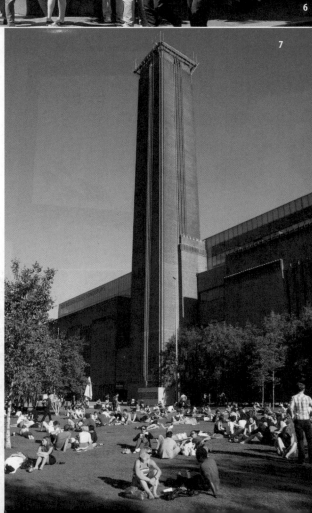

7

15

16

17

BUS OUTSIDE ST PAUL'S

Basics

Getting there

Unless you're coming from elsewhere in Britain, or from northwest Europe, the quickest and easiest way to get to London is by plane. The city has five airports (see p.20) and is a major destination for most international airlines, so airfares tend to be keenly competitive. How much you pay to fly to London depends on how far in advance you book, and how flexible you need your ticket to be.

Flights from the US and Canada

All major US and Canadian airlines run direct services from North America to London, Europe's busiest gateway. Two of London's airports – Heathrow and Gatwick – handle transatlantic flights, and in terms of convenience they're about equal.

Figure on around six hours' flying time from New York; it's an hour extra going the other way, due to headwinds. Add three or four hours more for travel from the West Coast. Most eastbound flights cross the Atlantic overnight, arriving the next morning; flying back, departure times tend to be morning or afternoon, arriving in the afternoon or evening of the same day.

The cheapest return fares (including taxes) from New York or Chicago (and even LA) start from around $500; or from around Can$800 from Toronto; and from around Can$1000 from Vancouver.

Flights from Australia and New Zealand

Flight time from Australia and New Zealand to London is at least 22 hours, and can be more depending on routes and transfer times. There's a wide variety of routes, with those touching down in Southeast Asia the quickest and cheapest on average. Given the length of the journey involved, you might be better off including a night's stopover in your itinerary; some airlines include one in the price of the flight.

The cheapest direct scheduled flights to London are usually to be found on one of the Asian airlines. Average return fares (including taxes) from eastern gateways to London are Aus$1500–2500 depending on the season. Fares from Perth or Darwin cost around Aus$200 less. Return fares from Auckland to London range between NZ$2000 and NZ$3000 depending on the season, route and carrier.

By plane or train from Ireland

Travel from Ireland is quickest by plane, with the likes of Aer Lingus and Ryanair offering return tickets from Dublin, Derry, Cork or Shannon to London Stansted or Gatwick for as little as €50. From Belfast International, easyJet has return fares to London Luton, Gatwick or Stansted from around £60, if you book far enough in advance; flybe has similar fares from Belfast City to London Gatwick. A fully flexible fare can cost three or four times that amount, but will allow you to change your plans after purchasing the ticket.

Flying may be quick, but the ferry and train fares are pretty competitive and much more flexible, with Irish Ferries (🖤 irishferries.com) offering SailRail return fares of around €80 to London (via Holyhead) from anywhere in the Republic; from Belfast (via Stranraer or Holyhead) returns start from £90. Journey time is eight hours from Dublin, ten from Belfast.

AGENTS AND OPERATORS

North South Travel UK ☎ 01245 608 291, 🖤 northsouthtravel .co.uk. Friendly, competitive travel agency, offering discounted fares worldwide. Profits are used to support projects in the developing world, especially the promotion of sustainable tourism.

STA Travel UK ☎ 0871 2300 040, US ☎ 1800 781 4040, Australia ☎ 134 782, New Zealand ☎ 0800 474 400, South Africa ☎ 0861 781 781, 🖤 statravel.co.uk. Worldwide specialists in independent travel; also student IDs, travel insurance, car rental, rail passes, and more. Good discounts for students and under-26s.

Trailfinders UK ☎ 0845 054 6060, Ireland ☎ 021 464 8800, Australia ☎ 1300 780 212, 🖤 trailfinders.com. One of the best-informed and most efficient agents for independent travellers.

A BETTER KIND OF TRAVEL

At Rough Guides we are passionately committed to travel. We feel that travelling is the best way to understand the world we live in and the people we share it with – plus tourism has brought a great deal of benefit to developing economies around the world over the last few decades. But the growth in tourism has also damaged some places irreparably, and climate change is exacerbated by most forms of transport, especially flying. All Rough Guides' trips are carbon-offset, and every year we donate money to a variety of charities devoted to combating the effects of climate change.

Arrival

The majority of visitors arrive in London at one of its five airports, all but one of which can involve an expensive trip to the centre. Those arriving by train or bus are dropped right in the middle of the city, with easy access to public transport.

By plane

Flying into London, you'll arrive at Heathrow, Gatwick, Stansted, Luton or City airport, each of which is less than an hour from the city centre.

Heathrow

Heathrow (Wheathrowairport.com) lies around fifteen miles west of central London, and is the city's busiest airport, with five terminals and three train/tube stations: one for terminals 1, 2 and 3, and separate ones for terminals 4 and 5. The fastest trains into London are the nonstop Heathrow Express services to Paddington station (daily 5am–midnight; journey 15–23min); online tickets cost £16.50 one way or £32 return (more if you purchase your ticket at the ticket office or on board the train). Heathrow Connect (Wheathrowconnect .com) trains stop at some intermediate stations (Mon–Sat 5am–midnight, Sun 6am–11pm; every 30min; journey 25–30min) but tickets cost just £8.50 single and £16.50 return. An even cheaper alternative is to take the Piccadilly Underground line (Wtfl.gov.uk), which connects the airport to numerous tube stations across central London (Mon–Sat 5.45am–11.45pm, Sun 6am–11.30pm; every 5min; journey 50min–1hr); tickets cost just £5 single – less if you have an Oyster card – or you can buy a Day Off-Peak Travelcard (Zones 1–6) for £8 (see p.22).

National Express bus services (Wnationalexpress .com) run from Heathrow direct to Victoria Coach Station (5am–9.30pm every 15–30min; journey 40–55min); tickets cost £5 single, £9 return. From 11.30pm, you can take night bus #N9 to Trafalgar Square for a bargain fare of £2.20 (every 20min; journey 1hr 10min). Taxis are plentiful, but will set you back between £50 and £80 to central London, and take around an hour (much longer in the rush hour).

Gatwick

Gatwick (Wgatwickairport.com) is around thirty miles south of London, and has a train station at the South Terminal. Nonstop Gatwick Express trains (Wgatwickexpress.com) run between the airport

and London Victoria (daily 4.30am–1.30am; every 15min; journey 30–35min); tickets cost around £18 single, £30 return (less online). A cheaper option is to take a Southern train service (Wsouthernrailway .com) to Victoria (every 15min; journey 35min, which stops at a couple of intermediate stations, or a First Capital Connect train (Wfirstcapitalconnect .co.uk) to various stations within London (every 15–30min; journey 30–45min), including London Bridge and St Pancras; tickets for either cost around £12 single.

From the North and South terminals easyBus (Weasybus.co.uk) runs buses to West Brompton tube near Earls Court (daily 4.30am–midnight every 20min; 1hr 10min), with online tickets going for as little as £2 single (£10 if you buy on board). National Express buses run from Gatwick direct to central London (daily 5am–9.30pm hourly; 1hr 30min); tickets cost around £7 single, £12.50 return. A taxi will set you back £100 or more, and take over an hour.

Stansted

Designed by Norman Foster, Stansted (Wstansted airport.com) is London's best-looking international airport, and lies roughly 35 miles northeast of the capital. The fastest trains are run by Stansted Express (Wstanstedexpress.com) to Liverpool Street (daily 5.30am–12.30am; every 15–30min; journey 45min), and cost £20 single, £27 return if you book online. All year round, 24 hours a day, easyBus runs buses to Baker Street tube (every 20–30min; 1hr 15min), with online tickets going for as little as £2 single (£10 if you buy on board). National Express runs buses 24 hours a day calling at various places in London en route to Victoria Coach Station (every 30min; journey 1hr 30min–1hr 45min), with tickets £10 single, £17 return. Terravision (Wterravision.eu) also run coaches to Liverpool Street and Victoria (daily 7.15am–1am every 30min; journey time 1hr 15min), with tickets £9 single, £14 return. A taxi will set you back £100, and take at least an hour.

City Airport

City Airport (Wlondoncityairport.com), London's smallest, used primarily by business folk, is situated in the Royal Albert Docks, ten miles east of central London, and handles European flights only. The Docklands Light Railway (DLR) takes you straight into Bank in the City (Mon–Sat 5.30am–12.15am, Sun 7am–11.15pm; every 8–15min; journey 20min), where you can change to the tube; single tickets cost around £4 (less if you have an Oyster card). A taxi from the airport to the City's financial sector will cost around £20, and take half an hour or so.

Luton

Luton Airport (ⓦlondon-luton.co.uk) is roughly thirty miles north of London and mainly handles charter flights. A free shuttle bus (every 10min) takes five minutes to transport passengers to Luton Airport Parkway station, which is connected by train to St Pancras (every 15–30min; journey 25–35min) and other stations in central London; single tickets cost around £12.50 single, £21.50 return. All year round, 24 hours a day, Green Line and easyBus run the #757 coach from Luton Airport to Victoria Coach Station (every 20–30min; journey 1hr 20min), stopping at several locations en route, including Baker Street. Tickets cost as little as £2 (or as much as £10) if you book with easyBus online. A taxi will cost in the region of £70–80 and take at least an hour to central London.

Arriving by train or bus

Eurostar (ⓦeurostar.com) trains arrive at St Pancras International next door to King's Cross. Trains from the Channel ports arrive at Charing Cross or Victoria, while boat trains from Harwich arrive at Liverpool Street. Arriving by train from elsewhere in Britain, you'll come into one of London's numerous mainline stations, all of which have adjacent Underground stations linking into the city centre's tube network. Coming into London by coach, you're most likely to arrive at Victoria Coach Station, a couple of hundred yards south down Buckingham Palace Road from Victoria train station and tube.

City transport

The city's highly complex transport system has improved over the last decade. The congestion charge has reduced traffic within central London, and much of the money has been ploughed into improving the bus and tube network. That said, London still has one of the most expensive transport systems in the world.

Transport for London (TfL) provides excellent free maps and details of bus and tube services from its six Travel Information Centres: the most central one is at Piccadilly Circus tube station (daily 9.15am–7pm); there are other desks at the arrivals at Heathrow (terminals 1, 2 & 3), Victoria, Euston, King's Cross and Liverpool Street train stations. There's also a 24-hour helpline and website for information on all bus and tube services (☎0843 222 1234, ⓦtfl.gov.uk).

> ### TRAIN INFORMATION
> For up-to-date information on all train services and ticket prices, contact National Rail Enquiries (☎0845 748 4950, ⓦnationalrail.co.uk).

For transport purposes, London is divided into six concentric zones (plus a few extra in the northwest), with fares calculated depending on which zones you travel through: the majority of the city's accommodation, pubs, restaurants and sights lie in zones 1 and 2. If you cannot produce a valid ticket for your journey, or travel further than your ticket allows, you will be liable to a Penalty Fare of £50, reduced to £25 if you pay within 21 days. Try and avoid travelling during the rush hour (Mon–Fri 8–9.30am & 5–7pm), if possible, when tubes become unbearably crowded and hot, and some buses get so full they won't let you on.

The tube

Except for very short journeys, the Underground – or tube, as it's known to Londoners – is by far the quickest way to get about. Eleven different lines cross much of the metropolis, although London south of the river is not very well covered. Each line has its own colour and name – all you need to know is which direction you're travelling in: northbound, eastbound, southbound or westbound (this gets tricky when taking the Circle Line). As a precaution, it's also worth checking the final destination displayed on the front of the train, as some lines, such as the District and Northern lines, have several different branches.

Services are frequent (Mon–Sat 5.30am–12.30am, Sun 7.30am–11.30pm), and you rarely have to wait more than five minutes for a train between central stations. Tickets must be bought in advance from automatic machines or from a ticket booth in the station entrance hall. Single fares are expensive – a journey in the central zone costs £4 – so if you're intending to make more than one journey, an Oyster card or a Travelcard is by far your best option (see p.22).

Buses

London's famous red double-decker buses are fun to ride on, but tend to get stuck in traffic jams, which prevents their running to a regular timetable. The standard walk-on fare is £2.20 without an Oyster card (see box, p.22), £1.30 with one. If this is the type of journey you'll be making more than a few times, it might be worth buying a One-Day Bus Pass, which costs £4 and can be used on all buses any time anywhere in London.

A lot of bus stops are request stops (easily recognizable by their red sign), so if you don't stick your arm out to hail the bus you want, it will pass you by, and if you don't ring the bell for the bus to stop, it will just keep on going. Some buses run a 24-hour service, but most run between 5am and midnight, with a network of night buses (prefixed with the letter "N") operating outside this period. Night-bus routes depart every twenty to thirty minutes, more frequently on Friday and Saturday nights. Tickets are £2.20 from central London, and Travelcards (see below) are valid until 4.30am. All stops are treated as request stops, so you must signal to get the bus to stop, and press the bell in order to get off.

Suburban trains

Large areas of London's suburbs are only served by the suburban train network. Wherever a sight can only be reached by train, we've indicated the nearest train station (and, if relevant, the central terminus from which trains depart). Oyster cards and Travelcards are valid on all suburban train services within Greater London. For information on

services, phone National Rail Enquiries on ☎0845 748 4950, or visit ⓦnationalrail.co.uk.

The most useful train line to cross the capital is the Overground, which connects, among other places, Richmond and Stratford, via Hampstead Heath, Camden and Islington (daily every 10–15min), and is slowly transforming into an orbital railway, and the First Capital Connect service (ⓦfirstcapitalconnect.co.uk), which runs north–south via King's Cross and Blackfriars (Mon–Sat every 15min, Sun every 30min).

Docklands Light Railway

The Docklands Light Railway, or DLR (☎020 7363 9700), runs driverless trains from Bank in the City, and from Tower Gateway (close to Tower Hill tube and the Tower of London) above ground to the financial centre of Docklands, plus other areas in the East End and also below ground to Greenwich and Woolwich. Oyster cards and Travelcards (see below) are valid on the network.

Boats

Unfortunately, boat services on the Thames are not fully integrated into the public transport system. If you have a valid Travelcard (either in paper or

---

OYSTER CARDS AND TICKETS

The cheapest, easiest way to get about London is to use an **Oyster card**, London's transport smartcard, available from all tube stations and Travel Information Centres, and valid on the bus, tube, Docklands Light Railway (DLR), Tramlink, Overground and all suburban rail services. You can use an Oyster card in one of two ways: you can use it simply to store a weekly/monthly/yearly season ticket, or you can use it as a pay-as-you-go – you can top-up your card at all tube stations and at most newsagents. As you enter the tube or bus, simply touch in your card at the card reader – if you're using pay-as-you-go, the fare will be taken off your card. If you're using the tube or train, you need to touch out again or a maximum cash fare of up to £7.40 will be deducted. A pay-as-you-go Oyster operates daily price-capping so that when you've paid the equivalent of a Day Travelcard, it will stop taking money off your card, though you still need to touch in (and out). Oyster cards are free for those purchasing monthly or yearly tickets; everyone else needs to hand over a £5 refundable deposit; visitors can buy a pay-as-you-go Oyster card for just £3.

If you don't have an Oyster card, you can still buy a paper **Travelcard** from machines and booths at all tube and train stations (and at many newsagents too – look for the sign). Anytime Day Travelcards start from £7.30 (zones 1 & 2); Day Off-Peak Travelcards are valid after 9.30am on weekdays and all day at the weekend, and cost £6.60 (zones 1 & 2), rising to £8 (zones 1–6). If you need to travel before 9.30am, it's worth considering a 7 Day Travelcard for £27.60 (zones 1 & 2).

Children under 11 travel for free; children aged 11–15 travel free on all buses and trams and at child-rate on the tube; children aged 16 or 17 can travel at half the adult rate on all forms of transport. However, all children over 10 must have an Oyster photocard to be eligible for the discounts – these should be applied for in advance online and will cost £10. Railcard holders can buy a Day Off-Peak Travelcard (zones 1–9) for children aged 11–15 for just £2, providing they're travelling with an adult.

Oyster form), you're entitled to a third off, but if you have a pay-as-you-go Oyster card, you get just ten percent off. Timetables and services are complex, and there are numerous companies and small charter operators – for a full list pick up a booklet from a TfL information centre (see p.21) or visit ⓦtfl.gov.uk.

One of the largest companies is Thames Clippers (ⓦthamesclippers.com), who run a regular commuter service (Mon–Fri 6am–10.30pm, Sat & Sun 9am–10.30pm; every 20–30min) between Waterloo and Greenwich (including the Dome), with some boats going as far as Woolwich. Typical fares are £5.50 single, with an unlimited hop-on, hop-off River Rover Pass costing £12.60, and a weekly ticket costing £36. A Rail (DLR) River Rover Pass (including unlimited travel on the DLR and hop-on, hop-off on City Cruises services) costs £15.

Other companies run boats upstream to Kew, Richmond and Hampton Court (see p.329). Look out, too, for the MV *Balmoral* and paddle steamer *Waverley*, which make regular visits to Tower Pier in the summer and autumn (☎0845 130 4647, ⓦwaverleyexcursions.co.uk).

Taxis

Compared to most capital cities, London's metered black cabs are an expensive option unless there are three or more of you. The minimum fare is £2.20, and a ride from Euston to Victoria, for example, costs around £12–15 (Mon–Fri 6am–8pm). After 8pm on weekdays and all day during the weekend, a higher tariff applies, and after 10pm, it's higher still. Tipping is customary. An illuminated yellow light over the windscreen tells you if the cab is available – just stick your arm out to hail it. London's cabbies are the best-trained in Europe; every one of them knows the shortest route between any two points in the capital, and they won't rip you off by taking another route. They are, however, a blunt and forthright breed, renowned for their generally reactionary opinions. To order a black cab in advance, phone ☎0871 871 8710, and be prepared to pay an extra £2.

Minicabs

Minicabs look just like regular cars and are considerably cheaper than black cabs, but they cannot be hailed from the street. All minicabs should be licensed and able to produce a TfL ID on demand. There are hundreds of minicab firms in the phone book, but the best way to pick is to take the advice of the place you're at, unless you want to be certain of a woman driver, in which case book a cab from Ladycabs (☎020 7272 3300), or a gay/lesbian-friendly driver, in which case call Freedom Cars (☎020 7739 9080). Avoid illegal taxi touts, who hang around outside venues alongside licensed cabs, and always establish the fare beforehand, as minicabs are not metered.

Pedicabs

Last, and definitely least, there's currently a plague of pedicabs or bicycle taxis in the West End. The oldest and biggest of the bunch are Bugbugs (☎020 7353 4028, ⓦbugbugs.com), who have rickshaws operating Monday to Saturday from 7pm until the early hours of the morning. The rickshaws take up to three passengers and fares are negotiable, so you should always agree a price beforehand based on a fare of around £3–5 per person.

Driving

Given the traffic jams, parking hassle and pollution caused, driving in London – especially central London – is by far the worst transport option available. However, if you must drive, bear in mind the rules of the road (even if no one else does). Seatbelts are compulsory front and back and the speed limit is 30mph, unless it says otherwise.

Your biggest nightmare as a driver is undoubtedly parking. The basic rules are that double red and double yellow lines mean no waiting or stopping, as do the zigzag lines that you'll see near a pedestrian crossing. Single yellow and single red lines mean that you can park on them after 6pm or 7pm, and at the weekends, but times vary from borough to borough, so read the signs before

---

CONGESTION CHARGE

All vehicles entering central London on weekdays between 7am and 6pm are liable to a **congestion charge** of £10 per vehicle. Drivers can pay the charge online, over the phone and at garages and shops, and must do so before midnight the same day or incur a £2 surcharge – 24 hours later, you'll be liable for a £120 Penalty Charge Notice (reduced to £60 if you pay within 14 days). Disabled travellers, motorcycles, minibuses and some alternative-fuel vehicles are exempt from the charge, and local residents get a 90 percent discount, but you must register in order to qualify. For more details, visit ⓦtfl.gov.uk.

leaving your vehicle. Parking at a meter or pay-and-display will cost you £4 an hour or more (up to 2hr), though again meters are often free in the evenings and at weekends. In some boroughs, you'll need a mobile phone and credit card with you to pay for your parking. Finally, you can go to a car park – NCP are the largest operators Ⓦncp.co.uk – which costs up to £10 for two hours during the day. If you park your car illegally, you will get a Penalty Charge Notice (usually £80), possibly get clamped (another £80) or get towed away (£125 and upwards). If you suspect your vehicle has been towed away, phone the police on ☎020 7747 4747.

Cycling

Cycling is more popular than ever in London, not least because it's the cheapest and – in the centre, at least – fastest way to get around. The easiest way to get cycling is to use the city's free cycle hire scheme or **Boris Bikes**, as they're universally known, after Boris Johnson, the Mayor of London at the time they were introduced. There are over 400 docking stations across central London. With a credit or debit card, you can buy 24 hours' access to the bikes for just £1, after which you get the first half hour free, so if you hop from docking station to docking station, you don't pay another penny. Otherwise, it's £1 for the first hour, increasing rapidly after that to £15 for three hours. If you're going to use the Boris Bikes a lot, you're best off becoming a member and getting a key – for more details see Ⓦtfl.gov.uk.

If you want to rent a better bike for longer than an hour or so, try London Bicycle Tour Company, on the South Bank at 1a Gabriel's Wharf, SE1 (☎020 7928 6838, Ⓦlondonbicycle.com), which has hybrid and mountain bikes for rent at £3–4 an hour or £20 for the first day, £10 per day thereafter, £50 for the week; On Your Bike, 52–54 Tooley St, SE1 (☎020 7378 6669, Ⓦonyourbike.com), which has a whole range of bikes for rent for £18 a day, £10 per day thereafter.

There are restrictions on taking **bikes on public transport**: no bikes other than folding bikes are allowed on any part of the system (with a few minor exceptions) from Monday to Friday between 7.30am and 9.30am, and from 4pm to 7pm. Bikes are also restricted on the tube, being only allowed on the District, Circle, East London, Hammersmith & City and Metropolitan lines, plus certain Overground sections of other tube lines. Bicycles are not allowed on the Docklands Light Railway, and restrictions on the suburban trains vary from company to company, so check before you set out.

Festivals

London hosts an enormous number of festivals throughout the year, several of which are worth planning a trip around. The biggest street festival is still the Notting Hill Carnival, which takes place at the end of August, and the longest-running event is still the Proms, whose series of classical music concerts takes place for around eight weeks over the summer. There are also regular free events held throughout the year on Trafalgar Square, funded by the Mayor of London. The list of events below really just skims the surface – there is also an excellent range of sporting events (see Chapter 31) and music festivals (see p.401).

JANUARY

London Parade Jan 1. Ⓦ londonparade.co.uk; admission charge for grandstand seats in Piccadilly, otherwise free. A procession of floats, marching bands, cheerleaders and clowns wends its way from Parliament Square, at noon, to Green Park.

London International Mime Festival Late Jan. Ⓦ mimefest .co.uk. Annual mime festival that takes place over a fortnight at the South Bank Centre, the ICA and other funky venues. It pulls in some very big names in mime, animation and puppetry.

Chinese New Year Late Jan/early Feb. Ⓦ londonchinatown.org; free. Celebrations in Soho's Chinatown, Leicester Square and even Trafalgar Square erupt in a riot of dancing dragons and firecrackers – expect serious human congestion.

FEBRUARY

Clowns Service First Sun of month 3pm. Holy Trinity Church, Beechwood Road, E8; Ⓦ clowns-international.com; Dalston Kingsland or Junction Overground; free. The Joseph Grimaldi Memorial Service for clowns, commemorating the great clown, with a clown show afterwards in the church hall.

Pancake Day Shrove Tuesday. Free. There are several places to enjoy a public pancake race: go to Brick Lane for frivolity, and the Guildhall for seriously silly costumes courtesy of the Poulterers' Guild.

MARCH

St Patrick's Day March 15. Ⓦ london.gov.uk; free. Events all over London and a parade that sets off at noon and ends up at Trafalgar Square, where there's a festival of Irish culture; also plenty of events in the week building up to the day.

Head of the River Race Late March or early April Sat. Ⓦ horr .co.uk; free. Less well known than the Oxford and Cambridge race, but much more fun, since there are over 400 crews setting off on the ebb tide at 10-second intervals and chasing each other from Mortlake to Putney.

The Boat Race Last Sat in March or first Sat in April. Ⓦ theboatrace.org; free. Since 1829 rowers from Oxford and

Cambridge universities have battled it out over four miles from Putney to Mortlake, setting off on the flood tide. The pubs at prime vantage points pack out early.

APRIL

Alternative Fashion Week Late April. W alternativearts.co.uk. Lots of new designers and no exclusive guest lists at this week-long fashion show, with 15 shows a day held in Spitalfields.

London Marathon Third or fourth Sun in month. W london -marathon.co.uk; free. The world's most popular marathon, with around 40,000 masochists sweating the 26.2 miles from Greenwich to central London. A handful of world-class athletes enter each year, but most of the competitors are running for charity, often in ludicrous costumes.

MAY

IWA Canal Cavalcade May Bank Holiday weekend. Little Venice; W waterways.org.uk; ⊖ Warwick Avenue; free. Lively three-day celebration of the city's inland waterways, with scores of decorated narrow boats, Morris dancers and lots of children's activities.

May Fayre and Puppet Festival Sun nearest May 9. St Paul's Churchyard; W alternativearts.co.uk.; ⊖ Covent Garden; free. The gardens of Covent Garden's St Paul's Church play host to puppet booths to commemorate the first recorded Punch and Judy show in England, seen by diarist Samuel Pepys in 1662.

Chestnut Sunday Sun nearest May 11. Bushy Park; W royalparks .gov.uk.; Hampton Court train station; free. Parade of antique bicycles, classic cars, motorcycles and carriages along Chestnut Avenue, with the trees in full blossom.

Baishakhi Mela Second Sun in month. Weavers Fields, Allen Gardens and Brick Lane; W baishakhimela.org.uk; ⊖ Bethnal Green, Whitechapel or Aldgate East; free. A colourful Bengali New Year open-air festival with vast crowds (120,000 and up), street entertainment, fun fairs and lots of food on Brick Lane.

Chelsea Flower Show Late May. Royal Hospital, Chelsea; W rhs.org.uk/Chelsea; ⊖ Sloane Square. The world's finest horticultural event with over 150,000 visitors over five days, is a solidly bourgeois affair. RHS members only on the first two days.

JUNE

Beating Retreat Two consecutive eves in early June 9pm. Horse Guards Parade; W army.mod.uk; ⊖ Charing Cross, Embankment or Westminster. Annual military display on Horse Guards' Parade over three evenings, marking the old custom of drumming and piping the troops back to base at dusk. Soldiers on foot and horseback provide a colourful ceremony which precedes a floodlit performance by the Massed Bands of the Foot Guards and the Mounted Bands of the Household Cavalry.

Spitalfields Summer Music Festival Mid-June. W spitalfieldsfestival.org.uk. The festival is held over two weeks in various venues across the East End, the festival focuses on early classical music, with the odd nod to world music.

Trooping the Colour Second Sat in month. W army.mod.uk; ⊖ Charing Cross, Embankment or Westminster. Celebration of the

Queen's official birthday (her real one is on April 21) featuring massed bands, gun salutes, fly-pasts and crowds of tourists and patriotic Britons. The royal procession along the Mall allows you a glimpse for free, and there are rehearsals (minus Her Majesty) on the two preceding Saturdays.

Meltdown Last two weeks of month. Southbank Centre; W southbankcentre.co.uk; ⊖ Waterloo. Fortnight of groovy gigs, films and other events on the South Bank, chosen and presided over by a different seminal musician each year.

City of London Festival Late June to mid-July. W colf.org. For three weeks, churches (including St Paul's Cathedral), livery halls, corporate buildings and even the streets around the City play host to classical and jazz musicians, theatre companies and other guest performers.

JULY

Hampton Court Palace Flower Show Early July. Hampton Court Palace; W rhs.org.uk/hamptoncourt; Hampton Court train station. Six-day international flower extravaganza that's beginning to eclipse its sister show in Chelsea. RHS members only on the first two days.

Doggett's Coat & Badge Race Mid-July. W pla.co.uk; free. World's oldest rowing race from London Bridge to Chelsea, established by Thomas Doggett, an eighteenth-century Irish comedian, to commemorate George I's accession to the throne.

Lambeth Country Show Sat in mid-July. Brockwell Park; W lambeth.gov.uk; free; Herne Hill train station. A traditional country show comes to Brixton's Brockwell Park, with traction engines, best-jam competitions, farm animals and a cider tent.

London Literature Festival Mid-July. W southbankcentre .co.uk. The capital's chief wordfest is held over a fortnight at the Southbank Centre, with music, poetry and debate.

The Proms or Henry Wood Promenade Concerts Mid-July to early Sept. W bbc.co.uk/proms. This series of nightly classical concerts at the Royal Albert Hall (and elsewhere) is a well-loved British institution. See p.413.

Italian Procession Sun nearest July 16. St Peter's Italian Church; W italianchurch.org.uk; ⊖ Farringdon; free. Big, boisterous Italian Catholic parade, party and stalls, which starts on Clerkenwell Road and roams the streets of what used to be London's very own Little Italy (see p.151).

Cart Marking Wed 11am in mid-July. Guildhall; W thecarmen .co.uk; ⊖ Bank; free. Recalling a 1681 Act which restricted to 421 the number of horse-drawn carts allowed in the City, this arcane ceremony involves vintage vehicles congregating in Guildhall Yard in a branding ceremony organized by the Worshipful Company of Car Men.

AUGUST

Great British Beer Festival Early Aug. Earls Court Exhibition Centre; W gbbf.camra.org.uk; ⊖ Earls Court. A five-day binge organized by the Campaign for Real Ale (CAMRA). With up to 700 brews to sample, the entrance fee is a small price to pay to drink yourself silly.

Carnaval del Pueblo Sun in early Aug. Burgess Park; ⓦ carnavaldelpueblo.co.uk; bus #63, #172, #343 or #363 from ⊖ Elephant & Castle; free. All-day Latino street party with a parade from Elephant & Castle and a festival in Burgess Park, with dancing and music from samba to hip-hop.

London Mela Sun in Aug or early Sept. Gunnersbury Park; ⓦ londonmela.org; ⊖ Gunnersbury; free. Nearly 100,000 revellers come to this big open-air Asian festival of live music, dance and the arts, washed down with the best festival food in the capital.

Notting Hill Carnival Sun & Mon of August Bank Holiday weekend. ⓦ thenottinghillcarnival.com; free. World-famous two-day street festival. Carnival is a tumult of imaginatively decorated floats, eye-catching costumes, thumping soundsystems, live bands, irresistible food and huge crowds (see p.278).

SEPTEMBER

Great River Race Sat in mid-Sept. ⓦ greatriverrace.co.uk; free. Hundreds of boats are rowed or paddled for 21 miles from Island Gardens on the Isle of Dogs to Ham House, Richmond. Starts are staggered and any number of weird and wonderful vessels take part.

Thames Festival Sat & Sun in early Sept. ⓦ thamesfestival.org; ⊖ Southwark; free. The Mayor of London's very own family-orientated community festival that takes place on both banks of the river, with river races, a Thames beach, dancing, music, fireworks and a night-time parade.

Sky Ride London Third Sun in month. ⓦ goskyride.com; free. A good excuse to jump on a bike for this traffic-free 15km ride around the capital – more than 80,000 people take part every year.

Open House Third weekend in month. ⓦ londonopenhouse .org; free. A once-a-year opportunity to peek inside over 700 buildings around London, many of which don't normally open their doors to the public. You'll need to book in advance for some of the more popular places.

Great Gorilla Run Last Sat in month. ⓦ greatgorillarun.org; free (to watch). Don a gorilla suit and join (or simply watch) 750 gorillas running 7km through the City for mountain gorilla conservation.

Costermongers Harvest Festival Parade Service Last Sun in month 1pm. Guildhall to St Mary-le-Bow; ⓦ pearlysociety.co.uk; ⊖ Bank or St Paul's; free. Cockney festival in the City, with donkeys and carts, marching bands and Pearly Kings and Queens in their traditional pearl-button-studded outfits.

OCTOBER

Judges' Service First Mon in month. Westminster Abbey; free. To mark the opening of the legal year the judiciary, in full regalia, attends a service at 10am in the abbey. Afterwards they process to the House of Lords for their "Annual Breakfast".

London Film Festival Mid to late Oct. ⓦ bfi.org.uk/lff. A two-week cinematic season with scores of new international films screened at the BFI Southbank and some West End venues.

Return to Camden Town Late Oct & early Nov. London Irish Centre, 50–52 Camden Square; ⓦ returntocamden.org; Camden Road Overground. Two long weekends of traditional Irish music, song and dance featuring a great line-up of performers as well as talks and workshops.

State Opening of Parliament Late Oct. ⓦ parliament.uk; free. The Queen arrives by coach at the Houses of Parliament at 11am accompanied by the Household Cavalry and gun salutes. The ceremony itself takes place inside the House of Lords and is televised; it also takes place whenever a new government is sworn in.

NOVEMBER

London to Brighton Veteran Car Run First Sun in month. Hyde Park; ⓦ veterancarrun.com; free. In 1896 Parliament abolished the Act that required all cars to crawl along at 2mph behind someone waving a red flag. A rally was set up to mark the occasion, and more than a century later 500 or so pre-1905 vehicles still set off from Hyde Park at sunrise and travel the 58 miles to Brighton along the A23 at the heady average speed of 20mph.

Bonfire Night Nov 5 or nearest weekend. Free. In memory of Guy Fawkes – executed for his role in the 1605 Gunpowder Plot to blow up King James I and the Houses of Parliament – effigies of the hapless Fawkes are burned on bonfires all over the capital. See local listings or head for Alexandra Palace, which provides a good vantage point from which to take in several displays at once.

London Jazz Festival Mid-Nov. ⓦ londonjazzfestival.org.uk. Big ten-day international jazz fest held in all London's jazz venues, large and small.

Lord Mayor's Show Second Sat in month. ⓦ lordmayorsshow .org; free. The Lord Mayor begins his or her day of investiture at Westminster, leaving there at around 9am for Guildhall. At 11.10am, the vast ceremonial procession, headed by a gilded coach, begins its journey from Guildhall to the Law Courts in the Strand, where the oath of office is taken at 11.50am. From there the coach and its train of 140-odd floats make their way back towards Guildhall, arriving at 2.20pm. After dark, there's a fireworks display on the Thames.

Remembrance Sunday Sun nearest Nov 11. Free. A day of commemorative ceremonies for the dead and wounded of the two world wars and other conflicts. The principal ceremony, attended by the Queen and the prime minister, takes place at the Cenotaph in Whitehall, beginning with a march-past of veterans and building to a one-minute silence at the stroke of 11am.

Christmas Lights Late Nov to Jan 5. Free. Assorted celebrities flick the switches, and Bond, Oxford and Regent streets are bathed in festive illumination from dusk to midnight until January 6. Also, each year since the end of World War II, Norway has acknowledged its gratitude to the country that helped liberate it from the Nazis with the gift of a mighty spruce tree that appears in Trafalgar Square in early December. Decorated with lights, it becomes the focus for carol singing versus traffic noise each evening until Christmas Eve.

DECEMBER

Ice rinks Dec–Jan. Ice rinks have become all the rage. You can skate outside the Natural History Museum, at Somerset House, Marble Arch, Kew Gardens and elsewhere.

Christmas Day Race Christmas Day. Serpentine Lido; ⓦ serpentineswimmingclub.com; ⊖ Knightsbrdge; free. Brave (or foolhardy) members of the Serpentine Swimming Club have taken an icy 100yd plunge and competed for the Peter Pan Cup in the Lido every year since 1864.

New Year's Eve Ⓦ london.gov.uk; free. New Year is welcomed by thousands of revellers who get to enjoy a spectacular firework display centred on the London Eye. Transport for London runs free public transport all night, sponsored by various public-spirited breweries.

Travel essentials

Addresses

London addresses come with postcodes at the end. Each street name is followed by a letter or letters giving the geographical location of the street in relation to the City (E for "east", WC for "west central" and so on) and a number that specifies its location more precisely. Unfortunately, this number doesn't correspond to the district's distance from the centre (as in most cities). So W11 (Notting Hill) for example, is closer to the centre of town than W4 (Chiswick), and SE3 (Blackheath) lies beyond the remote-sounding SE10 (Greenwich). Full postal addresses end with a digit and two letters, which specify the individual block, and will locate a building on Google Maps or a Sat Nav.

Climate

Despite the temperateness of the English climate, it's impossible to say with any degree of certainty that the weather will be pleasant in any given month. English summers rarely get unbearably hot, while the winters don't get very cold – though they're often wet. However, whenever you come, be prepared for all eventualities: it has been known to snow at Easter and rain all day on August Bank Holiday weekend.

Costs

The high cost of accommodation, and food and drink, makes London a **very expensive** place to visit. The minimum expenditure for a couple staying in a budget hotel and eating takeaway meals, pizzas or other such basic fare would be in the region of at least £50 per person per day. You only

TIPPING

There are no fixed rules for **tipping** in London. However, there's a certain expectation in restaurants or cafés that you should leave a tip of about ten percent of the total bill – check first, though, that "optional" service has not already been included. Taxi drivers also expect tips – add about ten percent to the fare – as do traditional barbers. The other occasion when you'll be expected to tip is in upmarket hotels where porters, bellboys and table waiters rely on being tipped to bump up their often dismal wages.

have to add in the odd better-quality meal, plus some major tourist attractions, a few films or other shows, and you're looking at around £75–100 as a daily budget, even in decidedly average accommodation. For more details on the costs of accommodation and eating, see chapters 23 and 24.

Most attractions and many cinemas and theatres offer **concessions** for senior citizens, the unemployed, full-time students and under-16s, with under-5s being admitted free almost everywhere – although proof of eligibility will be required in most cases.

Once obtained, **youth/student ID cards** soon pay for themselves in savings. Full-time students are eligible for the International Student Identity Card or **ISIC**, which costs around £10 and entitles the bearer to reduced air, rail and bus fares, and discounts at museums, theatres and other attractions. If you're not a student, but you're 25 or younger, you can get an International Youth Travel Card or **IYTC**, which costs the same as the ISIC and carries the same benefits. Visit Ⓦ isiccard.com for more details.

Crime and personal safety

The traditional image of the friendly British "bobby" is a bit of a tired old cliché, but in the normal run of

AVERAGE MONTHLY TEMPERATURES AND RAINFALL

	Jan	Feb	Mar	Apr	May	Jun	Jul	Aug	Sep	Oct	Nov	Dec
LONDON												
Max/min (°C)	6/2	7/2	10/3	13/6	17/8	20/12	22/14	21/13	19/11	14/8	10/5	7/4
Max/min (°F)	43/36	44/36	50/37	56/43	62/46	69/53	71/57	71/56	65/52	57/45	50/41	44/39
Rainfall (mm)	54	40	37	37	46	45	57	59	49	57	64	48

ENGLISH HERITAGE AND NATIONAL TRUST

A few of London's historic properties come under the control of the private National Trust (📞0844 800 1895, 🌐nationaltrust.org.uk), or the state-run English Heritage (📞0870 333 1181, 🌐english-heritage.org.uk). These properties are denoted in the guide by "NT" or "EH" after the opening times. Annual membership for each organization is around £50 and allows free entry to their respective properties, though if you're only visiting London for a short time, it may not be worth it.

events the police continue to be approachable, helpful and, for the most part, unarmed. If you're lost in London, asking a police officer is generally the quickest way to pinpoint your destination – police officers on street duty wear a distinctive domed hat with a silver tip. Like any other capital, London has its dangerous spots, but these tend to be obscure parts of the city where no tourist has any reason to go. The chief risk on London's streets is pickpocketing, and there are some virtuosos at work on the big shopping streets and the Underground (tube). Carry only as much money as you need for the day, and keep all bags and pockets fastened.

Should you have anything stolen or be involved in an incident that requires reporting, go to the local police station or phone 📞0300 123 1212; the 📞999 number should only be used in emergencies. Central 24hr Metropolitan police stations include: Charing Cross, Agar St, WC2 (🚇 Charing Cross); Holborn, 10 Lambs Conduit St, WC1 (🚇 Holborn); Marylebone, 1–9 Seymour St, W1 (🚇 Marble Arch); West End Central, 27 Savile Row, W1 (🚇 Oxford Circus); 🌐met .police.uk. The City of London Police are separate from the Metropolitan Police and have a police station at 182 Bishopsgate, EC2 (📞020 7601 2222, 🌐cityof-flondon.police.uk; 🚇 Liverpool Street). If there's an incident on public transport, you should call the British Transport Police, 55 Broadway SW1 (📞0800 405 040, 🌐btp.police.uk). If you have a complaint

against the police, take the officer's number and report it to the Independent Police Complaints Commission (📞0845 300 2002, 🌐ipcc.gov.uk).

Electricity

Electricity supply in London conforms to the EU standard of approximately 230V. Sockets are designed for British three-pin plugs, which are totally different from those in the rest of the EU and North America.

Entry requirements

Citizens of all European countries – except Albania, Bosnia, Macedonia, Montenegro, Serbia and the former Soviet republics (other than the Baltic states) – can enter Britain with just a passport, for up to three months (indefinitely if you're from the EU). US, Canadian, Australian and New Zealand citizens can stay for up to six months, providing they have a return ticket and adequate funds to cover their stay. Citizens of most other countries require a visa, obtainable from the British consular or mission office in the country of application.

Note that visa regulations are subject to frequent changes, so it's always wise to contact the nearest British embassy or High Commission before you travel. If you visit 🌐ukvisas.gov.uk, you can download the full range of application forms and information leaflets and find out the contact details of your nearest embassy or consulate. In addition, an independent charity, the Immigration Advisory Service (IAS), County House, 190 Great Dover St, London SE1 4YB (📞020 7967 1296, 🌐iasuk.org), offers confidential legal advice to anyone applying for entry clearance into the UK.

For visa extensions, you should write, before the expiry date given in your passport, to the UK Border Agency, Lunar House, 40 Wellesley Rd, Croydon CR9 2BY (📞0870 606 7766).

EMERGENCIES

Alcoholics Anonymous 📞0845 769 7555, 🌐alcoholics-anonymous.org.uk
Police, fire and ambulance 📞999
Rape crisis 📞0808 802 9999 (daily noon–2.30pm & 7–9.30pm), 🌐rapecrisis.org.uk
Samaritans 24hr counselling helpline 📞0845 790 9090, 🌐samaritans.org; or drop-in (daily 9am–9pm) at 46 Marshall St, W1 📞020 7734 2800; 🚇 Piccadilly Circus or Oxford Circus
Sexual Healthline 📞0845 122 8690, 🌐fpa.org.uk

EMBASSIES AND HIGH COMMISSIONS

Australian High Commission Australia House, Strand, WC2 📞020 7379 4334, 🌐uk.embassy.gov.au; 🚇 Charing Cross

24 HOUR ACCIDENT AND EMERGENCY

Charing Cross Hospital Fulham Palace Rd, W6 ☎020 3311 1005; ⊖ Hammersmith.
Chelsea & Westminster Hospital 369 Fulham Rd, SW10 ☎020 8746 8000; bus #14 or #414 from ⊖South Kensington.
Guy's Hospital Great Maze Pond, SE1 ☎020 7188 7188; ⊖ London Bridge.
Royal Free Hospital Pond St, NW3 ☎020 7794 0500; ⊖ Hampstead.
Royal London Hospital Whitechapel Rd, E1 ☎020 7377 7000; Whitechapel.
St Mary's Hospital Praed St, W2 ☎020 3312 6330; ⊖ Paddington.
University College London Hospital 235 Euston Rd, NW1 ☎0845 155 5000; ⊖ Euston Square or Warren Square.
Whittington Hospital Highgate Hill, N19 ☎020 7272 3070; ⊖ Archway.

Canadian High Commission 1 Grosvenor Square, W1 ☎020 7258 6600, ⓦunitedkingdom.gc.ca; ⊖ Bond Street
Irish Embassy 17 Grosvenor Place, SW1 ☎020 7235 2171, ⓦembassyofireland.co.uk; ⊖ Hyde Park Corner
New Zealand High Commission New Zealand House, 80 Haymarket, SW1 ☎020 7930 8422, ⓦnzembassy.com; ⊖ Piccadilly Circus
South African High Commission South Africa House, Trafalgar Square, WC2 ☎020 7451 7299, ⓦsouthafricahouseuk.com; ⊖ Charing Cross
US Embassy 24 Grosvenor Square, W1 ☎020 7499 9000, ⓦlondon.usembassy.gov; ⊖ Bond Street

Health

For minor complaints, pharmacists (known as chemists in England) can dispense a limited range of drugs without a doctor's prescription. Most pharmacies are open standard shop hours, though some stay open later: Zafash, 233–235 Old Brompton Rd, SW5 ☎020 7373 2798, ⓦzafash.com (⊖ Earl's Court), is open 24 hours; while Bliss, at 5–6 Marble Arch, W1 ☎020 7723 6116, ⓦblisslife.co.uk (⊖ Marble Arch), is open daily 9am till 11.30pm.

EU and EEA citizens are entitled to free medical treatment within the National Health Service, on production of an EHIC (European Health Insurance Card). Australia, New Zealand, Russia and several other non-EU countries also have reciprocal health-care arrangements with the UK. If it's an emergency, go to the Accident and Emergency (A&E) department of your local hospital, or phone for an ambulance (☎999). A&E services are free to all. You can also go to a Minor Injuries Clinic such as the one at St Bartholomew's Hospital, West Smithfield, EC1 ☎020 3465 5869 (Mon–Fri 8am–8pm; ⊖ Farringdon), or get free medical advice from NHS Direct, the health service's 24-hour helpline ☎0845 4647, ⓦnhsdirect.nhs.uk.

For an emergency dentist turn up as early as possible to the Dental Emergency Care Service at Guy's Hospital, St Thomas St (☎020 7188 7188; Mon–Fri 9am–5pm).

Insurance

Even though EU health-care privileges apply in the UK, it's as well to take out an insurance policy before travelling to cover against theft, loss and illness or injury. Non-EU citizens should check whether they are already covered before buying a new policy.

Internet access

Most hotels and hostels in London have internet access. Otherwise, your best bet is to find a café with wi-fi like the café in Foyles bookshop at 113–119 Charing Cross Rd (⊖ Tottenham Court Road). The

ROUGH GUIDES TRAVEL INSURANCE

Rough Guides has teamed up with **WorldNomads.com** to offer great travel insurance deals. Policies are available to residents of over 150 countries, with cover for a wide range of adventure sports, 24hr emergency assistance, high levels of medical and evacuation cover and a stream of travel safety information. Roughguides.com users can take advantage of their policies online 24/7, from anywhere in the world – even if you're already travelling. And since plans often change when you're on the road, you can extend your policy and even claim online. Roughguides.com users who buy travel insurance with WorldNomads.com can also leave a positive footprint and donate to a community development project. For more information go to ⓦroughguides.com/shop.

British Library and St Pancras Station both have free wi-fi, too. Some public libraries also offer free access.

Laundry

Most hotels offer a laundry service and most hostels have washing machines. Self-service laundrettes exist all over London, although they are harder to find in the centre – there's one at 78 Marchmont St, WC1 (daily 6.30am–10.30pm; ♦ King's Cross). For a central dry cleaners, try Valentino Dry Cleaners, 56b New Oxford St, WC1 ☎020 7436 1660 (Mon–Fri 8am–6pm, Sat 9am–1pm; ♦ Tottenham Court Road).

Left luggage

Airports Gatwick ☎ 01293 569900: North Terminal (daily 5am–9pm); South Terminal (24hr). Heathrow ☎ 020 8759 3344: Terminal 1 (daily 6am–11pm); Terminal 3 (daily 5am–11pm); Terminal 4 (daily 5.30am–11pm); Terminal 5 (daily 5.30am–11pm). London City ☎ 020 7646 0000 (daily 6am–10pm). Luton ☎ 01582 405100 (24hr). Stansted ☎ 01279 663213 (24hr). **Train stations** Excess Baggage Company (☎ 020 72620344, ⓦ left-baggage.co.uk): Charing Cross ☎ 020 7930 5444 (daily 7am–11pm); Euston ☎ 020 7387 1499 (daily 7am–11pm); King's Cross ☎ 020 7837 4334 (daily 7am–11pm); Liverpool Street ☎ 020 7247 4297 (daily 7am–11pm); Paddington ☎ 020 7262 0344 (daily 7am–11pm); St Pancras ☎ 020 7833 1596 (Mon–Sat 6am–10pm, Sun 7am–10pm); Victoria ☎ 020 7963 0957 (daily 7am–midnight); Waterloo ☎ 020 7401 8444 (daily 7am–11pm).

Lost property

Airports Gatwick (South Terminal) ☎ 01293 503162 (daily 10am–4pm); Heathrow (Terminals 3 & 5) ☎ 020 8634 4130 (daily 8am–7pm); London City ☎ 020 7646 0000 (daily 6am–10pm); Luton ☎ 01582 395219; Stansted ☎ 01279 663293 (daily 9.30am–4.30pm). **Eurostar** ☎ 0870 160 0052, ⓦ eurostar.com. **Train stations** ☎ 0870 000 5151, ⓦ networkrail.co.uk: Euston ☎ 020 7387 8699 (Mon–Fri 9am–5.30pm); King's Cross ☎ 020 7278 3310 (Mon–Sat 9am–5pm); Liverpool Street ☎ 020 7247 4297 (Mon–Fri 9am–5.30pm); Paddington ☎ 020 7313 1514 (Mon–Fri 9am–5.30pm); St Pancras ☎ 020 7833 1596 (Mon–Sat 6am–10pm, Sun 7am–10pm); Victoria ☎ 020 7963 0957 (Mon–Fri 9am–5.15pm); Waterloo ☎ 020 7401 7861 (Mon–Fri 7.30am–7pm). **Transport for London** Lost Property Office, 200 Baker St, NW1 (Mon–Fri 8.30am–4pm) ☎ 0845 330 9882, ⓦ tfl.gov.uk; ♦ Baker Street; map p.89. Contact TfL about property lost on buses, tubes or in black cabs.

Mail

The postal service is pretty efficient. First-class stamps to anywhere in the UK currently cost 46p and should arrive the next day; if the item is anything approaching A4 size, it will be classed as a "Large Letter" and will cost 75p; if you want to guarantee next day delivery, ask for Special Delivery (from £5.45). Second-class stamps cost 36p, taking three days; airmail to the rest of Europe costs 68p and should take three days; to the rest of the world stamps cost from 76p and should take five days. Stamps can be bought at post offices, and from newsagents and supermarkets, although they usually only sell books of four or ten first-class UK stamps.

For general postal enquiries phone ☎0845 774 0740 (Mon–Fri 8am–6pm, Sat 8am–1pm), or visit the website ⓦ royalmail.com. Almost all London's post offices are open Monday to Friday 9am–5.30pm, Saturday 9am–noon. The exception is the Trafalgar Square Post Office (24–28 William IV St, WC2N 4DL; Mon–Fri 8.30am–6.30pm, Tues opens 9.15am, Sat 9am–5.30pm), to which poste restante mail should be sent. In the suburbs you'll find sub-post offices operating out of shops, but these are open the same hours as regular post offices, even if the shop itself is open for longer. To find out your nearest post office, contact ☎0845 722 3344, ⓦ postoffice.co.uk (Mon–Fri 8.15am–6pm, Sat 8.30am–7pm).

Maps

The maps in this book should be adequate for sightseeing purposes. Alternatively, the Geographers' A–Z map series produces a whole range of street-by-street maps of London, from pocket-sized foldouts to giant atlases. Virtually every newsagent in London stocks them, but the best map shop in London is Stanford's, 12–14 Long Acre, WC2 (☎020 7836 1321, ⓦ stanfords.co.uk; ♦ Leicester Square). Free maps of the Underground and bus networks can be picked up at tourist offices and TfL information offices – see p.21.

Media

The most useful listings magazine for visitors is *Time Out*, which comes out every Tuesday and has a virtual monopoly on listings. It carries critical appraisals of all the week's theatre, film, music, exhibitions, children's events and more. London's only daily newspapers are both tabloids: the *Metro* is available on the public transport system, and the *Evening Standard* all over town – both are free. Each of the London boroughs has a local paper, usually printed twice weekly and filled mostly with news of local crimes and cheap adverts.

Money

The currency in the UK is the pound sterling (£), divided into 100 pence (p). Coins come in denominations of 1p, 2p, 5p, 10p, 20p, 50p, £1 and £2. Notes come in denominations of £5, £10, £20 and £50. Many shopkeepers may not accept £50 notes – the best advice is to avoid having to use them. At the time of writing, £1 was worth $1.60, €1.15, Can$1.60, Aus$1.60 and NZ$2. For the most up-to-date exchange rates, visit ⓦxe.com.

The easiest way to get hold of your cash is to use your **credit/debit card** in a "cash machine" (ATM); check in advance whether you will be subject to a daily withdrawal limit. There are ATMs all over the city, outside banks, supermarkets and post offices – beware of stand-alone ATMs in small shops, which charge up to £2 for each withdrawal. The opening hours for most **banks** are Monday to Friday 9.30am–4.30pm, with some branches opening on Saturday mornings. Post offices charge no commission, and are therefore a good place to change money and cheques. Lost or stolen credit/debit cards should be reported to the police and the following numbers: MasterCard ☎0800 964767, Visa ☎0800 895082.

Opening hours and public holidays

Generally speaking, shop opening hours are Monday to Saturday 9am or 10am to 5.30pm or 6pm – with some places in central London staying open till 7pm, and later on Thursdays and Fridays (around 9pm) – and Sundays and Bank Holidays

---

UK OPERATOR SERVICES

Domestic operator ☎100
International operator ☎155

---

noon to 6pm. There are still plenty of stores that close completely on Sundays and Bank Holidays. That said, numerous family-run corner shops stay open late every day of the year. The big supermarket chains tend to open Monday to Saturday from 8am to 10pm, Sunday 10am or 11am to 4pm or 5pm. Note that many petrol (gas) service stations in London are open 24 hours and have small shops.

Most tourist attractions and museums are typically open daily 10am to 6pm, occasionally with shorter hours on Sundays and public holidays (see box, above). Most places are closed on December 25 and 26. Several museums now have late-night openings until 9pm or 10pm, once or twice a week. Individual opening hours are given in the main text of this guide.

Phones

Public payphones are ubiquitous on the streets of London. Most take coins from 10p upwards (minimum charge 40p) and credit cards. Discount phonecards with a PIN number, available from newsagents, are the cheapest way to make international calls.

If you're taking your mobile/cellphone with you, check with your provider that roaming is activated (if you're coming from America, you will need a multi-band phone, unless you have a smart phone). Mobiles in Australia and New Zealand generally use the same system as the UK so should work fine. If you're staying for a while, it's easier to buy a handset and SIM card when you arrive – a basic pay-as-you-go phone can cost as little as £20.

London phone numbers are prefixed by the area code ☎020. Mobile numbers are prefixed with ☎07; numbers with ☎0800, 0808 and 0500 prefixes are free of charge (unless calling from a mobile); ☎0845 numbers are charged at local rates and ☎0870 up to the national rate, irrespective of where in the country you are calling from. Beware of premium-rate numbers which usually have the prefix ☎09, as these are charged at anything up to £1.50 a minute.

For directory enquiries, there are numerous companies offering the service, all with six-figure

---

PUBLIC HOLIDAYS

You'll find all banks and offices closed on the following Bank Holidays, while everything else pretty much runs to a Sunday schedule (except on Christmas Day when most places shut down): **New Year's Day** (January 1); **Good Friday** (late March/early April); **Easter Monday** (late March/early April); **Spring Bank Holiday** (first Monday in May); **May Bank Holiday** (last Monday in May); **August Bank Holiday** (last Monday in August); **Christmas Day** (December 25); **Boxing Day** (December 26). Note that if January 1, December 25 or December 26 falls on a Saturday or Sunday, the holiday falls on the following weekday.

PHONING HOME

To Australia ☎0061 + area code without the zero + number
To Ireland ☎00353 + area code without the zero + number
To New Zealand ☎0064 + area code without the zero + number
To South Africa ☎0027 + area code without the zero + number
To US and Canada ☎001 + area code + number

---

numbers beginning with ☎118. Whichever one you choose, the minimum charge you'll get away with is 40p. The best known is ☎118 118; for an online UK phone directory, visit ⓦukphonebook.com.

Smoking

Smoking is banned in all indoor public spaces including all cafés, pubs, restaurants, clubs and public transport.

Tax

Most goods in Britain are subject to Value Added Tax (VAT), which increases the cost of an item by 20 percent. Visitors from non-EU countries can save money through the Retail Export Scheme (tax-free shopping), which allows a VAT refund on goods taken out of the country. Note that not all shops participate in this scheme (those doing so will display a sign to this effect) and that you cannot reclaim VAT charged on hotel bills or other services. See ⓦhmrc.gov.uk for more details.

Time

Greenwich Mean Time (GMT) is used from the end of October to the end of March; for the rest of the year the country switches to British Summer Time (BST), one hour ahead of GMT. GMT is five hours ahead of the US East Coast; eight ahead of the US West Coast; and nine behind Australia's East Coast.

Toilets

There are surprisingly few public toilets in London. All mainline train and major tube stations have toilets. Department stores and free museums and galleries are another good option.

Tourist information

The chief tourist office in London is the Britain & London Visitor Centre, 1 Regent St, SW1 (April–Sept Mon 9.30am–6.30pm, Tues–Fri 9am–6.30pm, Sat 9am–5pm, Sun 10am–4pm; Oct–March Mon 9.30am–6pm, Tues 9am–6pm, Sat & Sun 10am–4pm; ☎0870 156 6366, ⓦvisitlondon.com; ⊖ Piccadilly Circus). There's also the London Information Centre, a tiny window in the tkts kiosk on Leicester Square, WC2 (daily 8am–midnight; ☎020 7292 2333, ⓦlondoninformationcentre.com; ⊖ Leicester Square).

Some London boroughs have tourist information offices, and every borough has its own tourism/leisure department, which can be consulted via the local council website. The most useful borough tourist offices are: Greenwich in the old Royal Naval College (daily 10am–5pm; ☎0870 608 2000; Cutty Sark DLR); and the City of London on the south side of St Paul's Cathedral (Mon–Sat 9.30am–5.30pm, Sun 10am–4pm; ☎020 7332 1456, ⓦvisitthecity.co.uk; ⊖ St Paul's).

Tours and walks

Standard sightseeing tours are run by several rival bus companies, their open-top double-deckers setting off every thirty minutes from Victoria station, Trafalgar Square, Piccadilly and other conspicuous tourist spots. You can hop on and off several different routes as often as you like with The Original Tour for around £25 (☎020 8877 2120, ⓦtheoriginaltour.com; daily 8.30am–6pm; every 15–20min;). Alternatively, for around £20 you can climb aboard one of the bright-yellow World War II D-Day amphibious vehicles used by London Duck Tours (☎020 7928 3132, ⓦlondonducktours.co.uk), which offers a combined bus and boat tour (daily 9.30am–6pm or dusk). After departing from Chicheley St (⊖ Waterloo), you spend 45 minutes driving round the usual sights, before plunging into the river for a 30-minute cruise; advance booking essential.

The cheapest option is to hop on a real London double-decker – the #11 bus from Victoria station, for example, will take you past Westminster Abbey, the Houses of Parliament, up Whitehall, round Trafalgar Square, along the Strand and on to St Paul's Cathedral. You can also take an old double-decker Routemaster, with open rear platform and roving conductor, on two "heritage" routes (daily every 15min 9.30am–6.30pm): #9 from the

THE LONDON PASS

If you're thinking of visiting a lot of fee-paying attractions in a short space of time, it's worth considering buying a **London Pass** (Ⓦ londonpass.com), which gives you free entry to a mixed bag of attractions including Hampton Court Palace, Kensington Palace, Kew Gardens, London Zoo, St Paul's Cathedral, the Tower of London and Windsor Castle. You can choose to buy the card with an **All-Zone Travelcard** thrown in; the extra outlay is relatively small, and this does include free travel out to Windsor. The pass costs around £39 for one day (£25 for kids), rising to £87 for six days (£60 for kids), or £46 with a Travelcard (£27 for kids) rising to £129 (£82 for kids). The London Pass can be bought online or in person from tourist offices and London's mainline train or chief underground stations.

Kensington High Street to Trafalgar Square and #15 from Trafalgar Square to Tower Hill.

Walking tours are infinitely more appealing and informative, mixing solid historical facts with juicy anecdotes in the company of a local specialist. Walks on offer range from a literary pub crawl round Bloomsbury to a roam around the East End. You'll find most of them detailed in *Time Out* magazine; as you'd imagine, there's more variety on offer in the summer months. Tours cost around £7–10 and take around two hours; normally you can simply show up at the starting point and join. If you want to plan – or book – walks in advance, contact the most reliable and well-established company, Original London Walks (Ⓣ 020 7624 3978, Ⓦ walks.com).

Travellers with disabilities

London is an old city, not well equipped for disabled travellers, though all public venues are obliged to make some effort towards accessibility. Even public transport is slowly improving, with most buses now wheelchair-accessible. The ancient tube and rail systems, designed, for the most part, in the nineteenth century, are still a trial for those with mobility problems. Around 25 percent of all

tube stations are step-free – the majority on the Docklands Light Railway – and are indicated by a blue symbol on the tube map. For a more detailed rundown, get hold of the free *Tube Access Guide* or use the TfL website to plan a step-free journey (Ⓦ tfl.gov.uk).

Tourism For All has lots of useful information on accessibility for visitors to London (Ⓣ 0845 124 9971, Ⓦ tourismforall.org.uk). Another valuable service is provided by Artsline (Ⓣ 020 7388 2227, Ⓦ artsline .org.uk), who can give up-to-date information and advice by phone on access to arts venues and events in London: theatres, cinemas, galleries and concert halls.

Websites

Aside from the aforementioned tourist authority and local borough websites, there's a vast quantity of useful London-related information online. Below are a handful of good general sites:

Ⓦ **culture24.org.uk** Useful national website, with up-to-date information on virtually every single museum, large or small, in London (and the UK).

Ⓦ **derelictlondon.co.uk** Pictorial catalogue of the city's abandoned cinemas, pubs, theatres and even toilets, plus other forgotten derelict gems.

Ⓦ **londonnet.co.uk** Web guide to London with useful up-to-date listings on eating, drinking and nightlife.

Ⓦ **gumtree.com** Very useful website for anyone living in London, looking for a job, a flat, or to buy or sell anything.

Ⓦ **thisislocallondon.co.uk** Local news website with links to all the capital's local papers.

Working in London

All Swiss nationals and EEA citizens (except those from Bulgaria and Romania) can work in London without a permit, although citizens of Czech Republic, Estonia, Hungary, Latvia, Lithuania, Poland, Slovakia or Slovenia must register under the Worker Registration Scheme. Other nationals need a work permit in order to work legally in the UK, with eligibility worked out on a points-based system. There are exceptions to the above rules, although these are constantly changing, so for the latest regulations visit Ⓦ ukvisas.gov.uk.

Whitehall and Westminster

The monuments and buildings in Westminster include some of London's most famous landmarks – Nelson's Column, Big Ben, the Houses of Parliament and Westminster Abbey, plus two of the city's top permanent art collections, the National Gallery and Tate Britain and its finest architectural set piece, Trafalgar Square. Although the area is a well-trodden tourist circuit for the most part, there are only a few shops or cafés and little commercial life (nearby Soho and Covent Garden, covered in chapters 5 & 8, are far better areas for this). It's also one of the easiest parts of London to walk round, with all the major sights within a mere half-mile of each other, and linked by one of London's most triumphant – and atypical – avenues, Whitehall.

Political, religious and regal power has emanated from **Whitehall** and **Westminster** for almost a millennium. It was King Edward the Confessor (1042–66) who first established Westminster as a royal and ecclesiastical power base, some three miles west of the City of London. The embryonic English parliament used to meet in the abbey and eventually took over the old royal palace of Westminster when Henry VIII moved out to Whitehall. Henry's sprawling Whitehall Palace burnt down in 1698 and was slowly replaced by government offices, so that by the nineteenth century Whitehall had become the "heart of the Empire", its ministries ruling over a quarter of the world's population. Even now, though the UK's world status has diminished and its royalty and clergy no longer wield much real power or receive the same respect, the institutions that run the country inhabit roughly the same geographical area: Westminster for the politicians, Whitehall for the ministers and civil servants.

Trafalgar Square

⊖ Charing Cross

As one of the few large public squares in London, **Trafalgar Square** has been both a tourist attraction and the main focus for political demonstrations for over a century and a half (see box below). Nowadays, most folk come here to see **Nelson's Column**, or to visit the **National Gallery**, though there are also various events, commemorations and celebrations staged here throughout the year. Each December, the square is graced with a giant Christmas tree covered in fairy lights, donated by Norway in thanks for Britain's support during World War II, and carol singers battle nightly with the traffic.

For centuries, Trafalgar Square was the site of the **King's Mews**, established in the thirteenth century by Edward I, who kept the royal hawks and the falconers here (the term "mews" comes from falconry: the birds were caged or "mewed up" there whilst changing their plumage). Chaucer was Clerk of the Mews for a time, and by Tudor times there were stables here, too. During the Civil War they were turned into barracks and later used as a prison for Cavaliers. In the 1760s, George III began to move the mews to Buckingham Palace, and by the late 1820s, **John Nash** had designed the new square (though he didn't live to see his plan executed). The Neoclassical National Gallery filled up the northern side in 1838, followed shortly afterwards by the central focal point, Nelson's Column, though the famous bronze lions didn't arrive until 1868. The development of the rest of the square was equally haphazard, though the overall effect is unified by the safe Neoclassical style of the buildings, and the square remains one of London's grandest architectural highlights.

A HISTORY OF PROTEST

Installed in 1845 in an attempt to deter the gathering of urban mobs, the Trafalgar Square fountains have failed supremely to prevent the square from becoming a focus of **political protest**. The first major demo was held in 1848 when the Chartists assembled to demand universal suffrage before marching to Kennington Common. Protests were banned until the 1880s, when the emerging Labour movement began to gather here, culminating in **Bloody Sunday, 1887**, when hundreds of demonstrators were injured, and three killed, by the police. To allow the police to call quickly for reinforcements, a police phone box was built into one of the stone bollards in the southeast corner of the square, with a direct link to Scotland Yard.

Throughout the 1980s, there was a continuous **anti-apartheid demonstration** outside South Africa House, and in 1990, the square was the scene of the **Poll Tax Riot**, which helped bring about the downfall of Margaret Thatcher. Some of the largest demonstrations London has ever seen were the anti-war protests against military intervention in Iraq and Afghanistan, though these simply passed through, en route to the more spacious environs of Hyde Park.

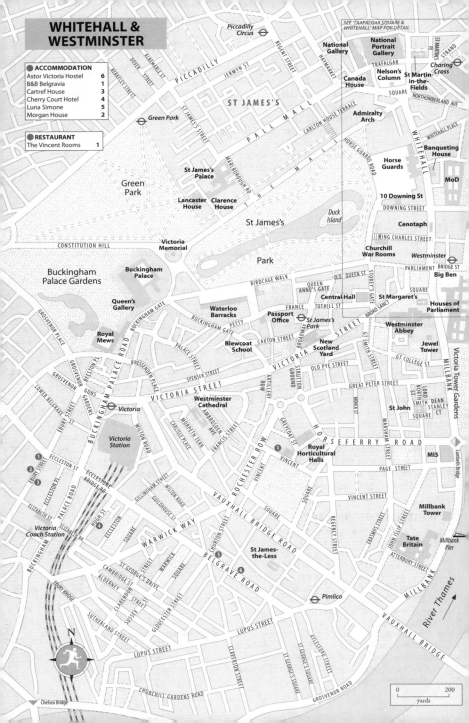

THE FOURTH PLINTH

The **fourth plinth**, in the northwest corner Trafalgar Square, was originally earmarked for an equestrian statue of William IV. In the end, it remained empty until 1999, since when it has been used to display works of modern sculpture, which are changed annually (Ⓦ london.gov .uk/fourthplinth). Highlights have included Rachel Whiteread's inverted plinth, Marc Quinn's *Alison Lapper Pregnant*, a nude statue of a woman without arms, and Anthony Gormley's *One & Other*, where several thousand individuals each had an hour to occupy the plinth.

Nelson's Column

Raised in 1843 and now one of London's best-loved monuments, **Nelson's Column** commemorates the one-armed, one-eyed admiral who defeated the French at the Battle of Trafalgar in 1805, but paid for it with his life. The sandstone statue which surmounts a 151-foot granite column is more than triple life-size but still manages to appear minuscule. The acanthus leaves of the capital are cast from British cannons, while bas-reliefs around the base – depicting three of Nelson's earlier victories as well as his death aboard HMS *Victory* – are from captured French armaments. Edwin Landseer's four gargantuan **bronze lions** guard the column and provide a climbing frame for kids (and demonstrators).

Keeping Nelson company at ground level, on either side of the column, are bronze **statues** of Napier and Havelock, Victorian major-generals who helped keep India British; against the north wall are busts of Beatty, Jellicoe and Cunningham, admirals from the last century. To the right of them are the imperial standards of length – inch, foot and yard – "accurate at 62 degrees Fahrenheit", as the plaque says, and still used by millions of Brits despite the best efforts of the European Union. Above this is an equestrian statue of George IV (bareback, stirrup-less and in Roman garb), which he himself commissioned for the top of Marble Arch, but which was later erected here "temporarily".

South Africa House and Canada House

There's an unmistakable whiff of empire about Trafalgar Square, with **South Africa House** erected in 1935 on the east side, complete with keystones featuring African animals, and **Canada House** (Mon–Fri 10am–6pm; free) constructed in warm Bath stone, on the opposite side of the square. Canada House was originally built by Robert Smirke in the 1820s, as a gentlemen's club and home for the Royal College of Physicians. It retains much of its original Neoclassical interior, and is now in the hands of the Canadian High Commission, who put on excellent temporary exhibitions.

St Martin-in-the-Fields

Trafalgar Sq • Mon, Tues & Fri 8.30am–1pm & 2–6pm, Wed 8.30am–1.15pm & 2–5pm, Thurs 8.30am–1.15pm & 2–6pm, Sat 9.30am–6pm, Sun 3.30–5pm • Free • ☎ 020 7766 1100, Ⓦ stmartin-in-the-fields.org • ⊖ Charing Cross

At the northeastern corner of Trafalgar Square stands the church of **St Martin-in-the-Fields**, fronted by a magnificent Corinthian portico and topped by an elaborate tower and steeple, designed in 1721 by James Gibbs – it was subsequently copied widely in the American colonies. The barrel-vaulted interior features ornate, sparkling white Italian plasterwork and is best appreciated while listening to one of the church's **free lunchtime concerts** (Mon, Tues & Fri) or ticketed, candle-lit evening performances. As the official parish church for Buckingham Palace, St Martin's maintains strong royal and naval connections – there's a royal box on the left of the high altar, and one for the admiralty on the right. Down in the newly expanded **crypt** – accessible via an entrance north of the church – there's a licensed **café** (see p.367), shop, gallery and **brass-rubbing centre**.

National Gallery

1

Trafalgar Sq • Daily 10am–6pm, Fri till 9pm • Free • ☎ 020 7747 2885, ⓦ nationalgallery.org.uk • ⊖ Charing Cross

Taking up the entire north side of Trafalgar Square, the sprawling Neoclassical hulk of the **National Gallery** houses one of the world's greatest art collections. Unlike the Louvre or the Hermitage, the National Gallery is not based on a former royal collection, but was begun as late as 1824 when the government reluctantly agreed to purchase 38 paintings belonging to a Russian émigré banker, John Julius Angerstein. The collection was originally put on public display at Angerstein's old residence, on Pall Mall, until today's purpose-built edifice was completed in 1838. A hostile press dubbed the gallery's diminutive dome and cupolas "pepperpots", and poured abuse on the Greek Revival architect, William Wilkins, who retreated into early retirement and died a year later.

The gallery now boasts a collection of more than 2300 paintings, whose virtue is not so much its size as its range, depth and quality. Among the 1000 paintings on permanent display are **Italian masterpieces** by the likes of Botticelli and Michelangelo, dazzling pieces by Velázquez and Goya, and an array of **Rembrandt** paintings that features some of his most searching portraits. In addition, the gallery has a particularly strong showing of **Impressionists**, with paintings by Monet, Degas, Van Gogh and Cézanne, plus several early Picassos. There are also showpieces by Turner, Reynolds and Gainsborough, but for a wider range of British art, head for Tate Britain (see p.60). **Special exhibitions** are held in the basement of the Sainsbury Wing and usually charge admission.

INFORMATION AND TOURS

Arrival There are four entrances to the National Gallery: Wilkins' original Portico Entrance up the steps from Trafalgar Square, the Getty Entrance on the ground floor to the east, the Sainsbury Wing to the west, and the back entrance on Orange Street. The Getty Entrance and the Sainsbury Wing both have an information–desk, which hands out free plans, and disabled access, with lifts to all floors.

Tours Plans (£1) and audioguides (£3.50) are available – much better, though, are the gallery's free guided tours,

which set off from the Sainsbury Wing foyer (daily 11.30am & 2.30pm, plus Fri 7pm; 1hr).

Eating To the right of the Getty Entrance is the *National Café* (Mon–Fri 8am–11pm, Sat 10am–11pm, Sun 10am–6pm), which has a self-service area, and a large brasserie, with an entrance on St Martin's Place. More formal dining is available at the *National Dining Rooms*, serving excellent British cuisine, over in the Sainsbury Wing (☎ 020 7747 2525).

The Sainsbury Wing

The original design for the gallery's modern **Sainsbury Wing** was dubbed by Prince Charles "a monstrous carbuncle on the face of a much-loved and elegant friend". So instead, the American husband-and-wife team of Venturi and Scott-Brown were commissioned to produce a softly-softly, postmodern adjunct, which playfully imitates elements of William Wilkins' Neoclassicism and even Nelson's Column and, most importantly, got the approval of Prince Charles, who laid the foundation stone in 1988.

Chronologically the gallery's collection begins in this wing, which houses the National's oldest paintings from the thirteenth to the fifteenth centuries, mostly early Italian Renaissance masterpieces, with a smattering of early Dutch, Flemish and German works.

Giotto to Van Eyck

The gallery's earliest works by **Giotto**, "the father of modern painting", and **Duccio**, a Sienese contemporary, are displayed in room 52. Meanwhile, next door, you can admire the extraordinarily vivid **Wilton Diptych**, one of the few English late medieval altarpieces to survive the Puritan iconoclasm of the Commonwealth. It was painted by an unknown fourteenth-century artist for the boy king Richard II, who is depicted being presented by his patron saints to the Virgin, Child and assorted angels.

TEN PAINTINGS NOT TO MISS

Wilton Dyptych Room 53
Battle of San Romano Paolo Uccello. Room 54
Arnolfini Portrait Jan van Eyck. Room 56
The Ambassadors Hans Holbein. Room 4
Self-Portrait at the Age of 63 Rembrandt van Rijn. Room 23
A Young Woman standing at a Virginal Johannes Vermeer. Room 25
The Cornfield John Constable. Room 34
Gare St Lazare Claude Monet. Room 43
After the Bath Edgar Degas. Room 46
Van Gogh's Chair Vincent Van Gogh. Room 45

Whatever you do, don't miss **Paolo Uccello**'s brilliant, blood-free *Battle of San Romano*, which dominates room 54. The painting commemorates a recent Florentine victory over her bitter Sienese rivals and once decorated a Medici bedroom as part of a three-panel frieze. Another Medici commission is *The Annunciation* by **Fra Filippo Lippi**, a beautifully balanced painting in which the poses of Gabriel and Mary carefully mirror one another, while the hand of God releasing the dove of the Holy Spirit provides the vanishing point.

Room 56 explores the beginnings of oil painting, and one of its early masters, **Jan van Eyck**, whose intriguing *Arnolfini Portrait* is celebrated for its complex symbolism. The picture has often been interpreted as a depiction of a marriage ceremony, though the theory is now strongly criticized, and the "bride" is thought simply to be fashionably round-bellied, rather than actually pregnant.

Botticelli to Piero della Francesca

Two contrasting Nativity paintings by **Botticelli** hang in room 57: the *Mystic Nativity* is unusual in that it features seven devils fleeing back into the Underworld, while in his *Adoration of the Kings*, Botticelli himself takes centre stage, as the best-dressed man at the gathering, resplendent in bright-red stockings and giving the audience a knowing look. Next door, in room 58, is his much-loved *Venus and Mars*, depicting a naked and replete Mars in deep postcoital sleep, watched over by a beautifully calm Venus, fully clothed and somewhat less overcome.

Further on, in room 62, hangs one of **Mantegna**'s best early works, *The Agony in the Garden*, which demonstrates a convincing use of perspective. Close by, the dazzling dawn sky in the painting on the same theme by his brother-in-law, **Giovanni Bellini**, shows the artist's celebrated mastery of natural light. Also in this room is one of Bellini's greatest portraits of the Venetian Doge *Leonardo Loredan*. Elsewhere, there are paintings from Netherlands and Germany, among them **Dürer**'s sympathetic portrait of his father (a goldsmith in Nuremberg), in room 65, which was presented to Charles I in 1636 by the artist's home town.

Finally, at the far end of the wing, in room 66, your eye will probably be drawn to **Piero della Francesca**'s monumental *Baptism of Christ*, one of his earliest surviving pictures, dating from the 1450s and a brilliant example of his immaculate compositional technique. Blindness forced Piero to stop painting some twenty years before his death, and to concentrate instead on his equally innovative work as a mathematician.

The main building

The collection continues in the gallery's **main building** with paintings from the sixteenth century to the early twentieth century. The account overleaf follows the collection more or less chronologically.

1

Veronese, Titian and Giorgione

The first room you come to from the Sainsbury Wing is the vast Wohl Room (room nine), containing mainly large-scale Venetian works. The largest of the lot is **Paolo Veronese**'s lustrous *Family of Darius before Alexander*, its array of colourfully clad figures revealing the painter's remarkable skill in juxtaposing virtually the entire colour spectrum in a single canvas. Here too, at opposite ends of the room, are all four of Veronese's slightly discoloured *Allegories of Love* canvases, designed as ceiling paintings, perhaps for a bedchamber.

More Venetian works hang in room 10, including **Titian**'s consummate *La Schiavona*, a precisely executed portrait within a portrait. His colourful early masterpiece *Bacchus and Ariadne*, and his much gloomier *Death of Actaeon*, painted some fifty years later, amply demonstrate the painter's artistic development and longevity. *The Virgin and Child* is another typical late Titian, with the paint jabbed on and rubbed in. Also here are two perplexing paintings attributed to the elusive **Giorgione**, a highly original Venetian painter, only twenty of whose paintings survive.

Bronzino, Michelangelo, Raphael and da Vinci

In room 8, **Bronzino**'s strangely disturbing *Venus, Cupid, Folly and Time* is a classic piece of Mannerist eroticism, once owned by François I, the decadent, womanizing, sixteenth-century French king. (Incidentally, Cupid's foot features in the opening animated titles of *Monty Python's Flying Circus*.) Here too is **Michelangelo**'s early, unfinished *Entombment*, which depicts Christ's body being carried to the tomb, and the National's major paintings by **Raphael**. These range from early works such as *St Catherine of Alexandria*, whose sensuous serpentine pose is accentuated by the folds of her clothes, and the richly coloured *Mond Crucifixion*, both painted when the artist was in his twenties, to later works like *Pope Julius II* – his (and Michelangelo's) patron – a masterfully percipient portrait of old age.

To continue with the Italians, skip through the next couple of rooms to room 2, which boasts **Leonardo da Vinci**'s melancholic *Virgin of the Rocks* (the more famous *Da Vinci Code* version hangs in the Louvre) and the "Leonardo Cartoon" – a preparatory drawing for a painting which, like so many of Leonardo's projects, was never completed. The cartoon was known only to scholars until the gallery bought it for £800,000 in the mid-1960s. In 1987, it gained further notoriety when an ex-soldier blasted the work with a sawn-off shotgun in protest at the political status quo.

Holbein, Cranach, Bosch and Bruegel

Room 4 contains several masterpieces by **Hans Holbein**, most notably his extraordinarily detailed double portrait, *The Ambassadors* – note the anamorphic skull

---

BORIS ANREP'S FLOOR MOSAICS

One of the most overlooked features of the National Gallery is the mind-boggling **floor mosaics** executed by Russian-born Boris Anrep between 1927 and 1952 on the landings of the main staircase leading to the Central Hall (and now in need of some restoration). The *Awakening of the Muses*, on the halfway landing, features a bizarre collection of famous figures from the 1930s – Virginia Woolf appears as Clio (Muse of History) and Greta Garbo plays Melpomene (Muse of Tragedy). The mosaic on the landing closest to the Central Hall is made up of fifteen small scenes illustrating the *Modern Virtues*: Anna Akhmatova is saved by an angel from the Leningrad Blockade in *Compassion*; T.S. Eliot contemplates the Loch Ness Monster and Einstein's Theory of Relativity in *Leisure*; Bertrand Russell gazes on a naked woman in *Lucidity*; Edith Sitwell, book in hand, glides across a monster-infested chasm on a twig in *Sixth Sense*; and in the largest composition, *Defiance*, Churchill appears in combat gear on the white cliffs of Dover, raising two fingers to a monster in the shape of a swastika.

in the foreground. Among the other works by Holbein is his intriguing *A Lady with a Squirrel and a Starling*, and his striking portrait of the 16-year-old Christina of Denmark, part of a series commissioned by Henry VIII when he was looking for a potential fourth wife. Look out, too, for Holbein's contemporary, **Lucas Cranach the Elder**, whose *Cupid Complaining to Venus* is a none-too-subtle message about dangerous romantic liaisons – Venus's wonderfully fashionable headgear only emphasizes her nakedness.

Next door, in room 5, hangs the National's one and only work by **Hieronymus Bosch**, *Christ Mocked*, in which four manic tormentors (one wearing an Islamic crescent moon and a Jewish star) bear down on Jesus. The painting that grabs most folks' attention, however, is **Massys**'s caricatured portrait of an old woman looking like a pantomime dame. Nearby, in room 14, you'll find the gallery's only **Bruegel**, the tiny *Adoration of the Magi*, with some very motley-looking folk crowding in on the infant; only the Black Magus looks at all regal.

Claude, Poussin and Dutch landscapes

The English painter **J.M.W. Turner** left specific instructions in his will for two of his **Claude**-influenced paintings to be hung alongside a couple of the French painter's landscapes. All four now hang in the octagonal room 15, and were slashed by a homeless teenager in 1982 in an attempt to draw attention to his plight. Claude's dreamy classical landscapes and seascapes, and the mythological (often erotic) scenes of **Poussin**, were favourites of aristocrats on the Grand Tour, and made both artists very famous in their time. Claude's *Enchanted Castle*, in particular, caught the imagination of the Romantics, allegedly inspiring Keats' *Ode to a Nightingale*. Nowadays, rooms 19 and 20, which are given over entirely to these two French artists, are among the quietest in the gallery.

Of the Dutch landscapes in rooms 21 and 22, those by **Aelbert Cuyp**'s stand out due to the warm Italianate light which suffuses his works, but the finest of all is, without a doubt, **Hobbema**'s tree-lined *Avenue, Middelharnis*. The market for such landscapes at the time was limited, however, and Hobbema quit painting at the age of just 30. **Jacob van Ruisdael**, Hobbema's teacher, whose works are on display nearby, also went hungry for most of his life.

Rembrandt and Vermeer

Rooms 23 and 24 feature mostly works by **Rembrandt**, including the highly theatrical *Belshazzar's Feast*, painted for a rich Jewish patron. Look out also for two of Rembrandt's searching self-portraits, painted thirty years apart, with the melancholic *Self Portrait Aged 63*, from the last year of his life, making a strong contrast to the sprightly early work. Similarly, the joyful portrait of Saskia, Rembrandt's wife, from the most successful period of his life, contrasts with his more contemplative depiction of his mistress, Hendrickje, who was hauled up in front of the city authorities for living "like a whore" with Rembrandt. The portraits of Jacob Trip and his wife, Margaretha de Geer, are among the most painfully realistic depictions of old age in the entire gallery.

Room 25 harbours **de Hooch**'s classic *A Woman and her Maid in a Courtyard*, and a self-portrait by Carel Fabritius, one of Rembrandt's pupils. Fabritius died in the explosion of the Delft gunpowder store, the subject of another painting in the room. Also here is the seventeenth-century **van Hoogstraten Peepshow**, a box of tricks which reflects the Dutch obsession of the time with perspectival and optical devices. Two typically serene works by **Vermeer** hang nearby and provide a counterpoint to one another: each features a *Young Woman at a Virginal*, but where she stands in one, she sits in the other; she's viewed from the right and then the left, in shadow and then in light and so on.

1

Rubens

Three adjoining rooms, known collectively as room 29, are dominated by the expansive, fleshy canvases of **Peter Paul Rubens**, the Flemish painter whom Charles I summoned to the English court. The one woman with her clothes on is the artist's future sister-in-law, Susanna Fourment, whose delightful portrait became known as *Le Chapeau de Paille* (*The Straw Hat*) – though the hat is actually made of black felt and decorated with white feathers. At the age of 54, Rubens married Susanna's younger sister, Helena (she was just 16), the model for all three goddesses posing in the later 1630s version of *The Judgement of Paris*. Also displayed here are Rubens' rather more subdued landscapes, one of which, the *View of Het Steen*, shows off the very fine prospect from the Flemish country mansion Rubens bought in 1635.

Velázquez, El Greco, Van Dyck and Caravaggio

The cream of the National Gallery's Spanish works are displayed in room 30, among them **Velázquez**'s *Rokeby Venus*, one of the gallery's most famous pictures. Velázquez is thought to have painted just four nudes in his lifetime, of which only the *Rokeby Venus* survives, an ambiguously narcissistic image that was slashed in 1914 by suffragette Mary Richardson, who loved the picture but was revolted by the way "men gaped at it all day".

Another Flemish painter summoned by Charles I was **Anthony van Dyck**, whose *Equestrian Portrait of Charles I*, in room 31, is a fine example of the work that made him a favourite of the Stuart court, romanticizing the monarch as a dashing horseman. Nearby is the artist's double portrait of *Lord John and Lord Bernard Stuart*, two dapper young cavaliers about to set out on their Grand Tour in 1639, and destined to die fighting for the royalist cause shortly afterwards in the Civil War.

Caravaggio's art is represented in the vast room 32 by the typically salacious *Boy Bitten by Lizard*, and the melodramatic *Christ at Emmaus*. The latter was a highly influential painting: never before had biblical scenes been depicted with such naturalism – a beardless and haloless Christ surrounded by scruffy disciples. At the time it was deemed to be blasphemous, and, like many of Caravaggio's religious commissions, was eventually rejected by the customers. One of the most striking paintings in this room is Giordano's *Perseus turning Phineas and his Followers to Stone*, in which the hero is dramatically depicted in sapphire blue, with half the throng already petrified.

British art 1750–1850

When the Tate Gallery opened in 1897, the vast bulk of the National's British art was transferred there, leaving just a few highly prized works behind. Among these are several superb late masterpieces by **Turner**, two of which herald the new age of steam: *Rain, Steam and Speed* and *The Fighting Temeraire*, in which a ghostly apparition of the veteran battleship from Trafalgar is pulled into harbour by a youthful, fire-snorting tug, a scene witnessed first-hand by the artist in Rotherhithe. Here, too, is **Constable**'s *Hay Wain*, painted in and around his father's mill in Suffolk, as is the irrepressibly popular *Cornfield*. There are landscapes, as well as the portraits, by **Thomas Gainsborough** – his feathery, light technique is seen to superb effect in *Morning Walk*, a double portrait of a pair of newlyweds. **Joshua Reynolds**' contribution is a portrait, *Lady Cockburn and her Three Sons*, in which the three boys clamber endearingly over their mother. And finally, the most striking portrait in the whole room is George Stubbs's pin-sharp depiction of the racehorse Whistlejacket rearing up on its hindlegs.

More works by Gainsborough and Reynolds hang in room 35, including the only known self-portrait of the former with his family, painted in 1747 when he was just 20 years old. On the opposite wall are the six paintings from **Hogarth**'s *Marriage à la Mode*, a witty, moral tale that allowed the artist to give vent to his pet hates: bourgeois hypocrisy,

1

snobbery and bad (ie Continental) taste. In the ornate, domed Central Hall (room 36) hangs Reynolds' dramatic portrait of the extraordinarily effeminate Colonel Tarleton.

French art 1700–1860

The large room of British art (room 34) is bookended with two small rooms of French art. In room 33, among works by the likes of Fragonard, Boucher and Watteau, there's a portrait of Louis XV's mistress in the year of her death and a spirited self-portrait by the equally well-turned-out Elisabeth Louise **Vigée-Lebrun**, one of only three women artists in the National Gallery.

In room 41, the most popular painting is **Paul Delaroche**'s slick and pretentious *Execution of Lady Jane Grey*, in which the blindfolded, white-robed, 17-year-old queen stoically awaits her fate. Look out, too, for **Gustave Courbet**'s languorous *Young Ladies on the Bank of the Seine*, innocent enough to the modern eye, scandalous when it was first shown in 1857 due to the ladies' "state of undress".

Impressionism and beyond

Among the gallery's busiest section are the four magnificent rooms (43–46) of Impressionist and post-Impressionist paintings, where rehangings are frequent. The National boasts several key works by **Manet**, including his famous *Music in the Tuileries Gardens*, and the unfinished *Execution of Maximilian*, one of three versions he painted. There are also canvases from every period of **Monet**'s long life: from early works like *The Thames below Westminster* and *Gare St Lazare* to the late, almost abstract paintings executed in his beloved garden at Giverny.

Other major Impressionist works include **Renoir**'s *Umbrellas*, **Seurat**'s classic pointillist canvas, *Bathers at Asnières* – one of the National's most reproduced paintings – and **Pissarro**'s *Boulevard Montmartre at Night*. There are also several townscapes from Pissarro's period of exile, when he lived in south London, during the Franco-Prussian War. There's a comprehensive showing of **Cézanne** with works spanning the great artist's long life. *The Painter's Father*, one of his earliest extant works, was originally painted onto the walls of his father's house outside Aix. *The Bathers*, by contrast, is a late work, whose angular geometry exercised an enormous influence on the Cubism of Picasso and Braque.

Van Gogh's famous, dazzling *Sunflowers* hangs here, the beguiling *Van Gogh's Chair*, dating from his stay in Arles with Gauguin, and *Wheatfield with Cypresses*, which typifies the intense work he produced shortly before his suicide. Finally, look out for **Picasso**'s sentimental Blue Period *Child with a Dove*; **Rousseau**'s imagined junglescape, *Surprised!*; Klimt's *Hermine Gallia*, in which the sitter wears a dress designed by the artist; and a trio of superb **Degas** canvases: *Miss La-La at the Cirque Fernando*, the languorous pastel drawing *After the Bath* and the luxuriant red-orange *La Coiffure*.

National Portrait Gallery

St Martin's Place • Daily 10am–6pm, Thurs & Fri till 9pm • Free • ☏ 020 7312 2463, ⊕ npg.org.uk • ⊖ Charing Cross

Around the east side of the National Gallery lurks the **National Portrait Gallery** founded in 1856 to house uplifting depictions of the good and the great. Though it undoubtedly has some fine works among its collection of over 10,000 portraits, many of the studies are of less interest than their subjects. Nevertheless, it's interesting to trace who has been deemed worthy of admiration at any one time: aristocrats and artists in previous centuries, warmongers and imperialists in the early decades of the twentieth century, writers and poets in the 1930s and 1940s. The most popular part of the museum by far is the contemporary section, where the whole thing degenerates into a sort of thinking person's Madame Tussauds, with photos and some very dubious portraits of today's celebrities.

INFORMATION

Arrival There are two entrances to the NPG: disabled access is from Orange Street, while the main entrance is on St Martin's Place. Once inside, head straight for the Ondaatje Wing, where there's an information desk – here you can pick up a Sound Guide (£3.50) which gives useful biographical background on many of the pictures.

Exhibitions The gallery's special exhibitions (for which there is often an entrance charge) are well worth seeing – the photography shows, in particular, are often excellent. **Eating** There's a little café in the basement, and the excellent but pricey rooftop *Portrait* restaurant on Floor 3, with incredible views over Trafalgar Square (☎ 020 7312 2490).

The Tudors and Stuarts

To follow the collection chronologically, take the escalator to the trio of **Tudor Galleries**, on Floor 2. Here, you'll find Tudor portraits of pre-Tudor kings as well as Tudor personalities: a stout **Cardinal Wolsey** looking like the butcher's son he was and the future **Bloody Mary** looking positively benign in a portrait celebrating her reinstatement to the line of succession in 1544. Pride of place goes to Holbein's larger-than-life cartoon of **Henry VIII**, showing the king as a macho buck against a modish Renaissance background, with his sickly son and heir, **Edward VI**, striking a deliberately similar pose close by. The most eye-catching canvas is the anamorphic portrait of Edward, an illusionistic painting that must be viewed from the side.

Also displayed here are several classic propaganda portraits of the formidable Elizabeth I and her dandyish favourites. Further on hangs the only known painting of **Shakespeare** from life, a subdued image in which the Bard sports a gold-hoop earring; appropriately enough, it was the first picture acquired by the gallery. To keep to the chronology, you must turn left here into room 5, where the quality of portraiture goes up a notch thanks to the appointment of Van Dyck as court painter. Among all the dressed-to-kill Royalists in room 5, **Oliver Cromwell** looks dishevelled but masterful, while an overdressed, haggard **Charles II** hangs in room 7 alongside his long-suffering Portuguese wife and several of his mistresses, including the orange-seller-turned-actress **Nell Gwynne**.

The eighteenth century

The **eighteenth century** begins in room 9, with members of the **Kit-Kat Club**, a group of Whig patriots, painted by one of its members, Godfrey Kneller, a naturalized German artist, whose self-portrait can be found in room 10. Next door, room 11 contains a hotchpotch of visionaries including a tartan-free **Bonnie Prince Charlie** and his saviour, the petite Flora MacDonald. In room 12 there are several fine self-portraits, including a dashing one of the Scot Allan Ramsay. Room 14 is dominated by *The Death of Pitt the Elder*, who collapsed in the House of Lords having risen from his sickbed to try and save the rebellious American colonies for Britain – despite the painting's title, he didn't die for another month.

In room 17, you'll find a bold likeness of **Lord Nelson**, unusually out of uniform, along with an idealized portrait of Nelson's mistress, **Lady Emma Hamilton**, painted by the smitten George Romney. Also here is a portrait of **George IV** and the twice-widowed Catholic woman, Maria Fitzherbert, whom he married without his father's consent. His official wife, **Queen Caroline**, is depicted at the adultery trial at which she was acquitted, and again, with sleeves rolled up, ready for her sculpture lessons, in an audacious portrait by Thomas Lawrence, who was called to testify on his conduct with the queen during the painting of the portrait.

The Romantics dominate room 18, with the ailing **John Keats** painted posthumously by Joseph Severn, in whose arms he died in Rome. Elsewhere, there's **Lord Byron** in Albanian garb, an open-collared **Percy Bysshe Shelley**, with his wife, Mary, nearby, and her mother, **Mary Wollstonecraft**, opposite.

The Victorians

Down on the first floor, the **Victorians** feature rather too many stuffy royals, dour men of science and engineering, and stern statesmen such as those lining the corridor of

1

room 22. Centre stage, in room 21, is a comical statue of **Victoria and Albert** in Anglo-Saxon garb. The best place to head for is room 24, which contains a deteriorated portrait of the **Brontë sisters** as seen by their disturbed brother Branwell; you can still see where he painted himself out, leaving a ghostly blur between Charlotte and Emily. Nearby are the poetic duo, **Robert** and **Elizabeth Barrett Browning**, looking totally Gothic in their grim Victorian dress.

In room 28, it's impossible to miss the striking Edwardian portrait of **Lady Colin Campbell**, posing in a luxuriant black silk dress. Finally, in room 29, where there are some excellent **John Singer Sargent** portraits, and several works by students of the Slade: **Augustus John**, looking very confident and dapper at the age of just 22, his sister, Gwen John, **Walter Sickert** (by Philip Wilson Steer) and Steer (by Sickert). Steer founded the New English Arts Club, at which the last two portraits were originally exhibited.

The twentieth century and beyond

The **twentieth-century** collection begins in room 30, with Sargent's group portrait of the upper-crust generals responsible for the slaughter of World War I. The interwar years are then generously covered in room thirty one. The faces on display here are frequently rotated, but look out for Sickert's excellent small, smouldering portrait of **Churchill**, Augustus John's portrayal of a ruby-lipped Dylan Thomas, Ben Nicolson's double portrait of himself and Barbara Hepworth and a whole host of works by, or depicting, the **Bloomsbury Group**.

Out on the Balcony Gallery, there's a who's who (or was who) of **Britain 1960–90**. Even here, amid the photos of the Swinging Sixties, there are quite a few genuine works of art by the likes of Leon Kossoff, R.B. Kitaj, Lucien Freud and Francis Bacon. The **Contemporary Galleries** occupy the ground floor, and are a constantly changing, unashamedly populist trot through the media personalities of the last decade or so. As well as a host of photo portraits, you can sample such delights as Michael Craig Martin's LCD portrait of architect Zaha Hadid, or the cartoon-like quadruple portrait of pop band Blur by Julian Opie.

Whitehall

Whitehall, the unusually broad avenue connecting Trafalgar Square to Parliament Square, is synonymous with the faceless, pinstriped bureaucracy charged with the day-to-day running of the country. Yet during the sixteenth and seventeenth centuries, it was, in fact, the chief London residence of the kings and queens of England. **Whitehall Palace** started out as the London seat of the Archbishop of York, but was confiscated and enlarged by Henry VIII

TRAFALGAR SQUARE & WHITEHALL

● **CAFÉ**
Café in the Crypt — 1
● **RESTAURANT**
National Dining Rooms — 2

● **ACCOMMODATION**
Northumberland House — 1
Sanctuary House — 2

● **PUBS & BARS**
The Chandos — 1
St Stephen's Tavern — 2

CHARLES I

Stranded on a traffic island to the south of Nelson's Column, on the site of the medieval **Charing Cross** (see p.136), an equestrian statue of **Charles I** gazes down Whitehall to the place of his execution in 1649, outside the Banqueting House. The king wore several shirts in case he shivered in the cold, which the crowd would take to be fear, and once his head was chopped off, it was then sewn back on again for burial in Windsor – a very British touch. The statue itself was sculpted in 1633 and was originally intended for a site in Roehampton, but was sold off during the Commonwealth to a local brazier, John Rivett, with strict instructions to melt it down. Rivett made a small fortune selling bronze mementoes, allegedly from the metal, while all the time concealing the statue in the vaults of St Paul's, Covent Garden. After the Restoration, in 1675, the statue was erected on the very spot where eight of those who had signed the king's death warrant were disembowelled in 1660. Until 1859, "King Charles the Martyr" Holy Day (Jan 30) was a day of fasting, and his execution is still commemorated here on the last Sunday in January with a parade by the royalist wing of the Civil War Society.

after a fire at Westminster Palace forced the king to find alternative accommodation; it was here that he celebrated his marriage to Anne Boleyn in 1533, and here that he died fourteen years later. Described by one contemporary chronicler as nothing but "a heap of houses erected at diverse times and of different models, made continuous", it boasted some two thousand rooms and stretched for half a mile along the Thames. Very little survived the fire of 1698 and, subsequently, the royal residence shifted to St James's and Kensington.

Since then, all the key governmental ministries and offices have migrated here, rehousing themselves on an ever-increasing scale. The **Foreign & Commonwealth Office**, for example, occupies a palatial Italianate building, built by George Gilbert Scott in 1868, and well worth a visit if you can gain access (☎020 7008 1500). The process reached its apogee with the grimly bland **Ministry of Defence (MoD)** building, completed in 1957, underneath which is Britain's most expensive military bunker, £125 million Pindar.

Banqueting House

Whitehall • Mon–Sat 10am–5pm • £5 • ☎ 020 3166 6154, ⓦ hrp.org.uk • ⊜ Charing Cross

The only sections of Whitehall Palace to survive the 1698 fire were Cardinal Wolsey's wine cellars (now beneath the Ministry of Defence) and Inigo Jones's **Banqueting House**, the first Palladian (or Neoclassical) building to be built in central London. Opened in 1622 with a performance of Ben Jonson's *Masque of Angers*, the Banqueting House is still used for state occasions (and, therefore, may be closed at short notice). The one room open to the public – the main hall upstairs – is well worth seeing for the superlative ceiling paintings, commissioned by Charles I from **Rubens** and installed in 1635. A glorification of the divine right of kings, the panels depict the union of England and Scotland, the peaceful reign of Charles's father, James I and, finally, his apotheosis.

Given the subject of the paintings, it's ironic that it was through the Banqueting House that **Charles I** walked in 1649 before stepping onto the executioner's scaffold from one of its windows. **Oliver Cromwell** moved into Whitehall Palace in 1654, having declared himself Lord Protector, and kept open table in the Banqueting House for the officers of his New Model Army; he died here in 1658. Two years later **Charles II** celebrated the Restoration here, and kept open house for his adoring public – Samuel Pepys recalls seeing the underwear of one of his mistresses, Lady Castlemaine, hanging out to dry in the palace's Privy Garden. (Charles housed two mistresses and his wife here, with a back entrance onto the river for courtesans.) To appreciate the place fully, it's worth getting hold of one of the free audioguides.

1

Horse Guards: Household Cavalry Museum

Whitehall • Daily March–Sept 10am–6pm; Oct–Feb 10am–5pm • £6 • ☎ 020 7930 3070, ⓦ householdcavalrymuseum.org.uk • ⊖ Charing Cross or Westminster

During the day, two mounted sentries and two horseless colleagues are posted to protect **Horse Guards**, a modest building begun in 1745 by William Kent, and originally the main gateway to St James's and Buckingham Palace. The black dot over the number two on the building's clock face denotes the hour at which Charles I was executed close by in 1649. Round the back of the building, you'll find the **Household Cavalry Museum** where you can try on a trooper's elaborate uniform, complete a horse quiz and learn about the regiments' history. With the stables immediately adjacent, it's a sweet-smelling place, and – horse-lovers will be pleased to know – you can see the beasts in their stalls through a glass screen. Don't miss the pocket riot act on display, which ends with the wise warning: "must read correctly: variance fatal".

Downing Street

ⓦ number10.gov.uk • ⊖ Westminster

London's most famous address, **10 Downing Street**, is the terraced house that was presented to the First Lord of the Treasury, Robert Walpole, Britain's first prime minister or PM, by George II in the 1730s. It has been the PM's residence ever since, with no. 11 home of the Chancellor of the Exchequer (in charge of the country's finances) since 1806, and no. 12 home of the government's Chief Whip (in charge of party discipline). These three are the only remaining bit of the original seventeenth-century cul-de-sac, though all are now interconnected and house much larger complexes than might appear from the outside. The public have been kept at bay since 1990, when Margaret Thatcher ordered a pair of iron gates to be installed at the junction with Whitehall, an act more symbolic than effective – a year later the IRA lobbed a mortar into the street from Horse Guards Parade, coming within a whisker of wiping out the entire Tory cabinet.

Churchill War Rooms

King Charles Street • Daily 9.30am–6pm • £14.50 • ☎ 020 7930 6961, ⓦ cwr.iwm.org.uk • ⊖ Westminster

In 1938, in anticipation of Nazi air raids, the basement of the Treasury building on King Charles Street was converted into the **Churchill War Rooms**, protected by a three-foot-thick concrete slab, reinforced with steel rails and tramlines. It was here that Winston Churchill directed operations and held cabinet meetings for the duration of

---

CHANGING OF THE GUARD

Changing the Guard takes place at two London locations: the Foot Guards hold theirs outside Buckingham Palace (May–July daily 11.30am; Sept–April alternate days; no ceremony if it rains; ⓦ changing-the-guard.com), but the more impressive one is held on Horse Guards Parade, behind Horse Guards, where a squad of mounted Household Cavalry arrives from Hyde Park to relieve the guards at the Horse Guards building on Whitehall (Mon–Sat 11am, Sun 10am) – alternatively, if you miss the whole thing, turn up at 4pm for the daily inspection by the Officer of the Guard, who checks the soldiers haven't knocked off early. If you want to see something grander, check out **Trooping the Colour**, and the **Beating Retreat**, which both take place in June (see p.25).

The Queen is colonel-in-chief of the seven **Household Regiments**: the Life Guards (who dress in red and white) and the Blues and Royals (who dress in blue and white) – princes William and Harry were both in the Blues and Royals – are the two Household Cavalry Regiments; while the Grenadier, Coldstream, Scots, Irish and Welsh guards make up the Foot Guards. The Foot Guards can only be told apart by the plumes (or lack of them) in their busbies (fur helmets), and by the arrangement of their tunic buttons. The three senior regiments (Grenadier, Coldstream and Scots) date back to the seventeenth century, as do the Life Guards and the Blues and Royals. All seven regiments still form part of the modern army as well as performing ceremonial functions such as the Changing of the Guard.

WHITEHALL STATUES AND THE CENOTAPH

The **statues** dotted along Whitehall recall the days of the empire. Kings and military leaders predominate, starting outside Horse Guards with the **2nd Duke of Cambridge** (1819–1904), whose horse was shot from under him in the Crimean War. As commander-in-chief of the British Army, he was so resistant to military reform that he had to be forcibly retired. Next stands the **8th Duke of Devonshire** (1833–1908), who failed to rescue General Gordon from the Siege of Khartoum in 1884–85. Appropriately enough, **Lord Haig** (1861–1928), who was responsible for sending thousands to their deaths in World War I, faces the Cenotaph, his horse famously poised ready for urination. Before you get to the Cenotaph, there's a striking new memorial to the **Women of World War II**, featuring seventeen uniforms hanging on a large bronze plinth.

At the end of Whitehall, in the middle of the road, stands Edwin Lutyens' **Cenotaph**, built in 1919 in wood and plaster to commemorate the Armistice, and rebuilt in Portland stone the following year. The stark monument, which eschews Christian imagery, is inscribed simply with the words "The Glorious Dead" – the lost of World War I, who, it was once calculated, would take three and a half days to pass by the Cenotaph marching four abreast. The memorial remains the focus of the **Remembrance Sunday** ceremony held on the Sunday nearest November 11. Between the wars, however, a much more powerful, two-minute silence was observed throughout the entire British Empire every year on November 11 at 11am, the exact time of the armistice at the end of World War I.

World War II. By the end of the war, the six-acre site included a hospital, canteen and shooting range, as well as sleeping quarters; tunnels fan out from the complex to outlying government ministries, and also, it is rumoured, to Buckingham Palace itself, allowing the Royal Family a quick getaway to exile in Canada (via Charing Cross station) in the event of a Nazi invasion.

The rooms remain much as they were when they were abandoned on VJ Day, August 15, 1945, and make for an atmospheric underground trot through wartime London. To bring the place to life, pick up an audioguide, which includes various eyewitness accounts by folks who worked here. The best rooms are Winnie's very modest emergency bedroom (though he himself rarely stayed here, preferring to watch the air raids from the roof of the building, or rest his head at the *Savoy Hotel*), and the Map Room, left exactly as it was on VJ Day, with its rank of multicoloured telephones, copious ashtrays, and floor-to-ceiling maps covering every theatre of war.

Churchill Museum

When you get to Churchill's secret telephone hotline direct to the American president, signs direct you to the self-contained Churchill Museum, which begins with his finest moment, when he took over as PM and Britain stood alone against the Nazis. You can hear snippets of Churchill's speeches and check out his trademark bowler, spotted bow tie and half-chewed Havana, not to mention his wonderful burgundy zip-up "romper suit". Fortunately for the curators, Churchill had an extremely eventful life and was great for a soundbite, so there are plenty of interesting anecdotes to keep you engaged.

Houses of Parliament

Parliament Square • ☎ 020 7219 4272, ⓦ parliament.uk • ⊖ Westminster

The Palace of Westminster, better known as the **Houses of Parliament**, is among London's best-known icons. The city's finest Victorian edifice and a symbol of a nation once confident of its place at the centre of the world, it's best viewed from the south side of the river, where the likes of Monet and Turner once set up their easels. The building's most famous feature is its ornate, gilded clock tower popularly known as **Big Ben**, at its most impressive when lit up at night. Strictly speaking, "Big Ben" refers only to the thirteen-ton bell that strikes the hour (and is broadcast across the world by the

1

BBC), and takes its name from either the former Commissioner of Works, Benjamin Hall, or a popular heavyweight boxer of the time, Benjamin Caunt.

The original Palace of Westminster was built by **Edward the Confessor** in the eleventh century to allow him to watch over the building of his abbey. Westminster then served as the seat of all the English monarchs until a fire forced Henry VIII to decamp to Whitehall. The Lords have always convened at the palace, but it was only following Henry's death that the House of Commons moved from the abbey's Chapter House into the palace's St Stephen's Chapel.

In 1834, a fire reduced the old palace to rubble. Today, save for Westminster Hall, and a few pieces of the old structure buried deep within the interior, everything you see today is the work of **Charles Barry**, who wanted to create something that expressed national greatness through the use of Gothic and Elizabethan styles. The resulting orgy of honey-coloured pinnacles, turrets and tracery is the greatest achievement of the Gothic Revival. Inside, the Victorian love of mock-Gothic detail is evident in the maze of over one thousand committee rooms and offices, the fittings of which were largely the responsibility of Barry's assistant, **Augustus Pugin**.

INFORMATION AND TOURS

Sitting times To find out exact "sitting times" and the dates of "recesses" (holiday closures), phone ☎ 020 7219 4272, or visit ⊛ parliament.uk. If Parliament is in session a Union flag flies from the southernmost tower, the Victoria Tower; at night there's a light above the clock face on Big Ben.

Public galleries To watch proceedings in either the House of Commons – the livelier of the two – or the House of Lords, simply join the queue for the public galleries outside St Stephen's Gate. The public are let in slowly from about 4pm onwards on Mondays and Tuesdays, from around 1pm Wednesdays, noon on Thursdays, and 10am on Sitting Fridays. Security is tight and the whole procedure can take an hour or more, so to avoid the queues, turn up an hour or so later or on a Sitting Friday.

Question Time UK citizens can attend Question Time – when the House of Commons is at its liveliest – which takes place in the first hour (Mon–Thurs) and Prime Minister's Question Time (Wed only), but they must book in advance with their local MP (☎ 020 7219 3000).

Guided tours Throughout the year there are also weekly guided tours (Sat 9.15am–4.30pm; 1hr 15min; £15); with daily ones during the summer opening (Mon–Sat) – in both cases it's a good idea to book in advance (☎ 0844 847 1672). All year round, UK residents are entitled to a free guided tour of the palace, as well as up Big Ben (Mon–Fri 9.15am, 11.15am & 2.15pm; 1hr 15min; no under-11s); both need to be organized through your local MP.

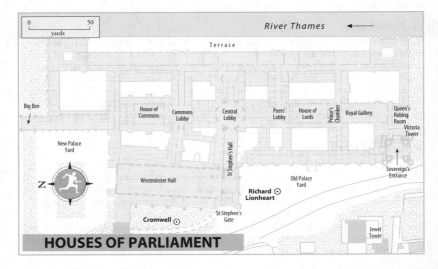

HOUSES OF PARLIAMENT

Westminster Hall

Virtually the only relic of the medieval palace is the bare expanse of **Westminster Hall**, which you enter after passing through security. Built by William II in 1099, it was saved from the 1834 fire by the timely intervention of the PM, Lord Melbourne, who took charge of the firefighting himself. The sheer scale of the hall – 240ft by 60ft – and its huge oak hammerbeam roof, added by Richard II in the late fourteenth century, make it one of the most magnificent secular medieval halls in Europe. It has also witnessed some 900 years of English history and been used for the lying-in-state of members of the Royal Family and a select few non-royals. Until 1821 every royal coronation banquet was held here and during the ceremony, the Royal Champion would ride into the hall in full armour to challenge any who dared dispute the sovereign's right to the throne.

Until the nineteenth century the hall was also used as the country's highest court of law: **William Wallace** had to wear a laurel crown during his treason trial here; **Thomas More** was sentenced to be hung, drawn and quartered (though in the end was simply beheaded); **Guy Fawkes**, the Catholic caught trying to blow up Parliament on November 5, 1605, was also tried here and actually hanged, drawn and quartered in Old Palace Yard. The trial of **Charles I** took place here, but the king refused to take his hat off, since he did not accept the court's legitimacy. **Oliver Cromwell**, whose statue now stands outside the hall, was sworn in here as Lord Protector in 1653, only to have his head stuck on a spike above the hall after the Restoration – it remained there for several decades until a storm dislodged it. It now resides in a secret location at Cromwell's old college in Cambridge University.

St Stephen's Hall

From Westminster Hall, visitors pass through the tiny **St Stephen's Hall**, designed by Barry as a replica of the Gothic chapel built by Edward I, where the Commons met from 1550 until the 1834 fire. It was into that chapel that Charles I entered with an armed guard in 1642 in a vain attempt to arrest five MPs who had made a speedy escape down the river – "I see my birds have flown", he is supposed to have said. Shortly afterwards, the Civil War began, and no monarch has entered the Commons since.

Central Lobby

Next you come to the bustling, octagonal **Central Lobby**, where constituents can "lobby" their MPs. In the tiling of the lobby Pugin inscribed the Biblical quote in Latin: "Except the Lord keep the house, they labour in vain that build it". In view of what happened to the architects, the sentiment seems like an indictment of parliamentary morality – Pugin ended up in Bedlam mental hospital and Barry died from overwork within months of completing the job. It was in the previous lobby, in 1812, that Spencer Perceval, the only British prime minister to be assassinated, was shot by a merchant whose business had been ruined by the Napoleonic Wars.

The House of Commons

If you're going to listen to proceedings in the **House of Commons**, you'll be asked to sign a form vowing not to cause a disturbance and then led up to the Public Gallery. Protests from the gallery were, in fact, once a fairly regular occurrence: suffragettes have poured flour, farmers have dumped dung, Irish Nationalists have lobbed tear gas, and lesbians have abseiled down into the chamber. Since an incendiary bomb in May 1941 destroyed Barry's original chamber, what you see now is a rather lifeless postwar reconstruction. Barry's design was modelled on the palace's original St Stephen's Hall, hence the choir-stall arrangement of the MPs' benches. Members of the cabinet (and the opposition's shadow cabinet) occupy the two "front benches"; the rest are "backbenchers". To avoid debates degenerating into physical combat, MPs are not allowed to cross the red

1

lines – which are exactly two swords' length apart – on the floor of the chamber during a debate, hence the expression "toeing the party line". The chamber is at its busiest during Question Time, though if too many of the 646 MPs turn up, a large number have to remain standing, as the House only has 427 seats. For much of the time, however, the chamber is almost empty, with just a handful of MPs present from each party.

The House of Lords

On the other side of the Central Lobby, a corridor leads to the **House of Lords** (or Upper House), a far dozier establishment peopled by unelected Lords and Ladies, plus a smattering of bishops. Their home boasts much grander decor than the Commons, full of regal gold and scarlet, and dominated by a canopied gold throne where the Queen sits for the state opening of Parliament in November. Directly in front of the throne, the Lord Chancellor runs the proceedings from the scarlet Woolsack, an enormous cushion stuffed with wool, which harks back to the time when it was England's principal export. Until 1999, there were 1000-plus hereditary Lords (over a quarter of whom had been to Eton) in the House. Most rarely bothered to turn up, but in emergencies, they could be (and were) called upon by the Conservatives, to ensure a right-wing victory in a crucial vote. Today, just ninety hereditary peers sit in the House, along with 26 senior bishops, while the rest are made up of life peers, appointed by the Queen on the advice of the Prime Minister. However, for the most part, the Lords have very little real power, as they can only advise and review parliamentary bills.

The royal apartments

If the House of Lords appeals, you can see more pomp and glitter by going on a **guided tour** (see p.50). You'll be asked to enter at the **Sovereign's Entrance** below Victoria Tower, where the Queen arrives in her coach for the state opening. Then, it's up the Royal Staircase to the Norman Porch, every nook of which is stuffed with busts of eminent statesmen. Next door is the **Queen's Robing Chamber**, which boasts a superb coffered ceiling and lacklustre Arthurian frescoes. As the name suggests, this is the room where the monarch dons the crown jewels before entering the Lords for the opening of Parliament. Beyond here you enter the **Royal Gallery**, a cavernous writing room for the House of Lords, hung with portraits of royals past and present, and two 45-foot-long frescoes of Trafalgar and Waterloo. Before entering the House of Lords itself, you pass through **Prince's Chamber**, commonly known as the Tudor Room after the numerous portraits that line the walls, including Henry VIII and all six of his wives. The tour then takes you through both Houses, St Stephen's Hall and finally Westminster Hall (all described above).

Jewel Tower

Daily April–Oct 10am–5pm; Nov–March 10am–4pm • EH • £3.20 • ☎ 020 7222 2219 • ⊖ Westminster

The **Jewel Tower** across the road from the Sovereign's Entrance, is the only other major remnant of the medieval palace apart from Westminster Hall. Constructed in 1365 by Edward III as a giant strongbox for his most valuable possessions, the tower formed the southwestern corner of the original exterior fortifications (there's a bit of moat left, too), and was called the King's Privy Wardrobe. Later, it was used to store the records of the House of Lords, and then as a testing centre by the Board of Trade's Standards Department. Nowadays, the tower houses an exhibition on the history of Parliament on the first floor and on the history of the tower itself on the second floor.

Victoria Tower Gardens

To the south of Parliament's Victoria Tower are the leafy **Victoria Tower Gardens**, which look out onto the Thames. Visitors are greeted by a statue of Emmeline Pankhurst, leader of the suffragette movement, who died in 1928, the same year women finally got the vote on equal terms with men; medallions commemorating her daughter

Christabel, and a WPSU Prisoners' Badge, flank the statue. Round the corner, a replica of Rodin's famous sculpture, *The Burghers of Calais*, makes a surprising appearance here, while at the far end of the gardens stands the **Buxton Memorial**, a neo-Gothic fountain, made from a real potpourri of exotic materials, erected in 1865 to commemorate the 1834 abolition of slavery.

Westminster Abbey

Parliament Square • Hours can vary: Mon–Fri 9.30am–4.30pm, Wed until 6pm, Sat 9.30am–2.30pm • £16 • ☎ 020 7654 4900,
Ⓦ westminster-abbey.org • ⊖ Westminster

The Houses of Parliament dwarf their much older neighbour, **Westminster Abbey**, which squats awkwardly on the western edge of Parliament Square. Yet this single building embodies much of the history of England: it has been the venue for every coronation since the time of William the Conqueror, and the site of just about every royal burial for some five hundred years between the reigns of Henry III and George II. Scores of the nation's most famous citizens are honoured here, too – though many of the stones commemorate people buried elsewhere – and the interior is cluttered with literally hundreds of monuments, reliefs and statues.

INFORMATION AND TOURS

Information If you have any questions, ask the vergers in the black gowns, the marshals in red or the abbey volunteers in green. Note that you can visit the Chapter House, the Cloisters and the College Garden (free admission), without buying an abbey ticket, by entering via Dean's Yard.

Guided tours There are guided tours by the vergers, which allow access to the Confessor's Tomb (Mon–Sat, times vary; ring ahead for details; 1hr 30min; £3). An audioguide to the abbey is available for free.

Services Admission to the daily services at the abbey (check website for details) is, of course, free.

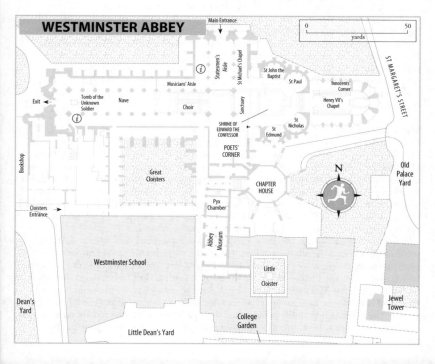

1

Brief history

Legend has it that the first church on the site was consecrated by St Peter himself, who was rowed across the Thames by a fisherman named Edric, who granted him a giant salmon as a reward. More verifiable is that there was a small Benedictine monastery here by the tenth century, for which **Edward the Confessor** built an enormous church. Nothing much remains of Edward's church, which was consecrated on December 28, 1065, just eight days before his death. The following January his successor, Harold, was crowned, and, on Christmas Day, William the Conqueror rode up the aisle on horseback, thus firmly establishing the tradition of royal coronation within the Confessor's church.

It was in honour of Edward (who had by now been canonized) that **Henry III** began to rebuild the abbey in 1245, in the French Gothic style of the recently completed Rheims Cathedral. The monks were kicked out during the Reformation, but the church's status as the nation's royal mausoleum saved it from any physical damage. In the early eighteenth century, Nicholas Hawksmoor designed the quasi-Gothic west front, while the most recent additions can be seen above the west door: a series of statues representing twentieth-century martyrs, from Dietrich Bonhöffer to Martin Luther King.

Statesmen's Aisle and the Sanctuary

With over 3300 people buried beneath its flagstones and countless others commemorated here, the abbey is, in essence, a giant mausoleum. It has long ceased to be simply a working church, and hefty admission charges are nothing new: Oliver Goldsmith complained about being charged three pence in 1765. A century or so later, so few people used the abbey as a church that, according to George Bernard Shaw, one foreign visitor kneeling in prayer was promptly arrested because the verger thought he was acting suspiciously. Despite protestations to the contrary, the abbey is now more mass tourist attraction than House of God.

The north transept, where you enter, is littered with overblown monuments to long-forgotten empire-builders and nineteenth-century politicians, and traditionally known as **Statesmen's Aisle**. From here, you can go straight to the central **Sanctuary**, site of the royal coronations. The most precious work of art here is the thirteenth-century Italian floor mosaic known as the **Cosmati pavement**. It depicts the universe with interwoven circles and squares of Purbeck marble, glass, and red and green porphyry, though it's sometimes covered by a carpet to protect it. The richly gilded high altar, like the ornately carved **choir stalls**, is, in fact, a neo-Gothic construction from the nineteenth century.

The side chapels

Some of the best funereal art is tucked away in **St Michael's Chapel**, east of the Statesmen's Aisle, where you can admire the remarkable monument to **Francis Vere** (1560–1609), one of the greatest soldiers of the Elizabethan period, made out of two slabs of black marble, between which lies Sir Francis; on the upper slab, supported by four knights, his armour is laid out, to show that he died away from the field of battle. The most striking grave, by Roubiliac, is that in which **Elizabeth Nightingale**, who died from a miscarriage, collapses in her husband's arms while he tries to fight off the skeletal figure of Death, who is climbing out of the tomb.

In the **north ambulatory**, two more chapels contain ostentatious Tudor and Stuart tombs that replaced the altarpieces that had graced them before the Reformation. One of the most extravagant tombs is that of Lord Hunsdon, Lord Chancellor to Elizabeth I, which dominates the **Chapel of St John the Baptist**, and, at 36ft in height, is the tallest in the entire abbey. More intriguing, though, are the sarcophagi in the neighbouring **Chapel of St Paul**: one depicts eight "weepers", kneeling children along the base of the tomb – the two holding skulls predeceased their parents – while the red-robed Countess of Sussex has a beautiful turquoise and gold porcupine (the family emblem) as her prickly footrest.

Henry VII's Chapel

At this point, you can climb the stairs and enter the Lady Chapel, better known as **Henry VII's Chapel**, the most dazzling architectural set piece in the abbey. Begun by Henry VII in 1503 as a shrine to Henry VI and as his own future resting place, it represents the final gasp of the English Perpendicular style, with its beautiful, light, intricately carved vaulting, fan-shaped gilded pendants and statues of nearly one hundred saints, high above the choir stalls. The stalls themselves are decorated with the banners and emblems of the Knights of the Order of the Bath, established by George I. **George II**, the last king to be buried in the abbey, lies in the burial vault under your feet, along with Queen Caroline – their coffins were fitted with removable sides so that their remains could mingle.

Beneath the altar is the grave of Edward VI, the single, sickly son of Henry VIII, while behind lies the chapel's *raison d'être*, the black marble **sarcophagus of Henry VII** and his spouse – their lifelike gilded effigies, modelled from death masks, are obscured by an ornate Renaissance grille by Pietro Torrigiano, who fled from Italy after breaking Michelangelo's nose in a fight. James I is also interred within Henry's tomb, while the first of the apse chapels, to the north, hosts a grand monument by Hubert le Sueur to James's lover, George Villiers, Duke of Buckingham, the first non-royal to be buried in this part of the abbey, who was killed by one of his own disgruntled soldiers.

The side chapels

The easternmost **RAF Chapel** sports a stained-glass window depicting airmen and angels in the Battle of Britain and a small piece of bomb damage from World War II. In the floor, a plaque marks the spot where Oliver Cromwell rested, briefly, until the Restoration, whereupon his mummified body was disinterred, dragged through the streets, hanged at Tyburn and beheaded. And the last of the apse chapels contains another overblown Le Sueur monument, in which four caryatids, holding up a vast bronze canopy, weep for Ludovic Stuart, another of James I's "favourites".

North aisle: Elizabeth I and the Innocents

Before descending the steps back into the ambulatory, pop into the chapel's north aisle, which is virtually cut off from the chancel. Here James I erected a huge ten-poster tomb to his predecessor, **Elizabeth I**. Unless you read the plaque on the floor, you'd never know that Elizabeth's Catholic half-sister, "Bloody Mary", is also buried here, in an unusual act of posthumous reconciliation. The far end of the north aisle, where James I's two infant daughters lie, is known as **Innocents' Corner**: Princess Sophia, who died aged three days, lies in an alabaster cradle, her face peeping over the covers, just about visible in the mirror on the wall; while Princess Mary, who died the following year aged 2, is clearly visible, casually leaning on a cushion. Set into the wall between the two is the Wren-designed urn containing (what are thought to be) the bones of the **Princes in the Tower**, Edward V and his younger brother, Richard (see p.183).

South aisle: Mary Queen of Scots

The south aisle of Henry VII's chapel contains a trio of stellar tombs, including James I's mother, **Mary, Queen of Scots**, whom Elizabeth I had beheaded. James had Mary's remains brought from Peterborough Cathedral in 1612, and paid significantly more for her extravagant eight-postered tomb, bristling with Scottish thistles and complete with a terrifyingly aggressive Scottish lion, than he had done for Elizabeth's (see above); the 27 hangers-on (including the Cavalier Prince Rupert and the "Winter Queen", Elizabeth of Bohemia) who are buried with her are listed on the nearby wooden screen. The last of the tombs here is that of **Lady Margaret Beaufort**, Henry VII's mother, her face and hands depicted wrinkles and all by Torrigiano. Below the altar, commemorated by simple modern plaques, lie yet more royals: **William and Mary**, **Queen Anne** and **Charles II**.

1

The Coronation Chair

As you leave Henry VII's Chapel, look out for Edward I's **Coronation Chair**, a decrepit oak throne dating from around 1300. The graffiti-covered chair, used in every coronation since 1308, was custom-built to incorporate the **Stone of Scone**, a great slab of red sandstone which acted as the Scottish coronation stone for centuries before Edward pilfered it in 1296. The stone remained in the abbey for the next seven hundred years, apart from a brief interlude in 1950, when some Scottish nationalists managed to steal it back and hide it in Arbroath. In a futile attempt to curry favour with the Scots before the 1997 election, the Conservatives returned the stone to Edinburgh Castle, where it now resides.

The Shrine of Edward the Confessor

Behind the chair lies the tomb of **Henry V**, who died of dysentery in France in 1422 at the age of just 35, and was regarded as a saint in his day. Above him rises the highly decorative, H-shaped Chantry Chapel, where the body of Henry's wife, Catherine of Valois, was openly displayed for several centuries – Pepys records kissing her corpse on his 36th-birthday visit to the abbey. The chapel acts as a sort of gatehouse for the **Shrine of Edward the Confessor**, the sacred heart of the building, and site of some of the abbey's finest tombs, now only accessible on a guided tour (see p.53). With some difficulty, you can just about make out the battered marble casket of the Confessor's tomb and the niches in which pilgrims would kneel.

Poets' Corner

In the south transept, you'll find the increasingly popular **Poets' Corner**. The first occupant, **Geoffrey Chaucer**, was buried here in 1400, not because he was a poet, but because he lived nearby, and his battered tomb, on the east wall, wasn't built for another 150-odd years. When **Edmund Spenser** chose to be buried close to Chaucer in 1599, his fellow poets – Shakespeare among them (possibly) – threw their own works and quills into the grave. Nevertheless, it wasn't until the eighteenth century that this zone became an artistic pantheon, since when the transept has been filled with tributes to all shades of talent.

Among those who are actually buried here, you'll find – after much searching – grave slabs or memorials for everyone from John Dryden and Samuel Johnson to **Charles Dickens** and Thomas Hardy (though his heart was buried in Dorset). Among the merely commemorated is **William Shakespeare**, whose dandyish statue is on the east wall. Even mavericks like Oscar Wilde, commemorated in the Hubbard window, are acknowledged here, though William Blake was honoured by a Jacob Epstein sculpture only in 1957, and Byron was refused burial for his "open profligacy", and had to wait until 1969.

Among the non-poets buried here is the great eighteenth-century actor **David Garrick**, depicted parting the curtains for a final bow, and the German composer **Georg Friedrich Handel**, who spent most of his life at the English court, and wrote the coronation anthem *Zadok the Priest*, first performed at George II's coronation, and performed at every subsequent one. There's even one illiterate, Thomas Parr, a Shropshire man who arrived in London as a celebrity in 1635 at the alleged age of 152, but died shortly afterwards, and whose remains were brought here by Charles II.

South choir aisle

Before you enter the cloisters, it's worth seeking out several wonderful memorials to undeserving types in the **south choir aisle**, though you may have to ask a verger to allow you to see them properly. The first is to **Thomas Thynne**, a Restoration rake, whose tomb incorporates a relief showing his assassination in his coach on Pall Mall by three thugs, hired to kill him by his Swedish rival in love. Further along lies **Admiral Clowdisley Shovell**, lounging in toga and wig. One of only two survivors of a shipwreck

1

in 1707, he was washed up alive on a beach in the Scilly Isles, off southwest England, only to be killed by a fisherwoman for his emerald ring. Above Shovell is a memorial to the court portrait painter **Godfrey Kneller**, who declared, "By God, I will not be buried in Westminster – they do bury fools there". In the event, he has the honour of being the only artist commemorated in the abbey (most are in St Paul's); the tomb is to his own design, but the epitaph is by Pope, who admitted it was the worst thing he ever wrote – which is just as well, as it's so high up you can't read it.

The cloisters

Cloisters daily 8am–6pm; Chapter House daily 10.30am–4pm • Free via Dean's Yard entrance

Doors in the south choir aisle lead to the **Great Cloisters**, rebuilt after a fire in 1298 and paved with yet more funerary slabs, including, at the bottom of the ramp, that of the proto-feminist writer **Aphra Behn**, upon whose tomb "all women together ought to let flowers fall", according to Virginia Woolf, "for it was she who earned them the right to speak their minds".

At the eastern end lies the octagonal **Chapter House**, built in 1255 for Henry III's Great Council or putative parliament. The House of Commons continued to meet here until 1395, though the monks were none too happy about it, complaining that the shuffling and stamping wore out the expensive tiled floor. Despite their whingeing, the thirteenth-century decorative paving tiles have survived well, as have sections of the remarkable apocalyptic wall-paintings, which were executed in celebration of the eviction of the Commons. Be sure to check out the southern wall, where the Whore of Babylon rides the scarlet seven-headed beast from *The Book of Revelation*.

Abbey Museum

Daily 10.30am–4pm • Free

The nearby high-security **Pyx Chamber** (daily 10.30am–4pm; free) is one of the few surviving Norman sections of the abbey, along with the neighbouring **Abbey Museum**. The museum contains a real mixed bag of exhibits, from replica coronation regalia used during rehearsals to the ring given by Elizabeth I to her lover, the Earl of Essex. The most bizarre items, though, are the lifelike wood and wax royal funereal effigies (several of which are wigless), used in royal burials (1307–1660) instead of an open coffin, including that of Lady Frances Stuart, the Duchess of Richmond and Lennox and model for Britannia on the old penny coin, complete with her pet parrot, which died a few days after she did.

College Garden

Tues–Thurs: April–Sept 10am–6pm; Oct–March 10am–4pm • Free

From the cloisters you can make your way via **Little Cloister**, where sick or elderly monks used to live, to the little-known **College Garden**, a 900-year-old stretch of green, originally used as a herb garden by the monastery's doctor. The garden now provides a quiet retreat and a croquet lawn for pupils of Westminster School; brass-band concerts take place in the summer (July & Aug Wed 12.30–2pm).

The nave

It's only when you finally leave the cloisters that you get to enter the **nave** itself. Narrow, light and, at over a hundred feet in height, by far the tallest in the country, the nave is an impressive space. The first monument to head for is the **Tomb of the Unknown Soldier**, by the west door, with its garland of red poppies commemorating the million British soldiers who died in World War I. Close by is a large floor slab dedicated to **Winston Churchill**, though he chose to be buried in his family plot in Bladon, Oxfordshire.

A tablet in the floor near the Unknown Soldier marks the spot where **George Peabody**, the nineteenth-century philanthropist whose housing estates in London still provide homes for those in need, was buried for a month before being exhumed and removed to Massachusetts; he remains the only American to have been buried in the abbey. On the pillar by St George's Chapel, right by the west door, is a doleful fourteenth-century portrait of **Richard II**, painted at his coronation at the age of 10, and the oldest known image of an English monarch painted from life. Above the west door, **William Pitt the Younger**, prime minister at just 23, teaches Anarchy a thing or two, while History takes notes.

The choir screen and the side aisles

The dried and salted body of the explorer and missionary **David Livingstone** is buried in the centre of the nave – except for his internal organs, which, following the tradition of the African people in whose village he died, were buried in a box under a tree. To the left of the gilded neo-Gothic choir screen is a statue of **Isaac Newton**, who, although a Unitarian by faith, would no doubt have been happy enough to be buried in such a prominent position. Other scientists' graves cluster nearby, including non-believer **Charles Darwin**, who, despite being at loggerheads with the Church for most of his life over *On the Origin of Species*, was given a religious burial in the abbey.

In the far corner of the south aisle, the eighteenth-century marble memorial to **General Hargrave** by Roubiliac, has the deceased rising from the grave in response to the Last Trumpet; at the time there was a public outcry that such an undistinguished man – he was Governor of Gibraltar – should receive such a vast memorial. Another controversial grave is that of poet and playwright **Ben Jonson**, who, despite being a double murderer, was granted permission to be buried here, upright so as not to exceed the eighteen square inches he'd been allowed; his epitaph reads simply, "O Rare Ben Jonson". The so-called **Musicians' Aisle** lies to the east, beyond a barrier, so you'll need to ask a verger for access. In fact, just two musicians of great note are buried here: Ralph Vaughan Williams and Henry Purcell, who served as the abbey's organist. Of the statues lining the aisle, only the tireless anti-slavery campaigner **William Wilberforce**, slouching in his chair, is actually buried in the abbey.

Parliament Square

Parliament Square was laid out in the mid-nineteenth century to give the new Houses of Parliament and the adjacent Westminster Abbey a grander setting, though nowadays it functions primarily as a traffic roundabout and as a favoured (though now illegal) on-off protest camp. Statues of notables – Abraham Lincoln, Benjamin Disraeli and Jan Smuts, to name but a few – are scattered amid the swirling cars and buses, with Winston Churchill stooping determinedly in the northeast corner of the central green. At the beginning of Westminster Bridge, you can also spot Boudicca, depicted keeping her horses and daughters under control without the use of reins – the imperialist boast "regions Caesar never knew, thy posterity shall sway" adorns the plinth.

St Margaret's Church

St Margaret Street • Mon–Fri 9.30am–3.30pm, Sat 9.30am–1.30pm, Sun noon–4.45pm • Free • ⊖ Westminster

Sitting directly in the shadow of Westminster Abbey, **St Margaret's Church** has been the unofficial parliamentary church since 1614 when Puritan MPs decided to shun the elaborate liturgy of the neighbouring abbey. St Margaret's has also long been a fashionable church to get married in – Pepys, Milton and Shakespeare were followed in the twentieth century by Churchill and Mountbatten – and it gets a steady stream of visitors simply by dint of being so close to the abbey (and because it's free, unlike the abbey). The present building dates back to 1523, and features some colourful Flemish stained glass above the altar, commemorating the marriage of Henry VIII and Catherine of Aragon (depicted in the bottom left- and right-hand corners). Constructed in 1526, the window was never intended for St Margaret's, and was only bought by the church in 1758 to replace those smashed by the Puritans. The west window commemorates Walter Raleigh, who was beheaded in

1

Old Palace Yard and buried in the old churchyard. Also interred here is William Caxton, who audited the parish accounts and set up the country's first printing press in the abbey close in 1476.

Supreme Court

Parliament Square • Mon–Fri 9.30am–4.30pm • Free • ☎ 020 7960 1500, ⓦ www.supremecourt.gov.uk • ⊖ Westminster

The House of Lords was the country's final court of appeal from medieval times until 2009, when the **Supreme Court** took over and housed itself in the former Middlesex Guildhall, a quasi-medieval Edwardian town hall that sits on the west side of Parliament Square, replete with lugubrious gargoyles and sculptures. With the abolition of the county of Middlesex in 1965, the building became a courthouse, and has recently been totally refurbished. The public are welcome to explore the building, view an exhibition on the Supreme Court and sit in on any sessions going on – plus there's a very nice **café** in the tiled and roofed inner light well.

Central Hall Westminster

Storey's Gate • ☎ 020 7222 8010, ⓦ c-h-w.com • ⊖ Westminster

Set back from Parliament Square, on Storey's Gate, the Methodists established their national headquarters, **Central Hall**, in 1912. In order to avoid the Gothic of the abbey, and the Byzantine of the nearby Catholic cathedral (see p.63), the Methodists opted for Edwardian Beaux-Arts – as a result, it looks rather like a giant continental casino, which is hardly appropriate given the Methodists' views on gambling and alcohol. Central Hall has been used over the years as much for political meetings as religious gatherings, and was the unlikely venue for the inaugural meeting of the **United Nations** in 1946. If there's no event on, you're free to wander round the building and – after donning black gloves – to look at the Historic Roll, a fifty-volume list of the folk who donated a guinea towards the cost of the building. Free **guided tours** are also available, and allow you to climb the stone balustrade atop the reinforced concrete dome.

Tate Britain

Millbank • Daily 10am–6pm; first Fri of month until 10pm • Free • ☎ 020 7887 8888, ⓦ tate.org.uk • ⊖ Pimlico or Vauxhall

Originally founded in 1897 with money from Henry Tate, inventor of the sugar cube, **Tate Britain** showcases British art from 1500 to the present day. In addition, the gallery has a whole wing devoted to Turner, as well as putting on large-scale temporary exhibitions (for which there is a charge) and sponsoring the **Turner Prize**, the country's most infamous modern-art award. Works by a shortlist of four artists under 50 are displayed in the gallery a month or two prior to the December prize-giving.

Tate Britain is currently undergoing some fairly major building work due to be completed in 2013. Until the work is completed, the curators have decided to eschew the gallery's traditional, chronological approach and embrace a thematic approach in its permanent displays. What you see on any one visit is a tiny fraction of Tate's collection, and the paintings are frequently re-hung. What follows, therefore, is a general rundown of the artists usually featured, plus some of the best works Tate owns, many of which stay on show more or less permanently.

INFORMATION AND TOURS

Arrival The traditional entrance on Millbank leads up the steps to a small information desk beneath a glass-domed rotunda. A larger entrance with disabled access is on nearby Atterbury Street, and leads down to information desks and the cloakroom. Tate's Clore Gallery extension, which houses the Turner Bequest, can be reached via the modern-art galleries, but it also has its own entrance and information desk to the right of the original gallery entrance.

Tate Boat If you're coming from, or going to, Tate Modern, there's a Tate Boat that plies between the two galleries (every 40min; 20min; ⓦ thamesclippers.com; £5).

Guided tours There are free guided tours (Mon–Fri 11am, noon, 2 & 3pm, Sat & Sun noon & 3pm) and you can rent one of the gallery's multimedia guides for £3.50.

British art from 1500 to 1800

The collection's earliest works are richly bejewelled portraits of the Elizabethan and Jacobean nobility, the most striking being the *Cholmondeley Ladies*, who were born on the same day, married on the same day and "brought to bed" on the same day, but are not now thought to be twins. Despite a smattering of English talent, such as **William Dobson**, whose portrait of courtier *Endymion Porter* is a perennial favourite, the Stuarts relied heavily on imported Dutch talent such as Van Dyck, Peter Lely – several of whose "lovelies" are usually on display – and the German Godfrey Kneller, who used to sign himself "Pictor Regis" such was the longevity of his royal patronage.

Hogarth and Constable

You can be guaranteed a good selection of works by the first great British artist, **William Hogarth**, including *O the Roast Beef of Old England*, a particularly vicious visual dig at the French, whom Hogarth loathed. **John Constable**'s most famous work, *Hay Wain*, hangs in the National Gallery, but the same location – Flatford Mill in his native Stour valley in Suffolk – features in many of the paintings owned by the Tate. Another painter to look out for is **George Stubbs**, for whom "nature was and always is superior to art", and who portrayed animals – horses in particular – with a hitherto unknown anatomical precision.

Gainsborough and Reynolds

Works by **Thomas Gainsborough** and **Joshua Reynolds** are sprinkled throughout the collection. Of the two, Reynolds, first president of the Royal Academy, was by far the more successful, elevating portraiture to pole position among the genres and flattering his sitters by surrounding them with classical trappings as in *Three Ladies adorning a Term of Hymen*. Gainsborough was equally adept at flattery, but preferred instead more informal settings, concentrating on colour and light. At the outset of his career, Gainsborough was also a landscape artist, often painting the Stour valley in Suffolk, where he – like Constable – was born.

William Blake

One room in the gallery is regularly devoted to the visionary works of the poet **William Blake**, who was considered something of a freak by his contemporaries. He rejected oil painting in favour of watercolours, and often chose unusual subject matter which matched his highly personal form of Christianity. He earned a pittance producing illuminated books written and printed entirely by himself, and painted purely from his own visions: "Imagination is My World; this world of Dross is beneath my notice", he wrote. He also executed a series of twelve large colour prints on the myth of the Creation, now considered among his finest works, several examples of which are normally on display here. Blake's works were originally intended for room 16, which is decorated by Boris Anrep's floor mosaics, accompanied by quotes from Blake's poem *The Marriage of Heaven and Hell*.

The Pre-Raphaelites

Tate is justifiably renowned for its vast collection of paintings by the **Pre-Raphaelites**, seven of whom formed their Brotherhood, the PRB, in 1848 in an attempt to re-create the humble, pre-humanist, pre-Renaissance world. One of the first PRB paintings to be exhibited was **Rossetti**'s *Girlhood of Mary Virgin*, which was well received by the critics, but his *Annunciation*, with its emaciated heroin-chic Virgin, the model for which was his sister, caused outrage. So too did **Millais**' *Christ in the House of His Parents*; Dickens described the figure of Jesus as "a hideous, wry-necked, blubbering, red-headed boy in a bed-gown". Millais also got into trouble for *Ophelia*, after his model, Elizabeth Siddal, caught a chill from lying in the bath to pose for the picture, prompting threats of a lawsuit from her father. Siddal later married Rossetti, and is also the model in his

1

Beata Beatrix, painted posthumously, after she died of an opium overdose in 1862. Other classic PRB paintings in the collection are Arthur Hughes' *April Love*, Henry Wallis's Romantic hero *Chatterton*, John William Waterhouse's *The Lady of Shalott*, and Burne-Jones' *King Cophetua and the Beggar Maid*, all inspired by poems by Lord Tennyson.

The Academy and the Impressionists

Throughout Tate Britain, the term "British" is very loosely applied, so you'll find several works by the French artist, **James Tissot**, whose Impressionist take on English life (and, in particular, English ladies in frilly frocks) was very popular. Lord Leighton's *Bath of Psyche* is a typical piece of Victorian soft porn, the likes of which made him by far the most successful Royal Academician of his generation. Other popular Victorian paintings to look out for include **John Singer Sargent**'s well-known *Carnation, Lily, Lily-Rose* and the American-born **Whistler**'s portrait of the precocious *Miss Cecily*, who looks as pissed off as she clearly felt after interminable sittings.

Twentieth-century British art

You'll find works by the same twentieth-century and contemporary British artists displayed in both Tate Modern and Tate Britain, so it's very hard to predict what will be on show here. Works by sculptors **Barbara Hepworth**, Jacob Epstein, Giacometti and **Henry Moore** usually feature prominently, while paintings by Walter Sickert and Francis Bacon crop up regularly. Vanessa Bell and Duncan Grant, from the Bloomsbury Group, are represented more often than not, and there are nearly always several paintings by **Stanley Spencer**, who saw his home village of Cookham, on the Thames, as paradise and depicted Christ preaching at the local regatta.

There's usually a good selection of work, too, by established living artists such as **Lucian Freud**, R.B. Kitaj, Frank Auerbach, **David Hockney** and op-art specialist Bridget Riley, as well as contemporary artists such as Rachel Whiteread, Tracey Emin, Chris Ofili and the ever-popular Anthony Gormley. Some less well-known artists to look out for include the Vorticist **David Bomberg**, who forged his own brand of Cubo-Futurism before World War I and pursued a more subdued Expressionism thereafter; **Ivon Hitchens**, whose distinctive use of blocks of colour harks back to the late works of Cézanne; and the self-taught St Ives painter **Alfred Wallis**.

The Turner Collection

J.M.W. Turner, possibly the greatest artist Britain has ever produced, bequeathed over 100 oil paintings to the nation, and the gallery now has 300, plus a staggering 19,000 watercolours and drawings. Turner's one condition was that the paintings should be housed and exhibited together – the original idea behind the Clore Gallery, the strangely childish building by James Stirling from 1987. The Turner Galleries still exhibit probably the world's largest collection of works by Turner, but you'll also find other artists' works here, and several of Turner's major works hang in the National Gallery.

J.M.W. TURNER (1775–1851)

Born in **Covent Garden**, Turner's childhood was blighted by the death of his younger sister, and the mental illness of his mother, who died in Bedlam in 1804. Nevertheless, he became an extremely successful artist, exhibiting his first watercolours in the window of his father's barbershop in Maiden Lane, while still a boy, and at the **Royal Academy** when he was just 14. He travelled widely in Europe, but when returning to England, lived increasingly as a recluse. He never married, but had two children with an older widow, and lived for thirty years with his father who worked as his studio assistant. Turner's only known **self-portrait** (he had no pretensions as a portraitist and was rather ashamed of his ruddy complexion) is usually on display, as are his personal belongings, such as his pocket watercolour kit and fishing rod, and his toothless death mask.

1

Marine scenes appealed to Turner throughout his life, and one of the finest examples is *The Shipwreck*. Natural cataclysms also feature strongly in Turner's works, either for their own sake, as in *Deluge*, or as part of a grand historical painting like *Snow Storm: Hannibal and His Army Crossing the Alps*. His financial independence allowed him to develop his own style freely and it's worth seeking out Turner's late works, great smudges of colour that seem to anticipate Monet in their almost total abandonment of linear representation. *Snow Storm – Steam Boat off a Harbour's Mouth* is a classic late Turner, a symbolic battle between the steam age and nature's primeval force. It was criticized at the time as "soapsuds and whitewash", though Turner himself claimed he merely painted what he saw, having been "lashed to a mast" for four hours.

From Millbank to Victoria Street

The area between **Millbank** – the busy riverside road that runs past Tate Britain – and **Victoria Street** – the link forged in the 1860s between Parliament and the newly built Victoria train station – is home to various governmental ministries that can't quite fit into Whitehall. It's also a favourite place for MPs to have their London bases, and many of the restaurants and pubs in the area have "division bells", which ring eight minutes before any vote in the House of Commons. As for sights, the area boasts one of the city's most exotic and unusual churches, the Roman Catholic Westminster Cathedral.

St John's, Smith Square

Smith Square • ☎ 020 7222 1061, ⓦ sjss.org.uk • ⊖ Westminster

Hidden away in the backstreets west of Millbank is the beautiful early Georgian architectural ensemble of **Smith Square**, home to the church of **St John**, a rare and totally surprising slice of full-blown Baroque, completed in 1728. With its four distinctive towers topped by pineapples, it was dubbed the "footstool church" – the story being that Queen Anne, when asked how she would like the church to look, kicked over her footstool. Bombed in 1941, the interior was totally gutted and has since been restored as a classical music venue, so to visit you'll have to go to a concert. The church's atmospheric restaurant is in the brick-vaulted crypt beyond the box office (access from Dean Stanley Street).

St James-the-Less

Thorndike Street • Mon–Fri 9.30am–1pm • Free • ☎ 020 7630 6282, ⓦ sjtl.org • ⊖ Pimlico

Another sight worth seeking out is the remarkable High Victorian church of **St James-the-Less**, designed by George Edmund Street in the 1860s, which lies to the south of Vincent Square, on the far side of Vauxhall Bridge Road, amid an unprepossessing 1960s Lillington Gardens housing estate. The red-and-black brickwork patterning on the exterior is exceptional, but pales in comparison to the red, black, cream and magenta tiling inside. The capitals of the church's rounded pillars hide biblical scenes amidst their acanthus-leaf foliage, and the font boasts similarly rich adornments, while above the chancel arch there's a wonderfully colourful fresco by G.F. Watts.

Westminster Cathedral

Victoria Street • **Campanile** Mon–Fri 9.30am–5pm, Sat & Sun 9.30am–6pm • £3 **Cathedral** Mon–Fri 7am–7pm, Sat 8am–7pm, Sun 8am–8pm • Free • ☎ 020 7798 9055, ⓦ westminstercathedral.org.uk • ⊖ Victoria

Set back from the stark 1960s architecture of Victoria Street, you'll find one of London's most surprising churches, the stripy neo-Byzantine concoction of the Roman Catholic **Westminster Cathedral**. Begun in 1895, it's one of the last and wildest monuments to the Victorian era: constructed from more than twelve million terracotta-coloured bricks, decorated with hoops of Portland stone, it culminates in a magnificent tapered campanile which rises to 274ft. From the small piazza to the

1

> ## THE SECRET SERVICE
>
> The green-and-beige postmodernist ziggurat across the water is Vauxhall Cross, the indiscreet Secret Intelligence Service or **MI6 headquarters** (🌐 sis.gov.uk), designed in the 1990s by Terry Farrell. It has featured in several Bond films and is connected by tunnel to Whitehall. Such conspicuousness comes at a price, however, and in 2000, the building, known as "Legoland" to those who work there, was hit by a rocket attack courtesy of some dissident Irish-republican terrorists. **MI5** (🌐 mi5.gov.uk), the UK's domestic Security Service, occupies the much more anonymous Thames House on the corner of Horseferry Road and Millbank.

northwest, you can admire the cathedral and the neighbouring mansions on Ambrosden Avenue, with their matching brickwork.

The **interior** is still only half-finished, and the domed ceiling of the nave – the widest in the country – remains an indistinct blackened mass, free of all decoration. To get an idea of what the place will look like when it's eventually completed, explore the series of **side chapels** – in particular the Holy Souls Chapel, the first one in the north aisle – whose rich, multicoloured decor makes use of over one hundred different marbles from around the world. Further down the north aisle is the Chapel of St George and the English Martyrs, where lies the enshrined body of St John Southworth, who was hanged, drawn and quartered as a traitor at Tyburn in 1654. Be sure, too, to check out the striking baldachin, held up by mustard-yellow pillars, and the low-relief Stations of the Cross sculpted by the controversial Eric Gill during World War I. The view from the **campanile** is definitely worth taking in as well, especially as you don't even have to slog up flights of steps, but can simply take a lift; the entrance is in the north aisle.

North of Victoria Street

The one tower block north of Victoria Street that deserves special mention is the Metropolitan Police headquarters, **New Scotland Yard**, on Broadway. The revolving sign alone should be familiar to many from countless British TV detective serials and news reports. Further up Broadway, at no. 55, is the austere **Broadway House**, home to the city's public transport body, Transport for London (TfL) and St James's Park tube station, and the tallest building in London when it was built in 1929 by Charles Holden. It gained a certain notoriety at the time for its nude statues by Jacob Epstein, in particular the boy figure in *Day*, whose penis had to be shortened to appease public opinion.

Round the corner, standing on its own in Caxton Street, is the former **Blewcoat School** (now a National Trust shop), a lovely little red-brick building built in 1709 by a local brewer as a charity school for the poor and used as such until 1926; a statue of a blue-coated charity boy still stands above the doorway.

There's more delightful Queen Anne architecture just to the north in **Queen Anne's Gate** and **Old Queen Street**, two exquisite streets, originally separated by a wall, whose position is indicated by a weathered statue of Queen Anne herself. Queen Anne's Gate is the older and more interesting of the two, each of its doorways surmounted by a rustic wooden canopy with pendants in the shape of acorns. It's worth walking round the back of the houses on the north side to appreciate the procession of elegant bow windows that look out onto St James's Park.

St James's

An exclusive little enclave sandwiched between St James's Park and Piccadilly, St James's was laid out in the 1670s close to the royal seat of St James's Palace. Even today, regal and aristocratic residences overlook nearby Green Park and the stately avenue of The Mall; gentlemen's clubs cluster along Pall Mall and St James's Street; and jacket-and-tie restaurants and expense-account shops line Jermyn Street. Hardly surprising, then, that most Londoners rarely stray into this area, though plenty of folk frequent St James's Park, with large numbers heading for the Queen's chief residence, Buckingham Palace. If you're not in St James's for the shops, the best time to visit is on a Sunday, when it's quieter, the nearby Mall is closed to traffic, and the royal chapels, plus the one accessible Palladian mansion, are open to the public.

St James's Park

St James's Park is the oldest of London's royal parks, having been drained and turned into a deer park by Henry VIII. It was redesigned and opened to the public by Charles II, who used to stroll through the grounds with his mistresses and courtiers, feed the ducks and even take a dip in the canal. By the eighteenth century, when some 6500 people had access to night keys for the gates, the park had become something of a byword for robbery and prostitution: diarist James Boswell was among those who went there specifically to be accosted "by several ladies of the town". The park's current landscaping was devised by Nash in the 1820s in an elegant style that established a blueprint for later Victorian city parks.

Today, the banks of the tree-lined lake are a favourite picnic spot for the civil servants of Whitehall and an inner-city reserve for wildfowl. James I's two crocodiles have left no descendants, alas, but the pelicans (which have resided here ever since a pair was presented to Charles II by the Russian ambassador) can still be seen at the eastern end of the lake, and there are exotic ducks, swans and geese aplenty. From the bridge across the lake there's a fine view over to Westminster and the jumble of domes and pinnacles along Whitehall – even the dull facade of **Buckingham Palace** looks majestic from here.

The Mall

⊖ St James's Park, Charing Cross or Westminster

The tree-lined sweep of **The Mall** – London's nearest equivalent to a Parisian boulevard (minus the cafés) – is at its best on Sundays, when it's closed to traffic. It was laid out in the first decade of the twentieth century as a memorial to Queen Victoria, and runs along the northern edge of St James's Park. The bombastic **Admiralty Arch** was erected to mark the entrance at the Trafalgar Square end of The Mall, while at the other end stands the ludicrous **Victoria Memorial**, Edward VII's overblown 2300-ton marble tribute to his mother: *Motherhood* and *Justice* keep Victoria company around the plinth, which is topped by a gilded statue of *Victory*, while the six outlying allegorical groups in bronze confidently proclaim the great achievements of her reign.

The Mall's most distinctive building is John Nash's **Carlton House Terrace**, whose graceful, cream-coloured Regency facade lines the north side of The Mall from Admiralty Arch. Among other things, it serves as the unlikely home of the **Institute of Contemporary Arts** or **ICA** (Wed noon–11pm, Thurs–Sat noon–1am, Sun noon–9pm; free; ☎ 020 7930 3647, ⊛ ica.org.uk), London's official headquarters of the avant-garde, so to speak, which moved here in 1968 and has put on a programme of regularly provocative exhibitions, films, talks and performances ever since.

Wellington Barracks, Guards' Chapel and Museum

Birdcage Walk • Museum Daily 10am–4pm • £4 • ☎ 020 7414 3271, ⊛ theguardsmuseum.com • ⊖ St James's Park

Named after James I's aviary, which once stood here, Birdcage Walk runs along the south side of St James's Park, with the Neoclassical facade of the **Wellington Barracks**, built in 1833 and fronted by a parade ground, occupying more than half its length. Of the various buildings here, though, it's the modernist lines of the **Guards' Chapel** that come as the biggest surprise. Hit by a V1 rocket bomb on the morning of Sunday, June 18, 1944 – killing 121 worshippers – the chapel was rebuilt in the 1960s. Inside, it's festooned with faded military flags, and retains the ornate Victorian apse, with Byzantine-style gilded mosaics, from the old chapel.

In a bunker opposite is the **Guards' Museum**, which displays the glorious scarlet-and-blue uniforms of the Queen's Foot Guards (see p.48). The museum also attempts to explain the Guards' complicated history, and gives a potted military history of the country since the Civil War. Among the exhibits here are a lock of Wellington's hair and a whole load of war booty, from Dervish prayer mats plundered from Sudan in

1898 to items taken from an Iraqi POW during the first Gulf War. The museum also displays (and sells) an impressive array of toy soldiers.

Buckingham Palace

The Mall • Late July to early Oct daily 9.45am–6.30pm • £17.50; advance booking fee £1.25 per ticket • ☏ 020 7766 7300, ⓦ royalcollection.org.uk • ⊖ Green Park

The graceless colossus of **Buckingham Palace**, popularly known as "Buck House", has served as the monarch's permanent London residence only since Queen Victoria's reign. It began its days in 1702 as the Duke of Buckingham's city residence, built on the site of a notorious brothel, and was sold by the duke's son to George III in 1762. The building was overhauled by Nash in the late 1820s for the Prince Regent, and again by Aston Webb in 1913 for George V, producing a palace that's about as bland as it's possible to be.

For ten months of the year there's little to do here, with the Queen in residence and the palace closed to visitors – not that this deters the crowds who mill around the railings all day, and gather in some force to watch the **Changing of the Guard** (see box, p.48), in which a detachment of the Queen's Foot Guards marches to appropriate martial music from St James's Palace (unless it rains, that is). If the Queen is at home, the Royal Standard flies from the roof of the palace and four guards patrol; if not, the Union flag flutters aloft and just two guards stand out front.

Traditionally, unless you were one of the select 30,000 society debutantes attending a "coming out" party, you had little chance of ever seeing inside Buckingham Palace. The debutantes were given the boot in 1958 and more democratic garden parties were established. Since 1993, however, the hallowed portals have been grudgingly opened for two months of the year. **Timed tickets** can be purchased in advance or from the box office on the south side of the palace; queues vary enormously, but you may have some time to wait before your allocated slot.

The interior

Of the palace's 775 rooms you get to see 19 of the grandest ones, but with the Queen and her family in Scotland, there's usually very little sign of life. The visitors' entrance is via the **Ambassadors' Court** on Buckingham Palace Road, which lets you into the enormous **Quadrangle**, from where you can see the Nash portico, built in warm Bath stone, that used to overlook St James's Park.

Through the courtyard, you hit the **Grand Hall**, decorated like some gloomy hotel lobby, from where Nash's rather splendid winding, curlicued **Grand Staircase**, with its floral gilt-bronze balustrade and white plaster friezes, leads past a range of very fine royal portraits, all beautifully lit by Nash's glass dome. Beyond, the small Guard Room leads into the **Green Drawing Room**, a blaze of unusually bright green silk walls, framed by lattice-patterned pilasters, and a heavily gilded coved ceiling. It was here that the Raphael Cartoons used to hang, until they were permanently loaned to the V&A.

The scarlet and gold **Throne Room** features a Neoclassical plaster frieze in the style of the Elgin Marbles, depicting the Wars of the Roses. The thrones themselves are disappointingly un-regal – just two pink his 'n' hers chairs initialled ER and P – whereas George IV's outrageous sphinx-style chariot seats, nearby, look more the part.

From the Picture Gallery to the Ballroom

Nash originally designed a spectacular hammerbeam ceiling for the **Picture Gallery**, which stretches right down the centre of the palace. Unfortunately, it leaked and was eventually replaced in 1914 by a rather dull glazed ceiling. Still, the paintings on show here are excellent and include several Van Dycks, two Rembrandts, two Canalettos, a Poussin,

FROM TOP BUCKINGHAM PALACE (P.68); ST JAMES'S PARK (P.67) >

Royal Parks
Constabulary

Cabinet War Rooms

a de Hooch and a wonderful Vermeer. Further on, in the East Gallery, check the cherub-fest in the grisaille frieze, before heading into the palace's rather overwrought **Ballroom**. It's here that the Queen holds her State Banquets, where the annual Diplomatic Reception takes place, and where folk receive their honours and knighthoods.

The west facade rooms

Having passed through several smaller rooms, you eventually reach the **State Dining Room**, whose heavily gilded ceiling, with its three saucer domes, is typical of the suite of rooms that overlooks the palace garden. Next door lies Nash's not very blue, but incredibly gold, **Blue Drawing Room**, lined with flock wallpaper interspersed with thirty fake onyx columns. The room contains one of George IV's most prized possessions, the "Table of the Grand Commanders", originally made for Napoleon, whose trompe-l'oeil Sèvres porcelain top features cameo-like portraits of the military commanders of antiquity.

Beyond the domed Music Room with its enormous semicircular bow window and impressive parquet floor, the **White Drawing Room** features yet another frothy gold and white Nash ceiling and a superb portrait of Queen Alexandra, wife of Edward VII. This room is also the incongruous setting for an annual royal prank: when hosting the reception for the diplomatic corps, the Queen and family emerge from a secret door behind a mirror to greet the ambassadors. Before you leave the palace, be sure to check out the Canova sculptures: *Mars and Venus* at the bottom of the Ministers' Staircase, and the pornographic *Fountain Nymph with Putto* in the Marble Hall. There's a **café** overlooking the palace gardens – the city's largest private gardens – if you want to linger before being ejected onto busy Grosvenor Place.

Queen's Gallery

Daily 10am–5.30pm • £9 • ☎ 020 7766 7301 • ⊖ Victoria

A Doric portico on the south side of the palace forms the entrance to the **Queen's Gallery**, which puts on temporary exhibitions drawn from the **Royal Collection**, a superlative array of art that includes works by Michelangelo, Raphael, Holbein, Reynolds, Gainsborough, Vermeer, Van Dyck, Rubens, Rembrandt and Canaletto, as well as the world's largest collection of Leonardo drawings, the odd Fabergé egg and heaps of Sèvres china. The Queen holds the Royal Collection, which is three times larger than the National Gallery, "in trust for her successors and the nation" – note the word order. However, with over 7000 works spread over the numerous royal palaces, the Queen's Gallery, and other museums and galleries around the country, you'd have to pay a king's ransom to see the lot.

Royal Mews

Jan–March Mon–Fri 11am–4pm; April–Oct daily 10am–5pm; Nov & Dec 10am–4pm • £8 • ☎ 020 7766 7302 • ⊖ Victoria

On the south side of the palace, further down Buckingham Palace Road, you'll find the **Royal Mews**, built by Nash in the 1820s. The horses – or at least their backsides – can be viewed in their luxury stables, along with an exhibition of equine accoutrements, but it's the royal carriages, lined up under a glass canopy in the courtyard, that are the main attraction. The most ornate is the **Gold State Coach**, made for George III in 1762, smothered in 22-carat gilding, panel paintings by Cipriani, and weighing four tons, its axles supporting four life-size Tritons blowing conches. Eight horses are needed to pull it and the whole experience apparently made Queen Victoria feel quite sick; since then it has only been used for coronations and jubilees. The mews also house the Royal Family's fleet of five Rolls Royce Phantoms and three Daimlers, none of which is obliged to carry numberplates.

Pall Mall

Running west from Trafalgar Square to St James's Palace, the wide thoroughfare of **Pall Mall** is renowned for its gentlemen's clubs, whose discreet Italianate and Neoclassical

THE ROYAL FAMILY

The popularity of the **royal family** to foreign tourists never seems to flag, but at home it has always waxed and waned. The Queen herself, in one of her few memorable Christmas Day speeches, accurately described 1992 as her **annus horibilis** (or "One's Bum Year" as the *Sun* put it). That was the year that saw the marriage break-ups of Prince Charles and Prince Andrew, the divorce of Princess Anne, and ended with the fire at Windsor Castle. Misjudging the public mood, the Conservative government offered taxpayers' money to foot the £50 million repair bill. After a furore, the royals offered to raise some of the money by opening Buckingham Palace to the public for the first time (and by cranking up the admission charges on all the royal residences).

To try and deflect some of the flak from that year, the Queen agreed to reduce the number of royals paid out of the state-funded Civil List, and, for the first time in her life, pay **taxes** on her personal fortune. The death of Princess Diana in 1997 caused a further drop in popularity, but the royals' ratings have improved steadily since the new millennium, partly because the family have got much better at PR. Efficiencies and cost-cutting have also taken place, though public subsidy is still considerable, with millions still spent by government departments on **luxuries** such as the Royal Squadron (for air travel) and the Royal Train (estimated at around £50,000 per trip), not to mention annual £15 million budget for the upkeep of the palaces.

With the **Royal Wedding** of Prince William to Kate Middleton in 2011, and the Queen's **Diamond Jubilee** in 2012, the Windsors are currently riding high on a wave of good publicity at home. No doubt there'll be plenty of royal gaffes in the future to keep the tabloids and republicans happy, but, with none of the mainstream political parties currently advocating scrapping the monarchy, the royal soap opera looks safe to run for many years to come.

2

facades, fronted by cast-iron torches, still punctuate the street. It gets its bizarre name from the game of *pallo a maglio* (ball to mallet) – something like modern croquet – popularized by Charles II and played here and on The Mall. Crowds gathered here in 1807 when it became London's first gas-lit street – the original lampposts (erected to reduce the opportunities for crime and prostitution) are still standing.

Lower Regent Street

Lower Regent Street, a quarter of the way down Pall Mall, was the first stage in John Nash's ambitious plan to link the Prince Regent's magnificent Carlton House with Regent's Park. Like so many of Nash's grandiose schemes, it never quite came to fruition, as George IV, soon after ascending the throne, decided that Carlton House – the most expensive palace ever to have been built in London – wasn't quite luxurious enough, and had it pulled down. Its Corinthian columns now support the main portico of the National Gallery.

Waterloo Place

Lower Regent Street opens into **Waterloo Place**, which Nash extended beyond Pall Mall once Carlton House had been demolished. At the centre of the square stands the **Crimean War Memorial**, fashioned from captured Russian cannons in 1861, and commemorating the 2152 Foot Guards who died during the Crimean War. The horrors of that conflict were witnessed by Florence Nightingale (see p.219), whose statue – along with that of Sidney Herbert (Secretary at War at the time) – were added in 1914.

South of Pall Mall, Waterloo Place is flanked by St James's two grandest gentlemen's clubs: the former **United Services Club** (now the Institute of Directors), to the east, and the **Athenaeum**, to the west. Their almost identical Neoclassical designs are by Nash's protégé Decimus Burton: the better-looking is the Athenaeum, its portico sporting a garish gilded statue of the goddess Athena and, above, a Wedgwood-type frieze inspired by the Elgin Marbles, which had just arrived in London. The Duke of Wellington was a regular at the United Services Club, and the horse blocks

– confusingly positioned outside the Athenaeum – were designed so the duke could mount his steed more easily.

Appropriately enough, an equestrian statue of that eminently clubbable man, **Edward VII** stands between the two clubs. More statues line the railings of nearby Waterloo Gardens: **Captain Scott** was sculpted by the widow he left behind after failing to complete the return journey from the South Pole; New Zealander **Keith Park**, the World War I flying ace and RAF commander who organized the fighter defence of London and southeast England during the Battle of Britain, was erected in 2010.

Duke of York's Column

To the south of Waterloo Place, overlooking St James's Park, is the **Duke of York's Column**, erected in 1833, ten years before Nelson's more famous one. The "Grand Old Duke of York", second son of George III, is indeed the one who marched ten thousand men "up to top of the hill and…marched them down again" in the famous nursery rhyme. The 123ft column was paid for by stopping one day's wages of every soldier in the British Army, and it was said at the time that the column was so high because the duke was trying to escape his creditors, since he died £2 million in debt.

Carlton House Terrace

Having pulled his old palace down, George IV had Nash build **Carlton House Terrace**, whose monumental facade now looks out onto St James's Park. No. 4, by the exquisitely tranquil Carlton Gardens, was handed to de Gaulle for the headquarters of the Free French during World War II; while nos. 7–9, by the Duke of York steps, served as the German embassy until World War II. Albert Speer designed the interior under the Nazis, while outside a tiny grave for *ein treuer Begleiter* (a true friend) lurks behind the railings near the column – it holds the remains of **Giro**, the Nazi ambassador's pet Alsatian, accidentally electrocuted in February 1934.

St James's Square

Around the time of George III's birth at no. 31 in 1738, **St James's Square** boasted no fewer than six dukes and seven earls, and over the decades it has maintained its exclusive air: no. 10 was occupied in turn by prime ministers Pitt the Elder, Lord Derby and Gladstone; at no. 16 you'll find the silliest-sounding gentlemen's club, the East India, Devonshire, Sports and Public Schools Club; no. 4 was home to Nancy Astor, the first woman MP, in 1919; while no. 31 was where Eisenhower formed the first Allied HQ. The narrowest house on the square (no. 14) is the **London Library**, a private library founded in 1841 by Thomas Carlyle, who got sick of waiting up to two hours for books to be retrieved from the British Library shelves only to find he couldn't borrow them (he used to steal them instead).

The square is no longer residential and, architecturally, it's not quite the period piece it once was, but its proportions remain intact, as do the central **gardens**, which feature an equestrian statue of **William III**, depicted tripping over on the molehill that killed him at Hampton Court. In the northeastern corner, there's a memorial marking the spot where police officer **Yvonne Fletcher** was shot dead in 1984, during a demonstration by Libyan dissidents outside what was then the Libyan embassy, at no. 5. Following the shooting, the embassy was besieged by armed police for eleven days, but in the end the diplomats were simply expelled and no one has ever been charged.

Schomberg House

80–82 Pall Mall

The unusual seventeenth-century mansion of **Schomberg House** is one of the few to stand out on Pall Mall, thanks to its Dutch-style red brickwork and elongated caryatids. In 1769, the house was divided into three, and the artist, Thomas

Gainsborough, who was at the height of his fame, lived in no 80, the western portion until his death in 1788. Next door, at no. 81, a Scottish quack doctor, James Graham, ran his Temple of Health and Hymen, where couples having trouble conceiving could try their luck in the "grand celestial bed" for £50 a night (a fortune in those days).

79 Pall Mall

Charles II housed **Nell Gwynne** here, and even gave her the freehold, so that the two of them could chat over the garden wall, which once backed onto the grounds of St James's Palace. It was from one of the windows overlooking the garden that Nell is alleged to have dangled her 6-year-old, threatening to drop him if Charles didn't acknowledge paternity and give the boy a title, at which Charles yelled out "Save the Earl of Burford!"; another, more tabloid-style version of the story alleges that Charles was persuaded only after overhearing Nell saying "Come here, you little bastard", then excusing herself on the grounds that she had no other name by which to call him.

Marlborough House

Pall Mall • Visits only by guided tour of groups of ten or more • ☎ 020 7747 6491, ⓦ thecommonwealth.org • ⊖ Green Park

Marlborough House itself is hidden from Marlborough Road by a high, brick wall, and only partly visible from The Mall. Queen Anne sacrificed half her garden in granting this land to her lover, Sarah Jennings, Duchess of Marlborough, in 1709. The duchess, in turn, told Wren to design her a "strong, plain and convenient" palace, only to sack him later and finish the plans off herself. The highlight of the interior is the **Blenheim Saloon**, with its frescoes depicting the first duke's eponymous victory, along with ceiling paintings by Gentileschi transferred from the Queen's House in Greenwich. The royals took over in 1817, though the last one to live here was Queen Mary, wife of George V. Since 1965, the palace has been the headquarters of the Commonwealth Secretariat, and can only be visited on a guided tour.

THE GENTLEMEN'S CLUBS

The **gentlemen's clubs** of Pall Mall and St James's Street remain the final bastions of the male chauvinism and public-school snobbery for which England is famous. Their origins lie in the coffee- and chocolate-houses of the eighteenth century, though the majority were founded in the post-Napoleonic peace of the early nineteenth century by those who yearned for the life of the officers' mess; drinking, whoring and gambling were the major features of early club life. **White's** – the oldest of the lot, and with a list of members that still includes numerous royals (Prince Charles held his [first] stag party here), prime ministers and admirals – used to be the unofficial Tory party headquarters, renowned for its high gambling stakes, while, opposite, was the Whigs' favourite club, **Brooks's**. Bets were wagered over the most trivial of things to relieve the boredom – "a thousand meadows and cornfields were staked at every throw" – and in 1755 one MP, Sir John Bland, shot himself after losing £32,000 in one night.

In their day, the clubs were also the battleground of sartorial elegance, particularly **Boodle's**, where the dandy-in-chief Beau Brummell set the fashion trends for the London upper class and provided endless fuel for gossip. It was said that Brummell's greatest achievement in life was his starched neckcloth, and that the Prince Regent himself wept openly when Brummell criticized the line of his cravat. More serious political disputes were played out in clubland, too. The **Reform Club** on Pall Mall, from which Phileas Fogg set off in Jules Verne's *Around the World in Eighty Days*, was the gathering place of the liberals behind the 1832 Reform Act, and remains one of the more "progressive" – it was one of the first to admit women as members in 1981. The Tories, led by Wellington, countered by starting up the **Carlton Club** for those opposed to the Act – bombed by the IRA in 1990, it's still the leading Conservative club, and only admitted women as full members in 2008 (Mrs Thatcher was made an honorary member).

St James's Palace

St James's Palace was built on the site of a lepers' hospital which Henry VIII bought in 1532. Bloody Mary died here in 1558 (her heart and bowels were buried in the Chapel Royal), and it was here that Charles I chose to sleep the night before his execution, so as not to have to listen to his scaffold being erected. When Whitehall Palace burnt down in 1698, St James's became the principal royal residence and even today it remains the official residence, with every ambassador to the UK accredited to the "Court of St James's", even though the monarchy moved over to Buckingham Palace in 1837. The main red-brick gate-tower, which looks out onto St James's Street, is a survivor from Tudor times; the rest of the modest, rambling, crenellated complex was restored and remodelled by Nash, and now provides a home for Princess Anne and Princess Alexandra and for the staff of Princes William and Harry.

Chapel Royal

Open for services only: Oct to Easter Sun 8.30am & 11.15am · ⊖ Green Park

St James's Palace is off-limits to the public, with the exception of the **Chapel Royal**, which is accessed from Cleveland Row. Charles I took Holy Communion in the chapel on the morning of his execution, and here, too, the marriages of William and Mary, George III and Queen Charlotte, Victoria and Albert, and George V and Queen Mary took place. One of the few remaining sections of Henry VIII's palace, it was redecorated in the 1830s, though the gilded strap-work ceiling matches the Tudor original erected to commemorate the brief marriage of Henry and Anne of Cleves (and thought to have been the work of Hans Holbein). The chapel's musical pedigree is impressive, with Tallis, Byrd, Gibbons and Purcell all having worked here as organists. Purcell even had rooms in the palace, which the poet Dryden used to use in order to hide from his creditors.

Queen's Chapel

Open for services only: Easter to July Sun 8.30am & 11.15am · ⊖ Green Park

Despite being on the other side of Marlborough Road, the **Queen's Chapel** is officially part of St James's Palace. A perfectly proportioned classical church, it was designed by Inigo Jones (with Gibbons and Wren helping with the decoration) for the Infanta of Spain, intended child bride of Charles I, and later completed for his French wife, Henrietta Maria, who was also a practising Catholic. A little further down Marlborough Road is the glorious Art-Nouveau memorial to **Queen Alexandra** (wife of Edward VII), the last work of Alfred Gilbert (of Eros fame), comprising a bronze fountain crammed with allegorical figures and flanked by robust lampposts.

Clarence House

Aug Mon–Fri 10am–4pm, Sat & Sun 10am–5.30pm · £8.50 · ☎ 020 7766 7303, ⓦ royalcollection.org.uk · ⊖ Green Park

John Nash was also responsible for **Clarence House**, which is attached to the southwest wing of St James's Palace. Built in the 1820s for William IV and used as his principal residence, it was occupied by various royals until the death of George VI, after which it became the home of the Queen Mother, George's widow for nearly sixty years. It's currently the official London home of Charles and Camilla (ⓦ princeofwales.gov.uk), but a handful of rooms can be visited over the summer when the royals are in Scotland. Visits (by guided tour) must be booked in advance, as they are extremely popular. The rooms are pretty unremarkable, so apart from a peek behind the scenes in a working royal palace, or a few mementoes of the Queen Mum, the main draw is the twentieth-century British paintings on display by the likes of Walter Sickert and Augustus John.

Jermyn Street

Jermyn Street (pronounced "German Street"), which runs parallel with Piccadilly, has been, along with Savile Row in Mayfair, the spiritual home of English gentlemen's fashion since the advent of the clubs (see box, p.73). Its window displays and wooden-panelled interiors still evoke an age when mass consumerism was unthinkable, and when it was considered that gentlemen "should either be a work of art or wear a work of art", as Oscar Wilde put it.

Antiquated epithets are part of the street's quaint appeal: Turnbull & Asser, at nos. 71–72, describe themselves as "Hosiers & Glovers"; Bates the hatters have found refuge in Hadditch & Key, the shirtmakers at no. 73, along with Binks, the stray cat which entered the shop in 1921 and never left, having been stuffed, sporting a cigar and top hat, and displayed in a glass cabinet; Taylor, a barber's at no. 74, are dubbed "Gentlemen's Court Hairdresser"; Foster & Son, a shoe shop at no. 85, style themselves as "Bootmakers since 1840"; while Floris, at no. 89, covers up the Royal Family's body odour with its ever-so-English fragrances, and Paxton & Whitfield, at no. 93, boasts an unrivalled selection of English and foreign cheeses.

Green Park

Green Park was established by Henry VIII on the burial ground of the old lepers' hospital that became St James's Palace. It was left more or less flowerless – hence its name (officially "The Green Park") – and, apart from the springtime swaths of daffodils and crocuses, it remains mostly meadow, shaded by graceful London plane trees. In its time, however, it was a popular place for duels (banned from neighbouring St James's Park), ballooning and fireworks displays. One such display was immortalized by Handel's *Music for the Royal Fireworks*, performed here on April 27, 1749, to celebrate the Peace of Aix-la-Chapelle, which ended the War of the Austrian Succession – over ten thousand fireworks were let off, setting fire to the custom-built Temple of Peace and causing three fatalities. The music was a great success, however.

Along the east side of the park runs the wide, pedestrian-only **Queen's Walk**, laid out for Queen Caroline, wife of George II, who had a little pavilion built nearby. At its southern end, there's a good view of **Lancaster House** (closed to the public), a grand Neoclassical palace built in rich Bath stone in the 1820s by Benjamin Wyatt, and used for government receptions and conferences since 1913. It was here that the end of white rule in Southern Rhodesia was negotiated in the late 1970s.

Spencer House

St James's Place • Feb–July & Sept–Dec Sun 10.30am–5.45pm • £9, no under-10s • ☎ 020 7499 8620, ⊛ spencerhouse.co.uk • ⊖ Green Park

A sign in one of the gardens backing onto Queen's Walk announces Princess Diana's ancestral home, **Spencer House**, one of London's finest Palladian mansions. Erected in the 1750s, its best-looking facade looks out over Queen's Walk onto Green Park, though access is from St James's Place. Inside, tour guides take you through nine of the state rooms, returned to something like their original condition by current owners, the Rothschilds. The Great Room features a stunning coved and coffered ceiling in green, white and gold, while the adjacent Painted Room is a feast of Neoclassicism, decorated with murals in the "Pompeian manner". The most outrageous decor, though, is to be found in Lord Spencer's Room, with its astonishing gilded palm-tree columns.

PICCADILLY CIRCUS

Mayfair

Although shops, offices, embassies and hotels outnumber aristocratic pieds-à-terre nowadays, the social cachet of the luxury apartments and mews houses of Mayfair has remained much the same. This is, after all, where the fictional Bertie Wooster – the perfect upper-class Englishman – and his faithful valet Jeeves, of P.G. Wodehouse's interwar novels, lived. Piccadilly may not be the fashionable promenade it once was, but a whiff of exclusivity still pervades Bond Street and its tributaries, where designer clothes emporia jostle for space with jewellers, bespoke tailors and fine art dealers. Most Londoners, however, stick to Regent and Oxford streets, home to the flagship branches of the country's most popular chain stores. It's here that Londoners are referring to when they talk of "going shopping up the West End".

Along with neighbouring St James's and Marylebone, **Mayfair** emerged in the eighteenth century as one of London's first real residential suburbs. Sheep and cattle were driven off the land by the area's big landowners (the largest of whom were the Grosvenor family, whose head is the Duke of Westminster, Britain's richest man) to make way for London's first major planned development: a web of brick-and-stucco terraces and grid-plan streets feeding into grand, formal squares, with mews and stables round the back. The name comes from the infamous fifteen-day fair, which bit the dust in 1764 after the newly ensconced wealthy residents complained of the "drunkenness, fornication, gaming and lewdness". Mayfair quickly began to attract aristocratic London away from hitherto fashionable Covent Garden and Soho, and set the westward trend for upper-middle-class migration.

Piccadilly Circus

Tacky and congested it may be, but Piccadilly Circus is, for many Londoners, the nearest their city comes to having a centre. A much-altered product of Nash's grand 1812 **Regent Street** plan, and now a major bottleneck, with traffic from Piccadilly, Shaftesbury Avenue and Regent Street all converging, it's by no means a picturesque place, and is probably best seen at night, when the spread of illuminated signs (a feature since the Edwardian era) gives it a touch of Times Square dazzle, and when the human traffic flow is at its most frenetic.

As well as being the gateway to the West End, this is also prime tourist territory, thanks mostly to the celebrated Shaftesbury Memorial, popularly known as **Eros**. The fountain's aluminium archer is one of London's top tourist attractions, a status that baffles all who live here – when it was first unveiled in 1893, it was so unpopular that the sculptor, Alfred Gilbert, lived in self-imposed exile for the next thirty years. The figure depicted is not Eros, but his lesser-known brother Anteros, who was the god of unrequited love, although in this case he commemorates the selfless philanthropic love of the Earl of Shaftesbury, a Bible-thumping social reformer who campaigned against child labour.

Behind Eros, it's worth popping in to **The Criterion** restaurant, at no. 224 Piccadilly, just for a drink, so you can soak in probably the most spectacular Victorian interior in London, with Byzantine-style gilded mosaic ceiling.

Trocadero

Piccadilly Circus · Daily 10am–midnight, Fri & Sat until 1am · ⓦ londontrocadero.com · ⊖ Piccadilly Circus

Just east of the Circus, **Trocadero** was originally an opulent restaurant, from 1896 until its closure in 1965. Since then, millions have been poured into this glorified amusement arcade, casino and multiplex cinema, in an unsuccessful attempt to find a winning formula. Much of the building is currently being gutted and redeveloped to include London's first pod hotel.

Ripley's Believe It or Not!

Piccadilly Circus · Daily 10am–midnight · £25 · ⓣ 020 3238 0022, ⓦ ripleyslondon.com · ⊖ Piccadilly Circus

Meanwhile, next door, in what was once the London Pavilion music hall, you'll find the world's largest branch of **Ripley's Believe It or Not!**, which bills itself as an odditorium. It's half waxworks, half old-fashioned Victorian freak show, with a mirror maze thrown in for good measure. Delights on display include shrunken heads and dinosaur eggs, a chewing gum sculpture of the Fab Four, and Tower Bridge rendered in 264,345 matchsticks. Booking online will save you a few pounds off the stratospheric admission charge.

Regent Street

Regent Street was drawn up by John Nash in 1812 as both a luxury shopping street and a triumphal way between George IV's Carlton House and Regent's Park to the north. It was the city's first stab at slum clearance, creating a tangible borderline to shore up fashionable Mayfair against the chaotic maze of neighbouring Soho. Today, it's still possible to admire the stately intentions of Nash's plan, even though the original arcading of the **Quadrant**, which curves westwards from Piccadilly Circus, is no longer there.

Regent Street enjoyed eighty years as Bond Street's nearest rival, before the rise of the city's middle classes ushered in heavyweight stores catering for the masses. Two of the oldest established stores can be found close to one another on the east side of the street: **Hamleys**, which claims to be the world's largest toy shop, and **Liberty**, the department store that popularized Arts and Crafts designs. Liberty features a central roof-lit well, surrounded by wooden galleries carved from the timbers of two old naval battleships; an overhead walkway leads to the eye-catching mock-Tudor extension, added in the 1920s.

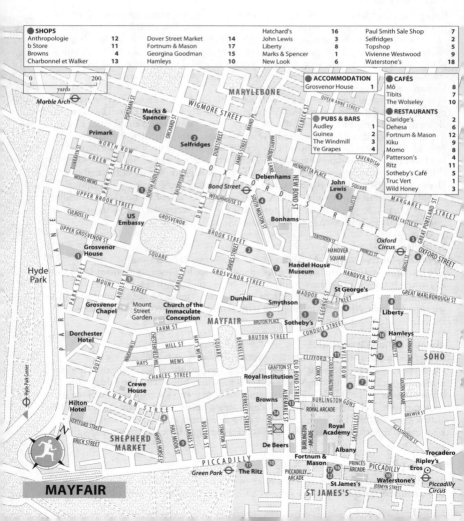

● SHOPS						
Anthropologie	12	Dover Street Market	14	Hatchard's	16	Paul Smith Sale Shop	7
b Store	11	Fortnum & Mason	17	John Lewis	3	Selfridges	2
Browns	4	Georgina Goodman	15	Liberty	8	Topshop	5
Charbonnel et Walker	13	Hamleys	10	Marks & Spencer	1	Vivienne Westwood	9
				New Look	6	Waterstone's	18

● ACCOMMODATION	
Grosvenor House	1

● CAFÉS	
Mô	8
Tibits	7
The Wolseley	10

● PUBS & BARS	
Audley	1
Guinea	2
The Windmill	3
Ye Grapes	4

● RESTAURANTS	
Claridge's	2
Dehesa	6
Fortnum & Mason	12
Kiku	9
Momo	8
Patterson's	4
Ritz	11
Sotheby's Café	5
Truc Vert	1
Wild Honey	3

MAYFAIR

MONOPOLY

Although **Monopoly** was patented during the Depression by an American, Charles Darrow, the British really took to the game, and the UK version was the one used in the rest of the world outside of the US. In 1935, to choose appropriate streets and stations for the game, the company director of Waddington's in Leeds sent his son, Norman Watson, and his secretary, Marjorie Phillips, on a day-trip to London. She came up with an odd assortment, ranging from the bottom-ranking Old Kent Road (still as tatty as ever) to an obscure dead-end street in the West End (Vine Street), and chose only northern train stations. All the properties have gone up in value since the board's inception (six zeros need to be added to most), but Mayfair and Park Lane (its western border), the most expensive properties on the Monopoly board, are still aspirational addresses.

Piccadilly

Piccadilly apparently got its name from the ruffs or "pickadills" worn by the dandies who promenaded here in the late seventeenth century. Despite its fashionable pedigree, it's no place for promenading in its current state, with three lanes of traffic careering down its nose to tail most of the day and night. Infinitely more pleasant places to window-shop are the **nineteenth-century arcades**, originally built to protect shoppers from the mud and horse dung on the streets, but now equally useful for escaping exhaust fumes.

Waterstone's and Hatchards

One of the most striking shops on Piccadilly, at nos. 203–206, is the sleek modernist 1930s facade of Simpsons department store, now the multi-storey flagship store of **Waterstone's** chain of bookshops. While Piccadilly may not be the shopping heaven it once was, it still harbours several old firms that proudly display their royal warrants. London's oldest bookshop, **Hatchards**, at no. 187, was founded in 1797, as a cross between a gentlemen's club and a library, with benches outside for servants and daily papers for the gentlemen inside to peruse. Today, it's a sister branch of Waterstone's, elegant still, but with its old traditions marked most overtly by a large section on international royalty.

St James's Church

197 Piccadilly • ☎ 020 7734 4511, ⊛ st-james-piccadilly.org • ⊖ Piccadilly Circus

Halfway along the south side of Piccadilly stands **St James's Church**, Wren's favourite parish church (he built it himself). The church has rich furnishings, with the limewood reredos, organ-casing and marble font all by the master sculptor **Grinling Gibbons**. St James's is a radical campaigning church, which runs a daily craft market (Tues–Sat) and a café at the west end of the church; it also puts on top-class, free lunchtime concerts and regularly displays contemporary outdoor sculptures in the churchyard.

Fortnum & Mason

181 Piccadilly • Mon–Sat 10am–8pm, Sun noon–6pm • ☎ 020 7734 8040, ⊛ fortnumandmason.com • ⊖ Green Park or Piccadilly Circus

One of Piccadilly's oldest institutions is **Fortnum & Mason**, the food emporium established in the 1770s by Charles Fortnum, one of George III's footmen. Over the main entrance, the figures of its founders bow to each other on the hour as the clock clanks out the Eton school anthem – a kitsch addition from 1964. The store is most famous for its opulent food hall and its picnic hampers, first introduced as "concentrated lunches" for hunting and shooting parties, and now *de rigueur* for Ascot, Glyndebourne, Henley and other society events. Fortnum's is credited with the invention of the Scotch Egg in 1851, and was also the first store in the world to sell Heinz baked beans in 1886.

Albany

One palatial Piccadilly residence which has avoided redevelopment is **Albany**, a plain, H-shaped Georgian mansion, designed by William Chambers, neatly recessed behind

THE SUMMER EXHIBITION

The most famous event in the Royal Academy's calendar is the **Summer Exhibition**, which has been held annually since 1769, and runs from June to mid-August. It's an odd event: anyone can enter paintings in any style. Around 10,000 entries are surveyed (at considerable speed) by the RA's Hanging Committee (great name) and around 1000 lucky winners get hung, in extremely close proximity, and sold. In addition, the eighty "Academicians" are allowed to display up to six of their own works – no matter how awful. The result is a bewildering display, which gets annually panned by the critics. However, with thirty percent of the purchase price going to the RA, it generates at least £2 million in income.

its own iron railings and courtyard, next door to the Royal Academy. Built in the 1770s for Lord Melbourne, it was divided in 1802 into a series of self-contained bachelor "sets" for members of the nearby gentlemen's clubs too drunk to make it home. Only those who had no connections with trade, and did not keep a musical instrument or a wife, were permitted to live here, and over the years they have been occupied by such literary figures as Byron, Gladstone, J.B. Priestley, Aldous Huxley, Patrick Hamilton and Graham Greene.

Royal Academy of the Arts

Burlington House, Piccadilly • Daily 10am–6pm, Fri until 10pm • £10–12 • John Madejski Fine Rooms guided tours Tues 1pm, Wed–Fri 1 & 3pm, Sat 11.30am; Free • ☎ 020 7300 8000, ⓦ royalacademy.org.uk • ⊖ Green Park

The **Royal Academy of Arts** occupies Burlington House, one of the few survivors from the ranks of aristocratic mansions that once lined the north side of Piccadilly. Rebuilding in the nineteenth century destroyed the original curved colonnades beyond the main gateway, but the complex has kept the feel of a Palladian *palazzo*. The academy itself was the country's first formal art school, founded in 1768 by a group of painters including Thomas Gainsborough and Joshua Reynolds. Reynolds went on to become the academy's first president, and his statue now stands in the courtyard, palette in hand ready to paint the cars hurtling down Piccadilly.

The academy's alumni range from Turner and Constable to Hockney and Tracey Emin, though the college has always had a conservative reputation for both its teaching and its shows. As well as hosting exhibitions, the RA has a small selection of works from its permanent collection in the white and gold **John Madejski Fine Rooms**. Highlights include a Rembrandtesque self-portrait by Reynolds, plus works by the likes of Constable, Hockney and Stanley Spencer. To see the gallery's most valuable asset, Michelangelo's marble relief, the *Taddei Tondo*, head for the glass atrium of Norman Foster's Sackler Galleries, at the back of the building.

The Wolseley and the Ritz

Further along Piccadilly, on the corner of Arlington Street, **The Wolseley** is a superb Art Deco building, originally built as a Wolseley car showroom in the 1920s, now a café (see p.368). The most striking original features are the zigzag inlaid marble flooring, the chinoiserie woodwork and the giant red Japanese lacquer columns. Across St James's Street, with its best rooms overlooking Green Park, stands the **Ritz Hotel**, famous for its afternoon teas (see p.377) and a byword for decadence since it first wowed Edwardian society in 1906. The hotel's design, with its two-storey French-style mansard roof and long arcade, was based on the rue de Rivoli in Paris.

Burlington Arcade

Mon–Wed & Fri 8am–6.30pm, Thurs 8am–7pm, Sat 9am–6.30pm, Sun 11am–5pm • Free • ⓦ burlington-arcade.co.uk • ⊖ Green Park

Along the side of the Royal Academy runs the **Burlington Arcade**, built in 1819 for Lord Cavendish, then owner of Burlington House, to prevent commoners throwing rubbish into his garden. Today, it's London's longest and most expensive nineteenth-century arcade, lined with mahogany-fronted jewellers, gentlemen's outfitters and the like. Upholding Regency decorum, it's still illegal to whistle, sing, hum, hurry or carry large packages or open umbrellas on this small stretch, and the arcade's beadles (known as Burlington Berties), in their Edwardian frock coats and gold-braided top hats, take the prevention of such criminality very seriously.

Piccadilly and Princes arcades

ⓦ piccadilly-arcade.com • ⊖ Green Park or Piccadilly Circus

Neither of Piccadilly's other two arcades can hold a torch to the Burlington, though they are still worth exploring if only to marvel at the strange mixture of shops. The finer of the two is the **Piccadilly Arcade**, an Edwardian extension to the Burlington on the south side of Piccadilly whose squeaky-clean bow windows display, among other items, Russian icons, model soldiers and buttons and cufflinks supplied to Prince Charles. The **Princes Arcade**, to the east, exudes a more discreet Neoclassical elegance and contains Prestat, purveyors of handmade, hand-packed chocolates and truffles to the Queen.

Bond Street

Bond Street runs more or less parallel to Regent Street, extending north from Piccadilly all the way to Oxford Street. It is, in fact, two streets rolled into one: the southern half, laid out in the 1680s, is known as **Old Bond Street**; its northern extension, which followed less than fifty years later, is known as **New Bond Street**. In contrast to their international rivals, rue de Rivoli and Fifth Avenue, both Bond streets are pretty unassuming architecturally – a mixture of modest Georgian and Victorian townhouses – but the shops that line them are among the flashiest in London.

Shopping

Unlike its overtly masculine counterpart, Jermyn Street (see p.75), **Bond Street** caters for both sexes, and although it has its fair share of old-established names, it's also home to flagship branches of multinational **designer clothes** outlets like Prada, D&G, Versace, Chanel and so on. This designer madness also spills over into **Conduit Street**, home to Issey Miyake, Vivienne Westwood and Moschino, not to mention Rigby & Peller, corsetieres to the Queen, as well as into neighbouring Dover Street, where Comme des Garçons have a vast indoor fashion bazaar at nos. 17–18.

Bond Street also has its fair share of perfumeries and **jewellers**, many of them long-established outlets that have survived the vicissitudes of fashion, and some, like De Beers, relatively recent arrivals. One of the most famous is **Asprey**, founded in 1781 by a family of Huguenot craftsmen, and now jewellers to the royals. The facade of the store, at no. 167, features a wonderful parade of arched windows, flanked by slender Corinthian wrought-iron columns. Close by is "Allies", a popular double statue of **Winston Churchill and President Roosevelt**, enjoying a chat on a bench – you can squeeze between the two of them, in the space where Stalin should be, for a photo opportunity.

Auction houses and art galleries

In addition to fashion, Bond Street is renowned for its **auction houses** (see box, p.82) and **art galleries**, although the latter are actually outnumbered by those on neighbouring **Cork Street**. The main difference between the two is that the Bond Street dealers are basically heirloom offloaders, where you might catch an Old Master or an Impressionist masterpiece, whereas Cork Street galleries sell largely contemporary art. Both have somewhat intimidating staff, but if you're interested, walk in (or ring the bell) and look around. They're only shops, after all.

3

3

AUCTION HOUSES

A very Mayfair-style entertainment lies in visiting the area's trio of auction houses. **Sotheby's**, 34–35 New Bond St (☎020 7293 5000, ⓦsothebys.com), was founded in 1744 and is the oldest of the three (and the fourth oldest in the world), though its pre-eminence only really dates from the last war. Above the doorway of Sotheby's is London's oldest outdoor sculpture, an Egyptian statue dating from 1600 BC. **Bonhams**, founded in 1793 (and now merged with Phillips), is at 101 New Bond St (☎020 7447 7447, ⓦbonhams.com); and **Christie's**, founded in 1766, is actually over in St James's at 8 King St (☎020 7839 9060, ⓦchristies.com).

Viewing takes place from Monday to Friday, and also occasionally at the weekend, and entry to the galleries is free of charge, though if you don't buy a catalogue, the only information you'll glean is the lot number. Thousands of the works that pass through the rooms are of museum quality, and, if you're lucky, you might catch a glimpse of a masterpiece in transit between private collections. Anyone can attend the auctions themselves, though remember to keep your hands firmly out of view unless you're bidding.

Sotheby's is probably the least intimidating: there's an excellent **café**, and staff offer free valuations, if you have an heirloom of your own to check out. There's always a line of people unwrapping plastic bags under the polite gaze of valuation staff, who call in the experts if they see something that sniffs of real money. Of the three, only Bonhams remains British-owned; Christie's and Sotheby's, once quintessentially English institutions, are now under French and US control, and both were found guilty of price-fixing in 2002.

Smythson

40 New Bond St • Mon–Wed & Fri 9.30am–6pm, Thurs 10am–7pm, Sat 10am–6pm • ⓦsmythson.com • ⊖ Bond Street

One Bond Street institution you can feel free to walk into is **Smythson**, the bespoke stationers, founded in 1887, who made their name printing Big Game books for colonialists to record what they'd bagged out in Africa and India. At the back of the shop is a small octagonal museum encrusted with shells and mirrors, and a few artefacts: photos and replicas of the book of condolence Smythson created for JFK's funeral, and the cherry calf-and-vellum diary given to Princess Grace of Monaco as a wedding gift.

Albemarle Street

Running parallel to Bond Street, to the west, is **Albemarle Street**, connected by the **Royal Arcade**, a small, but full-blown High Victorian shopping mall with tall arched bays and an elegant glass roof, with garish orange-and-white plasterwork entrances at either end. It was designed so that the wealthy guests of **Brown's** hotel in Albemarle Street could have a sheltered and suitably elegant approach to the shops on Bond Street. Apart from being a posh hotel opened in the 1830s by James Brown, Byron's former valet, *Brown's* is famous as the place where the country's first telephone call was placed by **Alexander Graham Bell** in 1876, though initially he got a crossed line with a private telegraph wire. Also in Albemarle Street, at no. 50, are the offices of **John Murray**, the publishers of Byron and of the oldest British travel guides. It was here in 1824 that Byron's memoirs were burnt to cinders, after Murray persuaded Tom Moore, to whom they had been bequeathed, that they were too scurrilous to publish.

Royal Institution

21 Albemarle Street • Mon–Fri 9am–9pm • Free • ☎020 7409 2992 • ⓦrigb.org • ⊖ Green Park

The weighty Neoclassical facade at 21 Albermarle Street heralds the **Royal Institution**, a scientific body founded in 1799 "for teaching by courses of philosophical lectures and experiments the application of science to the common purposes of life". The RI is best known for its six Christmas Lectures, begun by Michael Faraday and designed to popularize science among schoolchildren, but it also houses an enjoyable interactive **museum** aimed at both kids and adults. In the basement, you can learn about the ten chemical elements that have been discovered at the RI, and about the famous experiments that have taken place here: Tyndall's blue-sky tube, Humphry Davy's early lamps and Faraday's explorations into electromagnetism – there's even a reconstruction of Faraday's lab from the 1850s. The ground floor has displays on the fourteen Nobel Prize winners who have worked at the RI, while on the first floor, you can visit the semi circular hall where the Christmas Lectures take place and see some of the apparatus used in lectures over the decades.

Savile Row

Running parallel with New Bond Street, to the east, is another classic address in sartorial matters, **Savile Row**, *the* place to go for bespoke tailors since the early nineteenth century. Gieves & Hawkes, at no. 1, were the first tailors to establish themselves here back in 1785, with Nelson and Wellington among their first customers – they made the military uniform worn by Prince William at his wedding. More modern in outlook, Kilgour, at no. 8, famously made Fred Astaire's morning coat for *Top Hat*, helping to popularize Savile Row tailoring in the US. Henry Poole & Co, who moved to no. 15 in 1846 and has cut suits for the likes of Napoleon III, Dickens, Churchill and de Gaulle, invented the short smoking jacket (originally designed for the future Edward VII), later popularized as the "tuxedo".

Savile Row also has connections with the pop world. **The Beatles** used to buy their suits from Tommy Nutter's House of Nutter established in 1968 at no. 35, and in the same year set up the offices and recording studio of their record label **Apple** at no. 3, until the building's near physical collapse in 1972. On January 30, 1969, The Beatles gave an impromptu gig (their last live performance) on the roof here, stopping traffic and eventually attracting the attentions of the local police – as captured on film in *Let It Be*.

Mayfair's squares

Mayfair has three showpiece Georgian squares: **Hanover**, the most modest of the three and **Berkeley** and **Grosvenor**, the most grandiose, named after the district's two big private landowners. Planned as purely residential, all have suffered over the years, and have nothing like the homogeneity of the Bloomsbury squares. Nevertheless, they are still impressive urban spaces, and their social lustre remains more or less untarnished. Each one is worth visiting, and travelling between them gives you a chance to experience Mayfair's backstreets and, en route, visit one or two slightly more hidden sights.

St George's Church, Hanover Square

1–2 Hanover Square • Mon–Fri 8am–4pm, Sun 8am–noon • Free • ⓦ stgeorgeshanoversquare.org • ⊖ Bond Street

At the very southern tip of **Hanover Square** stands the Corinthian portico of **St George's Church**, much copied since, but the first of its kind in London when it was built in the 1720s. Nicknamed "London's Temple of Hymen", it has long been Mayfair's most fashionable church for weddings. Among those who tied the knot here are the Shelleys, Benjamin Disraeli, Teddy Roosevelt and George Eliot. The composer, Handel, a confirmed bachelor, was a warden here for many years and even had his own pew. North of the church, the funnel-shaped St George Street splays into the square itself, which used to boast the old Hanover Square Rooms venue, where Bach, Liszt, Haydn and Paganini all performed before the building's demolition in 1900.

Handel House Museum

25 Brook St • Tues–Sat 10am–6pm, Thurs till 8pm, Sun noon–6pm • £6 • ☏ 020 7495 1685 • ⓦ handelhouse.org • ⊖ Bond Street

The **Handel House Museum**, one block west of Hanover Square, is where the composer, Handel, lived for 36 years from 1723 until his death. He used the ground floor as a shop where subscribers could buy scores, while on the first floor, there was a rehearsal and performance room, plus a composition room at the back. The museum has few original artefacts, but the house has been redecorated to how it would have looked in Handel's day. Further atmosphere is provided by the harpsichord students who often practise in the rehearsal room; to find out about the regular recitals, visit the website. Access to the house is via the chic, cobbled yard at the back of the house.

Berkeley Square

Berkeley Square is where, according to the music-hall song, nightingales sing (though it's probable they were, in fact, blackcaps). Laid out in the 1730s, only the west side of the square has any surviving Georgian houses to boast of, and nowadays any birds would have trouble being heard over the traffic. However, what saves the square is its wonderful parade of 200-year-old **London plane trees**. With their dappled, exfoliating trunks, giant lobed leaves and globular spiky fruits, these pollution-resistant trees are a ubiquitous feature of the city, and Berkeley Square's specimens are among the finest. The square also has royal connections, as the Queen was born just off it, at 17 Bruton St, and then lived at 145 Piccadilly until 1936.

3

Bourdon House: Alfred Dunhill

Ⓦ dunhill.com • ⊖ Bond Street

Just north of Berkeley Square, it's possible to see inside **Bourdon House**, a lovely Georgian mansion on the corner of Davies and Bourdon streets. Former private residence of the Duke of Westminster, the house is now the flagship store of **Alfred Dunhill**. Don't be put off by the intimidating staff, but head for the first floor, where a few items are displayed from the days of Dunhill Motorities, gadget suppliers to Rolls Royce, whose slogan was "everything but the motor". This wonderful range made hip

---

HANDEL AND HENDRIX

Born **Georg Friedrich Händel** (1685–1759) in Halle, Saxony, Handel first visited London in 1710, composing *Rinaldo* in fifteen days flat. The furore it produced – not least when Handel released a flock of sparrows for one aria – made him a household name. The following year he was commissioned to write several works for Queen Anne, eventually becoming court composer to George I, his one-time patron in Hanover.

London quickly became Handel's permanent home: he anglicized his name and nationality and lived out the rest of his life here, producing all the work for which he is now best known, including the *Water Music*, the *Fireworks Music* and his *Messiah*, which failed to enthral its first audiences, but which is now one of the great set pieces of Protestant musical culture. George II was so moved by the *Hallelujah Chorus* that he leapt to his feet and remained standing for the entire performance. Handel himself fainted during a performance in 1759, and died shortly afterwards in his home, now a museum (see p.83); he is buried in Westminster Abbey. Today, Handel's birthday is celebrated with a concert at the Foundling Museum (see p.123), and an annual Handel Festival (Ⓦ london-handel-festival.com) takes place annually at St George's Church, Hanover Square (see p.83).

Two centuries later, **Jimi Hendrix** (1942–70) moved into the top floor flat of 23 Brook St, next door to Handel's old address, and lived there for eighteen months or so. Born in Seattle in 1942, Hendrix was persuaded to fly over to London in 1966 by The Animals. Shortly after arriving, he teamed up with two other British musicians, Noel Redding and Mitch Mitchell, and formed The Jimi Hendrix Experience. It was at the beginning of 1969 that Hendrix moved into Brook Street with his girlfriend, Kathy Etchingham; apparently he was much taken with the fact that it was once Handel's residence, ordering Kathy to go and buy the albums for him. It was also in London that Hendrix met his untimely death, on September 18, 1970. At the *Samarkand Hotel* in Notting Hill, after a gig at *Ronnie Scott's* in Soho, Hendrix, with alcohol still in his system, swallowed a handful of sleeping pills, later vomiting in his sleep and slipping into unconsciousness. He was pronounced dead on arrival at St Mary's Hospital, Paddington, and is buried in Seattle.

flasks disguised as books, "Bobby Finders" for detecting police cars, in-car hookahs and even a motorist's pipe with a windshield for open-top toking.

Grosvenor Square

To the northwest of Bourdon House, **Grosvenor Square**, is the largest of Mayfair's squares, and was known during World War II as "Little America" – General Eisenhower, whose statue stands in the square, ran the D-Day campaign from no. 20. The American presence is still pretty strong, thanks to the Roosevelt Memorial, the Ronald Reagan Statue, the 9/11 memorial garden dedicated to the 67 British victims of the 2001 attack, and the monstrously ugly and heavily guarded **US Embassy**, built in 1960, which occupies the entire west side of the square. The embassy is watched over by a giant gilded eagle plus a posse of armed police, and has been the victim of numerous attacks over the decades. The first major incident occurred in 1967 when Spanish anarchists machine-gunned the embassy in protest against US collaboration with Franco. The most famous (and violent) protest took place in 1968, when a demonstration against US involvement in Vietnam turned into a riot. Mick Jagger, so the story goes, was innocently signing autographs in his Bentley as the 1968 riot began, and later wrote *Street Fighting Man*, inspired by what he witnessed. Most weeks, there's some group or other camped out objecting to US foreign policy – in fact, American security concerns are such that they plan to move the embassy to a purpose-built $1 billion complex in Vauxhall in 2016.

3

Claridge's

49 Brook St • ☎ 020 7629 8860 • ⓦ claridges.co.uk • ➌ Bond Street

Claridge's started out in 1812 as Mivart's Hotel in a small terraced house, but has grown considerably larger since those days. The current building dates from 1898, has over 200 rooms, a Gordon Ramsay restaurant, and still attracts Hollywood and pop glitterati from Brad Pitt to U2. Its royal connections are also second to none. Most famously, King Peter II of Yugoslavia spent most of World War II in exile at the hotel – suite 212 was ceded to Yugoslavia for a day on June 17, 1945 so that his son and heir, Crown Prince Alexander, could be born on Yugoslav soil. A room in the hotel, painted "whorehouse pink", served as General Eisenhower's initial wartime pied-à-terre, and it was also the wartime hangout of the OSS, forerunner of the CIA. It was here in 1943 that Szmul Zygielbojm from the Polish government-in-exile, was told that Roosevelt had refused his request to bomb the rail lines leading to Auschwitz; the following day he committed suicide.

Grosvenor Chapel

24 South Audley St • Mon–Fri 9am–12.30pm • Free • ⓦ grosvenorchapel.org.uk • ➌ Bond Street, Green Park or Hyde Park Corner

American troops stationed over here used to worship at the **Grosvenor Chapel** two blocks south of Claridge's on South Audley Street, a simple classical building that formed the model for early settlers' churches in New England and still popular with the American community. The church's most illustrious corpse is radical MP John Wilkes ("Wilkes and Liberty" was the battle cry of many a mid-eighteenth-century riot). The interior comes as something of a surprise, however, as it was redesigned in Anglo-Catholic style by Ninian Comper in 1912, and features an elaborate tableau of gilded statuary: Christ crucified is flanked by Mary and one of the disciples, with two angels kneeling below with chalices ready to catch the sacred blood.

Mount Street Gardens: Church of the Immaculate Conception

Farm Street • Daily 8am–7pm • Free • ⓦ farmstreet.org.uk • ➌ Bond Street or Green Park

Built in ostentatious neo-Gothic style in the 1840s, the **Church of the Immaculate Conception Farm Street** is the London stronghold of the Jesuits, and as such is a fascinating and unusual church. Every surface is covered in decoration, but the reredos of gilded stone by Pugin (of Houses of Parliament fame) is particularly impressive.

3

THE CATO STREET CONSPIRACY

British history is disappointingly short on political assassinations: one prime minister, no royals and only a handful of MPs. One of the most dismal failures was the 1820 **Cato Street Conspiracy**, drawn up by sixteen revolutionaries in an attic off the Edgware Road in Marylebone. Their plan was to decapitate the entire Cabinet as they dined with Lord Harrowby at 44 Grosvenor Square. Having beheaded the Home Secretary and another of the ministers, they then planned to sack Coutts Bank, capture the cannon on the Artillery Ground, take Gray's Inn, Mansion House, the Bank of England and the Tower, torching the barracks in the process, and proclaiming a provisional government.

As it turned out, one of the conspirators was an *agent provocateur*, and the entire mob was arrested in the Cato Street attic on the night of the planned coup, February 23. In the melee, one Bow Street Runner was killed but eventually eleven of the conspirators were arrested and charged with high treason. Five of the ringleaders were hanged at Newgate, and another five were transported to Australia. Public sympathy for the uprising was widespread, so the condemned were spared being drawn and quartered, though they did have their heads cut off afterwards. (The hangman was later attacked in the streets and almost castrated.)

Behind the chapel are the beautifully secluded **Mount Street Gardens**, dotted with 200-year-old plane trees and enclosed by nineteenth-century red-brick mansions.

Oxford Street

As wealthy Londoners began to move out of the City during the eighteenth century, in favour of the newly developed West End, so **Oxford Street** – the old Roman road to Oxford – gradually replaced Cheapside as London's main shopping street. Today, despite successive recessions and sky-high rents, this two-mile hotchpotch of shops is still one of the world's busiest streets, its Christmas lights switched on by the briefly famous, and its traffic controllers equipped with loud-hailers to prevent the hordes of Christmas shoppers from losing their lives at the busy road junctions. The stretch west of Oxford Circus is slightly more upmarket; east of Oxford Circus, the street forms a scruffy border between Soho and Fitzrovia.

Selfridges

400 Oxford St • Mon–Wed & Sat 9.30am–8pm, Thurs & Fri 9.30am–9pm, Sun noon–6pm • ⓦ selfridges.com • ⊖ Bond Street

The one long-standing landmark on Oxford Street is **Selfridges**, a huge Edwardian department store fronted by giant Ionic columns, with the Queen of Time riding the ship of commerce and supporting an Art Deco clock above the main entrance. Opened in 1909 by Chicago millionaire Harry Gordon Selfridge, Selfridges is the second largest shop in London (after Harrods), and is credited with selling the world's first television set, as well as introducing the concept of the "bargain basement", "the customer is always right", the irritating "only ten more shopping days to Christmas" countdown, and the nauseous bouquet of perfumes from the cosmetics counters, strategically placed at the entrance to all department stores. Selfridge himself was a big spender and eventually died in Putney in poverty in 1947 at the age of 90. Today, while Harrods may have the snob value and the longer pedigree, it's a conservative institution compared to Selfridges, which keeps reinventing itself and successfully remains ahead of the field, particularly in fashion – the window displays alone are worth the journey here.

Marylebone

Marylebone may not have quite the social pedigree and snob value of neighbouring Mayfair, but it's still a wealthy and aspirational area. This is where the city's leading private specialists in medicine and surgery have had their practices since they gravitated here in the nineteenth century. And it was here that The Beatles (and many others since) took up residence when they hit the big time in the 1960s. Compared to the brashness of Oxford Street, which forms its southern border, Marylebone's backstreets are a pleasure to wander, especially the chi-chi village-like quarter around Marylebone High Street. The area's more conventional sights include the free art gallery and aristocratic mansion of the Wallace Collection, Sherlock Holmes old stamping ground around Baker Street, and the massively touristy Madame Tussauds.

Marylebone was once the outlying village of St Mary-by-the-Bourne (the bourne in question being the Tyburn stream) or St Marylebone (pronounced "marra-le-bun"), and when Samuel Pepys walked through open countryside to reach its pleasure gardens in 1668, he declared it "a pretty place". During the course of the next century, the gardens were closed and the village was swallowed up as its chief landowners – among them the Portlands and the Portmans – laid out a mesh of uniform Georgian streets and squares, much of which survives today.

Langham Place

North of Oxford Circus, Regent Street forms the eastern border of Marylebone, but stops abruptly at **Langham Place**, which formed an awkward twist in John Nash's triumphal route to Regent's Park in order to link up with the pre-existing Portland Place. Nash's solution was to build his unusual All Souls Church, now the only Nash building left in this star-studded chicane that's home to the BBC's Broadcasting House and the historic Langham Hotel.

All Souls Church

Langham Place • Mon–Sat 9.30am–5.30pm, Sun 9am–2pm & 5.30–8.30pm • Free • ☎ 020 7580 3522, ⓦ allsouls.org • ⊖ Oxford Circus

John Nash's simple and ingenious little **All Souls Church** was built in warm Bath Stone in the 1820s, and is the architect's only surviving church. The unusual circular Ionic portico and conical stone spire, which caused outrage in its day, are cleverly designed to provide a visual full stop to Regent Street and lead the eye round into Portland Place and ultimately to Regent's Park.

Broadcasting House

Langham Place • Guided tours Sun; £9.95; no under 12s • ☎ 0370 901 1227, ⓦ bbc.co.uk/tours • ⊖ Oxford Circus

Behind All Souls lies the totalitarian-looking **Broadcasting House**, BBC radio headquarters since 1932. The figures of Prospero and Ariel (pun intended) above the entrance are by Eric Gill, who caused a furore by sculpting Ariel with overlarge testicles, and, like Epstein a few years earlier at Broadway House, was forced in the end to cut the organs down to size. Broadcasting House is now the headquarters of BBC News (both TV and radio) and you can sign up for a guided tour (1hr 30min) – much more popular, however, are the more regular tours of the **BBC TV Centre**, out in west London (Mon–Sat; £9.50; no under-9s; ☎0370 901 1227; ⊖ White City or Wood Lane).

Langham Hotel

Opposite Broadcasting House stands the **Langham Hotel**, built in grandiose Italianate style and opened by the Prince of Wales in 1865 as the city's most modern hotel, with over one hundred water closets. It features in several

---

DOCTORS AND DENTISTS

Harley Street was an ordinary residential Marylebone street until the nineteenth century when doctors, dentists and medical specialists began to colonize the area in order to serve London's wealthier citizens. Private medicine survived the threat of the postwar National Health Service, and the most expensive specialists and hospitals are still to be found in the streets around here.

The national dental body, the **British Dental Association (BDA)** has its headquarters at nearby 64 Wimpole St, and a **museum** (Tues & Thurs 1–4pm; free; ☎020 7935 0875, ⓦbda.org; ⊖Bond Street) displaying the gruesome contraptions of early dentistry, and old prints of agonizing extractions. Although dentistry is traditionally associated with pain, it was, in fact, a dentist who discovered the first anaesthetic.

4

Sherlock Holmes mysteries, and its former guests have included Antonín Dvořák (who courted controversy by ordering a double room for himself and his daughter to save money), exiled emperors Napoleon III and Haile Selassie, Oscar Wilde, and the writer Ouida (aka Marie Louise de la Ramée), who threw outrageous parties for young Guards officers and wrote many of her bestselling romances in her dimly lit hotel boudoir. Following World War II, it was taken over by the BBC and used to record legendary shows such as *The Goons*, only returning to use as a luxury hotel in 1991.

Portland Place

After the chicane around All Souls, you enter **Portland Place**, laid out by the Adam brothers in the 1770s and incorporated by Nash in his grand route. Once the widest street in London, it's still a majestic avenue, lined exclusively with Adam-style houses, boasting wonderful fanlights and iron railings. At the northern end of Portland Place, Nash originally planned a giant "circus" as a formal entrance to Regent's Park (see p.283). Only the southern half – two graceful arcs of creamy terraces known collectively as **Park Crescent** – was completed, and it is now cut off from the park by the busy thoroughfare of Marylebone Road.

● CAFÉS		● RESTAURANTS		● ACCOMMODATION	
Abu Ali	5	Caffè Caldesi	4	International Students House	1
Comptoir Libanais	8	Phoenix Palace	1	Lincoln House	2
Golden Hind	6	The Providores and Tapa Room	2	Minotel Wigmore Court	3
Patisserie Valerie at Sagne	3			Sumner Hotel	4
Paul Rothe & Son	7				

● PUBS & BARS	
Dover Castle	2
Golden Eagle	3
Gunmakers	1

● SHOPS	
Daunt Books	2
Le Labo	1
Tracey Neuls	3

MARYLEBONE

Chinese Embassy

Several embassies occupy properties on Portland Place, but the most prominent is the **Chinese Embassy** at no. 49, opposite which there's usually a small group of protesters permanently positioned objecting either to Chinese policies in Tibet or Chinese suppression of Falun Gong. It was here in 1896 that the exiled republican leader Sun Yat-sen was kidnapped and held incognito, on the orders of the Chinese emperor. Eventually Sun managed to send a note to a friend, saying "I am certain to be beheaded. Oh woe is me!". When the press got hold of the story, Sun was finally released; he went on to found the Chinese Nationalist Party and became the first president of China in 1911.

Royal Institute of British Architects (RIBA)

66 Portland Place • Mon–Fri 8am–6pm, Sat 8am–5pm; exhibitions Mon–Sat 10am–5pm • Free • ☎ 020 7580 5533 • ⓦ architecture.com • ⊖ Regent's Park or Great Portland Street

The **Royal Institute of British Architects** or RIBA at no. 66, is arguably the finest building on Portland Place, with its sleek Portland-stone facade built in the 1930s amid the remaining Adam houses. The main staircase remains a wonderful period piece, with its etched glass balustrades and walnut veneer, and with two large black marble columns rising up on either side. You can view the interior en route to the institute's excellent ground floor bookshop, first-floor exhibition galleries and café.

Wallace Collection

Manchester Square • Daily 10am–5pm • Free • ☎ 020 7563 9500, ⓦ wallacecollection.org • ⊖ Bond Street

4

It comes as a great surprise to find the miniature eighteenth-century French chateau of Hertford House in the quiet Georgian streets just to the north of busy Oxford Street. Even more remarkable is the house's splendid **Wallace Collection** within, a public museum and art gallery combined, which boasts paintings by Titian, Rembrandt and Velázquez, the finest museum collection of Sèvres porcelain in the world and one of the finest displays of Boulle marquetry furniture, too. The collection was originally bequeathed to the nation in 1897 by the widow of Richard Wallace, an art collector and the illegitimate son of the fourth Marquess of Hertford. The museum has preserved the feel of a grand stately home, an old-fashioned institution with exhibits piled high in glass cabinets and paintings covering every inch of wall space. However, it's the combined effect of the exhibits set amid superbly restored eighteenth-century period fittings – and a bloody great **armoury** – that makes the place so remarkable. Labelling is deliberately terse, so as not to detract from the aristocratic ambience, but there are information cards in each room and audioguides available.

Ground floor

The ground-floor rooms begin with the **Front State Room**, to the right as you enter, where the walls are hung with several fetching portraits by Reynolds, and Lawrence's typically sensuous portrayal of the author and society beauty, the Countess of Blessington, which went down a storm at the Royal Academy in 1822. The decor of the **Back State Room** is a riot of Rococo, and houses the cream of the house's gaudily spectacular Sèvres porcelain. Centre stage is a period copy of Louis XV's desk, which was the most expensive piece of eighteenth-century French furniture ever made. On the other side of the adjacent Dining Room, in the **Billiard Room**, you'll find an impressive display of outrageous, gilded oak and ebony Boulle marquetry furniture. From the Dining Room, with its Canalettos, you can enter the covered courtyard, home to *The Wallace* restaurant, and head down the stairs to the temporary exhibition galleries and the **Conservation Gallery** where folk of all ages can try on some medieval armour.

Back on the ground floor, the **Sixteenth-Century Gallery** displays a wide variety of works ranging from *pietre dure*, bronze and majolica to Limoges porcelain and Venetian

WALLACE COLLECTION>

glass. In the **Smoking Room**, a small alcove at the far end survives to give an idea of the effect of the original Minton-tiled decor Wallace chose for this room. The next three rooms house the extensive **European Armoury** bought *en bloc* by Wallace around the time of the Franco-Prussian War. (It was in recognition of the humanitarian assistance Wallace provided in Paris during that war that he received his baronetcy.) A fourth room houses the **Oriental Armoury**, collected by the fourth Marquess of Hertford, including a cabinet of Asante gold treasure, a sword belonging to Tipu Sultan and one of the most important Sikh treasures in Britain, the sword of Ranjit Singh (1780–1839).

First floor

The main staircase, with its incredible Parisian wrought-iron balustrade and its gilded, fluted columns is overlooked by **Boucher**'s sumptuous mythological scenes. In the gloriously camp pink **Boudoir**, off the landing and conservatory, you'll find Reynolds' doe-eyed moppets, while the adjacent passageway boasts an unbelievably rich display of gold snuff boxes and miniatures. The **Study** features more Sèvres porcelain, Greuze's soft-focus studies of kids and a lovely portrait by Elisabeth Vigée-Lebrun, one of the most successful portraitists of pre-Revolutionary France. Next door, in the sky-blue **Oval Drawing Room**, one of Fragonard's coquettes flaunts herself to a smitten beau in *The Swing*, alongside more Boucher nudes – the soft porn of the *ancien régime*. There's plenty more Rococo froth in the other rooms on this floor, plus classic Grand Tour vistas from Canaletto and Guardi in the **West Room**.

In addition to all this French finery a good collection of Dutch paintings hangs in the **East Galleries**, including de Hooch's *Women Peeling Apples*, oil sketches by Rubens and landscapes by Ruisdael, Hobbema and Cuyp. On the opposite side of the house, the **West Galleries** feature works by the British landscape artist Richard Parkes Bonington and Delacroix, his great friend and admirer.

Great Gallery

Finally, you reach the largest room in the house, the **Great Gallery**, specifically built by Wallace to display his finest paintings, including works by Murillo and Poussin, several vast Van Dyck portraits, Rubens' *Rainbow Landscape* and **Frans Hals'** *Laughing Cavalier*. Here, too, are *Perseus and Andromeda*, a late work by **Titian**, and **Velázquez's** *Lady with a Fan*. At one end of the room are three portraits of the actress Mary Robinson as Perdita: one by Romney, one by Reynolds and, best of the lot, **Gainsborough**'s deceptively innocent portrayal, in which she insouciantly holds a miniature of her lover, the 19-year-old Prince of Wales (later George IV), who is portrayed in a flattering full-length portrait by Lawrence. Look out, too, for **Rembrandt**'s affectionate portrait of his teenage son, Titus, who helped administer his father's estate after bankruptcy charges and died at the age of just 28.

Marylebone High Street

Marylebone High Street is all that's left of the village street that once ran along the banks of the Tyburn stream. It's become considerably more upmarket since those bucolic days, though the pace of the street is leisurely by central London standards. A couple of shops, in particular, deserve mention: the branch of *Patisserie Valerie*, at no. 105, is decorated inside with the same mock-Pompeian frescoes that adorned it when it was founded as *Maison Sagne* in 1921 by a Swiss pastry-cook; at no. 83 is Daunt, a purpose-built bookshop from 1910, which specializes in travel books, and has a lovely, long, galleried hall at the back, with a pitched roof of stained glass.

St James's Church, Spanish Place

22 George St • Mon–Fri 7am–7pm, Sat 10am–7pm, Sun 8am–8pm • ⓦ sjrcc.org.uk • ⊖ Bond Street or Baker Street

Despite its name, **St James's Church, Spanish Place,** is actually tucked away on

neighbouring George Street, just off Marylebone High Street. A Catholic chapel was
built here in 1791 thanks to the efforts of the chaplain at the Spanish embassy, though
the present neo-Gothic building dates from 1890. Designed in a mixture of English
and French Gothic, the interior is surprisingly large and richly furnished, from the
white marble and alabaster pulpit to the richly gilded heptagonal apse. The Spanish
connection continues to this day: Spanish royal heraldry features in the rose window,
and there are even two seats reserved for the royals, denoted by built-in gilt crowns
high above the choir stalls.

Baker Street

Running north–south through Marylebone, **Baker Street**, is a fairly nondescript
one-way highway. Despite its unprepossessing nature, its associations with the fictional
detective Sherlock Holmes are, naturally, fully exploited. At the northern edge of
Marylebone Baker Street is bisected by the six-lane highway of **Marylebone Road**. Built
in the 1750s, along with Euston Road, to provide London with its first bypass, it
remains one of London's major traffic arteries, and is no place for a casual stroll. There
are, however, a couple of minor sights, such as **St Marylebone Church** and the **Royal
Academy of Music**, and one major tourist trap, **Madame Tusssauds**, that are all an easy
stroll from Baker Street tube.

Madame Tussauds

Marylebone Road • Mon–Fri 9.30am–5.30pm, Sat & Sun 9am–6pm • Online tickets from £26 • ☎ 0871 894 3000, ⓦ madametussauds
.com • ⊖ Baker Street

The wax models at **Madame Tussauds** have been pulling in the crowds ever since the
good lady arrived from France in 1802 bearing the sculpted heads of guillotined
aristocrats (she was lucky to escape the same fate – her uncle, who started the family
business, was less fortunate). The entrance fee might be extortionate and the likenesses
dubious, but London's biggest queues form here – to avoid joining them, book online,
or whizz round after 5pm for half-price.

There are **photo opportunities** galore in the first few sections, which are peppered
with contemporary celebrities from the BBC to Bollywood. Look out for the
diminutive Madame Tussaud herself, and the oldest wax model, Madame du Barry,
Louis XV's mistress, who gently respires as Sleeping Beauty – in reality she was
beheaded in the French Revolution. The **Chamber of Horrors** is irredeemably tasteless,
and – in the section called "Scream" – features costumed actors who jump out at you
in the dark (you can opt out of this). All the "great" British serial killers are here, and it
remains the murderer's greatest honour to be included. There's a reconstruction of John
Christie's hanging, a tableau of Marat's death in the bath, and the very guillotine that
lopped off Marie Antoinette's head, just for good measure.

Tussauds also features the **Spirit of London**, an irreverent five-minute romp through
the history of London in a miniaturized taxicab, taking you from Elizabethan times to
a postmodern heritage nightmare of tourist tat (not unlike much of London today).
The tour of Tussauds ends with a short hi-tech "experience", often inspired by a recent
Hollywood flick, including a 4D 360-degree film projected onto the ceiling of the
domed auditorium of the former London Planetarium.

Sherlock Holmes Museum

239 Baker St • Daily 9.30am–6pm • £6 • ☎ 020 7224 3688, ⓦ sherlock-holmes.co.uk • ⊖ Baker Street

Baker Street, which cuts across Marylebone Road, is synonymous with English
literature's languid super-sleuth, Sherlock Holmes, who lived at no. 221b. The
detective's address was always fictional, although the most likely inspiration was, in
fact, no. 21, at the south end of the street. However, the statue of Holmes's creator,
Arthur Conan Doyle, is at the north end of the street, outside Baker Street tube, round

MARYLEBONE STATION

Probably London's most discreet train terminal, **Marylebone Station** is hidden in the backstreets north of Marylebone Road on Melcombe Place, where a delicate and extremely elegant wrought-iron canopy links the station to the former *Great Central Hotel* (now *The Landmark*). Opened in 1899, Marylebone was the last and most modest of the Victorian terminals, originally intended to be the terminal for the Channel tunnel of the 1880s, a scheme abandoned after only a mile or so of digging, when Queen Victoria got nervous about foreign invasions. The station enjoyed a brief moment of fame after appearing in the opening sequence of The Beatles film *A Hard Day's Night* and now serves the Birmingham and Buckinghamshire commuter belt.

the corner from the **Sherlock Holmes Museum**, at no. 239 (the sign on the door says 221b). Unashamedly touristy – you can have your photo taken in a deerstalker – the museum is nevertheless a competent exercise in period reconstruction, stuffed full of Victoriana and life-size models of characters from the books.

St Marylebone Church

Marylebone Road • ☎ 020 7935 7315, ⓦ www.stmarylebone.org.uk • ⊖ Baker Street or Regent's Park

Completed in 1817, **St Marylebone Church** is only open fitfully for services and recitals, though the church's most attractive feature – the gilded caryatids holding up the beehive cupola on top of the tower – is visible from Marylebone High Street. It was at this church that **Elizabeth Barrett** and **Robert Browning** were secretly married in 1846 (there's a chapel dedicated to Browning), after which Elizabeth – six years older than Robert, an invalid, morphine addict and virtual prisoner in her father's house on Wimpole Street – returned home and acted as if nothing had happened. A week later the couple eloped to Italy, where they spent most of their married life. The church crypt houses a small chapel, a healing centre, an NHS health centre and a café.

Royal Academy of Music

Marylebone Road • Mon–Fri 11.30am–5.30pm, Sat noon–4pm • Free • ☎ 020 7873 7373, ⓦ ram.ac.uk • ⊖ Baker Street or Regent's Park

On the other side of Marylebone Road from St Marylebone Church stands the **Royal Academy of Music**, which was founded in 1823, and taught the likes of Arthur Sullivan, Harrison Birtwistle, Dennis Brain, Evelyn Glennie, Michael Nyman and Simon Rattle. As well as putting on free lunchtime and evening concerts, the academy houses a small **museum** at 1 York Gate. Temporary exhibitions are held on the ground floor, while in the String Gallery on the first floor, there's a world-class collection of Cremonese violins including several by Stradivari. The exhibition on the second floor in the Piano Gallery follows the development of the grand piano in England and gives you a peek into the resident luthier's workshop. Listening-posts on each floor allow you to experience the instruments in live performance.

CHINATOWN

Soho and Fitzrovia

Bounded by Regent Street to the west, Oxford Street to the north and Charing Cross Road to the east, Soho is very much the heart of the West End. It's been the city's premier red-light district for centuries and retains an unorthodox and slightly raffish air that's unique for central London. It has an immigrant history as rich as that of the East End and a louche nightlife that has attracted writers and revellers of every sexual persuasion since the eighteenth century. Conventional sights in Soho are few and far between, yet there's probably more street life here than anywhere else in the city centre. Most folk head to Soho to go the cinema or theatre, and to have a drink or a bite to eat in the innumerable bars, cafés and restaurants that pepper the tiny area and Fitzrovia, the quieter Soho spillover, north of Oxford Street.

5

Soho

Soho's historic reputation for tolerance made it an obvious place of refuge from dour, postwar Britain. **Jazz** and skiffle proliferated in the 1950s, folk and **rock** in the 1960s, and punk at the end of the 1970s. London's artistic (and alcoholic) cliques still gather here and the **media**, film and advertising industries have a strong presence. The area's most recent transformation has seen it become a very upfront gay enclave, especially around Old Compton Street. The attraction, though, remains in the unique mix of people who drift through Soho. There's nowhere else in the city where such diverse slices of London come face to face: businessmen, clubbers, drunks, theatregoers, fashion victims, market-stallholders, pimps, prostitutes and politicians. Take it all in, and enjoy – for better or worse, most of London is not like this.

Leicester Square

A short hop east of Piccadilly Circus, most Londoners tend to avoid **Leicester Square** unless they're heading for one of the cinemas. It's actually a fairly pleasant leafy square – at least by day – and was, in the eighteenth century, home to the fashionable "Leicester House set", headed by successive Hanoverian princes of Wales who didn't get on with their fathers at St James's. Busts of celebrities from those days can be found in the gardens, though most people are more impressed by the statues of Shakespeare and Charlie Chaplin, neither of whom have any real connection with the area. By night – and especially at weekends – Leicester Square resembles city centres across the country, a playground for the drunk and underdressed.

The square has been an **entertainment zone** since the mid-nineteenth century, when it boasted Turkish baths and music halls such as the grandiose Empire and, close by, the Hippodrome – designed by Frank Matcham in 1900 – edifices which survive today as a cinema and casino. Movie houses moved in during the 1930s, a golden age evoked by the sleek black lines of the Odeon on the east side, and maintain their grip on the area. The aforementioned **Empire** is the favourite for London's red-carpet premieres and, in a rather half-hearted imitation of the Hollywood tradition, there are even handprints-of-the-stars indented into the pavement of the square's southwestern corner.

SOHO'S WHO'S WHO

When **Soho** – named after the cry that resounded through the district when it was a popular place for rabbit hunting – was built over in the seventeenth century, its streets were among the most sought-after addresses in the capital. Princes, dukes and earls built their mansions around Soho and Leicester squares, which became the centre of high-society nightlife, epitomized by the wild masquerades organized by Viennese prima donna Theresa Cornelys (who had a daughter by Casanova), which drew "a riotous assembly of fashionable people of both sexes", a traffic jam of hackney chairs and a huge crowd of onlookers. By the end of the eighteenth century, however, the party was over, the rich moved west, and Soho began its inexorable descent into poverty and overcrowding. Even before the last aristocrats left, Soho had become one of the city's main dumping grounds for **immigrants**. French Huguenots were followed by Italians, Irish, Jews, and eventually the Chinese.

For several centuries, Soho has also been a favourite haunt of the capital's creative bohos and **literati**. It was at Soho's *Turk's Head* coffee shop, in 1764, that Joshua Reynolds founded "The Club", to give Dr Johnson unlimited opportunities for talking. Thomas de Quincey turned up in 1802, and was saved from starvation by a local prostitute, an incident later recalled in his *Confessions of an English Opium Eater*. Wagner arrived destitute in 1839, Marx lived in poverty here after the failure of the 1848 revolution, and Rimbaud and Verlaine pitched up after the fall of the Paris Commune in 1871. "Such noise and chaos. Such magnificent and terrible abandon. It's like stepping into the future", wrote Verlaine.

SOHO & FITZROVIA

Regent's Park
PARK CRESCENT
Great Portland Street
EUSTON ROAD
Warren Street
Euston Square
PARK CRESCENT
WARREN STREET
GREENWELL ST
FITZROY SQ
GRAFTON WAY
CARBURTON ST
London Foot
Hospital
MAPLE STREET
Post Office
Tower
HOWLAND STREET
FITZROVIA
American
Church
Habitat
Heal's
BLOOMSBURY
Pollock's
Toy Museum
Goodge
Street
MORTIMER STREET
All
Saints
CAVENDISH
SQUARE
GREAT CASTLE STREET
Getty
Images
Oxford
Circus
Marks and
Spencer
OXFORD STREET
Photographers'
Gallery
SEE 'CENTRAL SOHO'
MAP FOR DETAIL
HANOVER
SQUARE
London
Palladium
Liberty
Hamleys
SOHO
Tottenham
Court Road
Centrepoint
St Patrick's
St Giles
Ronnie
Scott's
St Martin's
School of Art
MAYFAIR
St Anne
Palace
Theatre
Seven Dials
Trocadero
Empire
CHINATOWN
Hippodrome
Leicester
Square
Coliseum
Piccadilly
Circus
ST JAMES'S
Odeon
National
Gallery

0   150
yards

5

THE SWISS CORNER

For no particularly good reason, the area in the northwest corner of Leicester Square has a Swiss theme to it. The impetus was the building of the Swiss Centre – a sort of trade centre-cum-tourist office – in 1968 and the renaming of the area as Swiss Court. After forty years of alpine theming, the much unloved Swiss Centre was finally demolished in 2008, leaving behind a slightly surreal **Swiss glockenspiel**. This tall steel structure is topped by a Swiss railway clock and features a glass drum decorated with the 26 cantonal flags which lower on the hour (Mon–Fri noon & 5–8pm, Sat & Sun 2–4pm), to sound a 27-bell carillon, thus revealing a procession of Helvetic cows and peasants making their way up the mountain.

Notre-Dame de France

5 Leicester Place • Mon–Fri noon–6pm, Sun 10am–6pm • Free • ☎ 020 7437 9363, ⓦ ndfchurch.org • ➔ Leicester Square

One little-known sight, north of Leicester Square, is the modern Catholic church of **Notre-Dame de France**, heralded by an entrance flanked by two pillars decorated with biblical reliefs. The main point of interest within the unusual circular interior is the Chapelle de la Vierge Marie, which contains a series of simple frescoes of the Annunciation, Crucifixion and Assumption by Jean Cocteau from 1960 and an altar mosaic of the Nativity by Boris Anrep (originally covered by a new panel by Cocteau much to Anrep's annoyance).

Chinatown

Hemmed in between Leicester Square and Shaftesbury Avenue, **Chinatown**'s self-contained jumble of **shops**, **cafés** and **restaurants** makes up one of London's most distinct ethnic enclaves. Only a minority of the capital's Chinese live in the three small blocks of Chinatown, with its ersatz touches – telephone kiosks rigged out as pagodas and formal entrances or *paifang* – yet the area remains a focus for the community, a place to do business or the weekly shopping, celebrate a wedding or just meet up on Sundays for dim sum. Most Londoners come to Chinatown simply to eat, but if the mood takes you, you can easily while away several hours sorting through the Chinese trinkets, ceramics and ornaments in the various arts and crafts shops, or amassing the perfect ingredients for a demon stir-fry.

The first Chinese immigrants were sailors who arrived here from the late eighteenth century onwards on the ships of the East India Company. London's first Chinatown grew up around the docks at Limehouse and eventually boasted over thirty Chinese shops and restaurants. Predominantly male, this closed community achieved a quasi-mythical status in Edwardian minds as a hotbed of criminal dives and opium dens, a reputation exploited in Sax Rohmer's novels (later made into films) featuring the evil Doctor Fu Manchu. Wartime bomb damage, postwar demolition and protectionist union laws all but destroyed Limehouse Chinatown. However, following the Communist takeover in China, a new wave of Chinese refugees began to buy up cheap property around **Gerrard Street**, establishing the nucleus of today's Chinatown.

Charing Cross Road

Created in the 1880s as part of the Victorians' slum clearance drive, **Charing Cross Road** boasts the highest concentration of **bookshops** anywhere in London: chain and discounted stores north of Cambridge Circus; smaller, independent and secondhand stores to the south. One of the first to open here, in 1906, was **Foyles**, a vast book emporium at no. 119, where Éamon de Valera, George Bernard Shaw, Walt Disney and Arthur Conan Doyle were all once regular customers. Once famous for its antiquated system for selling books that required customers to queue three times, it's now a vibrant place, with a busy café and regular live jazz and classical music gigs.

Two of the nicest places for secondhand-book browsing are **Cecil Court** and **St Martin's Court**, connecting the southern end of Charing Cross Road and St Martin's Lane.

These short, civilized, late-Victorian paved alleys boast specialist bookshops, such as the Italian Bookshop and Watkins Books, home of the occult, plus various antiquarian dealers selling modern first editions, old theatre posters, coins and notes, cigarette cards, maps and children's books.

Coliseum

St Martin's Lane • ☎ 0871 911 0200, ⓦ eno.org • ⊖ Leicester Square or Charing Cross

At the southern end of St Martin's Lane stands the **Coliseum**, an extravagant variety theatre built in 1904 by Frank Matcham, where the likes of Lillie Langtry, Sarah Bernhardt and the Ballets Russes all performed. Now home to the English National Opera (see p.415), it remains London's largest theatre, its cutest feature the revolving illuminated globe that crowns the building.

Shaftesbury Avenue

Sweeping through the southern part of Soho, the gentle curve of **Shaftesbury Avenue** is the heart of the West End's **Theatreland**, with theatres and cinemas along its entire length. Built in the 1870s, ostensibly to relieve traffic congestion but with the dual purpose of destroying the slums that lay in its path, the street was ironically named after Lord Shaftesbury, whose life had been spent trying to help the likes of those dispossessed by the road. The most impressive theatre architecturally is the grandiose terracotta **Palace Theatre**, overlooking Cambridge Circus, which opened in 1891 as the Royal English Opera House; it folded after just one year, and, since the 1920s, has mostly hosted musicals. Just off Cambridge Circus, hidden away down West Street, is St Martin's Theatre, where Agatha Christie's record-breaking murder-mystery *The Mousetrap* has been on non-stop since 1952, notching up over 24,000 performances.

Central Soho

If Soho had an official main drag, it would be **Old Compton Street**, which runs parallel with Shaftesbury Avenue, and forms the heart of **Central Soho**. The shops, boutiques and cafés in the narrow, surrounding streets are typical of the area and a good barometer of the latest Soho fads. Several places have survived the vicissitudes of fashion, including the original *Patisserie Valerie*, opened by the Belgian-born Madame Valerie in 1926, the Algerian Coffee Store, the Italian deli, I Camisa & Son, The Vintage House off-licence, and Gerry's, whose spirit-window display is a paean to alcohol.

The liberal atmosphere of Soho has made it a permanent fixture on the **gay scene** since the last century: gay servicemen frequented the *Golden Lion*, on Dean Street, from World War II until the end of National Service, while a succession of gay artists found refuge here during the 1950s and 1960s. Nowadays the scene is much more upfront, with every type of gay business jostling for position on and off Old Compton Street.

Greek Street

The streets off Old Compton Street are lined with Soho institutions past and present, starting in the east with **Greek Street**, named after the Greek church that once stood nearby. South of Old Compton Street, at no. 29, stands *Maison Bertaux*, London's oldest French patisserie, founded in 1871. The *Coach and Horses*, one door down at no. 29, was lorded over for years by the boozy gang of writer Jeffrey Bernard, painter Francis Bacon and jazz man George Melly, as well as the staff of the satirical magazine, *Private Eye*.

Frith Street

Frith Street is home to **Ronnie Scott's**, London's longest-running jazz club, founded in 1958 and still pulling in the big names. Opposite is *Bar Italia*, a tiny, quintessentially

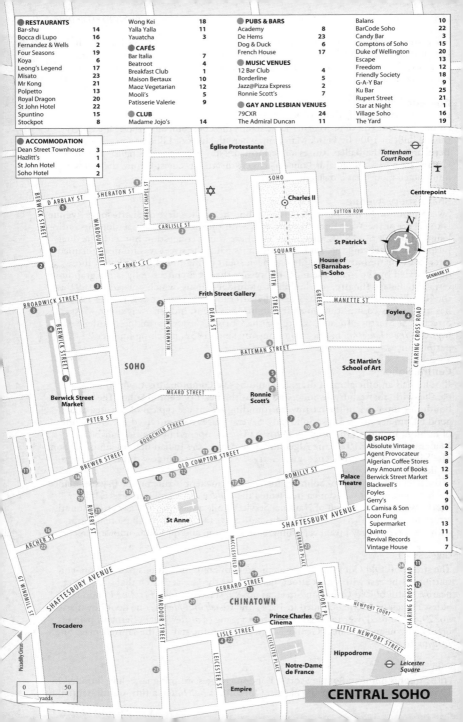

RESTAURANTS

Bar-shu	14
Bocca di Lupo	16
Fernandez & Wells	2
Four Seasons	19
Koya	6
Leong's Legend	17
Misato	23
Mr Kong	21
Polpetto	13
Royal Dragon	20
St John Hotel	22
Spuntino	15
Stockpot	8
Wong Kei	18
Yalla Yalla	11
Yauatcha	3

CAFÉS

Bar Italia	7
Beatroot	4
Breakfast Club	1
Maison Bertaux	10
Maoz Vegetarian	12
Mooli's	5
Patisserie Valerie	9

CLUB

Madame Jojo's	14

PUBS & BARS

Academy	8
De Hems	23
Dog & Duck	6
French House	17

MUSIC VENUES

12 Bar Club	4
Borderline	5
Jazz@Pizza Express	2
Ronnie Scott's	7

GAY AND LESBIAN VENUES

79CXR	24
The Admiral Duncan	11

Balans	10
BarCode Soho	22
Candy Bar	3
Comptons of Soho	15
Duke of Wellington	20
Escape	13
Freedom	12
Friendly Society	18
G-A-Y Bar	9
Ku Bar	25
Rupert Street	21
Star at Night	1
Village Soho	16
The Yard	19

ACCOMMODATION

Dean Street Townhouse	3
Hazlitt's	1
St John Hotel	4
Soho Hotel	2

SHOPS

Absolute Vintage	2
Agent Provocateur	3
Algerian Coffee Stores	8
Any Amount of Books	12
Berwick Street Market	5
Blackwell's	6
Foyles	4
Gerry's	9
I. Camisa & Son	10
Loon Fung Supermarket	13
Quinto	11
Revival Records	1
Vintage House	7

CENTRAL SOHO

SOHO ON RECORD

Soho has been a popular meeting point for the capital's up-and-coming pop stars since the late 1950s, when the likes of Cliff Richard, Tommy Steele and Adam Faith used to hang out at the **2 i's coffee bar**, 59 Old Compton St, and perform at the rock'n'roll club in the basement. Marc Bolan, whose parents ran a market stall on Berwick Street, also worked at the café in the early 1960s. The Rolling Stones first met in a pub on Broadwick Street in early 1962 and, by the mid-1960s, were playing Soho's premier rock venue, the **Marquee**, originally at 90 Wardour St. David Bowie performed there (as David Jones) in 1965, Pink Floyd played their "Spontaneous Underground" sessions the following year, Led Zeppelin had their first London gig there in 1968, and Phil Collins worked for some time as a cloakroom attendant.

In November 1975, The Sex Pistols played their first gig at **St Martin's School of Art** on Charing Cross Road, during which Sid Vicious (in the audience, and not the band, at the time) made his contribution to dance history when he began to "pogo". The classic punk venue, however, was the **100 Club** on Oxford Street, where the Pistols, The Clash, Siouxsie, The Damned and The Vibrators all played. The Pistols used to rehearse in the studios on **Denmark Street**, London's own version of New York's Tin Pan Alley, off Charing Cross Road, (still lined with music shops today). The Rolling Stones, The Kinks and Genesis all recorded songs there, and Elton John got his first job at one of the street's music publishers in 1963.

Italian café established in 1949, whose late-night hours make it a clubbers' favourite. It was in this building, appropriately enough for such a media-saturated area, that **John Logie Baird** made the world's first public television transmission in 1926. Next door, a plaque recalls that the 7-year-old Mozart stayed here in 1763, having wowed George III and London society.

Soho Square

Soho Square is one of the few patches of green amid the neighbourhood's labyrinth of streets and alleys. It began life as a smart address, surrounded by the houses of the nobility and centred on an elaborate fountain topped by a statue of Charles II. Charles survives, if a little worse for wear, on one of the pathways, but the fountain is now an octagonal, mock-Tudor garden shed. As for the buildings around the square, they are a typical Soho mix: 20th Century-Fox; the Victorian Hospital for Sick Women (now a walk-in health centre); Paul McCartney's discreet corporate headquarters, mpl; the British Board of Film Classification (the national guardians of movie censorship); and Bloomsbury, publishers of Harry Potter. There are also two square, red-brick churches. The most prominent is the Italianate **St Patrick's**, on the east side of the square, first consecrated in 1792 and thus the first Catholic church built in England after the Reformation; the current building dates from the 1890s and serves the Irish, Italian and Chinese communities. Concealed on the north side of the square, the **Église Protestante**, also from the 1890s, is the sole survivor of London's once numerous Huguenot churches; the 1950 tympanum relief depicts the French refugees crossing the Channel and being granted asylum by Edward VI.

House of St Barnabas-in-Soho

1 Greek St • By appointment Tues & Thurs 9–11am • Donation requested • ☎ 020 7437 1894, ⓦ hosb.org.uk • ⊖ Tottenham Court Road

If you're finding it difficult to imagine Soho ever having been an aristocratic haunt, arrange a visit to the **House of St Barnabas-in-Soho**, a Georgian mansion in the southeastern corner of the square. Built in the 1740s, the house retains some exquisite Rococo plasterwork on the main staircase and in the Council Chamber, which has a lovely view onto Soho Square. Since 1861, the building has been a Christian charity house for the destitute, so the rest of the interior is much altered and closed off. You can, however, visit the paved garden, whose plane trees inspired Dickens, and whose

5

twisted and gnarled mulberry tree was planted by silk-weaving Huguenots. On the south side of the garden is a cute little Byzantine-style chapel, built for the residents and used by Serbian refugees during World War I.

Dean Street

One block west of Frith Street runs **Dean Street**, once home to *The Colony Room*, a private drinking club that was at the heart of Soho's postwar bohemian scene, and still home to the members-only *Groucho Club*, at no. 45, where today's literati and media types preen themselves. Nearby, at no. 49, *The French House* is an open-to-all bohemian landmark, where the most popular drink is Ricard, and they only serve beer in halves. Opened by a German as the *York Minster* pub, it was bought by a Belgian, Victor Berlemont, in 1914, when the German owner was deported, and transformed into a French émigré haunt. Dylan Thomas and Brendan Behan were both regulars, and during World War II it was frequented by de Gaulle and the Free French forces.

Soho's most famous Jewish immigrant was **Karl Marx**, who in 1850 moved into two "evil, frightful rooms" on the top floor of no. 28, with his wife and maid (both of whom were pregnant by him) and four children, having been evicted from his first two addresses for failing to pay the rent. There's a plaque commemorating his stay (with incorrect dates), and the waiters at *Quo Vadis* restaurant below, will show diners round the rooms on request (☏020 7437 9585).

Wardour Street

A kind of dividing line between the busier eastern half of Soho and the marginally quieter western zone, **Wardour Street** is largely given over to the film and TV industry. Just north of Shaftesbury Avenue, there's a small park laid out on what used to be **St Anne's Church**, bombed in the last war, with only its tower now standing. The ashes of Dorothy L. Sayers are buried under the tower, and Baron von Neuhoff, a Westphalian adventurer who managed to get himself elected King of Corsica in 1736, is also interred here. His reign lasted eight months, after which he was forced to flee to try and raise more money and men to fight the

---

SOHO VICE

Prostitution is nothing new to Soho. Way back in the seventeenth and eighteenth centuries, prince and prole alike used to come here (and to Covent Garden) for paid sex. Several prominent courtesans were residents of Soho, their profession recorded as "player and mistress to several persons", or, lower down on the social scale, "generally slut and drunkard; occasionally whore and thief". *Hooper's Hotel*, a high-class Soho brothel frequented by the Prince of Wales, even got a mention in the popular, late eighteenth-century book *The Mysteries of Flagellation*. By Victorian times, the area was described as "a reeking home of filthy vice", where "the grosser immorality flourishes unabashed from every age downwards to mere children". And it was in Soho that Prime Minister Gladstone used to conduct his crusade to save prostitutes – managing "to combine his missionary meddling with a keen appreciation of a pretty face", as one perceptive critic observed.

By World War II, **organized gangs** like the notorious Messina Brothers from Malta controlled a huge vice empire in Soho, later taken over by one of their erstwhile henchmen, Bernie Silver, Soho's self-styled "Godfather". In the 1960s and 1970s, the sex trade threatened to take over the whole of Soho, aided and abetted by the police themselves, who were involved in a massive protection racket. The complicity between the gangs and the police was finally exposed in 1976, when ten top-ranking Scotland Yard officers were charged with bribery and corruption on a massive scale and sentenced to prison for up to twelve years. (Silver himself had been put inside in 1974.) The combined efforts of the Soho Society and Westminster Council has enormously reduced the number of sex establishments, but, with the rise of the lap-dancing club, the area's vice days are not quite over yet.

ART AND HERESY IN SOHO

The streets around Poland Street have more than their fair share of artistic and heretical associations. A blue plaque at 74 Broadwick St records that **William Blake** was born there in 1757, above his father's hosiery shop, and where, from the age of nine, he had visions of "messengers from heaven, daily and nightly". He opened a print shop of his own next door to the family home, and later moved nearby to 28 Poland St, where he lived six years with his "beloved Kate" and wrote perhaps his most profound work, *The Marriage of Heaven and Hell*, among other poems. Poland Street was also **Shelley**'s first halt after having been kicked out of Oxford in 1811 for distributing *The Necessity of Atheism*, and **Canaletto** ran a studio just south on Beak Street for a couple of years while he sat out the Seven Years' War in exile in London. And it was in the *Old King's Arms* pub on Poland Street in 1781 that the **Ancient Order of Druids** was revived.

Genoese. He lived out his exile on Dean Street and was eventually imprisoned for debt in 1750; when asked what assets he had, he declared "nothing but the Kingdom of Corsica".

Brewer Street

West of Wardour Street, along **Brewer Street**, the sex industry has a long history and firm foothold. It was at the **Windmill Theatre**, on nearby Great Windmill Street, that the famous "Revuedeville" shows, featuring static nude performers (movement was strictly forbidden by the censor), were first staged in the 1930s. The shows continued pretty much uninterrupted right through World War II – the subject of the 2005 film *Mrs Henderson Presents* – eventually closing in 1964. Meanwhile, back on Brewer Street, the **Raymond Revuebar** opened in 1952 as a "World Centre of Erotic Entertainment", finally succumbing, in 2004, to competition from the slick **lap-dancing clubs** that have rejuvenated the West End sex industry.

Broadwick Street

It was a water pump on **Broadwick Street** that caused the deaths of some 500 Soho residents in the **cholera epidemic** of 1854. Dr John Snow, Queen Victoria's obstetrician, traced the outbreak to the pump, thereby proving that the disease was waterborne rather than airborne, as previously thought. No one believed him, however, until he removed the pump handle and effectively stopped the epidemic. The original pump stood outside the pub now called the *John Snow*, on which there's a commemorative plaque and an easily missed red-granite kerbstone.

Carnaby Street

Until the 1950s, **Carnaby Street** was a backstreet on Soho's western fringe, occupied, for the most part, by sweatshop tailors who made up the suits for nearby Savile Row in Mayfair. Then, in 1954, Bill Green opened a shop in neighbouring Newburgh St, selling outrageous clothes to the gay men who were hanging out at the local baths. He was followed by **John Stephen**, a Glaswegian grocer's son, who opened His Clothes in Beak Street. In 1960, Stephen moved his operation to Carnaby Street and within a couple of years owned a string of trendy boutiques catering for the new market in flamboyant men's clothing, including the wonderfully named I Was Lord Kitchener's Valet. By 1964 – the year of the official birth of the Carnaby Street myth – Mods, West Indian Rude Boys and other "switched-on people", as the *Daily Telegraph* noted, had begun to hang out in Carnaby Street. By the time Mary Quant sold her first miniskirt here, the area had become the epicentre of London's **Swinging Sixties**, its street sign the capital's most popular postcard. A victim of its own hype, Carnaby Street quickly declined into an avenue of overpriced tack. Nowadays, it's pedestrianized and smart again, but dominated by chains – for any sign of

5

contemporary London fashion, you have to go round the corner to Fouberts Place and Newburgh Street.

Photographers' Gallery

16–18 Ramillies St • Tues–Sun 11am–6pm, Thurs & Fri until 8pm • Free • ☎ 0845 262 1618, ⓦ photonet.org.uk • ⊖ Oxford Circus

Established in 1971, the **Photographers' Gallery** was the first independent gallery devoted to photography in London. It moved from Great Newport Street to much enlarged premises in 2008 and now hosts three floors of free exhibitions that are invariably worth a visit, as are the bookshop and café.

Fitzrovia

Fitzrovia is the very much quieter northern extension of Soho, beyond Oxford Street. Like its neighbour, it has a raffish, cosmopolitan history, attracting its fair share of writers and bohemians over the last hundred years or so, including the Pre-Raphaelites and members of the Bloomsbury Group. That said, it's a lot less edgy than Soho, with just two real sights to visit – an ornate Victorian church on Margaret Street and Pollock's Toy Museum – and one unavoidable landmark, the former Post Office Tower.

All Saints, Margaret Street

Margaret Street • Mon–Sat 7.30am–7pm, Sun 8am–7.30pm • ⓦ allsaintsmargaretstreet.org.uk • ⊖ Oxford Circus

Few London churches are as atmospheric as **All Saints, Margaret Street**, built by William Butterfield in the 1850s. Patterned brickwork characterizes the entire ensemble of clergy house, choir school (Laurence Olivier sang here as a boy) and church, set around a small courtyard entered from the street through a pointed arch. The church interior – one of London's gloomiest – is best visited on a sunny afternoon when the light pours in through the west window, illuminating the fantastic polychrome marble and stone which decorates the place from floor to ceiling. Several of the walls are also adorned with Pre-Raphaelite Minton-tile paintings, the east window is a neo-Byzantine quasi-iconostasis with saintly images nestling in gilded niches, and the elaborate pulpit is like the entire church in miniature. Surrounded by such iconographical clutter, you would be forgiven for thinking you were in a Catholic church – but then that was the whole idea of the Victorian High Church movement, which sought to re-Catholicize the Church of England without actually returning it to the Roman fold.

Charlotte Street

Fitzrovia's main street, **Charlotte Street** is lined with cafés and restaurants, a boutique hotel and the headquarters of Saatchi & Saatchi, the advertising agency that made its name working for Mrs Thatcher in the 1980s. It's a lively street, but its real heyday was in the 1930s, when it was home to the *Tour Eiffel*, where Wyndham Lewis and Ezra Pound launched the Vorticist magazine *Blast*. *L'Étoile*, further up, was patronized by the likes of Dylan Thomas and T.S. Eliot, while *Bertorelli's* was where Eliot, John Berger and Christopher Isherwood, used to meet at the Wednesday Club in the 1950s. The same crowd would get plastered in the nearby *Fitzroy Tavern* – from which the area got its sobriquet – along with rather more outrageous bohemians, like the hard-drinking Nina Hamnett, the self-styled "Queen of Bohemia", who used to boast that Modigliani once told her she had the best tits in Europe.

Pollock's Toy Museum

1 Scala St • Mon–Sat 10am–5pm • £3 • ☎ 020 7636 3452, ⓦ pollockstoymuseum.com • ⊖ Goodge Street

Housed above a wonderful toy shop in the backstreets of Fitzrovia is the highly atmospheric, doll's-house-like **Pollock's Toy Museum**. Its collections include a fine example of the Victorian paper theatres popularized by Benjamin Pollock, who sold them under the slogan "a penny plain, two pence coloured". The other exhibits range from vintage teddy bears to Sooty and Sweep, and from Red Army soldiers to wax dolls, filling every nook and cranny of the museum's six tiny, rickety rooms and the stairs – be sure to look out for the dalmatian, Dismal Desmond.

Post Office Tower

Exploring Fitzrovia, it's impossible to ignore the looming presence of the former **Post Office Tower** (officially known as the BT Tower), a glass-clad pylon on Cleveland Street, designed in the early 1960s by a team of bureaucrats in the Ministry of Works. The city's tallest building until the NatWest Tower topped it in 1981, it's still a prominent landmark north of the river. Sadly, after a bomb attack in 1971, the tower closed to the public, and the revolving restaurant followed in 1980.

Fitzroy Square

Near the top of Fitzroy Street is **Fitzroy Square**, a Bloomsbury-style square begun by the Adam brothers in the 1790s and faced, unusually, with light Portland stone (or stucco) rather than the ubiquitous dark Georgian brickwork. Traffic is excluded, but few pedestrians come here either – except those hobbling to the London Foot Hospital – yet it's a square rich in artistic and revolutionary associations.

The painter **Ford Madox Brown** had fortnightly singsongs at no. 37 with his Pre-Raphaelite chums, and guests such as Turgenev and Liszt. **Virginia Woolf**'s blue plaque is at no. 29 (a house previously lived in by George Bernard Shaw): her Bloomsbury mates considered it a disreputable neighbourhood, when she moved with her brother in 1907, after first checking with the police. Later, in 1913, artist Roger Fry set up his **Omega Workshops** at no. 33, padding the walls with seaweed to keep out the noise. In the 1890s the square was home to the **International Anarchist School for Children**, run by 60-year-old French anarchist Louise Michel. The police eventually raided the building and closed down the school after finding bombs hidden in the basement.

A revolutionary of more international fame – the Venezuelan adventurer **General Francisco de Miranda** (1750–1816) – is commemorated with a statue at the eastern corner of the London Foot Hospital situated on the southern side of the square. De Miranda lived nearby for a few years at 58 Grafton Way, and in 1810 he met up in Fitzrovia with fellow revolutionary Simón Bolívar; de Miranda ended his days in a Spanish prison, while Bolívar went on to liberate much of South America.

Tottenham Court Road

It's been centuries since there was a stately mansion – the original Tottenham Court – at the northern end of **Tottenham Court Road**, which consistently makes a strong challenge for London's least prepossessing, central shopping street. A rash of stores flogging discount-priced electrical equipment pack out the southern end, while furniture-makers – the street's original vendors – from Habitat and Heal's to cheap sofa outlets, pepper its northern stretch. The London listings magazine *Time Out* has its base here, too.

The British Museum

Housed in London's grandest Greek Revival building, fronted by a giant Ionic colonnade and portico designed by Robert Smirke in the 1820s, the British Museum is one of the great museums of the world. With over 70,000 exhibits ranged over several miles of galleries, it boasts one of the largest collections of antiquities, prints and drawings housed under one roof – over 13 million objects (and growing). Its assortment of Roman and Greek art is unparalleled, its Egyptian collection is the best outside Egypt and there are fabulous treasures from Anglo-Saxon and Roman Britain, from Africa, China, Japan, India and Mesopotamia. You'll clearly never manage to see everything in one visit, so the best advice is to concentrate on a couple of areas of interest, or else sign up with one of the museum's excellent guided tours of a single room.

The origins of the BM (as it's known) lie in the 70,000 curios – from fossils and flamingo tongues to "maggots taken from a man's ear" – collected by **Hans Sloane**, a Chelsea physician who bequeathed them to George II in 1753 for £20,000. The king couldn't (or wouldn't) pay, so the collection was purchased by an unenthusiastic government to form the world's first public secular museum, housed in a mansion bought with the proceeds of a dubiously conducted public lottery. Soon afterwards, the BM began to acquire the antiquities that have made it, in many ways, the world's largest museum of plundered goods. The "robberies" of Lord Elgin are only the best known; countless others engaged in sporadic looting throughout the Empire and the BM itself sent out archeologists to strip classical sites bare. Despite calls from countries around the world for the return of their national treasures, the BM looks unlikely to shift its stance.

The BM can get very crowded, particularly at weekends, so get here as early as possible. It's all a far cry from the museum's beginnings in 1759, when it was open for just three hours a day, entry was by written application, and tickets for "any person of decent appearance" were limited to ten per hour. Nowadays, the BM can tire even the most ardent museum lover. J.B. Priestley, for one, wished "there was a little room somewhere in the British Museum that contained only about twenty exhibits and good lighting, easy chairs, and a notice imploring you to smoke". Short of such a place, the best advice is to visit the Enlightenment gallery and the adjacent room 2, tick off one or two of the **highlights** (see box, p.109), or concentrate on one or two sections.

6

INFORMATION AND TOURS

Opening hours Daily 10am–5.30pm, Fri until 8.30pm
Admission Free
Contact details ☎ 020 7323 8000, ⓦ britishmuseum.org
Tube Tottenham Court Road, Russell Square or Holborn
Orientation The BM has two entrances: the main entrance on Great Russell Street and a back entrance on Montague Place. You can pick up a museum plan from the main information desk in the Great Court, but even equipped with a plan, it's easy enough to get confused – don't hesitate to ask the helpful and knowledgeable museum staff.

Tours The BM offers daily guided tours, known as eyeOpener tours (30–40min; free), which concentrate on just one room. Look out, too, for the Hands-On desks (daily 11am–4pm; free), where you can handle some of the museum's artefacts. Another option is to pick up one of the audio tours (available daily 10am–4.30pm; £5).
Eating The museum's best café and restaurant is the *Gallery Café* beyond room 12; the *Court Café* in the Great Court itself is more snacky, though it has a spectacular setting; the *Court Restaurant* on the upper floor is pricier, and best booked in advance (☎ 020 7323 8990).

Ancient Greece and Rome

The BM's **Ancient Greece and Rome galleries** make up the largest section in the museum. The ground floor (rooms 11–23) is laid out along broadly chronological lines, from the Bronze Age to Hellenistic times; the upper floor (rooms 69–73) concentrates on the Roman Empire.

THE GREAT COURT

At the centre of the British Museum is the spectacular **Great Court** – the largest covered square in Europe – with its startling glass-and-steel curved roof, designed in 2000 by Norman Foster. And at the centre of the Great Court, newly encased in stone, is the domed, round **Reading Room**, designed by Sydney Smirke, Robert's younger brother, in 1857 to house the British Library. Numerous writers from Oscar Wilde to Virginia Woolf, have frequented the place, and it was here at padded leather desk O7 that Karl Marx wrote *Das Kapital*. Since the British Library moved out to St Pancras (see p.127), and the BM have stopped using the place to stage temporary exhibitions, the reading room is once again open to the public – and spectacular it is, too.

6

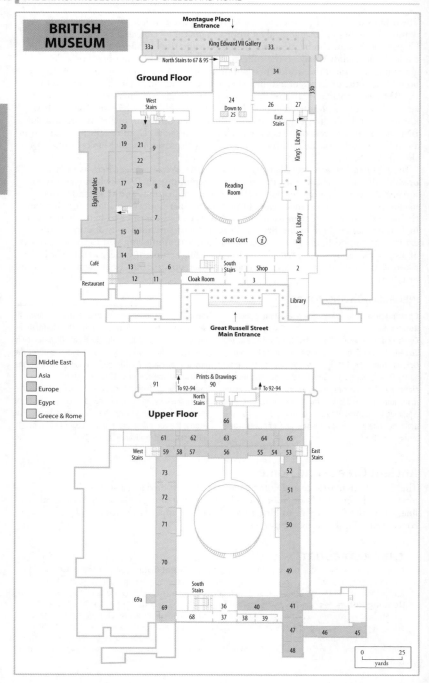

Classical Greece

The twin half-columns that once flanked a beehive tomb at Mycenae now herald the beginning of the Greek antiquities. There's a lot of fabulous stuff in the first few rooms, but the real highlights begin in room 15, whose centrepiece is the marble relief from the **Harpy Tomb**, an imposing 30ft funerary pillar from Xanthos in Turkey. Its name derived from the strange birdwomen which appear on two sides of the relief, carrying children in their arms.

The most important monument from Xanthos can be seen, partially reconstructed, in room 17. The fourth-century BC **Nereid Monument** is a mighty temple-like chieftain's tomb, fronted with Ionic columns interspersed with figures, once identified as Nereids (sea nymphs), now thought to be Aurae, or wind goddesses. The monument was brought back from the BM's first overseas excavations in 1842 by Charles Fellows, along with the greater part of the site's moveable art (including the Harpy Tomb relief).

6

Elgin Marbles

Dull is the eye that will not weep to see
Thy walls defaced, thy mouldering shrines removed
By British hands, which it had best behoved
To guard those relics ne'er to be restored.
Curst be the hour when from their isle they roved,
And once again thy hapless bosom gored,
And snatch'd thy shrinking gods to northern climes abhorred!   *Childe Harold's Pilgrimage*, Lord Byron

The large, purpose-built room 18 houses the museum's most famous relics, the **Parthenon sculptures**, better known as the **Elgin Marbles**, after Lord Elgin, who removed them from the Parthenon in Athens between 1801 and 1812. As British ambassador, Elgin claimed he had permission from the Ottoman authorities (who ruled Greece at the time) to remove them. There were justifications for Elgin's action – a Venetian missile had caused considerable damage in 1687 when it landed on a pile of gunpowder the Turks had thoughtfully stored there – though Byron was not the only one to protest at the time. The Greek government has asked for the sculptures to be sent back so they can be displayed, along with the rest of the sculptures, at the Acropolis Museum in Athens – so far, to no avail.

The frieze and the statues

Despite their grand setting (and partly due to all the hype), first impressions of the marble friezes, carved between 447 and 432 BC under the supervision of the sculptor **Pheidias**, can be a little disappointing. The long, repetitive queues of worshippers lack the vigorous immediacy of high-relief sculptural friezes. To prepare yourself, head into the adjacent interpretive rooms to learn more about the context of the marbles. The main frieze, for example, would actually have been situated virtually out of sight behind the first set of columns, and would originally have been picked out in red, blue and gold paint.

Next, head for the traffic jam of horsemen on the north frieze, which is well preserved and exhibits superb compositional dexterity – it's worth remembering that the frieze is carved to a depth of only two inches, yet manages to convey a much greater feeling of

---

THE BM HIGHLIGHTS

Assyrian reliefs Ground floor, rooms 7–10
African galleries Lower floor, room 25
Egyptian mummies Upper floor, rooms 62–63
Elgin Marbles Ground floor, room 18

Enlightenment Ground floor, room 1
Lewis chessmen Upper floor, room 40
Rosetta Stone Ground floor, room 4
Sutton Hoo Treasure Upper floor, room 41

6

GREEK VASES

The BM boasts an exhausting array of **Greek vases**: Mycenaean vases (1300 BC) in room 12 and Geometric (around 800 BC) and Athenian black-figure vases (around 600 BC) in room 13. Among the red-figure vases from Greece's Classical age (500 BC onwards) in rooms 14 and 15, check out the satyrs balancing wine coolers on their erect penises (room 15, cabinet 7). There are further hoards of mostly red-figure vases in room 19 and the mezzanine gallery in room 20, not to mention various examples dotted about rooms 68–73 and in the King's Library (room 1).

---

perspective. Another superlative slice stands directly opposite, where the oxen are being led to the gods (said to have inspired Keats to write *Ode on a Grecian Urn*). At each end of the room are the freestanding pedimental sculptures: the figures from the east pediment, which depict the extraordinary birth of Athena – she emerged full-grown and armed from the head of Zeus – are the most impressive, though most are headless.

Tomb of Payava

Two of Lord Elgin's even less defensible appropriations stand forlornly in room 19: a single column and one of the six caryatids from the portico of the **Erechtheum**, on the Acropolis. Further on, in room 20, is another large relic from Xanthos, the **Tomb of Payava**, built during the incumbent's lifetime in the fourth century BC; the reliefs on the tomb's steep roof would have been out of view of earthbound mortals, and are best viewed from the mezzanine (room 20a).

Wonders of the Ancient World

Room 21 contains fragments from one of the Seven Wonders of the Ancient World: two huge figures, an Amazonian frieze and a marble horse the size of an elephant from the self-aggrandizing tomb of **King Mausolus at Halikarnassos** (source of the word "mausoleum") from the fourth century BC. However, the real gem is the sculpted column drum, decorated in high relief, in room 22, from another Wonder, the colossal **Temple of Artemis at Ephesus**. The rest of the room is devoted to Hellenistic culture and features a fabulously delicate, gold oak wreath with a bee and two cicadas.

The upper floors

The remainder of the Greek and Roman collection is situated on the **upper floors** (rooms 69–73), best approached from the west stairs, which are lined with rich **mosaics**. For the most part, the best stuff is displayed in room 70, and includes a dazzling display of silverware from Roman Gaul and an intriguing, warty, crocodile-skin suit of armour worn by a Roman follower of the Egyptian crocodile cult (cabinet 18). Don't miss the first-century AD silver **Warren Cup** (cabinet 12a), whose graphic depictions of gay sex were deemed too risqué to be shown to the public until the 1990s. Next to it stands the **Portland Vase**, made from cobalt-blue blown glass, and decorated with opaque white cameos. The vase was famously smashed into over 200 tiny pieces by a drunken Irishman in 1845, for which he was fined £3.

Middle East

The **Middle Eastern collection** covers all the lands east of Egypt and west of India. The majority of exhibits on the ground floor (rooms 6–10) come from the Assyrian Empire, centred on modern-day Iraq; upstairs (rooms 52–59) you'll find more rich pickings from Mesopotamia and the surrounding region; in the north wing of the building, on the ground floor is a room devoted to Islam (room 34).

CLOCKWISE FROM TOP GREAT COURT (P.107); MOSAIC, WEST STAIRS (ABOVE); STANDARD OF UR (P.112) >

Assyrian sculpture and reliefs

A colossal guardian lion, smothered in inscriptions, signals the beginning of the BM's remarkable collection of **Assyrian sculptures and reliefs** (room 6). Close by stands a small black obelisk carved with images of foreign rulers paying tribute to Shalmaneser III (858–824 BC), interspersed with **cuneiform inscriptions**. Ahead lies the Egyptian sculpture gallery (room 4), but to continue with Assyria, turn left and pass between the two awesome five-legged, human-headed winged lions that once flanked the doorway of the throne room in the palace in Nimrud (now in northern Iraq), built by Ashurnasirpal II (883–859 BC). Beyond is a full-scale reconstruction of the colossal wooden **Balawat Gates** from the palace of Shalmaneser III, bound together with bronze strips decorated with low-relief friezes, depicting the defeat and execution of Shalmaneser's enemies.

Nimrud and Nineveh reliefs

The vast corridor of **Nimrud reliefs**, in room 7, were originally brightly coloured, appearing rather like stone tapestries, and adorned the interior of Ashurnasirpal II's palace. There are some great snapshots of Assyrian life – a review of prisoners, a bull hunt and so on – but the most memorable scene, located towards the middle of the room, is of the soldiers swimming across the sea on inflated animal bladders. The **Nineveh reliefs** in room 9 record the stupendous effort involved in transporting some gargantuan winged bulls from their quarry to the palace of Sennacherib (704–681 BC). The Assyrians moved these carved beasts in one piece; not so the British, who cut the two largest winged bulls into four pieces before transporting them – the joins are still visible on the pair, which now stand at the northern entrance to room 10.

Room 10 itself is lined with even more splendid Assyrian friezes from Sennacherib's palace in Nineveh. On one side (10b) the reliefs portray the chaos and carnage during the capture of Lachish (a city in modern-day Israel); the friezes were damaged, and Sennacherib's face smashed in, by Babylonian soldiers when the Assyrian capital later fell to its southern neighbours in 612 BC. On the other side (10a) are the **royal lion hunts** of Ashurbanipal (668–631 BC), which involved rounding up the beasts before letting them loose, one at a time, in an enclosed arena for the king's sport, a practice which effectively eradicated the species in Assyria; the succession of graphic death scenes features one in which the king slaughters the cats with his bare hands.

Mesopotamia

Upstairs, in room 59, are the Neolithic **Ain Ghazal statues**, the oldest large-scale representations of humans in the world, dating from the eighth millennium BC. Further on, in room 56, are some more of the BM's oldest artefacts, dating from Mesopotamia in the third millennium BC. The most extraordinary treasures hail from Ur, the first great city on earth, (now in Iraq): the enigmatic **Ram in the Thicket** (cabinet 17), a deep-blue lapis lazuli and white shell statuette of a goat on its hind legs, peering through gold-leaf branches; beside it, the equally mysterious **Standard of Ur**, a small hollow box showing scenes of battle on one side, with peace and banqueting on the other, all fashioned in shell, red limestone and lapis lazuli, set in bitumen; and the **Royal Game of Ur** (cabinet 16), one of the earliest known board games.

In room 55, a selection of tablets scratched with infinitesimal cuneiform script includes lists, receipts, prescriptions, the **Flood Tablet** (cabinet 8), a fragment of the Epic of Gilgamesh, the world's oldest story, and, in room 52, the **Cyrus Cylinder** (cabinet 4), recounting the Persian leader's capture of Babylon in 539 BC. Finally, also in room 52, there's the **Oxus Treasure** (cabinet 3), the most important surviving hoard of Persian goldwork from the Achaemenid Empire (550–330 BC), discovered in Tajikistan in 1877 and eventually picked up from the bazaar in Rawalpindi. The most celebrated pieces are the miniature four-horse chariot and the pair of armlets sprouting fantastical horned griffins.

6

Islam

The museum's fairly modest **Islamic collection** is tucked away in room 34, by the Montague Place entrance. Among the highlights are the **Damascus and Iznik ceramics** in greens, tomato-reds and no fewer than five shades of blue. Also worth seeking out at the far end of the room, are the medieval astrolabes, celestial globes and a **geomantic instrument** used to tell the future. The most striking exhibit is a naturalistic **jade terrapin**, discovered in Allahabad in 1600; close by is a silver-filigree cosmetic box said to be from Tipu Sultan's palace, and a couple of jade Mughal hookah bases encrusted with lapis lazuli and rubies set in gold.

6

Ancient Egypt

The BM's collection of **Egyptian antiquities**, ranging from Pre-dynastic times to Coptic Egypt, is one of the finest in the world, rivalled only by Cairo's; the highlights are the **Rosetta Stone**, the vast hall of Egyptian **sculpture** (room 4) and the large collection of **mummies** (rooms 61–66).

Egyptian sculpture

On the ground floor, just past the entrance to the Assyrian section (see opposite), two black-granite statues of **Amenophis III**, also known as Amenhotep III (c.1417–1379 BC), whose rule coincided with the zenith of Egyptian power, guard the entrance to the BM's large hall of **Egyptian sculpture** (room 4). The name "Belzoni", scratched behind the left heel of the larger statue, was carved by the Italian circus strongman responsible for dragging some of the heftiest Egyptian treasures to the banks of the Nile. Further on, a colossal pink-speckled granite head of Amenophis III stands next to his enormous dislocated arm. Nearby are four seated statues of the goddess Sakhmet, the half-lion, half-human bringer of destruction, who was much loved by Amenophis III – each sports solar discs and clutches the *ankh*, the Egyptian symbol of life.

North of here, another giant head and shoulders, comprised of two-coloured granite, bears the hole drilled by Napoleon's soldiers in an unsuccessful attempt to remove it from the mortuary temple of Rameses II – it was this relic that inspired Shelley's poem *Ozymandias*. Moving towards the end of the room, make sure you seek out the bronze Gayer-Anderson cat goddess **Bastet**, with gold nose- and ear-rings, and the colossal granite scarab beetle by the exit.

The mummies and other funerary art

Upstairs in room 61, eleven large fragments of the colourful wall-paintings from the **tomb-chapel of Nebamun** from 1350 BC are displayed, depicting the idealized life of wealthy Egyptians of the period. Next door, in room 62, is the popular **Egyptian**

THE ROSETTA STONE

There's usually a little huddle of people in the centre of the Egyptian sculpture hall crowded round the **Rosetta Stone**, officially the most visited object in the BM. This slab of dark granodiorite, found in Rashid (Rosetta) in the Nile delta in 1799 by French soldiers, is inscribed with a decree extolling the virtues of the new ruler Ptolemy V in 196 BC. What made the Rosetta Stone so famous, however, was that it was a trilingual text: Ancient Greek at the bottom, demotic Egyptian script in the middle and, most importantly of all, **Egyptian hieroglyphs** at the top. It was surrendered to the Brits in 1801, after they had defeated the French at Alexandria, and brought to the British Museum, where it has been on more or less continuous display since 1802. However, it was a French professor, Champollion, who eventually unlocked the secret of Egyptian hieroglyphs, and produced an accurate translation some twenty years later. A full-size replica, displayed as the Stone would have been in the nineteenth century (open to the elements and free to touch) is on display in the Enlightenment gallery.

mummy collection, including numerous mummified corpses, embalmed bodies, and inner and outer **coffins** richly decorated with hieroglyphs. In cabinet 29, there are mummies of animals, including cats, apes, crocodiles, falcons and an eel, along with their highly ornate coffins. Also on display are colourful funerary **amulets**, which were wrapped with the mummy, and **scarabs**, which were placed on the chest of the mummy to prevent the deceased's heart from bearing witness against him or her after death. And don't miss the diminutive, glazed turquoise hippo, one of the museum's most popular items (cabinet 23). The contents of Egyptian tombs included food, drink, clothing, furniture, weapons and dozens of **shabti figures** designed to perform any task the gods might require in the afterlife. In room 63, there are miniature boats to provide transport in the afterlife, beer brewers, butchers and even an entire model granary.

At this point, pop into room 66 to admire the joyful depiction of the Battle of Adwa (1896), when **Ethiopia** trounced Italy, the nearby Falasha (Jewish) dolls and the "chestlet" of beetle wings. Lastly, the 5000-year-old sand-preserved corpse in room 64 (cabinet 15) always comes in for ghoulish scrutiny, and there's a limestone building block (cabinet 14) from the Great Pyramid of Khufu (Cheops), another of the Seven Wonders of the Ancient World.

Europe

The BM fulfils its less controversial role as national treasure house of antiquities in the **Europe** section on the upper floor (rooms 40–51). Here, you'll find a vast range of exhibits from Iron Age jewellery to twentieth-century objets d'art.

Prehistoric/Roman Britain

One of the BM's most sensational finds is the well-preserved leathery half-corpse **Lindow Man**, in room 50, thought to have been clubbed and garrotted during a Druid sacrificial ceremony. Several impressive Iron Age treasure troves are also displayed in room 50, among them the **Snettisham Hoard** (cabinet 19) of gold and silver torcs (neck-rings). Look out, too, for the two most distinctive examples of **Celtic artistry**, the French Basse-Yutz wine flagons made from bronze and inlaid with coral, with happy little ducks on the lip and rangy dogs for handles. Room 49 displays finds from **Roman Britain**, many, like the bronze head (and hand) of the Roman emperor Hadrian (cabinet 14), dredged out of the Thames. The most impressive display is the fourth-century AD **Mildenhall Treasure** (cabinet 22), a 28-piece silver tableware set, whose Great Dish is decorated with Bacchic images in low relief.

Europe: Dark Ages to Medieval

Visitors entering room 40 are greeted by the incredible, fourteenth-century French **Royal Gold Cup** (cabinet 2), given by James I to the Constable of Castille, only to find its way back to England in later life – the scenes enamelled on its surface depict the gruesome story of St Agnes. Beyond lie the celebrated **Lewis chessmen** (cabinet 5), wild-eyed, thick-set, twelfth-century Scandinavian figures carved from walrus ivory, discovered in 1831 by a crofter in the Outer Hebrides. Don't miss, too, the large and graphic twelfth-century "Sheela-na-gig" from Ireland, thought to have been carved to ward off evil spirits. Room 41 houses the Anglo-Saxon **Sutton Hoo Treasure**, which includes silver bowls, gold jewellery and an iron helmet bejewelled with gilded bronze and garnets, all buried along with a forty-oar open ship in East Anglia around 625 AD, and discovered by accident in 1939.

Europe: Renaissance to Modern

Room 47 kicks off the **European nineteenth-century** section, and reflects the era's eclectic tastes, with everything from quasi-medieval jewellery to Neoclassical porcelain vases, much of it inspired by the BM itself. Look out for the Arts and Crafts De Morgan and Minton tiles (cabinet 12) and Christopher Dresser's outstanding geometric metalwork (cabinet 15). In room 48, the best of the museum's **twentieth-century exhibits** are displayed, including stunning examples of iridescent Tiffany glass, a copper vase by Frank Lloyd Wright and a lovely, chequered oak clock with a mother-of-pearl face, designed by Charles Rennie Mackintosh. There's also usually an impressive array of avant-garde Russian ceramics celebrating the achievements of the 1917 revolution.

Renaissance and Baroque art fills room 46, with a bafflingly wide range of works from all over Europe (though much of it of British origin). Highlights include a collection of eighteenth-century Huguenot silver, two pure-gold ice pails that belonged to Princess Diana's family and the Armada Service, a Tudor silver dining set.

The purple-walled room 45 contains the **Waddesdon Bequest**, curiosities amassed by Baron Rothschild in the nineteenth century: a mixed bag of silver gilt, enamelware, glassware and hunting rifles. Two of the finest works are the Holy Thorn Reliquary (cabinet 1), with its wonderfully macabre depiction of the Resurrection and a Flemish sixteenth-century boxwood altarpiece of Christ's Life and Passion (cabinet 8), just 6 inches high and carved with staggering detail.

King's Library – Enlightenment
The **Enlightenment gallery** (room 1) runs the length of the east wing. Built to house George III's library (now in the British Library in St Pancras), it's like a snapshot of the BM of old, lined with antique display cases stuffed with books and artefacts, illustrating the magpie tastes of the eighteenth-century colonial collector, epitomized by Hans Sloane himself, the BM's founder.

Sloane's own collection features everything from priapic statuettes to a black obsidian mirror used by the magician, John Dee, to conjure up spirits (case 20). And he was not alone in falling for the bizarre and magical to augment his "cabinet of curiosities": the rhino-horn cup which protected the drinker from poison and the Japanese "merman" (opposite case 14) – a dried monkey sewn onto a fish tail – are not atypical. Displayed here, too, are some of the museum's earliest acquisitions, brought back from the far reaches of the expanding British Empire: a piece of bark cloth made by Fletcher Christian's Tahitian partner (case 22); Tipu Sultan's sword and ring, and a whole variety of Javanese puppets and dolls (case 23) collected by Stamford Raffles.

Don't neglect to pop into the adjacent room 2, where some of the museum's **oldest exhibits** are usually displayed, like the 13,000-year-old ivory sculpture of swimming reindeer and the 11,000-year-old sculpture of two lovers entwined, found in the Judean desert.

TIME AND MONEY

The BM has a number of themed rooms, the largest of which is the Enlightenment gallery on the ground floor (see above). On the upper floor, rooms 38 & 39 resound to the tick-tocks and chimes of every type of timepiece from pocket watches to grandfather clocks. One of the best party pieces is the Polish clock from 1600 (room 38) featuring a cow that produced liquid from its udders on the hour, and the spectacular ship from 1585 (room 39) whose concealed organ would announce a banquet.

The **money** gallery (room 68) traces the history of filthy lucre from the use of grain in Mesopotamia around 2000 BC, to the advent of coins in around 625 BC in Greek cities in Asia Minor. There are pound-coin moulds and punches (cabinet 14), a geometric lathe for old £1 notes (cabinet 16) and a wonderful Tiffany-designed National Cash Register till (cabinet 13). The largest denomination bill is the 10 trillion Zimbabwe dollar note (cabinet 17), from 2008, which couldn't even pay for the price of a taxi ride. The most unusual exhibit, however, is the one million dollar note issued by the Hong Kong "Bank of Hell" (cabinet 18), featuring the face of Harold Wilson, and designed to be burnt as an offering to keep the deceased happy in the afterlife.

Americas

The BM's two American galleries lie to the side of the **Living and Dying gallery** (room 24), which features Hoa Hakananai'a, the giant basalt **Easter Island statue** (originally painted red and white), and four modern apocalyptic papier-mâché skeletons from the Mexican Day of the Dead festival. Close by is the famous crystal skull, thought to have been Aztec when the BM bought it in 1897, but now known to be a fake.

Next door is the **North American gallery** (room 26), whose precise exhibits change regularly, due to the delicate, organic nature of the materials used. However, you can be sure to find feather headdresses, masks, basketry, bead and shell currency and zoomorphic stone pipes. From the Arctic, there are Inuit furs and skins, including a caribou-skin parka and bone sled, and from the Southwest, the ever-popular Pueblo pottery made by the Hopi.

The **Mexican gallery** (room 27) covers Mexican art from the second millennium BC to the sixteenth century AD. The centrepiece is an Aztec fire serpent, Xiuhcoatl, carved in basalt: on one side is a collection of Huaxtec female deities in stone, sporting fan-shaped headdresses; on the other are an Aztec stone rattlesnake, the squatting figure of the sun-god, Xochipili, and the death-cult god, Mictlantecuhtli. A series of limestone Mayan reliefs from Yaxchilan, depicting blood-letting ceremonies, lines one wall and, elsewhere, there are some fifteenth-century turquoise mosaic masks and figurines.

Africa

The BM's **Africa** collection is housed on the lower floor (room 25). As you enter, you'll see the "Throne of Weapons", made from decommissioned weapons, as is the "Tree of Life" further on. Nearby there are **woodcarvings** from a whole range of African cultures: everything from a large stool from Ghana to backrests from the Congo. Further to the left, you'll find the Yoruba royal palace doors, carved in high relief and depicting, among other things, lazy British imperialists arriving on a litter to collect taxes.

To the right, there's a section on **masquerades**, with elaborate crocodile, buffalo, warthog and hippo masks from the last two centuries, and a video of contemporary initiation ceremonies in Nigeria. Perhaps the most famous of the BM's African exhibits are the so-called "**Benin Bronzes**", looted by the British in 1897. Confusingly, these are neither bronzes (they are, in fact, brass), nor from modern-day Benin, but from the former Benin Empire within modern-day Nigeria. Among the most impressive are the fifty or so ornate sixteenth-century brass plaques, nine hundred of which once decorated the royal palace in Benin City. Other Benin exhibits, such as the eye-catching ivory leopards studded with copper gun caps, were actually commissioned by Europeans.

Asia

The BM's Chinese collection is unrivalled in the West, and the Indian sculpture is easily as good as anything at the V&A. The Asian galleries (rooms 33, 67 & 92–95) are in the museum's north wing, by the Montague Place entrance.

China

The **Chinese collection** occupies one half of room 33. Immediately striking are the large pieces of garishly glazed **three-colour statuary**, particularly the three seated sages at the far end of the room, and the central cabinet of horses, camels, kings, officials and fabulous beasts. However, take time for the smaller pieces: the miniature landscapes (cabinet 56), popular among bored Chinese bureaucrats, or the incredible array of **snuff bottles** (cabinet 54), made from lapis lazuli, jade, crystal, tortoiseshell, quartz and amber. The Chinese invented **porcelain**, and there's a whole range on display here, but for an even more impressive collection of Chinese ceramics, head for room 95 (see below). Lastly, don't miss the **Chinese jade**, on display in the adjacent corridor (room 33b).

South and Southeast Asia

The other half of room 33 starts with a beautiful gilt-bronze statue of Tara, the goddess of good fortune, who was born from one of the tears wept by Avalokiteshvara (who embodies compassion and stands on the east side of the marble well). She heralds the beginning of the **South and Southeast Asian** antiquities, a bewildering array of artefacts from places as far apart as India and Indonesia. It's worth seeking out cabinet 55 with its Tibetan depictions of tantric sex, its *dakinis* (fierce minor goddesses who dance on demons), and Chitipati, lord of the graveyard. Cabinet 39 features a whole set of ivory figures from Kandy, representing the local royal family and officials, including the all-important umbrella-bearer. Beyond are larger-scale **Indian stone sculptures**, featuring a bevy of intimidating goddesses such as Durga, depicted killing a buffalo demon with her eight hands (cabinet 25).

Korea

The centrepiece of the BM's Korea gallery (room 67), up the north stairs from room 33, is a nail-free reconstruction of a *sarangbang* or scholar's study, a serene, minimalist space set aside for the gentleman of the house. Among the other exhibits, which range from illuminated Buddhist manuscripts to contemporary Korean objets d'art, look out for the bamboo fans (cabinet 21), used by dapper Korean gentlemen, their woven horsehair hats (cabinet 19), and the *paduk* gaming board (better known in the West as Go). There's a seventeenth-century white porcelain "full-moon" jar, admired for both its irregularity and its Confucian austerity, along with a modern version.

Chinese ceramics – Sir Percival David Collection

Next door is an entire room given over to **Chinese ceramics** (room 95), with nearly 1700 objects on display, dating from the third to the twentieth centuries. A few star exhibits get labels, like the "David vases", by the entrance, from 1351, in the blue-and-white Ming style that became so popular in Europe – touch-screen computers will help you identify the rest. What is so striking about many of the pieces is their apparent modernity – the bold single-colour porcelain wares at the far side of the room wouldn't look out of place in the 1960s, though in fact they date from the Ming and Qing dynasties. Among the most celebrated Chinese ceramics are the *Ru* wares whose "crackling" glaze was seen as a merit rather than a defect from the Song dynasty onwards.

Japan

The sensitive materials used in Japanese art mean that the items on display in the **Japan** (rooms 92–94) galleries change frequently. What you get is an educational sample laid out chronologically from the Neolithic Jomon period to the manga culture of contemporary Japan. In between, you get to inspect colourful Buddhist scrolls, Shinto shrines, nineteenth-century woodblock prints by artists such as Hokusai and Hiroshige, examples of *netsuke* (ornamental toggles) and *inro* (cases for holding small objects). Centre stage, there's a wonderfully ornate suit of Samurai armour, complete with the sort of horned helmet and mask that Darth Vadar might wear. There's also a section on the traditional tea ceremony alongside a reconstructed tea house, where the museum puts on regular demonstrations.

PRINTS AND DRAWINGS

The sheer volume of the BM's **prints and drawings** – 2 million prints and 50,000 drawings – means there's only space for a changing display in room 90. However, with an incredible collection of drawings by Leonardo, Raphael, Michelangelo, Rubens and Rembrandt, plus prints by Dürer and works by Hogarth, Constable, Turner and Blake – to mention but a few – the exhibitions are always worth exploring.

EUROSTAR, ST PANCRAS STATION

Bloomsbury

Bloomsbury was built over in grid-plan style from the 1660s onwards, and the formal, bourgeois Georgian squares laid out then remain the area's main distinguishing feature. In the last century, Bloomsbury acquired the reputation it continues to hold, as the city's most learned quarter, dominated by the dual institutions of the British Museum and London University. Today, the British Museum is clearly Bloomsbury's main draw – it has its own chapter (see p.106) – but the real pleasure in Bloomsbury is simply strolling through its leafy squares which, still provide some of the nicest picnic spots in central London. Only in its northern border, formed by busy Euston Road, does the character of the area change dramatically, with the hustle and bustle of the mainline train stations of St Pancras and King's Cross.

South of the British Museum

Over the years, there have been moves to demolish the small grid of Georgian streets to the south of the British Museum to give the BM (as it's known) a more triumphal approach. Thankfully, none have come to fruition and **Museum Street** and **Bury Place** remain a pleasure to explore, thriving on a mixture of antiquarian and secondhand print and book shops, and cafés and sandwich shops which feed the museum hordes. It's worth looking in at **Jarndyce**, the booksellers at 46 Great Russell St, whose left window is renowned for its display of bizarre antiquarian books, with titles such as *Correctly English in Hundred Days* and *The Art of Faking Exhibition Poultry*.

Cartoon Museum

35 Little Russell St · Tues–Sat 10.30am–5.30pm, Sun noon–5.30pm · £5.50 · ☎ 020 7580 8155, ⓦ cartoonmuseum.org · ♻ Tottenham Court Road

As well as putting on excellent temporary exhibitions, the **Cartoon Museum**, one block south of the BM, also has a permanent display of over two hundred works spanning two centuries, beginning with Hogarth's moralistic engravings and the caricatures of Gillray, Rowlandson and Cruickshank. The emphasis is very much on British cartoons from the likes of *Punch*, one of the earliest and longest-lasting satirical magazines, to *Private Eye*, which helped launch the careers of, among others, Ralph Steadman and Gerald Scarfe. The comic strips range from Ally Sloper, Britain's first regular comic-strip character who appeared in 1884, through D.C. Thompson (publisher of *Beano*), to *Viz*, the country's best-selling comic ever, which at its peak sold over a million copies each edition.

Church of St George's Bloomsbury

Bloomsbury Way · Daily 1–4pm · ☎ 020 7242 1979, ⓦ stgeorgesbloomsbury.org.uk · ♻ Tottenham Court Road or Holborn

A couple of blocks south of the BM is Hawksmoor's **Church of St George's Bloomsbury**, built to serve Bloomsbury's respectable residents. Its main point of interest is the unusual steeple – Horace Walpole called it "a masterpiece of absurdity" – a stepped pyramid based on Pliny's description of the tomb of Mausolus at Halikarnassos (fragments of which now reside in the BM), with lions and unicorns clinging precariously to the base. The tower is topped by a statue of the unpopular German-speaking monarch, George I, dressed in a Roman toga. Recently restored to its original, gleaming-white Georgian state, the interior is tall and wide, with a large clerestory, its best features the flaming pentecostal tongues on the keystones and an unusual semicircular apse, complete with a scallop-shell recess. There's an interesting multimedia exhibition on the history of the church and the whole area in the crypt.

Bloomsbury Square

A little further along Bloomsbury Way lies **Bloomsbury Square**, laid out in 1665 and the first of the city's open spaces to be officially called a "square". John Evelyn thought it "a noble square or piazza – a little towne", but sadly, little remains of its original or later Georgian appearance. At the south end of the square, however, you'll find **Sicilian Avenue**, a beautifully preserved architectural set piece from 1910. This unusually continental promenade leads diagonally onto Southampton Row and is separated from the main roads by slender Ionic screens. On Southampton Row itself, you can see the only **tram lines** left uncovered in central London from what was, between World Wars I and II, the world's largest tram system: to catch a glimpse, you must dodge the traffic and peek through the wrought-iron railings to the tracks as they descend into the former Kingsway tram subway.

Bedford Square

The most handsome of the Bloomsbury squares is **Bedford Square**, to the west of the BM. Some of Bloomsbury's best-known publishing houses – among them Hodder & Stoughton, Bodley Head, Jonathan Cape and Chatto & Windus – had their offices here until the 1980s. Architecturally, what you see now is pretty much as it was in the 1770s when it was built by the Russells (who still own it), though the gates which sealed the square from traffic have unfortunately been removed, as have all but one of the mews that once accommodated the coaches and servants of the square's wealthy

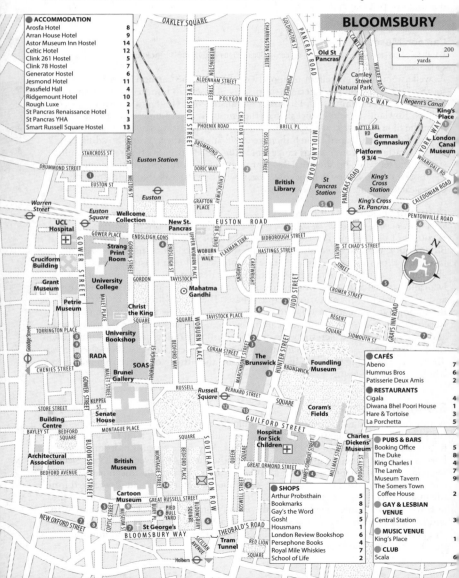

BLOOMSBURY

0   200
yards

inhabitants. Today, it's a perfect example of eighteenth-century symmetry and uniformity: each doorway arch is decorated with rusticated Coade stones; each side of the square is broken only by the white-stuccoed central houses; and the central garden is for residents of the square only.

Architectural Association

36 Bedford Sq · Term time Mon–Fri 10am–7pm, Sat 11am–5pm · ☎ 020 7887 4076, ⓦ aaschool.ac.uk · ⊖ Tottenham Court Road

The best way to get a look inside one of Bloomsbury's Georgian mansions is to head for the **Architectural Association**, which puts on occasional exhibitions, and has a bookshop in the basement and a studenty café-bar on the first floor, with a roof terrace open in fine weather.

Building Centre

26 Store St · Mon–Fri 9.30am–6pm, Sat 10am–5pm · Free · ☎ 020 7692 4000, ⓦ buildingcentre.co.uk · ⊖ Goodge Street

If you've got even a passing interest in London's architecture and planning, it's a good idea to pop into the **Building Centre**, which has a café and a bookshop and which stages topical exhibitions on the future of London's built environment. Its centrepiece is a vast model of London, including as-yet unrealized City skyscrapers and the 2012 Olympic Village.

Russell Square

The largest Bloomsbury square – indeed one of the largest in London – is **Russell Square**, to the northeast of the BM. Apart from its monumental scale, little remains of the Georgian scheme, though the gardens, with their gargantuan plane trees, are good for a picnic, and there's a café in the northeastern corner. The Bloomsbury figure most closely associated with the square is T.S. Eliot, who worked at no. 24, then the offices of Faber & Faber, from 1925 until his death in 1965. The only architectural curiosity is the **Russell Hotel**, on the eastern side; twice as high as everything around it, it's a no-holds-barred Victorian terracotta fancy, concocted in a bewildering mixture of styles in 1898 by Fitzroy Doll.

Gordon Square

Gordon Square is owned by the University of London, which surrounds it on three sides. With its winding paths and summer profusion of roses, it remains one of Bloomsbury's quietest sanctuaries and is predictably popular with students. Between the wars, it was at the centre of the Bloomsbury Group (see p.122): on the east side, where the Georgian houses stand intact, plaques mark the residences of writer Lytton Strachey (no. 51) and economist John Maynard Keynes (no. 46), while another (no. 50) commemorates the group as a whole.

Church of Christ the King

Gordon Square · Mon–Fri 8am–4pm · Free · ☎ 020 7388 3588, ⓦ fifparish.com · ⊖ Euston Square or Goodge Street

Looking like a miniature cathedral, in the southwest corner of the square, stands the strangely towerless **Church of Christ the King**, built in neo-Gothic style in the 1850s. The five-bay nave is cathedralesque – the nave of Westminster Abbey is only 13ft taller – with a hammerbeam roof, full triforium and clerestory, and the unbuilt spire was to have been nearly 150ft high. It was originally built for (and still belongs to) the Catholic Apostolic Church, a prayer sect within the Anglican Church who were utterly convinced that the Second Coming was imminent (and who were renowned for elaborate rituals, for speaking in tongues and for miraculous healing). It's currently the home of Forward in Faith, the conservative wing of the Church of England.

Tavistock Square

One block east is **Tavistock Square**, laid out by Thomas Cubitt in the early nineteenth century. Though the west side of the square survives intact, the house at no. 52, where the Woolfs lived from 1924 until shortly before Virginia's suicide in 1941, and from which they ran the Hogarth Press, is no longer standing. It was here that Woolf wrote her most famous novels – *To the Lighthouse*, *Mrs Dalloway*, *Orlando* and *The Waves* – in a little studio decorated by her sister Vanessa and Duncan Grant. At the centre of the square's gardens is a statue of **Mahatma Gandhi**, whose presence has transformed the square into something of a garden for peace, with various trees and benches dedicated to the cause. That peace, however, was shattered on the morning of **July 7, 2005**, when a suicide bomber blew himself up on bus #30 as it approached the northeast corner of the square, killing thirteen people. The blast occurred shortly after the city's tube system had been hit by three other terrorist bombs (see p.461) – a plaque on the railings commemorates the victims.

7

Woburn Walk

A short distance up Upper Woburn Place, not far from where the July 7, 2005, blast occurred, is the beautifully preserved Georgian terrace of **Woburn Walk**, designed in 1822 by Cubitt as London's first purpose-built pedestrianized shopping street. **W.B. Yeats** moved into no. 5 in 1895, shortly afterwards losing his virginity at the age of 31 to fellow writer Olivia Shakespear. He and Olivia went to Heal's to order a bed before consummating the relationship, and Yeats found the experience (of ordering the bed) deeply traumatic, as "every inch added to the expense". The same address was later occupied by the unrequited love of Yeats' life, Irish nationalist Maud Gonne, reputedly the most beautiful woman in Ireland, with, in Yeats' own words, "the carriage and features of a goddess".

THE BLOOMSBURY GROUP

The **Bloomsbury Group** were essentially a bevy of upper-middle-class friends who lived in and around Bloomsbury, at that time "an antiquated, ex-fashionable area", in the words of Henry James. The group revolved around siblings Virginia, Vanessa, Thoby and Adrian Stephen, who moved into 46 Gordon Square in 1904. Thoby's Thursday-evening gatherings and Vanessa's Friday Club for painters attracted a whole host of Cambridge-educated types who subscribed to Oscar Wilde's theory that "aesthetics are higher than ethics". Their diet of "human intercourse and the enjoyment of beautiful things" was hardly revolutionary, but their behaviour, particularly that of the two sisters (unmarried, unchaperoned, intellectual and artistic), succeeded in shocking London society, especially through their louche sexual practices (most of the group swung both ways).

All this, though interesting, would be forgotten were it not for their individual work. In 1922, Virginia declared, without too much exaggeration, "Everyone in Gordon Square has become famous": Lytton Strachey was the first to make his name with a series of unprecedentedly frank biographies; Vanessa, now married to the art critic Clive Bell, became involved in Roger Fry's prolific design firm, **Omega Workshops**; and the economist John Maynard Keynes became an adviser to the Treasury. (He later went on to become the leading economic theorist of his day.) The group's most celebrated figure, Virginia, now married to Leonard Woolf, had become an established novelist; she and Leonard had also founded the **Hogarth Press**, which published T.S. Eliot's *Waste Land* in 1922.

Eliot was just one of a number of writers, such as Aldous Huxley, Bertrand Russell and E.M. Forster, who were drawn to the Bloomsbury set, but others, notably D.H. Lawrence, were repelled by the clan's narcissism and narrow-mindedness. Whatever their limitations, the Bloomsbury Group were certainly Britain's most influential intellectual coterie of the interwar years, and their appeal shows little sign of waning.

Coram's Fields

Guilford Street · Daily 9am–7pm or dusk · Free · ☎ 020 7837 6138, ⓦ coramsfields.org · ⊖ Russell Square

Halfway along Guilford Street stands the old entrance to the **Foundling Hospital**, founded in 1756 by **Thomas Coram**, a retired sea captain. Coram campaigned for seventeen years to obtain a royal charter for the hospital, having been shocked by the number of dead or dying babies left by the wayside on the streets of London during the gin craze. (At the time, 75 percent of London's children died before they were 5.) All that remains of the original eighteenth-century buildings is the alcove where the foundlings used to be abandoned and the whitewashed loggia which forms the border to **Coram's Fields**, an inner-city haven for children, with swings and slides, plus a whole host of hens, horses, sheep, goats and ducks. Adults are not allowed into the grounds unless accompanied by a child.

Foundling Museum

40 Brunswick Sq · Tues–Sat 10am–5pm, Sun 11am–5pm · £7.50 · ☎ 020 7841 3600, ⓦ foundlingmuseum.org.uk · ⊖ Russell Square

The **Foundling Museum**, north of Coram's Fields, tells the fascinating story of the Foundling Hospital (see above). As soon as it opened, it was besieged, and forced to introduce a ballot system. After 1801 only illegitimate children were admitted, and even then only after the mother had given a verbal statement confirming that "her good faith had been betrayed, that she had given way to carnal passion only after a promise of marriage or against her will". Among the most tragic exhibits are the tokens left by the mothers in order to identify the children should they ever be in a position to reclaim them: these range from a heart-rending poem to a simple enamel pot label reading "ale".

One of the hospital's governors – he even fostered two of the foundlings – was the artist **William Hogarth**, who established London's first-ever public art gallery at the hospital to give his friends somewhere to display their works and to attract potential benefactors. As a result the museum boasts works by artists such as Gainsborough and Reynolds, as well as Hogarth's splendid *March of the Guards to Finchley*. Upstairs, the Court Room, where the governors still hold their meetings, has been faithfully reconstructed, with all its fine stuccowork. The fireplace features a wonderful relief depicting the trades of navigation and agriculture, into which the foundling boys were apprenticed before being sent out to the colonies. (The girls went into service.) On the top floor, there's a room dedicated to **Georg Friedrich Handel**, who gave annual charity performances of the *Messiah*, wrote an anthem for the hospital (basically a rehash of the *Hallelujah Chorus*) and donated an organ for the chapel, the keyboard of which survives. Today, the museum continues to put on regular lunchtime concerts and family events.

Charles Dickens Museum

48 Doughty St · Daily 10am–5pm · £7 · ☎ 020 7405 2127, ⓦ dickensmuseum.com · ⊖ Russell Square

Despite its plethora of blue plaques, Bloomsbury boasts just one literary museum, the **Charles Dickens Museum**, the only one of the writer's fifteen London addresses to survive intact. Dickens moved here in 1837 – when it was practically on the northern outskirts of town – soon after his marriage to Catherine Hogarth, and they lived here for two years, during which time he wrote *Nicholas Nickleby* and *Oliver Twist*. Although Dickens painted a gloomy Victorian world in his books, the drawing room here, in which Dickens entertained his literary friends, was decorated (and has since been restored) in a rather upbeat Regency style. Letters, manuscripts and first editions, the earliest known portrait (a miniature painted by his aunt in 1830) and the reading copies he used during extensive lecture tours in Britain and the States are the rewards for those with more than a passing interest in the novelist. On the ground floor, there's a café with free wi-fi.

CHARLES DICKENS

Few cities are as closely associated with one writer as London is with **Charles Dickens** (1812–70). The recurrent motifs in his novels have become the clichés of Victorian London – the fog, the slums and alleys, the prisons and workhouses, and of course the stinking river. Drawing on his own personal experience, he was able to describe the workings of the law and the conditions of the poor with an unrivalled accuracy.

Born in Portsmouth, the second of eight children, Dickens spent a happy early childhood in Chatham and then London. This was cut short at the age of 12 when his father was imprisoned in Marshalsea debtors' prison, and Charles was forced to work in a boot-blacking factory on the site of Charing Cross Station. The experience scarred him for life – he was hurt further when his mother forced him to keep the job even after his father's release – and was no doubt responsible for Dickens' strong philanthropic convictions. After two years as a solicitor's clerk at Gray's Inn, he became a parliamentary reporter and wrote *Sketches by Boz* (Dickens' journalistic pen name) and *The Pickwick Papers*, the two works that propelled him to fame and fortune in 1836.

The same year he married **Catherine Hogarth**, and there followed ten children – "the largest family ever known with the smallest disposition to do anything for themselves", as Dickens later described them – and sixteen novels, each published in monthly (or weekly) installments, which were awaited with bated breath by the Victorian public. Then in 1857, at the peak of his career, Dickens fell in love with the actress, **Ellen Ternan**; Dickens was 45, Ternan just 18. His subsequent separation from his wife, and his insistence that she leave the family house (while her sister Georgina and most of the children stayed), scandalized society and forced the author to retreat to Rochester.

Dickens died at his desk at the age of 58, while working on *The Mystery of Edwin Drood*. According to his wishes, there was no public announcement of his burial, though he was interred in Westminster Abbey (at Queen Victoria's insistence) rather than in Rochester (as he had requested). The twelve people present at the early-morning service were asked not to wear a black bow, long hatband or any other accessories of the "revolting absurdity" of Victorian mourning.

If you're on the Dickens trail, there are one or two other sights worth checking out: the Old Curiosity Shop (see p.145), on Lincoln's Inn Fields, the (possible) inspiration for Dickens' novel of the same name; the atmospheric Inns of Court (see p.143), which feature in several Dickens novels; "Nancy's Steps", where Nancy tells Rose Maylie Oliver's story in *Oliver Twist*, on the west side of London Bridge on the South Bank; and the evocative dockland area of Shad Thames (see p.235), where Bill Sykes has his hide-out.

London University

Ⓦ lon.ac.uk

London only organized its own **University** in 1826, but was the first in the country to admit students regardless of race, class, religion or gender. The university started life in Bloomsbury, but it wasn't until after World War I that it really began to take over the area. Nowadays, the various colleges and institutes have spread their tentacles to form an almost continuous academic swathe from the British Museum all the way to Euston Road. Despite this, the university's piecemeal development has left it with only a couple of distinguishing landmarks in the form of **Senate House** and **University College**. Several of the university departments run their own small, specialist **museums and galleries**, scattered across the campus.

Senate House

Looming over central Bloomsbury is the skyscraper of **Senate House**, a "bleak, blank, hideous" building, according to Max Beerbohm, now housing the university library. Designed with discreet Art Deco touches by Charles Holden in 1932, and austerely clad in Portland stone, it's best viewed from Malet Street. During the war it served as the Ministry of Information, where the likes of Evelyn Waugh, Graham Greene, Dorothy L. Sayers and George Orwell worked. Orwell later modelled the Ministry of

Truth in *1984* on it: "an enormous pyramidal structure of glittering white concrete, soaring up, terrace after terrace, 300 metres into the air".

SOAS (School of Oriental and African Studies)
Thornhaugh St • Brunei Gallery and Treasures of SOAS Tues–Sat 10.30am–5pm • Free • Ⓦ soas.ac.uk • ➡ Russell Square or Goodge Street

To the north of Senate House, the **School of Oriental and African Studies**, or **SOAS**, puts on fascinating temporary exhibitions of photography, sculpture and art at the rather snazzy **Brunei Gallery**, funded by the immensely rich Sultan of Brunei. In addition, there's a small permanent display of the **Treasures of SOAS**, a mere snapshot of their collection, but containing an incredible range of artefacts from a Korean "moon jar" to a fortune-teller's book from Thailand. The school's prize possession, though, is a sixteenth-century illustrated Mughal manuscript of *Anvar-i Suhayli*, a Persian adaptation of the Panchatantra, a set of Indian animal fables. There's also a tiny but excellent bookshop and a café on the ground floor, and a secluded Zen-like **roof garden** dedicated to Forgiveness.

Petrie Museum of Egyptian Archeology
Malet Place • Tues–Sat 1–5pm • Free • ☎ 020 7504 2884, Ⓦ petrie.ucl.ac.uk • ➡ Euston Square or Goodge Street

The **Petrie Museum**, next door to the Science Library, has a handful of rooms jam-packed with Egyptian antiquities, the bulk of them from excavations carried out from the 1880s onwards by Flinders Petrie, UCL's first Professor of Egyptology. The first large room is crammed with objects, including huge slabs of stonework – look out for Min, the god of fertility, depicted with a particular type of lettuce which, when rubbed, secreted a milky substance. Other cabinets are crammed full of tiny objects including weights and measures, *shabti* figures, combs, bottle stoppers, sandals, legs from a toy table, a mummified bird and a pair of tweezers. At the back of the room is the richly decorated wooden coffin of Nairytisitnefer from 750 BC, while down the back stairs are frog amulets, ivory spoons and a giant sandstone jackal's paw. To the nonspecialist, the adjacent room appears to contain little more than broken bits of pottery (a speciality of Professor Petrie's). Look more closely, however, and you'll also find the world's oldest dress, an understandably ragged, pleated garment worn by an Ancient Egyptian teenager around 3000 BC. More intriguing still is the very revealing bead-net dress made for a 12-year-old, from around 2400 BC.

Grant Museum of Zoology
21 University St • Mon–Fri 1–5pm • Free • ☎ 020 3108 2052, Ⓦ grant.museum.ucl.ac.uk • ➡ Warren Street or Euston Square

Another museum piled high with exhibits – in this case skeletons – is the **Grant Museum of Zoology**, named after Robert E. Grant (1793–1874), the university's first Professor of Zoology and Comparative Anatomy, a pre-Darwinian transmutationist who always wore full evening dress when delivering lectures and later risked his career by teaching evolution at UCL. Among the numerous specimens here, don't miss the jar of pickled moles, the walrus penis bone, the skeletons of a dugong, a dodo, a quagga (an extinct zebra) and a thylacine (an extinct marsupial wolf).

University College London (UCL)
Gower St • Art collections Mon–Fri 1–5pm • Free • ☎ 020 7679 2540, Ⓦ ucl.ac.uk • ➡ Euston Square

The oldest part of **University College London** is the rather prosaically named **Main Building**, William Wilkins' Neoclassical edifice from the 1820s, with its handsome Corinthian portico and fine quadrangle, set back (and well hidden) from busy Gower Street. UCL is home to one of London's most famous art schools, the **Slade**, which puts on small, but excellent temporary exhibitions drawn from its collection of over ten thousand works of art, by the likes of Dürer, Rembrandt, Turner and Constable, as well as works by former students, such as Stanley Spencer, Paul Nash, Wyndham Lewis,

> ### JEREMY BENTHAM'S SKELETON
>
> Also on display at UCL, in the south cloisters of the Main Building, is the philosopher **Jeremy Bentham** (1748–1832), one of the university's founders. Bentham bequeathed his fully clothed skeleton so that he could be posthumously present at board meetings of the University College Hospital governors, where he was duly recorded as "present, but not voting". Bentham's **Auto-Icon**, topped by a wax head and wide-brimmed hat, is in "thinking and writing" pose as the philosopher requested, and can be seen in a hermetically sealed mahogany booth. Close by is a pair of watchful Ancient Egyptian lions, reconstructed from several thousand fragments belonging to the Petrie Museum (see p.125).

Augustus John and Raymond Briggs. These are held at the **Strang Print Room**, situated in the south cloister of the main quadrangle.

There's more artwork on display in the octagon beneath the Main Building's central dome, in an area known as the **Flaxman Gallery** – follow the signs to the library and ask the guards to let you through. John Flaxman (1755–1826) made his name producing Neoclassical funerary sculpture – his works feature prominently in Westminster Abbey and St Paul's – and the walls here are filled with scaled-down, high-relief, plaster models worked on by Flaxman himself for his marble monuments. The gallery's centrepiece is a dramatic, full-size plaster model of St Michael overcoming Satan.

Euston

The northern boundary of Bloomsbury is defined by **Euston Road**, laid out in 1756 as the city's first bypass. This was the northern limit of London until the mid-nineteenth century when rival companies built Euston, King's Cross and St Pancras, termini serving the industrial boom towns of the north of England. Since those days, Euston Road has had some of the city's worst office architecture foisted on it, which, combined with the current volume of traffic, makes this an area for selective viewing only.

Amidst all the hubbub of Euston Road, it's easy to miss the depressingly functional **Euston Station**, descendant of London's first great train terminus, originally built with just two platforms way back in 1837. Philip Hardwick's original Neoclassical ensemble – including the famous Euston Arch – was demolished in the face of fierce protests in the 1960s – British Rail claimed it needed the space in order to lengthen the platforms, which it never did. All that remains of the Euston Arch are the sad-looking lodge-houses, which flanked it, though there are moves afoot to rebuild the arch if and when the over-stretched station is reconstructed.

Wellcome Collection

183 Euston Rd • Tues–Sat 10am–6pm, Thurs till 8pm, Sun 11am–6pm • Free • ☎ 020 7611 2222, ⓦ wellcomecollection.org • ⊖ Euston or Euston Square

Despite its unpromising location, the **Wellcome Collection** puts on thought-provoking temporary exhibitions on topical scientific issues on the ground floor, where there's also an excellent café and bookshop. The permanent collection is on the first floor and begins with **Medicine Now**, which focuses on contemporary medical questions such as the body, genomes, obesity and malaria. Each subject has an "art cube" which displays contemporary artists' responses to the issues: a world map traced out in mosquitoes by Alastair Mackie; Chris Drury's collage of maps and an echocardiogram; and a giant jelly baby "clone" by Mauro Perucchetti. Next door, **Medicine Man** showcases the weird and wonderful collection of historical and scientific artefacts amassed by American-born pharmaceutical magnate Henry Wellcome (1853–1936). These range from Florence Nightingale's moccasins and Napoleon's toothbrush to a sign for a Chinese doctor's hung with human teeth, from erotic figurines and phallic amulets to Inuit snow goggles and a leper clapper – in other words, this section is an absolute must.

St Pancras New Church

Euston Road • Open for services and recitals only • ☏ 020 7388 1461, Ⓦ stpancraschurch.org • ⊖ Euston

Euston Road's oldest edifice is **St Pancras New Church**, built at enormous expense in the 1820s on the corner of Upper Woburn Place. Designed in Greek Revival style, it is notable for its octagonal tower, based on the Tower of the Winds in Athens, and for the caryatids, tacked onto the east end, which are modelled on the Erechtheion on the Acropolis – though the Euston Road ladies had to be truncated at the waist after they were found to be too tall. The best time to visit the interior, which features a dramatically lit Ionic colonnade in the apse, and some lovely Victorian stained glass, is during one of the free Thursday lunchtime recitals. There are also regular art exhibitions held in the atmospheric **Crypt Gallery** (Ⓦ cryptgallery.org.uk), with access from Duke's Road.

King's Cross St Pancras

The area around **King's Cross** and **St Pancras** stations is always buzzing with buses, cars, commuters, tourists and, with the massive development going on around King's Cross station, construction workers. Architecturally, it's dominated by **St Pancras Station**, the most glorious of London's red-brick Victorian edifices, which overshadows its two neighbours: workaday **King's Cross Station** and the brick brutalist **British Library**, home to some of the nation's most precious books and documents.

British Library

96 Euston Rd • Mon–Fri 9.30am–6pm, Tues till 8pm, Sat 9.30am–5pm, Sun 11am–5pm • ☏ 020 7412 7332, Ⓦ bl.uk • ⊖ King's Cross St Pancras

As one of the country's most expensive public buildings, the **British Library** took flak from all sides during its construction: few readers wanted to move out of the splendid Round Reading Room in the British Museum, where the library had been since the 1850s; the number of extra readers' seats was negligible and the shelving inadequate; and, to top it all, the design was criticized by Prince Charles, who compared it to an academy for secret policemen. Yet, while it's true that Colin St John Wilson's penchant for red-brick brutalism is horribly out of fashion, the library has proved popular both with the scholars who use it and the public who visit the superb galleries.

The new **piazza**, in front of the library, features Eduardo Paolozzi's giant statue of Isaac Newton bent double over his protractor, inspired by William Blake – just one of a number of specially commissioned artworks. Look out, too, for Bill Woodrow's *Book, Ball & Chain* sofa and R.B. Kitaj's unsettling giant tapestry, *If not, not*, both in the main foyer, and Patrick Hughes' optical illusion, *Paradoxymoron*, in the basement cloakroom. The spiritual heart of the building is a multistorey glass-walled tower housing the vast **King's Library**, collected by George III, and donated by George IV in 1823. The library puts on a wide variety of events, including talks, films and occasional live performances, and has several cafés, a restaurant and free wi-fi.

John Ritblat Gallery; Treasures of the British Library

The dimly lit **John Ritblat Gallery** is where the BL's ancient manuscripts and precious books are permanently displayed. The sheer variety of sacred texts displayed is overwhelming, from illuminated Torahs to richly decorated Qur'ans (Korans), from a tiny palm-leaf glorification of the Hindu goddess Jagannatha in the shape of a cow to folding books on the life of the Buddha. The richly illustrated **Lindisfarne Gospels**, begun in 698 AD, is always on display, and you turn its pages – and those of other selected texts – on the touch-screen computers. In the section on printing, you can see the world's earliest-dated printed document, along with the **Gutenberg Bible**, from 1454–55, the first Bible printed using movable type (and therefore capable of being mass-produced).

The most famous of the **historical documents** is the **Magna Carta**, King John's letter to his subjects in 1215, on display in a room of its own. Other exhibits change from time to time, and could be anything from Thomas More's last letter to Henry VIII to Lenin's application for a British Library pass. Among the **literature**, there's Shakespeare's First Folio from 1623, Jane Austen's notebooks and writing desk and the touchingly beautiful handwritten and illustrated copy of *Alice in Wonderland* given by Lewis Carroll to Alice Liddell. While examining the literary masterpieces, you can also hear several authors reading extracts from their works. Similarly, in the **music** section, which contains oddities such as Mozart's marriage contract and Beethoven's tuning fork, you can listen to works ranging from Bach and The Beatles while perusing Purcell's autographed score.

The other galleries

The BL has several other galleries in which it stages temporary exhibitions (occasionally with an entrance charge), employing more of the library's wonderful texts, supplemented by items from the British Museum. Stamp lovers should make their way up to the BL's gargantuan **Philatelic Collections**, made up of over eight million items, eighty thousand of which are displayed in vertical pull-out drawers just outside the John Ritblat Gallery. The Tapling Collection kicks off the proceedings, as it did the collection when it was bequeathed in 1891, and in drawer number one you'll find the famous "Penny Black", the birthmark of modern philately. After that you get a world tour of stamps from long-forgotten mini-kingdoms such as Mecklenburg-Schwerin and Nowanugger. Those with a political interest should head for the Bojanowicz Collection, which covers Polish stamps from 1939 to 1946, including ones from the German and Russian occupations, and even POW and displaced persons' camps. The Kay Collection consists of stamps from the colonies, but real boffins should head for the Turner Collection of railway letter stamps from the likes of the Pembroke & Tenby Railway.

St Pancras Old Church

Pancras Rd • Daily 9am to dusk • Free • ☎ 020 7387 4193, ⓦ oldstpancrasteam.wordpress.com • ⊖ King's Cross St Pancras

Allegedly the first parish church built in London, **St Pancras Old Church** lies hidden and neglected behind iron railings on raised ground behind the British Library, up Midland Road. Apart from a little exposed Norman masonry and the sixth-century Roman altar stone, most of the church dates from the nineteenth century. The **churchyard**, which is overlooked by the lugubrious Victorian Hospital for Tropical Diseases, was partially destroyed by the arrival of the railway, with the majority of graves being heaped around an ash tree under the supervision of the writer Thomas Hardy. **John Soane's mausoleum** from 1816 – designed initially for his wife, and the inspiration for Giles Gilbert Scott's traditional red phone box – still stands in its original location, to the north of the church. Also buried here was Britain's great protofeminist, **Mary Wollstonecraft Godwin**, who died a few days after giving birth to her daughter, Mary. At the age of 16, the younger Mary was spotted visiting her mother's grave by the poet Percy Bysshe Shelley, who immediately declared his undying love, before eloping with her to Italy – both Marys are now buried in Bournemouth. A list of the graveyard's most illustrious corpses is inscribed on the monumental sundial erected by Baroness Burdett-Coutts, below which sits a statue of her collie dog, and there's a map of the prominent graves by the entrance.

St Pancras Station

Euston Rd • For guided tours contact the hotel's historian Royden Stock on ☎ 07778 932359; £20 • ⊖ King's Cross St Pancras

Among London's greatest Victorian follies is the former Midland Grand Hotel, whose majestic sweep of lancets, dormers and chimneypots forms the facade of **St Pancras Station**, now London's Eurostar terminus. Completed in 1876 by George Gilbert Scott, this masterpiece of neo-Gothic architecture enjoyed a brief heyday in the 1890s when the ratio of staff to guests was 3:1, but with few private bathrooms and no central heating, the hotel couldn't survive long into the modern age. For fifty years from 1935, it languished as underused British Rail offices, but has now been refurbished partly as private apartments and partly as the luxury *St Pancras Renaissance Hotel*.

King's Cross Station

Compared to St Pancras, **King's Cross Station**, opened in 1850 as the terminus for the Great Northern Railway, is a mere shed. Legend has it that Boudicca's bones lie under platform 10 – the area used to be known as Battle Bridge, and was believed to have been the site of the final set-to between the Iceni and the Romans. More famously, the fictional **Harry Potter** and his wizarding chums leave for school on the Hogwarts Express each term from platform 9¾. (The scenes from the films are, in fact, shot between platforms 4 and 5.) The whole area beside and behind King's Cross is undergoing major redevelopment, with new flats, shops and a campus for the University of the Arts.

Camley Street Natural Park

12 Camley St · Daily 10am–5pm · Free · ☎ 020 7833 2311, ⓦ wildlondon.org.uk · ⊖ King's Cross St Pancras

The oasis amongst all the King's Cross redevelopment is **Camley Street Natural Park**, transformed from a rubbish dump into a canalside wildlife haven, and run by the London Wildlife Trust. Pond, meadow and woodland habitats have been re-created and provide a natural environment for birds, butterflies, frogs, newts, toads and even the odd heron, plus a rich variety of plant life.

Kings Place

90 York Way · ☎ 020 7520 1490, ⓦ kingsplace.co.uk · ⊖ King's Cross St Pancras

A definite plus in the King's Cross redevelopment has been the arrival of **Kings Place**, a glassy new arts centre overlooking the Regent's Canal. As well as housing two state-of-the-art concert halls – home to the London Sinfonietta and the Orchestra of the Age of Enlightenment – the venue puts on regular art exhibitions, talks and events and has a swanky canalside café and restaurant to boot. The most famous resident, however, is *The Guardian* newspaper, which occupies the southern portion of the building.

London Canal Museum

12–13 New Wharf Rd · Tues–Sun 10am–4.30pm · £3 · ☎ 020 7713 0836, ⓦ canalmuseum.org.uk · ⊖ King's Cross St Pancras

Packed with traditional narrowboats, Battlebridge Basin, behind Kings Place, is a thoroughly appropriate location for the **London Canal Museum**. The museum testifies to the hard life boat families endured and includes a restored "butty" (an engine-less narrowboat used for storage) and some of the unusual Measham Ware pottery and crockery that was popular with canal-boat families. Other exhibits relate to the building itself, built as an icehouse by Swiss-Italian entrepreneur Carlo Gatti, London's main ice trader in the nineteenth century. Gatti single-handedly popularized ice cream in London, supplying most of the city's vendors, who became known as "Hokey-Pokey Men" – a corruption of the street cry *Ecco un poco*, "Just try a little". Upstairs there's video footage of the canal from the 1920s and the 1990s.

THE GERMAN GYMNASIUM AND THE GASHOLDERS

King's Cross is undergoing its biggest transformation since it was built over 150 years ago, and although a whole host of lovely old buildings have bitten the dust, a number of venerable structures have survived, among them *Die Turnhalle* or the **German Gymnasium** (Tues–Thurs 10am–5.30pm, Fri 10am–4.30pm; free; ⓦ kingscrosscentral.com) on St Pancras Road, built in the 1860s for the German Gymnastics Society and currently housing a model of the new development and an exhibition on the history of King's Cross. Also still standing are the brooding skeletal **King's Cross Gasholders**, Victorian monsters that hark back to an era when nothing was too lowly to be given Neoclassical decoration, hence the wrought-iron Doric pillars and red triglyphs. And without doubt the most beautiful slice of heritage is George Gilbert Scott's ornate **St Pancras Waterpoint**, which is earmarked to become a viewing tower, and has been moved to just beyond Camley Street Natural Park (see above).

Covent Garden and the Strand

Covent Garden's transformation from a workaday fruit and vegetable market into a fashionable *quartier* is one of the most miraculous and successful developments of the 1980s. More mainstream and commercial than neighbouring Soho, it's also a lot more popular thanks to the buskers, street entertainers and human statues that make the traffic-free Covent Garden Piazza an undeniably lively place to be. As its name suggests, the Strand, on the southern border of Covent Garden, once lay along the riverbank until the Victorians created the Embankment to shore up the banks of the Thames. One showpiece river palace, Somerset House, remains, its courtyard graced by a lovely fountain in summer, and its chambers home to the Courtauld Gallery's superb collection of Impressionist and Post-Impressionist paintings.

Covent Garden

Covent Garden has come full circle: what started out in the seventeenth century as London's first luxury neighbourhood is once more an aspirational place to live, work and shop. Boosted by buskers and street entertainers, the piazza is now one of London's major tourist attractions, and the streets to the north – in particular, Long Acre, Neal Street and Floral Street – are home to fashionable clothes and shoe shops.

Most visitors are happy enough simply to wander around watching the street life, having a coffee and doing a bit of shopping, but there are a couple of specific sights worth picking out. One of the old market buildings houses the enjoyable **London Transport Museum**, while another serves as the public foyer for the **Royal Opera House** and boasts a great roof terrace overlooking the piazza.

The piazza

Covent Garden's **piazza** – London's oldest planned square – was laid out in the 1630s, when the Earl of Bedford commissioned Inigo Jones to design a series of graceful Palladian-style arcades based on the main square in Livorno, Tuscany, where Jones had helped build the cathedral. Initially it was a great success, its novelty value alone attracting a plutocratic clientele, but over time the tone of the place fell as the **market** (set up in the earl's back garden) expanded and theatres, coffee houses and brothels began to proliferate.

By the onset of the nineteenth century, the market dominated the area, and so in the 1830s the piazza was cleaned up, slums were torn down and a proper market hall built in the Greek Revival style. A glass roof was added in the late Victorian era, but otherwise the building stayed unaltered until the market's closure in 1974, and only public protests averted yet another office development. Instead, the elegant Victorian market hall and its environs were restored to house shops, restaurants and arts-and-crafts stalls. In its early days, the area had an alternative hippy vibe, a legacy of the area's numerous squats. Nowadays, upmarket chain stores occupy much of the market hall and the arcades, with the arrival of the world's largest Apple Store, on the north side of the piazza, perhaps a sign of the direction in which the area is heading.

8

St Paul's Church

Covent Garden Piazza • Mon–Fri 8.30am–5pm, Sat times vary, Sun 9am–1pm • ☏ 020 7836 5221, Ⓦ actorschurch.org • ⊖ Covent Garden or Leicester Square

The piazza is overlooked from the west by **St Paul's Church**. The Earl of Bedford allegedly told Inigo Jones to make St Paul's no fancier than a barn, to which the

---

COFFEE HOUSES AND BROTHELS

By the eighteenth century the piazza was known as "the great square of Venus", home to dozens of gambling dens, bawdy houses and so-called "bagnios". Some bagnios were plain Turkish baths, but most doubled as **brothels**, where courtesans stood in the window and, according to one contemporary, "in the most impudent manner invited passengers from the theatres into the houses".

London's most famous **coffee houses** were concentrated here, too, attracting writers such as Sheridan, Dryden and Aphra Behn. The rich and famous frequented places like the *Shakespeare's Head*, whose cook made the best turtle soup in town, and whose head waiter, John Harrison, was believed to be the author of the anonymously published "Who's Who of Whores", *Harris's List of Covent Garden Ladies*, which sold over a quarter of a million copies in its day.

The *Rose Tavern*, on Russell Street (immortalized in Hogarth's *Rake's Progress*), was one of the oldest brothels in Covent Garden – Pepys mentions "frigging with Doll Lane" at the *Rose* in his diary of 1667 – and specialized in "Posture Molls", who engaged in flagellation and striptease, and were deemed a cut above the average whore. Food was apparently excellent, too, and despite the frequent brawls, men of all classes, from royalty to ruffians, made their way there.

architect replied, "Sire, you shall have the handsomest barn in England". It's better known nowadays as the **Actors' Church**, and is filled with memorials to thespians from Boris Karloff to Gracie Fields. The cobbles in front of the church's Tuscan portico – where Eliza Doolittle was discovered selling violets by Henry Higgins in George Bernard Shaw's *Pygmalion* – are now a legalized venue for buskers and street performers, who must audition for a slot.

The piazza's history of entertainment goes back to May 1662, when the first recorded performance of Punch and Judy in England was staged by Italian puppeteer Pietro Gimonde, and witnessed by Pepys. To celebrate this a **Punch and Judy Festival** is held on the second Sunday in May, in the gardens behind the church; for the rest of the year the **churchyard** provides a tranquil respite from the activity outside.

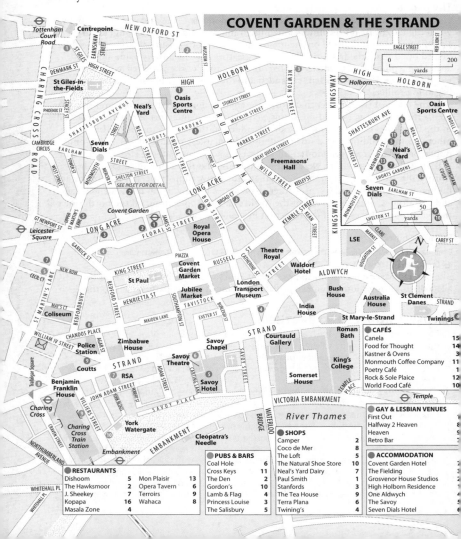

COVENT GARDEN & THE STRAND

CAFÉS
Canela	15
Food for Thought	14
Kastner & Ovens	3
Monmouth Coffee Company	11
Poetry Café	1
Rock & Sole Plaice	12
World Food Café	10

GAY & LESBIAN VENUES
First Out	
Halfway 2 Heaven	8
Heaven	9
Retro Bar	

SHOPS
Camper	2
Coco de Mer	8
The Loft	5
The Natural Shoe Store	10
Neal's Yard Dairy	7
Paul Smith	1
Stanfords	3
Terra Plana	6
Twining's	4

ACCOMMODATION
Covent Garden Hotel	
The Fielding	
Grosvenor House Studios	
High Holborn Residence	
One Aldwych	
The Savoy	
Seven Dials Hotel	

PUBS & BARS
Coal Hole	6
Cross Keys	11
The Den	2
Gordon's	10
Lamb & Flag	4
Princess Louise	3
The Salisbury	5

RESTAURANTS
Dishoom	5	Mon Plaisir	13
The Hawksmoor	2	Opera Tavern	6
J. Sheekey	7	Terroirs	9
Kopapa	16	Wahaca	8
Masala Zone	4		

London Transport Museum

Covent Garden Piazza • Daily 10am–6pm, Fri from 11am • Adults £13.50, under-16s free • ☎ 020 7379 6344, ⓦ ltmuseum.co.uk •
⊖ Covent Garden

A former flower-market shed on the piazza's east side houses the ever-popular **London Transport Museum**. A sure-fire hit for families with kids under 10, it's a must-see for any transport enthusiast, though restrictions of space mean that there are only a handful of large exhibits.

Still, the story of London's transport is a fascinating one – to follow it chronologically, head for Level 2, where you'll find a reconstructed 1829 Shillibeer's Horse Omnibus, which provided the city's first regular **horse-bus** service, and a horse-drawn tram, first introduced in the 1860s. Level 1 tells the story of the world's first underground system and contains a lovely 1920s Metropolitan Line carriage, fitted out in burgundy and green with pretty, drooping lamps. Down on the ground floor, the museum's one double-decker electric **tram** is all that's left to pay tribute to the world's largest tram system, which was dismantled in 1952. Look out, too, for the first **tube** train, from the 1890s, whose lack of windows earned it the nickname "the padded cell". Most of the interactive stuff is aimed at kids, but visitors of all ages should check out the tube driver simulator.

The artistically inclined can buy reproductions of London Transport's stylish **maps and posters**, many commissioned from well-known artists, at the shop on the way out. Real transport enthusiasts should check out the reserve collection at the **Museum Depot** in Acton (details on the website), which is open occasional weekends throughout the year.

Bow Street

8

Covent Garden's dubious reputation was no doubt behind the opening of **Bow Street** magistrates' office in 1748. The first two magistrates were Henry Fielding, author of *Tom Jones*, and his blind half-brother John – nicknamed the "Blind Beak" – who, unusually for the period, refused to accept bribes. Finding "lewd women enough to fill a mighty colony", Fielding set about creating London's first police force, the **Bow Street Runners**. Never numbering more than a dozen, they were employed primarily to combat prostitution, and they continued to exist a good ten years after the establishment of the uniformed Metropolitan Police in 1829. Bow Street police station (which closed in 1989, followed by the magistrates court in 2006) had the honour of incarcerating Oscar Wilde after he was arrested for "committing indecent acts" in 1895 – he was eventually sentenced to two years' hard labour. In 1908 Emmeline Pankhurst appeared here, charged with leafleting supporters to "rush" the House of Commons, and, in 1928, Radclyffe Hall's lesbian novel *The Well of Loneliness* was deemed obscene by Bow Street magistrates and remained banned in this country until 1949.

Royal Opera House

Bow St • Foyer: daily 10am–3.30pm • Backstage tours (1hr 30min) take place regularly and can be booked in advance; Mon–Fri 10.30am,
12.30 & 2.30pm, Sat 10.30am, 11.30am, 12.30 & 1.30pm; £10 • ☎ 020 7212 9389, ⓦ royaloperahouse.org • ⊖ Covent Garden

The main entrance to the **Royal Opera House** – a splendid Corinthian portico – stands opposite the former Bow Street magistrates' court. The original theatre witnessed the premieres of Goldsmith's *She Stoops to Conquer* and Sheridan's *The Rivals* before being destroyed by fire in 1808. To offset the cost of rebuilding, ticket prices were increased; riots ensued for 61 performances until the manager finally backed down. The current building dates from 1858, and is the city's main opera house, home to both the Royal Ballet and Royal Opera. A covered passageway connects the piazza with Bow Street, and allows access to the ROH box office, and upstairs to the beautiful wrought-iron-and-glass **Floral Hall**. Continuing up the escalators, you reach the *Amphitheatre* bar-restaurant, with a glorious terrace overlooking the piazza.

Drury Lane

One block east of Bow Street runs **Drury Lane**, nothing to write home about in its present condition, but in Tudor and Stuart times a very fashionable address. During the Restoration, it became a permanent fixture in London's theatrical and social life, but by the eighteenth century, it had become a notorious slum rife with prostitution. Nevertheless, it was at no. 179 that J Sainsbury opened his first food store in 1869 – "Quality perfect, prices lower" – and it is here, of course, that the Muffin Man lives in the children's nursery rhyme.

Theatre Royal, Drury Lane

Drury lane • Backstage tours of the theatre are great fun and are led by actors: Mon, Tues, Thurs & Fri 2.15 & 4.15pm, Wed & Sat 10.15 & 11.45am; £9 • ☎ 0870 890 1109 • ⊖ Covent Garden

The most famous building in the street is the **Theatre Royal, Drury Lane** first established here in 1663 (the current one dates from 1812 and faces onto Catherine Street). It was at the original theatre that women were first permitted to appear on stage in England (their parts having previously been played by boys), but critics were sceptical about their competence at portraying the fairer sex and thought their profession little better than prostitution – most had to work at both to make ends meet (as the actress said to the bishop). The scantily clad women who sold oranges to the audience were considered even less virtuous, the most famous being **Nell Gwynne** who from the age of fourteen was playing comic roles on stage. At the age of eighteen, she became Charles II's mistress, the first in a long line of Drury Lane actresses who made it into royal beds.

It was also at the Theatre Royal that **David Garrick**, as actor, manager and part-owner from 1747, revolutionized the English theatre, treating the text with more reverence than had been customary, insisting on rehearsals and cutting down on improvisations. The rich, who had previously occupied seats on the stage itself, were confined to the auditorium, and the practice of refunding those who wished to leave at the first interval was stopped. However, an attempt to prevent half-price tickets being sold at the beginning of the third act provoked a riot and had to be abandoned. Despite Garrick's

---

COVENT GARDEN'S SHOPPING STREETS

Apple may have arrived on the piazza, but the shopping streets to the north still hold one or two surprises. **Floral Street**, a quiet cobbled backstreet, running east–west one block north of the Piazza, is a good place to start. At the eastern end is a strange helix-shaped walkway connecting the Royal Ballet School with the Royal Opera House. In the western half you can inspect the tongue-in-cheek window displays of three adjoining shops run by top-selling British designer Paul Smith (nos. 40–44). Another quirky outlet is the shop entirely dedicated to Tintin, the Belgian boy-detective (no. 34). Meanwhile, squeezed beside a very narrow alleyway off Floral Street is the **Lamb and Flag**, the pub where the Poet Laureate, John Dryden, was beaten up in December 1679 by a group of thugs, hired most probably by his rival poet, the Earl of Rochester, who mistakenly thought Dryden was the author of an essay satirizing him.

One block north, **Long Acre** has long been Covent Garden's main shopping street, though it originally specialized in coach manufacture. The most famous shop on the street is **Stanford's**, the world's oldest and largest map shop (see p.430), packed to the rafters with Rough Guides. Look out, too, for **Carriage Hall**, an old stabling yard originally used by coachmakers (now converted into shops), surrounded by cast-iron pillars and situated between Long Acre and Floral Street. Running north from Long Acre, **Neal Street** features some fine Victorian warehouses, complete with stair towers for loading and shifting goods between floors, from the days of the fruit, vegetable and flower market. The street is currently dominated by shoe stores, with only a few alternative shops left: *Food for Thought*, the veggie café founded in 1971, is a rare survivor, as is **Neal's Yard**, a tiny little courtyard off Shorts Gardens, stuffed with cafés and prettily festooned with flower boxes and ivy.

reforms, the Theatre Royal remained a boisterous and often dangerous place of entertainment: George II and George III both narrowly escaped assassination attempts, and the orchestra often had cause to be grateful for the cage under which they were forced to play. The theatre has one other unique feature: two royal boxes, instigated in order to keep George III and his son, the future George IV, apart, after they had a set-to in the foyer.

Freemasons' Hall

60 Great Queen St • Mon–Fri 10am–5pm • Free • Guided tours Mon–Fri usually 11am, noon, 2, 3 & 4pm; free • ☎ 020 7395 9257, Ⓦ ugle.org.uk • ⊖ Covent Garden

Looking east off Drury Lane, down Great Queen Street, it's difficult to miss the austere, Pharaonic mass of the **Freemasons' Hall**, built as a memorial to all the Masons who died in World War I. Whatever you may think of this reactionary, secretive, male-dominated organization, the interior is worth a peek for the **Grand Temple** alone, whose pompous, bombastic decor is laden with heavy symbolism. To see the Grand Temple, sign up for one of the **guided tours** and bring some ID with you. The Masonically curious might also take a look at the shop, which sells Masonic merchandise – aprons, wands, rings and books about alchemy and the cabbala – as do several shops on Great Queen Street.

The Strand

As its name suggests the **Strand** – the main road from Westminster to the City – once ran along the banks of the River Thames. From the twelfth century onwards, it was famed for its riverside residences, owned by bishops, noblemen and courtiers, which lined the south side of the street, each with their own river gates opening onto the Thames. In the late 1860s, the Victorians built the **Embankment**, simultaneously relieving congestion along the Strand, cutting the aristocratic mansions off from the river and providing an extension for the tube and a new sewerage system. By the 1890s, the mansions on the Strand had given way to **theatres**, giving rise to the music-hall song *Let's All Go Down the Strand* (have a banana!), and prompting Disraeli to declare it "perhaps the finest street in Europe". A hundred years later, several theatres survive, from the sleek Adelphi to the Lyceum, but the only surviving Thames palace is **Somerset House**, which houses gallery and exhibition space, and boasts a wonderful fountain-filled courtyard.

Charing Cross Station

The Strand begins at **Charing Cross Station**, fronted by the French Renaissance-style *Charing Cross Hotel*, built in the 1860s. Acting as a mini-roundabout for taxis in the station's cobbled forecourt, is a Victorian replica of the medieval **Charing Cross**, removed from nearby Trafalgar Square by the Puritans. The original thirteenth-century cross was the last of twelve erected by Edward I, to mark the overnight stops on the funeral procession of his wife, Eleanor, from Nottinghamshire to Westminster Abbey in 1290.

Zimbabwe House

Opposite Charing Cross Station, on the corner of Agar Street, is the Edwardian-era former British Medical Association building, now **Zimbabwe House**, housing the Zimbabwean embassy, outside which there are now regular protests against the Mugabe regime. Few passers-by even notice the eighteen naked figures by Jacob Epstein that punctuate the second-floor facade, but at the time of their unveiling in 1908, they caused enormous controversy – "a form of statuary which no careful father would wish his daughter and no discriminating young man his fiancée to see", railed the press. When the Southern Rhodesian government bought the building in 1937 they pronounced the sculptures to be "undesirable" and a potential hazard to passers-by, and proceeded to hack at the genitals, heads and limbs of all eighteen, which remain mutilated to this day.

The Savoy

On the south side of the Strand, the blind side street of Savoy Court – the only street in the country where the traffic drives on the right – leads to **The Savoy**, London's grandest hotel, built in 1889 by Richard D'Oyly Carte. César Ritz was the original manager, Auguste Escoffier the chef, who went on to invent the *pêche Melba* at the hotel. The hotel's *American Bar* introduced cocktails into Europe in the 1930s, Guccio Gucci started out as a dishwasher here and the list of illustrious guests is endless: Monet and Whistler both painted the Thames from one of the south-facing rooms, Sarah Bernhardt nearly died here, and Strauss the Younger arrived with his own orchestra. It's worthwhile strolling up Savoy Court to check out the hotel's Art Deco foyer, the polygonal glass fish fountain and the silver and gold statue of John of Gaunt. The adjacent **Savoy Theatre**, with its outrageous 1930s silver and gold fittings, was originally built in 1881 to showcase Gilbert and Sullivan's comic operas, witnessing eight premieres, including *The Mikado* – the theatre's profits helped fund the building of the hotel.

Savoy Chapel

Savoy Hill • Tues–Thurs 11.30am–3.30pm, Fri 11.30am–1pm • Free • ☎ 020 7379 8088, ⓦ duchyoflancaster.org.uk • ⊖ Charing Cross or Embankment

Nothing remains of John of Gaunt's medieval Savoy Palace, which stood here until it was burnt down in the 1381 Peasants' Revolt, though the **Savoy Chapel** (or The Queen's Chapel of the Savoy to give its full title), hidden round the back of the hotel down Savoy Street, dates from the time when the complex was rebuilt as a hospital for the poor in 1505. The chapel is much altered, but it became a fashionable venue for weddings when the hotel and theatre were built next door – all three were the first public buildings in the world to be lit by electricity. And talking of lighting, don't miss the **Patent Sewer Ventilating Lamp**, erected in the 1880s halfway down Carting Lane, and still powered by methane collected in a U-bend in the sewers below.

Victoria Embankment

To get to the **Victoria Embankment**, from the Strand, head down Villiers Street, beside Charing Cross Station. Completed in 1870, the embankment was the inspiration of French engineer **Joseph Bazalgette**, who used the reclaimed land for a new tube line, new sewers, and a new stretch of riverside parkland – now filled with an eclectic mixture of statues and memorials from Robbie Burns to the Imperial Camel Corps. The 1626 **York Watergate**, in the Victoria Embankment Gardens to the east of Villiers Street, gives you an idea of where the banks of the Thames used to be: the steps through the gateway once led down to the river.

Cleopatra's Needle

London's oldest monument, **Cleopatra's Needle**, languishes little noticed on the Thames side of the busy Victoria Embankment, guarded by two Victorian sphinxes (facing the wrong way). In fact, the sixty-foot-high, 180-ton stick of granite has nothing to do with Cleopatra – it's one of a pair erected in Heliopolis (near Cairo) in 1475 BC (the other one is in New York's Central Park) and taken to Alexandria by Emperor Augustus fifteen years after Cleopatra's suicide. This obelisk was presented to Britain in 1819 by the Turkish viceroy of Egypt, but nearly sixty years passed before it finally made its way to London. It was erected in 1878 above a time capsule containing, among other things, the day's newspapers, a box of hairpins, a railway timetable and pictures of the country's twelve prettiest women.

8

Royal Society of Arts (RSA)

6–8 John Adam St • Tours by appointment only • ☎ 020 7930 5115 • ⓦ thersa.org • ⊖ Charing Cross or Embankment

Founded in 1754, the "Society for the encouragement of Arts, Manufactures and Commerce", better known now as the Royal Society of Arts or **RSA**, moved into a purpose-built, elaborately decorated house designed by the Adam brothers in 1774. The building contains a small display on the Adelphi (see below) and retains several original Adam ceilings and chimneypieces. The highlight, however, is The Great Room, with six paintings on *The Progress of Human Knowledge and Culture* by James Barry, forming a busy, continuous pictorial frieze around the room, punctuated by portraits of two early presidents by Reynolds and Gainsborough. The RSA is one of a number of Adam houses that survive from the magnificent riverside development built between 1768 and 1772 by the Adam brothers and known as the **Adelphi**, which was, for the most part, demolished in 1936.

Benjamin Franklin House

36 Craven St • Tours (45 min) must be booked in advance; Wed–Sun noon–5pm; £7 • ☎ 020 7925 1405, ⓦ benjaminfranklinhouse.org •
⊖ Charing Cross or Embankment

From 1757 to 1775, **Benjamin Franklin** (1706–90) had "genteel lodgings" here. While Franklin was espousing the cause of the British colonies (as the US then was), the house served as the first de facto American embassy; eventually, he returned to America to help draft the Declaration of Independence and frame the US Constitution. Wisely, the curators have left the **Benjamin Franklin House** pretty much empty, eschewing any attempt to install period furniture. Instead, aided by a costumed guide and a series of impressionistic audiovisuals, visitors are transported back to the time of Franklin, who lived here with his "housekeeper" in cosy domesticity, while his wife and daughter languished in Philadelphia.

Aldwych

The wide crescent of **Aldwych**, forming a neat "D" on its side with the eastern part of the Strand, was driven through the slums of this zone in the early twentieth century. A confident ensemble occupies the centre, with the enormous Australia House and India House sandwiching **Bush House**, home of the BBC's World Service from 1940 to 2012. Despite its thoroughly British associations, Bush House was actually built by the American speculator Irving T. Bush, whose planned trade centre flopped in the 1930s. The giant figures on the north facade and the inscription, "To the Eternal Friendship of English-Speaking Nations", thus refer to the friendship between the US and Britain, and are not, as many people assume, the World Service's declaratory manifesto.

Not far from these former bastions of Empire, up Houghton Street, lurks that erstwhile hotbed of left-wing agitation, the **London School of Economics**. Founded in 1895, the LSE gained a radical reputation in 1968, when a student sit-in protesting against the Vietnam War ended in violent confrontations that were the closest London came to the heady events in Paris that year. Famous alumni include Carlos the Jackal, Cherie Booth (wife of ex-Prime Minister Tony Blair) and Mick Jagger.

Somerset House

Strand • **Fountain Court** Daily 7.30am–11pm • Free **Riverside terrace** Daily 8am–6pm • Free **Embankment galleries** Daily
10am–6pm • £6 • ☎ 020 7845 4600, ⓦ somersethouse.org.uk • ⊖ Temple or Covent Garden

Somerset House is the sole survivor of the grandiose river palaces that once lined the Strand, its four wings enclosing a large courtyard rather like a Parisian *hôtel*. Although it looks like an old aristocratic mansion, the present building was, in fact, purpose-built in 1776 by William Chambers, to house numerous learned societies and governmental offices (including the Navy Office). Nowadays, Somerset House's granite-paved courtyard is a great place to relax thanks to its fab 55-jet **fountain** that spouts straight from the cobbles, and does a little syncopated dance every half-hour. The courtyard is also used for open-air performances, concerts, installations and, in winter, an ice rink.

The north wing houses the permanent collection of the **Courtauld Institute**, best known for its outstanding Impressionist and Post-Impressionist paintings. The south wing has a lovely riverside terrace with a café-restaurant and the **Embankment Galleries**, which host innovative special exhibitions on contemporary art and design. Before you head off to one of the collections, however, make sure you go and admire the Royal Naval Commissioners' superb gilded eighteenth-century barge in the **King's Barge House**, below ground level in the south wing.

Courtauld Gallery

Somerset House, Strand • Daily 10am–6pm, occasional Thurs until 9pm • £6 (free Mon 10am–2pm) • ☎ 020 7848 2526,
Ⓦ courtauld.ac.uk • ⊖ Temple or Covent Garden

Founded in 1931 as part of the University of London, the Courtauld Institute was the first body in Britain to award degrees in art history as an academic subject. It's most famous, however, for the **Courtauld Gallery**, which displays its priceless art collection, whose virtue is quality rather than quantity. Best known for its superlative Impressionist and Post-Impressionist works, the Courtauld also owns a fine array of earlier works by the likes of Rubens, Botticelli, Bellini and Cranach the Elder and gives regular talks throughout the year.

The displays currently start on the **ground floor** with a small room devoted to medieval religious paintings. Next, you ascend the beautiful, semicircular **staircase** to the first-floor galleries, whose exceptional plasterwork ceilings recall their original use as the learned societies' meeting rooms. This is where the cream of the Courtauld's collection is currently displayed: rehangings have become more frequent, however, so ask if you can't find a particular painting.

The first floor galleries

To follow the collection chronologically, start in room 2, where you'll find two splendid fifteenth-century Florentine *cassoni* (chests), with their original backrests, and a large **Botticelli** altarpiece commissioned by a convent and refuge for repentant prostitutes; hence Mary Magdalene's pole position below the Cross. You can also admire **Lucas Cranach the Elder**'s *Adam and Eve*, one of the highlights of the collection, with the Saxon painter revelling in the visual delights of Eden. Works by **Rubens** dominate room 3, ranging from oil sketches for church frescoes to large-scale late works, plus a winningly informal portrait of his close friend Jan Brueghel the Elder and family. Also in this room hangs **Pieter Bruegel the Elder**'s *Landscape with Flight into Egypt*, a small canvas once owned by Rubens. Further on, there are works by Goya, Reynolds, Romney, Tiepolo and an affectionate portrait by **Gainsborough** of his wife, painted in his old age.

The cream of the gallery's **Impressionist** works occupy the next few rooms, and include **Renoir**'s *La Loge*, **Degas**' *Two Dancers*, pointillist works by **Seurat**, several **Monet** landscapes and a view of Lordship Lane by **Pissarro** from his days in exile in London. There's also a small-scale version of **Manet**'s bold *Déjeuner sur l'herbe*, and his atmospheric *A Bar at the Folies-Bergère*, a nostalgic celebration of the artist's love affair with Montmartre, painted two years before his death. **Cézanne**'s works include one of his series of *Card Players*, while **Gauguin**'s Breton peasants *Haymaking* contrasts with his later Tahitian works, including the sinister *Nevermore*. Look out, too, for *Child with a Dove*, from 1901, which heralded Picasso's "Blue Period", and **Van Gogh**'s *Self-Portrait with Bandaged Ear*, painted shortly after his remorseful self-mutilation, following an attack on his housemate Gauguin.

Second floor: twentieth-century works

The **second floor** is used primarily to display the Courtauld's twentieth-century works, which bring a wonderful splash of colour and a hint of modernism to the galleries.

There isn't the space to exhibit the entire collection, so it's impossible to say for definite what paintings will be on show at any one time. Room 8 is home to several magnificent, late, geometrical but lush Provençal landscapes by **Cézanne**. In room 9, you hit the bright primary colours of the Courtauld's superb collection of **Fauvist** paintings, by the likes of Derain, Vlaminck, Braque, Dufy and Matisse, which spill over into room 10. You'll also find *Yellow Irises*, a rare early Picasso from 1901, and one of **Modigliani**'s celebrated nudes.

Elsewhere on this floor, there's usually a selection of works by **Roger Fry**, who helped organize the first Impressionist exhibitions in Britain, and went on to found the Omega Workshops in 1913 with Duncan Grant. Fry bequeathed his private collection to the Courtauld, including several paintings by Grant, his wife Vanessa Bell, and Fry himself. The last few rooms contain works by the likes of Kokoschka, Jawlensky, Kirchner, Delaunay and Léger, and an outstanding array of works by **Kandinsky**, the Russian-born artist who was thirty when he finally decided to become a painter and moved to Munich. He's best known for his pioneering abstract paintings, such as *Improvisation on Mahogany* from 1910, where the subject matter begins to disintegrate in the blocks of colour.

King's College

Strand • Roman Bath visits by appointment only: April to mid-Oct Wed 1–4pm; free • ☎ 020 7641 5264 • ⊖ Temple or Covent Garden

Adjacent to Somerset House, the ugly concrete facade of **King's College** (part of the University of London) conceals Robert Smirke's much older buildings, which date from its foundation in 1829. Rather than entering the college itself, stroll down Surrey Street and turn right down Surrey Steps, which are in the middle of the old *Norfolk Hotel*, whose terracotta facade is worth admiring. This should bring you out at one of the most unusual sights in King's College: the **"Roman" Bath**, a 15ft-long tub (actually dating from Tudor times at the earliest) with a natural spring that produces 2000 gallons a day. It was used in Victorian times as a cold bath (Dickens' David Copperfield "had many a cold plunge" here). The bath is visible through a window (daily 9am to dusk), but you can only get a closer look by appointment.

St Mary-le-Strand

Strand • Mon–Sat 11am–4pm, Sun 10am–1pm; recitals Wed 1pm • Free • ☎ 020 7836 3126 • ⓦ stmarylestrand.org, • ⊖ Temple or Covent Garden

St Mary-le-Strand, completed in 1724 in Baroque style and topped by a delicately tiered tower, was the first public building of James Gibbs, who went on to design St Martin-in-the-Fields. Nowadays, the church sits ignominiously amid the traffic hurtling westwards down the Strand, though even in the eighteenth century, parishioners complained of the noise from the roads, and it's incredible that recitals are still given here. The entrance is flanked by two lovely magnolia trees, and the interior has a particularly rich plastered ceiling in white and gold. It was in this church that Bonnie Prince Charlie allegedly renounced his Roman Catholic faith and became an Anglican, during a secret visit to London in 1750.

St Clement Danes

Strand • Daily 9am–4pm • Free • ☎ 020 7242 8282 • ⓦ raf.mod.uk/stclementdane • ⊖ Temple or Covent Garden

St Clement Danes, designed by Wren, occupies a traffic island in the Strand. Badly burnt out in the Blitz (the pock marks are still visible in the exterior north wall), the church was handed over to the RAF, who turned it into a memorial to those killed in World War II. Glass cabinets in the west end of the church contain some poignant mementoes, such as a wooden cross carved from a door hinge in a Japanese POW camp. The nave and aisles are studded with over eight hundred squadron and unit badges, while heavy tomes set in glass cabinets record the 120,000 RAF service personnel who died. The church's carillon plays out various tunes, including the nursery rhyme *Oranges and*

Lemons (daily 9am, noon, 3, 6 & 9pm), though St Clement's Eastcheap in the City is more likely to be the church referred to in the rhyme.

In front of the church, the statue of **Gladstone**, with his four female allegorical companions, is flanked by two air chiefs: **Lord Dowding**, the man who oversaw the Battle of Britain, and "**Bomber**" **Harris**, architect of the saturation bombing of Germany which killed 500,000 civilians (and over 55,000 Allied airmen commemorated on the plinth). Although Churchill was ultimately responsible, the opprobrium was left to fall on Harris, who was denied the peerage all the other service chiefs received, while his forces were refused a campaign medal. The unveiling of this privately funded statue to honour Harris, in 1992, on the anniversary of the bombing of Cologne, drew widespread protests in Britain and Germany.

Twinings

216 Strand • Mon–Fri 9am–5pm, Sat 10am–4pm • ☎ 020 7383 1359, ⓦ twinings.com • ⊖ Temple, Chancery Lane or Covent Garden

In 1706, Thomas Twining, tea supplier to Queen Anne, bought Tom's Coffee House and began serving tea as well as coffee, thereby effectively opening the world's first tea room. A branch of **Twinings**, which sells limited edition long leaf tea, still occupies the site and its slender Neoclassical portico features two reclining Chinamen, dating from the time when all tea came from China. At the back of the shop is a small **museum** with a fine display of ornate caddies, photos of the Twining family and some historic packaging and advertising.

Lloyd's Bank's Law Courts

222 Strand • Mon, Tues, Thurs & Fri 9am–5pm, Wed 10am–5pm • ⊖ Temple, Chancery Lane or Covent Garden

Much of the extravagant decor of the short-lived *Palsgrave Restaurant*, which was built at 222 Strand in 1883, is preserved in **Lloyds TSB**'s Law Courts branch. The foyer features acres of Doulton tiles, hand-painted in blues and greens, and a flying-fish fountain that was originally supplied with fresh water from an artesian well sunk 238ft below the Strand. The interior of walnut and sequoia wood panelling is worth a look, too, and features ceramic portrait panels. The Law Courts themselves stand opposite (see pp.142–147).

8

ROYAL COURTS OF JUSTICE

Holborn and the Inns of Court

Strategically placed between the royal and political centre of Westminster and the mercantile and financial might of the City, Holborn (pronounced "Ho-bun") became the hub of the English legal system in the thirteenth century. Hostels, known as Inns of Court, were established where lawyers could eat, sleep and study law. Hidden away from the general hubbub of London, the Inns make for an interesting stroll, their archaic, cobbled precincts exuding the rarefied atmosphere of an Oxbridge college, and sheltering one of the city's oldest churches, the twelfth-century Temple Church. Elsewhere, Holborn boasts two of London's most enjoyable small museums: the Sir John Soane's Museum, with its architectural illusions and eclectic array of curios, and the Hunterian Museum, home of freakish medical curiosities.

Temple

Temple, the largest of the Inns of Court, was once the headquarters of the Knights Templar, a military order of monks whose job was to protect pilgrims en route to Jerusalem. The Templars became very powerful, the Crown took fright and the order was suppressed in 1307, with the land passing to another order, the Knights Hospitaller. Legal London already had a foothold here by this point, so when the monks left during the Reformation, the lawyers simply took over the whole precinct. Temple actually consists of two Inns – **Middle Temple** and **Inner Temple** – both of which lie south of the Strand and Fleet Street. It's difficult to tell which Inn you're in, unless you check the coat of arms on each building: the Lamb of God (for Middle Temple) and the Pegasus (for Inner Temple). Nevertheless, the maze of courtyards and passageways is fun to explore – especially after dark, when the Temple is gas-lit – and a welcome haven from London's traffic. There are several points of access, simplest of which is Devereux Court, which leads south off the Strand, but at the weekend, you can only enter from Tudor Street to the east.

Middle Temple Hall

Mon–Fri 10–11.30am & 3–4pm, though sometimes closed for events • Free • ☎ 020 7427 4800 • ⊖ Temple or Blackfriars

Medieval students ate, attended lectures and slept in the **Middle Temple Hall**, on Fountain Court, and it remains the Inn's main dining room. The present building was constructed in the 1560s and provided the setting for many Elizabethan masques and plays – including Shakespeare's *Twelfth Night*, which was premiered here in 1602. The hall is worth a visit for its fine hammerbeam roof, wood panelling and decorative Elizabethan screen, and the small wooden table said to have been carved from the hatch from Francis Drake's ship, the *Golden Hind*.

Temple Church

Mon–Fri 2–4pm, but times vary • £3 • ☎ 020 7353 3470, ⓦ templechurch.com • ⊖ Temple or Blackfriars

Despite wartime damage, the original round **Temple Church** – built by the Templars in 1185 and modelled on the Church of the Holy Sepulchre in Jerusalem – still stands. The interior features striking Purbeck marble piers, recumbent marble effigies of medieval knights and tortured grotesques grimacing in the spandrels of the blind arcading. At the northwestern corner of the choir, behind the decorative altar tomb of Edmund Plowden, builder of Middle Temple Hall, stairs lead up to a cell, less than 5ft long, in which disobedient knights were confined. The church makes an appearance in both the book and the film of *The Da Vinci Code* by Dan Brown.

Inner Temple

Garden May–Sept: Mon–Fri noon–3pm

The millennium column, to the south of Temple Church, marks the point where the Great Fire of 1666 was extinguished; it's topped by a diminutive statue of two

---

THE INNS

Even today, every aspiring barrister in England and Wales must study at one of the four Inns – **Inner Temple**, **Middle Temple**, **Lincoln's Inn** and **Gray's Inn** – in order to qualify and be "called to the Bar". It's an old-fashioned system of patronage (you need contacts to get accepted at one of the Inns) and one that has done much to keep the judiciary overwhelmingly white, male, public school- and Oxbridge-educated. The most bizarre stipulation is that to qualify as a barrister, you must attend a dozen formal dinners. Dress code is strict – "dark lounge suit, plain collar and sober tie/white blouse" or "genuine ethnic dress" – although the meals are heavily subsidized: under £20 for a four-course meal with wine and port. Back in medieval times, aspiring lawyers would take part in mock courts and dine together in the main halls. Today barristers' professional training is conducted by private law schools, but the dinners live on.

9

knights sharing a horse, a reference to the fact that Knights Templar were often too poor to have a horse each. **Inner Temple Hall**, to the south of the column, is a postwar reconstruction, as is clear from the brickwork. This was the Inn where Mahatma Gandhi studied law in 1888, living as a true Englishman, dressing as a dandy, dancing, taking elocution lessons and playing the violin, while his close associate Jawaharlal Nehru spent two even wilder years here a decade or so later, gambling, drinking and running up considerable debts. The public are also permitted to explore the **Inner Temple Garden**, which slopes down to the

HOLBORN & THE INNS OF COURT

0 — 100
yards

THEOBALD'S ROAD

JOCKEY'S FIELD

BEDFORD ROW

PORTPOOL LANE

Gray's Inn Gardens

GRAY'S INN ROAD

Gray's Inn

CLERKENWELL

LEATHER LANE

HATTON GARDEN

THEOBALD'S ROAD

RED LION SQUARE

GRAY'S INN SQUARE

FIELD CT

SOUTH SQUARE

Chancery Lane ❶

Prudential Assurance

St Etheldreda

Holborn ⊖ HIGH HOLBORN

HOLBORN

❷

ELY PLACE

CHARTERHOUSE STREET

❸

Sir John Soane's Museum

STONE BUILDINGS

London Silver Vaults

Staple Inn

HOLBORN CIRCUS

St Andrew

Lincoln's Inn

REMNANT ST

LINCOLN'S INN FIELDS

Lincoln's Inn Fields

OLD SQUARE

ST ANDREW ST

NEW FETTER LANE

SHOE LANE

KINGSWAY

Old Hall

Hunterian Museum

PORTUGAL ST

SERLE STREET

NEW SQUARE

CHANCERY LANE

Former Public Records Office

FETTER LANE

CITY

LINCOLN'S INN FIELDS

Old Curiosity Shop

PORTUGAL STREET

CAREY STREET ❹

LSE

Royal Courts of Justice

St Dunstan-in-the-West

Temple Bar ❺

FLEET STREET

ALDWYCH

Bush House

STRAND

Prince Henry's Room

Temple Church

DEVEREUX COURT

Twinings

BRICK COURT

MIDDLE TEMPLE LANE

St Clement Danes

FOUNTAIN COURT

Temple

N

St Mary-le-Strand

ARUNDEL STREET

SURREY ST

KING'S BENCH WALK

TUDOR STREET

Somerset House

TEMPLE PLACE

Temple ⊖

Inner Temple Gardens

VICTORIA EMBANKMENT

Middle Temple

VICTORIA EMBANKMENT

River Thames

● PUBS & BARS	
Bar Polski	3
Cittie of Yorke	1
Old Bank of England	5
Seven Stars	4
Ye Olde Mitre	2

Embankment and is where Shakespeare set the fictional scene of the plucking of red and white roses in *Henry VI Part One*.

9

Royal Courts of Justice

Strand · Mon–Fri 9am–4.30pm; no cameras allowed · Free · ☎ 020 7947 6000 · ⊖ Temple

On the north side of the Strand, the **Royal Courts of Justice** are home to the Court of Appeal and the High Court, where the most important civil cases are tried (criminal cases are heard at the Old Bailey). It was through the main portal and steps of this daunting Gothic Revival complex, designed in the 1870s, that the Guildford Four and Birmingham Six walked to freedom, and it's where countless public figures have battled it out with the tabloids. In the intimidating Main Hall, where bewigged barristers are busy on their mobiles, you can pick up a plan and a short guide to the complex, while the glass cabinets in the centre of the hall list which cases are being heard and where. In the minstrels' gallery, there's a small exhibition on the history of legal dress codes.

Lincoln's Inn Fields

To the north of the Law Courts lies **Lincoln's Inn Fields**, London's largest square. Originally simply pasture land and a playground for Lincoln's Inn students, it was used as a place of execution in Tudor times, would-be assassin Anthony Babington and his Catholic accomplices being hanged, drawn and quartered here for high treason in 1586. Laid out in the early 1640s, the square's most arresting statue is that of Margaret MacDonald (wife of the first Labour prime minister Ramsay MacDonald, who died at no. 3), amid a brood of nine children (she herself had six), commemorating her social work among the young. In the southwest corner of the square is one of London's few surviving timber-framed buildings, the sixteenth-century **Old Curiosity Shop** in Portsmouth Street (currently a shoe shop), which claims to be the inspiration for Dickens' sentimental tale of the same name.

Hunterian Museum

Lincoln's Inn Fields · Tues–Sat 10am–5pm · Free · ☎ 020 7869 6560, ⊕ rcseng.ac.uk · ⊖ Holborn

The **Hunterian Museum** is on the first floor of the imposing Royal College of Surgeons building on the south side of Lincoln's Inn Fields. First opened in 1813, the museum contains the unique specimen collection of the surgeon-scientist John Hunter (1728–93). The centrepiece of the museum is the Crystal Gallery, a wall of jars of pickled skeletons and body pieces – from the gall bladder of a puffer fish to the thyroid of a dromedary – prepared by Hunter himself. Among the most prized exhibits are the skeleton of the "Irish giant", Charles Byrne (1761–83), who was seven feet ten inches tall, and the Sicilian dwarf Caroline Crachami (1815–24), who stood at only one foot ten and a half inches when she died at the age of nine. You'll find Crachami in the McCrae Gallery, where a series of gruesome dental instruments herald the odontological collection. Upstairs, you can have a go at simulated minimal-access surgery, and examine Joseph Lister's cumbersome carbolic-acid spray machine, known as the "donkey engine", with which he pioneered antiseptic surgery, performing operations obscured in a cloud of phenol (he even conducted a foggy operation on Queen Victoria – who had an abscess in the royal armpit – accidentally spraying her in the face in the process).

Sir John Soane's Museum

13 Lincoln's Inn Fields · Tues–Sat 10am–5pm, candle-lit eve on first Tues of month 6–9pm (note that the museum is very popular and you may have to queue to get in) · Free · Guided tours Sat 11am; £5 · ☎ 020 7405 2107, ⊕ soane.org · ⊖ Holborn

A group of buildings on the north side of the square houses the fascinating **Sir John Soane's Museum**. Soane (1753–1837), a bricklayer's son who rose to be architect of the Bank of England, gradually bought up three adjoining Georgian properties here between 1792 and 1824, altering them to serve not only as a home but also as a place

9

to stash his large collection of art and antiquities. No. 13, the central house with the stone loggia, is arranged much as it was in his lifetime, with an ingenious ground plan and an informal, treasure-hunt atmosphere. Few of Soane's projects were actually built, and his home remains the best example of what he dubbed his "poetry of architecture", using mirrors, domes and skylights to create wonderful spatial ambiguities.

The most unusual part of the house is the colonnaded **monument court**, built over the former stables at the back of the house. All around are antique busts and masonry; above is the wooden chamber on stilts from which Soane supervised his students. To your right is the **picture room**, whose false walls swing back to reveal another wall of pictures, which itself opens to reveal a window and a balcony looking down onto the crypt. The star paintings are **Hogarth**'s satirical *Election* series and his merciless morality tale *The Rake's Progress*.

The flagstoned **crypt** features a "monk's parlour", a Gothic folly dedicated to a make-believe padre, Giovanni, complete with tomb (containing Soane's wife's dog, Fanny), cloister and eerie medieval casts and gargoyles. The hushed sepulchral chamber continues the morbid theme with its wooden mummy case, a model of an Etruscan tomb (complete with skeleton), and the tombstones of Soane's wife and son. You then emerge into the colonnaded atrium, home to an Egyptian **sarcophagus**, rejected by the British Museum and bought by Soane.

Back on the ground floor, make your way to the **breakfast parlour**, which features all Soane's favourite architectural features: coloured skylights, a canopied dome and ranks of tiny convex mirrors. A short stroll up the beautiful cantilevered staircase brings you to the first-floor **drawing rooms**, whose airiness and bright colour scheme come as a relief after the ancient clutter of the downstairs rooms.

Lincoln's Inn

Lincoln's Inn Fields • **Inn** Mon–Fri 9am–6pm; **Chapel** Mon–Fri noon–2pm; **Gardens** Mon–Fri noon–2.30pm • Free • First Fri of month guided tour 2pm; £5 • ☎ 020 7405 1393, ⓦ lincolnsinn.org.uk • ⊖ Holborn

Lincoln's Inn, on the east side of Lincoln's Inn Fields, is in many ways the prettiest of the Inns of Court – famous alumni include Thomas More, Oliver Cromwell and Margaret Thatcher. The oldest building is the fifteenth-century Old Hall (by appointment only), where the lawyers used to live and where Dickens set the case Jarndyce versus Jarndyce, the opening scene in *Bleak House*.

Beyond the Old Hall is the sixteenth-century **gatehouse** – best viewed from Chancery Lane – impressive for its age and bulk, not to mention its characteristic diamond-patterned brickwork. Adjacent is the **chapel**, built in 1620, with its unusual fan-vaulted open undercroft; on the first floor, the nave, rebuilt in 1880, hit by a Zeppelin in World War I and much restored since, still boasts its original ornate pews. North of the chapel lie the Palladian **Stone Buildings**, best appreciated from the manicured lawns of the Inn's gardens; the strange miniature castle near the garden entrance is the gardeners' tool shed, a creation of George Gilbert Scott, designer of London's old red telephone boxes.

Chancery Lane

Running along the eastern edge of Lincoln's Inn is legal London's main thoroughfare, **Chancery Lane**, home of the Law Society (the solicitors' regulatory body for England and Wales) and lined with shops where barristers, solicitors and clerks can buy their wigs, gowns, legal tomes, stationery and champagne.

London Silver Vaults

Chancery Lane • Mon–Fri 9am–5.30pm, Sat 9am–1pm • Free • ☎ 020 7242 3844, ⓦ thesilvervaults.com • ⊖ Chancery Lane

On the east side of Chancery Lane are the **London Silver Vaults**, which began life in 1876 as the Chancery Lane Safe Deposit for London's wealthy elite, but now house a strange, claustrophobic lair of subterranean shops selling every kind of silverware – mostly antique, mostly English and often quite tasteless.

Gray's Inn

South Square • Mon–Fri 10am–4pm; gardens open to the public weekday lunchtimes • Free • ☎ 020 7458 7800, Ⓦ graysinn.info • ⊖ Chancery Lane

The last of the four Inns of Court, **Gray's Inn** lies hidden away off High Holborn, at the top of Chancery Lane; access is next to the venerable *Cittie of Yorke* pub. Established in the fourteenth century, the Inn took its name from the de Grey family, who owned the original mansion used as student lodgings; most of what you see today, however, was rebuilt after the Blitz. The **Hall** (by appointment only), with its fabulous Tudor screen and stained glass, witnessed the premiere of Shakespeare's *Comedy of Errors* in 1594. The north side of the Inn, taken up by the wide green expanse of **Gray's Inn Gardens**, is entirely and impressively visible through its wrought-iron railings from Theobald's Road.

Holborn

Confusingly, **Holborn** is also the name of a street – an eastern continuation of High Holborn – with two remarkable buildings, one on either side of the road. The first, on the south side, is **Staple Inn**, a former Inn of Chancery (a less prestigious version of the Inns of Court). Its overhanging half-timbered facade and gables date from the sixteenth century and are the most extensive in the whole of London; they survived the Fire, but had to be extensively rebuilt after the Blitz. More or less opposite stands the palatial, terracotta-red **Prudential Assurance Building**, begun in 1879 by Alfred Waterhouse. This fortress of Victorian capitalism has its very own Bridge of Sighs, harbours a dramatic memorial to the Prudential men who fell in World War I (plus a more sober one for World War II) and retains much of its original Doulton-tiled interior. At the eastern end of Holborn lies **Holborn Circus**, a vast traffic intersection centred on London's politest statue, in which a cheerful Prince Albert doffs his hat to passers-by.

Ely Place

Just off Charterhouse Street, which runs northeast from Holborn Circus, is the cul-de-sac of **Ely Place**, named after the Bishop of Ely, whose London residence used to stand here from 1290 to 1772. John of Gaunt lived in the bishop's palace for a while after his own house on the Strand was burnt down in the 1381 Peasants' Revolt. It's from the palace that Shakespeare has John of Gaunt say his "this sceptre'd isle" speech in *Richard II*, and the strawberries produced by the palace gardens get a positive recommendation in *Richard III* – a strawberry fair is held each June in honour of this. The street remained technically part of Cambridgeshire until the 1930s, and even today it is gated and guarded by a beadle, lodge and wrought-iron gates.

St Etheldreda's Church

14 Ely Place • Daily 8am–5pm, Sun till 12.30pm • Free • ☎ 020 7405 1061, Ⓦ stethelreda.com • ⊖ Chancery Lane

All that remains of the bishop's palace now is **St Etheldreda's Church**, the bishop's former private chapel, halfway down the street on the left. First built in the thirteenth century, the chapel was bought in 1874 by the Roman Catholic Rosminian Order in 1874. The Upper Church, though much restored, retains much of its medieval masonry, and features two spectacularly huge postwar stained-glass windows; the west window depicts several English Catholic martyrs, including the Carthusian Prior John Haughton, whose statue also occupies the first niche on the south wall. The atmospherically gloomy medieval crypt contains a model of the pre-Reformation church complex.

CLERKENWELL GREEN

Clerkenwell

Situated slightly uphill from the City and, more importantly, outside its jurisdiction, Clerkenwell (pronounced "Clark-unwell") began life as a village serving the various local monastic foundations. In the nineteenth century, the district's population trebled, mostly through Irish and Italian immigration, and the area acquired a reputation for radicalism exemplified by the Marx Memorial Library, where the exiled Lenin plotted revolution. Nowadays, Clerkenwell is a typical London mix of Georgian and Victorian townhouses, housing estates, old warehouses, loft conversions and art studios. It lies very much off the conventional tourist trail, but over the last two decades, it has emerged as one of the city's most vibrant and fashionable areas, with a host of shops, cafés, restaurants and pubs.

Following the Great Fire, Clerkenwell was settled by craftsmen, including newly arrived French Huguenots, excluded from the City guilds. At the same time, the springs that give the place its name were rediscovered (and are still visible through the window of 14–16 Farringdon Lane), and Clerkenwell became a popular **spa resort** for a century or so. During the nineteenth century, the district's springs and streams became cholera-infested sewers, and the area became an overpopulated **slum area**, home to three prisons and the setting for Fagin's Den in Dickens' *Oliver Twist*. Victorian slum clearances and wartime bombing took their toll, the population declined and by the 1980s, the area's traditional trades – locksmithing, clockmaking, printing and jewellery – all but disappeared. Nowadays, the area is characterized by media and design companies (particularly architects), with trendy bars and restaurants catering for the area's loft-dwelling residents.

10

Hatton Garden

Ⓦ hatton-garden.net

Hatton Garden, connecting Holborn Circus (see p.147) with Little Italy (see p.151), is no beauty spot, but, as the centre of the city's **diamond and jewellery trade** since medieval times, it's an intriguing place to visit during the week. There are over fifty shops and, as in Antwerp and New York, ultra-orthodox Hasidic Jews dominate the business here as middlemen. Near the top of Hatton Garden, there's a plaque commemorating **Hiram Maxim** (1840–1916), the American inventor who perfected the automatic gun named after him in the workshops at no. 57.

East of Hatton Garden, off Greville Street, lies **Bleeding Heart Yard**, a key location in Dickens' *Little Dorrit*. The name refers to the gruesome 1626 murder of Lady Hatton, who sold her soul to the devil, so the story goes. One night, during a ball at nearby Hatton House, the devil came to collect, and all trace of her vanished except her heart, which was found bleeding and throbbing on the pavement.

Parallel to Hatton Garden, take a wander through **Leather Lane Market**, a weekday lunchtime market selling everything from fruit and veg to clothes and electrical gear.

Mount Pleasant and the British Postal Museum

Rosebery Avenue • Postal Museum Mon–Fri 10am–5pm, Thurs until 7pm, plus second Sat of month 10am–5pm (closed the following Mon) • Free • ☎ 020 7239 2570, Ⓦ postalheritage.org.uk • ⊖ Farringdon

Halfway up Rosebery Avenue – built in the 1890s to link Clerkenwell Road with Islington to the north – stands **Mount Pleasant**, opened in 1889 and at one time the largest sorting office in the world. A third of all inland mail passes through here, and originally much of it was brought by the post office's own underground railway network, **Mail Rail** (Ⓦ mailrail.co.uk). Opened in 1927 and similar in design to the tube, the railway was fully automatic, sending driverless trucks between London's sorting offices and train stations at speeds of up to 35mph. Unfortunately, all 23 miles of this two-foot-gauge railway was mothballed in 2003, with no immediate plans to reactivate it. Philatelists, meanwhile, should head to the **British Postal Museum**, by the sorting office on Phoenix Place, which puts on small exhibitions drawn from its vast archive.

Exmouth Market

Food market Mon–Fri noon–3pm • Ⓦ exmouth-market.com • ⊖ Farringdon

Opposite Mount Pleasant is **Exmouth Market**, now at the epicentre of trendy Clerkenwell. Apart from a surviving pie-and-mash shop, the street has been colonized by modish shops, bars and restaurants, and there's now a small **foodie market**. A blue plaque at no.56 pays tribute to **Joey Grimaldi** (1778–1837), son of Italian immigrants and the "Father of Clowns", who first appeared on stage at nearby Sadler's Wells at the age of 3. Close by, the street's **Church of the Holy Redeemer** sports a fetching Italianate campanile, while the groin-vaulted interior features a large baldachin and stations of the cross – yet despite appearances, it belongs to the Church of England.

Sadler's Wells

Rosebery Avenue • ⓦ sadlerswells.com • ⊖ Angel

Clerkenwell's days as a fashionable spa began when Thomas Sadler rediscovered a medicinal well in his garden in 1683 and established a music house to entertain visitors. The well has since made a comeback at the **Sadler's Wells Theatre**, further up Rosebery Avenue, the seventh theatre here since 1683, and now one of London's main opera and ballet venues. A borehole sunk into the old well provides all non-drinking supplies, helps cool the building and produces bottled drinking water for the punters.

CLERKENWELL

● RESTAURANTS		● CAFÉS	
Fish Central	1	Caravan	5
Medcalf	2	Clark & Sons	4
The Modern Pantry	7	Clerkenwell	
Morito	3	Kitchen	6
Moro	3	Kurz & Lang	10
St John	9	Pho	8
Smiths of Smithfield	12	Prufrock's	11

● SHOPS	
Brill	1
G. Gazzano & So	2

● CLUB	
Fabric	8

● PUBS & BARS	
Café Kick	1
Dovetail	6
The Eagle	3
Jerusalem Tavern	7
The Peasant	2
Slaughtered Lamb	4
The Three Kings	5

● ACCOMMODATION	
The Rookery	3
Rosebery Hall	1
The Zetter Hotel & Townhouse	2

Victoria Miro Gallery

LITTLE ITALY

In the late nineteenth century, London experienced a huge influx of Italian immigrants who created their own **Little Italy** in the triangle of land now bounded by Clerkenwell Road, Rosebery Avenue and Farringdon Road; craftsmen, artisans, street performers and musicians were later joined by ice-cream vendors, restaurateurs and political refugees. Between the wars the population peaked at around 10,000 Italians, crammed into overcrowded, insanitary slums. The old streets have long been demolished, and few Italians live here these days; nevertheless, the area remains a focus for a community that's now spread right across the capital.

The main point of reference is **St Peter's Italian Church** (☎020 7837 1528, ✺italianchurch .org.uk), built in 1863 and still the favourite venue for Italian weddings and christenings, as well as for Sunday Mass. It's rarely open outside of the daily Mass, though you can view the World War I memorial in the main porch, and, above it, the grim memorial to the seven hundred Anglo-Italian internees who died aboard the *Arandora Star*, a POW ship which sank en route to Canada in 1940. St Peter's is the starting point of the annual Italian Procession, begun in 1883 and now a permanent fixture on the Sunday nearest July 16 (see p.25).

A few old-established Italian businesses survive, too: the Scuola Guida driving school at 178 Clerkenwell Rd, and the deli, G. Gazzano & Son, at 167–169 Farringdon Rd. There's also a plaque to **Giuseppe Mazzini** (1805–72), the chief protagonist in Italian unification, above the barbers at 10 Laystall St. Mazzini lived in exile in London for many years and was very active in the Clerkenwell community, establishing a free school for Italian children in Hatton Garden.

Islington Museum

245 St John St · Daily except Wed & Sun 10am–5pm · Free · ☎ 020 7527 2837 · ✺ Angel or Farringdon

If you're keen to learn some more about Clerkenwell, Finsbury or the wider borough of Islington (see p.288), it's worth seeking out the **Islington Museum**, housed in the basement of the Finsbury Library (access is down the steps on the north side). There's a dressing-up box for the kids and some fascinating sections on the area's radical politics for the adults. Highlights include the bust of Lenin, part of a memorial designed by Lubetkin, that was erected in 1942 in Holford Square (see p.153), but had to be removed after the war, after it was targeted by Fascists; you can also view some of the library books embellished by Joe Orton and Kenneth Halliwell (see p.290).

Clerkenwell Green

There hasn't been any green on **Clerkenwell Green** for at least three centuries. By contrast, poverty and overcrowding were the main features of nineteenth-century Clerkenwell, and the Green was well known in the press as "the headquarters of republicanism, revolution and ultra-non-conformity" and a popular spot for **demonstrations**. The most violent of these was the "Clerkenwell Riot" of 1832, when a policeman was stabbed to death during a clash between unemployed demonstrators and the newly formed Metropolitan Police Force. In 1871, a red flag was flown from a lamp post on the Green in support of the Paris Commune. London's first **May Day** march set off from here in 1890, and the tradition continues to this day. In 1900, the Labour Party was founded at a meeting on nearby Farringdon Road; in 1903 Lenin and Stalin first met at the *Crown & Anchor* (now the *Crown Tavern*); the Communist Party had its headquarters close by on St John Street for many years; and the Party's *Daily Worker* (and later *Morning Star*), *The Guardian* and *The Observer* were all printed on Farringdon Road.

Marx Memorial Library

Clerkenwell Green · Mon–Thurs 1–2pm or by appointment; closed Aug · Free · ☎ 020 7253 1485, ✺ marx-memorial-library.org · ✺ Farringdon

The oldest building on the Green is the former Welsh Charity School, at no. 37a, built in 1737 and now home to the **Marx Memorial Library**. Headquarters of the left-wing

10

THE PEOPLE'S REPUBLIC OF FINSBURY

The Borough of Finsbury was subsumed into Islington in 1965, but the former **Finsbury Town Hall** (now a dance academy) still stands, an attractive building from 1899, whose name is spelt out in magenta glass on the delicate wrought-iron canopy that juts out into Rosebery Avenue. As the plaque outside states, the district was the first to boast an Asian MP, **Dadabhai Nairoji**, who was elected (after a recount) as a Liberal MP in 1892 with a majority of five. In keeping with its radical pedigree, the borough went on to elect several Communist councillors and became known popularly as the "People's Republic of Finsbury". The council commissioned Georgian-born Berthold Lubetkin to design the modernist **Finsbury Health Centre** on Pine Street, off Exmouth Market, described by Jonathan Glancey as "a remarkable outpost of Soviet thinking and neo-Constructivist architecture in a part of central London wracked with rickets and TB". Lubetkin's later **Spa Green Estate**, the council flats further north on the opposite side of Rosebery Avenue from Sadler's Wells, featured novelties such as rubbish shutes and an aerofoil roof to help tenants dry their clothes.

London Patriotic Society from 1872, and later the Social Democratic Federation's Twentieth Century Press, this is where **Lenin** edited seventeen editions of the Bolshevik paper *Iskra* in 1902–03. The library itself, founded in 1933 in response to the book burnings in Nazi Germany, is open to members only. However, visitors are welcome to view the "workerist" *Hastings Mural* from 1935, and the poky little back room where Lenin worked on *Iskra*. Stuffed with busts, the latter is maintained as a kind of shrine, and there's a copy of Rodchenko's red and black chess set for good measure, too.

St James's Church

Clerkenwell Close • Mon–Fri 9.30am–5.30pm • Free • ☎ 020 7251 1190, ⓦ jc-church.org • ⊖ Farringdon

The area north of the Green was once occupied by the Benedictine nunnery of St Mary. The buildings have long since vanished, though the current church of **St James** on Clerkenwell Close, from 1792, is the descendant of the convent church. A plain, galleried building decorated in Wedgwood blue and white, its most interesting features are the twin staircases for the galleries at the west end, both of which were fitted with wrought-iron guards to prevent parishioners from glimpsing any ladies' ankles as they ascended.

St John's Gate

St John's Lane • Mon–Sat 10am–5pm • Free • ☎ 020 7324 4005, ⓦ museumstjohn.org.uk • ⊖ Farringdon

St John's Gate was built in Kentish ragstone in 1502 as the southern entrance to the Priory of the Order of St John of Jerusalem, the oldest of Clerkenwell's religious establishments. The Knights of St John, or Knights Hospitaller, were responsible for the defence of the Holy Land, and the Clerkenwell priory was established as the order's headquarters in the 1140s. The priory was sacked by Wat Tyler's poll-tax rebels in 1381 on the lookout for the prior, Robert Hales, who was responsible for collecting the tax; Hales was eventually discovered at the Tower, dragged out and beheaded on Tower Hill. Following the Reformation, the Knights moved to Malta, and the Gate housed the Master of Revels, the Elizabethan censor, and later a coffee house run by Richard Hogarth, father of the painter, William. Today, the gatehouse is the headquarters of the **St John Ambulance**, a voluntary first-aid service, established in 1877.

The main room of the gatehouse **museum** traces the development of the Order before its expulsion in 1540 by Henry VIII. There's masonry from the old priory, crusader coins and a small arms collection salvaged from the knights' armoury on Rhodes. The museum's other gallery tells the story of the St John Ambulance, featuring a display of early uniforms and equipment. And if you're lucky, there'll be a uniformed nurse on hand to bring the exhibition to life.

Crypt of the Grand Priory Church

Guided tours Tues, Fri & Sat 11am & 2.30pm • Donation requested

Of the original twelfth-century church, all that remains is the **Norman crypt**, which contains two outstanding monuments: a sixteenth-century Spanish alabaster effigy of a Knight of St John, and the emaciated effigy of the last prior, who died of a broken heart in 1540 following the Order's dissolution. Above ground, the curve of the church's walls – it was circular, like Temple Church – is traced out in cobblestones on St John's Square. To visit the Grand Priory Church, you must take a **guided tour**, which also allows you to explore the gatehouse, including the mock-medieval Chapter Hall.

10

Charterhouse

Charterhouse Square • By guided tour only April–Aug Wed 2.15pm; advance booking essential • £10 • ☎ 020 7253 9503,
Ⓦ thecharterhouse.org • ➔ Barbican or Farringdon

In the southeast corner of Clerkenwell lies **Charterhouse**, founded in 1371 as a Carthusian monastery. The Carthusians were the most respected of the religious orders in London and the only one to put up any significant resistance to the Dissolution of the Monasteries, for which the prior was hanged, drawn and quartered at Tyburn, and his severed arm nailed to the gatehouse as a warning to the rest of the community. The gatehouse, on Charterhouse Square, which retains its fourteenth-century oak doors, is the starting point for the excellent, exhaustive two-hour **guided tours**.

Very little remains of the original buildings, as the monastery was rebuilt as a Tudor mansion after the Dissolution. The monks lived in individual cells, each with its own garden and were only allowed to speak to one another on Sundays; three of their tiny cells can still be seen in the west wall of **Preachers' Court**. The larger of the two enclosed courtyards, **Masters' Court**, retains the wonderful Great Hall, which boasts a fine Renaissance carved screen and a largely reconstructed hammerbeam roof, as well as the Great Chamber where Elizabeth I and James I were once entertained. The **Chapel**, with its geometrical plasterwork ceiling, is half-Tudor and half-Jacobean, and contains the marble and alabaster tomb of **Thomas Sutton**, whose greyhound-head emblem crops up throughout the building. It was Sutton, deemed "the richest commoner in England" at the time, who bought the place in 1611 and converted it into a charity school for boys (now the famous public school in Surrey) and an **almshouse** for gentlemen – known as "brothers" – forty of whom continue to be cared for here.

LENIN IN CLERKENWELL

Virtually every Bolshevik leader spent at least some time in exile in London at the beginning of the twentieth century, to avoid the attentions of the Tsarist secret police. **Lenin** (1870–1924) and his wife, Nadezhda, arrived in April 1902 and found unfurnished lodgings at 30 Holford Square, off Great Percy Street, under the pseudonyms of Mr and Mrs Jacob Richter. Like Marx, Lenin did his studying in the British Library – L13 was his favourite desk.

The couple also entertained other exiles – including **Trotsky**, whom Lenin met for the first time at Holford Square in October 1902 – but Lenin's most important job was his editing of *Iskra* with Yuli Martov (later the Menshevik leader) and Vera Zasulich (one-time revolutionary assassin). The paper was set in Cyrillic script at a Jewish printer's in the East End and run off on the Social Democratic Federation presses on Clerkenwell Green.

In May 1903, Lenin left to join other exiles in Geneva, though over the next eight years he visited London on five more occasions. The Holford Square house was destroyed in the Blitz, so, in 1942, the local council erected a (short-lived) **monument** to Lenin (now in the Islington Museum). A blue plaque at the back of the hotel on the corner of Great Percy Street commemorates the site of 16 Percy Circus, where Lenin stayed in 1905.

BANK OF ENGLAND

The City

The City is where London began. It was here, nearly 2000 years ago that the Romans first established a settlement on the Thames; later the medieval city emerged as the country's most important trading centre; and it remains one of the world's leading financial hubs. When you consider what's happened here, it's amazing that anything has survived. Yet Wren's spires still punctuate the skyline, as does his masterpiece, St Paul's Cathedral. Other relics, such as the City's few remaining medieval alleyways and Wren's Monument to the Great Fire, are less conspicuous, and even the locals have problems finding the Museum of London and the Barbican arts complex. It's also worth checking out the modern architecture, including Richard Rogers' mould-breaking Lloyd's Building, and Norman Foster's eye-catching Gherkin.

The City currently stretches from Temple Bar in the west to the Tower of London in the east – administrative boundaries only slightly larger than those marked by the Roman walls and their medieval successors. However, in this **Square Mile** (as the City is often called) you'll have to dig hard to find leftovers of London's early days: four-fifths of the area burnt down in the Great Fire. What you see on the ground is mostly the product of three fairly recent building phases: the Victorian construction boom; the overzealous reconstruction that followed the Blitz; and the building frenzy that began in the 1980s, and which has since seen over half the City's office space rebuilt.

The biggest change of all, though, has been in the City's **population**. Until the eighteenth century, the vast majority of Londoners lived and worked in or around the City; nowadays, while more than 340,000 commuters spend Monday to Friday here, less than 10,000 actually live here, mostly cooped up in the Barbican complex. The result of this shift is that the City is only fully alive during office hours, with many pubs, restaurants and even some tube stations and tourist sights closing at the weekend.

Fleet Street

11

Fleet Street offers one of the grandest approaches to the City, thanks to the view across to Ludgate Hill and beyond to St Paul's Cathedral, but it's best known for its associations with the printed press and particularly the newspaper industry (see box, p.158).

Temple Bar

Temple Bar, at the western end of Fleet Street, is the latest in a long line of structures marking the boundary between the City of Westminster and the City of London. It began as a simple chain between two posts but a Wren-designed triumphal arch stood here by the 1670s. The heads of executed traitors were displayed on the arch until the mid-eighteenth century – one could even rent a telescope for a closer look. Then, in 1878, the arch was removed to ease traffic, exiled for over a century to a park in Hertfordshire, only to be re-erected near St Paul's (see p.163). The current monument, topped by a winged dragon, marks the spot where the sovereign must ask for the Lord Mayor's permission to enter the City, a tradition that began when Elizabeth I passed through on her way to St Paul's to give thanks for the defeat of the Spanish Armada.

Prince Henry's Room

17 Fleet St • Mon–Fri 11am–2pm • Free • ⓦ cityoflondon.gov.uk • ⊖ Blackfriars or Temple

The western part of Fleet Street was spared from the Great Fire, which stopped at the junction with Fetter Lane, just short of **Prince Henry's Room**, a fine Jacobean house with timber-framed bay windows on the first floor, and the gateway to Inner Temple at street level. Originally a pub, later a waxworks, the first-floor room now contains material relating to the diarist Samuel Pepys (see box, p.159), who was born and baptized in the area. Even if you've no interest in Pepys, the wood-panelled room is worth a look as it contains a very fine Jacobean plasterwork ceiling and original stained glass.

THE CORPORATION

The one unchanging aspect of the City is its special status, conferred on the area by William the Conqueror to win favour with its powerful burghers, and extended and reaffirmed by successive rulers ever since. Even today, with its own Lord Mayor, its Beadles, Sheriffs and Aldermen, its separate police force and its select electorate of freemen and liverymen, the City is an anachronistic, one-party mini-state. It's run by the **City of London Corporation** (ⓦ cityoflondon.gov.uk), an unreconstructed old-boys network whose medievalist pageantry camouflages the very real power and wealth that it holds. Its anomalous status is all the more baffling when you consider that the area was an early bastion of British democracy: it was the City that traditionally stood up to bullying sovereigns.

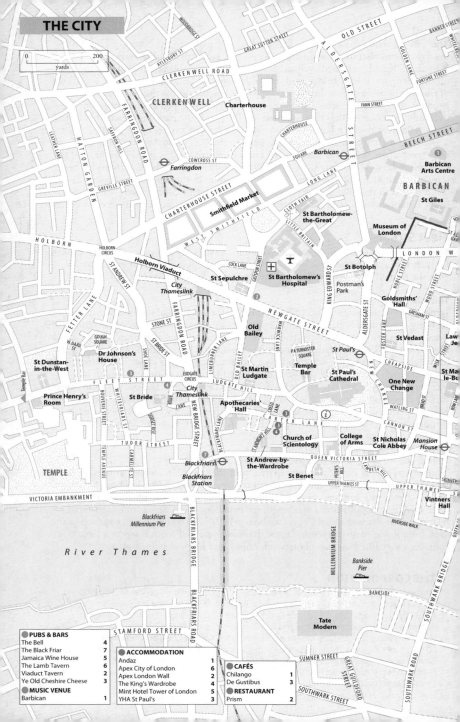

THE CITY

0   200
yards

WOODBRIDGE ST

OLD STREET

BANNER ST

WHITECROSS ST

GREAT SUTTON STREET

AYLESBURY ST

CLERKENWELL ROAD

ALDERSGATE STREET

GOLDEN LANE

FORTUNE STREET

CLERKENWELL

Charterhouse

FANN STREET

BEECH STREET

LEATHER LANE

FARRINGDON ROAD

SAFFRON HILL

HATTON GARDEN

COWCROSS ST

Farringdon

CHARTERHOUSE

SQUARE

Barbican

LONG LANE

Barbican Arts Centre

BARBICAN

St Giles

GREVILLE STREET

CHARTERHOUSE STREET

Smithfield Market

CLOTH FAIR

LITTLE BRITAIN

St Bartholomew-the-Great

CHARTERHOUSE

Museum of London

HOLBORN

HOLBORN CIRCUS

WEST SMITHFIELD

LONDON W

ST ANDREW ST

Holborn Viaduct

COCK LANE

GILTSPUR STREET

St Bartholomew's Hospital

St Botolph

St Sepulchre

KING EDWARD ST

Postman's Park

NOBLE STREET

Goldsmiths' Hall

WOOD STREET

City Thameslink

FARRINGDON ROAD

STONE ST

NEWGATE STREET

ALDERSGATE ST

FOSTER LANE

GRESHAM ST

FETTER LANE

GOUGH SQUARE

W. HARD ST

Dr Johnson's House

SHOE LANE

ST BRIDE ST

Old Bailey

WARWICK LANE

OLD BAILEY

PATERNOSTER SQUARE

Temple Bar

St Vedast

St Paul's

CHEAPSIDE

Law Je

St Dunstan-in-the-West

FLEET STREET

LUDGATE CIRCUS

City Thameslink

LUDGATE HILL

St Martin Ludgate

St Paul's Cathedral

St Ma le-Bo

Prince Henry's Room

BOUVERIE STREET

WHITEFRIARS ST

St Bride

DORSET RISE

NEW BRIDGE STREET

LIMEBURNER LANE

CREED LANE

One New Change

BREAD ST

BOW LANE

WATLING ST

Apothecaries' Hall

STANDBROOK HILL LANE

CARTER LANE

CANNON ST

Church of Scientology

College of Arms

St Nicholas Cole Abbey

Mansion House

TEMPLE

TUDOR STREET

CARMELITE ST

TEMPLE AVENUE

BLACKFRIARS LANE

Blackfriars

St Andrew-by-the-Wardrobe

QUEEN VICTORIA STREET

PETER'S HILL

LAMBETH HILL

SKINNER

Blackfriars Station

St Benet

UPPER THAMES ST

UPPER THAMES ST

Vintners Hall

VICTORIA EMBANKMENT

Blackfriars Millennium Pier

BLACKFRIARS BRIDGE

RIVERSIDE WALK

SOUTHWARK BRIDGE

QUEEN

River Thames

MILLENNIUM BRIDGE

Bankside Pier

BANKSIDE

BLACKFRIARS ROAD

STAMFORD STREET

Tate Modern

GREAT GUILDFORD STREET

SOUTHWARK ROAD

SUMNER STREET

SOUTHWARK STREET

11

THE FLEET STREET PRESS

Fleet Street's associations with the printed press began in 1500, when Wynkyn de Worde, William Caxton's apprentice (and the first man to print italics), moved the Caxton presses here from Westminster to be close to the lawyers of the Inns of Court (his best customers) and to the clergy of St Paul's, London's largest literate group. In 1702, the world's first daily newspaper, the now defunct **Daily Courant**, began publishing here, and by the nineteenth century, all the major national and provincial dailies had moved their presses to the area. Then in 1985, Britain's first colour tabloid, *Today*, appeared, using computer technology that rendered the Fleet Street presses obsolete. It was left to media tycoon Rupert Murdoch to take on the printers' unions in a bitter year-long dispute that changed the newspaper industry for ever.

The press headquarters that once dominated the area have all now relocated, leaving just a handful of small publications and a few architectural landmarks to testify to 500 years of printing history. The former **Daily Telegraph** building, at nos. 135–141, is one of London's few truly Art Deco edifices, built in a Greco-Egyptian style in 1928, with a striking polychrome clock and a great stone relief above the doorway depicting Mercury's messengers sending news around the world. It was upstaged a few years later, however, by the city's first glass curtain-wall construction, the former **Daily Express** building at no. 127, with its sleek black Vitrolite facade. It's worth peering inside the cinema-like foyer, which features a silver-leaf sunburst ceiling, ocean-wave floor tiles, shiny silver serpent handrails, and remarkable chrome and gold relief panels extolling the British Empire.

There's a tiled wall in Magpie Alley, off Bouverie Street, which illustrates the history of Fleet Street's presses, and some metal information panels nearby in the windows of the old *Daily Mail* building at Ashentree Court, off Whitefriars Street. Another account of Fleet Street's history is the exhibition in the crypt of **St Bride's Church** (Mon–Fri 8am–6pm, Sat 11am–3pm, Sun 10am–6.30pm; free; ☎ 020 7427 0133, ⓦ stbrides.com), the "journalists' and printers' cathedral", situated behind the former Reuters building. The church also boasts Wren's tallest, and most exquisite, spire (said to be the inspiration for the traditional tiered wedding cake).

St Dunstan-in-the-West

186a Fleet St • Mon–Fri 11am–2pm • ☎ 020 7405 1929, ⓦ stdunstaninthewest.org • ⓔ Temple or Blackfriars

The church of **St Dunstan-in-the-West**, with a distinctive neo-Gothic tower and lantern, from the 1830s, dominates the top of Fleet Street. To the side is the much earlier clock temple, erected in 1671 by the parishioners in thanks for escaping the Great Fire; inside the temple, the legendary British giants Gog and Magog, in gilded loincloths, nod their heads and clang their bells on the hour. The statue of Queen Elizabeth I, in a niche in the vestry wall, and the crumbling statues of the legendary King Lud and his two sons in the porch, originally stood over Ludgate, the City gateway that once stood halfway up Ludgate Hill. The church's unusual, octagonal, neo-Gothic interior features a huge wooden iconostasis, used during the regular Romanian Orthodox services.

Dr Johnson's House

17 Gough Square • Mon–Sat: May–Sept 11am–5.30pm; Oct–April 11am–5pm • £4.50 • ☎ 020 7353 3745, ⓦ drjohnsonshouse.org • ⓔ Blackfriars

Numerous narrow alleyways lead off the north side of Fleet Street beyond Fetter Lane, concealing legal chambers and offices. Two of the narrow alleyways that lead north off Fleet Street – Bolt Court and Hind Court – eventually open out into cobbled Gough Square, which features a statue of Dr Johnson's cat, Hodge, enjoying an oyster. The square's one authentic eighteenth-century building is **Dr Johnson's House,** where the great savant, writer and lexicographer lived from 1748 to 1759 while compiling the 41,000 entries for the first English dictionary.

Johnson rented the house on Gough Square with the £1575 advance he received for the dictionary. Despite his subsequent fame, Johnson was in and out of debt all his life – his famous philosophical romance, *Rasselas*, was written in less than a week to raise funds for his mother's funeral. The house itself is a lovely Georgian period piece peppered with quotes by the great man and portraits of his contemporaries, including Johnson's servant Francis Barber, to whom he left most of his wordly goods. On the second floor, you can watch a video on Johnson's life, after which you get to see the open-plan attic, in which Johnson and his six clerks put together the dictionary, and where kids can try on some replica Georgian garb.

Ludgate Circus

Fleet Street terminates at **Ludgate Circus**, built in the 1870s to replace a bridge over the **River Fleet**, which had already been buried under the roads after a drunken butcher got stuck in the river mud and froze to death. The Fleet originally marked the western boundary of the walled City, and was once an unmissable feature of the landscape, as the tanneries and slaughterhouses of Smithfield, to the north, used to turn the water red with entrails. The Fleet's western bank was the site of the notoriously inhumane **Fleet Prison**, where the poet John Donne was imprisoned in 1601 for marrying without his father-in-law's consent. Until 1754, Fleet Prison was renowned for its clandestine "**Fleet Marriages**", performed by priests (or impostors) who were imprisoned there for debt. These marriages, in which couples could marry without a licence, attracted people of all classes, and took place in the prison chapel until 1710, when they were banished to the neighbouring taverns, the fee being split between clergyman and innkeeper.

11

St Paul's Cathedral

Cathedral Mon–Sat 8.30am–4.30pm; galleries Mon–Sat 9.30am–4.15pm • £14.50 • ☎ 020 7236 4128, ⓦ www.stpauls.co.uk • ⊖ St Paul's

The enormous lead-covered dome of **St Paul's Cathedral** has dominated the City skyline since it was built after the Great Fire – and remains so despite the encroaching tower blocks. Its showpiece west facade is particularly magnificent, fronted by a wide flight of steps, a double-storey portico and two of London's most Baroque towers. While it can't compete with Westminster Abbey for celebrity corpses, pre-Reformation sculpture, royal connections and sheer atmosphere, St Paul's is nevertheless a perfectly calculated architectural space, a burial place for captains rather than kings, artists not poets, and a popular wedding venue for the privileged few (including Charles and Diana).

SAMUEL PEPYS

Born to a humble tailor and a laundress in Salisbury Court, off Fleet Street, **Samuel Pepys** (1633–1703) was baptized in St Bride's (see opposite) and buried in St Olave's, having spent virtually his entire life in London. Family connections secured an education at St Paul's School, a scholarship to Cambridge and a career in the civil service. He was an MP, served as Secretary to the Admiralty, and was instrumental in the establishment of a professional British navy. In 1679 he was imprisoned for six weeks in the Tower on suspicion of treason, but returned to office, only to be forced out again in 1689, following the overthrow of James II.

Of course, it's not Pepys' career, but his **diaries**, written between 1660 and 1669, that have immortalized him. This rollicking journal includes eyewitness accounts of the Restoration, the Great Plague and the Great Fire, giving an unparalleled insight into London life at the time. Ultimately, Pepys emerges from the pages, warts and all, as an eminently likeable character, who seems almost imperturbable – he gives as much space to details of his pub meals as he does to the Great Fire, and finishes most entries with his catchphrase "and so to bed".

Pepys was also a notorious womanizer, detailing his philanderings in his diary in Spanish so as to avoid detection by his French Huguenot wife. Nevertheless he was caught *in flagrante* with one of her best friends, and his slow reconciliation with his spouse is recorded in a novelist's detail, the diary ending in 1669 as they sail off to the Continent to patch things up. In the event, his wife died later that year and he never remarried. Pepys bequeathed his vast library to his old college in Cambridge, where his diaries lay undiscovered until the nineteenth century, when they were finally published (with the erotic passages omitted) in 1825.

THE CITY'S CHURCHES

The City of London is crowded with **churches** (ⓦ visitthecity.co.uk), the majority of them built or rebuilt by Christopher Wren after the Great Fire. Prompted by the decline in the City's population, the Victorians demolished a fair few, but over forty remain intact. The **opening times** given in the text should be taken with a pinch of salt, since most rely on volunteers to keep their doors open. As a general rule, weekday lunchtimes are the best time to visit, since many City churches put on free lunchtime concerts. Below is a list of the six most interesting:

St Bartholomew-the-Great Cloth Fair. This is the oldest surviving pre-Fire church in the City and by far the most atmospheric. It was also the first church in the country to charge an entrance fee. See p.167.

St Mary Abchurch Abchurch Lane. Uniquely for Wren's City churches, the interior features a huge, painted, domed ceiling, plus the only authenticated Gibbons reredos. See p.174.

St Mary Aldermary Queen Victoria Street. Wren's most successful stab at Gothic, with fan vaulting in the aisles and a panelled ceiling in the nave. See p.164.

St Mary Woolnoth Lombard Street. Hawksmoor's only City church, sporting an unusually broad, bulky tower and a Baroque clerestory that floods the church with light from its semicircular windows. See p.175.

St Olave Hart Street. Built in the fifteenth century, and one of the few pre-Fire Gothic churches in the City. See p.179.

St Stephen Walbrook Walbrook. Wren's dress rehearsal for St Paul's, with a wonderful central dome and plenty of original woodcarving. See p.175.

The current building is the fifth on this site, its immediate predecessor being **Old St Paul's**, a huge Gothic cathedral built by the Normans, whose 489ft spire (destroyed by lightning in 1561) was one of the wonders of medieval Europe. St Paul's was just one of over fifty church commissions Christopher Wren received in the wake of the Great Fire. Hassles over his initial plans, and wrangles over money plagued the project throughout, but Wren remained unruffled and the world's first Protestant cathedral was officially completed in 1710 under Queen Anne, whose statue stands below the steps. The cathedral achieved iconic status during the **Blitz**, when it stood defiantly unscathed amid the carnage (as in the famous wartime propaganda photo), and a monument to the south of the cathedral commemorates both the **St Paul's Watch** – who patrolled the cathedral roof every night to combat the incendiary bombs – and all those firefighters who have died since while carrying out their duties.

INFORMATION AND TOURS

Entry Admission charges are nothing new at St Paul's – they were first introduced in 1709, before the cathedral was even finished. Once inside, pick up a free plan, and simply ask the vergers if you're having trouble locating a particular monument; alternatively, multimedia guides are available free of charge.

Tours Introductory talks run regularly throughout the day, and longer guided tours (1hr 30min), that allow you access to one or two areas off limits to the public, set off at 10.45am, 11.15am, 1.30pm and 2pm. If you're in a group of five or more, you can also pay an extra £5 each to go on a full-on behind-the-scenes triforium tour (Mon & Tues 11.30am & 2pm, Fri 2pm; book in advance on ☎ 020 7246 8357).

Services It's worth attending one of the cathedral's services, if only to hear the choir, who perform during most evensongs (Mon–Sat 5pm), and on Sundays at 10.15am, 11.30am and 3.15pm. Strictly speaking, on Sundays St Paul's is only open for services and consequently there's no admission charge. However, in between services, you're free to wander round the cathedral and crypt (though not the galleries).

The interior

Queen Victoria thought the **nave** "dirty, dark and undevotional", though since the destruction of the stained glass in the Blitz, it is once again light and airy, as Wren intended. Burials are confined to the crypt, and memorials were only permitted after 1790 when overcrowding at Westminster Abbey had become intolerable. Unfortunately, what followed was a series of overblown funerary monuments to the military heroes of the Napoleonic Wars. Some are simply ludicrous, like the virtually naked statue of

11

Captain Burges, in the south aisle, holding hands with an angel over a naval cannon; others are more offensive, such as the monument to Thomas Fanshaw Middleton, first Protestant Bishop of India, depicted baptizing "heathen" locals. The best of the bunch are Flaxman's **Nelson** memorial, in the south transept, with its seasick lion, and, in the north aisle, the bombastic bronze and marble monument – the cathedral's largest – to the **Duke of Wellington**, begun in 1857 but only topped with the statue of the duke astride his faithful steed, Copenhagen, in 1912. Both men are buried in the crypt.

The best place from which to appreciate the glory of St Paul's is beneath the **dome**, which was decorated (against Wren's wishes) by Thornhill's monochrome trompe-l'oeil frescoes, now rather upstaged by the adjacent gilded spandrels. St Paul's most famous work of art, however, hangs in the north transept: the crushingly symbolic *Light of the World* by the Pre-Raphaelite **Holman Hunt**, depicting Christ knocking at the handleless, bramble-strewn door of the human soul, which must be opened from within. The original is actually in Keble College, Oxford, though this copy was executed by the artist himself, some fifty years later in 1900.

11

The chancel

By far the most richly decorated section of the cathedral is the **chancel**, in particular the spectacular, swirling, gilded Byzantine-style mosaics of birds, fish, animals and greenery, from the 1890s. The intricately carved oak and limewood choir stalls, and the imposing organ case, are the work of Grinling Gibbons. The north choir-aisle contains Henry Moore's *Mother and Child* sculpture and allows you to admire Jean Tijou's ornate black-and-gold **wrought-iron gates** that separate the aisles from the high altar. The latter features an extravagant Baroque baldachin, held up by barley-sugar columns and wrapped round with gilded laurel, created after the war to a design by Wren. Behind the high altar stands the **American Memorial Chapel**, dedicated to the 28,000 Americans based in Britain who lost their lives in World War II (check out the space rocket hidden in the carved wooden foliage of the far right-hand panel, a tribute to America's postwar space exploration). Leaving via the south choir-aisle, you'll find the upstanding shroud of **John Donne**, poet, preacher and one-time Dean of St Paul's, the only complete effigy to have survived from Old St Paul's.

The galleries

From the south transept, a series of stairs lead to the dome's three **galleries**, and they're well worth the climb. The initial 259 steps take you to the **Whispering Gallery**, so called because of its acoustic properties – words whispered to the wall on one side are audible 100ft away on the other, though it's often so busy you can't hear much above the hubbub. Another 119 steps up bring you to the exterior **Stone Gallery**, around the base of the dome, while the final 152 steel steps take you inside the dome's inner structure to the **Golden Gallery**, just below the golden ball and cross which top the cathedral. The views of the City and along the Thames are unbeatable – you should be able to identify the distinctive white facade of Wren's London house, next to the Globe Theatre, from which he could contemplate his masterpiece. Before you ascend the last flight of stairs, be sure to look through the peephole in the floor, onto the monochrome marble floor beneath the dome, a truly terrifying sight.

The crypt

The entrance to the cathedral's vast **crypt** is on your left as you leave the south choir-aisle. The whitewashed walls make this one of the least atmospheric mausoleums you could imagine – a far cry from the nineteenth century, when visitors were shown around the tombs by candlelight.

The crypt boasts as many painters and architects as Westminster Abbey has poets, most of them stuffed into the southern aisle, known as **Artists' Corner**. Appropriately enough, it was Wren himself who started the trend, with a tomb inscribed: "*lector, si*

PATERNOSTER SQUARE

The Blitz destroyed the area immediately to the north of St Paul's, including Paternoster Row, which had been the centre of the book trade since 1500. The postwar office complex that replaced it was torn down in the 1980s and supplanted by the softer, post-classical development of **Paternoster Square**, centred on a Corinthian column topped by a gilded urn, and, since 2004, home to the London Stock Exchange. One happy consequence of the square's redevelopment is that **Temple Bar**, the last surviving City gateway which once stood at the top of Fleet Street (see p.155), found its way back to London after a century of languishing in a park in Hertfordshire. Designed by Wren himself, the triumphal arch now forms the entrance to Paternoster Square from St Paul's, with the Stuart monarchs, James I and Charles II, and their consorts, occupying the niches.

monumentum requiris, circumspice" (reader, if you seek his monument, look around). Close to Wren are the graves of Reynolds, Turner, Millais, Holman Hunt, Lord Leighton and Alma-Tadema; nearby there's a bust of Van Dyck, whose monument perished along with Old St Paul's. Over in the north aisle is the grave of Alexander Fleming, the discoverer of penicillin.

The crypt's two star tombs – those of **Nelson** and **Wellington** – occupy centre stage. Wellington's porphyry and granite monstrosity is set in its own mini-chapel, surrounded by memorials to illustrious British field marshals, while Nelson lies in a black marble sarcophagus originally designed for Cardinal Wolsey and later intended for Henry VIII and his third wife, Jane Seymour. As at Trafalgar Square, Nelson lies close to later admirals Jellicoe and Beatty (the last person to be buried in the cathedral, in 1936). Beyond are the cathedral shop, a café and the exit.

St Paul's Churchyard

St Paul's Churchyard, to the northeast of the cathedral, was also destroyed in the Blitz. The churchyard's most arresting feature now is a column, erected in 1910, topped by a gilded statue of St Paul, and diplomatically inscribed "amid such scenes of good and evil as make up human affairs, the conscience of the church and nation through five centuries found public utterance". This is a reference to **Paul's Cross**, a polygonal open-air pulpit – its groundplan is marked out in the paving – from which official proclamations and religious speeches were made. Heretics were regularly executed on this spot, and in 1519 Luther's works were publicly burnt here, before Henry VIII changed sides and demanded the "preaching down" of papal authority from the same spot. The cross was destroyed by the Puritans in 1643.

Cheapside

It's difficult to believe that **Cheapside**, which connects St Paul's with Bank, was once London's foremost shopping street, the widest thoroughfare in the City, and site of the medieval marketplace. Nowadays only the names of the nearby streets – Bread Street, Milk Street, Honey Lane, Poultry – recall its former prominence, which faded when the shops and their customers moved to the West End from the eighteenth century.

One New Change

1 New Change · Daily 7am–10pm · ⓦ onenewchange.com · ⊖ St Paul's

Commerce has recently returned to Cheapside in the form of **One New Change**, an uncompromisingly modern building by Jean Nouvel, whose opaque brown glass facade is reminiscent of a Stealth bomber. Even if you've no interest in the formulaic franchises which fill this multistorey shopping mall, it has one great thing going for it: a sixth-floor, sun-trap roof terrace that's open to the public and has views over to St Paul's, Tate Modern and the Shard.

11

11

DICK WHITTINGTON

The City's Lord Mayor is elected on an annual basis, and the most famous Lord Mayor of the lot is **Dick Whittington** (c.1350–1423) of pantomime fame. The third son of a wealthy Gloucestershire family, Whittington was an apprentice mercer, dealing in silks and velvets, who rose to become one of the richest men in the City by the age of just 21. He was an early philanthropist, establishing a library at Greyfriars' monastery and a refuge for single mothers at St Thomas' Hospital, and building one of the city's first public lavatories, a unisex 128-seater known as "Whittington's Night Soil House of Easement". The pantomime story appeared some 200 years after Whittington's death, though quite how he became the fictional ragamuffin who comes to London after hearing the streets are paved with gold, no one seems to know. Traditionally, Whittington is leaving London with his knapsack and cat, when he hears the Bow Bells ring out "Turn again, Whittington, thrice Lord Mayor of London" (he was, in fact, mayor on four occasions and was never knighted as the story claims). The theory on the cat is that it was a common name for a coal barge at the time, and Whittington is thought to have made much of his fortune in the coal trade. There's a statue on Highgate Hill commemorating the very spot where Dick allegedly heard the Bow Bells, and a stained-glass window in St Michael Paternoster Royal, on Skinner's Lane, near where he lived.

St Mary-le-Bow

Cheapside • Mon–Thurs 7am–6pm, Fri 7am–4pm • ⓦ stmarylebow.co.uk • ⊖ St Paul's

One of the distinguishing features of Cheapside is Wren's church of **St Mary-le-Bow**, whose handsome tower features a conglomeration of pilasters, a circular colonnade, a granite obelisk and a dragon weather vane. The tower also contains postwar replicas of the famous "Bow Bells", which sounded the 9pm curfew for Londoners from the fourteenth to the nineteenth centuries, and within whose earshot all true Cockneys are born. The original interior was totally destroyed in the Blitz and is a postwar re-creation, but the church's medieval crypt survived and is home to the atmospheric *Café Below* (see p.376).

St Mary Aldermary

Bow Lane • Mon–Fri 11am–3pm • ⓦ stmaryaldermary.co.uk • ⊖ Mansion House or Bank

At the southern end of Bow Lane lies the church of **St Mary Aldermary**, whose interior is a rare foray into the perpendicular Gothic style by Wren, based on the original church – the plaster fan-vaults and saucer domes in the aisles are the highlight. **Bow Lane** itself is lovely, narrow, pedestrianized street redolent of the pre-Fire City, jam-packed at weekday lunchtimes with office workers heading for its sandwich bars and pubs.

Blackfriars

Most folk heading south from St Paul's are aiming for the **Millennium Bridge** (see p.227), to cross over the river to Tate Modern and Bankside. However, instead of simply heading for the bridge, it's worth taking time to venture into the backstreets and alleyways, or go for a stroll along the **Riverside Walk** which now extends all the way from Blackfriars railway bridge to Tower Bridge.

    Blackfriars, the district between Ludgate Hill and the river, is named after the Dominican monastery that stood here until the Dissolution. The monks' old refectory became Blackfriars Theatre, where Shakespeare and his fellow actors performed in the winter months. Although the area was destroyed in the Great Fire, it suffered little from wartime bombing and remains a warren of alleyways, courtyards and narrow streets, conveying something of the plan of the City before the Victorians, the German bombers and the 1960s brutalists did their worst. The best place to go for a taste of the monastic is *The Black Friar*, 174 Queen Victoria Street, which boasts a fantastically ornate **Arts and Crafts** pub interior (see p.391).

Church of Scientology

146 Queen Victoria St · Daily 9am–10pm · Free · ☎ 020 7246 2700, Ⓦ scientology-london.org · ⊖ Blackfriars

Built in the 1860s for the British and Foreign Bible Society, the London headquarters of the Church of Scientology look like an Italian *palazzo*. If you're prepared to put up with the slightly creepy attendants, the building itself is worth admiring, and there's a whole exhibition on **L. Ron Hubbard**, the American pulp-fiction writer and hypnotist who founded the Scientology cult.

College of Arms

Queen Victoria St · Mon–Fri 10am–4pm · Free · ☎ 020 7248 2762, Ⓦ college-of-arms.gov.uk · ⊖ Blackfriars or Mansion House

Originally built round a courtyard in the 1670s, the red-brick mansion of the **College of Arms** was opened up to the south with the building of Queen Victoria Street in the 1870s. The college is the headquarters of heraldry in England, and even today is in charge of granting coats of arms to those who can prove they've been "a benefit to the community". The Earl Marshal's Court – featuring a gallery, copious wooden panelling and a modest throne – is the only room open to the public, unless you apply to trace your family or study heraldry in the college library.

11

Old Bailey

Old Bailey · Mon–Fri 10am–1pm & 2–5pm · Free · ☎ 020 7248 3277, Ⓦ cityoflondon.gov.uk · ⊖ St Paul's

The Central Criminal Court is better known as the **Old Bailey**, after the street on which it stands, which used to run along the medieval city walls. The court's pompous, domed, Edwardian building – "Defend the Children of the Poor & Punish the Wrongdoer" the entrance proclaims – is topped by a gilded statue of Justice, unusually depicted without blindfold, holding her sword and scales. The country's most serious criminal court cases take place here, and have included, in the past, the trials of Lord Haw-Haw, the Kray Twins, the Angry Brigade (see p.292), and all Britain's multiple murderers. You can watch the proceedings from the visitors' gallery

PUBLIC EXECUTIONS AND BODY SNATCHERS

After 1783, when hangings at Tyburn were stopped, **public executions** at Newgate began to draw crowds of 100,000 and more. The last public beheading took place here in 1820 when five Cato Street Conspirators (see p.86) were hanged and decapitated with a surgeon's knife. It was in hanging, however, that Newgate excelled, its most efficient gallows dispatching twenty criminals simultaneously. Unease over the "robbery and violence, loud laughing, oaths, fighting, obscene conduct and still more filthy language" that accompanied public hangings drove the executions inside the prison walls in 1868. The night before an execution, a handbell was tolled outside the condemned's cell, while the jailer recited the Newgate verse that began: "All you that in the condemned hole do lie/Prepare you, for tomorrow you shall die… And when St Sepulchre's bell in the morning tolls/The Lord above have mercy on your souls." Until Newgate got its own bell, the "Great Bell of Old Bailey" was in the church of **St Sepulchre** (Mon–Fri 11.30am–2.30pm, Ⓦ st-sepulchre.org.uk), and tolled the condemned to the scaffold at eight in the morning. The handbell and verse are displayed inside the church, opposite the Old Bailey.

The bodies of the executed were handed over to the surgeons of St Bartholomew's for dissection, but body snatchers also preyed on non-criminals buried in St Sepulchre churchyard. Such was the demand for corpses that relatives were forced to pay a nightwatchman to guard the graveyard in a specially built watch-house – still visible to the north of the church – to prevent the "Resurrection Men" from retrieving their quarry. Successfully stolen stiffs were taken to the nearby *Fortune of War* tavern, which stood on Pie Corner, by Cock Lane, to be sold to the surgeons. Today, Pie Corner is marked by a gilded overfed cherub known as **Fat Boy**, who commemorates the "staying of the Great Fire" of 1666, which, when it wasn't blamed on the Catholics, was ascribed to the sin of gluttony, since it had begun in Pudding Lane and ended at Pie Corner.

(no under-14s), but you're not allowed to take anything into the court (and that includes mobiles) and there's no cloakroom. Sadly, visitors do not get to see the Grand Hall, with its swirling marble floor and walls, succession of domes, and grandiloquent frescoes.

The site of the Old Bailey was originally occupied by **Newgate Prison**, which began life as a small lock-up above the medieval gateway of Newgate. Burnt down in the 1780 Gordon Riots, it was rebuilt as "a veritable Hell, worthy of the imagination of Dante", as one of its more famous inmates, Casanova, put it. Earlier well-known temporary residents included Thomas Malory, who wrote *Le Morte d'Arthur* while imprisoned here for murder (among other things); Daniel Defoe, who was put inside for his *The Shortest Way with Dissenters*; Ben Jonson, who served time for murder; and Christopher Marlowe, who was on a charge of atheism.

Smithfield

11

The ground was covered, nearly ankle-deep with filth and mire; a thick steam perpetually rising from the reeking bodies of the cattle, and mingling with the fog. Oliver Twist, Charles Dickens

Originally open ground outside the City walls, **Smithfield** is a corruption of "Smooth Field". It was used as a horse fair in Norman times, and later became the site for **Bartholomew Fair**, established in 1133 by Rahere, prior and founder of St Bartholomew's priory and hospice to raise funds. Rahere himself used to perform juggling tricks, while Pepys reports seeing a horse counting sixpences and, more reliably, a puppet show of Ben Jonson's play *Bartholomew Fair*. Predictably enough, it was the Victorians who closed it down to protect public morals.

The meat **market**, with which Smithfield is now synonymous, grew up as a kind of adjunct to the fair. Live cattle continued to be herded into Smithfield until 1852, when the fair was suppressed and the abattoirs moved out to Islington. A new covered market hall was erected in 1868, along with the "Winkle", a spiral ramp at the centre of West Smithfield, linked to the market's very own (now defunct) tube station. Smithfield subsequently tripled in size and remains London's main meat market – the action starts around 4am and is all over by noon.

St Bartholomew's Hospital

West Smithfield • Museum Tues–Fri 10am–4pm • Free • Guided tours Fri 2pm; £5 • ☎ 020 3465 5798 • Ⓥ www.bartsandthelondon .nhs.uk • ⊖ St Paul's

St Bartholomew's Hospital – affectionately known as Bart's – is the oldest hospital in London. It began as an Augustinian priory and hospice in 1123, founded by Rahere, courtier, clerk and even court jester to Henry I, on the orders of St Bartholomew, who

---

BLOOD AND GUTS AT SMITHFIELD

Blood was spilled at **Smithfield** long before the meat market was legally sanctioned here in the seventeenth century. During the 1381 Peasants' Revolt, the poll-tax rebels under **Wat Tyler** assembled here to negotiate with the boy-king Richard II. At the meeting, Lord Mayor Walworth pulled Tyler from his horse and stabbed him, after which he was bustled into St Bartholomew's for treatment, only to be dragged out by the king's men and beheaded.

Smithfield subsequently became a regular venue for **public executions**. The Scottish hero, William Wallace, was dragged behind a horse from the Tower, then hanged, drawn and quartered here in 1305, and the Bishop of Rochester's cook was boiled alive in 1531, but the local speciality was **burnings**. These reached a peak during the reign of "Bloody" Mary in the 1550s, when hundreds of Protestants were burnt at the stake for their beliefs, in revenge for the Catholics who had suffered a similar fate under Henry VIII and Edward VI; a plaque on the side of Bart's commemorates some of those who died.

appeared to him in a vision while he was in malarial delirium on a pilgrimage to Rome. The priory was dissolved by Henry VIII, but in 1546, with just two weeks left to live, the king agreed to re-found the hospital.

The **Henry VIII Gate**, built in 1702, features a statue of the king, with a lame man on the right and a diseased man on the left lounging on the broken pediment above. Further along, you can make out shrapnel marks left from a 1916 Zeppelin air raid. Behind the Henry VIII Gate stands the church of **St Bartholomew-the-Less** (daily 7am–8pm), sole survivor of the priory's four chapels. The tower and vestry are fifteenth-century, the octagonal interior is neo-Gothic, though it does contain a Tudor memorial to Elizabeth I's surgeon. Beyond the church lies three-quarters of **The Square** created for the hospital by James Gibbs in the mid-eighteenth century, with the **Great Hall** on the north side, accessed by the **Grand Staircase**, its walls decorated with biblical murals that were painted free of charge by Hogarth, who was born and baptized nearby and served as one of the hospital's governors.

St Bartholomew's Museum

You can get a glimpse of the aforementioned Grand Staircase from inside **St Bartholomew's Museum**, on the left, under the archway into the courtyard. Among the medical artefacts, there are some fearsome amputation instruments, a pair of leather "lunatic restrainers", some great jars with labels such as "poison – for external use only", and a cricket bat autographed by W.G. Grace, who was a student at Bart's in the 1870s. To see the Great Hall join one of the fascinating weekly **guided tours**, which take in the surrounding area as well; the meeting point is the Henry VIII Gate.

11

St Bartholomew-the-Great

Cloth Fair • Mon–Fri 8.30am–5pm, Sat 10.30am–4pm, Sun 8.30am–8pm; mid-Nov to mid-Feb Mon–Fri closes 4pm • £4 • ☎ 020 7606 5171, Ⓦ greatstbarts.com • ⊖ Barbican

Hidden in the backstreets north of the hospital, **St Bartholomew-the-Great** is London's oldest and most atmospheric parish church. Begun in 1123 as the main church of St Bartholomew's priory and hospice, it was partly demolished in the Reformation, and gradually fell into ruins: the cloisters were used as a stable, there was a boys' school in the triforium, a coal and wine cellar in the crypt, a blacksmith's in the north transept and a printing press (where Benjamin Franklin once worked) in the Lady Chapel. From 1887, Aston Webb restored what remained, and added the chequered patterning and flintwork that now characterizes the exterior. Much beloved of film companies, in 2007 it became the first parish church in the country to charge an entrance fee.

To get an idea of the scale of the original church, approach it through the half-timbered Tudor **gatehouse**, on Little Britain Street. A wooden statue of St Bartholomew stands in a niche; below is the thirteenth-century arch that once formed the entrance to the nave. The churchyard now stands where the nave itself would have been, and one side of the **cloisters** survives to the south, now housing the delightful *Cloister Café* (closed Sat). The rest of the church is a confusion of elements, including portions of the transepts and, most impressively, the **chancel**, where thick Norman pillars separate the main body from the ambulatory. There are various pre-Fire monuments, the most prominent being the tomb of Rahere (see opposite), which shelters under a fifteenth-century canopy north of the altar, with an angel at his feet and two canons kneeling beside him reading from the prophets. Beyond the ambulatory lies the large Lady Chapel, mostly nineteenth-century, though with original stonework here and there.

Barbican

Silk Street • Arts Centre Mon–Sat 9am–11pm, Sun noon–11pm • Free • ☎ 020 7638 8891, Ⓦ barbican.org.uk • ⊖ Barbican

The City's only large residential complex is the concrete brutalist ghetto of the **Barbican**, built on the heavily bombed Cripplegate area. It's a classic 1970s urban dystopia, a maze of pedestrian walkways and underground car parks, pinioned by three 400ft tower blocks. At the centre of the complex is the **Barbican Arts Centre**, home to the London Symphony Orchestra, two performance spaces, a three-screen cinema, a rooftop garden, a public library and an art gallery. Sadly, the arts centre's obtusely confusing layout continues to prove user-repellent; just finding the main entrance on Silk Street is quite a feat, even for Londoners.

St Giles-without-Cripplegate

Fore St • Mon–Fri 11am–4pm • Free • ☎ 020 7638 1997, ⓦ stgilescripplegate.com • ⊖ Barbican

The Barbican's solitary prewar building is the heavily restored early Tudor church of **St Giles-without-Cripplegate**, now bracketed between a pair of artificial lakes, and overlooking an impressive corner bastion of the old Roman fort. It was in this church that Oliver Cromwell was married in 1620 and John Milton buried in 1674 – he was subsequently exhumed in 1793, his teeth knocked out as souvenirs and his corpse exhibited to the public until the novelty wore off.

Museum of London

150 London Wall • Daily 10am–6pm • Free • ☎ 020 7001 9844, ⓦ museumoflondon.org.uk • ⊖ Barbican or St Paul's

Hidden in the southwestern corner of the Barbican complex is the **Museum of London,** whose permanent galleries are basically an educational trot through London's past from prehistory to the present day, illustrated by the city's major archeological finds and some great scale models. The real strength of the museum, however, lies in the excellent temporary exhibitions, gallery tours, lectures, walks and videos it organizes throughout the year.

London until 1666

The permanent displays start on floor E (where visitors enter), with a section on **London Before London**. Here, you'll find a cave-bear skull from half a million years ago, Neolithic flint tools, not to mention a lion skull, a hippo's tooth, an auroch's skull and an elephant's foot. The **Roman London** section includes the Bucklersbury mosaic floor, displayed in a mock-up of a wealthy Roman dining room, gold coins, marble busts from the Temple of Mithras (see p.174), and mock-up Roman shop displays. Highlights in the **Medieval London** section include a reconstructed Saxon home, a model of Old St Paul's and a wonderfully over-the-top video on the Black Death. Look out, too, for the Cheapside Hoard, found by workmen in 1912, and containing the finest collection of 400 Elizabethan and Jacobean jewels in the world.

Modern London

The museum's new, hi-tech, post-1666 **Modern London** galleries are all on the ground floor (L2), and include revealing sections on how slavery helped increase the city's wealth, the history of the suffragette movement and the political struggles of the 1930s.

POSTMAN'S PARK

Opposite the former General Post Office building, southeast of Smithfield, lies **Postman's Park**, one of the most curious and little-visited corners of the City. Here, in 1900, in the churchyard of St Botolph, Aldersgate, the painter and sculptor George Frederick Watts paid for a national memorial to "heroes of everyday life", a patchwork wall of majolica tiles protected by a canopy and inscribed with the names of ordinary folk who had died in the course of some act of bravery. It exhibits the classic Victorian sentimental fascination with death, and makes for macabre but compelling reading: "Drowned in attempting to save his brother after he himself had just been rescued" or "Saved a lunatic woman from suicide at Woolwich Arsenal station, but was himself run over by the train". In 2009, the first new addition for 78 years was added to the wall.

LONDON'S WALLS

London was a bona fide **walled city** from the time of the Romans until the Great Fire of 1666. For another hundred years, it still had its **seven gateways** – the last one, Temple Bar, was only removed in 1878, and now stands near St Paul's Cathedral. Several sections of wall were still being dismantled in the eighteenth and nineteenth centuries, and, if you know where to look, there are still several substantial sections of the city walls in situ today.

In 120 AD, the Romans built a grid-plan **military fort** to house around one thousand soldiers, just east of the Museum of London – the wall is visible from the museum, and one of the corner bastions (complete with section of moat) can be seen from St Giles Cripplegate in the Barbican. However, it wasn't until 200 AD that the Romans threw up a proper two-mile long curtain wall, 20ft high and 9ft thick. The walls fell into decay in Saxon times, but were repaired and restored in the medieval and Tudor periods. On **Noble Street**, just southeast of the museum, one of the most interesting sections came to light after the Blitz, showing where the new city walls joined the older wall of the military fort.

There's an official **London Wall Walk**, which starts outside Tower Hill tube, by the remains of the medieval Postern Gate, although the only other really impressive sections of wall are in nearby Cooper's Row (see p.187).

11

One of the most popular sections is the **Victorian Walk**, several streets of reconstructed period shops from a toyshop to a barbers. You can relax in a mock-up interwar cinema and watch old footage of prewar London, admire the wonderful Art Deco bronze lifts from Selfridges, or play on the interactive Charles Booth map which plotted the city's poverty in 1889.

The postwar section features snapshots from each decade: a model of the Skylon from the 1951 Festival of Britain, some groovy Swinging Sixties clothes, punk and Silver Jubilee memorabilia from 1977. There's a great section paying tribute to London's ethnic diversity and a vast model of some 1990s squats on Hackney's London Fields. Finally, you reach the space reserved for the **Lord Mayor's Coach**, which rivals the Queen's in sheer weight of gold decoration. Built in 1757, it's still used to parade the new Lord Mayor at the annual Lord Mayor's Show (see p.26).

Guildhall

Gresham St • Daily 10am–5pm; Oct–April closed Sun • Free • ☎ 020 7606 3030, ⓦ cityoflondon.gov.uk • ⊖ Bank

Despite being the seat of the City governance for over 800 years, **Guildhall** doesn't exactly exude municipal wealth. Nevertheless, it's worth popping inside the **Great Hall** which miraculously survived both the Great Fire and Blitz – you must approach from the reception on the west side of the courtyard, not the quasi-Indian porch, tacked on by George Dance the Elder in the eighteenth century, to the north. The hall is still used for functions, though only the walls survive from the original fifteenth-century building, which was the venue for several high-treason trials, including those of Lady Jane Grey and her husband, Lord Dudley, and, three years later, Archbishop Cranmer. As you leave, be sure to check out the crazy pagan giants Gog and Magog, who look down from the minstrels' gallery, and who feature every year in the Lord Mayor's Show (see p.26).

Guildhall Art Gallery

Mon–Sat 10am–5pm, Sun noon–4pm • Free • ☎ 020 7332 3700, ⓦ cityoflondon.gov.uk • ⊖ Bank

Occupying the eastern side of the Guildhall courtyard is the **Guildhall Art Gallery**. Some of the best works are the Pre-Raphaelite pictures displayed in the first gallery you enter: **Holman Hunt**'s *The Eve of St Agnes* (inspired by Keats' poem), painted while he was still a student, and bought by the gallery's first director out of his own pocket; **Rossetti**'s *La Ghirlandata*, a typically lush portrait, in intense blues and greens, of a model who's a dead ringer for Jane Morris, with whom the artist was infatuated; **Millais**' two portraits of his daughter Effie in her Sunday best – *My First Sermon*, in which she sits attentively listening, and *My Second Sermon*, when the novelty has worn off and she has dozed off.

Also hiding up here is **Constable**'s full-sized oil sketch of *Salisbury Cathedral*, characterized by loose brushwork and an air of foreboding, and a marble statue of **Margaret Thatcher**, now surrounded by a protective glass cabinet after the head was knocked off by a protester in 2002.

The Copley painting, London pictures and Victorian galleries

The layout of the entire gallery is designed around the gigantic and very dramatic painting *The Defeat of the Floating Batteries at Gibraltar, September 1782* by **John Singleton Copley**, depicting the Brits magnanimously saving the drowning enemy

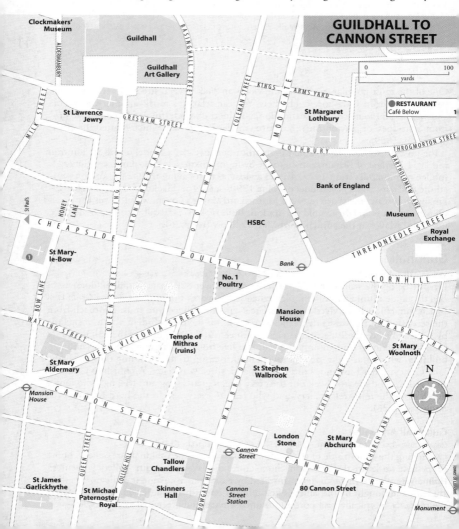

from flaming barques. Commissioned by the Corporation, poor old Copley had to redo the entire thing when the garrison officers insisted on having more prominence.

One of the gallery's strengths is its wide range of **London** pictures – depicting City ceremonies, bygone vistas of old London, postwar bomb sites and so on – which you'll find sprinkled throughout the collection. On the ground floor, you'll also find a small sample of works by the English artist **Matthew Smith** (1879–1959), who was heavily influenced by Cézanne's late works and Matisse's Fauvist phase. Confusingly, it's in the **Victorian galleries** that you'll find one of the 22 portraits, commissioned by the Corporation, of the Fire Judges who assessed property claims in the wake of the Great Fire.

Roman amphitheatre

During the gallery's construction in the 1990s, a **Roman amphitheatre**, dating from around 120 AD, was discovered in the Guildhall courtyard. The foundations of the eastern entrance are all that remain, displayed in the basement, but they give you a hint of the vast size of the original arena, which would have held up to six thousand. (The outline of the amphitheatre is marked out on the pavement in the courtyard.)

11

Clockmakers' Museum

Aldermanbury • Mon–Sat 9.30am–4.45pm • Free • ☏ 020 7332 1868, ⓦ clockmakers.org • ⊖ Bank

Access to the **Clockmakers' Museum**, run by the Worshipful Company of Clockmakers, is from Aldermanbury, on the west side of Guildhall. Here, you'll find everything from Tudor pocket watches to grandfather clocks, which ring out in unison on the hour. Highlights include an orrery clock, a rolling ball clock (of the kind invented by William Congreve), a water clock, the ghoulish skull watch, once believed to have been given by Mary Queen of Scots to her maid-of-honour, and the watch used by Edmund Hillary on Everest. Of particular interest is the collection of marine chronometers including the earliest known clock made by **John Harrison** (1693–1776), along with his brother, when he was only 20. Pride of place, though, goes to H5, which looks like an oversized pocket watch, was tested by George III himself at Richmond observatory, and won Harrison the Longitude Prize (see p.320).

St Lawrence Jewry

Mon–Fri 8am–4pm • Recitals Mon & Tues 1pm • ☏ 020 7600 9478, ⓦ stlawrencejewry.org.uk • ⊖ Bank

Across the courtyard from the Guildhall stands Wren's church of **St Lawrence Jewry**, whose smart interior reflects its role as the official City of London Corporation church. Opened in 1677 in the presence of Charles II, but gutted during the Blitz, the church's handsome, wide, open-plan interior is well worth a peek for its richly gilded plasterwork ceiling. The church's gilded gridiron weathervane recalls St Lawrence's martyrdom – he was slow-roasted, but still managed to crack jokes, hence why he's the patron saint of comedians. The name "Jewry" recalls the site of London's **Jewish ghetto**. Old Jewry, the street two blocks east, was the nucleus of the community, who suffered a bloody expulsion on the orders of Edward I.

Bank and around

Bank lies at the heart of the City's financial district and is the busy meeting point of eight streets. It's an impressive architectural ensemble, overlooked by a handsome collection of Neoclassical buildings – among them the Bank of England, the Royal Exchange and Mansion House – each one faced in Portland stone.

Royal Exchange

Mon–Fri: **shops** 10am–6pm; **cafés, bars and restaurants** 8am–11pm • ⓦ theroyalexchange.com • ⊖ Bank

By far the most graceful of Bank's buildings is the **Royal Exchange**, first built in 1570 at the personal expense of the fabulously wealthy businessman, Thomas Gresham (his gilded

11

THE CITY LIVERY COMPANIES

The hundred or so **City Livery Companies** in the Square Mile are descended from the craft guilds of the Middle Ages, whose purpose was to administer apprenticeships and take charge of quality control, in return for which they were granted monopolies. Over time, the guilds grew prodigiously wealthy, built themselves ever more opulent halls and staged lavish banquets at which they would wear elaborate "livery" (or uniforms). Many – though not all – of the old guilds now have very little to do with their original trade, though this is not the case with the guilds that have been formed in the last hundred years. It's fair to say the livery companies remain deeply undemocratic and anomalous, but their prodigious wealth and charitable works have helped pacify the critics. As with the Freemasons, the elaborate ceremonies serve to hide the very real power that these companies still hold. Liverymen dominate the Court of Common Council, the City's ruling body, and as Aldermen, they take it in turns to be first a Sheriff, and eventually Lord Mayor – a knighthood is virtually guaranteed.

The City boasts numerous Livery Company halls, many with enticing names such as the Tallow Chandlers and Cordwainers. Few survived the Great Fire, fewer still the Blitz, but a handful are worth visiting for their ornate interiors. The problem is gaining **admission**. The City tourist office (☎ 020 7332 1456) has tickets to some halls; other halls will allow you to join a pre-booked group tour for around £5–10 per person. It's not something you can do on the spur of the moment, though some livery halls are used during the City of London Festival and others are open on Open House weekend (see p.26). Below is a selection of the most interesting Livery halls:

Apothecaries' Hall Blackfriars Lane ☎ 020 7236 1189, ⓦ apothecaries.org; ⊖ Blackfriars. The seventeenth-century courtyard is open to the public, but entry to the magnificent staircase and the Great Hall – with its musicians' gallery, portrait by Reynolds and collection of leech pots – is by appointment only.

Fishmongers' Hall London Bridge ☎ 020 7626 3531, ⓦ fishhall.org.uk; ⊖ Monument. A prominent Greek Revival building on the riverfront, with a grand staircase hall, and the very dagger with which Mayor Walworth stabbed Wat Tyler (see p.448).

Goldsmiths' Hall Foster Lane ☎ 020 7606 7010, ⓦ thegoldsmiths.co.uk; ⊖ St Paul's. One of the easiest to visit as there are regular exhibitions allowing you to see the sumptuous central staircase built in the 1830s.

Skinners' Hall 8 Dowgate Hill ☎ 020 7236 5629, ⓦ skinnershall.co.uk; ⊖ Cannon Street. The seventeenth-century staircase and courtroom survive, while the wood-panelled hall contains a wonderful series of Frank Brangwyn murals from 1902.

Tallow Chandlers' Hall 4 Dowgate Hill ☎ 020 7248 4726, ⓦ tallowchandlers.org; ⊖ Cannon Street. Set back from the street around an attractive courtyard, the Candlemakers' Company retains its seventeenth-century courtroom, complete with original seating.

Vintners' Hall 68 Upper Thames St ☎ 020 7236 1863, ⓦ vintnershall.co.uk; ⊖ Mansion House. The oldest hall in the City, dating from 1671, with a period-piece staircase with "fabulously elaborate balusters".

grasshopper flies from the roof), as a meeting place for City merchants. The current building, fronted by a massive eight-column portico and a very convenient set of steps for lunching office workers, is the third on the site and was built in the 1840s. Nowadays, the building is filled with expense account shops, but it's still worth exploring the inner courtyard, with its beautifully tiled floor, glazed roof and half-columns in three classical orders. The swish *Grand Café* occupies both the courtyard and the mezzanine floor, from which you can view a series of frescoes illustrating the history of the City.

Mansion House

Guided tours Tues 2pm; closed Aug • £6 • ☎ 020 7937 9307, ⓦ cityoflondon.gov.uk • ⊖ Bank

Mansion House, the Lord Mayor's sumptuous Neoclassical lodgings during his or – on the odd, rare occasion – her term of office, is open to the public once a week. Designed in 1753 by George Dance the Elder, the building's grandest room is the columned **Egyptian Hall**, with its high, barrel-vaulted, coffered ceiling. Also impressive is the vast collection of gold and silver tableware, the mayor's 36-pound gold mace and the pearl sword given by Elizabeth I and held out to the sovereign on visits to the City. Scattered about the rooms are an impressive array of Dutch and Flemish paintings by the likes of

Hals, Ruisdael, Cuyp, Hobbema and de Hooch. Places are allocated on a first-come, first-served basis, so turn up at the Walbrook entrance in good time.

Bank of England

Threadneedle St • Mon–Fri 10am–5pm • Free • ☎ 020 7601 5545, ⓦ bankofengland.co.uk • ⊖ Bank

Established by William III in 1694 to raise funds for his costly war against France, the **Bank of England** – the so-called "Grand Old Lady of Threadneedle Street" – wasn't erected on its present site until 1734. The bank was attacked during the 1780 Gordon Riots, but never sacked thanks to the bank's clerks, who melted down their inkwells into bullets. Subsequently a detachment of the Foot Guards, known as the Bank Picquet, was stationed outside until 1973. Security remains pretty tight at the bank, which still acts as a giant safe-deposit box, storing the official gold reserves of many of the world's central banks (though Britain's own were moved to the Federal Reserve Bank of New York during World War II).

The windowless, outer curtain wall, which wraps itself round the 3.5-acre island site, is pretty much all that remains of John Soane's late eighteenth-century design. However, you can view a reconstruction of Soane's Bank Stock Office, with its characteristic domed skylight, in the **museum,** whose entrance is on Bartholomew Lane. The exhibition traces the history of the bank, banknotes and banking in general. Beyond, beneath a reconstruction of Herbert Baker's interwar rotunda (wrecked in the Blitz), you can caress a 13kg gold bar, worth over £250,000, and, elsewhere, view specimens of every note issued by the Royal Mint over the centuries (including a million pound note).

11

St Mary Woolnoth

King William St • Mon–Fri 9.30am–4.30pm • Free • ⊖ Bank

Hidden from the bustle of Bank itself, a short distance down King William Street, stands **St Mary Woolnoth,** one of Nicholas Hawksmoor's six idiosyncratic London churches. The main facade is very imposing, with its twin turrets, Doric pillars and heavy rustication. Inside, in a cramped but lofty space, Hawksmoor manages to cram in a cluster of three big Corinthian columns at each corner, which support an ingenious lantern lit by semicircular clerestory windows. The most striking furnishing is the altar canopy, held up by barley-sugar columns and studded with seven golden cherubic faces. The church's projecting clock gets a brief mention in T.S. Eliot's *The Waste Land*.

St Stephen Walbrook

39 Walbrook.• Mon–Fri 10am–4pm • Free • ⓦ ststephenwalbrook.net • ⊖ Bank

Named after the shallow stream which provided Roman London with its fresh water, the church of **St Stephen Walbrook** is the Lord Mayor's official church and Wren's most spectacular after St Paul's. Faced with a fairly cramped site, Wren created a church of

---

FROM COFFEE HOUSE TO BOARDROOM

Several of the City's most important institutions have their origins in the **coffee houses** which sprung up in the second half of the seventeenth century. The first coffee house in London was established in St Michael's Alley, off Cornhill, in 1652 by **Pasqua Rosée**, the Armenian servant of a merchant who traded in Turkey. It was an instant success and in less than a century, there were literally hundreds of rival establishments, as the coffee house became the place the City's wheelers and dealers preferred to conduct their business. **Richard Lloyd's** coffee house – perhaps the best known – was where London's sailors, merchants and ship owners went for the latest maritime news, eventually evolving into Lloyd's Register of Shipping and Lloyd's of London insurance market. Meanwhile, **Jonathan's**, in Exchange Alley, posted up the price of stocks and commodities, attracting dealers who'd been ejected from the nearby Royal Exchange for rowdiness, and eventually became the London Stock Exchange.

LONDON STONE

Bank may have a good claim to being the heart of the City, or perhaps Guildhall as the administrative core, but London's real omphalos, its geomantic centre, is the **London Stone**, a small block of limestone lodged behind an iron grille set low into the exterior wall of 111 Cannon St, at the corner of St Swithin's Lane. Whatever your reaction to this bizarre relic, it has been around for some considerable time, certainly since the 1450 Peasants' Revolt, when the Kentish rebel Jack Cade struck it, declaring himself "Lord of the City".

---

great space and light, with sixteen Corinthian columns arranged in clusters around a central coffered dome, which many regard as a practice run for his cathedral. The furnishings are mostly original, but the modern beech-wood pews jar, as does Henry Moore's altar, an amorphous blob of Travertine stone – nicknamed "The Camembert". The Samaritans were founded here by the local rector in 1953, and their first helpline telephone serves as a memorial in the church's southwest corner.

11

St Mary Abchurch
Abchurch Lane, off King William St • Mon–Fri 11am–3pm • ⊖ Cannon Street

St Mary Abchurch is set in its own courtyard (the paved-over former graveyard), but nothing about the dour red-brick exterior prepares you for Wren's spectacular interior, which is dominated by a vast dome fresco painted by a local parishioner and lit by oval lunettes, with the name of God in Hebrew centre stage. The lime-wood reredos, festooned with swags and garlands, and decorated with gilded urns and a pelican, is a Grinling Gibbons masterpiece.

Temple of Mithras
The remains of a **Temple of Mithras** were discovered beside the old stream of the Walbrook in 1954 during the construction of an office block on Queen Victoria Street. Mithraism was a male-only cult popular among the Roman legions before the advent of Christianity. Its Persian deity, Mithras, is always depicted slaying a cosmic bull, while a scorpion grasps its genitals and a dog licks its wounds – the bull's blood was seen as life-giving, and initiates had to bathe in it. The foundations of the third-century temple give little impression of what the building would have been like – the reconstruction in the Museum of London offers a better idea.

Bishopsgate to the Tower
Financial institutions predominate in the easterly section of the Square Mile, many of them housed in the brashest of the City's new architecture. **Bishopsgate**, named after one of the seven gates in the old City walls, is dominated by bombastic skyscrapers such as the angular, glass-clad Broadgate Tower, at the northern end, Heron Tower, halfway along, and the Pinnacle – the City's tallest skyscraper so far, at the southern end. The area's two most obvious landmarks are both temples of Mammon: the groundbreaking **Lloyd's Building** and the unmissable **Gherkin**. These, plus the Victorian splendour of **Leadenhall Market**, the oldest **synagogue** in the country, several pre-Fire churches and Wren's famous **Monument** to the Great Fire make for an especially interesting sector of the City to explore.

Liverpool Street Station
Built in 1874 **Liverpool Street Station** stands on the site of the old Bethlem Royal Hospital (or Bedlam), the infamous lunatic asylum, where the public could pay a penny and laugh at the inmates. Liverpool Street is now the City's busiest terminal, renowned for its vibrantly painted wrought-iron Victorian arches. The station's Liverpool Street entrance features the **Kindertransport memorial**, erected in 2003 and

depicting some of the Jewish children who arrived at the station from Nazi Germany, without their parents, shortly before war broke out.

Adjoining Liverpool Street Station, to the west, are the traffic-free piazzas of the 1980s **Broadgate** complex. *Fulcrum*, Richard Serra's 55ft-high rusting steel sheets, acts as a kind of gateway to the **Broadgate Circle**, whose arena is used as an open-air ice rink in winter and as a performance space in summer. Continuing north to **Exchange Square**, you'll find a cascading waterfall, the hefty *Broadgate Venus* by Fernando Botero, and Xavier Corbero's *Broad Family* of obelisks, one of whose "children" reveals a shoe.

Bishopsgate Institute

230 Bishopsgate • Mon–Sat 10am–5.30pm, Wed until 8pm • Free • ☎ 020 7392 9200, Ⓦ bishopsgate.org.uk • ⊖ Liverpool Street

Across the road from Liverpool Street Station is the faïence facade of the diminutive **Bishopsgate Institute**, a graceful Art Nouveau building designed by Harrison Townsend. Townsend went on to design the excellent Whitechapel Art Gallery (see p.198) and the wonderful Horniman Museum (see p.313). Opened in 1895, the institute houses a public library and puts on courses and talks throughout the year.

11

St Ethelburga's

78 Bishopsgate • Fri 11am–3pm • Free • ☎ 020 7496 1610, Ⓦ stethelburgas.org • ⊖ Liverpool Street

Hemmed in by office blocks on either side is the "humble rag-faced front" of the pre-Fire church of **St Ethelburga**. All but totally destroyed by an IRA bomb in 1993, the church was totally rebuilt and now houses a Centre for Reconciliation and Peace, hosting regular inter-faith events and workshops, and hosting world music gigs on a Friday. The bare interior retains the nineteenth-century font inscribed with the Greek palindrome "Cleanse my sins, not just my face" and half the tiny garden round the back, houses a polygonal, multi-faith Bedouin tent covered in woven goat's hair.

St Helen's

Bishopsgate • Mon–Fri 9.30am–5pm • Free • ☎ 020 7283 2231, Ⓦ st-helens.org.uk • ⊖ Liverpool Street, Bank, Monument or Aldgate

Another pre-Fire church that suffered extensive damage in the IRA blasts of the 1990s is the late Gothic church of **St Helen**, set back to the east of Bishopsgate. With its undulating crenellations and Baroque bell turret, it's an intriguing building, incorporating the original pre-Reformation Benedictine nunnery church and containing five grand pre-Fire tombs. Since the bomb, the floor level has been raised, the church screens shifted, a new organ gallery added and the seating rearranged to focus on the pulpit, in keeping with the church's current evangelical bent.

The Gherkin

30 St Mary Axe • ⊖ Liverpool Street or Aldgate

The most famous of the new rash of tall buildings to puncture the City skyline is Norman Foster's iconic, glass-diamond-clad **Gherkin**, officially known as 30 St Mary Axe. It sits on the site of the old Baltic Exchange, destroyed in an IRA bomb in 1992 that killed three people, commemorated on a nearby wall. At 590ft, it's very tall, but most Londoners like it for its cheeky shape, and at street level it's a very modest building. You can't go up it, but you can grab a bite to eat on the ground floor.

Lloyd's Building

1 Lime St • Guided tours by appointment only; £10 • ☎ 020 7327 6586, Ⓦ lloyds.com • ⊖ Bank or Monument

Completed by Richard Rogers in 1986, the **Lloyd's Building**, opposite St Andrew Undershaft, remains probably the City's most innovative and remarkable office block. "A living, breathing machine", it's a vertical version of Rogers' Parisian Pompidou Centre, in which the jumble of blue-steel pipes and cables form the outer casing, with glass lifts zipping up and down the exterior. The portico of the previous, much more sedate, Lloyds' Building (c.1925) has been preserved on Leadenhall Street, so the current

CITY SKYSCRAPERS

The economic recession notwithstanding, the City skyline is sprouting a whole new generation of **skyscrapers**. From 1980, for thirty years, the City's tallest building was 600ft-high Tower 42, designed as the **NatWest Tower** by Richard Seifert (in the shape of the bank's logo). In 2010, this was topped by the **Heron Tower**, a fairly undistinguished 660ft skyscraper with a 144ft mast at 110 Bishopsgate, designed by Kohn Pedersen Fox – on the plus side, public access means you can check out the shark aquarium in the atrium, and pop into the bar-restaurant on the 40th floor. More hope to follow: Rafael Viñoly's 525ft **Walkie Talkie**, 20 Fenchurch St, so-called because it will get wider as it gets bigger, will include a public "sky garden" on the roof; **The Pinnacle**, 22–24 Bishopsgate, also by Kohn Pedersen Fox, will be a swirling 945ft helter-skelter of a tower (with a restaurant on the top floor); and **The Cheesegrater**, Richard Rogers' 737ft triangular-shaped office block at 122 Leadenhall St, is due for completion in 2013. With the Pinnacle, The City will have outreached Canary Wharf, but it will still be ousted for the prize of the country's tallest building by Renzo Piano's 1017ft **Shard**, near London Bridge (see p.232).

11

headquarters represented a bizarre leap into the modern by this most conservative of City institutions – the largest insurance and reinsurance market in the world. Some things never change, though, and the building is still guarded by porters in antiquated waiters' livery, in recognition of Lloyd's origins as Edward Lloyd's coffee house in 1688.

Lloyd's started out in shipping, but the famous **Lutine Bell**, salvaged from a captured French frigate in 1799 and traditionally struck once for bad news, twice for good, now only tolls once to commemorate more general disasters, twice for distinguished guests. The highlights of the interior are the **Underwriting Room**, centred on the aforementioned Lutine Bell, above which an incredible barrel-vaulted glass atrium rises almost 200ft, and the **Adam Room**, a dining room designed by Robert Adam in 1763 for Bowood House, Wiltshire, and now incongruously positioned on the eleventh floor. Dress code for visitors is jacket and tie for men and business-style for women.

Leadenhall Market

Gracechurch St • Market: Mon–Fri 11am–4pm • ⓦ leadenhallmarket.co.uk • ⊖ Bank or Monument

Occupying the very site where Roman London's basilica and forum once stood, **Leadenhall Market**'s graceful Victorian cast-ironwork is richly painted in cream and maroon, with each of the four entrances to the covered arcade topped by an elaborate stone arch. Inside, the traders cater mostly for the lunchtime City crowd, their barrows laden with exotic seafood and game, fine wines, champagne and caviar, while the surrounding shops and bars remain busy until the early evening.

Bevis Marks Synagogue

4 Heneage Lane • Mon, Wed & Thurs 10.30am–2pm, Tues & Fri 10.30am–1pm, Sun 10.30am–12.30pm • £4 • Guided tours Wed & Fri noon, Sun 11am; free • ⓣ 020 7626 1274, ⓦ bevismarks.org.uk • ⊖ Aldgate

Hidden away behind a red-brick office block in a little courtyard off Bevis Marks is the Bevis Marks Synagogue. Built in 1701 by Sephardic Jews who had fled the Inquisition in Spain and Portugal, this is the country's oldest surviving synagogue, and its roomy, rich interior gives an idea of just how wealthy the community was at the time. Although it seats over 600, it's only a third of the size of its prototype in Amsterdam, where many Sephardic Jews initially settled. The Sephardic community has since moved out to Maida Vale and Wembley, and the congregation has dwindled, though the synagogue's magnificent array of chandeliers makes it very popular for candle-lit Jewish weddings. Close by Bevis Marks, just past Creechurch Lane, a plaque commemorates the even larger **Great Synagogue** of the Ashkenazi Jews, founded in 1690 but destroyed by bombs in 1941.

St Katharine Cree

86 Leadenhall St • Mon–Fri 10.30am–4pm • Free • ⊖ Aldgate

The church of **St Katharine Cree**, completed in 1631, is a rare example of its period, having miraculously escaped the Great Fire of 1666. It's a transitional building with Neoclassical elements, such as the Corinthian columns of the nave and, above, a Gothic clerestory and ribbing. At the east end is a very lovely, seventeenth-century stained-glass Catherine-wheel window. The church was consecrated in 1631 by Bishop Laud, and the "bowings and cringings" he indulged in during the service, were later used as evidence of his Catholicism, at his trial and execution for heresy in 1645.

London Metal Exchange

56 Leadenhall St • Noon–1.30pm, 3.30–5pm • Free • ☎ 020 7264 5555, ⓦ lme.com • ⊖ Aldgate

The only place in the City where you can still witness the human scrum of share dealing – known as "open-outcry" – is at the **London Metal Exchange**, where metals – and even plastic – but not silver, gold or platinum are traded. The dealing takes place within the Ring, with each metal traded in five-minute bursts – to visit the public viewing gallery, you must phone ahead.

St Botolph-without-Aldgate

Aldgate High St • Tues 11am–3pm, Thurs 10am–3pm • Free • ⓦ stbotolphs.org.uk • ⊖ Aldgate

Built beside Aldgate, one of the old City gateways, and now surrounded by swirling traffic, **St Botolph-without-Aldgate** was designed in the 1740s by George Dance the Elder. Its bizarre interior, remodelled last century, features blue-grey paintwork, gilding on top of white plasterwork, some dodgy modern art, a batik reredos and a stunning, modern stained-glass rendition of Rubens' *Descent from the Cross* on a deep-purple background. Situated at the edge of the East End, this is a famously campaigning church, active on issues like gay priests and social exclusion.

Monument

Daily 9.30am–5.30pm • £3 • ☎ 020 7626 2717, ⓦ themonument.info • ⊖ Monument

In the 1670s, Wren's **Monument** commemorating the Great Fire of 1666 (see p.466) used to rise above the rooftops. No longer so prominent on the skyline, this plain 202-foot Doric column, crowned with spiky gilded flames, nevertheless remains the tallest isolated stone column in the world; if it were laid out flat it would touch the site of the bakery where the fire started, east of Monument. The bas-relief on the base depicts Charles II and the Duke of York in Roman garb conducting the emergency relief operation. The 311 steps to the gallery at the top – plagued by suicides until a cage was built around it in 1842 – once guaranteed an incredible view; nowadays it's dwarfed by the surrounding buildings.

St Magnus-the-Martyr

Lower Thames St • Tues–Fri 10am–4pm, Sun 10am–1pm • ☎ 020 7626 4481, ⓦ stmagnusmartyr.org.uk • ⊖ Monument

Not far from the Monument is another Wren edifice, the church of **St Magnus-the-Martyr**, whose octagonal spire used to greet all travellers arriving in the City across old London Bridge. Now it stands forlorn by busy Lower Thames Street, though the Anglo-Catholic interior holds, in T.S. Eliot's words, "an inexplicable splendour of Ionian white and gold". In addition, there's a wooden pier from an old Roman wharf in the porch, and a great model of the old London Bridge in the vestry.

Old Billingsgate Market

16 Lower Thames St • ☎ 020 7283 2800, ⓦ oldbillingsgate.co.uk • ⊖ Monument

Along the river from St Magnus is **Old Billingsgate Market**, a handsome Victorian market hall that once housed London's chief wholesale fish market, but has since been turned into a corporate events venue. It's difficult to imagine the noise and smell of old

LONDON BRIDGE

Unreal City
Under the brown fog of a winter dawn,
A crowd flowed over London Bridge, so many,
I had not thought death had undone so many.

The Waste Land, T.S. Eliot

At rush hour, you can still see Eliot's "undead" trudging to work across **London Bridge**, which was, until 1750, the only bridge across the Thames. The Romans were the first to build a permanent crossing here, a structure succeeded by a Saxon version that was pulled down by King Olaf of Norway in 1014, and commemorated in the popular nursery rhyme *London Bridge is Falling Down*. It was the medieval bridge, however, that achieved world fame: built of stone and crowded with timber-framed houses, it became one of London's greatest attractions. At the centre stood the richly ornate **Nonsuch House**, decorated with onion domes and Dutch gables, and a chapel dedicated to Thomas Becket; at the Southwark end was the Great Gatehouse, on which the heads of traitors were displayed, dipped in tar to preserve them. The houses were removed in the mid-eighteenth century, and a new stone bridge erected in 1831 – that one now stands in **Lake Havasu City**, in the Arizona desert, having been bought in the 1960s by a guy who, so the story goes, thought he'd purchased Tower Bridge. The present concrete structure – without doubt the ugliest yet – dates from 1972.

11

Billingsgate, whose porters used to carry the fish in towers of baskets on their heads, and whose wives were renowned for their bad language even in Shakespeare's day: "as bad a tongue…as any oyster-wife at Billingsgate" (*King Lear*). Next door stands the Neoclassical **Custom House**, from 1825, which has been collecting duties from incoming ships since around 1275.

St Olave

8 Hart St • Mon–Fri 10am–5pm • Free • ☎ 020 7488 4318, Ⓦ sanctuaryinthecity.net • ⊖ Tower Hill

Saved from the Fire, but left as an empty shell by the Blitz, the ragstone Gothic church of **St Olave**, was dubbed "St Ghastly Grim" by Dickens after the skulls and crossbones and vicious-looking spikes adorning the 1658 entrance to the graveyard on Seething Lane, a short stroll from St Dunstan's. Samuel Pepys lived in Seething Lane for much of his life, and he and his wife, Elizabeth, are both buried here amid the pre-Fire brasses and monuments – Elizabeth's monument was raised by Pepys himself; Pepys' own is Victorian.

All Hallows-by-the-Tower

Byward St • Mon–Fri 8am–6pm, Sat & Sun 10am–5pm • Brassrubbing Mon–Fri 2–4pm; £5 per brass • ☎ 020 7481 2928, Ⓦ ahbtt.org.uk • ⊖ Tower Hill

All Hallows-by-the-Tower, another pre-Fire church, only just survived the Blitz – most of the church is a postwar neo-Gothic pastiche wrought in concrete. The furnishings are fascinating, however, and include lots of maritime memorials, model ships, two wings of a Flemish triptych from around 1500, and, best of all, the exquisitely carved Gibbons limewood font cover, in the southwest chapel. Close by is an arch from the original seventh-century church; remains of a tessellated Roman pavement can also be found in the tiny Crypt Museum. All Hallows also has some superb pre-Reformation brasses, and offers brassrubbing.

Tower of London and around

Tower Hill is choked with tourists who flock here to see one of London's most famous landmarks, Tower Bridge and the adjacent Tower of London. Despite all the attendant hype and heritage claptrap, the Tower remains one of London's most remarkable buildings, site of some of the goriest events in the nation's history, and somewhere all visitors and Londoners should explore at least once. Sitting beside the river, at the eastern edge of the old city walls, the Tower is chiefly famous as a place of imprisonment and death, yet it's also been used as a royal residence, armoury, mint, menagerie, observatory and – a function it still serves – a safe-deposit box for the Crown Jewels. And, finally, it's easy to forget that the Tower is, above all, the most perfectly preserved (and restored) medieval fortress in the country.

Begun as a simple watchtower, built by **William the Conqueror** to keep an eye on the City, the Tower had evolved into a palace-fortress by 1100. The inner curtain wall and towers were built under Henry III, while the outer fortifications, and an even wider moat, were added by Edward I, on his return from the Crusades, which means that most of what's visible today was already in place by 1307, the year of Edward's death. The Tower has been besieged on a number of occasions – firstly, in 1191, when the unpopular Bishop Longchamp held out against Richard I's brother, John, after only three days – but sacked only once, during the 1381 Peasants' Revolt, when the Archbishop of Canterbury, among others, was dragged out and lynched.

The Tower's **first prisoner**, the Bishop of Durham, arrived in 1101, imprisoned by Henry I, and promptly escaped from the window of his cell by a rope, having got the guards drunk. Gruffydd ap Llywelyn Fawr, heir to the Welsh throne, attempted a similar feat from the White Tower in 1244, with less success: "his head and neck were crushed between his shoulders…a most horrid spectacle." – the window he used was subsequently bricked up and can still be seen on the south side of the Tower. Incidentally, the **most famous escapee** from the Tower was the Jacobite 5th Earl of Nithsdale, who, the night before his execution in 1716, managed to get past the guards dressed as his wife's maid (despite his red beard), and lived in poverty and happiness for almost thirty years in exile in Rome.

Following the Restoration in 1660, the general public were admitted to the tower for the first time to view the **coronation regalia** and the impressive displays of arms and armour – by the end of Victoria's reign, there were half a million visitors to the fortress each year. Nevertheless, during both of the world wars, the Tower was still used to hold prisoners: **Roger Casement**, the Irish nationalist, was held here briefly before his trial and hanging in 1916, and the last VIP inmate was **Rudolf Hess**, Hitler's deputy, who flew secretly into Britain to try to sue for peace in May 1941 and was held in the tower for a few days. The **last execution** took place on August 14, 1941, when Josef Jakobs, a German spy who (like Hess) had broken his ankle while parachuting into Britain, was given the privilege of being seated before the firing squad.

12

INFORMATION AND TOURS

Opening hours March–Oct Mon & Sun 10am–5.30pm, Tues–Sat 9am–5.30pm; Nov–Feb closes 4.30pm.
Admission £18. To avoid queuing (and save some money), buy your ticket online.
Contact Details ☎ 020 3166 6000, ⊕ hrp.org.uk.
Tube Tower Hill.
Eating There's a spacious and fairly decent café in the New Armouries building, and plenty of benches on which to

picnic. Alternatively, you can obtain a re-entry pass and have lunch outside the Tower.
Tours You can explore the Tower complex independently, or with an audioguide (£4), but it's a good idea to get your bearings by joining up with one of the free, entertaining hour-long guided tours, given at regular intervals by one of the Tower's Beefeaters – it's also the easiest way to visit the Chapel of St Peter-ad-Vincula.

BEEFEATERS

Formed in 1485 by Henry VII as a personal bodyguard, The Tower's Beefeaters are officially known as **Yeoman Warders** – the nickname "Beefeaters" was coined in the seventeenth century, when it was a term of abuse for a well-fed domestic servant. These self-assured, eminently photogenic guards are best known for their scarlet-and-gold Tudor costumes, but unless it's a special occasion you're more likely to see them in dark-blue Victorian "undress". The Beefeaters have all done at least 22 years' military service, and are aged between 40 and 55 on appointment. The first-ever woman Beefeater was appointed in 2007; two years on, two of her male colleagues were dismissed for harassing her. All the Beefeaters live in the Tower and one of their many duties is to give theatrically irreverent guided tours to the tourists, which many of them clearly relish.

Bell Tower

Visitors enter the Tower by the Middle Tower and the Byward Tower, in the southwest corner. Two of the first victims of the Reformation – Thomas More and John Fisher – were incarcerated nearby in the **Bell Tower**, from whose dinky wooden belfry a bell still signals the curfew hour (and used to toll to signal an execution). More was initially allowed writing materials, but later they were withdrawn; Fisher was kept in worse conditions ("I decay forthwith, and fall into coughs and diseases of my body, and cannot keep myself in health") and was so weak that he had to be carried to the scaffold on Tower Hill. The 20-year-old future Queen Elizabeth I arrived here in 1554, while her half-sister Queen Mary tried to find incriminating evidence against her. Catholic Mass was performed daily in Elizabeth's cell for the two months of her imprisonment, but she refused to be converted.

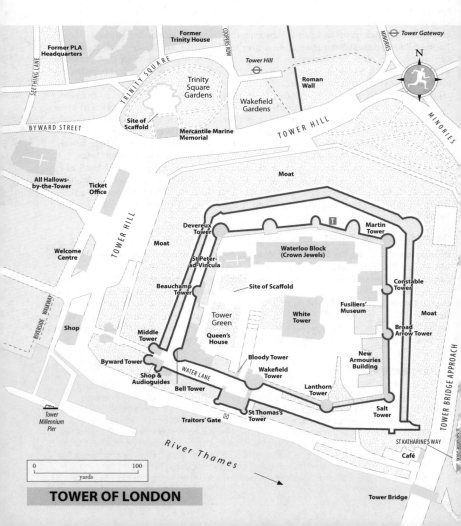

TOWER OF LONDON

Traitors' Gate

Most prisoners were delivered through **Traitors' Gate**, on the waterfront, which forms part of **St Thomas's Tower**, now partially reconstructed to re-create the atmosphere of Edward I's **medieval palace**. The King's Bedchamber has a beautiful little oratory in one of the turrets, while in the larger oratory of the Throne Room, in 1471, the "saintly but slightly daft" Henry VI was murdered at prayer, possibly on the orders of Edward IV or Richard III. Not long afterwards, Edward had his brother, the Duke of Clarence, executed in the Tower for high treason, drowned in a butt of malmsey wine (at his own request – according to Shakespeare).

Bloody Tower

The main entrance to the Inner Ward is beneath a 3.5-ton, 700-year-old portcullis, which forms part of the **Bloody Tower**, so called because it was here that the 12-year-old Edward V and his 10-year-old brother, Richard, were accommodated "for their own safety" in 1483 by their uncle, Richard of Gloucester (later Richard III), following the death of their father, Edward IV. Of all the Tower's many inhabitants, few have so captured the public imagination as the **Princes in the Tower**. According to Thomas More, they were smothered in their beds, and buried naked at the foot of the White Tower. In 1674, workmen discovered the skeletons of two young children close to the Tower; they were subsequently buried in Innocents' Corner in **Westminster Abbey**.

The study of **Walter Raleigh** (see box below) is re-created on the first floor, while his sleeping quarters upstairs, built to accommodate his wife, children and three servants, now house an exhibition on the Princes in the Tower and on the poisoning of the poet **Thomas Overbury**. Confined to the Bloody Tower in 1613 by James I, Overbury was slowly poisoned to death with arsenic concealed within the tarts and jellies sent by the wife of one of the king's favourites, Robert Carr, the Earl of Somerset. Two years later, Carr and his wife were themselves arrested, tried and condemned to death – in the end, they were simply incarcerated in the Tower for five years before being pardoned. The Lieutenant of the Tower was less fortunate, and was hanged for failing to protect his prisoners.

12

White Tower

William the Conqueror's central hall-keep, known as the **White Tower**, is the original "Tower", begun in 1076. Whitewashed (hence its name) in the reign of Henry III, it now

---

WALTER RALEIGH

The Bloody Tower's most illustrious inmate – even more famous in his time than the princes – was **Walter Raleigh** (1554–1618), who spent three separate periods in the Tower. His first misdemeanor was 1591 when he impregnated and secretly married Elizabeth Throckmorton, one of Elizabeth I's ladies-in-waiting, without the Queen's permission. A year later his crime was discovered and he was sent to the Tower (with his wife Bess); his second spell began in 1603, when he was found guilty of plotting against James I. He spent nearly thirteen years here, with his wife and kids, growing and smoking tobacco (his most famous import), composing poetry, concocting potions in his distillery and writing *The Historie of the World*, which outsold even Shakespeare, despite being banned by James I for being "too saucy in censuring princes". When Raleigh complained that the noise of the portcullis kept him awake at night, he was moved to much worse accommodation. In 1616 he was released and sent off to Guyana to discover gold, on condition that he didn't attack the Spanish; he broke his word and was sent straight back to the Tower on his return in 1618. For six weeks he was imprisoned in "one of the most cold and direful dungeons", before being beheaded at Westminster.

sports a Kentish ragstone exterior thanks to Wren, who added the large windows. Of the tower's four turrets, topped by stylish Tudor cupolas, only three are square: the fourth is rounded in order to encase the main spiral staircase, and for a short while was used by Charles II's royal astronomer, Flamsteed, before he moved to Greenwich. The main entrance to the Tower is the original one, high up in the south wall, out of reach of the enemy, and accessed by a wooden staircase which could be removed during times of siege.

Royal Armouries

The four floors of arms and armour displayed within the tower represent a mere smidgen of the **Royal Armouries** (the majority of which resides in Leeds), originally established by Henry VIII in Greenwich and on display here since the time of Charles II. If you're really keen on arms and armour, sign up for one of the regular free guided tours. Among the most striking armour displayed on the ground floor is the colossal garniture of 1540 made for Henry VIII (and famous for its protruding codpiece), juxtaposed with boy king Edward VI's tiny suit of armour. The collection takes a lurch into the present day with a polo helmet and knee pads belonging to Prince Charles.

The **Line of Kings**, on the first floor, is a display first recorded in 1660, originally depicting the monarchs of England on horseback. Also on show here is a suit of armour for a man six feet nine inches tall (once thought to have been John of Gaunt) and one for a boy just three feet one and a half inches high (possibly Charles I). Several exotic gifts presented to the royalty reside here, too, including the Japanese armour presented to King James I by the Shogun of Japan. On the top floor, there's an interesting exhibition on the executions that have taken place within the Tower and on Tower Hill over the years – the block and axe from the last beheading are here (see opposite).

Chapel of St John

Whatever your interests, you should pay a visit to the first-floor **Chapel of St John**, a beautiful Norman structure completed in 1080, making it the oldest intact ecclesiastical building in London. It was here that Henry VI's body was buried following his murder in 1471; that Henry VII's queen, Elizabeth of York, lay in state surrounded by 800 candles, after dying in childbirth, and that Lady Jane Grey came to pray on the night before her execution. Today, the once highly decorated blocks of

12

ROYAL MENAGERIE

The **Royal Menagerie** began in earnest in 1235 when the Holy Roman Emperor presented three "leopards" to Henry III; the keeper was initially paid sixpence a day for the sustenance of the beasts (they were, in fact, **lions**), and one penny for himself. From the 1330s, they were put on public display in the outer barbican (which became known as the Lion Tower), and joined some years later by a **polar bear** from the King of Norway (who was put on a leash and allowed to catch fish in the Thames) and an **elephant** from the King of France. James I was particularly keen on the menagerie, and used to stage regular animal fights on the green, but the practice was stopped in 1609 when one of the bears killed a child. In 1704, six lions, two leopards, three eagles, two Swedish owls "of great bigness", two "cats of the mountains" and a jackal were recorded. Visitors were advised not to "play tricks" after an orang-utan threw a cannonball at one and killed him.

The menagerie was transferred to the newly founded **London Zoo** in the 1830s, leaving the Tower with just its **ravens**, descendants of early scavengers attracted by waste from the palace kitchens. They have been protected by royal decree since the Restoration, and have their wings clipped so they can't fly away – legend says that the Tower (and therefore the kingdom) will fall if they do, though the Tower was in fact briefly raven-less during the last war after the Tower suffered heavy bombing. While the ravens may appear harmless, they are vicious, territorial creatures best given a wide berth. They live in coops in the south wall of the Inner Ward, are fed raw meat from Smithfield Market, have individual names and even have their own graveyard in the dry moat near the main entrance.

honey-coloured Caen limestone are free of all ecclesiastical excrescences, leaving the chapel's smooth curves and rounded apse perfectly unencumbered.

Tower Green

Despite appearances, the pretty little open space of **Tower Green** was the chief place of execution within the Tower for many centuries – the names of those beheaded here are recorded on an incongruous glass monument at the centre of the green. The bloody, headless corpses of the executed (from Tower Green and Tower Hill) were buried in the Tudor **Chapel of St Peter-ad-Vincula**, to the north, accessible only during the first and last hour the Tower is open, or on the Beefeaters' tours.

On the west side of the green, the **Beauchamp Tower** houses an exhibition on the Tower's prisoners on the ground floor. Beauchamp Tower itself accommodated only the wealthiest prisoners and boasts a better class of graffiti: Lord Dudley, husband of Lady Jane Grey, even commissioned a stonemason to carve the family crest on the first floor.

In the southwest corner of the green is the sixteenth-century **Queen's House** (closed to the public), distinguished by its swirling Tudor timber frames. These were the most luxurious cells in the Tower, and were used to incarcerate the likes of Catherine Howard and Anne Boleyn, who had also stayed there shortly before her coronation. Lady Jane Grey was cooped up here in 1553, and in the following year it was from here she watched the headless torso of her husband, Lord Dudley, being brought back from Tower Hill, only hours before her own execution. In 1688, William Penn, the Quaker and founder of Pennsylvania, was confined to the Queen's House, where he penned his most popular work, *No Cross, No Crown*.

Jewel House

The castellated Waterloo Block or Jewel House, north of the White Tower, now holds the **Crown Jewels**, the major reason so many people flock to the Tower. The Jewels include the world's three largest cut diamonds, but only a few of the exhibits could be described as beautiful – assertions of status and wealth are more important considerations. Queues can be long, and you only get to view the rocks from moving walkways. The vast majority of exhibits postdate the Commonwealth, when most of the royal riches were melted down for coinage or sold off.

Before you reach the walkway, look out for the twelfth-century **Coronation Spoon**, the oldest piece of regalia. The first piece along the walkway is **St Edward's Crown**, used in every coronation since the Restoration. The world's largest diamond, the 530-carat "First Star of Africa" or **Cullinan I** is set into the Sceptre with the Cross, while the legendary 105.6-carat **Koh-i-Nûr** (Mountain of Light) is set into the Queen Elizabeth, the Queen Mother's Crown from 1937. The last and most famous crown is the **Imperial State Crown,** worn by the Queen on state occasions, and sparkling with 2868 diamonds, 17 sapphires, 11 emeralds, 5 rubies and 273 pearls. The crown contains several very famous jewels: St Edward's Sapphire, taken from the ring of Edward the Confessor and set in the cross atop the crown; the Black Prince's Ruby, on the front cross; and Cullinan II, the 317-carat "Second Star of Africa".

Salt Tower to the Martin Tower

Visitors can walk along the Tower's eastern walls, starting at the **Salt Tower,** which features more prisoners' graffiti, including a stunningly detailed zodiac carved by Hugh Draper, incarcerated in 1561 on a charge of sorcery. This is where Edward I kept the Scottish King John Baliol prisoner for three years from 1296. Halfway along the walls, the **Constable Tower** contains a small exhibition on the 1381 Peasants' Revolt.

The **Martin Tower,** at the far end of the wall walk, houses a display of crowns with their gems taken out and relates the story of the most famous attempt to steal the Crown Jewels which took place here in 1671, when "Colonel" **Thomas Blood,** an Irish adventurer, made an attempt to make off with the lot, disguised as a parson. He was caught with the crown under his habit, the orb in one of his accomplices' breeches and the sceptre about to be filed in half. Charles II, good-humoured as ever, met and pardoned the felon, and even awarded him a pension and made him welcome at court.

12 Fusiliers' Museum

Last, and probably least, the Tower also contains the **Fusiliers' Museum** which tells the story of the Royal Fusiliers (City of London Regiment), now part of the Royal Regiment of Fusiliers. The original regiment was founded in 1685 from Tower guards and was called the Ordnance Regiment, as it was their job to escort the artillery. The museum trots through the regiment's various campaigns, displays its medals and spoils from across the Empire, and lists its most famous alumni, although it neglects to mention that East End gangsters, the Kray Twins, were once Fusiliers, and were in fact held prisoner in the Tower overnight in 1952 after having failed to turn up on time for their National Service call-up.

TOWER CEREMONIES

The Ceremony of the Keys is a 700-year-old, seven-minute floodlit ceremony. At 9.53pm daily, the Chief Yeoman Warder, accompanied by the Tower Guard, locks the Tower gates, and as he attempts to return to the Inner Ward, the following exchange then takes place: "Halt. Who comes there?" "The Keys." "Whose Keys?" "Queen Elizabeth's Keys." "Pass then, all's well." Then the Last Post is sounded and the ceremony ends. To find out how to witness this long-running drama, visit the website.

Gun Salutes are fired by the Honourable Artillery Company at 1pm at Tower Wharf on royal birthdays and other special occasions.

The Constable's Dues occurs once a year when a large Royal Navy ship moors alongside the Tower; the ship's captain and his escort march through the Tower and present a barrel of rum to the Constable of the Tower.

The Ceremony of the Lilies and Roses is carried out every year on May 21 by the provosts of Eton and King's College, Cambridge, who place white lilies and roses (their respective emblems) on the spot where King Henry VI, founder of both institutions, was murdered on May 21, 1471.

The Beating of the Bounds ceremony takes place once every three years (the next one is in 2014) on Ascension Day (forty days after Easter), outside the walls of the Tower. It used to be little boys who were beaten, but now it's the 29 stones that mark the limits of the Tower's jurisdiction that are thrashed with willow wands by local children, while the Chief Yeoman Warder gives the order "Whack it, boys! Whack it!"

OFF WITH HIS HEAD!

The first official beheading took place on Tower Hill in 1388 and the last in 1747, when the 80-year-old Jacobite **Lord Lovat** was dispatched. Lovat's beheading drew such a crowd that one of the spectators' stands collapsed, killing several bystanders, at which Lovat exclaimed: "The more mischief, the better sport." The Duke of Monmouth, beheaded in 1685 for his rebellion against James II, suffered the most botched execution: it took **Jack Ketch** (who lives on in Punch & Judy shows) five blows of the axe to sever his head, and even then the job had to be finished off with a surgeon's knife. Hangings continued for another thirty-odd years, ending with the execution of two prostitutes and a one-armed soldier arrested for attacking a Catholic-run pub in the 1780 Gordon Riots. Occasionally, over the centuries, the tables were turned: during the **1381 Peasants' Revolt**, rioters broke into the Tower, dragged out the Lord High Treasurer (the man responsible for the hated poll tax), and hacked him to death, along with the Archbishop of Canterbury.

Tower Hill

Perhaps it's fitting that traffic-blighted **Tower Hill** to the northwest of the Tower should be such a god-awful place, for it was here that the Tower's convicted "traitors" were executed. The actual spot for the executions, at what was the country's first permanent scaffold, is marked by a plaque on the west side of Trinity Square Gardens, which names a handful of the 125 executed here.

Close by stands the **Mercantile Marine Memorial**, designed by Edwin Lutyens, smothered with the names of the 12,000 merchant seamen who died in World War I, and subsequently enlarged with a vast, sprawling sunken section commemorating the 24,000 more who died in World War II.

The marine theme is continued in the buildings overlooking the gardens: the gargantuan temple-like former headquarters of the **Port of London Authority** (soon to be a hotel), an Edwardian edifice that exudes imperial confidence, with Neptune adorning the main tower; and, to the east, the elegant Neoclassical former headquarters of **Trinity House** (ⓦ trinityhouse.co.uk), the organization that oversees the upkeep of the lighthouses of England, Wales, the Channel Islands and Gibraltar – check out the reliefs of mermen, cherubs and lighthouses on the main facade, and the splendid gilded nautical weather vane.

Continuing east, you'll find perhaps the most impressive remaining section of London's **Roman walls** (see p.169) behind the *Grange City Hotel*, on Cooper's Row, and in Wakefield Gardens, close to Tower Hill tube station, along with an eighteenth-century copy of a Roman statue of Emperor Trajan, saved from a Southampton scrapyard by a local vicar.

Tower Bridge

Daily: April–Sept 10am–6.30pm; Oct–March 9.30am–6pm · £8 · ☎ 020 7403 3761, ⓦ towerbridge.org.uk · ⊖ Tower Hill

Tower Bridge ranks with Big Ben as the most famous of all London landmarks. Completed in 1894, its neo-Gothic towers are clad in Cornish granite and Portland stone, but conceal a frame of Scottish steel, which, at the time, represented a considerable engineering achievement, allowing a road crossing that could be raised to give tall ships access to the upper reaches of the Thames. The raising of the bascules (from the French for "seesaw") remains an impressive sight, and an event that takes place around a thousand times a year – visit the website for details. If you buy a ticket, you get to walk across the elevated walkways linking the summits of the towers, and visit the Tower's Engine Rooms, on the south side of the bridge, where you can see the now-defunct, giant coal-fired boilers which drove the hydraulic system until 1976, and play some interactive engineering games.

HOXTON SQUARE

The East End

The districts of Whitechapel, and in particular Spitalfields, within sight of the City skyscrapers, represent the old heart of the East End. If you visit just one area it should be this zone, which preserves mementoes from each wave of immigration. Most visitors come for the nightlife that has evolved around Brick Lane and Shoreditch, and for the Sunday markets: Spitalfields for fashion and food; Petticoat Lane for cheap clothes; Brick Lane for fashion, accessories and music; Columbia Road for flowers and plants. These apart, the area only repays selective sightseeing, and is no beauty spot – Victorian slum clearances, Hitler's bombs and postwar tower blocks have left large areas looking bleak. Of course the one part of the East End that has been totally transformed is the lower Lee Valley, a former industrial area, now home to the 2012 Olympic Park.

Few places in London have engendered so many myths as the **East End** (a catch-all title which covers just about everywhere east of the City, but has its historic heart closest to the latter). Its name is synonymous with slums, sweatshops and crime, epitomized by antiheroes such as Jack the Ripper and the Kray twins, and with rags-to-riches success stories of a whole generation of Jews who were born in these cholera-ridden quarters and then moved to wealthier pastures. Old East Enders will tell you that the area's not what it was – and it's true, as it always has been. The East End is constantly changing, as newly arrived **immigrants** assimilate and move out.

The first immigrants were **Huguenots**, French Protestants fleeing from religious persecution in the 1680s, who bequeathed the word "refugee" (from the French, *réfugié*). They were welcomed by all except the apprentice weavers whose work they undercut. Some settled in Soho, but the majority settled in Spitalfields, where they were operating thousands of silk looms by the end of the eighteenth century. Within three generations the Huguenots were almost entirely assimilated, and the **Irish** became the new immigrant population. Irish labourers, ironically enough, played a major role in building the area's Protestant churches, and later were crucial to the development of the docks. The perceived threat of cheap Irish labour provoked riots in 1736 and 1769, and their Catholicism made them easy targets during the 1780 Gordon Riots.

It was the influx of **Jews** escaping pogroms in eastern Europe and Russia that defined the character of the East End in the late nineteenth century. The Bishop of Stepney complained in 1901 that his churches were "left like islands in the midst of an alien sea". The same year, the MP for Stepney helped found the East End's first organized racist movement, the British Brothers League, whose ideology foreshadowed the British Union of Fascists, led by Oswald Mosley and famously defeated at the **Battle of Cable Street** (see p.196). The area's Jewish population has now dispersed throughout London, and gentrification has made serious inroads over the last decade or so, though the East End remains a deprived area. Despite the millions that have been poured into the nearby Docklands development, and the proximity of the wealth of the City, unemployment, racial tensions and housing problems persist.

Spitalfields

Ⓦ visitspitalfields.com

On the eastern edge of the City, **Spitalfields** started life as a cemetery, situated just outside the Roman walls. Its name derives from the medieval priory and hospital (hence "spital") of St Mary which stood here until the Dissolution – the old priory mortuary chapel has been preserved to the west of the old market. Nowadays, although Spitalfields continues to undergo a slow but steady gentrification, it retains a certain grittiness. The whole area is at its busiest and buzziest on Sundays, when there are no fewer than five **markets** all within a stone's throw of one another.

Spitalfields Market

Thurs & Fri 10am–4pm, Sun 9am–5pm • Ⓦ oldspitalfieldsmarket.com • ⊖ Liverpool Street

Originally established back in the seventeenth century in open countryside east of the City, **Spitalfields Market** was once the capital's premier fruit and vegetable market. Since the wholesale market moved out to Stratford in 1991, Spitalfields has become something of a hybrid. In the rather lugubrious Victorian red-brick and green-gabled

---

The East End of London is the hell of poverty. Like an enormous, black, motionless, giant kracken, the poverty of London lies there in lurking silence and encircles with its mighty tentacles the life and wealth of the City and of the West End...

J.H. Mackay, *The Anarchists* (1891)

13 building, a food, vintage clothes and crafts market continues to thrive. Meanwhile, the western, 1920s half of the market has been replaced by an anonymous glass-box mixed offices and shops development designed by Norman Foster. Part of the original facade survives on the north side of Brushfield Street; on the south side, the old fruiterers' shops are occupied by modishly retro businesses, such as Verde & Co, author Jeanette Winterson's deli venture (see p.378).

Christ Church

Mon–Fri 11am–4pm, Sun 1–4pm • ☏ 020 7377 6793, ⓦ ccspitalfields.org • ⊖ Liverpool Street

Christ Church is a characteristically bold church designed by Nicholas Hawksmoor, completed in 1729 and facing Spitalfields Market from across Commercial Street. The church's main features are its huge 225-foot-high broach spire and giant Tuscan portico, raised on steps and shaped like a Venetian window (a central arched opening flanked by two smaller rectangles), a motif repeated in the tower and doors. Inside, there's a forest of giant columned bays, a hexagonal, embossed ceiling, with a lion and a

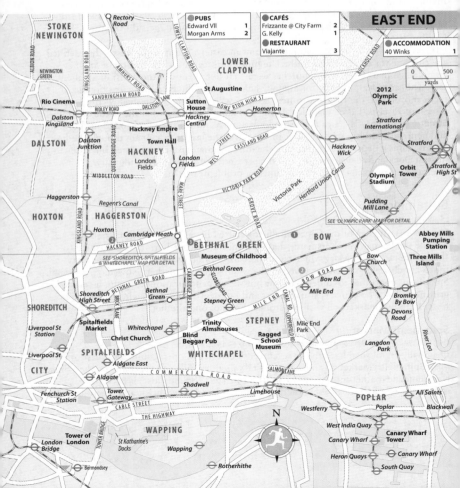

● PUBS	
Edward VII	1
Morgan Arms	2

● CAFÉS	
Frizzante @ City Farm	2
G. Kelly	1
● RESTAURANT	
Viajante	3

EAST END

● ACCOMMODATION	
40 Winks	1

13

unicorn playing peekaboo on the top of the chancel beam and, opposite, London's largest Georgian organ. The church's restoration has saved it from falling down; sadly, it's also removed all the atmosphere the old decaying interior once had.

South of Spitalfields Market

South of Spitalfields Market are several reminders of the old Jewish community: the **Soup Kitchen for the Jewish Poor**, on Brune Street, which opened in 1902 and closed in 1992 (the undulating stone lettering and the Christian and Jewish dates are still clearly visible), a mural opposite, and the **Sandys Row synagogue**, an old Huguenot chapel converted in 1870 for Dutch Jews and one of the few working synagogues left in the East End. The surrounding network of narrow streets is fascinating to walk around – unique survivors that give a strong impression of the old East End. From the bakery at 12 Widegate St, with its high-relief ceramic friezes, cross Sandys Row, and walk down Artillery Passage into **Artillery Lane**, which boasts a superb Huguenot shop front at no. 56. Incidentally, the ballistic connection dates from the reign of Henry VIII, when the Royal Artillery used to hold gunnery practice here.

Petticoat Lane (Middlesex Street)

Clothes market Sun 9am–2pm

Further south from Spitalfields Market lies **Petticoat Lane**, heavily bombed in the Blitz and not one of London's prettiest streets, but one with a rich history. The street originally lay outside the City walls, and was known as Hogs Lane; later, the area became known for its secondhand goods market, selling among other things the petticoats that gave the market and street its new name; the authorities then renamed it Middlesex Street in 1830 to avoid the mention of ladies' underwear (though the original name has stuck) and tried to prevent Sunday trading here (it was finally sanctioned by law in 1936). In the Victorian era the market grew into one of London's largest, and by the end of the century it was known as the Jews' Market, and stood at the heart of the Jewish East End, a "stronghold of hard-sell Judaism…into which no missionary dared to set foot", according to novelist Israel Zangwill. It remains the city's number-one cheap new clothes market, with a smaller lunchtime version in the week (Mon–Fri) on neighbouring Wentworth Street.

Dennis Severs' House, 18 Folgate Street

18 Folgate Street • Mon 6–9pm, Mon following the first and third Sun noon–2pm, Sun noon–4pm • Mon lunch £5, Mon eve £12, Sun £8 • ☏ 020 7247 4013, ⓦ dennissevershouse.co.uk • ⊖ Liverpool Street

You can visit one of Spitalfields' characteristic eighteenth-century terraced houses at 18 Folgate Street, where the American artist **Dennis Severs** lived until 1999. Eschewing all modern conveniences, Severs lived under candlelight, decorating his house as it would have been two hundred years ago. The public were invited to share in the experience which he described as like "passing through a frame into a painting". Today, visitors are free to explore the candle-lit rooms and are left with the distinct impression that the resident Huguenot family has literally just popped out: there's the smell of food, lots of clutter and the sound of horses' hooves on the cobbled street outside.

Brick Lane

Brick Lane gets its name from the brick kilns situated here after the Great Fire to help rebuild the City. By 1900, this was the high street of London's unofficial Jewish ghetto, but from the 1960s, Brick Lane became the heart of the Bangladeshi community. Racism has been a problem for each wave of immigrants, but nowadays it's City developers and bohemian gentrification that are changing the face of the street. For the moment, the southern half of Brick Lane remains pretty staunchly Bangladeshi: bright-coloured sari fabrics line the clothes-shop windows, and, in the evening, waiters from the numerous restaurants try to cajole you into their establishments. Along the

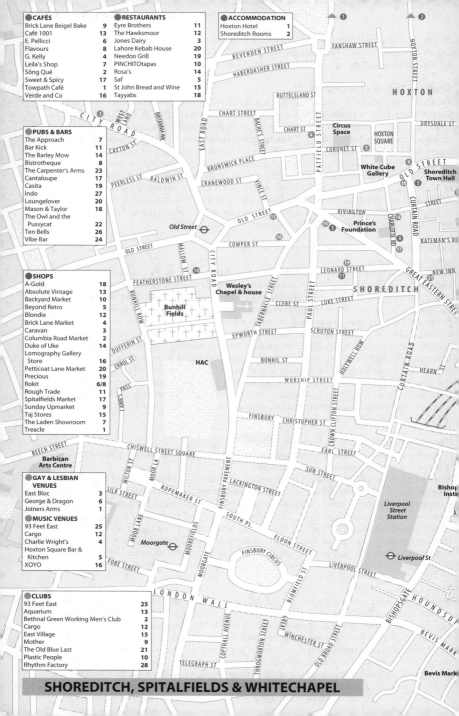

CAFÉS

Brick Lane Beigel Bake	9
Café 1001	13
E. Pellicci	6
Flavours	8
G. Kelly	4
Leila's Shop	7
Sông Quê	2
Sweet & Spicy	17
Towpath Café	1
Verde and Co	16

RESTAURANTS

Eyre Brothers	11
The Hawksmoor	12
Jones Dairy	3
Lahore Kebab House	20
Needoo Grill	19
PINCHITOtapas	10
Rosa's	14
Saf	5
St John Bread and Wine	15
Tayyabs	18

ACCOMMODATION

Hoxton Hotel	1
Shoreditch Rooms	2

PUBS & BARS

The Approach	7
Bar Kick	11
The Barley Mow	14
Bistrotheque	8
The Carpenter's Arms	23
Cantaloupe	17
Casita	19
Indo	27
Loungelover	20
Mason & Taylor	18
The Owl and the Pussycat	22
Ten Bells	26
Vibe Bar	24

SHOPS

A-Gold	18
Absolute Vintage	13
Backyard Market	10
Beyond Retro	5
Blondie	12
Brick Lane Market	4
Caravan	3
Columbia Road Market	2
Duke of Uke	14
Lomography Gallery Store	16
Petticoat Lane Market	20
Precious	19
Rokit	6/8
Rough Trade	11
Spitalfields Market	17
Sunday Upmarket	9
Taj Stores	15
The Laden Showroom	7
Treacle	1

GAY & LESBIAN VENUES

East Bloc	3
George & Dragon	6
Joiners Arms	1

MUSIC VENUES

93 Feet East	25
Cargo	12
Charlie Wright's	4
Hoxton Square Bar & Kitchen	5
XOYO	16

CLUBS

93 Feet East	25
Aquarium	13
Bethnal Green Working Men's Club	2
Cargo	12
East Village	15
Mother	9
The Old Blue Last	21
Plastic People	10
Rhythm Factory	28

SHOREDITCH, SPITALFIELDS & WHITECHAPEL

SHIPTON ST

RAVENSCROFT ST

COLUMBIA ROAD

BAXENDALE ST

WIMBOLT ST

QUITTER ST

WARNER PL

MANSFORD ST

TEESDALE ST

CANROBERT ST

ELWIN ST

QUITTER ST

COLUMBIA ROAD

OLD BETHNAL GREEN RD

IVIRNEY ST

POLLARD ROW

FLORIDA ST

SQUIRRIES STREET

ROBERTA ST

WELLINGTON ROW

GOSSET STREET

COLUMBIA ROAD MARKET

HACKNEY ROAD

USTIN ST

eonard

VIRGINIA ROAD

AVENUE

NAVARE ST

Arnold
Circus

CLUB ROW

OLD NICHOL ST

SWANFIELD STREET

BARNET GROVE

BETHNAL GREEN ROAD

VALLANCE ROAD

Weavers
Fields

REDCHURCH STREET

Rich
Mix

BRICK LANE

BETHNAL GREEN ROAD

BETHNAL GREEN ROAD

VOSS ST

DERBYSHIRE ST

SCLATER ST

Brick Lane
Market

CHESHIRE STREET

DUNBRIDGE STREET

TENT ST

WHEELER ST

horeditch
gh Street

BRICK LANE

QUAKER STREET

Spitalfields
Farm

BUXTON

STREET

Old Truman
Brewery

DRAY'S LANE

SPITALFIELDS

HANBURY STREET

19 Princelet St

PRINCELET STREET

HANBURY STREET

Whitechapel

LAMB STREET

Old
pitalfields
Market

COMMERCIAL

Jamme Masjid

FOURNIER STREET

School

GREATOREX ST

Royal
London
Hospital

field
STREET

Christ Church

FASHION ST

BRICK LANE

OLD MONTAGUE STREET

East
London
Mosque

ndys Row

WHITES ROW

STREET

Fieldgate St

Fieldgate St

NEW ARK ST

Institute of
Cell & Molecular
Sciences

BRUNEL ST

TOYNBEE ST

Toynbee
Hall

WENTWORTH STREET

GUNTHORPE ST

OLD CASTLE STREET

ANGEL ALLEY

Whitechapel
Bell Foundry

ADLER STREET

WHITECHAPEL

NEW ROAD

BELL LANE

Women's Library

Aldgate
East

Whitechapel
Art Gallery

WHITECHAPEL

icoat Lane Market

GOULSTON STREET

WHITECHAPEL HIGH ST

LEMAN ST

COMMERCIAL ROAD

Aldgate

BRAHAM STREET

N

0   400

yards

13

northern half of Brick Lane, the pavements are busy with punters heading for the late-night cafés and clubs that have colonized the area.

The changing ethnic make-up of this part of Brick Lane is most clearly illustrated in the **Jamme Masjid** (Great Mosque) on the corner of Fournier Street. Established in 1743 as a Huguenot church, it became a Wesleyan chapel in 1809, the ultra-Orthodox Spitalfields Great Synagogue in 1897, and since 1976 has served as a mosque – it's impossible to miss thanks to the 90ft-high luminous, freestanding metal minaret, topped by a crescent moon, that was erected in 2009. Another example, a little further south, is **Christ Church primary school**, whose pupils are mostly Muslim; a hundred years ago they were mainly Jewish, as the Star of David on one of the drainpipes testifies.

The Old Truman Brewery
Brick Lane • ⓦ trumanbrewery.com

A red-brick chimney halfway up Brick Lane heralds the **Old Truman Brewery**, founded back in 1666 and once the largest in the world. It's now a creative centre for music, fashion, art and IT and forms the focal point of Brick Lane's current gentrification. In the brewery's **Dray's Lane**, the old stables have been turned into cafés and shops for independent designers and artists; on Sundays, market stalls fill the Up Market and Backyard Market buildings.

19 Princelet Street
Occasional open days • Free • ☎ 020 7247 5352, ⓦ 19princeletstreet.org.uk • ⊖ Liverpool Street

If you want to dig deeper into the area's past, try and visit on one of the open days at **19 Princelet Street**, just off Brick Lane, where there's a permanent exhibition on Spitalfields' rich history of immigration. This beautifully preserved eighteenth-century silk-weavers' house also houses a wonderfully evocative former synagogue, built by Polish Jews in the 1860s and entirely hidden behind the Georgian facade. The attic was home to the mysterious real-life main character in Rachel Lichtenstein's *Rodinsky's Room* (see p.463).

Shoreditch

Shoreditch, to the north of Spitalfields, has been colonized by artists, designers and architects and transformed into one of the city's most self-consciously artistic enclaves, despite the area's lack of obvious aesthetic charm. The area is rich in literary and artistic associations. Situated just outside the City, it was here that James Burbage established the country's **first public theatre** – called simply the Theatre – in 1576 (he later took it down and reassembled it on Bankside as the Globe). There are a couple of specific sights – the **Geffrye Museum** of period interiors and **Wesley's Chapel and House** – but the majority of folk come here for the area's **bars** (see p.392), **clubs** (see p.403) and **art galleries**.

St Leonard's, Shoreditch

The area's most prominent landmark is **St Leonard's**, the Neoclassical church designed by George Dance the Elder in 1740 and situated at the junction of Old Street,

13

LONDON'S JEWS

William the Conqueror invited the first **Jews** to England in 1066. After a period of relatively peaceful coexistence and prosperity, the small community increasingly found itself under attack, milked by successive monarchs and forced eventually to wear a distinguishing mark or *tabula* on their clothing. The Crusades whipped up further religious intolerance, the worst recorded incident taking place in 1189, when thirty Jews were killed by a mob during the coronation of Richard I. In 1278 Edward I imprisoned the entire community of around six hundred on a charge of "clipping coins" (debasing currency by shaving off bits of silver from coins), executing 267 at the Tower, and finally in 1290 expelling the rest.

For nearly four centuries thereafter, Judaism was outlawed in England. Sephardic (ie Spanish or Portuguese) Jews fleeing the Inquisition began arriving from 1540 onwards, though they had to become, or pretend to be, Christians until 1656, when Oliver Cromwell granted Jews the right to meet privately and worship in their own homes. The Jews who arrived immediately following this **Readmission** were in the main wealthy merchants, bankers and other businessmen. As a beacon of (relative) tolerance and economic prosperity, London quickly attracted further Jewish immigration by poorer Sephardi families and, increasingly, Ashkenazi settlers from eastern and central Europe.

By far the largest influx of **Ashkenazi Jews** arrived after fleeing pogroms that followed the assassination of Tsar Alexander II in 1881. The more fortunate were met by relatives at the Irongate Stairs by Tower Bridge; the rest were left to the mercy of the boarding-house keepers or, after 1885, found shelter in the Jewish Temporary Shelter. They found work in the sweatshops of the East End: cabinetmaking, shoemaking and, of course, tailoring – by 1901, over 45 percent of London's Jews worked in the garment industry.

Perhaps the greatest moment in Jewish East End history was the **Battle of Cable Street**, which took place on October 4, 1936, when Oswald Mosley and three thousand of his black-shirted fascists attempted to march through the East End. More than twice that number of police tried to clear the way for Mosley with baton charges and mounted patrols, but they were met with a barrage of bricks and stones from some 100,000 East Enders chanting the slogan of the Spanish Republicans: "*No pasaran*" (They shall not pass). Eventually the police chief halted the march – and another East End legend was born. A mural on the side of the old Shadwell town hall on Cable Street commemorates the event.

After World War II, more and more Jews moved out to the suburbs of North London, and the largest Orthodox Jewish communities are now to be found in Golders Green and Stamford Hill, with 200,000 Jews across the city as a whole.

Shoreditch High Street and Kingsland Road. Though it's usually closed, you can sometimes take a look inside on a Sunday morning and admire the memorial to Elizabeth Benson on the southeast wall, which depicts two skeletons tearing at the Tree of Life.

Shoreditch Town Hall

380 Old St • ☎ 020 7739 6176, ⓦ shoreditchtownhall.org.uk • ⊖ Old Street

The former **Shoreditch Town Hall** is a self-confident Victorian edifice, recently restored and now host to a whole number of events and exhibitions, private and public. The town hall's tower features Progress, torch and battleaxe in hand, and, in the pediment, Hope and Plenty, reclining beside the Shoreditch motto "More Light, More Power", adopted in recognition of the borough's progressive policy of creating power from rubbish incineration. The source of this power, the Shoreditch Electric Light Station, still stands on nearby Hoxton Market, sporting the wonderful motto *E pulvere lux et vis* (Out of the dust, light and power). The old refuse destructor now houses Circus Space (ⓦ thecircusspace.co.uk), a college for jugglers and acrobats.

Hoxton Square

The geographical focus of Hoxton's transformation is **Hoxton Square**, situated northeast of Old Street tube: a strange and not altogether happy assortment of light industrial units, many now artists' studios, arranged around a leafy, formal square. The square's chief landmark is the **White Cube** (Tues–Sat 10am–6pm; free; ⓦwhitecube.com) just the prominent of a whole number of art galleries in the area. It's a sort of miniature Tate Modern: an old piano factory, with a glass roof plonked on the top, that puts on shows by the likes of Damien Hirst, Tracey Emin and Sam Taylor-Wood.

Geffrye Museum

Kingsland Rd · **Almshouse** First Sat and first & third Wed of month, plus occasionally Thurs · £2 · **Museum** Tues–Sat 10am–5pm, Sun noon–5pm · Free · ☎ 020 7739 9893, ⓦ geffrye-museum.org.uk · Hoxton Overground

Hoxton's chief attraction is the **Geffrye Museum**, housed in a grandiose enclave of eighteenth-century ironmongers' almshouses, set back from Kingsland Road. In 1911, at a time when the East End furniture trade was centred on Shoreditch, the almshouses were converted into a museum for the "education of craftsmen". The Geffrye remains, essentially, a furniture museum, with the almshouses rigged out as period living rooms of the urban middle class, ranging from the oak-panelled seventeenth century, through refined Georgian to cluttered Victorian. You'll also pass through the original central Georgian **chapel**, with its tiny Neoclassical apse and archetypal stone-coloured wood panelling; round the back of the chapel, an enclosed balcony overlooking the garden serves as a reading room.

Further on is the museum's twentieth-century **extension**, with four "snapshots in time", beginning with an Edwardian drawing room in understated Arts and Crafts style, and finishing off with a minimalist 1990s loft conversion. The extension also houses a pleasant licensed **café-restaurant**, serving inexpensive British food, and hosts excellent temporary exhibitions on the lower ground floor. Out the back, the **gardens** show the transition in horticultural tastes from the seventeenth-century knot gardens to today's patio garden, culminating in a pungent, walled **herb garden** (April–Oct only).

To get a feel of what the living conditions in the **almshouses** were like, one of them has been restored to its original condition and can now be visited on certain days (see above), though numbers are limited and visits are by timed entry only.

Wesley's Chapel and House

49 City Rd · Mon–Sat 10am–4pm, Sun noon–1.45pm · Free · ☎ 020 7253 2262, ⓦ wesleychapel.org.uk · ⊖ Old Street

Striking an unusual note of calm on busy City Road is the largely Georgian ensemble of **Wesley's Chapel and House** set around a cobbled courtyard. A place of pilgrimage for Methodists from all over the world, the chapel was designed in 1778 by George Dance and heralded the coming-of-age of the followers of **John Wesley** (1703–91), who had started out in a small foundry east of the present building.

The **chapel** forms the centrepiece of the complex, though it is uncharacteristically ornate for a Methodist place of worship, with its powder-pink columns of French jasper and its superb, Adam-style gilded plasterwork ceiling, not to mention the colourful Victorian stained glass depicting, among other things, Wesley's night-time conversion, with his brother still in his dressing gown. The chapel has often attracted well-heeled weddings: one Margaret Hilda Roberts got married to divorcé Denis Thatcher here in 1951, and later paid for the new communion rail.

The **Museum of Methodism** (same hours) in the basement tells the story of Wesley and Methodism, and there's even a brief mention of Mrs Mary Vazeille, the 41-year-old, insanely jealous, wealthy widow he married, and who eventually left him. Wesley himself lived his last two years in the Georgian **house** to the right of the main gates, and inside you can see bits of his furniture and his deathbed, plus an early shock-therapy machine with which he used to treat members of his congregation. Wesley's **grave** is round the back of the chapel, in the shadow of a modern office block.

13

> ## JOHN WESLEY AND METHODISM
>
> The name "**Methodist**" was a term of abuse used by John Wesley's fellow Oxford students, but it wasn't until his "conversion" at a prayer meeting in Aldersgate (marked by a large memorial outside the Museum of London) in 1738, that Wesley decided to become an independent field preacher. More verbal and even physical abuse followed during which Wesley was accused of being, among other things, a papist spy and an illegal gin distiller. Yet despite his lifelong dispute with the Anglican church, despite commissioning preachers, and bequeathing more than 350 Methodist chapels serving over 130,000 worshippers, Wesley himself never left the Church of England and died within it, urging his followers, where possible, to do the same.

Bunhill Fields

City Road • April–Sept Mon–Fri 7.30am–7pm, Sat & Sun 9.30am–7pm; Oct–March Mon–Fri closes 4pm • ⊖ Old Street

Appropriately enough, **Bunhill Fields**, the main burial ground for Dissenters or Nonconformists (practising Christians who were not members of the Church of England), lies across the road from Wesley's Chapel. Following bomb damage in the last war, most of the graveyard is fenced off, though you can still stroll through on the public footpaths under a canopy of giant London plane trees. The three most famous graves have been placed in the central paved area: the simple tombstone of poet and artist **William Blake** stands next to a replica of writer **Daniel Defoe**'s, while opposite lies the recumbent statue of **John Bunyan**, seventeenth-century author of *The Pilgrim's Progress*.

Whitechapel High Street and Road

Whitechapel High Street lies at the heart of the old East End, and – along with its extension, Whitechapel Road – follows the route of the old Roman road from London to Colchester. Starting in the west at Aldgate, the City's eastern gateway, the street is still a good barometer for the current East End and is worth a stroll for a glimpse of London that's only a stone's throw (and yet light years) from the City.

Women's Library

Old Castle St • Mon–Fri 9.30am–5.30pm, Thurs until 8pm, Sat 10am–4pm • Free • ☎ 020 7320 2222, ⓦ thewomenslibrary.ac.uk • ⊖ Aldgate East or Aldgate

In the 1840s, the Victorians decided it was time to do something about "the great unwashed" and a grandly named Committee for Promoting the Establishment of Baths and Wash-Houses for the Labouring Classes was set up. Among the plushest public baths were the Goulston Square Wash Houses, opened by Prince Albert himself: "a penny for a cold bath, two for a hot bath for up to four children under eight". The grey-brick facade of the old wash houses survives on Old Castle Street, south of Wentworth Street, but the interior is now home to the **Women's Library**, which puts on excellent exhibitions covering a wide range of issues, with a feminist slant, on the ground floor. The actual library (Tues–Fri only) was set up by the suffragette Millicent Fawcett in 1926 and specializes in women's history; it also puts on regular talks and events, and has a café on the first floor.

Whitechapel Art Gallery

77–82 Whitechapel High St • Wed–Sun 11am–6pm, Thurs until 9pm • Free • ☎ 020 7522 7888, ⓦ whitechapel.org • ⊖ Aldgate East

The East End institution that draws in more outsiders than any other is the **Whitechapel Art Gallery**, housed in a beautiful, crenellated 1899 Arts and Crafts building by Charles Harrison Townsend. The gallery was founded by one of the East End's many Victorian philanthropists, **Samuel Barnett**. His motives may have been dubious – "The principle of our work is that we aim at decreasing not suffering but sin", he once claimed – but the legacy of his good works is still discernible across the East End. The gallery now puts on innovative exhibitions of contemporary art, as well as hosting the biennial East End Academy, a chance for local artists to get their work shown to a wider audience.

East London Mosque

82–92 Whitechapel Rd • ☎ 020 7650 3000, ⓦ eastlondonmosque.org.uk • ⊖ Whitechapel

Whitechapel Road boasts the most visible symbol of Muslim presence in the East End, the **East London Mosque**, a gaudy red-brick 1980s building, with a golden dome and minaret, which seats five thousand; it stands in marked contrast to the tiny **Fieldgate Street Great Synagogue**, behind the mosque, dating from 1899. Neither building is open to the public.

Whitechapel Bell Foundry

33–34 Whitechapel Rd • Mon–Fri 9am–4.15pm • Free • Guided tours occasionally Wed 5.30pm, Sat 10am & 1.30pm, £10; no under-14s • ☎ 020 7247 2599, ⓦ whitechapelbellfoundry.co.uk • ⊖ Whitechapel

On the south side of the street, the **Whitechapel Bell Foundry** occupies the short terrace of Georgian houses on the corner of Fieldgate Street. Big Ben, the Liberty Bell, the Bow Bells and numerous English church bells (including those of Westminster Abbey) all hail from the foundry, established in 1570. Inside, there's a small exhibition on the history of the foundry, which is the oldest manufacturing company in the country.

Whitechapel Market

Mon–Sat 8am–6pm • ⊖ Whitechapel

Whitechapel Road widens halfway along, at the beginning of **Whitechapel Market**, once one of the largest hay markets in London, now given over to everything from nectarines to net curtains, and including a large number of stalls catering for the

ANARCHISTS IN THE EAST END

Founded in 1886, the **Freedom Press** (Mon–Sat noon–6pm, Sun noon–4pm; ☎ 020 7247 9249, ⓦ freedompress.org.uk; ⊖ Aldgate East), a small anarchist bookshop and printing press in Angel Alley, by the side of the Whitechapel Art Gallery, is the lone survivor of an East End tradition of radical politics that reached its height at the end of the nineteenth century. For a roll call of famous anarchists, check out the stainless-steel portrait gallery in Angel Alley. East End anarchism found a strong following among the Jewish community especially, and supporters of the *Arbeter Fraynd* newspaper (whose editor was the wonderfully named Rudolf Rocker) staged atheist demonstrations outside Orthodox synagogues on the Sabbath, as well as making other gestures like ostentatiously smoking and eating ham sandwiches. In 1907, delegates to the Fifth Congress of the Russian Social Democratic Labour Party staged a meeting on the corner of Fulbourne Street attended by, among others, Lenin, Stalin, Trotsky, Gorky, Litvinov and Rosa Luxembourg. The local Jubilee Street Anarchist Club later loaned £1700 to the Bolsheviks, and were paid back in full by the Soviet government after the revolution.

The event for which the anarchists are best remembered, however, is the **Siege of Sidney Street**, which took place in January 1911. A gun battle occurred after a routine police enquiry at the back of a jeweller's on Houndsditch, and left one Russian anarchist and three policemen dead. Over the next few weeks, all but three of the anarchist gang were arrested; following a tip-off, the three were eventually cornered in a building on Sidney Street. A further gun battle ensued: a detachment of Scots Guards and two cannons were deployed, and even the Home Secretary, Winston Churchill, put in an appearance. By lunchtime the house was in flames, leaving two charred bodies in the burnt-out shell. However, the ringleader, nicknamed Peter the Painter, vanished without trace, to join the likes of Jack the Ripper as an East End legend.

13

THE WHITECHAPEL MURDERS

In eight weeks between August and November 1888, five prostitutes were stabbed to death in and around Whitechapel. Few of the letters received by the press and police, which purported to come from the murderer, are thought to have been genuine (including the one which coined the nickname **Jack the Ripper**), and the murderer's identity remains a mystery to this day. At the time, it was assumed he was a Jew, probably a *shochet* (a ritual slaughterman), since the mutilations on the corpses were obviously carried out with some skill. The theory gained ground when the fourth victim was discovered outside the (predominantly Jewish) Working Men's Club off Commercial Road, and for a while it was dangerous for Jews to walk the streets at night for fear of reprisals.

Ripperologists have trawled through the little evidence there is to produce **numerous suspects**, none of whom can be conclusively proven guilty. The most celebrated suspect is the Duke of Clarence, eldest son of the future Edward VII, an easy if improbable target, since he was involved in a scandal involving a male brothel and was a well-known homosexual. Crime writer Patricia Cornwell spent over a million dollars trying (and failing) to prove conclusively that the Ripper was the painter Walter Sickert, who exhibited an unhealthy fascination with the murders. The man who usually tops the lists, however, was a cricket-playing barrister named Druitt whose body was found floating in the Thames some weeks after the last murder, though, as usual, there is no evidence linking him with any of them.

The one **positive outcome** of the murders was that they focused the attention of the rest of London on the squalor of the East End. Philanthropist Samuel Barnett, for one, used the media attention to press for improved housing, streetlighting and policing to combat crime and poverty in the area. Today, the murders continue to be exploited in gory, misogynistic detail by the likes of Madame Tussauds and the London Dungeon, while guided walks retracing the Ripper's steps set off every week throughout the year (see p.33).

local Bangladeshi and Somali communities. In the 1890s, this was where casual workers used to gather to be selected for work in the local sweatshops, earning it the Yiddish nickname *Hazer Mark*, or "pig market". The sole reminder of those days is the Edward VII monument at the centre of the market, erected by the local Jewish community in 1911.

Royal London Hospital Museum

Newark St • Tues–Fri 10am–4.30p • Free • ☎ 020 7377 7608, ⓦ bartsandthelondon.nhs.uk • ⊖ Whitechapel

It was on the nearby Mile End Road that Joseph Merrick, better known as the **Elephant Man**, was discovered in a freak show in 1884 by Dr Treves, and subsequently admitted as a patient to the **Royal London Hospital** on Whitechapel Road. He remained there, on show as a medical freak, and was eventually allowed to live there until his death in 1890, at the age of just 27. There's an interesting twenty-minute documentary on Merrick, and a small section displaying, among other things, the veil and hat he wore, in the **Hospital Museum** on Newark Street. The museum also covers the history of the hospital and of nursing and medicine in general, with a section on Edith Cavell, who trained here before assisting Allied soldiers to escape from occupied Belgium; she was eventually arrested and shot as a spy by the Germans in 1915.

The Blind Beggar

337 Whitechapel Rd • Mon–Sat 11am–11pm, Sun noon–10.30pm • Free • ☎ 020 7347 6195, ⓦ theblindbeggar.com • ⊖ Whitechapel

At the eastern end of Whitechapel Road stands the handsome, gabled entrance to the former **Albion Brewery**, where the first bottled brown ale was produced in 1899. Next door is the former brewery tap, the **Blind Beggar**, the East End's most famous pub since March 9, 1966, when Ronnie Kray walked into the crowded bar and shot gangland rival George Cornell for calling him a "fat poof". This murder spelt the end of the infamous Kray Twins, Ronnie and Reggie, both of whom were sentenced to life imprisonment, though their well-publicized gifts to local charities created a Robin Hood image that still persists.

Bethnal Green and Bow

The East End spreads out east of Whitechapel into the districts of **Bethnal Green**, to the north, and **Bow**, to the east. The Mile End Road is just an extension of Whitechapel Road, and easily explored on foot, but to reach more mainstream sights such as the **Museum of Childhood**, you'll need to hop on public transport.

Mile End Road

The **Mile End Road** is an extension of Whitechapel Road, and the westernmost section, known as the Mile End Waste, is punctuated at the western end by a bust, and at the eastern by a more dramatic statue, of William Booth, founder of the Salvation Army (see below). There are also two unusual architectural features worth mentioning nearby. The more surprising is the **Trinity Almshouses**, a quaint courtyard of cottages with a central chapel, built in 1695 for "Twenty-eight decay'd Masters and Commanders and the widows of such". Further up, on the same side of the street, stands a large Neoclassical former department store, sporting a central domed tower, its facade of Ionic half-columns sliced in two by a small two-storey shop that used to belong to a Jewish watchmaker called **Spiegelhalter**. This architectural oddity is the result of a dispute between Spiegelhalter and his affluent Gentile neighbour, Thomas Wickham, who was forced to build his new store around the watchmaker's shop after he refused to be bought out.

Ragged School Museum

46–50 Copperfield Rd • Wed & Thurs 10am–5pm, first Sun of month 2–5pm • Free • ☎ 020 8980 6405, ⓦ raggedschoolmuseum.org.uk • ⊖ Mile End

South of the Mile End Road, on the bombed-out remains of Copperfield Road, the **Ragged School Museum** occupies a Victorian canalside warehouse originally used to store lime juice. Accommodating more than one thousand pupils from 1877 to 1908, this was the largest of London's numerous Ragged Schools, institutions that provided free education and two free meals daily to children with no means to pay the penny a week charged by most Victorian schools. This particular Ragged School was just one of innumerable projects set up by the East End's most irrepressible philanthropist, the diminutive and devout **Dr Thomas Barnardo**, whose tireless work for the children of the East End is the subject of the ground-floor exhibition. Upstairs, there's a reconstructed

---

EAST END PHILANTHROPISTS

The poverty of the East End has attracted numerous philanthropists over the years, particularly during the Victorian era, from Dr Barnardo, of Ragged School fame, to Lady Burdett-Coutts, whose fountain still stands in Victoria Park. The most famous of the lot, however, was **William Booth** (1829–1912), a pawnbroker by trade and a Methodist lay preacher. One June evening in 1865, Booth, moved by the sight of the crowds at the pubs and gin palaces, was evangelizing on the Mile End Road. He was invited by some fellow missioners to lead a series of meetings in a tent they had set up on the Mile End Waste. Booth and his wife then set up the Christian Mission, which eventually led to the foundation, in 1878, of the quasi-military Christian movement known as the **Salvation Army**. In contrast to many Victorian philanthropists, Booth never accepted the divisive concept of the deserving and undeserving poor – "if a man was poor, he was deserving". Booth railed against the laissez-faire economic policies of his era, while attending to the immediate demands of the poor, setting up soup kitchens and founding hostels, which, by the time of his death in 1912, had spread right across the globe. Booth is buried in Abney Park Cemetery (see p.292).

13

Victorian schoolroom, where period-dressed teachers, cane in hand, take today's schoolkids through the rigours of a Victorian lesson, and on the top floor you can see two contrasting mock-up kitchens from the 1890s and the 1950s. There are also further displays on the nearby docks and local sweatshops, and a canalside café back on the ground floor.

Victoria Park

Daily 6am–dusk • Cambridge Heath train station or Hackney Wick Overground; bus #277 from ⊖ Mile End or bus #8 from ⊖ Liverpool Street

London's first public park (as opposed to royal park) **Victoria Park** was opened in the heart of the East End in 1845, after a local MP presented Queen Victoria with a petition of 30,000 signatures. The only large open space in the area, "Viccy Park" immediately became a favourite spot for **political rallies**: Chartists congregated here in their thousands in 1848; Suffragette supporters of the ELFS gathered here, under the leadership of Sylvia Pankhurst; it even had its own Speakers' Corner attended by the likes of George Bernard Shaw and William Morris. Since the Anti-Nazi League played here in 1978, it's probably more famous for its regular use for music festivals.

The world's oldest **model boat club**, the Victoria Model Steam Boat Club, founded in 1904, still meets on most summer Sunday mornings at the park's lakes. Look out, too, for the (replica) **Dogs of Alcibiades**, two snarling sculpted beasts based on the Molossian hounds kept by the Athenian statesman and presented by Lady Regnart in 1912. The much larger eastern section of the park contains an extraordinarily lavish Gothic-cum-Moorish **drinking fountain**, decorated with oversized cherubs and paid for by Baroness Burdett-Coutts in 1861 – it hasn't functioned for years. At the park's eastern edge are two alcoves from Old London Bridge, brought here in 1860.

Museum of Childhood

Cambridge Heath Rd • Daily 10am–5.45pm • Free • ☎ 020 8983 5200, ⓦ www.vam.ac.uk • ⊖ Bethnal Green

The elegant, open-plan wrought-iron hall that houses the **Museum of Childhood** was, in fact, part of the original V&A building, and was transported to the East End from South Kensington in the late 1860s in order to bring art to the poor. The emphasis has changed since those pioneering days, and although the wide range of exhibits means that there's something here for everyone, the museum's most frequent visitors are children, with plenty of hands-on exhibits and special kids' events at weekends and during school holidays.

To the right as you enter, are the clockwork and moving **toys** – bring your 20p pieces for the bigger exhibits – everything from classic robots to a fully functioning model railway, early computer games and wooden toys – there's often a queue for the replica Victorian rocking horse. At the back, the museum has a great collection of marionettes and puppets, which brings you into the doll and figures section, ranging from teddies and Smurfs to Inuit dolls. The most famous exhibits are the remarkable antique **dolls' houses** dating back to 1673: they are displayed upstairs, where you'll also find antique dolls and prams, a play area for very small kids, the ever-popular Wallace the Lion gobbling up the little schoolboy Albert, and a space for temporary exhibitions.

Olympic Park

Focus of the 2012 Olympics, London's **Olympic Park** is situated in a most unlikely East End backwater, on a series of islands formed by the River Lee (or Lea) and various tributaries and canals. Before the Games, access is well nigh impossible, though you can get good views from the Greenway, an elevated cycle path to the south. After the Games, the park will undoubtedly eventually become a tourist destination, and somewhere worth exploring in its own right.

OLYMPIC PARK

New Spitalfields Market

RUCKHOLT ROAD

River Lea

HOMERTON ROAD

Eton Manor

A12

0   200
yards

N

EASTWAY

LOOP ROAD

Hockey
Centre

Velodrome

BMX
Circuit

Hockey
Warm-up
Area

TEMPLE MILL LANE

International Broadcast
Centre/
Main Press Area

Basketball
Arena

River Lea Navigation

LOOP ROAD

Olympic
Village

Handball
Arena

Hackney
Wick

Stratford
International
Station

Energy
Centre

Hertford Union
Canal

LOOP ROAD

Sponsors'
Hospitality
Zone

Stratford
City

Water
Polo
Arena

Aquatics
Centre

Stratford
Train Station

Olympic
Stadium

Stratford
Bus Station

LOOP ROAD

Orbit
Tower

City Mill River

Greenway (Cycle Path)

Waterworks River

WARTON ROAD

CARPENTER'S ROAD

Stratford
High St

Warm-up
Area

STRATFORD HIGH STREET

Pudding
Mill Lane

West Ham

13

2012 OLYMPICS

London is the only city in the world to have hosted the Olympics three times. In **1908**, the city saved the day when Vesuvius erupted and Rome had to pull out as host. In **1948**, London stepped in at short notice and staged the austerity games, where the athletes were told to bring their own food and were put up in RAF camps. Even given a background of economic cutbacks, however, **2012** is set to be a more extravagant affair, with the total spend likely to be in excess of £9 billion (three times the figure quoted during the bidding, but probably only a quarter of what was spent in Beijing).

The focus of the games is very much on the Olympic Park, but a number of events are taking place elsewhere in London, mostly in existing venues: **Wimbledon** for the tennis; **Wembley Stadium** for some of the football; **Wembley Arena** for badminton and rhythmic gymnastics; **ExCel**, by Royal Victoria Dock, for everything from fencing to table tennis. The (O2) Dome – known as the **North Greenwich Arena** during the Games – hosts the gymnastics and basketball finals, and **Earl's Court** stages the volleyball. Equestrian events are scheduled for **Greenwich Park**, while **Hyde Park** hosts the triathlon and **Regent's Park** the road cycling. Archery takes place at **Lord's** Cricket Ground, shooting at the **Royal Artillery Barracks** in Woolwich, canoe slalom at the White Water Centre further up the Lee valley, and – the one piece of planning that really grabbed the headlines – beach volleyball on **Horse Guards Parade**. Only rowing, sailing and mountain biking will take place any great distance from the capital.

The organizers have been at pains to brand 2012 as a "green" Games, successfully clearing up an industrial wasteland and using just a quarter of the steel used in Beijing for the main stadium. Nevertheless, the Olympics inevitably leave a pretty hefty **carbon footprint**. The games have certainly generated employment, though not necessarily for locals, and transport to the area has improved, but the London Olympic bid sold itself on its **legacy**. Whether the permanent venues will become a collection of expensive white elephants, and the park merely a rich enclave in a deprived area, remains to be seen.

The centrepiece of the park is the **Olympic Stadium**, surrounded on three sides by the River Lee and the City Mill River; seating 80,000 for the Olympics, the stadium is earmarked to become home to West Ham United football club, with a reduced capacity of 60,000. Standing close to the stadium, with a bird's-eye view of the whole site from its public observation deck, is the **Orbit** tower, a 377ft-high continuous loop of red recycled steel designed by Anish Kapoor, and dubbed the Helter Skelter. The most eye-catching venue, however, is Zaha Hadid's wave-like **Aquatics Centre**, to the east, which cost four times its original estimate, and will be very expensive to maintain, but at least it looks good. The other truly sexy building is the curvy **Velodrome**, with its banked, Siberian pine track and adjacent BMX circuit. Eton Manor, venue for the wheelchair tennis, and the Handball Arena, will eventually serve as multi-sports centres, but several of the venues will be dismantled after the Games, the largest being the 12,000-seat Basketball Arena. Overlooking the whole site, the **Olympic Village** sits on the eastern edge of the park, designed for 17,000 athletes during the Games, and thereafter to be converted into 2800 new homes. After the Olympics, the park is to be named after the Queen, though it's probably going to end up being known as "Lizzy Park".

ARRIVAL AND INFORMATION

Arrival Transport arrangements will be different during the Games, so visit ⓦ london2012.com for details. The nearest tube is Stratford; alternatively you can approach from Hackney Wick Overground or Pudding Mill Lane DLR station.

Moving on If you've had enough of sampling the Olympic site, you can head north up the River Lee, to the Hackney Marshes (see p.294), or downriver to Three Mills Islands (see opposite).

Three Mills Island

One good reason to head further east, beyond the A102 and the River Lee, is to visit the eighteenth-century architectural ensemble of **Three Mills Island**, an artificial island in the River Lee, close to the Olympic Park. Despite its name, there are now only two mills remaining, the most distinctive of which is the **Clock Mill**, with its conical oasts – kilns used to dry out grain – and its pretty white clock tower.

House Mill

May–Oct Sun 11am–4pm; March, April & Dec first Sun of month • £3 • ☎ 020 8980 4626, ⓦ housemill.org.uk • ⊖ Bromley-by-Bow

Opposite the Clock Mill stands the Dutch-style **House Mill**, built in 1776, around which you can take a guided tour, which explains the milling process and shows you the surviving mill wheels which were driven by the tide. Beyond the mills are later gin-distillery buildings, now converted into television and film studios. There's a café in the Miller's House and a craft market takes place outside on the first Sunday of the month (March–Dec).

Abbey Mills

Visible to the northeast of Three Mills Island is the new **Abbey Mills Pumping Station**, sporting a gleaming metal pitched roof, and, adjacent, its much more famous Victorian predecessor, a glorious Gothic-Italianate edifice nicknamed the "Cathedral of Sewage". The latter was built in the 1860s by Joseph Bazalgette and Edwin Cooper, and was originally flanked by two twin chimneys decorated in Moorish style, which were sadly demolished during World War II. Visible to the southeast of Three Mills are seven ornate, wrought-iron **Victorian gasholders**, built on the site of a rocket factory set up in the 1820s by William Congreve.

CANARY WHARF

Docklands

The architectural embodiment of smash-and-grab capitalism according to its critics or a blueprint for inner-city regeneration to its free-market supporters – the Docklands area has always provoked extreme reactions. Despite the catch-all name, however, Docklands is far from homogeneous. Canary Wharf, with its Manhattan-style skyscrapers, is the most visible landmark, but it's by no means typical; warehouse conversions, industrial-estate sheds, left-over council housing, and Costa del Thames apartments in a whole travesty of styles, are more indicative. Travelling through on the Docklands Light Railway (DLR), the area comes over as a fascinating open-air design museum, not a place one would choose to live or work necessarily – most see it as removed from the rest of London – but a spectacular sight nevertheless.

From the sixteenth century onwards the **Port of London** was the trading lynchpin of the British Empire and the key to the city's wealth. The "legal quays" – roughly the area between London Bridge and the Tower – were crowded with as many as 1400 seagoing vessels forced to wait for up to 6 weeks to be unloaded, with some 3500 cutters, barges and punts jostling between their hulls. It was to relieve such congestion that, from 1802 onwards, London constructed the largest enclosed **cargo-dock system** in the world. Each dock was surrounded by 40ft-high walls, patrolled by its own police force and geared towards a specific cargo. Casual dockers gathered at the dock gates each morning for the "call-on", a human scrummage to get selected for work. This mayhem was only stopped after World War II, when the Dock Labour Scheme was introduced, and by then it was too late. Since the mid-nineteenth century, competition from the railways eroded the river traffic, and with the development of container ships and the movement of the port to Tilbury in the 1960s, the old city docks began to wind down.

In 1981, the **London Docklands Development Corporation (LDDC)** was set up to regenerate the area, with the unfortunate slogan of "Looks like Venice, works like New York". By the time the LDDC was wound up in 1998, it had achieved more than many thought possible, though it's certainly easy to criticize its approach – ad hoc planning, and a lack of basic amenities, green spaces, civic architecture or public buildings, and consultation with the local community. Today, however, construction is continuing apace, with the end result destined to be, as one critic aptly put it, "a chain of highly polarized ghettos epitomizing the gulf between the rich and poor, home-owner and tenant". For the local community's views, visit ⓦwharf.co.uk.

ARRIVAL AND INFORMATION

Arrival and departure You can view Docklands from a distance on one of the boats that course up and down the Thames (see p.22). For a close-up you should take the driverless, overhead Docklands Light Railway or DLR (see p.22). If you're heading for Greenwich, and fancy taking a boat back into town, it might be worth considering a Rail River Rover Pass (£15), which gives you unlimited travel on the DLR and City Cruises services between Greenwich and Westminster. Note that bicycles are not allowed on the DLR, though you can walk them through the Greenwich Foot Tunnel.

The Thames Path You can walk the two miles from Wapping to Canary Wharf along, or close to, the riverbank, by following the Thames Path; there are also several pedestrian bridges linking the different quays around Canary Wharf.

Wapping

Once famous for its boatyards and its 36 riverside pubs (a handful of which remain), **Wapping** changed forever with the construction of the enclosed docks. Cut off from the East End by the high dock walls, its inhabitants crowded into unsanitary housing, the area became notorious for thieves, attracted by rolling drunk sailors and poorly guarded warehouses. With the destruction wrought during the Blitz and the commercial demise of the docks, Wapping was very run-down by the 1980s and an early candidate for regeneration. Restoration of existing property rather than demolition and redevelopment has been the rule, so something of Wapping's Victorian atmosphere remains, and, as it is a short walk from the Tower, this is easily the most satisfying part of Docklands to explore.

St Katharine Docks

ⓦ skdocks.co.uk • ⊖ Tower Hill or Tower Gateway DLR

St Katharine Docks were built in the late 1820s – in the process some 11,300 people were made homeless, and the medieval hospital of St Katharine demolished. The docks specialized in luxury goods such as ivory, spices, carpets and cigars, but were very badly bombed in the Blitz and, in the early 1970s, were turned into a luxury yacht marina.

With little of the original warehouse architecture surviving, the docks' redeeming qualities are the old **swing bridges**, the one or two old sailing ships and Dutch barges that moor here, and the central **Ivory House** warehouse, with its clock tower and wrought-iron colonnade. Built in 1854, at its peak this warehouse received over 200 tons of ivory annually (that's 4000 dead elephants), plus hippopotamus and walrus teeth and even mammoth tusks from Siberia. Halfway along East Smithfield, you can see the original gates with elephants on the pillars, and on the corner of Thomas More Street, a section of the **original dock wall** survives, plus the main entrance to the former London Docks, with two Neoclassical Customs and Excise offices from 1805.

Dickens Inn, an eighteenth-century timber-framed brewery warehouse, was air-lifted in 1969 from its original site several hundred yards to the east. At the centre of the docks is the ugly **Coronarium chapel** (now a *Starbucks*), built for Queen Elizabeth II's Silver Jubilee, and as near as possible to the church of St Katharine's, which was owned by the Crown.

DOCKLANDS

News International

East down the busy Highway lies the headquarters of Rupert Murdoch's **News International**, a complex dubbed "Fortress Wapping", on account of its high walls, barbed wire and security cameras. Murdoch was one of the first capitalist press barons to give Docklands his blessing, sacking his entire workforce of printers and journalists when he moved his newspapers – *The Times, Sunday Times, The Sun* and the former *News of the World* – out here to Wapping in 1986, sparking one of the most bitter trade-union disputes of the Thatcher era. Mounted police engaged in violent skirmishes with protesters for nearly a year – no prizes for guessing who won.

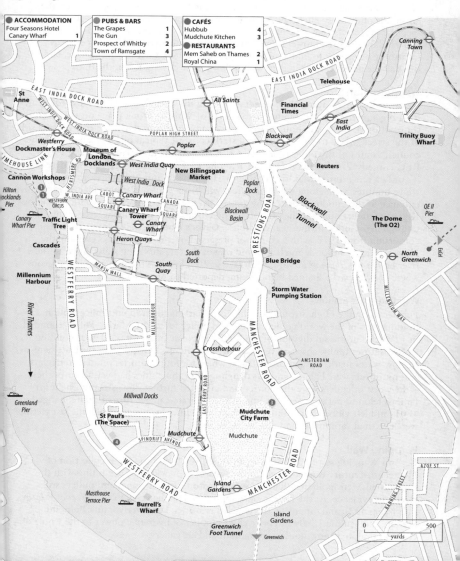

● ACCOMMODATION		● PUBS & BARS		● CAFÉS	
Four Seasons Hotel		The Grapes	1	Hubbub	4
Canary Wharf	1	The Gun	3	Mudchute Kitchen	3
		Prospect of Whitby	2	● RESTAURANTS	
		Town of Ramsgate	4	Mem Saheb on Thames	2
				Royal China	1

Tobacco Dock

Close by stands **Tobacco Dock**, a huge warehouse built in 1814 and initially used to store tobacco and wine. A fascinating combination of timber and early cast-iron framing, it was converted into a shopping complex in 1990 by postmodernist Terry Farrell, but the place closed soon afterwards and has been a dead mall for years. On the south of Tobacco Dock, a tree-lined **canal walk** – all that remains of the huge Western Dock that once stood here – will take you effortlessly back to Wapping High Street.

14

St George-in-the-East

The Highway • Daily 9am–5pm • ☎ 020 7481 1345, Ⓦ stgite.org.uk • Shadwell DLR

Nicholas Hawksmoor's church of **St George-in-the-East**, built in 1726, stands on the north side of the busy Highway. As bold as any of Hawksmoor's buildings, it boasts four "pepperpot" towers above the nave, built to house the staircases to the church's galleries, and a hulking west-end tower topped by an octagonal lantern. Within, it comes as something of a shock to find a miniature modern church squatting in the nave, but that's all the parish could come up with following the devastation of the Blitz.

Wapping High Street

If you arrive on **Wapping High Street** expecting the usual parade of shops, you're in for a big surprise. Traditionally, the business of Wapping took place on the river; thus tall brick-built warehouses, most now converted into flats, line the Thames side of the street, while to the north – in a stark contrast typical of Docklands – lie the council estates of the older residents. (Alf Garnett, the dockworker of the 1960s BBC comedy *Till Death Us Do Part*, lived here.) Few tourists make it out here, but it's only a ten-minute walk from St Katharine Docks, and well worth the effort.

Five minutes' walk along the High Street will bring you to **Wapping Pier Head**, former entrance to the London Docks, now grassed over but still flanked by grand, curvaceous Regency terraces built for the officials of the Dock Company. Further east is the unusual neo-Gothic former tea warehouse, **Oliver's Wharf**, a trailblazing apartment conversion from 1972, with a couple of preserved overhead gangways crossing the High Street just beyond. You'll also find one of the few surviving stairs down to the river beside the *Town of Ramsgate* pub (see p.392); beneath the pub are the dungeons where convicts were chained before being deported to Australia.

Wapping Police Station

Further along the High Street from Oliver's Wharf stands **Wapping Police Station**, headquarters of the world's oldest uniformed police force, the Marine Police, founded in 1798 and now a subdivision of the Met. The police boatyard is a 1960s building which features funky, abstract, vertical fibreglass friezes. Down by the riverside here, at the low-water mark, was **Execution Dock**, where for four centuries pirates, smugglers and mutineers were hanged and left dangling until three tides had washed over them – the worst offenders were then tarred and gibbeted further downstream. The most famous felon to perish here was Captain Kidd, pirate-catcher-turned-pirate, hanged in 1701, and left gibbeted in an iron cage by the Thames for twenty years; the last victims were executed for murder and mutiny in 1830.

Wapping Wall

Beyond Wapping station, along **Wapping Wall**, you'll find the finest collection of nineteenth-century warehouses left in the whole of Docklands, beginning with the gargantuan Metropolitan Wharf, its wrought-iron capstan cranes and pulleys still clearly in evidence. At the far end of Wapping Wall is the venerable *Prospect of Whitby* pub (see p.392), and, opposite, the ivy-clad red-brick **London Hydraulic Pumping Station**, built in the 1890s and once chief supplier of hydraulic power to the whole of central London; it now houses a restaurant and art gallery.

Shadwell Basin

Shadwell Basin, over the swing bridge to the north of the Pumping Station, is one of the last remaining stretches of water that once comprised three interlocking docks, known simply as London Docks and first opened in 1805. Now a water sports centre, it's enclosed on three sides by characteristically gimmicky new housing finished off in primary reds and blues. Rising up majestically behind the houses to the north is **St Paul's** (ⓦstpaulsshadwell.org), the "sea captains' church", with a Baroque tower.

14

Limehouse

East of Wapping, **Limehouse** was a major shipbuilding centre in the eighteenth and nineteenth centuries, hub of London's canal traffic and the site of the city's first **Chinatown**, a district sensationalized in Victorian newspapers as a warren of opium and gambling dens, and by writers such as Oscar Wilde, Arthur Conan Doyle, Sax Rohmer and Dickens: "Down by the docks the shabby undertaker's shop will bury you for next to nothing, after the Malay or Chinaman has stabbed you for nothing at all." Wartime bombing and postwar road schemes all but obliterated Limehouse: **Narrow Street**, the main thoroughfare, is sleepier than Wapping High Street and the only remnants of the Chinese community are the street names: Canton, Mandarin, Ming and Pekin among them. For London's contemporary Chinatown, see the Soho and Fitzrovia chapter (p.98).

St Anne's Church

Limehouse's major landmark is Hawksmoor's **St Anne's Church**, rising up just north of the DLR viaduct. Begun in 1714, and dominated by a gargantuan west tower, topped by an octagonal lantern, it boasts the highest church clock in London. The interior was badly damaged by fire in 1850, though it does contain a superb organ built for the Great Exhibition the following year. In the graveyard Hawksmoor erected a pyramidal structure carved with masonic symbols, now hopelessly eroded; opposite is a war memorial with relief panels depicting the horrors of trench warfare.

Limekiln Dock

A pedestrian bridge carries the Thames Path path over the entrance to Limehouse Basin and then the tidal inlet of **Limekiln Dock**, overlooked to the north by a picturesque gaggle of listed warehouses, and to the south by the gargantuan Dundee Wharf development, sporting a huge grey freestanding pylon of balconies. Beyond lies the mock-Egyptian development that houses the *Four Seasons Hotel* (see p.360). The Thames Path eventually ploughs its way right round the Isle of Dogs, but for now it's still a bit stop-start once you get past Canary Wharf Pier.

Isle of Dogs

A whole people toil at the unloading of the enormous ships, swarming on the barges, dark figures, dimly outlined, moving rhythmically, fill in and give life to the picture. In the far distance, behind the interminable lines of sheds and warehouses, masts bound the horizon, masts like a bare forest in winter, finely branched, exaggerated, aerial trees grown in all the climates of the globe.

Gabriel Mourey (1865–1943)

The Thames begins a dramatic horseshoe bend at Limehouse, thus creating the **Isle of Dogs**. The origin of the peninsula's strange name has been much debated: it could be a corruption of ducks, or of dykes, or, in fact, refer to the royal kennels which once stood here. In 1802, London's first enclosed trade docks were built here to accommodate rum and sugar from the West Indies. The demise of the docks was slow in coming, but rapid in its conclusion: in 1975, there were still 8000 jobs; five years later they were closed. Now at the heart of the new Docklands, the Isle of Dogs reaches its apotheosis in the skyscrapers of **Canary Wharf**. Yet while some

90,000 workers trek to Canary Wharf each weekday, the rest of the "island" remains surreally lifeless, an uneasy, socially divided community comprised of drab council housing, encompassed by a horseshoe of crass, super-rich, riverside developments.

Canary Wharf

The strip of land in the middle of the former West India Docks, **Canary Wharf** was originally a destination for rum and mahogany, and later tomatoes and bananas (from the Canary Islands, hence the name). It's the easiest bit of the Isle of Dogs to explore on foot, though the whole place feels a bit like a stage-set, a spotlessly clean business quarter policed by security guards, with make-believe streets like Wren Steps and Chancellor Passage. The most famous building is Cesar Pelli's 800ft-high stainless-steel **Canary Wharf Tower** (closed to the public) – the highest building in the country for two decades after it was completed in 1991. Officially known as One Canada Square, the tower is flanked by Norman Foster's HSBC and Pelli's Citigroup skyscrapers, both of which are 656ft high, glass-clad and rather dull.

ARRIVAL

By boat, bus or foot Arriving by boat, bus or foot, you come to Westferry Circus, the double-decker roundabout park at the western end of the tree-lined West India Avenue. This, in turn, leads to Cabot Square, centred on a graceful fountain and, beyond, to the colonnaded offices that terminate at Canada Square.

By DLR Arriving by DLR at Canary Wharf is spectacular, with the rail line cutting right through the middle of the office buildings, spanned by Pelli's parabolic steel-and-glass canopy.

By tube Arriving by tube, you get probably the best close-up view of the Pelli tower from the forest of public clocks on West Plaza, right outside Norman Foster's stingray-like entrance to the tube.

West India Quay and around

North of Cabot Square, you can cross a floodlit floating bridge to **West India Quay**, probably the most pleasing development on the Isle of Dogs. Here, two Georgian warehouses (out of nine) have survived and now house flats, bars, restaurants and the Museum of London Docklands (see opposite).

Immediately to the west of the warehouses is the old entrance to the West India Docks, heralded by the **Ledger Building** (now a pub), which sports a dinky Doric portico and, round the corner, a splendidly pompous plaque commemorating the opening of the docks from 1800. Opposite, across Hertsmere Road, stands a small, circular, domed building, the lone survivor of two guardhouses that flanked the main entrance to the docks; behind it lies the former cooperage, now the **Cannon Workshops**.

To the northeast, behind the Ledger Building, are more little-known remnants of the old docks, among them the stately **Dockmaster's House**, built in 1809 as the Excise Office and now a restaurant, with a smart white balustrade. Behind here, on Garford Street, there's a prim row of **Dock Constables' Cottages**, built in pairs in 1802, with the one for the sergeant slightly detached. Before you reach them, you'll pass **Grieg House**, a lovely yellow-and-red-brick building, built in 1903 as part of the Scandinavian Seamen's Temperance Home, with a little cupola and lovely exterior mouldings.

Nothing will convey to the stranger a better idea of the vast activity and stupendous wealth of London than a visit to these warehouses, filled to overflowing with interminable stores of every kind of foreign and colonial products; to these enormous vaults, with their apparently inexhaustible quantities of wine; and to these extensive quays and landing-stages, cumbered with huge stacks of hides, heaps of bales, and long rows of casks…Those who wish to taste the wines must procure a tasting-order from a wine merchant. Ladies are not admitted after 1pm. Visitors should be on their guard against insidious effects of "tasting" in the heavy, vinous atmosphere.

Baedeker's Handbook for London (1905)

Museum of London Docklands
West India Quay • Daily 10am–6pm • Free • ☎ 020 7001 9844, ⓦ www.museumindocklands.org.uk • West India Quay DLR

If you've any interest in the history of the docks or the Thames, then a visit to the **Museum of London Docklands** is well worth it. Housed in a warehouse built in 1803 for storing rum, sugar, molasses, coffee and cotton, the museum takes a chronological approach, beginning on the top floor, where you'll find a great model of old London Bridge, one side depicting it around 1450, the other around 1600. Also here is the Rhinebeck Panorama, an 8ft-long watercolour showing the "legal quays" in the 1790s, just before the enclosed docks were built. On the floor below are diverse sections on slavery, frost fairs and whaling, a reconstructed warren of late nineteenth-century shops and cobbled streets called "Sailortown", plus mock-ups of a cooperage, a bottling vault and a tobacco-weighing office. Look out, too, for the model of Brunel's *Leviathan*, the fascinating wartime film reel and the excellent even-handed coverage of the docks' postwar history. Those with kids should head for Mudlarks, where children can learn a bit about pulleys and ballast, drive a DLR train or just romp around the soft play area.

Westferry Road
Points of interest elsewhere on the Isle of Dogs are few and far between, but one or two monuments are worth pointing out around Westferry Road. One of Docklands' more playful monuments is Pierre Vivant's **Traffic Light Tree**, west of Heron Quays, at the top of Westferry Road, which features a cluster of traffic signals all flashing madly – a strangely confusing sight for drivers after dark. Impossible to miss, to the southwest, is **Cascades**, a wedge of high-rise triangular apartments that's become something of a Docklands landmark. Equally unavoidable is **Millennium Harbour**, a gated development whose weatherboarded top-floor penthouses jut out like air-traffic-control towers.

Burrell's Wharf
At the southern end of Westferry Road, you come to **Burrell's Wharf**, a residential development based around the industrial relics of the old Millwall Ironworks, built in the 1830s. The boiler-house chimney survives, as does the Italianate Plate House, where the steel plates for Isambard Kingdom Brunel's 19,000-ton steamship, the *Great Eastern* (aka the *Leviathan*), were manufactured. Built at a cost of £1 million, the *Leviathan* was four times larger than any other ship in the world at the time, but enjoyed a working life of just sixteen years as a passenger liner and cable-layer. The timber piles of the ship's 1857 launching site can still be seen, a little further upstream.

Island Gardens
The DLR now goes directly under the river to Greenwich, but it's worth considering getting out at **Island Gardens**, in the far south of the Isle of Dogs. From the eponymous park here, Christopher Wren used to contemplate his masterpieces, the Royal Naval College and the Royal Observatory, and you, too, can do the same, before heading across the river via the 1902 **Greenwich Foot Tunnel**.

Trinity Buoy Wharf
Hidden to the east of East India Dock is the bizarre little enclave of **Trinity Buoy Wharf**. Built in 1803, it is home to London's only lighthouse, one of a pair built by Trinity House for experiments in optics and used by, among others, Michael Faraday. The wharf also houses offices and flats, built out of old shipping containers, an original 1940s American mobile diner where you can get a bite to eat, and a whole array of boats. In the lighthouse itself, there's a musical installation called **Longplayer** (Sat & Sun 11am–5pm; Dec–March closes 4pm; free; ⓦlongplayer.org), a twenty-minute recording of Tibetan singing bowls, manipulated to create a 1000-year-long loop, and due to play until December 31, 2999. The wharf is a ten-minute walk from East India DLR station, at the end of Orchard Place, where the Bow Creek (part of the River Lee) winds its way into the Thames.

The South Bank

The South Bank has a lot going for it. As well as the massive waterside arts centre, it's home to a host of tourist attractions including the enormously popular London Eye, Europe's largest observation wheel, the adjacent London Aquarium and, further inland, the Imperial War Museum, which harbours the country's only permanent exhibition devoted to the Holocaust. With most of London sitting on the north bank of the Thames, the views from here are the best on the river, and thanks to the wide, traffic-free riverside boulevard, the whole area can be happily explored on foot. Buskers congregate here, as much as at Covent Garden, to entertain the crowds. And you can continue your wanderings eastwards along the riverside walkway towards Tate Modern and the regenerated districts of Bankside and Southwark (Chapter 16).

For centuries London stopped southwards at the Thames; the South Bank was a marshy, uninhabitable place, a popular place for duck-shooting, but otherwise seldom visited. Then, in the eighteenth century, wharves began to be built along the riverbank, joined later by factories, so that by 1905 the Baedeker guidebook characterized **Lambeth** (covered in this chapter) and Southwark (covered in the next chapter) as "containing numerous potteries, glass-works, machine-factories, breweries and hop-warehouses". Slums and overhead railway lines added to the grime until 1951, when a slice of Lambeth's badly bombed riverside was used as a venue for the Festival of Britain, the site eventually evolving into the **Southbank Centre**, a vibrant arts complex, encased in an unlovely concrete shell. What helped kick-start the South Bank's more recent rejuvenation was the arrival of the spectacular **London Eye**, and the renovation of **Hungerford Bridge**, which is now flanked by a majestic symmetrical double-suspension footbridge. To find out about the latest events and exhibitions on the South Bank (and in neighbouring Southwark) visit ⓦlondon-se1.co.uk.

15

Southbank Centre

ⓦ southbankcentre.co.uk

In 1951, the South Bank Exhibition, on derelict land south of the Thames, formed the centrepiece of the national **Festival of Britain**, an attempt to revive morale postwar by celebrating the centenary of the Great Exhibition (when Britain really did rule over half the world). The most striking features of the site were the Ferris wheel (now reincarnated as the London Eye), the saucer-shaped Dome of Discovery (inspiration for the Millennium Dome), the Royal Festival Hall (which still stands) and the cigar-shaped steel and aluminium Skylon tower.

The great success of the festival eventually provided the impetus for the creation of the **Southbank Centre** comprising the Royal Festival Hall, Queen Elizabeth Hall, the Purcell Room and the Hayward art gallery, all squeezed between Hungerford and Waterloo bridges. Unfortunately, however, it failed to capture the imagination of the public in the same way, and became London's much unloved culture bunker. The low point came in the 1980s when hundreds of homeless lived under the complex in a "Cardboard City". Since then, there have been considerable improvements, and the centre's unprepossessing appearance is softened, too, by its riverside location, its avenue of trees, fluttering banners, occasional buskers and skateboarders, and the weekend secondhand bookstalls outside nearby BFI Southbank. The nearest tube is Waterloo, but the most pleasant way to **approach** the Southbank Centre is via Hungerford Bridge from Embankment or Charing Cross tube.

Royal Festival Hall

Southbank Centre • Poetry Library Tues–Sun 11am–8pm; free; ⓦ poetrylibrary.org.uk • ⊖ Waterloo

The only building left from the 1951 Festival of Britain is the **Royal Festival Hall** or RFH, one of London's main concert venues, whose auditorium is suspended above the open-plan foyer – its curved roof is clearly visible above the main body of the building. The interior furnishings remain fabulously period, and exhibitions and events in the foyer are generally excellent, making this one of the most pleasant South Bank buildings to visit. You can also kill time before a concert in the little-known **Poetry Library** on Level 5, where you can either browse or, by joining (membership is free), borrow from the library's vast collection of poetry since 1912.

Architecturally, the most depressing parts of the Southbank Centre are the **Queen Elizabeth Hall** (QEH) and the more intimate **Purcell Room**, which share the same foyer and are built in uncompromisingly brutalist 1960s style. **The Hayward**, the art gallery which sits behind and on top of this concrete garbage, is equally repellent from the outside, with the exception of its strange rooftop neon sculpture.

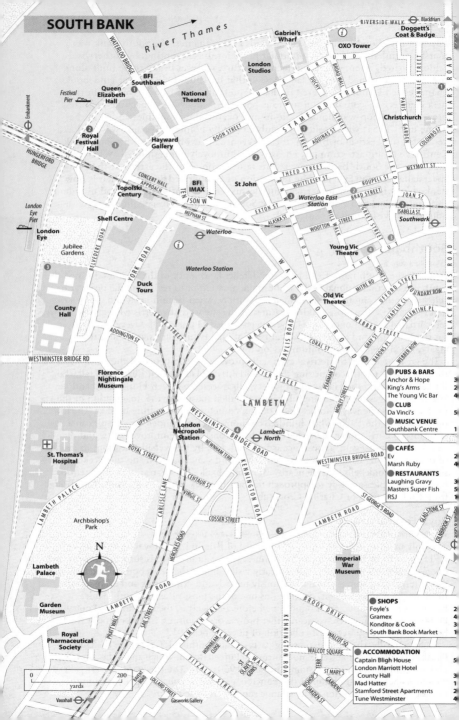

SOUTH BANK

River Thames

RIVERSIDE WALK · Blackfriars
Doggett's Coat & Badge

Gabriel's Wharf
OXO Tower

London Studios

Embankment

Festival Pier

BFI Southbank

Queen Elizabeth Hall

National Theatre

Christchurch

Royal Festival Hall

Hayward Gallery

HUNGERFORD BRIDGE

Topolski Century

CONCERT HALL APPROACH

Shell Centre

London Eye Pier

London Eye

Jubilee Gardens

County Hall

St John

Waterloo East Station

Southwark

Young Vic Theatre

Waterloo

Waterloo Station

Duck Tours

Old Vic Theatre

Florence Nightingale Museum

WESTMINSTER BRIDGE RD

St. Thomas's Hospital

London Necropolis Station

LAMBETH

Lambeth North

WESTMINSTER BRIDGE ROAD

Archbishop's Park

Lambeth Palace

Garden Museum

Royal Pharmaceutical Society

Imperial War Museum

0   200
yards

Vauxhall

Gasworks Gallery

PUBS & BARS
- Anchor & Hope **3**
- King's Arms **2**
- The Young Vic Bar **4**

CLUB
- Da Vinci's **5**

MUSIC VENUE
- Southbank Centre **1**

CAFÉS
- Ev **2**
- Marsh Ruby **4**

RESTAURANTS
- Laughing Gravy **3**
- Masters Super Fish **5**
- RSJ **1**

SHOPS
- Foyle's **2**
- Gramex **4**
- Konditor & Cook **3**
- South Bank Book Market **1**

ACCOMMODATION
- Captain Bligh House **5**
- London Marriott Hotel County Hall **3**
- Mad Hatter **1**
- Stamford Street Apartments **2**
- Tune Westminster **4**

TOPOLSKI CENTURY

An unusual and little-known sight on the South Bank is **Topolski Century** (150-152 Concert Hall Approach; tours by appointment only, £10; ☎020 7620 1275, ⓦtopolskicentury.org.uk; ⊖ Waterloo), hidden under the arches on the north side of Hungerford Bridge on Concert Hall Approach. This enormous work, by Polish-born artist Feliks Topolski (1907–89), consists of a series of murals, painted floor to ceiling on panels, telling the story of Topolski's life and that of the twentieth century. Painted from 1975 until the artist's death, it depicts many of the seminal events and the leading figures of the century, as well as containing a more light-hearted section entitled "One Hundred Hippies", featuring Mick Jagger and members of Hawkwind.

Waterloo Bridge and beyond

Waterloo Bridge, famous for being built mostly by women during World War II, marks the eastern limit of the Southbank Centre, but the next stretch of riverside to Blackfriars Bridge has cultural attractions of its own: from the city's leading arts cinema, **BFI Southbank**, to the retail-workshops of the renovated **Oxo Tower**. The bridge itself was the scene of the **assassination** of Georgi Markov, a Bulgarian dissident working at the BBC World Service, in 1978. He was shot in the leg with a ricin pellet fired from an umbrella by a member of the Bulgarian secret police and died three days later.

15

BFI Southbank

Belvedere Rd • Mediathèque Tues–Fri noon–8pm, Sat & Sun 12.30–8pm • Free • ⓦ bfi.org.uk • ⊖ Waterloo

Tucked underneath Waterloo Bridge is **BFI Southbank**, which screens London's most esoteric films, hosts a variety of talks, lectures and mini-festivals and also runs **Mediathèque**, where you can settle into one of the viewing stations and choose from a selective archive of British films, TV programmes and documentaries. The BFI also runs the **BFI IMAX**, housed within the eye-catching glass-drum, which rises up from the old "Bull Ring" beneath the roundabout at the southern end of Waterloo Bridge. Boasting the largest screen in the country, it's definitely worth experiencing a 3D film here at least once, but as with all IMAX cinemas, it suffers from the fact that very few movies are shot on 70mm film.

National Theatre

South Bank • Backstage tours daily 1hr 15min; £7.50 • ☎ 020 7452 3400, ⓦ nationaltheatre.org.uk • ⊖ Waterloo

Just east of Waterloo Bridge, looking like a multistorey car park, is Denys Lasdun's **National Theatre** (officially the Royal National Theatre). An institution first mooted in 1848, it was only finally realized in 1976, and, like the Southbank Centre, its concrete brutalism tends to receive a lot of critical flak, with Prince Charles likening it to a nuclear power station. That said, the three auditoriums within are superb, and the **backstage tours** here are excellent and popular, so book in advance if possible.

Gabriel's Wharf

Beyond the National Theatre, the riverside promenade brings you eventually to **Gabriel's Wharf**, an ad hoc collection of lock-up craft shops, brasseries and bars that has a small weekend craft market. It's a refreshing change from the franchises which have colonized much of the South Bank, and one for which Coin Street Community Builders (ⓦcoinstreet.org) must be thanked. With the population in this bomb-damaged stretch of the South Bank down from fifty thousand at the beginning of the century to four thousand in the early 1970s, big commercial developers were keen to step in and build hotels and office blocks galore. They were successfully fought off, and instead the emphasis has been on projects that combine commercial and community interests.

OXO Tower

South Bank · **Exhibition Gallery** Daily 11am–6pm · Free · **Public viewing gallery** Daily 10am–10pm · Free · ⊖ Blackfriars

East of Gabriel's Wharf stands the landmark **OXO Tower**, an old power station that was converted into a meat-packing factory in the 1930s by Liebig Extract of Meat Company, best known in Britain as the makers of OXO stock cubes. To get round the local council's ban on illuminated advertisements, the company cleverly incorporated the letters into the windows of the main tower, and then illuminated them from within. Nowadays, the building contains an exhibition gallery on the ground floor, plus flats for local residents, and a series of retail-workshops for designers on the first and second floors, and a swanky restaurant, bar and brasserie on the top floor. To enjoy the view, however, you don't need to eat or drink here: you can simply take the lift to the eighth-floor **public viewing gallery**.

Waterloo Station

Originally built in 1848, **Waterloo Station** is easily the capital's busiest station, serving the city's southwestern suburbs and the southern Home Counties. Its two finest features are easily missed: the station's ornate Edwardian facade is hidden behind the railway bridge on Mepham Street, while the snake-like, curving roof of the old Eurostar terminal, designed by Nicholas Grimshaw in 1993, is tucked away on the west side of the station.

Without doubt Waterloo's most bizarre train terminus was the former **London Necropolis Station**, whose early twentieth-century facade survives at 121 Westminster Bridge Rd, to the south of the station. Originally opened in 1854 following one of London's worst outbreaks of cholera, trains from this station took coffins and mourners to Brookwood Cemetery in Surrey (at the time, the world's largest cemetery). Brookwood Station even had separate platforms for Anglicans and Nonconformists and a licensed bar – "Spirits served here", the sign apparently read – but the whole operation was closed down after bomb damage in World War II.

Heading west from the main station concourse, an overhead walkway heads off to the South Bank, passing through the Stalinist-looking **Shell Centre** (officially and poetically entitled The Downstream Building). Built in the 1950s – and the tallest building in London at the time – it's still owned and operated by oil giant Shell, which started life as an East End sea-shell shop in 1833.

London Eye

Daily April–June 10am–9pm; July & Aug 10am–9.30pm; Sept–March 10am–8.30pm · From £17 online · ☎ 08701 871 3000, Ⓦ londoneye.com · ⊖ Waterloo or Westminster

Despite being little more than ten years old, the **London Eye** is already one of the city's most famous landmarks. Standing an impressive 443ft high, it's the largest Ferris wheel in Europe, weighing over 2000 tons, yet as simple and delicate as a bicycle wheel. It's constantly in slow motion, which means a full-circle "flight" in one of its 32 pods (one for each of the city's boroughs) should take around 30 minutes – that may seem a long time, though in fact it passes incredibly quickly. Not surprisingly, you can see right out to the very edge of the city – bring some binoculars if you can – where the suburbs slip into the countryside, making the wheel one of the few places (apart from a plane window) from which London looks a manageable size. Book online (to save money) – on arrival, you'll still have to queue to be loaded on unless you've paid extra – or you'll have to buy your ticket from the box office at the eastern end of County Hall.

County Hall

Ⓦ londoncountyhall.com

The colonnaded crescent of **County Hall** is the only truly monumental building on the South Bank. Designed to house the London County Council, it was completed in 1933 and enjoyed its greatest moment of fame in the 1980s as the headquarters of the GLC (Greater London Council), under the Labour leadership of Ken Livingstone, or "Red Ken", as the right-wing press called him at the time. The Tories moved in swiftly, abolishing the GLC in 1986, and leaving London as the only European city without an elected authority. In 2000, Livingstone had the last laugh when he was successfully elected to become London's first mayor, and head of the new Greater London Authority (GLA), housed in City Hall, near Tower Bridge. The building's tenants are constantly changing, but it's currently home to, among other things, several hotels and restaurants, an aquarium, a museum and an amusement arcade. None of the attractions that have gravitated here is an absolute must, and several have fallen by the wayside, but they prosper (as do the numerous buskers round here) by feeding off the vast captive audience milling around the London Eye.

London Aquarium

County Hall • Mon–Thurs 10am–6pm, Fri–Sun 10am–7pm • From around £17 online • ☎ 0871 663 1679, ⓦ visitsealife.com/London • ⊖ Waterloo or Westminster

The most enduring County Hall tenant is the **Sea Life London Aquarium**, housed in the basement across three subterranean levels. With some super-large tanks, and everything from dog-face puffers and piranhas to robot fish (seriously) and crocodiles, this is an attraction that's pretty much guaranteed to please kids, albeit at a price (book online to save a few quid or to avoid queuing). Impressive in scale, the aquarium boasts a thrilling Shark Walk, in which you have sharks swimming underneath you, as well as a replica blue whale skeleton encasing an underwater walkway. Ask at the main desk or check the website for details of the daily presentations and feeding times.

London Film Museum

County Hall • Mon–Wed & Fri 10am–5pm, Thurs 11am–5pm, Sat 10am–6pm, Sun 11am–6pm • £13.50 • ☎ 020 7202 7043, ⓦ londfilmmuseum.com • ⊖ Waterloo or Westminster

The **London Film Museum** occupies a labyrinth of rooms on the first floor of County Hall. It's not a particularly hi-tech exhibition, so the main draw is really the vast array of props and costumes from Hollywood franchises like *Alien*, *Star Wars* and *Batman*. And there's a firmly British bent to the place, with each exhibit chosen either because the studio, the designer, the writer or the director was a Brit. Appropriately enough, there's a whole section on Charlie Chaplin, a local Lambeth boy born in the borough in 1889, and naturally enough there's a room of Harry Potter props, from the Tri-Wizard Cup to Hogwarts school uniforms.

Lambeth

South of Westminster Bridge, you leave the South Bank proper behind (and at the same time lose the crowds) and head upstream to what used to be the village of Lambeth (now a large borough stretching as far south as Brixton). Vestiges of village atmosphere are notably absent, but there are a few minor sights worth considering, such as **Lambeth Palace** and the **Garden Museum**. It's also from this stretch of the riverbank that you get the best views of the Houses of Parliament. Inland lies London's most even-handed military museum, the **Imperial War Museum**, which has a moving permanent exhibition devoted to the Holocaust.

Florence Nightingale Museum

Lambeth Palace Rd • Daily 10am–5pm • £5.80 • ☎ 020 7620 0374, ⓦ florence-nightingale.co.uk • ⊖ Lambeth North, Waterloo or Westminster

On the south side of Westminster Bridge, a series of red-brick Victorian blocks and modern accretions make up **St Thomas' Hospital**, originally founded in the twelfth century, but only established here after being ejected from its Georgian premises by

London Bridge in 1862, when the railway came sweeping through Southwark. At the hospital's northeastern corner, off Lambeth Palace Road, is the **Florence Nightingale Museum**, celebrating the devout woman who single-mindedly revolutionized the nursing profession by establishing the first school of nursing at St Thomas' in 1860 and publishing her *Notes on Nursing*, emphasizing the importance of hygiene, decorum and discipline. The exhibition is imaginatively set out, aided by audioguides in the shape of a stethoscope. It hits just the right note by putting the two years she spent tending to the wounded of the Crimean War in the context of a lifetime of tireless social campaigning. Exhibits include the Turkish lantern she used in Scutari hospital, near Istanbul, that earned her the nickname "The Lady with the Lamp", and her pet owl, Athena, (now stuffed) who used to perch on her shoulder.

Lambeth Palace

Lambeth Palace Rd • By appointment only • Free • ☎ 020 7898 1200, ⓦ archbishopofcanterbury.org • ⊖ Westminster, Lambeth North or Vauxhall

A short walk south of St Thomas's stands the imposing red-brick Tudor Gate of **Lambeth Palace**, London residence of the Archbishop of Canterbury since 1197. The whole complex is well worth a visit, but guided tours are by appointment only and are extremely popular – you'll need to book this year for next year.

The most impressive room is, without doubt, the **Great Hall** (now the library), with its very late Gothic, oak hammerbeam roof, built after the Restoration by Archbishop Juxon, whose coat of arms, featuring African heads, can be seen on the bookshelves. Upstairs, the **Guard Room** boasts an even older, arch-braced timber roof from the fourteenth century, and is the room where Thomas More was brought for questioning before being sent to the Tower (and subsequently beheaded).

Among the numerous portraits of past archbishops, look out for works by Holbein, Van Dyck, Hogarth and Reynolds. The final point on the tour is the **palace chapel**, where the religious reformer and leader of the Lollards, John Wycliffe, was tried (for the second time) in 1378 for "propositions, clearly heretical and depraved". The door and window frames date back to Wycliffe's day, but the place is somewhat overwhelmed by the ceiling frescoes by Leonard Rosoman, added in the 1980s, telling the story of the Church of England. Best of all is the fact that you can see the choir screen and stalls put there in the 1630s by Archbishop Laud, and later used as evidence of his Catholic tendencies at his trial (and execution) in 1645.

Garden Museum

Lambeth Palace Rd • Mon–Fri & Sun 10.30am–5pm, Sat 10.30am–4pm; closed first Mon of month • £6 • ☎ 020 7401 8865, ⓦ gardenmuseum.org.uk • ⊖ Westminster, Lambeth North or Vauxhall

Next door to Lambeth Palace stands the Kentish ragstone church of **St Mary-at-Lambeth**, largely rebuilt in Victorian times, but retaining its fourteenth-century medieval tower. The church is now home to the **Garden Museum** which puts on excellent exhibitions on a horticultural theme in the ground-floor galleries, and has a small permanent exhibition in the "belvedere", reached by a new wooden staircase. There's a small section on John Tradescant, gardener to James I and Charles I who's buried in the churchyard (see below), including one of his curiosities – a "vegetable lamb" that's in fact a Russian fern – plus a few dibbers and grubbers, and some pony boots designed to prevent damage to your lawn.

You can visit the church's shop and café for free – what's more you can take your tea and cake out into the small graveyard, now laid out as a **seventeenth-century knot garden**, where two interesting sarcophagi lurk among the foliage. The first, topped by an ornamental breadfruit, is the resting place of **Captain Bligh** of *Mutiny on the Bounty* fame (see opposite). More intriguing is the **Tradescant memorial** which features several very unusual reliefs: a seven-headed griffin contemplating a skull and a crocodile sifting through sundry ruins flanked by gnarled trees. Tradescant was a tireless traveller in his

CAPTAIN BLIGH

Born in Cornwall, **William Bligh** (1754–1817) joined the navy at the age of seven. He was chosen in 1776 by Captain Cook to be sailing master on the *Resolution* for his third and fatal voyage to the Pacific, and, in 1787, was appointed commander of the *Bounty* when it set off to transport breadfruit trees from Tahiti to the West Indies. On the way home the crew mutinied and set Bligh and 18 others adrift in a 23ft open boat, with no charts and few provisions. Using just a quadrant and a compass, Bligh successfully navigated the craft 3600 miles to the Indonesian island of Timor, a journey of 47 days. He served under Nelson at the Battle of Copenhagen, and later became governor of New South Wales, where his subjects once again rebelled. On his return to England, he was promoted to vice-admiral, lived on Lambeth Road (his house is now a B&B) and was buried in the family plot at St Mary-at-Lambeth (now the Garden Museum).

search for new plant species, and set up a museum of curiosities known as "Tradescant's Ark" in Lambeth in 1629. Among the many exhibits were the "hand of a mermaid…a natural dragon, above two inches long…blood that rained on the Isle of Wight…and the Passion of Christ carved very daintily on a plumstone". The less fantastical pieces formed the nucleus of Oxford's Ashmolean Museum.

15

Imperial War Museum

Lambeth Road • Daily 10am–6pm • Free • ☎ 020 7416 5000, ⓦ london.iwm.org.uk • ⊖ Lambeth North or Elephant & Castle

From 1815 until 1930, the domed building at the east end of Lambeth Road was the infamous lunatic asylum of Bethlem Royal Hospital, better known as **Bedlam**. (Charlie Chaplin's mother was among those confined here – the future comedian was born and spent a troubled childhood in nearby Kennington.) When the hospital was moved to Beckenham on the southeast outskirts of London, the wings of the 700-foot-long facade were demolished, leaving just the central building, now home to the **Imperial War Museum**, by far the capital's best military museum. In addition to the permanent galleries described below, the IWM has several long-term temporary exhibitions, and a busy schedule of talks and films worth checking out.

The main galleries

The treatment of the subject is impressively wide-ranging and fairly sober, once you've passed through the **Large Exhibits Gallery**, with its militaristic display of guns, tanks, fighter planes and a giant V-2 rocket. On the **lower ground floor**, the array of documents and images attesting to the human damage of the last century of war is underlined by a clock which adds two more casualties every minute to its grand total. In addition to the static displays, a good deal of stagecraft is used to convey the misery of combat, with a walk-through World War I trench, and a re-creation of the Blitz in which you wander from an air-raid shelter through bomb-ravaged streets, accompanied by blaring sirens and human voices.

On the first floor, you'll find the permanent **Secret War** gallery, which follows the clandestine activities of MI5, MI6 and the SOE (the wartime equivalent of MI6) – expect exploding pencils, trip wires and spy cameras – though its finale is marred by an unrealistically glowing account of the SAS operations in the 1991 Gulf War.

The art galleries and Extraordinary Heroes

The museum's **art galleries**, on the second floor, puts on superb exhibitions taken from their vast collection of works by war artists, official and unofficial, including the likes of David Bomberg, Wyndham Lewis, Stanley Spencer and John Nash. One painting that's on permanent display in its own room, alongside three other similarly grand canvases, is *Gassed*, by John Singer Sargent, a painter better known for his portraits of society beauties.

Crimes Against Humanity, also on the second floor, features a harrowing half-hour film on genocide and ethnic violence in the last century. You can also pay a visit to the nearby **Explore History Centre** and peruse the museum's reference books, archive film clips and its online collection.

On the top floor, the **Extraordinary Heroes** exhibition displays the largest collection of Victoria Crosses in the world. However, this is much more than a medal gallery as touch screen computers tell the moving stories behind the decorations.

The Holocaust Exhibition

Many people come to the Imperial War Museum specifically to see the **Holocaust Exhibition** (not recommended for under-14s), which you enter from the third floor. Taking a fairly conventional, sober approach to the subject, the museum has made a valiant attempt to avoid depicting the victims of the Holocaust as nameless masses, by focusing on individual cases, and interspersing the archive footage with eyewitness accounts from contemporary survivors.

The exhibition pulls few punches, bluntly stating that the pope failed to denounce the anti-Jewish **Nuremberg Laws**, that writers such as Eliot and Kipling expressed anti-Semitic views, and that at the 1938 Evian Conference, the European powers refused to accept any more Jewish refugees. Despite the restrictions of space, there are sections on the extermination of the gypsies, Nazi euthanasia, pre-Holocaust Yiddish culture and the persecution of the Slavs. The **genocide**, which began with the *Einsatzgruppen* and ended with the gas chambers, is catalogued in painstaking detail, while the problem of "proving" the Final Solution is also addressed, in a room that emphasizes the complexity of the Nazi bureaucracy, which, allied to an ideology of extermination, made the Holocaust not just possible but inevitable.

The centrepiece of the museum is a vast, all-white, scale model of (what is, in fact, only a very small slice of) **Auschwitz-Birkenau**, showing what happened to the two thousand Hungarian Jews who arrived at the camp from the town of Beregovo in May 1944. The significance of this transport is that, uniquely, photographs taken by the SS, of the selection process meted out on these particular arrivals managed to survive the war. In the alcoves overlooking the model, which has a pile of discarded possessions from the camps as its backdrop, survivors describe their first impressions of Auschwitz. This section is especially harrowing, and it's as well to leave yourself enough time to listen to the reflections of camp survivors at the end, as they attempt to come to terms with the past.

15

Southwark

In Tudor and Stuart London, the chief reason for crossing the Thames, to what is now Southwark, was to visit the disreputable Bankside entertainment district around the south end of London Bridge. Four hundred years on, Londoners have rediscovered the habit of heading for the area, thanks to the traffic-free riverside path and a wealth of top attractions, with the charge led by the mighty Tate Modern. Tourist spots now pepper the riverside from Blackfriars Bridge to Bermondsey from the remarkable Shakespeare's Globe Theatre to the Gothic horror excesses of the London Dungeon. East of Tower Bridge is the thriving little warehouse development of Butler's Wharf, centred on the excellent Design Museum. And further east still, Rotherhithe clings onto its old seafaring identity despite the demise of its once extensive enclosed docks.

Bankside

Ⓦ visitbankside.com

Bankside is dominated by the awesome **Tate Modern**, while close by, the **Millennium Bridge** provides a wonderful pedestrian link from the City and St Paul's. To the east are two thoroughly researched reconstructions: **Shakespeare's Globe Theatre** and Drake's Tudor galleon, the **Golden Hinde**. At this point, the shops, cafés and stalls of nearby **Borough Market**, which becomes something of a gourmet food haven (Thurs–Sat), provide a welcome refuelling stop, before you check out some of the city's best-preserved Gothic architecture in **Southwark Cathedral**.

The reconstruction of Shakespeare's Globe Theatre is pretty much all there is above ground today to remind you of Southwark's pre-industrial golden age of entertainment under the Tudors and Stuarts. For centuries, however, Bankside was best known for its **brothels**, which were already doing a thriving trade under the Romans. In 1161, the brothels were licensed by royal decree, but made to adhere to various rules and restrictions: prostitutes could now be fined three shillings for "grimacing to passers-by", but were given Sunday mornings off in order to attend church. The women wore red-and-white-striped caps and white aprons, and were known as "Winchester Geese", since the land was owned by the Bishop of Winchester. The Church made a small fortune out of the rent until Henry VIII closed the bawdy houses down.

In Elizabethan times, Bankside once more became the most nefarious area in London, known as "Stew's Bank" for its brothels or "stewhouses", and was studded with **bull- and bear-pits**. Pepys recalls seeing "some good sport of the bulls tossing of the

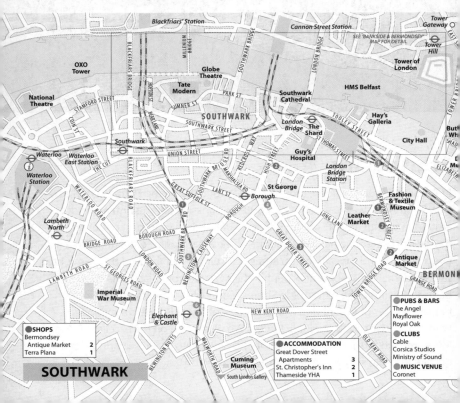

SHOPS
Bermondsey
Antique Market 2
Terra Plana 1

ACCOMMODATION
Great Dover Street
Apartments 3
St. Christopher's Inn 2
Thameside YHA 1

PUBS & BARS
The Angel
Mayflower
Royal Oak

CLUBS
Cable
Corsica Studios
Ministry of Sound

MUSIC VENUE
Coronet

SOUTHWARK

dogs; one into the very boxes", but opinion was by then inclining towards Evelyn's description of the sport as a "rude and dirty pastime" and in 1682 the last bear-garden was closed down. Most famous of all, of course, were Bankside's theatres (see p.228).

Tate Modern

Bankside • Daily 10am–6pm, Fri & Sat until 10pm • Free • ☎ 020 7887 8888, ⓦ tate.org.uk • ⊖ Southwark

Tate Modern is an absolute must for anyone visiting or living in London. Originally designed as an oil-fired power station by Giles Gilbert Scott, this austere, brick-built "cathedral of power" was closed down in 1981 and reopened as a modern art gallery in 2000. The masterful conversion, by the Swiss duo Herzog & de Meuron, has left plenty of the original industrial feel, while providing wonderfully light and spacious galleries to show off Tate's impressive collection of international twentieth-century artists, including Monet, Duchamp, Moore, Matisse, Mondrian, Picasso, Pollock, Rothko and Warhol.

Tate Modern receives around five million visitors a year, more than double what was envisaged. To alleviate this, the Tate has built a **new extension**, also designed by Herzog & de Meuron to the south of the power station. Open from 2012, its displays concentrate, in particular, on photography, video works and installations.

Tate's **permanent collection** dates back as far as 1900, but the curators have eschewed the old chronological approach, and gone instead for hanging works according to themes and -isms. So in amongst all the attention-grabbing conceptual stuff, you'll find some early twentieth-century paintings, looking terribly old-fashioned in their gilded frames. You'll need stamina to wade through more than one level in any one visit, so if

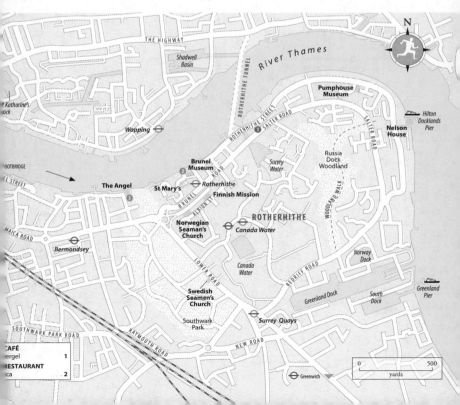

there's something you really want to see, go there first before you run out of energy. And remember that one of the joys of Tate Modern is coming across artists or artistic movements about which you may know very little.

ARRIVAL, INFORMATION AND TOURS

Arrival To appreciate the Tate's architecture fully, approach from the Millennium Bridge. The nearest entrance to the bridge is the North Entrance underneath the chimney, which brings you out at Level 2. The best way to enter, however, is via the ramp at the West Entrance, allowing you to fully appreciate the stupefying enormity of the main turbine hall, which sits on Level 1, below the Thames, and rises to a height of 115ft, and is used to display large-scale installations. There's also a Tate Boat, that plies between the two galleries (every 40min; 20min; ⓦ thamesclippers.com; £5).

Orientation Level 1 is also where you'll find the

information desk, and, on the opposite side, the museum's cloakroom and giant bookshop. Escalators from this floor lead straight up to Level 3, which, along with Level 5, contains the permanent collection; Level 4 is used for large-scale special exhibitions, for which there is an entrance fee.

Tours There are free guided tours (daily at 11am, noon, 2 & 3pm), multimedia guides (£3.50) and various apps available (Tate has free wi-fi).

Eating There's a pricey restaurant and bar on Level 7, with a great view over the river, and a more reasonably priced café on Level 2.

Level 3

Each level is divided into two distinct sections. On Level 3, **Poetry and Dream** concentrates, though by no means exclusively, on the interwar period. At the heart of the wing is a large room densely hung with works by the major Surrealists: **Miró**, **Magritte**, **Dalí** and the dreamlike **de Chirico**. Other rooms are given over to single artists like **Joseph Beuys**, whose bizarre choice of materials derives directly from his wartime experiences, when his plane crashed in the Crimea and he was saved by local Tartars, who cocooned him in felt and fat.

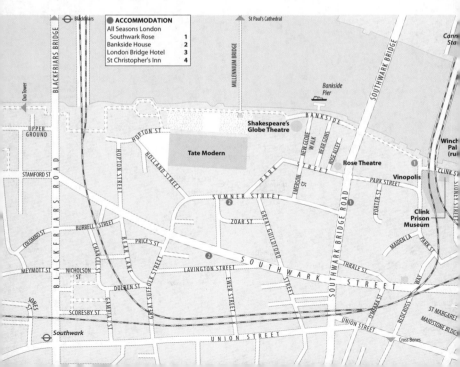

THE MILLENNIUM BRIDGE

The first new bridge to be built across the Thames since Tower Bridge opened in 1894, the sleek, stainless-steel **Millennium Bridge** is London's sole pedestrian-only crossing. A suspension bridge of innovative design – the high-profile triumvirate responsible were sculptor Anthony Caro, architect Norman Foster and engineers Ove Arup – it famously bounced up and down when it first opened in 2000 and had to be closed for another two years for repairs. It still wobbles a bit, but most people are too busy enjoying the spectacular views across to St Paul's Cathedral and Tate Modern to notice.

The Tate owns works from every period of **Picasso**'s life, including *Weeping Woman*, which is both a portrait of his lover Dora Maar and a heartfelt response to the Spanish Civil War. Throughout Tate Modern, you'll also find quite a bit of overlap with Tate Britain, with works by British artists like **Stanley Spencer**, whose unique Biblical visions and domestic scenes are all set in and around his home village of Cookham.

In **Material Gestures**, the emphasis is on the immediate postwar decades. Here, you catch perennial Tate favourites like **Mark Rothko**'s abstract "Seagram Murals". Commissioned by the swanky *Four Seasons* restaurant in New York, they were withheld by Rothko, who decided he didn't wish his art to be a mere backdrop to the recreation of the wealthy. Abstract expressionist works by **Jackson Pollock** are juxtaposed with *Waterlilies*, one of **Monet**'s much earlier experiments with abstraction. You'll also find the odd jaunty paper collage by **Matisse**, executed towards the end of his life when he was wheelchair-bound, plus a good selection of much earlier **Fauvist** works by the likes of Kandinsky, Derain and Kirchner.

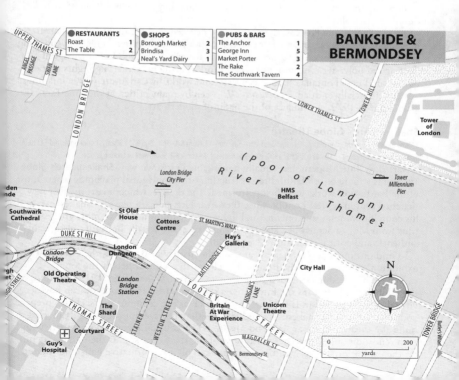

● RESTAURANTS	
Roast	1
The Table	2

● SHOPS	
Borough Market	2
Brindisa	3
Neal's Yard Dairy	1

● PUBS & BARS	
The Anchor	1
George Inn	5
Market Porter	3
The Rake	2
The Southwark Tavern	4

BANKSIDE & BERMONDSEY

SHAKESPEARE & CO

London's first purpose-built theatres emerged in Shoreditch in the 1570s, but they flourished on Bankside, with no fewer than four during the reign of James I: the **Swan**, built in 1587, with Edward Alleyn (founder of Dulwich College) as the lead actor and Christopher Marlowe as its main playwright; the **Rose**, built in 1595, its foundations still extant on Park Street; the **Hope**, built in 1613, which doubled as a bear garden and theatre; and the **Globe**, erected in 1599 on Park Street, where Shakespeare put on his greatest plays, now reconstructed on New Globe Walk. The theatres lasted barely half a century before being closed down by the Puritans, who considered them "chapels of Satan". With the Restoration, the focus of the theatre scene, and its accompanying vices, moved to Covent Garden, and Southwark faded from the limelight.

Level 5

Up on Level 5, in **States of Flux**, there's a wide range of works, with one of the central rooms given over to the -isms of Picasso and Braque's **Cubism**, the Italian **Futurism** of Severini and Dottori and the **Vorticism** of British artists like David Bomberg. Several examples of **Pop Art** by Andy Warhol and Roy Lichtenstein hang in one of the other large rooms, and further on, there are some characteristically uncompromising works by the queen of pop art Bridget Riley.

The gallery usually displays one or two works by **Marcel Duchamp**, whose seminal *Fountain*, a (disappointingly clean) urinal signed "R. Mutt, 1917" which was the world's first "readymade", a non-art object which becomes "art" only because it sits in a museum. Taking this idea one stage further, **Kurt Schwitters** put together works such as an "assemblage of discarded rubbish and printed ephemera", for as he himself said, "everything the artist spits is art" – a philosophy that logically led to Piero Manzoni's can of "Artist's Shit".

Over in **Energy and Process**, there's a gallery devoted to the little-known Italian art movement, *arte povera*, in which found objects played an important role. But this wing also brings the collection right up to date with Korean artist Do Ho Suh's magical floating red polyester evocation of his New York apartment. Other highlights to look out for are Lucio Fontana's slashed canvases, and works by **Carl André** whose infamous "Bricks" (officially entitled *Equivalent VIII*), seen by many critics, at the time Tate acquired it in 1972, as evidence of the nadir of modern art.

Shakespeare's Globe Theatre

21 New Globe Walk • Exhibition mid-April to mid-Sept Mon–Sat 9am–12.30pm & 1–5pm, Sun 9–11.30am & noon–5pm; mid-Oct to mid-April 9am–5.30pm; £11.50 • ☎ 020 7902 1500, ⓦ shakespearesglobe.com • ⊖ Southwark or London Bridge

Dwarfed by Tate Modern, but equally remarkable in its own way, **Shakespeare's Globe Theatre** is a more or less faithful reconstruction of the polygonal playhouse where most of the Bard's later works were first performed. The theatre, which boasts the first new thatched roof in central London since the Great Fire, puts on plays by Shakespeare and his contemporaries, using only natural light and the minimum of scenery. The season runs from May to September, and the performances are usually both fun, historically authentic and critically acclaimed (see p.418).

To find out more about Shakespeare and the history of Bankside, the Globe's stylish **exhibition**, to the west of the theatre, is well worth a visit. It details the long campaign by the single-minded American actor Sam Wanamaker (1919–93) to have the Globe rebuilt, but it's the interactive exhibits that hit the spot. You can have a virtual play on period musical instruments such as the crumhorn or sackbut, prepare your own edition of Shakespeare and feel the thatch, hazelnut shell and daub used to build the theatre. There are even booths in which you can record and compare your own rendition of key speeches with those of the stage greats, plus the odd live demo on the exhibition's stage. Visitors also get taken on an informative half-hour **guided** tour round the theatre itself; during the summer season, if you visit in the afternoon, you get to visit the nearby Rose Theatre instead for a reduced fee (see below).

Vinopolis

1 Bank End • Thurs & Fri 2–10pm, Sat noon–10pm, Sun noon–6pm • From £21 • ☎ 020 7940 3000, ⓦ vinopolis.co.uk • ⊖ London Bridge

Housed in the former wine vaults under the railway arches on Clink Street, **Vinopolis** is a strange fish: part wine bar-restaurant, part wine retailers (there's a branch of the excellent Majestic Wines round the back), part museum. The focus of the complex is the "Wine Odyssey", a light-hearted, rather disjointed trot through the world's wine regions with an audioguide. The visual gags – you get to tour round the Italian vineyards on a Vespa – are a bit lame, and tickets are pricey, but do include at least six wine tastings; you can also upgrade your ticket to include more tastings of wine and other alcoholic drinks. The staff diligently use spittoons, but most visitors seem quite happy to get slowly inebriated.

Clink Prison Museum

1 Clink St • Mon–Fri 10am–6pm, Sat & Sun 10am–7.30pm; July–Sept closes 9pm • £6 • ☎ 020 7403 0900, ⓦ clink.co.uk • ⊖ London Bridge

Housed in the suitably dismal confines of an old cellar is the **Clink Prison Museum**, built near the site of the former Clink Prison, and the origin of the expression "in the clink". The prison began in the twelfth century as a dungeon for disobedient clerics under the Bishop of Winchester's Palace – the rose window of the palace's Great Hall has survived just east of the prison – and later it became a dumping ground for heretics, debtors, prostitutes and a motley assortment of Bankside lowlife, before being burnt to the ground during the 1780 Gordon Riots. The exhibition features a handful of prison-life tableaux and dwells on the torture and grim conditions within, but, given the rich history of the place, it's a disappointingly lacklustre display.

16

Golden Hinde

1 & 2 Pickfords Wharf • Mon–Sat 10am–5.30pm, Sun 10am–5pm, but phone ahead • £6 • ☎ 020 7403 0123, ⓦ goldenhinde.com • ⊖ London Bridge

At the east end of Clink Street, in St Mary Overie Dock, sits an exact replica of the **Golden Hinde**, the galleon in which Francis Drake sailed around the world from 1577 to 1580. This version was launched in 1973, and circumnavigated the world for the next twenty years, before eventually settling here in Southwark. The ship is surprisingly small and, with a crew of eighty-plus, must have been cramped, to say the least. There's a refreshing lack of interpretive panels, so it's worth trying to coincide with one of the tours, during which costumed guides show you the ropes, so to speak, and demonstrate activities such as firing a cannon or using the ship's toilet. Always phone ahead, though, to check that a group hasn't booked the place up.

Southwark Cathedral

Mon–Fri 8am–6pm, Sat & Sun 8.30am–6pm • Free • ⓦ cathedral.southwark.anglican.org • ⊖ London Bridge

Built in the thirteenth century as the Augustinian priory church of St Mary Overie, it's a minor miracle that **Southwark Cathedral** survived the nineteenth century, which saw

---

THE ROSE THEATRE

The discovery of the remains of the **Rose Theatre** (☎ 020 7261 9565, ⓦ rosetheatre.org.uk), the Globe's great rival, beneath an office block on Park Street in 1989, helped enormously in the reconstruction of the Globe. The outline of the theatre can clearly be traced in the foundations, but most of the remains are currently flooded to preserve them while funds are gathered for a full excavation. Close by the Rose exhibition, there's a plaque showing where the Globe actually stood, before it was destroyed in a fire started by a spark from a cannon during a performance of Shakespeare's *Henry VIII*. The Rose can only be visited by tour, as part of the package offered by the Globe exhibition on summer afternoons (see opposite).

the east-end chapel demolished to make way for London Bridge, railways built within a few feet of the tower and some very heavy-handed Victorian restoration. As if in compensation, the church was given cathedral status in 1905, and has since gone from strength to strength – if you're feeling peckish, the cathedral refectory serves tasty food.

Of the original thirteenth-century **interior**, only the choir and retrochoir now remain, separated by a beautiful, high, stone Tudor screen; they are probably the oldest Gothic structures left in London and were used by the Bishop of Winchester as a court – those sentenced ended up in the Clink. The cathedral contains numerous intriguing **monuments**: from a thirteenth-century oak effigy of a knight, to the brightly painted tomb of poet John Gower, Chaucer's contemporary, in the north aisle, his head resting on the three books he wrote – one in Latin, one in French and one in English. The quack doctor Lionel Lockyer has a humorous epitaph in the north transept, and, nearby, there's a chapel dedicated to John Harvard, who was baptized here in 1607. In the south aisle, an early twentieth-century memorial to Shakespeare (he was a worshipper in the church and his brother is buried here) depicts the Bard in green alabaster lounging under a stone canopy. Above the memorial is a postwar stained-glass window featuring a whole cast of characters from the plays.

Borough Market

8 Southwark St • Thurs 11am–5pm, Fri noon–6pm, Sat 8am–5pm • ☎ 020 7407 1002, ⓦ boroughmarket.org.uk • ⊖ London Bridge

Medieval Southwark, also known as **The Borough**, was London's first suburb, clustered round the southern end of London Bridge, the only bridge over the tidal Thames until 1750, and thus the only route south. London Bridge was the most obvious place for the Kent farmers to sell their goods to the City grocers, and there's been a thriving market here since medieval times. The present **Borough Market** is squeezed beneath the railway arches between the High Street and the cathedral. The early-morning wholesale fruit and vegetable market winds up around 8am and is one of the few still trading under its original Victorian wrought-iron shed. But the market is best known nowadays for its busy, busy specialist food market (see p.433), with stalls selling top-quality produce from around the world, with permanent outlets such as Neal's Yard Dairy and Konditor & Cook, in the shops close by.

Borough High Street

As the main road south out of the City, **Borough High Street** was for centuries famous for its **coaching inns**. Chaucer's Canterbury pilgrims set off from *The Tabard* (in Talbot Yard), but by Dickens' time "these great rambling queer old places", as he called them, were closing down. The only extant coaching inn is the **George Inn**, situated in a cobbled yard east off the High Street, dating from 1677 and now owned by the National Trust. Unfortunately, the Great Northern Railway demolished two of the three original galleried fronts, but the lone survivor is a remarkable sight nevertheless, and is still run as a pub (see p.394).

Opposite Borough tube station, at the southernmost end of Borough High Street, is **St George the Martyr**, built in the 1730s, with four clock faces: three white and illuminated at night; one black and pointing towards Bermondsey, whose parishioners refused to give money for the church. To the north of St George's, a wall survives from the **Marshalsea**, the city's main debtors' prison, where Dickens' father (and family) was incarcerated for six months in 1824.

Redcross Way

Running parallel with Borough High Street, one block to the west, is **Redcross Way**, a little-visited backstreet that hides a couple of remarkable sights. The first is **Red Cross Garden**, the row of cottage-style model dwellings established by the social reformer (and founder of the National Trust) Octavia Hill, to house the workers of a local rag factory. The row of houses faces onto a miniature village green, complete with village pond and even a maypole. Meanwhile, on the opposite side of the street, is the site of the **Cross Bones cemetery** (Ⓦcrossbones.org.uk). It was on this unconsecrated land that the prostitutes who worked on Bankside were buried, and later, the local poor were interred. Local residents have turned the gates, leading to the plot of land, into an impromptu shrine of messages and tokens to those buried, and the plan is eventually to establish a Garden of Remembrance. A short vigil is held on the 23rd of every month around 7pm outside the gates.

Old Operating Theatre Museum and Herb Garret

St Thomas Street • Daily 10.30am–5pm; closed mid-Dec to early Jan • £5.90 • ☎ 020 7188 2679, Ⓦ thegarret.org.uk • ⊖ London Bridge

The most educative and the strangest of Southwark's museums is the **Old Operating Theatre Museum and Herb Garret**. Built in 1821 up a spiral staircase at the top of a church tower, where the hospital apothecary's herbs were stored, this women's operating theatre was once adjacent to the women's ward of St Thomas' Hospital (now in Lambeth). Despite being gore-free, the museum is as stomach-churning as the nearby London Dungeon, for this theatre dates from the pre-anaesthetic era.

The surgeons who used this room would have concentrated on speed and accuracy (most amputations took less than a minute), but there was still a thirty percent mortality rate, with many patients simply dying of shock, and many more from bacterial infection (about which very little was known). This much is clear from the design of the theatre itself, which has no sink and is made almost entirely of mahogany and pine, a breeding ground for bacteria. Sawdust was sprinkled on the floor to soak up the blood and prevent it dripping onto the congregation in the church below. In the herbarium section, you can read up on the medicinal uses of the herbs stored and have a go at making your own pills.

Guy's Hospital

St Thomas St • ☎ 020 7188 7188, Ⓦ guysandstthomas.nhs.uk • ⊖ London Bridge

Guy's Hospital was founded in 1726 by Thomas Guy, a governor of nearby St Thomas' Hospital, with the money he made in the City's South Sea Bubble fiasco. With its 469ft-high concrete brutalist tower, Guy's is the tallest hospital in the world, but it also retains several of its original eighteenth-century buildings: the courtyard on the south side of St Thomas Street, and a pretty little **Hospital Chapel**, on the west side of the courtyard. It's worth having a look at the interior with its cheerful light-blue paintwork, raked balconies on three sides, and its the giant marble and alabaster tomb of the founder, who's depicted welcoming a new patient to the hospital, though in fact Guy died a year before the first patients were admitted.

Bermondsey

Famous in the Middle Ages for its Cluniac abbey, **Bermondsey**, the area east of London Bridge, changed enormously in the nineteenth century. In 1836, the London and Greenwich Railway – the city's first – was built through the district, supported by 878 brick arches stretching for four miles. The area became famous for its wharves, its tanneries and its factories. So much of the city's food – teas, wines, grain, butter, bacon and cheese – was stored here that it was nicknamed "London's Larder". Bermondsey also became infamous for some of the worst social conditions in Victorian London, as Charles Kingsley discovered: "O God! What I saw! People having no water to drink but the water of the common sewer which stagnates full of…dead fish, cats and dogs."

Badly bombed in the Blitz, the docks had closed down by the 1960s. They have since undergone a Docklands-style regeneration, and much of the original warehouse architecture has been preserved, particularly east of Tower Bridge, around Butler's Wharf. **HMS Belfast**, the cruiser moored near City Hall, is the only permanent

16

maritime link. Nearby the curvaceous dock of Hay's Wharf, originally built to accommodate tea clippers like the *Cutty Sark*, has been filled and transformed into the **Hay's Galleria**, a shopping precinct whose (year-round) Christmas Shop is a must if you've got children. The area's most popular attraction, however, is the Hammer-horror **London Dungeon**, tucked under the railway arches under London Bridge Station, and the **London Bridge Experience**, opposite. And then there's **The Shard**....

The Shard

32 London Bridge • Ⓦ shardlondonbridge.com • ⊖ London Bridge

London's – and the country's – tallest building, **The Shard**, is squeezed in beside London Bridge Station. While there's a case to be argued for the City's skyscrapers, and for those at Canary Wharf, it's hard to justify such a hubristic (Qatari-funded) enterprise south of the river. On a more positive note, Renzo Piano's tapered, glass-clad tower block does at least have a public viewing platform on the top (72nd) floor, from which, of course, there are terrific views over London, and – thankfully – no view of the Shard itself.

London Bridge Experience

2–4 Tooley St • Mon–Fri 10am–5pm, Sat & Sun 10am–6pm • £23, or from £11 online • ☎ 0844 847 2287, Ⓦ thelondonbridgeexperience .com • ⊖ London Bridge

Inspired by the popular hammer horror mayhem of the nearby London Dungeons, some bright sparks have created the rival **London Bridge Experience**, in the railway vaults on the north side of Tooley Street. First off, you're led on a theatrical trot through the history of London Bridge, with guides in period garb hamming up the gory bits. Then, in case you're not scared enough yet, in the **London Tombs** section (no under-11s), more actors, dressed as zombies and murderers, leap out of the foggy gloom to frighten the wits out of you. Finally, in peace and quiet, you get to peruse some artefacts from (and a model of) old London Bridge.

London Dungeon

28–34 Tooley St • Daily: April–July, Sept & Oct 10am–5.30pm; Aug 9.30am–7pm; Nov–March 10am–5pm; longer hours in school holidays • £23, or £16 online • ☎ 020 7403 7221, Ⓦ thedungeons.com • ⊖ London Bridge

Housed under the railway arches of London Bridge Station, the **London Dungeon** is the original Gothic horror-fest, and remains one of the city's major crowd-pleasers – to avoid queuing (and save money), buy your ticket online. Young teenagers and the credulous probably get the most out of the various ludicrous live action scenarios, each one hyped up by the team of ham actors dressed in period garb. Expect a "Boat Ride to Hell" and a "Drop Ride to Doom", and be prepared to shoot ghosts in the "Vengeance 5D Lasar Ride", not to mention endure the latest "Jack the Ripper Experience".

Britain at War Experience

64–66 Tooley St • Daily: April–Oct 10am–5pm; Nov–March 10am–4.30pm • £12.95 • ☎ 020 7403 3171, Ⓦ britainatwar.co.uk • ⊖ London Bridge

Winston Churchill's Britain at War Experience is an illuminating insight into the stiff-upper-lip London mentality during the Blitz. It begins with a rickety elevator ride down to a mock-up of a tube air-raid shelter (minus the stale air and rats), in which a contemporary newsreel cheerily announces "a great day for democracy" as bombs drop indiscriminately over Germany. This is just a prelude to the museum's hundreds of wartime artefacts, posters and old shop fronts, all looking a bit worn around the edges, but still fascinating. You can sit in an Anderson shelter beneath the chilling sound of the V-1 "doodlebugs", tune in to contemporary radio broadcasts and walk through the chaos of a just-bombed street – pitch-dark, noisy and smoky.

CLOCKWISE FROM TOP LEFT BOROUGH MARKET (P.230); MILLENNIUM BRIDGE (P.227); SOUTHWARK CATHEDRAL (P.229); THE GLOBE (P.228) >

HMS Belfast

Morgan Lane, Tooley St · Daily March–Oct 10am–6pm; Nov–Feb 10am–5pm · £12.25 · ☎ 020 7940 6300, ⊛ hmsbelfast.iwm.org.uk ·
⊖ London Bridge

Permanently moored opposite Southwark Crown Court, the camouflage-painted **HMS Belfast** is an 11,550-ton Royal Navy cruiser. Launched in Belfast in 1938, the *Belfast* spent the first two years of the war in the Royal Naval shipyards, after being hit by a mine in the Firth of Forth. It later saw action in the 1943 Battle of North Cape and assisted in the D-Day landings before being decommissioned after the Korean War, and becoming an outpost of the Imperial War Museum.

The fun bit is exploring the maze of cabins and scrambling up and down the vertiginous ladders of the ship's seven confusing decks, which could accommodate a crew of over 900. Be sure to check out the punishment cells, in the most uncomfortable part of the ship, and to make it down to the airlocked Boiler Room, a spaghetti of pipes and valves, from which there was very little chance of escape in the event of the ship being hit. If you want to know more about the cruiser's history, head for the Exhibition Flat in Zone 5; next door, in the Life at Sea room, you can practise your Morse code and knots, and listen to accounts of naval life on board.

City Hall

The Queen's Walk · Mon–Thurs 8.30am–6pm, Fri 8.30am–5.30pm · Free · ☎ 020 7983 4000, ⊛ london.gov.uk · ⊖ London Bridge

East of the *Belfast*, overlooking the river, is Norman Foster's startling glass-encased **City Hall**, which looks like a giant car headlight or fencing mask. Headquarters for the Greater London Authority and the Mayor of London, visitors are welcome to stroll up the helical walkway, visit the café and watch proceedings from the second floor. For access to "London's Living Room" on the ninth floor, which boasts the best views over the Thames, contact City Hall. Before you leave the area, be sure to check out Fiona Banner's shiny black *Full Stops*, 3D renditions styled in different fonts and wrought in bronze.

Bermondsey Street

Once the area's high street, **Bermondsey Street** has been transformed over the last decade into a trendy strip of cafés, pubs and shops. This was also once the heart of the tanning industry – hence Tanner Street, Morocco Street (where much of the leather came from) and Leathermarket Road, which leads to the former **Leather Hide and Wool Exchange** of 1878, decorated with roundels depicting the process of tanning. Next door is the former Leather Market, built in 1833 and now converted into workshops, including one where you can watch **glassblowing** demonstrations (Mon–Fri 10am–1 & 2–5pm; free).

At the far end of the street, the Bermondsey **antique market** takes place on Friday mornings. The market is also known confusingly as the New Caledonian Market, after the prewar flea market that used to take place off Islington's Caledonian Road.

Fashion and Textile Museum

83 Bermondsey St · Wed–Sun 11am–6pm · £5 · ☎ 020 7407 8664, ⊛ ftmlondon.org · ⊖ London Bridge

The **Fashion and Textile Museum** is the lifelong dream of Zandra Rhodes, fashion *grande dame extraordinaire*. Designed by Mexican architect Ricardo Legorreta, and daubed in Rhodes' favourite colours of yellow, pink and orange, the FTM (a former cash-and-carry warehouse) is an arresting sight on an otherwise drab architectural street. Rhodes opened her first boutique in the 1960s, and reached the peak of her popularity during the punk era. Her own sartorial taste hasn't changed much in the intervening years, but thankfully FTM's exhibitions are more wide-ranging – from designer tea cosies to 1970s fashion – and are often drawn from her own vast collection.

Butler's Wharf

East of Tower Bridge, **Butler's Wharf** is one of the densest networks of Victorian warehousing left in London and one of the most enjoyable parts of Docklands to explore. From Tower Bridge itself (see p.187), you can get a really good view of the old **Anchor Brewhouse**, which produced Courage ales from 1789 until 1982. A cheery, ad hoc sort of building, with a boiler-house chimney at one end and malt-mill tower and cupola at the other, it has been sensitively converted into apartments. Next door is the original eight-storey **Butler's Wharf**, the largest warehouse complex on the Thames when it was built in 1873. Closed down in the 1970s, it became London's largest artists' colony, home to everyone from Derek Jarman to Sid Vicious. Nowadays, its flats, shops and restaurants form part of Terence Conran's gastronomic empire, but the wide promenade on the riverfront is open to the public.

Shad Thames, the narrow street at the back of Butler's Wharf, has kept the wrought-iron overhead gangways by which the porters used to transport goods from the wharves to the warehouses further back from the river; it's one of the most atmospheric alleyways in the whole of Docklands. For a totally different ambience, head for **Horsleydown Square**, to the south of Shad Thames, where terracotta-rendered flats, with striking blue balconies, overlook a piazza centred on a fountain encrusted with naked women, whose belongings are sculpted around the edge. Also worth a look, two blocks south on Queen Elizabeth Street, is the **Circle**, a modern take on the Victorian "circus", its street facades smothered in shiny cobalt-blue tiles.

Design Museum

Shad Thames • Daily 10am–5.45pm • £7 • ☏ 0870 833 9955, ⓦ designmuseum.org • ⊖ Tower Hill

East of Butler's Wharf is Terence Conran's superb riverside **Design Museum**. The stylish white edifice, a Bauhaus-like conversion of an old 1950s warehouse, is the perfect showcase for mass-produced industrial design from classic cars to Tupperware. The museum hosts a series of special exhibitions (up to four at any one time) on important designers, movements or single products. The museum shop is great for design classics and innovations, and the small coffee bar in the foyer serves delicious cakes and is a great place to relax; there's also the superb *Blue Print Café* on the top floor.

16

St Saviour's Dock

East of the Design Museum, a stainless-steel footbridge takes you across **St Saviour's Dock**, a tidal inlet overlooked by swanky warehouse offices. Incredible though it may seem, it really is still possible to smell the spices – cinnamon, nutmeg and cloves, mostly – which were stored here until the 1970s, especially in the last section of Shad Thames after a shower of rain. The footbridge takes you over to **New Concordia Wharf** on Mill Street, one of the first warehouse conversions in the area, completed in 1984. Next door stands the photogenic **China Wharf**, with its stack of semicircular windows picked out in red.

The area around St Saviour's Dock was dubbed by the Victorian press "the very capital of cholera". In 1849, the *Morning Chronicle* described it thus: "Jostling with unemployed labourers of the lowest class, ballast heavers, coal-whippers, brazen women, ragged children, and the very raff and refuse of the river, [the visitor] makes his way with difficulty along, assailed by offensive sights and smells from the narrow alleys which branch off." This was the location of Dickens' fictional **Jacob's Island**, a place with "every imaginable sign of desolation and neglect", where Bill Sikes met his end in *Oliver Twist*.

THE THAMES PATH

A leisurely way to reach Rotherhithe is to walk the mile-long **Thames Path** from Butler's Wharf, stopping en route at *The Angel*, a pub once frequented by Pepys and Captain Cook, which now stands all alone on Bermondsey Wall, with great views over to Wapping. Close by are the foundations of Edward III's moated manor house, begun in 1353, and the "Leaning Tower of Bermondsey", a precariously tilting riverside house just downstream from the pub.

Rotherhithe

Rotherhithe, the thumb of marshy land jutting out into the Thames east of Bermondsey, has always been slightly removed from the rest of London. It was a thriving shipbuilding centre even before the construction of the Surrey Commercial Docks in the nineteenth century. However, no other set of London dockyards took such a hammering in the Blitz, and the immediate postwar decades were years of inexorable decline. The docks have since been reclaimed for new housing estates and more upmarket Docklands developments. Despite its geographical isolation, you can reach Rotherhithe very easily via the tube and Overground network.

Around St Mary's Church

The bit of Rotherhithe worth visiting is the heart of the old eighteenth-century seafaring village around **St Mary's Church**, which stands in its own leafy square, northwest of the Overground station. The church itself is unremarkable, but it has rich maritime associations: several of the furnishings are made from the timber of the *Fighting Temeraire*, the veteran of Trafalgar which ended its days in a Rotherhithe breaker's yard (Turner's painting of its last voyage hangs in the National Gallery), and the master of the *Mayflower* was buried here. The **Mayflower** was Rotherhithe-owned and -crewed, and set off from outside the *Mayflower* pub in 1620 to transport the Pilgrim Fathers to the New World. (The ship had to call in at Plymouth for repairs after being damaged in the English Channel.) The pub (see p.394), north of the church, is a rickety white weatherboarded building, badly damaged in the last war, and a minor pilgrimage site for Americans.

Brunel Museum

Railway Avenue • Daily 10am–5pm, Tues until 9.30pm • £2 • ☎ 020 7231 3840, Ⓦ brunel-museum.org.uk • ⊖ Rotherhithe

To the northeast of St Mary's, the **Brunel Museum** is a brick-built shed that marks the site of the Thames Tunnel, the world's first under-river tunnel. It was begun in 1825 by Marc Brunel and his more famous son, Isambard, and was originally designed for horse-drawn carriages to travel between Rotherhithe and Wapping. The technology used was invented by Brunel senior and its basic principles have been used for all subsequent tunnelling. However, plagued by periodic flooding, labour unrest, fatalities and lack of funds, the tunnel took eighteen years to construct and was nicknamed "The Great Bore" by the press.

Funds ran out before the spiral ramps, which would have allowed horse-drawn vehicles actually to use the tunnel, could be built. Instead, in 1843, the tunnel was opened to pedestrians as a tourist attraction, pulling in two million visitors in its first year. It was visited by Queen Victoria herself, who knighted Brunel junior, but soon became the haunt of whores and "tunnel thieves". In 1869 it was taken over by the East London Railway (now the Overground) and remains the most watertight of all the rail tunnels under the Thames. The circular working shaft, which housed an engine to pump water out of the tunnel, survives to the east of the engine house. As well as telling the tunnel's fascinating story, the museum displays some of the old souvenirs sold in Victorian times.

Surrey Docks

The once marshy land of Rotherhithe peninsula, east of the old village, was chosen as the site for London's first wet dock, the Howland Great Dock, built in 1696 to take on any extra repair work and refitting emanating from the Royal Dockyards in nearby Deptford. Later renamed Greenland Dock, it became part of the network known as **Surrey Commercial Docks**. The main trade was timber, which was piled into stacks up to 80ft high by porters nicknamed "Flying Blondins" (after the tightrope walker), who wore distinctive leather pads on their heads and shoulders to protect them from splinters. The docks took a pounding in the Blitz, and on one

16

SCANDINAVIAN SEAMEN'S MISSIONS

One of the more unusual legacies of Rotherhithe's seafaring past is the trio of Scandinavian seamen's missions – a reminder of the former dominance of the timber trade in the nearby Surrey Docks – which survive to the south of the tube station, around Albion Street. The most prominent is the **Norwegian Seamen's Church**, by the approach road to the Rotherhithe Tunnel, which flies the Norwegian flag and features a longboat atop its weather vane. Albion Street itself still has a Scandinavian bent – even the nearby public toilets are bilingual – and further down you'll find the well-maintained **Finnish Seamen's Mission**, built in modernist style in 1958, with a freestanding belfry that looks more like a fire-station practice tower. The **Swedish Seamen's Church** (complete with hostel), further south at 120 Lower Rd, completes the trio but is architecturally undistinguished.

particular occasion, 350,000 tons of timber were set ablaze in one of the largest fires ever seen in Britain.

Rotherhithe Street

Rotherhithe Street, which hugs the riverbank, is the longest street in London at around a mile and a half. It's mainly residential, a mixture of new Docklands developments and council housing, but the **Thames Path**, which runs parallel to it for most of the way, is pleasant enough to walk or cycle along, with great views over to Limehouse and Canary Wharf.

Halfway along the street, you can learn more about the area's history at the **Pumphouse Museum** (Mon–Fri 10am–4pm; free; ☎020 7231 2976, ⓦthepumphouse.org.uk; bus #C10 from ⊖ Canada Water or Rotherhithe), housed in an old pumphouse on Lavender Road. Further along, you can catch a boat back into town or on to Greenwich, from the Nelson Dock Pier beside the *Hilton* hotel. If you've time to kill, check out the three-masted schooner (now a restaurant) built in the 1950s as a training ship for the French navy, and nearby **Nelson House**, a beautiful Georgian house built for one of the wealthy owners of Nelson Dock.

16

Hyde Park and Kensington Gardens

Most visitors are amazed at how green and pleasant so much of the city centre is, with three royal parks – St James's Park, Green Park and Hyde Park – forming a continuous grassy belt that stretches for four miles. Hyde Park, together with its westerly extension, Kensington Gardens, is the largest of the trio, covering a distance of a mile and a half from Speakers' Corner in the northeast to Kensington Palace in the southwest. You can jog, swim, fish, sunbathe or mess about in boats on the Serpentine, cross the park on horseback or mountain bike, or view the latest in modern art at the Serpentine Gallery. At the end of your journey, you've made it to one of London's most exclusive districts, the Royal Borough of Kensington and Chelsea, covered in the next two chapters.

Hyde Park

Daily 5am–midnight • ☎ 020 7298 2100, ⓦ royalparks.gov.uk • ⊖ Hyde Park Corner, Marble Arch, Knightsbridge or Lancaster Gate

Seized from the Church by Henry VIII to satisfy his desire for yet more hunting grounds, **Hyde Park** was first opened to the public by James I, when refreshments available included "milk from a red cow". Under Charles II, the park became a fashionable gathering place for the beau monde, who rode round the circular drive known as the Ring, pausing to gossip and admire each other's equipages. Its present appearance is mostly due to Queen Caroline, an enthusiast for landscape gardens, who spent a great deal of George II's money creating the park's main feature, the **Serpentine** lake.

Hangings, muggings and duels, the 1851 Great Exhibition and numerous public events have all taken place here – and it's still a popular gathering point for political demonstrations, as well as the location of **Speakers' Corner** (see below). For the most part, however, Hyde Park is simply a wonderful open space that allows you to lose all sight of the city beyond a few persistent tower blocks. The southeast corner of the park contains two conventional tourist attractions: **Apsley House**, housing a museum to the Duke of Wellington, and the triumphal **Wellington Arch**, which you can now climb.

Marble Arch

Marble Arch looks rather forlorn on a ferociously busy traffic island in the treeless northeastern corner of the park at the west end of Oxford Street. Designed in 1828 by John Nash as a triumphal entrance for Buckingham Palace, it has suffered over the years: the sculpted friezes intended to adorn it ended up on the palace, while the equestrian statue of George IV, intended to surmount it, was carted off to Trafalgar Square. When the palace was extended in the 1840s, the arch was moved to form an entrance to Hyde Park, its upper chambers used as a police observation post. During the 1855 riot (see below), a detachment of police emerged from the arch, like the Greeks from the Trojan Horse, much to the surprise of the demonstrators. The arch has been joined recently by a slightly surreal 33ft-high bronze sculpture of a horse's head by Nic Fiddian-Green.

Tyburn Convent

8 Hyde Park Place • Daily 6.30am–8.30pm • Guided tours 10.30am, 3.30 & 5.30pm • Free • ⓦ tyburnconvent.org.uk • ⊖ Marble Arch

Despite appearance, Marble Arch stands on the most historically charged spot in Hyde Park, as it marks the site of **Tyburn gallows**, the city's main public execution spot (until 1783, when the action moved to Newgate). There's a plaque on the traffic island in the middle of Edgware Road where it joins Bayswater Road marking the approximate site of the gallows, where around 50,000 lost their lives. Of these, some 105 were Catholics, martyred during the Reformation, in whose memory the **Tyburn Convent** was established at 8 Hyde Park Place in 1902. It's run by a group of cloistered French Benedictine nuns who are happy to show visitors round the basement shrine, which contains a mock-up of the Tyburn gibbet over the main altar, and various pictures and relics of the martyrs. The house next door to (and now part of) the convent, no. 10, is London's smallest, measuring just three and a half feet across.

Speakers' Corner

⊖ Marble Arch

In 1855 an estimated 250,000 people gathered in the northeastern corner of the park to protest against the Sunday Trading Bill (Karl Marx was among the crowd and thought it was the beginning of the English Revolution), and ever since it has been one of London's most popular spots for political demos. In 1872 the government licensed free assembly at **Speakers' Corner**, a peculiarly English Sunday-morning tradition that continues to this day, featuring a motley assortment of ranters and hecklers. The largest demonstration in London's history took place in this section of the park in 2003 when over a million people turned up to try and stop the war against Iraq.

HYDE PARK & KENSINGTON GARDENS

RESTAURANT
Lanesborough — 1

ACCOMMODATION
Astor Quest Hotel — 2
Baglioni — 4
Columbia Hotel — 3
Smart Hyde Park Inn — 1

0 — 200 — yards

Hyde Park Corner

17

The park's southeast corner, **Hyde Park Corner** is a better place to enter the park than Marble Arch. You'll still have to battle with one of London's busiest traffic interchanges, but at least you can actually visit **Wellington Arch** which stands at the centre of the roundabout. A statue of Wellington no longer graces the arch, but instead stands at ground level opposite his erstwhile residence, **Apsley House** (see p.242). Wellington is depicted seated astride his faithful steed, Copenhagen, who carried the field marshal for sixteen hours during the Battle of Waterloo; the horse eventually died in 1836 and was buried with full military honours at the duke's country pile in Hampshire.

Close by are two powerful war memorials unveiled in 1925: the first, the **Machine Gun Corps Memorial**, features the naked figure of David leaning on Goliath's sword and the chilling inscription, "Saul hath slain his thousands, but David his tens of thousands"; the larger of the two, the **Artillery Memorial**, includes a 9.2-inch howitzer rendered in Portland stone, realistic relief depictions of the brutality of war, and the equally blunt, Shakespearean epitaph, "Here was a royal fellowship of death". These two have recently been joined by two much larger memorials: the **Australian War Memorial** is a gargantuan curved wall of grey granite slabs inscribed with the names of the towns in which the soldiers were born and the battles they fought; opposite stand the sixteen bronze spikes of the **New Zealand Memorial**, each of which is inscribed with text, patterns and sculptures commemorating the bonds between New Zealand and the UK.

Wellington Arch

Hyde Park Corner • Wed–Sun: April–Oct 10am–5pm; Nov–March 10am–4pm • EH • £3.90 • ⊖ Hyde Park Corner

Designed by a youthful Decimus Burton in 1828 to commemorate Wellington's victories in the Napoleonic Wars, **Wellington Arch** originally served as the northern entrance to Buckingham Palace. Positioned opposite Burton's delicate Hyde Park Screen, the arch once formed part of a fine architectural ensemble with Apsley House,

---

TYBURN GALLOWS

For nearly 500 years, **Tyburn** was the capital's main **public execution** site, its three-legged gibbet known as the "Tyburn Tree" or the "Triple Tree", capable of dispatching over 20 people at one go. Dressed in their best clothes, the condemned were first processed through the streets in a cart (the nobility were allowed to travel in their own carriages) from Newgate Prison, often with the noose already in place. They received a nosegay at St Sepulchre, opposite the prison, and then a pint of ale at various taverns along the route, so that most were blind drunk by the time they arrived at Tyburn. The driver had to remain sober, however, hence the expression "on the wagon".

The condemned were allowed to make a speech to the crowd and were attended by a chaplain, though according to one eighteenth-century spectator he was "more the subject of ridicule than of serious attention". The same witness describes how the executioner, who drove the cart, then tied the rope to the tree: "This done he gives the horse a lash with his whip, away goes the cart and there swings my gentleman kicking in the air. The Hangman does not give himself the trouble to put them out of their pain but some of their friends or relations do it for them. They pull the dying person by the legs and beat his breast to dispatch him as soon as possible."

Not all relatives were so fatalistic, however, and some would attempt to support the condemned in the hope of a last-minute reprieve, or of reviving the victim when they were cut down. Fights frequently broke out when the body was cut down, between the relatives, the spectators (who believed the corpse had miraculous medicinal qualities), and the surgeons (who were allowed ten corpses a year for dissection). The executioner, known as "**Jack Ketch**" after the famous London hangman, was allowed to take home the victim's clothes, and made further profit by selling the hanging rope by the inch. Following the 1780 Gordon Riots, the powers-that-be took fright at unruly gatherings like Tyburn, and in 1783 the Tyburn Tree was demolished.

17

Wellington's London residence, and St George's Hospital to the west. Unfortunately the symmetry was destroyed when the arch was repositioned in 1883 to line up with Constitution Hill – named after the "constitutional" walks that Charles II used to take here. The arch's original statue was an enormous equestrian portrayal of the "Iron Duke" erected in 1846 while he was still alive. The duke was taken down in 1883, and eventually replaced by Peace and her four-horse chariot, erected in 1912. Inside, you can view an exhibition on the history of the arch, and of London's outdoor sculpture, and take a lift to the top of the monument (once London's smallest postwar police station) where the exterior balconies offer a bird's-eye view of the swirling traffic.

Apsley House: the Wellington Museum

149 Piccadilly • Wed–Sun: April–Oct 11am–5pm; Nov–March 11am–4pm • EH • £6.30 • ⊖ Hyde Park Corner

Known during the Iron Duke's lifetime as "Number One, London", **Apsley House** was once an immensely desirable residence, but nowadays, overlooking a very busy roundabout, it would be poor reward for any national hero. The interior isn't what it used to be either, but in this case it's Wellington himself who's to blame. Built and exquisitely decorated by Robert Adam in the 1770s for Baron Apsley, it was remodelled by Benjamin Wyatt after Wellington bought the place in 1817. Wyatt faced the red-brick exterior with Bath stone and more or less got rid of the Adam interiors. As a result, the house is very much as it would have been in Wellington's day, and the current duke still lives in the attic.

The art collection

The house is worth visiting for the **art collection** alone. Wellington acquired the paintings in 1813 after the Battle of Vittoria, when he seized the baggage train of Napoleon's

---

THE IRON DUKE

Perhaps if the **Duke of Wellington** had died, like Nelson, at his moment of greatest triumph, he too would enjoy an unsullied posthumous reputation. Instead, the famously blunt duke went on to become the epitome of the outmoded, reactionary conservative, earning his famous nickname, the "Iron Duke", not from his fearless military campaigning, but from the iron shutters he had to install at Apsley House after his windows were broken by demonstrators rioting in favour of the 1832 Reform Bill, to which the duke was vehemently opposed.

Born **Arthur Wesley** in Dublin in 1769 – the same year as Napoleon – he never considered himself Irish: "just because you're born in a stable, doesn't make you a horse" he is alleged to have said. He was educated at (but hated) Eton and the French military academy at Angers, and campaigned out in India, helping to defeat Tipu Sultan, and becoming Governor of Mysore. After continued military success in his Napoleonic campaigns, he eventually became Duke of Wellington in 1814, shortly before achieving his most famous victory of all at Waterloo.

With great reluctance he became **prime minister** in 1828, "a station, to the duties of which I am unaccustomed, in which I was not wished, and for which I was not qualified…I should have been mad if I had thought of such a thing". Despite his own misgivings, his government passed the Catholic Relief Act – allowing Catholics to sit in Parliament – thus avoiding civil war in Ireland, but splitting the Tory ranks. Accused of popery by the Earl of Winchelsea, Wellington challenged him to a duel in Battersea Park; the duke fired and missed (he was a notoriously bad shot), while the earl shot into the air and apologized for the slur.

Wellington's opposition to the Reform Bill brought down his government and allowed the Whigs (under Earl Grey, of tea fame) to form a majority government for the first time in sixty years. Despite retiring from public life in 1846, he was on hand to organize the defence of the capital against the Chartists in 1848, and strolled across to the Great Exhibition every day in 1851. Two million people lined the streets for his funeral in 1852 (more than for anyone before or since), and he has more outdoor statues (and pubs named after him) in London than any other historical figure. Despite this, his greatest legacy is, of course, the **Wellington boot**, originally made of leather, now rubber.

HYDE PARK STATUES AND MEMORIALS

17

Hyde Park is peppered with statues, none more colossal than the 18ft-high bronze of **Achilles**, in the southeastern corner of the park, designed in 1822 by Richard Westmacott to commemorate the Duke of Wellington, and cast from captured French cannon. As the country's first public nude statue it caused outrage, especially since many thought it a portrait of the duke himself, and the chief fundraisers were "the women of Great Britain". In actual fact, it represents neither the duke nor Achilles, but is a copy of one of the Horse Tamers from the Quirinal Hill in Rome. William Wilberforce led a campaign to have the statue removed for decency's sake; a fig leaf was placed in the appropriate place as a compromise.

Visible to the north is the **July 7 Memorial**, a simple, startling memorial, erected on the fourth anniversary of the 2005 suicide bombings. The 52 stainless steel pillars stand nearly 12ft high, and each one is inscribed with the victim's time and place of death. Only a short distance to the west, in The Dell, a couple of boulders set in gravel within a copse of silver birch, form an even more understated **Holocaust Memorial**.

To the north of the nearby Serpentine stands the park's over-manicured bird sanctuary, overlooked by the **Hudson Memorial**, sculpted by Jacob Epstein and featuring a low relief of Rima, a naked, female, South American version of Tarzan, and several exotic birds. (Rima the Jungle Girl is the main protagonist in the 1904 adventure novel *Green Mansions*, written by the naturalist and writer W.H. Hudson.) It's difficult to believe now, but when the memorial was unveiled in 1925, there was a campaign of protest against the statue, led by the *Daily Mail*. Rima was considered too butch, the art too "Bolshevist" and the memorial later became the victim of several (anti-semitic) attacks.

brother, Joseph, who was fleeing for France with 200 paintings belonging to the King of Spain. The best pieces, including works by de Hooch, Van Dyck, Goya, Rubens and Murillo, cover the red walls of the **Waterloo Gallery** on the first floor, where sliding mirrors cover the windows. The most prized works of all are a trio by Velázquez – *The Water-Seller of Seville*, *Portrait of a Gentleman* and *Two Young Men Eating at a Humble Table* – though Wellington preferred Correggio's *Agony in the Garden*, the key for which he used to carry round with him, so he could take the picture out of its frame and dust it fondly.

The rooms

Like several of the house's other rooms, the Waterloo Gallery was originally hung with yellow satin, which, as one of the duke's friends lamented, "is just the very worst colour he can have for the pictures and will kill the effect of the gilding". It was here that Wellington held his annual veterans' **Waterloo Banquet**, using the thousand-piece silver-gilt Portuguese service, now displayed in the rather lugubrious **Dining Room** at the other end of the house. Most of the Waterloo portraits are, in fact, hung in the adjacent **Striped Drawing Room**, which is decorated like a military tent in the manner of Napoleon's Loire chateau, Malmaison.

Canova's famous, more than twice life-sized, **nude statue of Napoleon** stands at the foot of the main staircase, having been bought by the government for the duke in 1816. It was disliked by the sitter, not least for the tiny figure of Victory in the emperor's hand, which appears to be trying to fly away. In the dimly lit **Plate and China Room**, also on the ground floor, you can view numerous gifts to the duke, including a 400-piece Prussian dinner service decorated with scenes of Wellington's life, and the bizarre Egyptian service, which was originally a divorce present from Napoleon to Josephine; unsurprisingly, she rejected it and Louis XVIII ended up giving it to the duke. In the basement there's plenty of Wellingtonia, a goodly selection of cruel, contemporary caricatures and a pair of the famous boots.

Rotten Row

From behind the Hyde Park Screen, which stands beside Apsley House, two roads set off west to Kensington: South Carriage Road, which is open to cars, and **Rotten Row**, which

17

THE GREAT EXHIBITION AND THE CRYSTAL PALACE

South of the Serpentine was the site of the **Great Exhibition** of the Works and Industry of All Nations, held between May 1 and October 15, 1851. The idea originated with Henry Cole, a minor civil servant in the Record Office, and was taken up enthusiastically by Prince Albert despite opposition from snooty Kensington residents, who complained it would attract an "invasion of undesirables who would ravish their silver and their serving maids". A competition to design the exhibition building produced 245 rejected versions, until Joseph Paxton, head gardener to the Duke of Devonshire, offered to build his "**Crystal Palace**", a wrought-iron and glass structure some 1848ft long and 408ft wide. The acceptance of Paxton's radical proposal was an act of faith by the exhibition organizers, since such a structure had never been built, and their faith was amply rewarded – 200 workers completed the building in just 4 months.

As well as showing off the achievements of the **British Empire** it was also a unique opportunity for people to enjoy the products of other cultures. Thousands of exhibits were housed in the Crystal Palace, including the Koh-i-Noor diamond (displayed in a birdcage), an Indian ivory throne, a floating church from Philadelphia, a bed which awoke its occupant by ejecting him or her into a cold bath, false teeth designed not to be displaced when yawning, a fountain running with eau de Cologne, and all manner of china, fabrics and glass.

To everyone's surprise, **six million visitors** came, and the exhibition made a profit, which was used to buy 87 acres of land south of Kensington Road, for the creation of a "Museumland" where "the arts and sciences could be promoted and taught in a way which would be of practical use to industry and make Britain the leading country of the industrialized world". The Crystal Palace itself was dismantled after the exhibition and rebuilt in southeast London in 1854, where it served as a concert hall, theatre, menagerie and exhibition space, only to be entirely destroyed by fire in 1936 (see p.313).

remains a bridle path. The name is thought to be a corruption of *route du roi* (king's way), after William III who established it as a bridle path linking Westminster and Kensington. William had 300 oil lamps hung from the trees to try to combat the increasing number of highwaymen active in the park, thus making Rotten Row the first road in the country to be lit at night. The measure was only partly successful – George II himself was later mugged here. To the south of Rotten Row, the **Hyde Park Barracks** are difficult to miss, thanks to Basil Spence's uncompromising 308ft-tall concrete residential tower block. Early in the morning, you might catch sight of the Household Cavalry exercising in the park, and at around 10.30am daily (Sun 9.30am) they set off for the Horse Guards building in Whitehall for the Changing of the Guard (see p.48).

The Serpentine

Rowing boats and pedalos Easter–Oct; Solarshuttle June–Aug daily every 30min noon–dusk

The Serpentine, Hyde Park's curvaceous lake, was created in 1730 by damming the Westbourne, a small tributary of the Thames, in order that Queen Caroline might have a spot for the royal yachts to mess about on. A miniature re-enactment of the Battle of Trafalgar was staged here in 1814, and two years later Shelley's pregnant wife, Harriet Westbrook, drowned herself in the lake after the poet had eloped with the 16-year-old Mary Wollstonecraft. The popular **Lido** (see p.439) is situated on the south bank, alongside the lovely Lido café, and rowing boats and pedalos can be rented from the **Boathouse** on the north bank. The solar-powered **Solarshuttle** boat ferries folk from one bank to the other in the summer.

Diana Fountain

Daily March & Oct 10am–6pm; April–Aug 10am–8pm; Sept 10am–7pm; Nov–Feb 10am–4pm • Free • ⊖ Knightsbridge or Lancaster Gate

Close to the Lido is the **Diana Fountain**, a memorial to the Princess of Wales which opened in 2004. Less of a fountain, and more of a giant oval-shaped mini-moat, the intention was to allow children to play in the running water, but, after three people suffered minor injuries, the fountain has been fenced off and supplied with security guards, making it

17

rather less fun for kids, who are now officially only allowed to dabble their feet. More fun for children is the **Princess of Wales Playground**, in the northwest corner of Kensington Gardens, featuring a ship stuck in sand, paving gongs and other groovy playthings.

Kensington Gardens

Daily 6am to dusk • ☎ 020 7298 2141, ⓦ royalparks.gov.uk • ⊖ Lancaster Gate, Queensway or High Street Kensington

The more tranquil half of the park, west of the West Carriage Drive, is known as **Kensington Gardens**, and is, strictly speaking, a separate entity from Hyde Park, though the only difference is that the gates of Kensington Gardens are locked at dusk. More exclusive because of the proximity of royalty at Kensington Palace, the gardens were first opened to the public in George II's reign, but only on Sundays and only to those in formal dress, not including sailors, soldiers or liveried servants. Unrestricted access was only granted in Victoria's reign, by which time, in the view of the Russian ambassador's wife, the park had already been "annexed as a middle-class rendezvous. Good society no longer [went] there except to drown itself."

Long Water

The upper section of the Serpentine – beyond the bridge – is, officially, actually known as the **Long Water**, and is by far the prettiest section of the lake. It narrows until it reaches the lovely **Italian Gardens**, which boasts a group of five fountains, laid out symmetrically in front of a pumphouse disguised as an Italianate loggia.

Pet Cemetery

To the east of the Italian Gardens, by Victoria Gate, lies the odd little **Pet Cemetery**, begun in the 1880s when Mr and Mrs J. Lewis Barnes buried their Maltese terrier, Cherry, here. When the Duke of Cambridge buried his wife's pet hound at the same spot after it had been run over on Bayswater Road, it became *the* place to bury your pooch; three hundred other cats and dogs followed, until the last burial in 1967. The cemetery – "perhaps the most horrible spectacle in Britain", according to George Orwell – is no longer open to the public, though you can peep over the wall.

Serpentine Gallery

Daily 10am–6pm; Teahouse July–mid-Oct • Free • ☎ 020 7402 6075, ⓦ serpentinegallery.org • ⊖ South Kensington

In the southeast corner of the park stands the **Serpentine Gallery**, built as a tearoom in 1908 because the park authorities thought "poorer visitors" might otherwise cause trouble if left without refreshments. An art gallery since the 1960s, it has a reputation for lively, and often controversial, contemporary art exhibitions, and contains an excellent bookshop. Each year, the gallery also commissions a leading architect to design a temporary **pavilion** for its summer-only teahouse extension.

From 2012, the gallery will have a second exhibition space called the **Serpentine Sackler Gallery**, housed in the Magazine, a former munitions depot, built in 1805, on the north side of the nearby Serpentine, so that the military could arm themselves in the event of a "foreign invasion or popular uprising". Designed in the style of a

---

ROYAL GUN SALUTES

At noon on February 6 (Accession Day), April 21 (Queen's Birthday), June 2 (Coronation Day) and June 10 (Duke of Edinburgh's Birthday), the Royal Horse Artillery wheel out cannons and the park resounds to a 41-round **Royal Gun Salute**. If a date falls on a Sunday, then the salute takes place the next day. Further gun salutes take place in Green Park, at 11am on the Queen's official birthday (a variable date in June), for London state visits and the State Opening of Parliament (Nov or Dec 11.08am) plus a two-gun salute on Remembrance Sunday at 11am and 11.02am.

17

PETER PAN & CO

The best-known of all the park's outdoor monuments is **Peter Pan**, the fictional character who enters London along the Serpentine and whose statue stands by the west bank of the Long Water; fairies, squirrels, rabbits, birds and mice scamper round the pedestal. It was in Kensington Gardens that the author, J.M. Barrie, used to walk his dog, and it was here that he met the five pretty, upper-class Llewellyn Davies boys, who wore "blue blouses and bright red tam o'shanters", were the inspiration for the "Lost Boys", and whose guardian he eventually became. Barrie himself paid for the statue, which was erected in secret during the night in 1912.

The rough-hewn muscleman struggling with his horse, to the southwest of Peter Pan, is G.F. Watts' **Physical Energy**, a copy of the Rhodes memorial in Cape Town; to the north is a granite obelisk raised to **John Hanning Speke**, who was the first non-African to find the source of the Nile, and who died in 1864 after accidentally shooting himself rather than the partridge he was aiming at. Just outside the Princess of Wales Playground is the **Elfin Oak**, a gnarled stump from Richmond Park, carved with little animals and mystical creatures by children's-book illustrator Ivor Innes in the late 1920s.

Palladian villa, it has been restored and extended by Zaha Hadid, of Olympic Aquatic Centre fame, and will feature two annual commissions: a large-scale, indoor light installation and an outdoor "playscape" designed for children and adults.

Albert Memorial

March–Dec first Sun of month 2pm & 3pm • 45min guided tours £6 • ☎ 020 7495 0916 • ⊖ South Kensington

Completed in 1876 by George Gilbert Scott, the **Albert Memorial**, on the south side of Kensington Gardens, is as much a hymn to the glorious achievements of Britain as to its subject, Queen Victoria's husband (who died of typhoid in 1861), who sits under its central canopy, gilded from head to toe, clutching a catalogue for the 1851 Great Exhibition. The pomp of the monument is overwhelming: the spire, inlaid with semiprecious stones and marbles, rises to 180ft; a marble frieze around the pediment is cluttered with 169 life-sized figures (all men) in high relief, depicting poets, musicians, painters, architects and sculptors from ancient Egypt onwards; the pillars are topped with bronzes of Astronomy, Chemistry, Geology and Geometry; mosaics show Poetry, Painting, Architecture and Sculpture; four outlying marble groups represent the four continents; and other statuary pays homage to Agriculture, Commerce and other aspects of imperial economics. Albert would not have been amused: "I can say, with perfect absence of humbug, that I would rather not be made the prominent feature of such a monument…it would upset my equanimity to be permanently ridiculed and laughed at in effigy", he once claimed.

Kensington Palace

Daily March–Oct 10am–6pm; Nov–Feb 10am–5pm • £12.50 • ☎ 020 3166 6000, ⓦ hrp.org.uk • ⊖ Queensway or High Street Kensington

On the western edge of Kensington Gardens stands **Kensington Palace**, a modestly proportioned, Jacobean brick mansion bought as an out-of-town residence by William and Mary in 1689 as the king's asthma and bronchitis were aggravated by Whitehall's damp and fumes. Wren, Hawksmoor and later William Kent were called in to embellish the place, though the palace was actually chief royal residence for barely fifty years.

KP – as it's fondly known in royal circles – is the official London residence of newly weds Prince William and Kate Middleton. It's also where William's mother, **Princess Diana** lived until her death in 1997. Occasionally Diana's dresses are on display, but there's no access to her rooms, which were on the west side of the palace, where the dukes and duchesses of Kent and Gloucester all still live. Today, the palace is undergoing a lengthy restoration and re-organization, so it's impossible to say exactly what route visitors will be made to take.

INFORMATION

Arrival KP's most handsome facade faces south, behind a flamboyant statue of William III, given to Edward VII by the Kaiser. The public entrance is on the east side, and must be approached from the Round Pond, where George I used to keep his edible turtles, and the Broad Walk, a favourite rollerblading avenue; both are overlooked by a flattering statue of Queen Victoria sculpted by her daughter, Princess Louise.

Eating To the north of the palace there's a lovely café in Hawksmoor's Orangery, built for Queen Anne as a summer dining room, and decorated with carving and statues by Grinling Gibbons.

Royal Ceremonial Dress Collection

The palace is home to the **Royal Ceremonial Dress Collection** and there are always plenty of frocks on display. The precise exhibits change from year to year but usually you get to see a few of the **Queen's dresses** – from the glamorous 1950s ball gowns, smothered in sequins and pearls, to her more suspect later penchant for apricot- and peach-coloured frocks – and a selection of **Princess Diana's dresses**. You may also get to look round the apartment where the Queen's sister, **Princess Margaret**, lived until her death in 2002. However, the place has been stripped bare of virtually all its original furnishings, except for a few rather peculiar portraits of Margaret, and the hagiographical exhibition shies away from anything seamy and dwells instead on her status as an amateur conchologist.

King's Apartments

The most impressive state apartments are the **King's Apartments**, beginning with the grandiose **King's Staircase**, designed by William Kent, with its Irish black marble steps, its Tijou wrought-iron balustrade and trompe-l'oeil crowds of courtiers and yeomen. Another great Kent creation is the "grotesque"-style painting on the ceiling of the **Presence Chamber**, which also features a lovely pear-wood Gibbons overmantle with weeping putti. Two rooms further on, the **Cupola Room**, with its monstrously ugly clock occupying centre stage, features another wonderful trompe-l'oeil fresco, which gives the effect of a coffered dome. The grandest room in the whole palace, is the **King's Gallery**, whose red damask walls are hung with paintings by, among others, Tintoretto. Also of interest is the wind dial above the fireplace, connected to the palace weather vane, built for William III and still fully functioning.

Queen's Apartments

The **Queen's Apartments** are much more modest, wood-panelled rooms hung with Dutch works reflecting the tastes of William and Mary. The best room is the **Queen's Bedchamber**, decked out in deep-blue velvet, with a four-poster bed that belonged to Queen Mary of Modena, James II's second wife. It was here that the diminutive Queen Anne died of gout; the toilet on which George II died of a heart attack, brought on by constipation, is, however, no longer in existence. **Queen Mary's Closet** was the scene of a furious quarrel between Queen Anne and her lover, the Duchess of Marlborough, after which they never saw each other again. And lastly, **Queen Mary's Gallery**, once magnificently decorated with 154 pieces of Oriental porcelain (now reduced to a mere handful), is lined with royal portraits. At the far end is one by Peter Lely, of Anne Hyde, mistress and later wife of the future James II; they officially married after she was already pregnant, causing something of a royal scandal even in the libidinous Restoration period.

Queen Victoria

Queen Victoria was born in Kensington Palace in 1819 and spent her dull, sad childhood cooped up here with her strict mother, the Duchess of Kent, who slept with her in the same room. According to her diary, her best friends were the palace's numerous "black beetles". Totally redecorated in 1836, **Queen Victoria's Bedroom** has been preserved, and you can also get to visit the gloomy **Red Saloon**, where the 18-year-old queen held her first Privy Council meeting, just hours after William IV's death on June 20, 1837.

South Kensington, Knightsbridge and Chelsea

The Royal Borough of Kensington and Chelsea, particularly the area around Knightsbridge, has been in vogue ever since royalty moved into Kensington Palace in the late seventeenth century. The popular tourist attractions lie in South Kensington, where three of London's top free museums – the Victoria and Albert, Natural History and Science museums – stand on land bought with the proceeds of the 1851 Great Exhibition. Chelsea, to the south, also has royal connections, though these date mostly from Tudor times and have left only a few scant remains. Since the nineteenth century, however, when artists and writers began to move here, Chelsea has been more bohemian than its neighbours – today, the Saatchi Gallery continues that tradition.

South Kensington

To everyone's surprise, the 1851 Great Exhibition was not only an enormous success, but actually yielded a profit, with which Prince Albert and his committee bought 87 acres of land in **South Kensington**. Institutions and museums, whose purpose was to "extend the influence of Science and Art upon Productive Industry", were to be established here to form a kind of "**Museumland**". Albert died of typhoid in 1861 at the age of just 41, and never saw his dream fully realized, but "Albertopolis", with its remarkable cluster of **museums and colleges**, plus the vast Albert Hall, now stands as one of London's most enlightened examples of urban planning.

With the founding of "Museumland", the surrounding area was transformed almost overnight into one of the most fashionable in town. Fields, farms and private estates were turned into street after street of ostentatious, whitewashed Italianate terraces, grandiose red-brick mansions and mews houses. Today, the borough remains among the world's most expensive slices of real estate, heartland of the privately educated, wealthy offspring of the middle and upper classes and the rich and famous.

18

Victoria and Albert Museum (V&A)

Cromwell Rd · Daily 10am–5.45pm, Fri until 10pm · Free · Various free tours set off from the main information desk in the Grand Entrance · ☎ 020 7942 2000, ⓦ vam.ac.uk · ⊖ South Kensington

For variety and scale, the **Victoria and Albert Museum** is the greatest museum of applied arts in the world. The range of exhibits on display means that whatever your taste, there's bound to be something to grab your attention: the finest collection of Italian sculpture outside Italy, the world's largest collection of Indian art outside India, plus extensive Chinese, Islamic and Japanese galleries; a gallery of twentieth-century objets d'art; and more Constable paintings than Tate Britain. In addition, the V&A's temporary shows on art, photography and fashion – some of which you have to pay for – are among the best in Britain. As Baedeker noted in 1905, "it can hardly be claimed that the arrangements of the [museum] are specially perspicuous". Beautifully but haphazardly displayed across a seven-mile, four-storey maze of rooms, the V&A's treasures are, however, impossible to survey in a single visit so get hold of a **free floor plan** to help you decide which areas to concentrate on.

The V&A began life in 1852 as the Museum of Manufactures – it being Albert's intention to bolster Britain's industrial dominance by inspiring factory workers, students and craftspeople with examples of excellence in applied art and design. Later it was renamed the South Kensington Museum, with Queen Victoria laying the foundation stone of the present, deeply colonial building in 1899 (her last major public engagement); ten years later Aston Webb's imposing main entrance, with its octagonal cupola, flying buttresses and pinnacles, was finished. The side entrance on Exhibition Road, originally built in 1873 for the School of Naval Architects, is equally ornate, with terracotta arcading and Minton tiles.

Raphael Cartoons

The most famous of the V&A's many exhibits are the **Raphael Cartoons** (room 48a) – from the Italian *cartone* meaning a large piece of paper. They comprise seven vast, full-colour paintings in distemper, which are, in fact, designs for tapestries ordered by Pope Leo X for the Sistine Chapel. The pictures – based on episodes from the New Testament – were bought by the future Charles I in 1623. They were subsequently reproduced in countless tapestries and engravings and became more familiar and influential than any of the artist's paintings. Alongside the paintings is an example of one of the tapestries woven at Mortlake.

At the far end of the room stands the **Retable of St George**, a huge fifteenth-century gilded altarpiece from Valencia, centred on a depiction of James I of Aragon defeating the Moors at the Battle of Puig in 1237. More alarming, though, are the bloodthirsty side panels, which feature the gross tortures endured by St George, with him having nails driven through his body before being placed in a cauldron of molten lead, dragged naked through the streets and finally beheaded and sawn in half.

South Asia

Such are the constraints of space that a mere fraction of the world-class **South Asia** collection is displayed (room 41), much of it derived from London's old East India

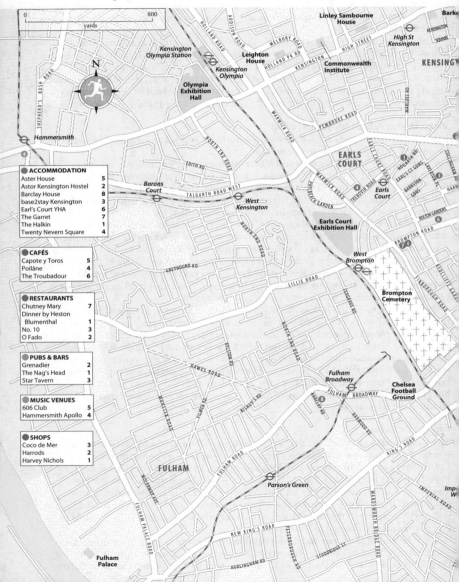

ACCOMMODATION

Aster House	5
Astor Kensington Hostel	2
Barclay House	8
base2stay Kensington	3
Earl's Court YHA	6
The Garret	7
The Halkin	1
Twenty Nevern Square	4

CAFÉS

Capote y Toros	5
Poilâne	4
The Troubadour	6

RESTAURANTS

Chutney Mary	7
Dinner by Heston Blumenthal	1
No. 10	3
O Fado	2

PUBS & BARS

Grenadier	2
The Nag's Head	1
Star Tavern	3

MUSIC VENUES

606 Club	5
Hammersmith Apollo	4

SHOPS

Coco de Mer	3
Harrods	2
Harvey Nichols	1

Company Museum. The most popular exhibit is **Tippoo's Tiger**, a life-sized wooden automaton of a tiger mauling an officer of the East India Company; the innards of the tiger feature a miniature keyboard which simulates the groans of the dying soldier. It was made for the amusement of Tipu Sultan, who was killed when the British took Seringapatam in 1799, and whose watch, telescope, brooch and sword are also displayed here. Close by is the **Golden Throne**, revered by the Sikh community as it belonged to **Ranjit Singh**, the first and last Sikh emperor, and was taken by the British when they

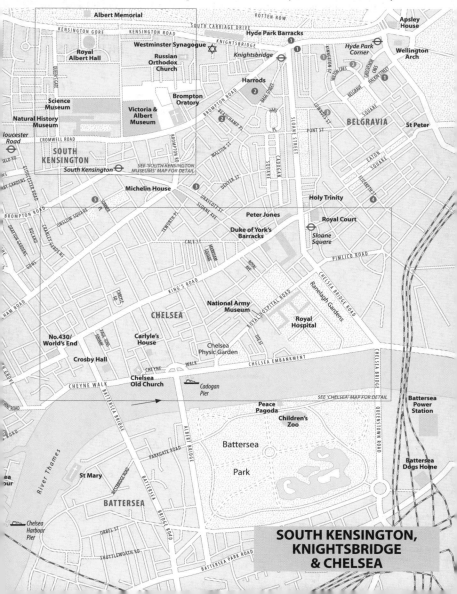

SOUTH KENSINGTON, KNIGHTSBRIDGE & CHELSEA

annexed the Punjab in 1849. Next to it is a conical turban decorated with quoits, which can be taken off and hurled at your enemy. Elsewhere, there's a superb white nephrite-jade wine cup, carved in the shape of a shell, made for the Mogul emperor Shah Jahan.

Islam

The **Islamic Middle East** gallery (room 42), next door, has, as its centrepiece, the silk-and-wool **Ardabil Carpet**, the world's oldest dated Persian carpet dating from 1540: copies have variously adorned the floors of 10 Downing Street and Hitler's Berlin

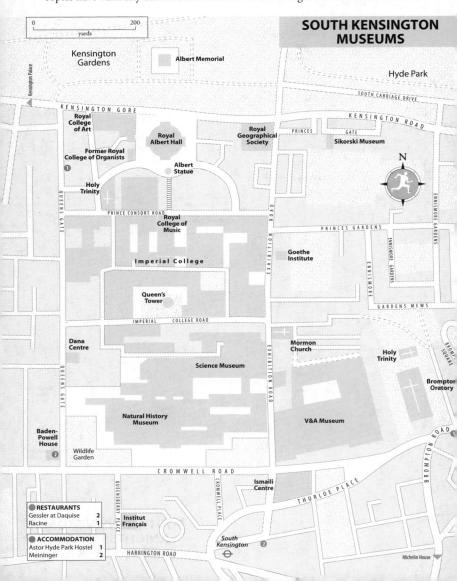

office. Unusually, on the west side of the gallery, there are several oil paintings of female acrobats, a harem's tea party and several full-length portraits from the Qajar dynasty in nineteenth-century Iran.

China and Japan

In the **China** gallery (room 44), the range of materials, from jade to rhino horn, lacquer to lapis lazuli, is more striking than any individual piece, though the pair of top-hatted gentlemen carved in marble stand out in the parade of Buddhas near the entrance – they are thought to represent Korean envoys. There's a surprising range, from a sixteenth-century Ming cupboard that's so minimalist, it could be modernist, to a great Art Deco clock from fashionable interwar Shanghai.

At the main entrance to the adjacent **Japan** gallery (room 45) is an incredible bronze incense burner, decorated with life-sized peacocks. Amid the wealth of silk, lacquer and samurai armour, look out for the tiny, elaborately carved, jade and marble *netsuke* (belt toggles) portraying such quirky subjects as "spider on aubergine", "starving dog on a bed of leaves" and "badger dressed in a lotus leaf".

Cast Courts

Two enormous **Cast Courts** (rooms 46a & 46b), filled with plaster casts of famous works of art and architecture, were created at the outset of the V&A so that ordinary Londoners could experience the glories of classical and ancient art. These barrel-vaulted, glass-roofed rooms remain an astonishing sight and will open after refurbishment in 2013. In room 46a, a copy of the colossal Trajan's Column, sliced in half to fit in the room, towers over the rest of the plaster casts, while over in room 46b, a life-sized replica of Michelangelo's *David* stands among the pulpits of Pisa cathedral and baptistry, and Ghiberti's celebrated bronze doors from the baptistry in Florence.

Sculpture

Along the south side of the central garden (rooms 21–24), in the V&A's showpiece **Sculpture** display, you'll find **Bernini**'s life-sized fountain sculpture, *Neptune and Triton*, amid a whole series of top-notch Italian pieces. Other highlights include Canova's depiction of Theseus astride the Minotaur, and his head of Helen of Troy about which Byron wrote an eight-line paean. **Auguste Rodin** donated several sculptures to the V&A in 1914, including his beautifully wrought *The Fallen Angel*, a swirling mass of rippling bronze, and his sensuous *Cupid and Psyche*, in which the lovers emerge half-hewn from the white marble. Look out, too, for a torso by Meštrovic, several strikingly simple works by Eric Gill and an Art Deco fireplace with a relief depicting society gossip.

Round the corner (rooms 17–20), the museum displays its impressive collection of **Buddhist sculpture**, from serene, gilded-copper seated figures from Tibet and Nepal to an entire Burmese shrine. There's also a corridor of **small-scale sculpture** on Level 3 in room 111, ranging from medieval religious ivories and English alabaster relief panels to German lime-wood masterpieces and a whole collection of works by Gilbert Bayes, who worked at Doulton, the ceramics company. (Bayes's Art Deco Doulton frieze from the company's headquarters in Lambeth is displayed in room 127.)

18

FUTURE PLANS

Like most big museums, the V&A is in a constant state of flux, with galleries opening and closing throughout the year. Brand new **Furniture** galleries are due to open in 2013 on level 6 to keep Ceramics company, the **Cast Courts** are also due to re open in 2013 after a thorough refurbishment and there will be new **Europe 1600–1800** galleries opening in 2014. And with Exhibition Road being made pedestrian-friendly, the V&A have commissioned a fancy new entrance which should be completed in 2016.

18

Medieval & Renaissance 300–1600

To visit the V&A's outstanding **Medieval & Renaissance** galleries chronologically, head for the lower level galleries (Level 0, room 8–10c), where the highlights include the **Gloucester Candlestick**, a mass of gilded foliage and figures commissioned for the city's Benedictine abbey around 1104, and the **Becket Casket**, a Romanesque reliquary in Limoges enamel designed to house the English saint's relics. Don't miss the German altarpiece, painted around 1400 and decorated with 45 vivid scenes from the Apocalypse.

The collection continues into the Renaissance upstairs (Level 2, rooms 62–64b), where you'll find the **Burghley Nef**, a slightly ludicrous sixteenth-century French gilded silver salt cellar in the shape of a ship. Even more incredible craftsmanship is on view in the Italian carved pearwood altarpiece, which features a complex crucifixion scene. Other highlights include a Tintoretto self-portrait, one of Leonardo's tiny notebooks, and Donatello's *Chellini Madonna*, a bronze roundel given by the artist to his doctor in lieu of payment – the reverse was designed to cast replicas in glass, and a bronze of the good doctor stands close by.

The galleries to the right of the information desk (Level 1, rooms 50a–50d) display the large-scale **Renaissance sculptures** such as Giambologna's expressively brutal *Samson Slaying a Philistine*. Passing through the immense marble and alabaster choirscreen from 's-Hertogenbosch cathedral, you'll find a series of full-scale altarpieces and an entire Florentine chapel, plus a new ambulatory-cum-treasury of monstrances, fold-away croziers, crosses and chalices.

British Galleries 1500–1760

The superbly designed **British Galleries** are a joy to visit. The first series of rooms covers **Britain 1500–1760** (Level 2, rooms 52–58), and begins in room 58 with Tudor times. Highlights include Torrigiani's bust of Henry VII, Holbein's miniature of Anne of Cleves, with its original ivory case, and the **Howard Grace Cup**, a medieval ivory cup associated with Thomas Becket, but given a Tudor silver-gilt makeover and crowned by a tiny St George and the dragon. At the other end of the scale is the **Great Bed of Ware**, a king-sized Elizabethan oak four-poster in which 26 butchers and their wives are said to have once spent the night, and which gets a mention in Shakespeare's *Twelfth Night*. Other specific items to look out for include the **Dark Jewel** given to Francis Drake by Queen Elizabeth I, the tapestries embroidered by **Mary, Queen of Scots** during her incarceration, James II's wonderfully camp wedding suit and the amazing high-relief lime-wood *Stoning of St Stephen* by Gibbons.

The galleries also contain a number of **period interiors** saved in their entirety from buildings that have since been demolished. These include a Jacobean panelled room from Bromley-by-Bow, a Georgian parlour from Henrietta Street in Covent Garden and a heavily gilded Rococo **Norfolk House Music Room** from St James's Square (where concerts are held on occasional Fridays at 6.30pm). Towards the end, you should pass Roubiliac's marble statue of **Handel**, carved in 1738 and the first statue in Europe of a living artist. It originally stood in the then-fashionable Vauxhall Gardens in south London, and caused a great stir in its day, with the composer depicted as Apollo slouching in inspired disarray, one shoe dangling from his foot.

British Galleries 1760–1900

Upstairs, **Britain 1760–1900** (Level 4, rooms 118–125) kicks off with a Chippendale four-poster made for the actor David Garrick, paintings by Gainsborough and Constable and Canova's erotic *Sleeping Nymph*. Again, period interiors are a big feature of the collection: Adam's Venetian-red Glass Drawing Room from Northumberland House and the fan-vaulted Strawberry Room from Lee Priory in Kent, which was inspired by Walpole's Gothic Revival masterpiece in Twickenham, Strawberry Hill. You'll also find plenty of outpourings from the **Arts and Crafts movement**, starting with a cabinet painted with medieval scenes by William Morris, inspired by Walter Scott's

THE WORLD'S FIRST MUSEUM CAFÉ

Whatever you do, make sure you pay a visit to the *V&A Café* in the museum's original refreshment rooms, the **Morris, Gamble & Poynter Rooms**, at the back of the main galleries.

Embellished by Edward Poynter with a wash of decorative blue tiling depicting the months and seasons of the year, the eastern **Poynter Room**, where the hoi polloi ate, was finished in 1881 and originally known as the Grill Room – the grill, also designed by Poynter, is still in place and was in use until 1939.

On the opposite side, the dark-green **Morris Room** (William Morris's first public commission), completed in 1868, accommodated a better class of diner. The decorative detail is really worth taking in – gilded Pre-Raphaelite panels and Burne-Jones stained glass, embossed olive-branch wallpaper and a running cornice frieze of dogs chasing hares.

The largest and grandest of the rooms lies between the two. The **Gamble Room**, completed in 1878 by the museum's own team of artists, boasts dazzling, almost edible decor, with mustard, gold and cream-coloured Minton tiles covering the walls and pillars from floor to ceiling. Fleshy Pre-Raphaelite nudes hold up the nineteenth-century chimneypiece from Dorchester House, while a ceramic frieze of frolicking cherubs accompanies a quote from Ecclesiastes, spelt out in decorative script around the cornice.

18

novels. Other highlights to look out for include *La Belle Iseult*, Morris's only known painting (of his future wife), and a whole room on the Scottish School, including several tables and chairs from Glasgow tearooms designed by Charles Rennie Mackintosh.

Silver, Gold, Mosaics and Ironwork

Like their centrepiece, the giant **Jerningham Wine Cooler**, smothered with images of Bacchic revelry, the vast **Silver** galleries (Level 3, rooms 65–70a) are almost overwhelming. More manageable is the wonderful nearby gallery of **Sacred Silver and Stained Glass** (rooms 83–84). The stained glass, all beautifully backlit, dates from around 1140 to the present day, while the silver includes reliquaries, crosses, crowns and medieval shrines from every era and from all over Europe.

The most remarkable exhibits in the **Gold, Silver & Mosaics** galleries (Level 3, rooms 70–73) are the **gold boxes**, used to hold snuff or sweets, which were the luxury item of choice in the eighteenth century. Equally mind-blowing are the nineteenth-century **micromosaics**, although the stupefying technique is more impressive than the end results: copies of the Old Masters. The Florentine *pietro dure* items, from the sixteenth century, represent another technically astounding artform – they're like stone collages – which verge on the kitsch.

Somewhat off the beaten path, it's worth persevering to find the V&A's **Ironwork** collection, a display of keys, locks, gates and grilles, ranged along a vast corridor (Level 3, rooms 113–114e). At the centre is George Gilbert Scott's Hereford Screen, an eight-ton neo-Gothic monster of copper and ironwork that was pulled out of the city's cathedral in 1967. Nearby, there are two great cabinets filled with every kind of tin, from a Huntley & Palmers biscuit-dispensing machine to a money box in the shape of a tea caddy.

Paintings

The V&A's collection of **Paintings** (Level 3, rooms 81, 82, 87–88a) includes minor works by Blake, Corot, Degas, Delacroix, Rembrandt, Tintoretto and Botticelli, a study for Ingres' *Odalisque*, a Tiepolo sketch, some Fantin-Latour flowers and several Pre-Raphaelite works, the best of which is Rossetti's verdant, emerald-green *The Day Dream*, one of his last great works. The V&A owns over four hundred works by John Constable, bequeathed by his daughter, including famous views of Salisbury Cathedral (in the British Galleries) and Dedham Mill, and full-sized preparatory oil paintings for *The Hay Wain* and *The Leaping Horse*, plus a whole host of his alfresco cloud studies and sketches. There are also several works by **Turner**, including a dreamy view of East

---

V&A'S HIDDEN GEMS

The V&A is so vast, it's very easy to miss one or two of its hidden gems. While you're on Level 3, make sure you see the spectacular Minton tiles of the **Ceramic Staircase**, designed by Frank Moody. Note the ceramic memorial to Henry Cole, the work of his niece, who has rendered her uncle in mosaic with "Albertopolis" in relief above. Make sure, too, that you get a close look at the grandiose **Leighton Frescoes** (Level 3, rooms 102 & 107), which used to look down onto the Cast Courts from on high.

The V&A's relatively small **20th Century** collection (Level 3, rooms 7 & 76) is easily overlooked, yet it's stuffed with high-quality artefacts: furniture by Otto Wagner, Charles Rennie Mackintosh, Bauhaus and the Wiener Werkstätte co-op; Constructivist fabrics and crockery; and a range of works by Finnish modernist supremo Alvar Aalto. Postwar design classics, from plywood chairs and melamine tableware to Olivetti typewriters and Dyson vacuum cleaners, are displayed in one half of the adjacent National Art Library.

18

Cowes Castle, painted for the castle's owner, John Nash, and **Gainsborough's Showbox**, in which he displayed the oil-on-glass landscapes he executed in the 1780s. Room 90 is used for temporary exhibitions of prints and drawings, and room 90a displays **portrait miniatures** by Holbein, Hilliard and others.

Theatre

The display areas of the **Theatre & Performance** galleries (Level 3, rooms 103–106) are divided into themes – producing, rehearsing, promotion and so on – and cover every theatrical genre from music hall to straight theatre, plus a surprisingly large amount of pop memorabilia. You may not learn much about the history of London theatre, but you do get to see some great individual exhibits, from the rotating hook, tunic and shorts used by Pansy Chinery in her teeth-spinning act to Pink Floyd's Azimuth Co-ordinator, which could produce an early form of surround sound. Perhaps the best section is "costume and make-up" where you can examine General Tom Thumb's waistcoat, Adam Ant's self-made Prince Charming get-up, Elton John's lurex Bicycle John outfit from the height of glam rock and an exact replica of Kylie Minogue's dressing room c.2007.

Jewellery

The justifiably popular **Jewellery** galleries (Level 3, rooms 91–93) display everything from a Bronze Age gold collar from Ireland to contemporary jewellery made from recycled materials. Amongst the earlier pieces, there are some pretty impressive gold papal rings – giant knuckle-dusters made from rock crystal – and some lovely gilded pomanders used to ward off evil. Specific highlights to look out for, further on, include the emeralds and diamonds given by Napoleon to his adopted daughter in 1806 (cabinet 15), the emeralds and rubies captured from Seringapatam in 1799, and the rare Siberian amethysts given by Tsar Alexander I to the wife of the Third Marquess of Londonderry (all in cabinet 24). Elsewhere, there are Art Nouveau pieces by René Lalique (cabinet 26), Arts and Crafts works by May Morris (cabinet 29) and the ostentatious personal jewellery of the eccentric Edith Sitwell (cabinet 30). Check out cabinet 56, too, for the Fabergé cigarette cases, the spectacular Manchester Tiara from 1903 (cabinet 55a) and the whole series of semiprecious carved animals that belonged to Queen Alexandra (cabinet 56).

Architecture, Glass and Ceramics

The V&A's **Architecture** gallery (Level 4, rooms 127–128) puts on special exhibitions, but also has a permanent display of architectural models in room 128. It's an eclectic array of realized and unrealized projects – everything from a fifteenth-century mosque and a Le Corbusier villa, to Spiral (Daniel Libeskind's now-shelved extension for the

V&A) and Bluewater, Britain's largest mall. Beyond, lies the relatively small **Glass Gallery** (Level 4, room 131), with its spectacular modern glass staircase and balustrade. The beauty and variety of the glass on display is staggering, and ranges from the Greek and Roman world to objets d'art by contemporary artists.

Finally, for those with stamina, or who wish to lose the crowds, there's an exhaustively encyclopaedic collection of **Ceramics** (Level 6, rooms 136–146) on the top floor. The best stuff for non-specialists is in room 140, where you'll find work by the Wiener Werkstatte and the Omega Workshops, Clarice Cliff crockery, a Suffragette tea-set and Communist ceramics. The contemporary pieces in room 141 range from manga to mad, while room 142 features one-off modern pieces by everyone from Picasso to Grayson Perry. And for a global overview of ceramics through the ages, continue to room 145, which has everything from Greek black-figure vases to Victorian de Morgan tiles.

18

Science Museum

Exhibition Rd • Daily 10am–6pm • Free • ☎ 0870 870 4868, ⓦ sciencemuseum.org.uk • ➡ South Kensington

The **Science Museum**, which broke away from the V&A in 1914, is undeniably impressive, filling seven floors with items drawn from every conceivable area of science, with hands-on galleries that appeal to adults and kids. The spectacular **Wellcome Wing** dragged the museum into the twenty-first century, and by 2015 pretty much all the old galleries will have been swept away. And replaced by new galleries on science, space, communications and climate change. The museum will also have a more arresting exterior, thanks to the planned Beacon – a glowing bulge in the museum's Neoclassical face on Exhibition Road.

INFORMATION AND TOURS

Tours and events Your first stop should be the information desk, in the Energy Hall, where you can pick up a museum plan and find out about the day's events and demonstrations; you can also sign up for a free guided tour on a specific subject. The museum's Dana Centre (165 Queen's Gate; ☎ 020 7942 4040, ⓦ danacentre.org.uk) puts on free talks, discussions and events aimed at adults.

Exhibitions The museum stages populist special exhibitions (for which you have to pay), often timed to coincide with the latest special-effects movie, and has flight simulators, and a 3D IMAX cinema (£8).

Eating Refreshment pit-stops include the *Revolution Café* off the Energy Hall, and the funky *Deep Blue Café* in the Wellcome Wing, plus several picnic areas.

The ground floor

The largest exhibit in the **Energy Hall**, by the entrance, is the bright red Burnley mill engine, whose enormous wheel used to drive 1700 looms and worked *in situ* until as late as 1970. To the side is an exhibition on **James Watt** (1736–1819), the Scot who was instrumental in kick-starting the Industrial Revolution in Britain. As well as inspecting examples of his inventions, you can view the perfectly preserved garret room workshop that Watt used in his retirement.

Beyond lies the **Exploring Space** exhibition, which follows the history of rockets from tenth-century China and Congreve's early nineteenth-century efforts, through the V-1 and V-2 wartime bombs, right up to the Apollo landings. There's a great, full-size replica of the Apollo 11 landing craft which deposited US astronauts on the moon in 1969.

Beyond, **Making the Modern World** displays iconic inventions of modern science and technology. These include *Puffing Billy*, the world's oldest surviving steam locomotive, used for hauling coal in 1815, and Robert Stephenson's *Rocket* of 1829, which pulled the Manchester–Liverpool passenger service. Other ground breaking inventions on display include a Ford Model T, the world's first mass-produced car, and a gleaming aluminium Lockheed 10A Electra airliner from 1935, which signalled the birth of modern air travel. Less glamorous discoveries, such as the brain scanner, occupy the sidelines, along with disasters such as the drug thalidomide.

18

Wellcome Wing

The darkened, ultra-violet **Wellcome Wing** beckons you on from Making the Modern World. The **Antenna** displays, on the ground floor, change regularly in order to cover contemporary science issues while they are topical. **Pattern Pod**, meanwhile, is for under-8s, and is basically a lot of interactive hi-tech fun. Kids can experiment with water ripples, footprints and the Penrose tessellation, and groove away in the multicoloured human shadow box.

On Floor 1, **Who am I?** is a guaranteed winner, as it concentrates on humans themselves. You can morph yourself into the opposite sex, watch a sperm race and test the gender of your brain. **Atmosphere**, on Floor 2, is a touch-screen exhibition exploring the causes and effects of climate change, and the possibilities for reducing carbon emissions. Floor 3 contains **In Future**, where you can play frivolous but fun multi-player educational games, and vote on contemporary socio-scientific questions, such as "Should you be able to choose the gender of your child?"

The basement

The basement houses two hands-on galleries perfect for children under 11. In the misleadingly entitled **Garden**, 3- to 6-year-olds don waterproofs to experiment with lock gates, and hard hats to play with pulleys. The imaginatively entitled **Things** is aimed at the natural curiosity of 7- to 11-year-olds about unidentifiable objects. A longer attention span and a fair bit of reading are involved, and there are the usual problems with crowds at the weekend and with the durability of the exhibits.

Floor 1

The **Challenge of Materials**, ranged around the balcony on the first floor, is an extremely stylish exhibition – the glass-floored suspension bridge is particularly cool – covering the use of materials ranging from aluminium to zerodur (used for making laser gyroscopes). As well as the excellent hands-on displays, there are aesthetically pleasing exhibits as diverse as a Bakelite coffin and an Axminster-carpet morning gown designed by Vivienne Westwood.

Further on, you'll find a very old-fashioned, little-visited section on **Agriculture**, perfect for those with a penchant for ploughs and tractors. Right next door, however, is **Plasticity**, a thought-provoking history of (and in some respects a paean to) plastic from Bakelite to PVC, hidden by an eye-catching curtain of giant red plastic strips.

Floor 2

The most popular section on Floor 2 is **Energy**, with its "do not touch" electric-shock machine that absolutely fascinates kids. Much of it is thought-provoking stuff – you can play computer games to learn how to reduce your carbon emissions – and the rest comprises more conventional displays, everything from a bird oil lamp to a clay stove from contemporary Kenya.

Elsewhere on Floor 2, there are sections on **Computing** and **Mathematics** now renamed "histories", as they were designed some years ago. Taking up quite some space are Charles Babbage's gargantuan Difference Engine 1, the world's first computer built in 1832, and his unrealized second version, which the museum completed in 1991.

Finally, you reach the little-visited **Ships** section, with its interminable glass cabinets of model vessels, from the *Great Harry* and the *Mayflower* to the *Great Eastern* and the *Cutty Sark*, not to mention Townsend Thoresen's ill-fated *Spirit of Free Enterprise*, which sank in the Zeebrugge disaster of 1987. Look out too for the model of the old London docks, at the point of their demise in the 1960s.

Floor 3

Floor 3 is now mobbed by kids having enormous fun at the **Launchpad**, the museum's chief interactive gallery where they can experiment with water, waves, light and sound

CLOCKWISE FROM TOP LEFT SCIENCE MUSEUM (P.257); V&A (P.249); NATURAL HISTORY MUSEUM INTERIOR AND EXTERIOR (P.260) >

and build a catenary arch (and knock it down again); "explainers" are on hand to try and impart some educational input.

If you're looking for peace and quiet, head next door for the exquisite scientific instruments, chiefly created by George Adams for George III, in **Science in the Eighteenth Century**. Close by, **Health Matters** dwells thoughtfully on modern medical history from the introduction of mass vaccination to the challenge of finding a cure for HIV.

Heading towards the Wellcome Wing, you eventually reach the giant hangar of **Flight**, festooned with aircraft of every description from a Spitfire to a modern executive jet. Look out for the scaled-down model of the Montgolfier balloon which recorded the first human flight in 1783, and the full-size model of the flimsy contraption in which the Wright brothers made their epoch-making power-assisted flight in 1903.

18

Floors 4 and 5

If old-fashioned displays are more your thing, head for **Glimpses of Medical History** on Floor 4. The exhibition features an attractive series of dioramas of medical operations, and larger mock-ups of surgeries and dentists' and chemists' premises through the ages, starting with Neolithic trepanning and finishing up with the gore-free spectacle of an open-heart operation c.1980.

Even more fascinating (but equally old-fashioned) is Wellcome's **Science and Art of Medicine** gallery on Floor 5. Using an anthropological approach, this is a visual and cerebral feast, galloping through ancient medicine, medieval and Renaissance pharmacy, alchemy, quack doctors, royal healers, astrology and military surgery. Offbeat artefacts include African fetish objects, an Egyptian mummy, numerous masks, an eighteenth-century Florentine model of a female torso giving birth, and George Washington's dentures.

Natural History Museum

Cromwell Rd · Daily 10am–5.50pm · Free · ☎ 020 7942 5000, ⓦ nhm.ac.uk · ⊖ South Kensington

Alfred Waterhouse's purpose-built mock-Romanesque colossus, with its 675-foot terracotta facade built in 1880, ensures the status of the **Natural History Museum** as London's most handsome museum. Its vast collections derive from a bequest by Hans Sloane to the British Museum, separated off in the 1860s after a huge power struggle. The founding director, Richard Owen, was an amazing figure, who arranged expeditions around the globe to provide everything from butterflies to dinosaurs for the museum's cabinets.

Nowadays, the museum copes manfully with the task of remaining an important resource for serious zoologists, and a major tourist attraction for the families with kids who flock here to check out the dinosaur collection. The **Central Hall** is dominated by "Dippy", a replica **Diplodocus** skeleton, 85ft from tip to tail, while the "side chapels" are filled with "wonders" of the natural world – a model of a sabre-toothed tiger, a stuffed Great Bustard, a dodo skeleton and so on. It's also worth pausing here to take in the architecture of this vast "nave", whose walls are decorated with moulded terracotta animals and plants.

INFORMATION AND TOURS

Arrival If the queues are long for the main entrance, you're better off heading for the Red Zone's side entrance on Exhibition Road. The museum is divided into four colour-coded zones, but all you really need to know is that the Red Zone is the old Geology Museum linked to the rest of the museum by the Birds section, and the Orange Zone is the new Darwin Centre.

Exhibitions and tours As well as large, very popular special exhibitions (for which there's a charge), the museum also puts on lots of free tours, talks, discussions, workshops and performances and in the winter there's an ice rink in front of the building.

Eating There's a café behind the stairs in the Central Hall, and in the Red Zone and a picnic area in the basement, or you can head out to the Wildlife Garden (April–Oct), west of the entrance.

Blue Zone

In **Dinosaurs**, a raised walkway leads straight to the highlight for many kids, the grisly life-sized animatronic dinosaur tableau, currently a roaring *Tyrannosaurus rex*. The rest of the displays are less theatrical and more informative, with massive-jawed skeletons and more conventional models.

The old-fashioned **Mammals** section is filled with stuffed animals and plastic models and dominated by a full-sized model of a blue whale juxtaposed with its skeleton. It usually goes down well enough with younger children, but it's showing its age somewhat.

18

Green Zone

Investigate Mon–Fri 2.30–5pm, Sat & Sun 11am–5pm; during school holidays daily 11am–5pm

The other firm favourite with kids is the arthropod room, known as **Creepy Crawlies**. Filled with giant models of bugs, arachnids and crustaceans, plus displays on spiders, mites and other unlovely creatures, it's here that you'll find the museum's only live exhibits, a colony of leaf-cutter ants from Trinidad, which feed on a fungus that they grow on the leaves they've gathered.

Meanwhile down in the basement is the excellent futuristic **Investigate**, aimed at children aged 7 to 14 – at busy times, you may need to obtain a timed ticket. Kids get to choose a tray of specimens and then play at being scientists, using microscopes, scales, a computer and various tools of the trade to examine and catalogue the items before them. There are one or two simpler hands-on exhibits too, as well as several plant species to look at.

Up on the first floor, **Minerals** features serried ranks of glass cabinets, culminating in a darkened chamber called **The Vault**. Here, the cream of the museum's rocks reside: a meteorite from Mars, a golden nugget weighing over 1000lb, one of the largest uncut emeralds in the world and the Star of South Africa, found in 1869, which triggered the South Africa diamond rush. Don't miss the 1300-year-old slice of **Giant Sequoia**, on the top floor, and while you're there, admire the view down onto the Central Hall, the moulded monkeys clinging to the arches and the ceiling panels depicting plant specimens.

Orange Zone

Little visited, compared to the rest of the museum, the **Orange Zone** is made up of the **Darwin Centre**, dominated by the giant concrete **Cocoon**, encased within the centre's glass-fronted atrium like a giant egg and home to over 20 million specimens. Visitors can take the lift to the seventh floor and enter the Cocoon to learn more about the history of the collection, about taxonomy and the research and field trips the museum funds.

In the nearby **Zoology spirit building**, you can view a small selection of bits and bobs pickled in glass jars, everything from silkworm larvae and a peculiar venomous snail that's killed more than one unwary collector, to a jar of parasitic worms from a sperm whale's stomach and a brown rat found during the building's construction. To join one of the **guided tours** that take you behind the scenes and allow you to talk to the museum's scientists, you need to book on the day at the information desk in Central Hall.

Red Zone

If you enter the museum from Exhibition Road, you enter the vast, darkened hall of the **Red Zone**, with the solar system and constellations writ large on the walls. Boarding the central escalator will take you through a partially formed globe to the top floor and **The Power Within**, an exhibition on volcanoes and earthquakes. The most popular section is the 1995 Kobe earthquake simulator, where you enter a mock-up of a Japanese supermarket and see the soy-sauce bottles wobble, while watching an in-store video of the real event. Despite the museum's protestations, the whole thing seems in very poor taste. On the same floor is **Restless Surface**, an interactive display on the earth's elements, soil and rock erosion and, of course, global warming.

Down one floor, **From the Beginning** covers the geological history of the planet from the Big Bang to the present day. The display ends with a crystal ball, which predicts the earth's future (bleak, but probably not within our lifetime). More alluring is **Earth's Treasury**, a dimly lit display of lustrous minerals and crystals, gemstones and jewels. Exhibits include rocks that shine in UV light, carved artefacts such as a lapis lazuli necklace, and even some recently discovered kryptonite (the mineral that weakens Superman).

Finally, **Earth Today and Tomorrow** (on the ground floor) is a look at how we are running down the earth's non-renewable natural resources, and polluting the planet in the process. Ironically, one of the chief sponsors is Rio Tinto, the distinctly environmentally unfriendly mining company.

Brompton Oratory

Brompton Rd • Mon–Fri 6.30am–8pm, Sat 6.30am–7.45pm, Sun 7.30am–8pm • Free • ☏ 020 7808 0900, ⊛ bromptonoratory.com • ⊖ South Kensington

London's most flamboyant and atmospheric Roman Catholic church, the **Brompton Oratory** stands just east of the Victoria and Albert Museum. The first large Catholic church to be built since the Reformation, it was begun by the young and unknown Herbert Gribble in 1880 and modelled on the Gesù church in Rome, "so that those who had no opportunity of going over to Italy to see an Italian church had only to come here to see a model of one". The ornate Italianate interior, financed by the Duke of Norfolk, is filled with gilded mosaics and stuffed with sculpture, much of it genuine Italian Baroque from the Gesù church and Siena cathedral, notably the seventeenth-century apostles in the nave and the main altar, and the reredos of the Lady Chapel. The pulpit is a superb piece of neo-Baroque from the 1930s, with a high cherub count on the tester. True to its architecture, the church practises a "rigid, ritualized, smells-and-bells Catholicism", as one journalist put it, with daily Mass in Latin, a top-notch choir on Sundays, and some very high-society weddings throughout the year.

Royal Albert Hall

Kensington Gore • Guided tours depart form Door 12 daily except Wed 10.30am–3.30pm; £8.50 • ☏ 020 7838 3105, ⊛ royalalberthall .com • ⊖ South Kensington or High Street Kensington

The funds raised on the death of the Prince Consort in 1861 were squandered on the nearby Albert Memorial (see p.246), and it took considerable effort by Henry Cole, his collaborator on the Great Exhibition, to get funding to complete the **Royal Albert Hall**. Plans for this splendid iron- and glass-domed auditorium had been drawn up during the prince's lifetime, with an exterior of red brick, terracotta and marble that was already the hallmark of South Ken architecture. Completed in 1871, the hall has been the venue for everything from Miss World to pop gigs, and is the main venue for London's most democratic classical music festival, the annual Henry Wood Promenade Concerts, better known as the **Proms** (see p.413).

Several other educational institutions congregate around the Albert Hall, as was Albert's intention. The most striking architecturally is the former **Royal College of**

FRENCH CONNECTIONS

Part of South Ken's cachet is thanks to its **French connections**, with a French school and crèche, a couple of bookshops, a deli and several genuine patisseries and brasseries clustered around the **Institut Français** (⊛ institut-francais.org.uk) on Queensberry Place, which itself maintains an interesting programme of theatre, cinema and exhibitions.

A further French sight worth checking out is the gorgeous Art Deco **Michelin House**, a short walk to the south down Brompton Road. Faced in white faïence and decorated with tyres and motoring murals by French artists in 1911, its ground floors now house the shop, café, oyster bar and restaurant of *Bibendum* (⊛ bibendum.co.uk), all run by Terence Conran.

Organists to the west of the Albert Hall, a strange neo-Jacobean confection, designed for free in 1875 by Henry Cole's eldest son and laced with cream, maroon and sky-blue sgraffito.

Also on the west side of the Albert Hall is the headquarters of the **Royal College of Art**, founded back in 1837 but now housed in a seven-storey concrete block, designed in the 1960s by RCA staff. A postgraduate art college, the RCA's past students range from Henry Moore and David Hockney to Adam Ant and Tracey Emin; student art exhibitions are held during term-time on the ground floor.

18

Royal College of Music

Prince Consort Rd • Term-time Tues–Fri 11.30am–4.30pm • Free • ☎ 020 7591 4346, ⓦ cph.rcm.ac.uk • ⊖ South Kensington

Behind the Albert Hall, flanked by the monumental **South Steps**, is a memorial to the Great Exhibition, featuring the Prince Consort. Predating the Royal Albert Hall (which Albert turns his back on), it originally stood amid the gardens and pavilions of the Royal Horticultural Society, which were replaced in the 1880s by the colossal **Imperial Institute** building. Of this only the 287ft **Queen's Tower** (closed to the public) remains, stranded amid the modern departments of Imperial College, the University of London's science faculty.

Instead, Albert now stands facing the splendid, neo-Gothic **Royal College of Music**, whose students have included Ralph Vaughan Williams and Benjamin Britten. The college houses a **museum** containing a collection of over 800 instruments, dating from the fifteenth to the twentieth centuries, including the world's oldest surviving keyboard instrument.

Royal Geographical Society

1 Kensington Gore • Mon–Fri 10am–5pm • Free • ☎ 020 7591 3000, ⓦ rgs.org • ⊖ South Kensington

East of the Albert Hall is the **Royal Geographical Society**, a wonderful brick-built complex in the Queen Anne style, with statues of two of the society's early explorers, David Livingstone and Ernest Shackleton, occupying niches along the outer wall. The society gives regular talks, maintains a remarkable library and map room and puts on excellent special exhibitions (entrance on Exhibition Road).

Sikorski Museum

20 Prince's Gate • Mon–Fri 2–4pm, first Sat of month 10.30am–4pm • Free • ☎ 020 7589 9249, ⓦ pism.co.uk • ⊖ South Kensington

South Ken's Polish connections are exemplified by the **Sikorski Museum** and Polish Institute, east of the Royal Geographical Society. World War II militaria form the bedrock of the museum, along with the personal effects of General Wladyslaw Sikorski, the prewar prime minister who fled to London in 1939, only to die in a mysterious plane accident in 1943. The absence of a non-Communist leader of Sikorski's standing after the war was lamented by exiled Poles for the next forty years.

Czech Memorial Scrolls Museum

Kent House, Rutland Gardens • By appointment Tues & Thurs 10am–4pm • Free • ☎ 020 7584 3741, ⓦ czechmemorialscrollstrust.org • ⊖ Knightsbridge

Another East European connection is contained within the **Westminster Synagogue** in Kent House, a spacious Victorian mansion in Rutland Gardens, off Kensington Road. The synagogue occupies the first floor, while the third floor houses the **Czech Memorial Scrolls Museum**, which tells the miraculous story of the 1564 Torah scrolls which were gathered from all over Bohemia and Moravia by the Nazis, possibly for their planned "Museum of an Extinct Race", survived the Holocaust, and were purchased from the Communist government in 1964 and brought here. The shelves have been gradually emptying as the scrolls are restored and sent out to Jewish communities all over the world, but the remainder are displayed here.

Knightsbridge

Knightsbridge is irredeemably snobbish, revelling in its reputation as the swankiest shopping area in London, with designer stores all the way down **Sloane Street**, and its pretty little mews streets, built to house servants and stables, but now inhabited by the rich themselves. However, most people come to Knightsbridge for just one reason: to visit Harrods, London's most famous department store. **Belgravia**, over to the east and strategically close to Buckingham Palace, is London's chief embassy land, with at least 25 scattered amongst the grid-plan stuccoed streets. All in all, it's a pretty soulless place, although there are one or two lovely pubs hidden in the various mews.

18

Harrods

Brompton Rd · Mon–Sat 10am–8pm, Sun noon–6pm · ☎ 020 7730 1234, ⓦ harrods.com · ⊖ Knightsbridge

Housed in a grandiose 1905 terracotta building, which turns into a palace of fairy lights at night, **Harrods** has come a long way since it started out as a family-run grocer's in 1849. Nowadays, it is the UK's largest shop, spread over 7 floors, 5 acres, with over 5000 staff, and over 15 million customers a year. If you are coming to visit, note that a "clean and presentable" **dress code** is enforced and backpacks either have to be carried in the hand or placed in the store's left luggage (£3). Once here, however, you can avail yourself of the first-floor "luxury washrooms" and splash on a range of perfumes for free.

Even if you don't want one of the distinctive olive-green Harrods carrier bags, the store has a few sections on the ground floor that are sights in their own right. Chief among these is the **Food Hall**, with its exquisite Arts and Crafts tiling. There's also an Egyptian Hall, with pseudo-hieroglyphs and sphinxes, and an Egyptian Escalator, with a **Di and Dodi fountain shrine**. Here, to the strains of Mahler (and the like), you can contemplate photos of the ill-fated couple, and, preserved in an acrylic pyramid, a used wine-glass from the couple's last evening and the engagement ring Dodi allegedly bought for Di the previous day. Another memorial has been erected at Door Three, a life-size bronze statue entitled *Innocent Victims*, depicting the couple dancing on a beach and clutching an albatross. Dodi's father, Mohamed Al-Fayed, sold Harrods to the Qatari royal family for £1.5 billion in 2010, but so far the memorials are still *in situ*.

Chelsea

Until the sixteenth century, **Chelsea** was nothing more than a tiny fishing village on the banks of the Thames, centred around Chelsea Old Church. It was Thomas More who started the upward trend by moving here in 1520, followed by members of the nobility, including Henry VIII himself. In the eighteenth century, Chelsea acquired its riverside houses along Cheyne Walk, which gradually attracted a posse of literary and intellectual types. However, it wasn't until the late nineteenth century that the area began to earn its reputation as London's very own Left Bank.

In the 1960s, Chelsea was at the forefront of "Swinging London", with the likes of David Bailey, Mick Jagger, George Best and the "Chelsea Set" hanging out in the boutiques and coffee bars. Later, the **King's Road** became a catwalk for hippies and in the late 1970s it was the unlikely epicentre of the punk explosion. Nothing so risqué goes on in Chelsea now, with franchise fashion rather than avant-garde fashion the order of the day, though some of its residents like to think of themselves as a cut above the purely moneyed types of Kensington. The area's other aspect, oddly enough considering its reputation, is a **military** one, with the former Chelsea Barracks, the Royal Hospital and the National Army Museum.

Sloane Square

A leafy nexus on the very eastern edge of Chelsea, **Sloane Square** is centred on a modern Venus fountain, featuring a relief of Charles II and Nell Gwynne. On the east

CHELSEA

CAFÉ
Mona Lisa   2

RESTAURANT
Hunan   1

PUBS & BARS
Anglesea Arms   2
Cooper's Arms   3
Fox & Hounds   1
Pig's Ear   4

SHOPS
Anthropologie   3
John Sandoe   2
Manolo Blahnik   4
Rigby & Peller   1
Vivienne Westwood/World's End   5

N

0   200
yards

EBURY BRIDGE ROAD
PIMLICO ROAD
ST BARNABAS STREET
PASSMORE ST
Royal Court Theatre
Sloane Square
CHESTER ROW
BOURNE STREET
GRAHAM TERRACE
HOLBEIN PLACE
SLOANE GARDENS
LOWER SLOANE STREET
Sloane Square
Holy Trinity
Peter Jones
Saatchi Gallery
CULFORD GDNS
LINCOLN ST
DRAYCOTT PLACE
DRAYCOTT AVENUE
BRAY PLACE
SLOANE AVENUE
WHITEHEAD'S GROVE
ELYSTAN STREET
CALE STREET
BRITTEN STREET
ST LUKE'S STREET
ELYSTAN PLACE
SYDNEY PL
FULHAM ROAD
SUMNER PLACE
SOUTH KENSINGTON
DOVEHOUSE STREET
SYDNEY STREET
MARKHAM STREET
MARKHAM SQUARE
SMITH STREET
WELLINGTON SQUARE
ROYAL AVENUE
CHELTENHAM TERR
WALPOLE ST
LEONARD'S TERR
FRANKLIN'S ROW
LUKE'S ROW
MON'S ROW
ST LEONARD'S TERRACE
WEST ROAD
ORMONDE GATE
SLOANE STREET
RANELAGH GROVE
CHELSEA
Old Town Hall
The Pheasantry
KING'S ROAD
RADNOR WALK
FLOOD STREET
SMITH TERRACE
TEDWORTH STREET
TEDWORTH SQUARE
CHRISTCHURCH ST
ST LOO AVENUE
REDBURN ST
FLOOD STREET
MARGARETTA TERR
MANOR STREET
OAKLEY STREET
Chelsea Antique Market
Chelsea Square
CARLYLE SQUARE
THE VALE
ELM PARK GARDENS
ELM PARK ROAD
ELM PARK WALK
MULBERRY WALK
MALLORD STREET
OLD CHURCH STREET
CARLYLE
Carlyle's House
Chelsea Old Church
Crosby Hall
Lindsay House
No. 430/World's End
DANVERS STREET
BEAUFORT STREET
MILMAN'S STREET
PARK WALK
PAULTONS SQUARE
LAWRENCE STREET
JUSTICE WALK
GLEBE PLACE
UPPER CHEYNE WALK
CHEYNE WALK
CHEYNE ROW
LAWRENCE STREET
CHEYNE WALK
ALBERT BRIDGE
Cadogan Pier
River Thames
CHELSEA EMBANKMENT
ROYAL HOSPITAL ROAD
CHELSEA BRIDGE ROAD
Ranelagh Gardens
Museum
Royal Hospital
National Army Museum
Chelsea Physic Garden
DILKE STREET
SWAN WALK
PARADISE WALK
TITE STREET
DILKE STREET
FLOOD STREET
Battersea Park
Peace Pagoda
CRANLEY PL
DE VERE STREET
SELWOOD TERRACE
NEVILLE STREET
EGERTON TERRACE
IXWORTH PLACE

side of the square, beside the tube station, stands the Victorian **Royal Court Theatre**, a bastion of new theatre writing since John Osborne's *Look Back in Anger* sent tremors through the establishment in 1956. On the opposite side is **Peter Jones**, a department store housed in London's finest glass-curtain building, built in the 1930s, which curves its way seductively into the King's Road.

Holy Trinity, Sloane Square

Sloane St • Mon–Sat 8.30am–5.30pm, Sun 8.30am–1.30pm • ☎ 020 7730 7270, ⓦ holytrinitysloanesquare.co.uk • ➔ Sloane Square

18

Just up Sloane Street from the square is another architectural masterpiece, **Holy Trinity**, created in 1890, and probably the finest Arts and Crafts church in London. The east window is the most glorious of the furnishings, a vast 48-panel extravaganza designed by Edward Burne-Jones, and the largest ever made by Morris & Co. Holy Trinity is very High Church, filled with the smell of incense and statues of the Virgin Mary, and even offering confession.

King's Road

The **King's Road**, Chelsea's main artery, was designed as a royalty-only thoroughfare by Charles II, in order – so the story goes – to avoid carriage congestion en route to Nell Gwynne's house. Lesser mortals could travel down it on production of a special copper pass but it wasn't opened to the public until 1830. This prompted a flurry of speculative building that produced the series of elegant, open-ended squares – Wellington, Markham, Carlyle and Paultons – which still punctuate the road. If you don't fancy walking down the King's Road, buses #11 and #22 run the length of it, and buses #19 and #319 run from Sloane Square partway down and then south across Battersea Bridge.

Saatchi Gallery

King's Rd • Daily 10am–6pm • Free • ☎ 020 7823 2363, ⓦ saatchi-gallery.co.uk • ➔ Sloane Square

Set back from the King's Road, a short stroll from Sloane Square, is the former **Duke of York's HQ**, built in 1801 and fronted by a solid-looking Tuscan portico. The building is now the unlikely home of the **Saatchi Gallery**, which puts on changing exhibitions of contemporary art in its fifteen equally proportioned, whitewashed rooms. Charles Saatchi, the collector behind the gallery, was the man whose clever advertising campaigns kept Mrs Thatcher in power in the 1980s and who introduced Young British Artists (YBAs) like Damien Hirst, Sarah Lucas and Rachel Whiteread to the world in the 1990s.

Royal Avenue

The first of the picturesque squares that open out onto the King's Road is **Royal Avenue**, on the south side. This particular one is rather like a Parisian *place*, with plane trees and gravel down the centre, and was originally laid out in the late seventeenth century as part of William III's ambitious (and unrealized) scheme to link Kensington Palace with the Royal Hospital to the south. The next square along is Wellington Square, suspected fictional London address of James Bond; Ian Fleming lived, on and off, in Chelsea and no. 30 is thought to have been the location of Bond's "comfortable ground-floor flat".

World's End

The stretch of the King's Road beyond Beaufort Street, known as **World's End**, was the epicentre of Chelsea's Swinging Sixties scene, with boutiques like Granny Takes a Trip and hippie shops like Gandolf's Garden and the Sweet Shop. In 1971, Malcolm McLaren and his school teacher girlfriend, Vivienne Westwood, opened a Teddy Boy-revival store called Let It Rock, located, with a neat sense of irony, right next door to the Chelsea Conservative Club, at no. 430. In 1975 they changed tack and renamed the shop SEX, stocking it with proto-punk fetishist gear, with simulated burnt limbs in the window. It became a magnet for the likes of John Lydon and John Simon Ritchie, better known as Johnny Rotten and Sid Vicious, and was renamed Seditionaries – the rest, as they say, is history. Now known as World's End, the shop, with its landmark backward-running clock, continues to flog Westwood's eccentric designer clothes.

Royal Hospital Chelsea

Royal Hospital Rd • April–Sept Mon–Sat 10am–noon & 2–4pm, Sun 2–4pm; Oct–March Mon–Sat only • Free • ☎ 020 7881 5200, ⓦ chelsea-pensioners.co.uk • ⊖ Sloane Square

18

Among the most nattily attired of all those parading down the King's Road are the scarlet- or navy-blue-clad Chelsea Pensioners, army veterans from the nearby **Royal Hospital** founded by Charles II in 1682. Designed by Wren, the hospital's plain, red-brick wings and grassy courtyards became a blueprint for institutional and collegiate architecture across the Empire. On Founder's Day (May 29), the Pensioners, wearing their traditional tricorn hats, festoon Grinling Gibbons' gilded statue of Charles with oak leaves to commemorate the day after the disastrous 1651 Battle of Worcester, when the future king hid in an oak tree to escape his pursuers.

The public are welcome to visit the hospital's austere **chapel**, with its huge barrel vaulting and Sebastiano Ricci's colourful apse fresco *Resurrection*, in which Jesus patriotically bears the flag of St George. Opposite lies the equally grand, wood-panelled **dining hall**, where the three hundred or so Pensioners still eat under portraits of the sovereigns and Antonio Verrio's vast allegorical mural of Charles II and his hospital. In the Secretary's Office, designed by John Soane, on the east side of the hospital, there's a small **museum**, displaying Pensioners' uniforms, medals and two German bombs. The playing fields to the south, from which you get the finest view of the hospital, are the venue for the annual **Chelsea Flower Show** (see p.25).

National Army Museum

Royal Hospital Rd • Daily 10am–5.30pm • Free • ☎ 020 7730 0717, ⓦ national-army-museum.ac.uk • ⊖ Sloane Square

The concrete bunker next door to the Royal Hospital houses the **National Army Museum**. There are plenty of interesting historical artefacts, plus an impressive array of uniforms and medals, but for a more balanced view of war, you're better off visiting the Imperial War Museum.

To follow the museum chronologically, start in the lower ground floor with **The Making of Britain** (1066–1783), which concentrates on the Civil War and the origins of the professional British Army, before heading for **Changing the World** (1784–1904), a

---

LONDON'S PLEASURE GARDENS

"…the fragrancy of the walks and bowers, with the choirs of birds that sung upon the trees, and the loose tribe of people that walked under their shades, I could not but look upon the place as a kind of Mahometan paradise."   The Spectator May 20, 1712

London's pleasure gardens were among the city's chief entertainments in the eighteenth century. **Vauxhall Gardens**, open from around 1660, on the south bank, provided the blueprint: formal, lantern-lit gardens, musical entertainments and "dark walks", perfect for secret assignations. Of Vauxhall, there is now no trace, but its nearest rival was **Ranelagh Gardens**, now a pleasant little landscaped park near the Royal Hospital. A couple of information panels in the gardens' Soane-designed shelter show what the place used to look like when Canaletto painted it in 1751. The main feature was a giant Rotunda, where the beau monde could promenade to musical accompaniment – the 8-year-old Mozart played here. Shortly after it opened in 1742, Walpole reported that "you can't set your foot without treading on a Prince or Duke". Fashion is fickle, though, and the rotunda was eventually demolished in 1805.

18

WILDE ABOUT CHELSEA

John Singer Sargent, Augustus John, James Whistler and Bertrand Russell all lived at one time or another in Tite Street, which runs alongside the National Army Museum, but the street's most famous resident was writer and wit **Oscar Fingal O'Flahertie Wills Wilde** (1856–1900), who moved into no. 1 in 1880 with an old Oxford chum, Frank Miles, only to be asked to leave the following year by the latter (under pressure from his father, Canon Miles), after the hostile reception given to Wilde's recently published poetry. Four years later, Wilde moved back into the street to no. 34, with his new bride Constance Lloyd. By all accounts he was never very good at "playing husband", though he was happy enough to play father to his two boys (when he was there). It was in Tite Street, in 1891, that Wilde first met **Lord Alfred Douglas**, son of the Marquis of Queensberry and known to his friends as "Bosie", who was to become his lover, and eventually to prove his downfall.

At the height of Wilde's fame, just four days after the first night of *The Importance of Being Earnest*, the marquis left a visiting card for Wilde, on which he wrote "To Oscar Wilde, posing as a somdomite [sic]". Urged on by Bosie, Wilde unsuccessfully sued Queensberry, losing his case when the marquis produced incriminating evidence against Wilde himself. On returning to the *Cadogan Hotel* on Sloane Street, where Bosie had rooms, Wilde was arrested by the police, taken to Bow Street police station, charged with homosexual offences and eventually sentenced to **two years' hard labour**. Bankrupt, abandoned by Bosie and separated from his wife, he served his sentence in Pentonville, Wandsworth and later Reading jail. On his release he fled abroad, travelling under the pseudonym of Sebastian Melmoth, and died three years later from a syphilitic infection. He is buried in Paris's Père Lachaise cemetery.

none-too-critical look at the British Empire. Here you can see a vast spot-lit model of the Battle of Waterloo (at 7pm before the Prussians arrived to save the day). The skeleton of Marengo, Napoleon's charger at the battle, the saw used to amputate the Earl of Uxbridge's leg and Richard Caton-Woodville's famous painting of *The Charge of the Light Brigade* are among the highlights of this section.

World Wars has sections on just about every conflict zone of the two global conflicts from a slice of the Somme to the POW camps of the Far East. **Conflicts of Interest**, on the top floor, and a good section on the Korean War, complete the story. Make sure you pop into the **Art Gallery**, where there are some excellent military portraits by the likes of Reynolds, Gainsborough, Romney and Lawrence, not to mention a suave self-portrait by a uniformed Rex Whistler, who died in action shortly after D-Day.

Chelsea Physic Garden

66 Royal Hospital Rd • April–Oct Wed–Fri noon–5pm, Sun noon–6pm; July & Aug also Wed until 10pm; plus occasional winter weekend openings • £8 • ☎ 020 7349 6458, ⓦ chelseaphysicgarden.co.uk • ⊖ Sloane Square

Founded in 1673 by the Royal Society of Apothecaries, the **Chelsea Physic Garden** is the oldest botanical garden in the country after Oxford's: the first cedars grown in this country were planted here in 1683, cotton seed was sent from here to the American colonies in 1732, England's first rock garden was constructed here in 1773, and the walled garden contains Britain's oldest olive tree. Unfortunately, it's a rather small garden, and a little too close to Chelsea Embankment to be a peaceful oasis, but keen botanists will enjoy it nevertheless. A statue of Hans Sloane, who presented the Society with the freehold, stands at the centre of the garden; behind him there's a teahouse, serving afternoon tea and delicious home-made cakes.

Cheyne Walk

Chelsea Physic Garden marks the beginning of **Cheyne Walk** (pronounced "chainy"), whose quiet riverside locale and succession of Queen Anne and Georgian houses drew artists and writers here in great numbers during the nineteenth century. Since the building of the Embankment and the increase in traffic, however, the character of this peaceful haven has been lost. Novelist Henry James, who lived at no. 21, used to take "beguiling drives" in his wheelchair along the Embankment; today, he'd be hospitalized in the process. An older contemporary of James, Mary Ann Evans (better known under her pen name George Eliot), moved into no. 4 – the first blue plaque you come to – in December 1880, five months after marrying an American banker 21 years her junior. Three weeks later she died of a kidney disease. Composer Ralph Vaughan Williams lived at no. 13; thirty or so years later, composers Mick Jagger and Keith Richards followed suit, at no. 48 and no. 3 respectively.

Chelsea Old Church

64 Cheyne Walk • Tues–Thurs 2–4pm • ☎ 020 7795 1019, ⓦ chelseaoldchurch.org.uk • Bus #19 or #319 from ⊖ Sloane Square

At the end of Cheyne Walk's gardens, there's a garish, gilded statue of **Thomas More**, "Scholar, Saint, Statesman", a local who used to worship in nearby **Chelsea Old Church** where he built his own private chapel in the south aisle (the hinges for the big oak doors are still visible). More is best known for his martyrdom in 1535, though he himself showed little mercy to heretics – he even had some tied to a tree in his Chelsea back garden and flogged. Badly bombed in the last war, the church nevertheless contains an impressive number of monuments. Chief among them is Lady Cheyne's memorial (possibly by Bellini) and More's simple canopied memorial to his first wife, Jane, in which he himself hoped to be buried. In the event, his torso ended up in the Tower of London, while his head was secretly buried in Canterbury by his daughter, Margaret Roper. More's second wife, Alice, is also buried here.

Crosby Hall

You can get a flavour of Chelsea in Thomas More's day from nearby **Crosby Hall**, part of a fifteenth-century wool merchant's house once owned by More, transferred in 1910 bit by bit from Bishopsgate in the City to the corner of Danvers Street, west of Chelsea Old Church, on the site of More's gardens. Once occupied by the future Richard III (and used as a setting by Shakespeare), it's now a private residence, so you can admire its brick exterior, but not the great hall's fine hammerbeam roof.

Beyond Crosby Hall

The continuation of **Cheyne Walk**, beyond Crosby Hall, is no less rich in cultural associations. Mrs Gaskell was born in 1810 at no. 93, while the painter James Whistler, who lived at ten different addresses in the 41 years he spent in Chelsea, lived for a time at no. 96, the house where the Provisional IRA and the British government met secretly in 1972, to discuss peace, some five months after Bloody Sunday. The Brunels, Marc and Isambard, both lived at no. 99, which form part of **Lindsey House**, built in 1674 on the site of Thomas More's farm – it's occasionally possible to visit the entrance hall, garden room and gardens (phone ☎020 7447 6605 for more details). Last but not least, the reclusive J.M.W. Turner lived at no. 119 for the last six years of his life under the pseudonym Booth, and painted many a sunset over the Thames.

Carlyle's House

24 Cheyne Row • April–Oct Wed–Fri 2–5pm, Sat & Sun 11am–5pm • NT • £4.90 • ☎ 020 7352 7087 • Bus #19 or #319 from ⊖ Sloane Square

Scottish historian **Thomas Carlyle** (1795–1881) set up home here with his wife, Jane, in 1834. Carlyle's full-blooded and colourful style of writing brought him great fame during his lifetime – a statue was erected to the "Sage of Chelsea" on Cheyne Walk less than a year after his death in 1881, and the house became a museum just fifteen years later. That said, the intellectuals and artists who visited Carlyle – among them Dickens, Tennyson, Chopin, Mazzini, Browning and Darwin – were attracted as much by the wit of his strong-willed wife, with whom Carlyle enjoyed a famously tempestuous relationship. The house itself is a typically dour Victorian abode, kept much as the

Carlyles would have had it – the historian's hat still hangs in the hall. Among the artefacts are a letter from Disraeli offering a baronetcy and Carlyle's reply, refusing it. The top floor contains the garret study where Carlyle tried in vain to escape the din of the street and the neighbours' noisy roosters, in order to complete his final magnum opus on Frederick the Great.

18

Brompton Cemetery

210 Old Brompton Rd • Daily summer 8am–8pm; winter 8am–4pm • Guided tours Sun 2pm & 3.30pm • Free • ⓦ royalparks.gov.uk •
⊖ West Brompton

Brompton Cemetery is the least overgrown of London's "Magnificent Seven" Victorian graveyards. Laid out on a grid plan in 1840 and now overlooked by the east stand of Chelsea Football Club, the cemetery's leafy central avenue leads south to an octagonal chapel. Here, you'll find the grave of Frederick Leyland, president of the National Telephone Company: designed by Edward Burne-Jones, it's a bizarre copper-green jewel box on stilts, smothered with swirling wrought-ironwork. Before you reach the chapel, eerie colonnaded catacombs, originally planned to extend the full length of the cemetery, open out into the Great Circle, a forest of tilted crosses.

Few really famous corpses grace Brompton, but enthusiasts might like to seek out Suffragette leader **Emmeline Pankhurst**; Henry Cole, the man behind the Great Exhibition and the V&A; Fanny Brawne, the love of Keats' life; and John Snow, Queen Victoria's anaesthetist, whose chloroform-fixes the monarch described as "soothing, quieting and delightful beyond measure". **Long Wolf**, a Sioux Indian chief, was a temporary resident here, after he died while on tour entertaining the Victorian masses with Colonel "Buffalo Bill" Cody. His body has since been returned to his descendants in America.

Fulham Palace

Bishop's Avenue • **Palace** By guided tour only second and fourth Sundays and third Tuesday at 2pm • £5 **Museum** Mon–Wed, Sat & Sun
1–4pm • Free • ☎ 020 7736 3233, ⓦ fulhampalace.org • ⊖ Putney Bridge

It's worth venturing as far as the New King's Road by Putney Bridge in order to visit **Fulham Palace**, in Bishop's Park. Once the largest moated site in England, it was the residence of the Bishop of London from 704 to 1973. The oldest section of the present-day complex is the modestly scaled Tudor courtyard, patterned with black diamonds; the most recent is William Butterfield's neo-Gothic chapel, which, with the other period interiors, can only be seen on the **guided tours**. You can also visit the small **museum** which traces the building's complex history, and displays a few archeological finds, including a mummified rat. In the palace grounds there's a lovely herb garden, with a Tudor gateway and a maze of miniature box hedges, but sadly no sign of the moat, which was filled in in 1921.

Battersea

Folk who want, but can't afford, to live in Chelsea have colonized the terraces and mansions across the river in **Battersea**. For most of its history, however, Battersea was a staunchly working-class enclave. In 1913 it elected the country's first black mayor, John Richard Archer, and in the 1920s returned Shapurji Saklatvala as its MP – first for the Labour Party, then as a Communist. Saklatvala was always in the news: he was banned from entry into the US and even to his native India. He was also the first person to be arrested during the 1926 General Strike, after a speech in Hyde Park urging soldiers not to fire on striking workers, for which he received a two-month prison sentence.

Physically, Battersea is dominated by the presence of **Battersea Power Station**, Giles Gilbert Scott's awesome cathedral of power from 1933, which looks like an upturned table and featured (along with an inflatable flying pig) on the Pink Floyd album cover

Animals. Closed down in 1983, every plan for subsequent resurrection has ended in failure – for the latest, visit ⓦbatterseapowerstation.org.uk.

Battersea Dogs and Cats Home

4 Battersea Park Rd • Daily 10.30am–4pm • £2 • ☎ 020 7622 3626, ⓦ battersea.org.uk • ⊖ Vauxhall or Battersea Park train station

After the power station, most Londoners know Battersea for just one thing: its Dogs Home, now the **Battersea Dogs and Cats Home**, established here in 1871 as the "Home for Lost Dogs and Cats". Cats are still catered for, though it's better known for its dogs, with up to 280 dogs and 80 cats accommodated at any one time, and over 16,000 passing through their doors each year. Visitors are welcome, even if they're not thinking of adopting a pet.

Battersea Park

Park Daily 8am–dusk • Free • ☎ 020 8871 7530, ⓦ batterseapark.org **Children's Zoo** Daily 10am–5pm • £7.95 • ☎ 0845 6016 679, ⓦ batterseaparkzoo.co.uk • Bus #19 or #319 from ⊖ Sloane Square or Battersea Park train station

Battersea being a place of great poverty, the Victorians decided, in the 1850s, to do something to help ameliorate the social conditions by establishing **Battersea Park**, connected to Chelsea by the Albert Bridge, one of the campest bridges to span the Thames, especially when lit up at night with fairy lights, like a seaside pier. Today, the park is probably best known for its two-tier **Peace Pagoda**, erected in 1985 by Japanese Buddhists. Made from a combination of reconstituted Portland stone and Canadian fir trees, the pagoda shelters four large gilded Buddhas. The park's **fountain lake**, to the southwest, is impressive in summer, and there's a small family-run **Children's Zoo**, established during the 1951 Festival of Britain, and home to monkeys, lemurs, mynah birds, otters and meerkats.

St Mary's Church

Battersea Church Rd • ⓦ stmarysbattersea.org.uk • Bus #170 from ⊖ Victoria or Imperial Wharf overground

The old village of Battersea was originally centred on **St Mary's Church,** half a mile upstream. In 1775, when the current church was built, Battersea was a peaceful place with a population of less than 2000, among them Catherine Boucher, who married the poet and visionary William Blake in the church in 1782. Another painter associated with St Mary's is Turner, who used to sit in the oriel vestry window and paint the clouds and sunsets (his favourite chair is now reverently preserved in the chancel) – both painters now have commemorative windows.

18

NOTTING HILL CARNIVAL

High Street Kensington to Notting Hill

Despite the smattering of aristocratic mansions and the presence of royalty in Kensington Palace, the village of Kensington remained surrounded by fields until well into the nineteenth century. The village has disappeared entirely now in the busy shopping district around Kensington High Street, and the chief attractions are the wooded Holland Park and the former artists' colony clustered around the exotically decorated Leighton House. Bayswater and Notting Hill, to the north, were for many years the bad boys of the borough, dens of vice and crime comparable to Soho. Gentrification has changed them out of all recognition, though they remain more cosmopolitan districts, with a strong Arab presence and vestiges of the African-Caribbean community who initiated and still run the Notting Hill Carnival, one of Europe's largest street festivals.

High Street Kensington

The village of Kensington was centred on Kensington Church Street, but once the area was transformed into a residential suburb in the nineteenth century, the commercial centre shifted to **Kensington High Street** – better known as **High Street Ken**, after the tube. The street is dominated architecturally by the twin presences of George Gilbert Scott's neo-Gothic church of **St Mary Abbots** (whose 250ft spire makes it London's tallest parish church) and the Art Deco colossus of **Barkers** department store, remodelled in the 1930s. The rest of the street is nothing special, but in the quieter backstreets, you'll find one or two hidden gems like **Holland Park**, the former gardens of an old Jacobean mansion, and **Leighton House**, the perfect Victorian artist's pad.

Kensington Roof Gardens

99 Kensington High St • Phone ☎ 020 7937 7994 for opening hours • ⓦ roofgardens.virgin.com • ⊖ High Street Kensington

A little-known feature of the High Street is Europe's largest **Roof Gardens**, which tops the former Derry & Toms department store, another monster 1930s building, next door to Barkers. To check the gardens are open, phone ahead; to gain access, head for the side entrance on Derry Street and take the lift. The nightclub at the centre of the garden is pretty tacky, but the mock-Spanish convent, the formal gardens, the four pink flamingoes, sundry ducks and the views across the rooftops are surreal.

Kensington Square

On the south side of the High Street lies **Kensington Square**, an early piece of speculative building laid out in 1685. Luckily for the developers, royalty moved into Kensington Palace shortly after its construction, and the square soon became so fashionable that it was dubbed the "old court suburb". By the nineteenth century, the courtiers had moved out and the bohemians had moved in: Thackeray wrote *Vanity Fair* at no. 16; the Pre-Raphaelite painter Burne-Jones lived at no. 41; the actress Mrs Patrick Campbell, for whom George Bernard Shaw wrote *Pygmalion*, lived at no. 33; and composer Hubert Parry (of *Jerusalem* fame) gave music lessons to Vaughan Williams at no. 17. John Stuart Mill, philosopher and champion of women's suffrage, lived next door, and it was here that the first volume of Thomas Carlyle's sole manuscript of *The French Revolution* was accidentally used by a maid to light the fire.

Holland Park

Hidden away in the backstreets north of High Street Kensington is the densely wooded **Holland Park**, popular with the neighbourhood's army of nannies and au pairs, who take their charges to the excellent adventure playground. To get there, take one of the paths along the east side of the former **Commonwealth Institute**, a bold 1960s building with a startling tent-shaped Zambian copper roof. The park is laid out in the former grounds of **Holland House** – only the east wing of the Jacobean mansion could be salvaged after World War II, but it gives an idea of what the place used to look like. A **youth hostel** is linked to the east wing (see p.363); the garden ballroom houses the spectacular *Belvedere* restaurant; and throughout the summer **outdoor performances** take place (ⓦ operahollandpark.com), continuing a tradition which stretches back to the first Lady Holland, who put on plays here in defiance of the puritanical laws of Cromwell's Commonwealth. Several formal **gardens** are laid out before the house, drifting down in terraces to the arcades, the orangery and the ice house, which have been converted into a café and an art gallery. The most unusual of the formal gardens, which are peppered with modern sculpture, is the **Kyoto Garden**, a Japanese-style sanctuary to the northwest of the house, complete with koi carp and peacocks.

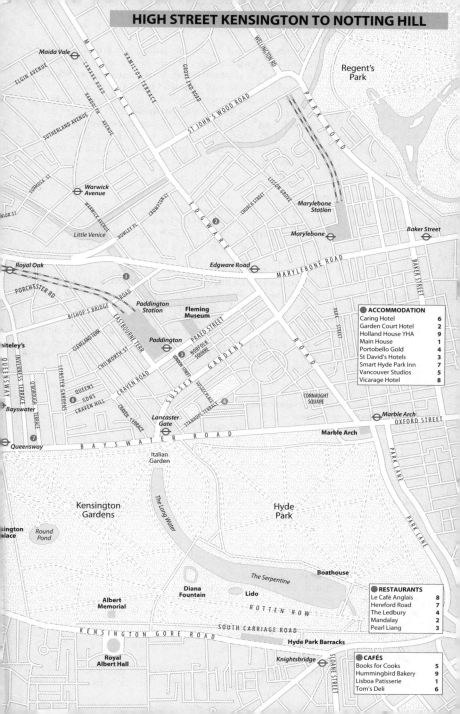

HIGH STREET KENSINGTON TO NOTTING HILL

Regent's Park

Maida Vale

Elgin Avenue

Sutherland Avenue

Warwick Avenue

Little Venice

Royal Oak

Porchester Rd.

Bishop's Bridge

Paddington Station

Fleming Museum

Paddington

Whiteley's

Queensway

Bayswater

Inverness Terrace

Leinster Gardens

Queensway

Italian Garden

Kensington Gardens

Kensington Palace

Round Pond

Albert Memorial

Royal Albert Hall

Diana Fountain

The Long Water

The Serpentine

Lido

Hyde Park

Boathouse

Rotten Row

South Carriage Road

Kensington Gore Road

Hyde Park Barracks

Knightsbridge

Marble Arch

Oxford Street

Park Lane

Baker Street

Marylebone Station

Marylebone

Edgware Road

Marylebone Road

Lancaster Gate

Bayswater Road

St John's Wood Road

Grove End Road

Maida Vale

Hamilton Terrace

Wellington Rd.

Park Road

Lisson Grove

Church Street

Edgware Road

Praed Street

Sussex Gardens

Craven Road

Connaught Square

Sloane Street

● ACCOMMODATION

Caring Hotel	6
Garden Court Hotel	2
Holland House YHA	9
Main House	1
Portobello Gold	4
St David's Hotels	3
Smart Hyde Park Inn	7
Vancouver Studios	5
Vicarage Hotel	8

● RESTAURANTS

Le Café Anglais	8
Hereford Road	7
The Ledbury	4
Mandalay	2
Pearl Liang	3

● CAFÉS

Books for Cooks	5
Hummingbird Bakery	9
Lisboa Patisserie	1
Tom's Deli	6

Holland Park artists' colony

Several wealthy Victorian artists rather self-consciously founded an **artists' colony** around the fringes of Holland Park, and a number of their highly individual mansions are still standing. First and foremost is **Leighton House**, now a museum (see below). Leighton's neighbours included G.F. Watts and Holman Hunt, Marcus Stone, illustrator of Dickens, and, in the most outrageous house of all, architect William Burges, who designed his own medieval folly, the **Tower House**, at 29 Melbury Rd. Slightly further afield, at 8 Addison Rd, is the Arts and Crafts **Debenham House**, designed by Halsey Ricardo in 1906 for the department-store Debenham family. The exterior is covered with peacock-blue and emerald-green tiles and bricks; the interior, which features a wonderful neo-Byzantine domed hall, is even more impressive. Sadly, both houses are closed to the public.

Leighton House Museum

12 Holland Park Rd • Daily except Tues 10am–5.30pm • £5 • ⓦ rbkc.gov.uk • ⊖ High Street Kensington

Leighton House, the "House Beautiful", was built for Frederic Leighton, president of the Royal Academy and the only artist to be made a peer (albeit on his deathbed). "It will be opulence, it will be sincerity", the artist opined before starting work on the house in the 1860s.

The entrance hall, with its walls of peacock-blue de Morgan tiles, is wonderfully lugubrious, but the star attraction is the remarkable domed **Arab Hall**, built in 1877. Based on a Moorish palace in Palermo, it resounds to the trickle of a central black marble fountain, and is decorated with Saracen tiles, gilded mosaics and latticework drawn from all over the Islamic world. The other rooms are less spectacular in comparison, but are hung with excellent paintings by Lord Leighton and his Pre-Raphaelite friends, Burne-Jones, Alma-Tadema, Watts and Millais – there's even a Tintoretto. Skylights brighten the upper floor, which contains a lovely gilded boudoir looking down onto the Arab Hall and Leighton's vast studio, where he used to hold evening concerts.

18 Stafford Terrace

18 Stafford Terrace • Guided tours Wed 11.15am & 2.15pm, Sat & Sun 11.15am, 1, 2.15 & 3.30pm • £6 • ☎ 020 7602 3316, ⓦ rbkc.gov.uk • ⊖ High Street Kensington

18 Stafford Terrace is where the successful *Punch* cartoonist, Linley Sambourne, lived until his death in 1910. A grand, though fairly ordinary stuccoed terrace house by Kensington standards, it's less a tribute to the artist (though it does contain a huge selection of Sambourne's works) and more a showpiece for the Victorian Society, which helps maintain the house in all its cluttered, late-Victorian excess, complete with stained glass, heavy furnishings and lugubrious William Morris wallpaper. The 90-minute guided tours are great fun, and, in the afternoons, are led by an actor in period garb; there are also occasional evening tours which re-create a night in with the Sambournes.

Bayswater and Paddington

It wasn't until the removal of the gallows at Tyburn (see p.241) that the area to the north of Hyde Park began to gain respectability. The arrival of the Great Western Railway at Paddington in 1838 further encouraged development, and the gentrification of **Bayswater**, the area immediately north of the park, began with the construction of an estate called Tyburnia. These days Bayswater is mainly residential, and a focus for London's widely dispersed Arab community, who are catered for by some excellent restaurants and cafés along the busy **Edgware Road**.

Paddington Station

Paddington Station, on Praed Street, is one of the world's great early train stations, its cathedral-scale wrought-iron sheds designed by Isambard Kingdom Brunel in 1851.

An earlier wooden structure was the destination of Victoria and Albert's first railway journey in 1842. The train, pulled by the engine *Phlegethon*, travelled at an average speed of 44mph, which the prince consort considered excessive – "Not so fast next time, Mr Conductor", he is alleged to have remarked. To the north and east of Paddington is **Paddington Basin**, built as the terminus of the Grand Union Canal in 1801. Now regenerated, it's worth exploring if only to admire the trio of funky footbridges which span the water. Funkiest of the lot is the **Rolling Bridge**, a hydraulic gangway that coils up into an octagon rather like a curled-up woodlouse – it curls up every Friday at noon. If you follow the basin to the northwest, you'll reach Little Venice in about five minutes (see p.281).

Fleming Museum
Praed St • Mon–Thurs 10am–1pm • £2 • ☎ 020 3312 6526, ⓦ www.imperial.nhs.uk • ⊖ Paddington

One block east of Paddington up Praed Street is St Mary's Hospital, home of the **Fleming Museum**, on the corner of Norfolk Place, where the young Scottish bacteriologist Alexander Fleming accidentally discovered penicillin in 1928. A short video, a small exhibition and a reconstruction of Fleming's untidy lab tell the story of the medical discovery that saved more lives than any other during the last century. Oddly enough, it aroused little interest at the time, until a group of chemists in Oxford succeeded in purifying penicillin in 1942. Desperate for good news in wartime, the media made Fleming a celebrity, and he was eventually awarded the Nobel Prize, along with several of the Oxford team.

19

Queensway
Bayswater's main drag is **Queensway**, a cosmopolitan street with Middle Eastern cafés, and, just up Moscow Road, the beautifully ornate Greek Orthodox Cathedral of **St Sophia** (ⓦstsophia.org.uk), boasting mosaics by Boris Anrep. Queensway is best known, however, for **Whiteley's**, opened in 1885 as the city's first real department store or "Universal Provider" with the boast that it could supply "anything from a pin to an elephant". The present building opened in 1907, and in the same year was the scene of the murder of the store's founder, William Whiteley, by a man claiming to be his illegitimate son. Whiteley's also had the dubious distinction of being Hitler's favourite London building – he planned to make it his HQ once the invasion was over. The store closed in 1981, and now houses shops, restaurants and a multiscreen cinema, but the original wrought-iron staircase, centaurs' fountain and glass-domed atrium all survive.

Notting Hill
Notting Hill is home to London's most popular market, **Portobello Road**, and its most famous annual street festival, the **Notting Hill Carnival**. It's also one of the city's most affluent neighbourhoods, characterized by leafy avenues, private garden squares, trendy shops and white stuccoed mansions. Back in the 1950s, however, it was described as "a massive slum, full of multi-occupied houses, crawling with rats and rubbish". Along with Brixton in south London, it was one of the main neighbourhoods settled by Afro-Caribbean immigrants, invited over to work in the public services. Tensions between the black families who'd moved into the area and the young white working-class "Teddy Boys" were exploited by far-right groups. And for four days in August 1958, Pembridge Road became the epicentre of the UK's first **race riots**.

The following year, the **Notting Hill Carnival** (see p.278) was begun as a response to the riots; in 1965 it took to the streets and has since grown into one of Europe's biggest street festivals. In the 1970s and early 1980s, tensions between the black community and the police came to a head at carnival time, but strenuous efforts on both sides have meant that such conflict has generally been avoided in the last two decades. However,

19

NOTTING HILL CARNIVAL

When it emerged in the 1960s, **Notting Hill Carnival** was little more than a few church-hall events and a carnival parade by Trinidadians. Today Carnival, held over the August Bank Holiday weekend, still belongs to West Indians (from all parts of the city), but there are participants too from London's Latin American and Asian communities, and Londoners of all descriptions turn out to watch the bands and parades, drink Red Stripe, eat curry goat and generally hang out.

The main sights of Carnival are the **costume parades**, which take place on the Sunday (for kids) and Monday (for adults) from around 10am until just before midnight. The parade makes its way around a three-mile route, and consists of big trucks which carry the soundsystems and *mas* (masquerade) bands, behind which the masqueraders dance in outrageous costumes. Most of the *mas* bands play a variety of soca or calypso featuring steel bands – the "pans" of the **steel bands** are one of the chief sounds of Carnival and have their own contest on the Saturday at Horniman's Pleasance, off Kensal Road by the canal. As well as the parade, there are several stages for live music and numerous soundsystems where you can catch reggae, ragga, drum'n'bass, jungle, garage, house and much more.

Over the last decade or so, the Carnival has generally been fairly relaxed, considering the huge numbers of people it attracts. However, this is not an event for you if you're at all bothered by very loud music or crowds – around a million people attend the festival each year and you can be wedged stationary during the parades. It's also worth taking more than usual care with yourself and your belongings. The static soundsystems are switched off at 7pm each day – if there's going to be any trouble it tends to come after that point or, if you feel at all uneasy, head home early.

Getting to and from the Carnival is quite an event in itself. Ladbroke Grove tube station is closed for the duration, while other stations have restricted hours or are open only for incoming visitors.

there are still plenty of doubters among the area's wealthier and mostly white residents, most of whom switch on the alarm system and leave town for the weekend.

Portobello Road

Portobello Road is a meandering, beguiling street that starts just up Chepstow Road from the tube and is famed for its market (see p.434), at its busiest on Saturdays. A short distance up the road stands the **Electric Cinema** (see p.420), London's oldest movie house, which opened in 1910 on the corner of Blenheim Crescent. Portobello Road is the chief location in the movie *Notting Hill*: Hugh Grant's travel bookshop is at 142 Portobello Rd (now a shoe shop) though the real Travel Bookshop is actually round the corner at Blenheim Crescent 13–15), his house is nearby at 280 Westbourne Park Rd and the private gardens he and Julia Roberts break into are on Rosmead Road.

Trellick Tower

Passing under the **Westway** flyover and east into Golborne Road, you come face-to-face with the awesome **Trellick Tower**, a 31-floor high-rise block of flats designed by Ernö Goldfinger in 1973. The separate service tower has arrow slits and an overhanging boiler tower, yet despite its uncompromising concrete brutalist appearance, it remains popular with its residents. Golborne Road itself is known for its Portuguese and Moroccan cafés, giving the road some of the bohemian feel of old Notting Hill, and making it the perfect place to wind up a visit to the market.

Museum of Brands, Packaging and Advertising

2 Colville Mews • Tues–Sat 10am–6pm, Sun 11am–5pm • £6.50 • ☎ 020 7908 0880, ⓦ museumofbrands.com • ⊖ Notting Hill Gate

Despite its rather unwieldy title, it's definitely worth popping into the **Museum of Brands, Packaging and Advertising**, hidden away off Lonsdale Road, one block east of

Portobello Road. The museum houses an awesome array of old British shop displays through the decades, based on the private collection of Robert Opie, a Scot whose compulsive collecting disorder has left him with 10,000 yoghurt pots alone. From Victorian ceramic pots of anchovy paste to the alcopops of the 1990s, the displays provide a fascinating social commentary on the times. Look out for the militarization of marketing during the last two world wars, with their bile beans "for radiant health and a lovely figure" and V for Victory mugs, and clock the irony of the glamorous early cigarette adverts or the posters for Blackpool "for happy, healthy holidays".

Kensal Green Cemetery

April–Sept Mon–Sat 9am–6pm, Sun 10am–6pm; Oct–March closes 5pm • Free • Guided tours: March–Oct Sun 2pm; Nov–Feb first & third Sun 2pm; £5 • ☎ 020 8969 0152, ⓦ kensalgreen.co.uk • ⬥ Kensal Green

Beside the gasworks, the Great Western Railway and the Grand Union Canal, lies **Kensal Green Cemetery**, the first of the city's commercial graveyards, opened in 1833 to relieve the pressure on overcrowded inner-city churchyards. Highgate may be the most famous of the "Magnificent Seven" Victorian cemeteries, but Kensal Green has by far the best funerary monuments. It's still owned by the founding company and remains a functioning cemetery, with services conducted daily in the central Greek Revival Anglican chapel. **Guided tours** of the cemetery also include a visit to the **catacombs** (bring a torch) on the first and third Sunday of the month.

The graves of the more famous incumbents – Thackeray, Trollope and the Brunels – are less interesting architecturally than those arranged on either side of the Centre Avenue, which leads from the easternmost entrance on Harrow Road. Vandals have left numerous headless angels and irreparably damaged the beautiful Cooke family monument, but still worth looking out for are Major-General Casement's bier, held up by four grim-looking turbaned Indians, circus manager Andrew Ducrow's conglomeration of beehive, sphinx and angels, and artist William Mulready's neo-Renaissance extravaganza. Other interesting characters buried here include Charles Wingfield, who invented lawn tennis; Mary Seacole, the "black Florence Nightingale"; Marcus Garvey, the black nationalist; Charles Blondin, the famous tightrope walker; Carl Wilhelm Siemens, the German scientist who brought electric lighting to London; and "James" Barry, Inspector-General of the Army Medical Department, who, it was discovered during the embalming of the corpse, was in fact a woman. Playwright Harold Pinter was buried here and Queen singer Freddie Mercury was cremated here, but his ashes were scattered in Mumbai.

19

KENWOOD, HAMPSTEAD HEATH

North London

Everything north of the Marylebone and Euston roads was, for the most part, open countryside until the mid-nineteenth century, and is now largely built up, right the way up to the "green belt" created in the immediate postwar period to try and limit the continuing urban sprawl. This North London chapter begins by following the Regent's Canal, which once traced the limit of the city's northern outskirts, and now passes through the heart of Camden Town, with its famous weekend market. It then concentrates on just a handful of the former satellite villages, now subsumed into the general mass of north London, and runs the gamut from wealthy Hampstead to gritty Hackney. Most of north London is easily accessible by tube; in fact, it was the expansion of the tube that encouraged the forward march of bricks and mortar in the outer suburbs.

The first section of the chapter traces the route of the **Regent's Canal**, built in 1820 on the city's northern periphery. Along the way, the canal passes one of London's finest parks, **Regent's Park**, framed by Nash-designed architecture and home to London Zoo. The canal forces its way into most Londoners' consciousness only at **Camden**, a rakish place even today, whose weekend market is one of the city's big attractions – a warren of stalls selling funky wares, street fashion, books and music.

Few visitors to the capital head out to neighbouring **Islington**, which has its own flourishing antiques trade, and **Hackney**, further east, with its ethnically diverse population, thus missing out on two of north London's defining areas. The real highlights, though, for visitors and residents alike, are **Hampstead** and **Highgate**, elegant, largely eighteenth-century developments, which still reflect their village origins. They have the added advantage of proximity to one of London's wildest patches of greenery, **Hampstead Heath**, where you can enjoy stupendous views, kite flying and outdoor bathing, as well as high art at the Neoclassical mansion of **Kenwood House**.

Also covered, at the end of this chapter, are a few sights in more far-flung suburbs: the nineteenth-century utopia of **Hampstead Garden Suburb**; the Orthodox Jewish suburb of **Golders Green**; the **RAF Museum** at Hendon; and the spectacular **Hindu temple** in Neasden.

Little Venice

↔ Warwick Avenue

The Regent's Canal starts out from the west the triangular leafy basin known as **Little Venice**, a nickname coined by one-time resident and poet Robert Browning. The title may be far-fetched, but the willow-tree Browning's Island is one of the prettiest spots on the canal, and the houseboats and barges moored hereabouts are brightly painted and strewn with tubs of flowers. While you're here, try and catch a marionette performance on the **Puppet Theatre Barge** (see p.441), moored on the Blomfield Road side of the basin, a unique and unforgettable experience; performances take place every weekend at 3pm, and daily throughout the school holidays (except Aug & Sept). You can also catch a **canal boat** to Camden (see p.217), or walk south to the newly developed Paddington Basin (see p.277).

20

REGENT'S CANAL

The **Regent's Canal**, completed in 1820, was constructed as part of a direct link from Birmingham to the newly built London Docks. After an initial period of heavy usage it was overtaken by the railway, and never really paid its way as its investors had hoped. By some miracle, however, it survived, and its nine miles, 42 bridges, twelve locks and two tunnels stand as a reminder of another age. The lock-less stretch of the canal **between Little Venice and Camden Town** is the busiest, most attractive section, tunnelling through to Lisson Grove, skirting Regent's Park, offering views of London Zoo, and passing straight through the heart of Camden Market. You can walk, jog or cycle along the towpath, but this section of the canal is also served by scheduled narrowboats.

Three companies run daily **boat services** between Camden and Little Venice, passing through the Maida Hill tunnel. Whichever you choose, you can board at either end; **tickets** cost around £10 return, and journey time is 50 minutes one-way.

Jenny Wren ☎020 7485 4433, ⓦwalkersquay .com. The narrowboat *Jenny Wren* starts off at Camden, goes through a canal lock (the only company to do so) and heads for Little Venice (with a live commentary). March Sat & Sun only; April–Oct daily.
Jason's Trip ☎020 7286 3428, ⓦjasons.co.uk. This 100-year-old traditional narrowboat has been running

trips since 1951; services set off three or four times a day from Little Venice. April to early Nov.
London Waterbus Company ☎020 7482 2660, ⓦlondonwaterbus.com. Services leave from both Camden and Little Venice, and call in at London Zoo en route. April–Sept daily; Oct Thurs–Sun only; Nov– March Sat & Sun only, weather permitting.

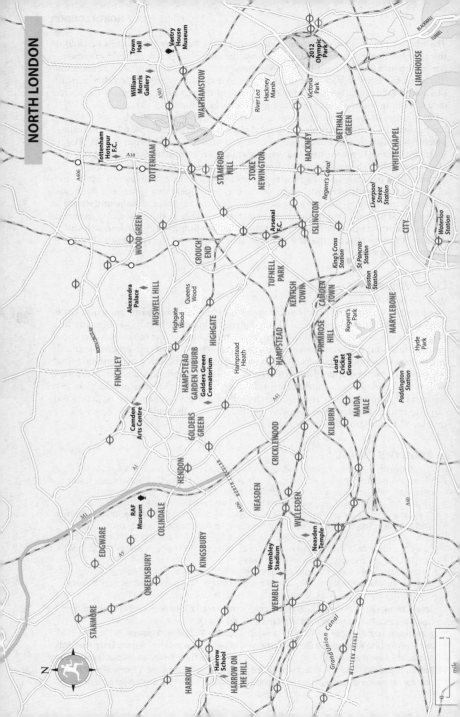

NORTH LONGON

Town Hall
Vestry House Museum

2012 Olympic Park

William Morris Gallery

WALTHAMSTOW

River Lea
Hackney Marsh

Victoria Park

BLACKWALL
TUNNEL

LIMEHOUSE

Tottenham Hotspur F.C.

A10

TOTTENHAM

STAMFORD HILL

STOKE NEWINGTON

HACKNEY

BETHNAL GREEN

Regent's Canal

WHITECHAPEL

WOOD GREEN

Arsenal F.C.

ISLINGTON

Liverpool Street Station

CITY

Waterloo Station

A406

CROUCH END

King's Cross Station

St Pancras Station

Alexandra Palace

Queens Wood

MUSWELL HILL

Highgate Wood

HIGHGATE

TUFNELL PARK

KENTISH TOWN

CAMDEN TOWN

Euston Station

Regent's Park

MARYLEBONE

Hyde Park

NORTH CIRCULAR

FINCHLEY

HAMPSTEAD

Hampstead Heath

PRIMROSE HILL

Lord's Cricket Ground

Paddington Station

HAMPSTEAD GARDEN SUBURB

Golders Green Crematorium

MAIDA VALE

A41

Camden Arts Centre

GOLDERS GREEN

KILBURN

A1

HENDON

CRICKLEWOOD

M1

RAF Museum

NEASDEN

WILLESDEN

Neasden Temple

A40

Grand Union Canal

EDGWARE

COLINDALE

A5

KINGSBURY

Wembley Stadium

WEMBLEY

WESTERN AVENUE

STANMORE

QUEENSBURY

HARROW

Harrow School

HARROW ON THE HILL

N

0   mile   1

St John's Wood

The residential district of **St John's Wood** was built over in the nineteenth century by developers hoping to attract a wealthy clientele with a mixture of semidetached Italianate villas, multi-occupancy Gothic mansions and white stucco terraces. Edwin Landseer (of Trafalgar Square lions fame), novelist George Eliot and Mrs Fitzherbert, the uncrowned wife of George IV, all lived here, while current residents include knights Richard Branson and Paul McCartney and supermodel Kate Moss.

Lord's Cricket Ground

St John's Wood Rd · Museum Non-match days: April–Oct Mon–Fri 10am–5pm; Nov–March Mon–Thurs 11.30am–5pm; £7.50 · Guided tours April–Sept daily 10am, noon, 2pm; £15 · ☎ 020 7616 8595, ⓦ lords.org · ⊖ St John's Wood

The Regent's Canal was bad news for Thomas Lord, who had only recently been forced to shift his cricket ground due to the construction of Marylebone Road. In 1813, with the canal coming, he once more upped his stumps and relocated, this time to St John's Wood Road, where **Lord's**, as the ground is now known, remains to this day. Lord's is, of course, home of the **MCC** (Marylebone Cricket Club), founded in 1787, and the most hallowed institution in the game, boasting a very long members waiting list (unless you're exceptionally famous or rich). Its politics were neatly summed up by Viscount Monckton, who said, "I have been a member of the Committee of the MCC and of a Conservative cabinet, and by comparison with the cricketers, the Tories seem like a bunch of Commies."

Lord's is home to the **MCC museum**, the world's oldest sports museum, which houses the minuscule pottery urn containing the Ashes (along with the complex tale of this odd trophy), numerous historic balls, bats and bails, and a sparrow which was "bowled out" by Jehangir Khan at Lord's in 1936. You can also visit the museum as part of a **guided tour**, which sets off from the Grace Gates at the southwest corner of the ground. On the tour, you also get to see the famous Long Room (from which the players walk onto the pitch), Lord's Real Tennis Court, the various stands and the futuristic aluminium Media Centre, cruelly nicknamed "Cherie Blair's Smile".

20

Regent's Park

Daily 5am to dusk · ☎ 020 7486 7905, ⓦ royalparks.gov.uk · ⊖ Regent's Park, Baker Street, Great Portland Street, St John's Wood or Camden Town

Regent's Park is one of London's smartest parks, with a boating lake, ornamental ponds and waterfalls and wonderful gardens all enclosed in a ring of magnificent nineteenth-century mansions. As with almost all of London's royal parks, we have Henry VIII to thank for Regent's Park which he confiscated from the Church for yet more hunting grounds. However, it wasn't until the reign of the Prince Regent (later George IV) that the park began to take its current form – hence its official title, The Regent's Park – and the public weren't allowed in until 1845 (and even then for just two days of the week). According to John Nash's 1811 master plan, the park was to be girded by a continuous belt of terraces, and sprinkled with a total of 56 villas, including a magnificent pleasure palace for the prince himself, linked by Regent Street to Carlton House in St James's. Inevitably, the plan was never fully realized, but enough was built to create something of the idealized garden city that Nash and the Prince Regent envisaged.

The eastern terraces

Nash's terraces form a near-unbroken horseshoe of cream-coloured stucco around the Outer Circle. By far the most impressive are the eastern terraces, especially **Cumberland Terrace**, completed in 1826, and intended as a foil for George IV's planned pleasure palace and tea pavilion. Its 800ft-long facade, hidden away on the eastern edge of the park, is punctuated by Ionic triumphal arches, peppered with classical alabaster statues and centred on a Corinthian portico with a pediment of sculptures set against a vivid sky-blue background. In 1936 an angry crowd threw bricks through the windows of no. 16, which belonged to American divorcée Mrs Wallis Simpson, whose relationship with Edward VIII was seen as a national calamity, and eventually led to his abdication.

Fifty-two more statues depicting British worthies were planned for the even longer facade of **Chester Terrace**, to the south, but Nash decided the ridicule they provoked was "painful to the ears of a professional man" and ditched them. Nevertheless, Chester Terrace is worth walking down if only to take in the splendid triumphal arches at each end, which announce the name of the terrace in bold lettering; the northern one features a bust of Nash.

To the north of Cumberland Terrace, the neo-Gothic **St Katharine's Precinct** provides a respite from the Grecian surroundings, though not one Nash was at all happy with. The central church serves the Danish community, who have erected a copy of the imposing tenth-century **Jelling Stone** in an alcove to the right.

The Inner Circle

Of the numerous villas planned for the park itself in Nash's master plan, only eight were actually built, and of those just two originals have survived around the **Inner**

●CAFÉS		●RESTAURANTS				● PUBS & BARS			
Afghan Kitchen	11	Elk in the Woods	13	Ottolenghi	8	The Albert	12	Edinboro Castle	20
Alpino	12	Gem	5	El Parador	6	Bridge House	25	The Engineer	10
Cà Phê	7	Mango Room	4	Trojka	3	Camden Head	29	The Enterprise	4
Garden Café	9	Manna	2			The Charles Lamb	35	Island Queen	34
M. Manze	10					The Crown	27	King's Head	26
Marine Ices	1					Duke of Cambridge	33	The Lansdowne	7

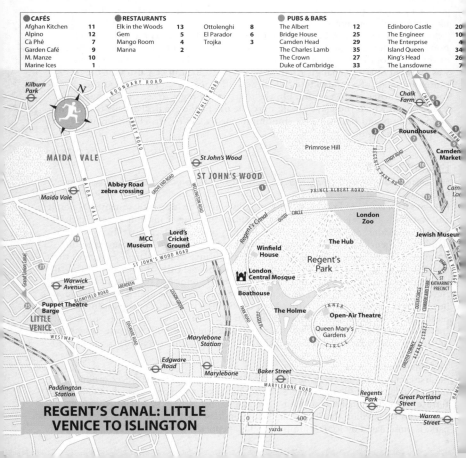

REGENT'S CANAL: LITTLE VENICE TO ISLINGTON

Circle: St John's Lodge, built in 1812 and currently owned by the Sultan of Brunei, and **The Holme**, Decimus Burton's first-ever work (he was just 18 at the time), which is picturesquely sited by the Y-shaped **Boating Lake** (open March–Oct). Within the Inner Circle is the Open Air Theatre (see p.419), and **Queen Mary's Gardens**, which is by far the prettiest section of the whole park. A large slice of the gardens is taken up with a glorious rose garden, featuring some four hundred varieties, surrounded by a ring of ramblers.

London Central Mosque

146 Park Rd · Daily 9am–10pm · Free · ☎ 020 7725 2213, ⓦ iccuk.org · ⊖ Marylebone or St John's Wood

A further surprise on the Regent's Park skyline is the shiny copper dome and minaret of the **London Central Mosque** (also known as the Islamic Cultural Centre), built in 1977, and an entirely appropriate addition given the Prince Regent's taste for the Orient (as expressed in the Brighton Pavilion). Non-Muslim visitors are welcome to look in at the information centre and the café, and glance inside the hall of worship, which can hold 5000 or more worshippers and which is dominated by an enormous, sparkling, central chandelier.

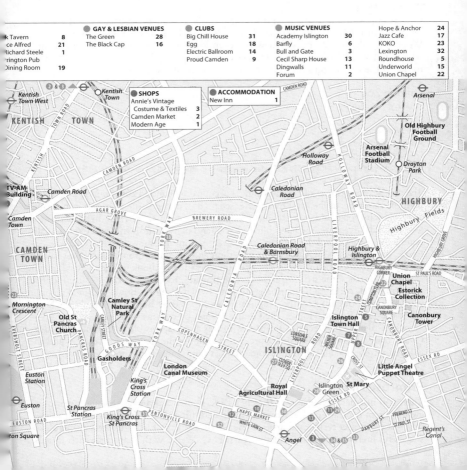

● GAY & LESBIAN VENUES		● CLUBS		● MUSIC VENUES			
The Green	28	Big Chill House	31	Academy Islington	30	Hope & Anchor	24
The Black Cap	16	Egg	18	Barfly	6	Jazz Cafe	17
		Electric Ballroom	14	Bull and Gate	3	KOKO	23
		Proud Camden	9	Cecil Sharp House	13	Lexington	32
				Dingwalls	11	Roundhouse	5
				Forum	2	Underworld	15
						Union Chapel	22

Partial venue labels at far left:
- k Tavern — 8
- ce Alfred — 21
- Richard Steele — 1
- rrington Pub —
- Dining Room — 19

● SHOPS
- Annie's Vintage
- Costume & Textiles — 3
- Camden Market — 2
- Modern Age — 1

⊖ ACCOMMODATION
- New Inn — 1

THE BEATLES IN LONDON

Since the Fab Four lived in London for much of the 1960s, it's hardly surprising that the capital is riddled with Beatle associations. The prime Beatles landmark is, of course, the **Abbey Road** zebra crossing featured on the album cover, located near the EMI studios, where the group recorded most of their albums. The nearest tube is St John's Wood – remember to bring three friends plus another to take the photos. Incidentally, Paul McCartney still owns the house at 7 Cavendish Ave, which he bought in 1966, two blocks east of the zebra crossing.

One (short-lived) nearby curiosity was the **Apple Boutique**, opened by The Beatles at 94 Baker St (⊖ Baker Street), in December 1967 as a "beautiful place where you could buy beautiful things". The psychedelic murals that covered the entire building were whitewashed over after a lawsuit by the neighbours, and eight months later The Beatles caused even more pandemonium when they gave the shop's entire stock away free in the closing-down sale.

Other Beatles locations include the old **Apple headquarters** in Savile Row, Mayfair, where the 1969 rooftop concert took place, while Macca has his current office on Soho Square (see p.101). Real devotees of the group should buy *The Beatles' England* by David Heron and Norman Maslov, or sign up for a Beatles tour, run by The Original London Walks (☎ 020 7624 3978, ⓦ walks.com).

Winfield House

On the opposite side of the road from the mosque is **Winfield House**, a dull 1930s replacement for Decimus Burton's Hertford House, built by the heiress to the Woolworth chain, Countess Haugwitz-Reventlow (better known as Barbara Hutton), who gifted Winfield House to the US government during World War II and went on to marry Cary Grant; it's now the American ambassador's residence.

London Zoo

The lion sits within his cage,
Weeping tears of ruby rage,
He licks his snout, the tears fall down
And water dusty London town.

The Zoo, Stevie Smith

Regent's park • Daily March–Oct 10am–5.30pm; Nov–Feb 10am–4pm • £18 depending on season • ☎ 020 7722 3333, ⓦ zsl.org/zsl-london-zoo • ⊖ Camden Town

The northeastern corner of Regent's Park is occupied by **London Zoo**. Founded in 1826 with the remnants of the royal menagerie (see p.184), the enclosures here are as humane as any inner-city zoo could make them, and kids usually enjoy themselves. In particular they love Animal Adventure, the new children's zoo (and playground) where they can actually handle the animals, and the regular "Animals in Action" live shows. The invertebrate house, now known as BUGS, Gorilla Kingdom and the walk-through Rainforest Life and Meet the Monkeys enclosures are also guaranteed winners – book online to avoid queuing.

The zoo boasts some striking architectural features, too, such as the 1930s modernist, spiral-ramped, concrete former penguin pool (where Penguin Books' original colophon was sketched), designed by the Tecton partnership, led by Berthold Lubetkin, who also made the zoo's Round House. The Giraffe House, by contrast, was designed in Neoclassical style by Decimus Burton, who was also responsible for the mock-Tudor Clock Tower. Other landmark features are the mountainous Mappin Terraces and the colossal tetrahedral aluminium-framed tent of Lord Snowdon's modern aviary.

Primrose Hill

The small northern extension of Regent's Park, known as **Primrose Hill**, commands a great view of central London from its modest summit. And it lends its name to the much sought-after residential area, to the northeast, which has attracted numerous successful literati and artists over the years: H.G. Wells, W.B. Yeats, Friedrich Engels,

Kingsley Amis and Morrissey have all lived here. You might catch the present denizens such as Jamie Oliver, Ewan McGregor, Alan Bennett or Martin Amis browsing the bookshops and galleries on **Regent's Park Road**, which skirts Primrose Hill to the east. Ted Hughes and Sylvia Plath lived in a flat at 3 Chalcot Square, just east of Regent's Park Road, and it was nearby at 23 Fitzroy Rd, the house that Yeats once lived in, that Plath committed suicide in 1963.

Camden Town

Until the canal arrived, **Camden Town** wasn't even a village, but by Victorian times it had become a notorious slum area, an image it took most of the past century to shed. In the meantime, it attracted its fair share of artists, most famously the Camden Town Group formed in 1911 by Walter Sickert, later joined by the likes of Lucian Freud, Frank Auerbach and Leon Kossoff. These days, you're more likely to bump into young foreign tourists heading for the market, and as-yet-unknown bands on the lookout for members of the local music industry.

For all the gentrification of the last thirty years, Camden retains a gritty aspect, compounded by the various railway lines that plough through the area, the canal and the large shelter for the homeless on Arlington Road. Its proximity to three mainline stations has also made it an obvious point of immigration over the years, particularly for the Irish, but also for Greek Cypriots during the 1950s. The **market**, however, gives the area a positive lift, especially at weekends, and is now the district's best-known attribute.

Camden Lock

20

If you've seen enough jangly earrings for one day, stand on the bowed iron footbridge by **Camden Lock** itself, and admire the castellated former lock-keeper's house, to the west. You can catch a boat to Little Venice, from the nearby lock inlet (see p.281); the flight of three locks to the east begins the canal's descent to Limehouse and the Thames. The first lock pound is overlooked by Terry Farrell's former **TV-AM Building**, now occupied by MTV, but still retaining its giant blue-and-white egg cups from breakfast television days. Here, too, are the covered basins of the Interchange Warehouse, linked by a disused railway line to the **Camden Catacombs**, built in the nineteenth century as stables for the pit ponies that used to shunt the railway wagons.

Roundhouse

Chalk Farm Road • ☎ 0844 482 8008, ⓦ roundhouse.org.uk • ⊖ Chalk Farm

Camden's pit pony stabling extended as far north as the brick-built **Roundhouse**, on Chalk Farm Road, now a performing arts venue, but originally built in 1846 as an engine repair shed for 23 goods engines, arranged around a central turntable. Within fifteen years the engines had outgrown the building, and for the next century it was used for storing booze. In 1964, Arnold Wesker established the place as a political

---

CAMDEN MARKET

Camden Market was confined to Inverness Street until the 1970s, when the focus shifted to the disused warehouses around Camden Lock. The tiny crafts market which began in the cobbled courtyard by the lock has since mushroomed out of all proportion, with stalls on both sides of Camden High Street and Chalk Farm Road. More than 100,000 shoppers turn up here each weekend and Camden Lock and the Stables Market now stay open all week long (see p.434). For all its tourist popularity, Camden remains a genuinely offbeat place. To avoid the crowds, which can be overpowering in the summer, aim to come either early (before noon) or late (after 4pm), or on a Friday. The nearest tube is Camden Town, though this is exit-only at peak times; Chalk Farm tube is only ten minutes' walk up Chalk Farm Road from Camden Lock.

theatre venue, and two years later, the Roundhouse began to stage rock gigs – everyone from Hendrix and The Doors to The Ramones and Kraftwerk – and other nonconformist happenings. In 1966, it held a launch party for the underground paper, *International Times*, at which Pink Floyd and Soft Machine both performed, later hosting a Dialectics of Liberation conference organized by R.D. Laing, not to mention performances by the anarchist Living Theatre of New York, featuring a naked cast.

Jewish Museum

129 Albert St • Daily except Fri 10am–5pm, Fri 10am–2pm • £7.50 • ☎ 020/7284 7384, ⓦ jewishmuseum.org.uk • ⊖ Camden Town

Despite having no significant Jewish associations, Camden is home to London's purpose-built **Jewish Museum**. On the mezzanine floor, there's an interactive exhibition explaining Jewish practices and illustrated by cabinets of Judaica, including a sixteenth-century Venetian Ark of the Covenant and treasures from London's Great Synagogue in the City, burnt down by Nazi bombers in 1941. On the first floor, an imaginatively designed exhibition tells the history of British Jews from 1066 onwards, plus a special Holocaust gallery on Leon Greenman (1920–2008), one of only two British Jews who suffered and survived Auschwitz. The museum also puts on a lively programme of special exhibitions, discussions and concerts, and has a café on the ground floor (closed Sat).

Islington

⊖ Angel

Since the 1960s, **Islington**'s picturesque but dilapidated Regency and early Victorian squares and terraces have been snapped up by professionals and City types and comprehensively renovated. The impact of this gentrification, however, has been relatively minor on the borough as a whole, which stretches as far north as Highgate Hill, and remains one of the city's poorest. **Chapel Street market** (Tues–Sun), to the west of Upper Street, selling cheap clothes, fruit and veg and Arsenal football memorabilia, is a salutary reminder of Islington's working-class roots. For more on the history of Islington, visit the borough's museum (see p.151).

There's little evidence of those roots on the main drag, **Upper Street**: the arrival of its antique market – confusingly known as **Camden Passage** – coincided with the new influx of cash-happy customers, and its pubs and **restaurants** reflect the wealth of its new residents. For entertainment, Islington boasts the long-established *King's Head* **pub theatre**, the Little Angel **puppet theatre** and the ever-popular Almeida plus several comedy and live-music venues (see chapters 26 & 29). All of which make Islington one of the liveliest areas of north London in the evening – a kind of off-West End.

Upper Street

Looking at the traffic fighting its way along **Upper Street**, it's hard to believe that "merry Islington", as it was known, was once a spa resort to which people would come to drink the pure water and breathe the clean air. And walking along Upper Street (and several of the surrounding streets), it's impossible not to be struck by one of the area's quirky

---

THE NEW RIVER

In 1613, **Hugh Myddelton** (1560–1631), Royal Jeweller to James I, revolutionized London's water supply by drawing fresh water direct from the River Lee, 38 miles away in Hertfordshire, via an aqueduct known as the **New River**. A weathered statue of Myddelton, unveiled by Gladstone in 1862, stands at the apex of Islington Green. Right up until the late 1980s the New River continued to supply most of north London with its water – the original termination point was at **New River Head**, near Sadler's Wells theatre (see p.416); the succession of ponds to the northeast of Canonbury Road is a surviving fragment of the scheme; north of Stoke Newington, much of the river remains in *situ*.

architectural features – the raised pavements which protected pedestrians from splattered mud. Such precautions were especially necessary since Islington was used as a convenient grazing halt for livestock en route to the Agricultural Hall or Smithfield.

Royal Agricultural Hall

The ugly modern glass frontage of the Business Design Centre hides the former **Royal Agricultural Hall**, Islington' finest Victorian building, completed in 1862, and known locally as the "Aggie". As well as hosting agricultural and livestock exhibitions, it used to host the World's Fair, the Grand Military Tournament, Cruft's Dog Show and such marvels as Urbini's performing fleas. During World War II, however, it was requisitioned by the government for use by the Post Office, who remained in residence until 1971. The interior is still magnificent – even if the exhibitions now held there are more prosaic (think packaging conferences and careers fairs) – with the best exterior view from Liverpool Road, where two large brick towers rise up either side of the roof, like a Victorian train station.

Islington Green to Cross Street

Today, Islington has fewer green spaces than any other London borough – one of the few being the minuscule **Islington Green**, just up from Angel tube. Twice a week (Wed & Sat), the pavements to the east of the green are occupied by the antique stalls of the **Camden Passage market**, although the antique shops in the market's narrow namesake and the surrounding streets stay open all week.

   Just north of the green stands **St Mary's Church**, originally built in the 1750s. Only the steeple survived the Blitz, though the light, spacious 1950s interior is an interesting period piece, with six fluted Egyptian-style columns framing the sanctuary. The churchyard opens out into Dagmar Passage, where in 1961 a former temperance hall was converted into the **Little Angel Puppet Theatre** (see p.441). The archway at the end of Dagmar Terrace brings you out onto **Cross Street**, Islington's loveliest street, with eighteenth-century houses sloping down to Essex Road and raised pavements on both sides.

20

Union Chapel

North of **Islington Town Hall**, a handsome 1920s Neoclassical Portland-stone building, set back from Upper Street, is the fancifully extravagant **Union Chapel**. Built in 1888, at the height of the Congregationalists' popularity, it remains a church, but is now also an innovative independent concert venue (see p.400). Its lugubrious, spacious, octagonal interior is designed like a giant Gothic auditorium, with raked seating and galleries capable of holding 1650 rapt worshippers (or concert goers) with the pulpit centre stage.

Highbury Fields

At the top of Upper Street lies the largest open space in the entire borough, the modestly sized park of **Highbury Fields**, where over 200,000 people gathered in 1666 to escape (and watch) the Great Fire. Now overlooked on two sides by splendid Georgian and Victorian terraces, it's probably Islington's most elegant green space. A plaque on the park's public toilets commemorates the country's first-ever gay rights demonstration (against police harassment) which took place here in 1970. Of course Highbury is also world famous as the former home of **Arsenal** football club, who now play at a new 60,000-seat stadium, ten minutes' walk away (see p.436).

Canonbury Square

Islington's most perfect Regency set piece, **Canonbury Square**, is centred on a smartly maintained flower garden, but blighted by traffic ploughing up Canonbury Road. In 1928, **Evelyn Waugh** moved into the first floor of no. 17 with his wife Evelyn Gardiner (they called themselves "He-Evelyn" and "She-Evelyn"). In those days, the square was

ORTON IN ISLINGTON

Playwright **Joe Orton** and his lover **Kenneth Halliwell** lived together for sixteen years, spending the last eight years of their lives in a top-floor bedsit at 25 Noel Rd, to the east of Upper Street, where the Regent's Canal emerges from the Islington tunnel. It's ironic that the borough council has seen fit to erect a plaque on the house commemorating the couple, when it was instrumental in pressing for harsh prison sentences after both men were found guilty of stealing and defacing local library books in 1962 (see p.151). A few of the wittily doctored books are now on display at the **Islington Museum**.

Six months in prison worked wonders for Orton's writing, as he himself said: "Being in the nick brought detachment to my writing". It also brought him success, with irreverent comedies like *Loot*, *Entertaining Mr Sloane* and *What the Butler Saw* playing to sell-out audiences in the West End and on Broadway. Orton's meteoric fame and his sexual profligacy drove Halliwell to despair, however, and on August 9, 1967, Halliwell finally cracked – beating Orton to death with a hammer and then killing himself with a drug overdose. Their ashes were mixed together and scattered over the grass at **Golders Green Crematorium** (see p.307). Apart from the local public toilets, Orton's favourite hangout was the appropriately entitled *Island Queen* pub, at the end of Noel Road.

nothing like as salubrious as it is now. In fact, it was precisely the square's squalor that appealed to **George Orwell**, who moved into the top floor of no. 27 in 1944, with his wife and son, having been bombed out of his digs in St John's Wood; he later used it as the prototype for Winston Smith's home in *1984*.

Immediately to the northeast of the square stands the last remaining relic of Islington's bygone days as a rural retreat, the red-brick **Canonbury Tower**, originally part of a Tudor mansion built for the prior of St Bartholomew in the City. The very top floor boasts three Elizabethan interiors, with carved oak panelling and fireplaces carved with Freemasonic and Rosicrucian symbols from when the rooms were used by Renaissance man Francis Bacon. The tower is currently occupied by the Canonbury Masonic Research Centre, who will occasionally show visitors round (☎ 020 7226 6256, ⊛ canonbury.ac.uk).

Estorick Collection of Modern Italian Art

Canonbury Road • Wed, Fri & Sat 11am–6pm, Thurs 11am–8pm, Sun noon–5pm • £5 • ☎ 020 7704 9522, ⊛ estorickcollection.com • ⊖ Highbury & Islington

Islington's most intriguing attraction is the **Estorick Collection of Modern Italian Art**, which occupies a Georgian mansion on Canonbury Square, with the entrance on Canonbury Road. The most exciting works in the gallery are those of the early Italian Futurists, although their founding manifesto of 1909 urged followers to "divert the canals to flood the museums!" Futurism's mouthpiece was the fascist Filippo Marinetti, a rich boy with a penchant for crashing fast cars, and, as evidenced by the photos, an eye for natty waistcoats, complete with appliqué hands patting the pockets.

The permanent collection, spread out over the two upper floors, ranges from the rainbow colours of *Music* by Luigi Russolo (inventor of the *intonarumori* – a sort of avant-garde hurdy-gurdy), which is firmly Futurist, to a few portraits by Modigliani, and a typically melancholic canvas by Symbolist painter, Giorgio de Chirico. One of the strangest works is Medardo Rosso's wax sculpture *Woman with a Veil*, from 1893, which had a profound influence on the Futurists. Other highlights include Giacomo Balla's *Hand of the Violinist*, a classic Futurist study of movement, speed and dexterity, and Gino Severini's Cubist *Dancer*. The gallery also features paintings by lesser-known Italian artists such as Giorgio Morandi, Massimo Campigli, Mario Sironi and Zoran Music, as well as by Italy's two leading postwar sculptors, Emilio Greco and Marino Marini. Excellent special exhibitions are held on the lower floors, and there's a pleasant Italian café that spills out into the back courtyard in good weather.

20

Hackney

The borough of **Hackney** stretches from Shoreditch (see p.194), on the East End edge of the City, to the north London suburb of **Stamford Hill**. One of the most ethnically diverse of all London boroughs, it comes as no surprise that the country's longest-serving black woman MP, Diane Abbott, has her constituency in Hackney. The fact that the borough has tourist signposts comes as a surprise to many visitors, yet Hackney repays selective visits: **Dalston** is now the home of cutting-edge nightlife; **Stoke Newington** is a haven of inexpensive restaurants and laidback cafés; and **Hackney Central** boasts the former music hall of the Hackney Empire, with the red-brick Tudor mansion of **Sutton House** a short stroll away.

Dalston

Dalston is undergoing a seismic transformation, and is currently vying with Shoreditch as London's hippest, grittiest new *quartier*. Among the early pioneers is the excellent *Vortex Jazz Club*, on the frankly quite sleazy Gillett Square, followed by the *Arcola Theatre*, one of the city's most dynamic fringe venues, which has recently occupied a former paint factory on Ashwin Street, next door to the avant-garde music venue *Café OTO*. This trio has been accompanied by bars and clubs dotted up and down the high street from Dalston Junction. With two refurbished Overground stations, and trains capable of whizzing you in all directions, Dalston's transport has vastly improved recently, too.

Kingsland High Street

Kingsland High Street had a history of entertainment long before the current crop of clubs came along, with four or five cinemas in close proximity. The lone survivor is the Art Deco **Rio Cinema**, at no. 107, opened in 1937 as the Dalston Classic, replacing the

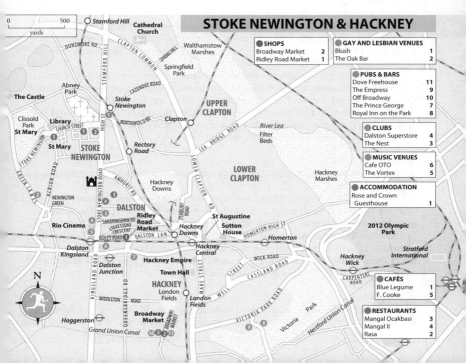

THE ANGRY BRIGADE

On August 20, 1971, six alleged members of the **Angry Brigade** – at the time Britain's only home-grown urban terrorist group – were arrested at 359 Amhurst Rd, off Stoke Newington High Street, along with (according to the police) a small arsenal of weapons and explosives. The police attempted to link the Angries with the explosives (despite the lack of forensic evidence) and a total of 25 bomb attacks on the homes of Tory politicians and other members of the Establishment, during which only one person had been slightly injured. After one of the longest criminal trials in English history, at which two other alleged members were also charged, four of the accused were sent to prison for conspiracy to cause explosions and four were acquitted.

1915 Kingsland Empire, and is still going strong. Dalston's other heritage sight is the *Shanghai* restaurant, which preserves the 1910 decor of tiles, marble and glass from its days as an eel and pie shop, founded in 1862 by the ubiquitous Cooke family.

Ridley Road Market

Mon–Thurs 6am–6pm, Fri & Sat 6am–7pm • Dalston Kingsland or Dalston Junction Overground

In the immediate postwar period, Dalston was a predominantly Jewish area, and **Ridley Road Market** (Mon–Sat) was the scene of battles between Mosley's fascists and Jewish ex-servicemen. The market is still in good health, and an accurate reflection of Dalston's ethnic diversity, with Cockney fruit and veg stalls, halal butchers, a 24-hour bagel bakery, West Indian grocers and African and Asian fabric shops. A Turkish/Kurdish supermarket marks the eastern end of the market, its railings still displaying the Star of David from its original Jewish occupants.

Stoke Newington

Bus #73 or #476 from ⊖ Angel or Stoke Newington train station from Liverpool St

Stoke Newington (or "Stokey") is probably the most immediately appealing area of Hackney, though like much of the borough, it's off the tube map. Stokey's best attribute is **Church Street**, a more or less franchise-free, former village high street of little independent shops and restaurants.

The whole area was, for several centuries, a haven for Nonconformists (Christians who were not members of the Anglican church), who were denied the right to live in the City. The most famous Dissenter to live in Stokey was **Daniel Defoe**, who wrote *Robinson Crusoe* on the corner of what is now Defoe Road and Church Street; his gravestone is displayed in the Hackney Museum – stolen from Bunhill Fields in the 1870s, it was discovered in Southampton in 1940.

Abney Park Cemetery

Stoke Newington High St • Park Dawn–dusk; Visitor Centre Mon–Fri 9.30am–4.30pm • Free • ☎ 020 7275 7557, ⊛ abney-park.org.uk • Stoke Newington train station

When Bunhill Fields (see p.198) became overcrowded, **Abney Park Cemetery**, became the "Campo Santo of English non-Conformists", in the words of the 1903 brochure. The most famous grave is that of **William Booth**, founder of the Salvation Army (see p.201), by the Church Street entrance, but the romantically overrun cemetery was originally planted as an A–Z arboretum, and is now an inner-city wildlife reserve (not to mention a gay cruising area). A **visitors' centre** is housed in one of the Egyptian-style lodges at the main entrance, on busy Stoke Newington High Street.

Clissold Park

Stoke Newington's two main churches, both dedicated to **St Mary**, reflect the changes wrought on the area in the last couple of centuries: the sixteenth-century village church

CLOCKWISE FROM TOP LEFT CHURCH STREET (P.292); HIGHGATE CEMETERY (P.305); SWAMINARAYAN TEMPLE (P.308); LITTLE VENICE (P.281) >

stands opposite a more urbane structure built by George Gilbert Scott in the 1850s, with a spire that outreached all others in London in its day. This pair marks the entrance to **Clissold Park**, founded in 1889 and centred on a porticoed mansion built in the 1790s as a country house for the Quaker Hoare banking family, now beautifully restored and housing the park café. The duck and terrapin pond in front was once part of the New River; elsewhere are goats, deer, a small aviary and a butterfly tunnel.

Stamford Hill

In the northern tip of the borough, **Stamford Hill** is home to a tight-knit, mostly Yiddish-speaking, community of Hasidic Jews, one of Hackney's oldest immigrant populations. The most visually striking aspect of this ultra-Orthodox community is the men's attire – frock coats, white stockings and elaborate headgear – which derives from that worn by the Polish nobility of the period. The shops on Stamford Hill and Dunsmure Road, running west, are where the Hasidim buy their kosher goods.

Springfield Park

On Sundays, large numbers of Hasidic families take the air at **Springfield Park**, opened in 1905 "to change the habits of the people and to keep them out of the public houses". The park boasts an awesome view east across the Lee Valley to the adjacent **Walthamstow Marshes**, a valuable stretch of wetland that's alive with butterflies and warblers in the summer. The park also has a decent **café** (ⓦsparkcafe.co.uk) in the White Lodge Mansion by the pond.

To reach Springfield Park from Stamford Hill, walk across Clapton Common, and down Spring Hill. En route, check out the four winged beasts (characters from the *Book of Revelation*) at the base of the spire of the **Cathedral Church of the Good Shepherd** on the corner of Rookwood Road, built for the sect of Spiritual Free Lovers, the Agapemonites, in 1892. Six thousand gathered outside here in 1902 to throw rotten tomatoes at the womanizing vicar, who had declared himself the Second Messiah, and drive him into Clapton Pond to see if he could walk on water.

Middlesex Filter Beds

Sat & Sun: Easter–Sept 10am–6pm; Oct–Easter 10am–4pm; summer holidays also Mon–Fri 10am–5pm • Free • Clapton train station

If you follow the River Lee south of Walthamstow Marshes, you will eventually reach the **Middlesex Filter Beds**, originally built in 1852 on the south side of Lea Bridge Road. Closed in 1969 and mostly drained, the filter beds now serve as a nature reserve – in the spring check out the noisy frogs in the pond by the main culvert. To the south of the filter beds lie the **Hackney Marshes**, best known as the venue for Sunday League football matches, beyond which is the 2012 Olympic Park (see p.202).

Hackney Central

The old parish of Hackney was originally centred around the dumpy fifteenth-century tower of the former parish church of **St Augustine**, and next to it, the Old Town Hall, built in 1802 (now a betting shop). At this point, Mare Street is still discernably a village high street, and is known, for obvious reasons, as the **Narroway**. The modern borough has its headquarters further south on Mare Street around **Hackney Town Hall**, built in a very restrained 1930s Art Deco style and set back from the high street. Close by is the ornate terracotta **Hackney Empire**, one of the last surviving music halls in London, built in typically extravagant style by Frank Matcham in 1899.

Hackney Museum

1 Reading Lane • Tues, Wed & Fri 9.30am–5.30pm, Thurs 9.30am–8pm, Sat 10am–5pm • Free • ☎ 020 8356 3500, ⓦ hackney.gov.uk • Hackney Central Overground

Beside the town hall stands the borough's new library and the **Hackney Museum**. As well as excellent temporary exhibitions, the museum has an interesting permanent

20

display with lots of personal accounts from local residents. Specific exhibits to look out for include the "upside-down" map of the borough and the Saxon log boat found in Springfield Park, thought to have been a ferry for taking folk across the River Lee.

Sutton House

2 & 4 Homerton High St • Feb to mid-Dec Mon–Fri 10am–4.30pm, Sat & Sun noon–4.30pm • NT • £3 • ☎ 020 8986 2264 • Hackney Central Overground

Hidden away, at the east end of the Georgian terrace of Sutton Place, stands **Sutton House**. Built in 1535 for Ralph Sadleir, a rising star at the court of Henry VIII, the house takes its name from Thomas Sutton, founder of Charterhouse, who lived in an adjacent building (he is buried at Charterhouse, minus his entrails, which you've probably just walked over in the graveyard by Mare Street). The National Trust have done their best to adapt to unfamiliar surroundings and have preserved not just the exquisite Elizabethan "linenfold" wooden panelling, but also a mural left by squatters in 1986. In addition to showing its rambling complex of period rooms, the house puts on classical concerts, hosts contemporary art exhibitions, and even runs a café.

Walthamstow

East of the River Lee and the marshes, the chief reason to head out to **Walthamstow** is to visit the William Morris Gallery, but there are one or two other points of interest in the district. **Walthamstow Market** (Mon–Sat) stretches for almost a mile along the old High Street, north of the tube station, and claims to be the country's longest street market. For a traditional East End snack, head for *Manzes*, at no. 76, one of London's finest pie-and-mash shops, with its traditional tiled walls and ceiling.

20

Vestry House Museum

2 Vestry Rd • Wed–Sun 10am–5pm • Free • ☎ 020 8496 4391, ⓦ walthamforest.gov.uk • ⊖ Walthamstow Central

At the peaceful heart of the old village of Walthamstow is the **Vestry House Museum**, built in 1730 and at one time the village workhouse. Later on, it became the police station, and a reconstructed police cell from 1861 is one of the museum's chief exhibits. Pride of place, however, goes to the tiny Bremer car, Britain's first-ever petrol-driven automobile, designed in 1892 by local engineer Fred Bremer, 20-year-old son of German immigrants. Victorian times are comprehensively covered, while the temporary exhibitions tend to focus on contemporary topics. The other point of interest nearby is the fifteenth-century half-timbered **Ancient House**, a short walk up Church Lane.

Civic Centre

Walthamstow's **Civic Centre** is an arresting sight, set back from Forest Road around a huge open courtyard. Designed in an unusual 1930s Scandinavian style, it is, without doubt, London's grandest town-hall complex. Indeed, there's a touch of Stalinism about the severe Neoclassical central portico and in the exhortation above the adjacent Assembly Hall: "Fellowship is life and the lack of fellowship is death." Sadly, construction of the law courts that would have completed the ensemble was interrupted by the war, but this remains one of the most startling public buildings in London.

William Morris Gallery

Forest Rd • ☎ 020 8527 3782, ⓦ walthamforest.gov.uk • ⊖ Walthamstow Central

The **William Morris Gallery** is housed in a lovely Georgian mansion with two big bay windows. This was the Morris family home from 1848 until the death of Morris's father, a successful businessman in the City, in 1856. Poet, artist, designer and socialist, William Morris (1834–96) was one of the most fascinating characters of Victorian

London. Closely associated with both the Pre-Raphaelite and Arts and Crafts movements, he went on to set up Morris & Co, whose work covered all areas of applied art: glasswork, tiles, metalwork, curtains, furniture, calligraphy, carpets, book illumination and (perhaps most famously) wallpaper.

As well as being a successful capitalist – the company's flagship store was on Mayfair's Hanover Square – Morris also became one of the leading political figures of his day, active in the Socialist League with Eleanor Marx, and publishing several utopian tracts, most famously *News from Nowhere*, in which he suggested that the Houses of Parliament be used as "a storage place for manure" (you can buy a copy in the bookshop for the tube journey back).

Closed at the time of writing, the gallery will hopefully have undergone a thorough refurbishment by the time you read this. In addition to housing a new exhibition about Morris himself, and a tearoom, the gallery has a small collection of paintings by his later followers and Pre-Raphaelite chums: Burne-Jones, Ford Madox Brown and Rossetti. You can also see several other works by Morris elsewhere in London: at the V&A, Holy Trinity Church, and the Red House.

Hampstead

Perched on a hill to the west of Hampstead Heath, **Hampstead** village developed into a fashionable spa in the eighteenth century, and was not much altered thereafter. Its sloping site, which deterred Victorian property speculators and put off the railway companies, saved much of the Georgian village from destruction. Later, it became one of the city's most celebrated literary *quartiers* and even now it retains its reputation as a bolt hole of the high-profile intelligentsia and discerning pop stars. You can get some idea of its tone from the fact that the local Labour MP is currently the actor-turned-politician Glenda Jackson.

The steeply inclined **High Street**, lined with trendy shops and arty cafés, flaunts the area's ever-increasing wealth without completely losing its charm, though the most appealing area is the extensive, picturesque and precipitous network of alleyways, steps and streets east and west of Heath Street. Proximity to **Hampstead Heath** is, of course, the real joy of the area, for this mixture of woodland, smooth pasture and landscaped garden is quite simply the most exhilarating patch of greenery in London.

Holly Bush Hill

If you wander into the backstreets north of Hampstead tube, you will probably end up at the small triangular green on **Holly Bush Hill**, where the white weatherboarded **Romney House** stands (closed to the public). In 1797, painter George Romney converted the house and stables into London's first purpose-built studio house, though he spent only two years here before returning to the Lake District and the wife he had abandoned thirty years earlier. Later, it served as Hampstead's Assembly Rooms, where Constable used to lecture on landscape painting. Several houses are set grandly behind wrought-iron gates, on the north side of the green, including the late seventeenth-century **Fenton House** (see below).

Fenton House

Hampstead Grove • March–Oct Wed–Sat 11am–5pm • NT • House £6.50; garden only £1 • Demonstration tours £12–18 • ⓘ 020 7435 3471 • ⊖ Hampstead

All three floors of **Fenton House** are decorated in the eighteenth-century taste and currently house a collection of **European and Oriental ceramics** bequeathed by the house's last private owner, Lady Binning. The house also contains a smattering of British twentieth-century paintings by the likes of Walter Sickert, Duncan Grant and Spencer Gore, plus a superb collection of **early musical instruments** – all displayed on the top floor, from which you can see right across London. Among the many spinets, virginals and clavichords is an early Broadwood grand piano and an Unverdorben lute from 1580 (one of only three in the world). Experienced keyboard players are occasionally let loose on some of the instruments during the day; **concerts** also take place, although tickets tend to sell out months in advance; alternatively, sign up for one of the occasional **demonstration tours**. Tickets for the house also allow you to take a stroll in the beautiful terraced garden, with an orchard, a kitchen garden and a formal **garden**, featuring some top-class topiary and herbaceous borders.

Admiral's House

Beyond Fenton House, up Hampstead Grove, is Admiral's Walk, so-called after its most famous building, **Admiral's House**, a whitewashed Georgian mansion with nautical excrescences. Once painted by Constable, it was later lived in by Victorian architect George Gilbert Scott, of Albert Memorial fame. Until his death in 1933 John Galsworthy lived in the adjacent cottage, **Grove Lodge** – "[it] wasn't cheap, I can tell you", he wrote to a friend on arrival – where he completed *The Forsyte Saga* and received the 1932 Nobel Prize, which was presented to him here since he was too ill to travel abroad. Opposite is **The Mount**, a gently sloping street descending to Heath Street, which has changed little since it was depicted in *Work* by Pre-Raphaelite artist (and local resident) Ford Madox Brown.

St John-at-Hampstead

Church Row • Daily 9am–5pm • Free • ☎ 020 7794 5808, ⓦ hampsteadparishchurch.org.uk • ➔ Hampstead

The Georgian terraces of tree-centred **Church Row**, at the south end of Heath Street, are where City gents would stay for the week when Hampstead was a thriving spa. The street forms a grand approach to **St John-at-Hampstead**, which has an attractive period-piece Georgian interior and a romantically overgrown cemetery. The chest-tomb of the clockmaker John Harrison lies in the churchyard; **John Constable** is buried in the southeastern corner; Hugh Gaitskill, Labour Party leader from 1955 to 1963, lies in the Churchyard Extension to the northeast. If you continue up Holly Walk, you'll come to **St Mary's Church**, whose Italianate facade is squeezed into the middle of a row of three-storey cottages. This was one of the first Catholic churches built in London after the Reformation, and the original facade from 1816 was much less conspicuous.

20

Hampstead Cemetery

Fortune Green Rd • Mon–Fri 7.30am–dusk, Sat 9am–dusk, Sun 10am–dusk • Free • ➔ Hampstead or Finchley Road & Frognal Overground

A good selection of Hampstead luminaries are buried in the rather more neatly maintained **Hampstead Cemetery**, half a mile west of central Hampstead, on the other side of Finchley Road, and founded in 1876 when St John's Churchyard Extension was full. The pioneer of antiseptic surgery Joseph Lister, music-hall star Marie Lloyd, children's book illustrator Kate Greenaway, Hollywood actress Lilli Palmer and the Hungarian Laszlo Biro, who invented the ballpoint pen in 1938, are among those buried here. The full-size stone organ monument to the obscure Charles Barritt is the most unusual piece of funerary art, while the most unlikely occupant is Grand Duke Mikhail Mikhailovitch of Russia, uncle to the last tsar, Nicholas II.

Freud Museum

20 Maresfield Gardens • Wed–Sun noon–5pm • £6 • ☎ 020 7435 2002, ⓦ freud.org.uk • ➔ Finchley Road

One of the most poignant of London's house museums is the **Freud Museum** in the leafy suburban streets of south Hampstead. Having fled Vienna after the Anschluss, **Sigmund Freud** arrived in London in the summer of 1938, and was immediately Britain's most famous Nazi exile. He had been diagnosed as having cancer way back in 1923 (he was an inveterate cigar-smoker) and given just five years to live. He lasted sixteen, but was a semi-invalid when he arrived in London, and rarely left the house except to visit his pet dog, Chun, who was held in quarantine for nearly a year. On

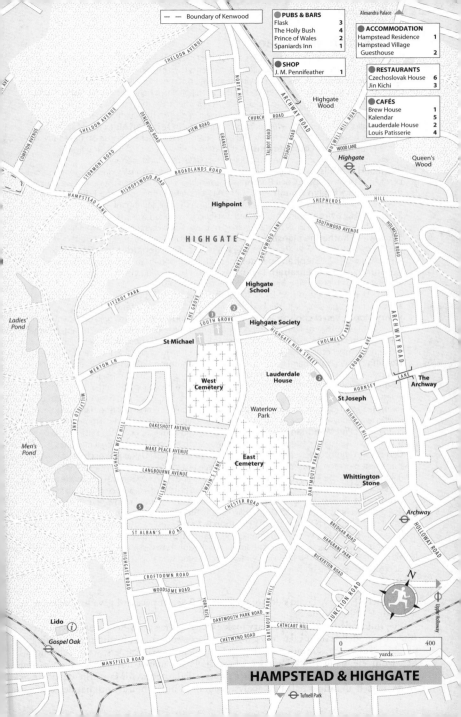

— — Boundary of Kenwood

PUBS & BARS
Flask   3
The Holly Bush   4
Prince of Wales   2
Spaniards Inn   1

SHOP
J. M. Pennifeather   1

ACCOMMODATION
Hampstead Residence   1
Hampstead Village
  Guesthouse   2

RESTAURANTS
Czechoslovak House   6
Jin Kichi   3

CAFÉS
Brew House   1
Kalendar   5
Lauderdale House   2
Louis Patisserie   4

Alexandra Palace

SHELDON AVENUE
NORTH HILL
CHURCH ROAD
ARCHWAY ROAD
Highgate Wood
MUSWELL HILL ROAD
WOOD LANE
Highgate
Queen's Wood

SHELDON AVENUE
DENEWOOD ROAD
VIEW ROAD
GRANGE ROAD
TALBOT ROAD
BISHOPS ROAD

COMPTON AVENUE
STORMONT ROAD
BROADLANDS ROAD

HAMPSTEAD LANE
BISHOPSWOOD ROAD

Highpoint

SHEPHERDS
HILL
SOUTHWOOD AVENUE
HOLMESDALE ROAD

HIGHGATE

NORTH ROAD
SOUTHWOOD LANE

Highgate School

FITZROY PARK

THE GROVE
SOUTH GROVE
Highgate Society
HIGHGATE HIGH STREET
CHOLMELEY PARK
CROMWELL AVE
ARCHWAY ROAD

Ladies' Pond

St Michael

MERTON LN

CHOLMELEY RD

HORNSEY LANE
The Archway

West Cemetery

Lauderdale House

St Joseph

MILLFIELD LANE

Waterlow Park

HIGHGATE HILL

Men's Pond

OAKESHOTT AVENUE
MAKE PEACE AVENUE
LANGBOURNE AVENUE

HIGHGATE WEST HILL
SWAIN'S LANE

East Cemetery

DARTMOUTH PARK HILL

Whittington Stone

HILLWAY

CHESTER ROAD

Archway
HOLLOWAY ROAD

ST ALBAN'S ROAD

HIGHGATE ROAD

BREDGAR ROAD
HARGRAVE PARK
BICKERTON ROAD

CROFTDOWN ROAD
WOODSOME ROAD

YORK RISE

DARTMOUTH PARK ROAD
DARTMOUTH PARK HILL
CATHCART HILL

JUNCTION ROAD

N

Lido (i)

Gospel Oak

CHETWYND ROAD

MANSFIELD ROAD

Upper Holloway

0   400
yards

HAMPSTEAD & HIGHGATE

Tufnell Park

HAMPSTEAD WHO'S WHO

Over the years, countless writers, artists and politicos have been drawn to Hampstead, which has more blue plaques commemorating its residents than any other London borough. **John Constable** lived here in the 1820s, trying to make ends meet for his wife and seven children and painting cloud formations on the Heath, several of which hang in the V&A. **John Keats** moved into Well Walk in 1817, to nurse his dying brother, then moved to a semidetached villa, fell in love with the girl next door, bumped into Coleridge on the Heath, and in 1821 went to Rome to die; the villa is now a museum (see opposite). In 1856, **Karl Marx** finally achieved bourgeois respectability when he moved into Grafton Terrace, a new house on the south side of the Heath. **Robert Louis Stevenson** stayed here when he was 23 suffering from tuberculosis, and thought it "the most delightful place for air and scenery".

Author **H.G. Wells** lived on Church Row for three years just before World War I. In the same period, the photographer **Cecil Beaton** was attending a local infants' school, and was bullied there by author **Evelyn Waugh** – the start of a lifelong feud. The composer **Edward Elgar**, who lived locally, became a special constable during the war, joining the Hampstead Volunteer Reserve. **D.H. Lawrence**, and his German wife Frieda, watched the first major Zeppelin raid on London from the Heath in 1915 and decided to leave. Following the war, Lawrence's friend and fellow writer, **Katherine Mansfield**, lived for a couple of years in a big grey house overlooking the Heath, which she nicknamed "The Elephant". Actor **Dirk Bogarde** was born in a taxi in Hampstead in 1921. **Stephen Spender** spent his childhood in "an ugly house" on Frognal, and went to school locally. **Elizabeth Taylor** was born in Hampstead in 1932, and came back to live here in the 1950s during her first marriage to Richard Burton.

In the 1930s, Hampstead's modernist Isokon Flats, on Lawn Road, became something of an artistic hangout, particularly its drinking den, the *Isobar*: architect **Walter Gropius**, and artists **Henry Moore**, **Ben Nicholson** and his wife **Barbara Hepworth** all lived here (Moore moved out in 1940, when his studio was bombed, and retired to Herefordshire); another tenant, **Agatha Christie**, compared the exterior to a giant ocean liner. Architect **Ernö Goldfinger** built his modernist family home at 2 Willow Rd, now a museum, (see opposite) and local resident **Ian Fleming** named James Bond's adversary after him. **Mohammed Ali Jinnah** abandoned India for Hampstead in 1932, living a quiet life with his daughter and sister, and working as a lawyer. **George Orwell** lived rent-free above Booklovers' Corner, a bookshop on South End Road, in 1934, in return for services in the shop in the afternoon; *Keep the Aspidistra Flying* has many echoes of Hampstead and its characters. **Sigmund Freud** spent the last year of his life in Hampstead, having reluctantly left Austria, following the Nazi Anschluss; his house is now a museum (see p.297). Artist **Piet Mondrian** also escaped to Hampstead from Nazi-occupied Paris, only to be bombed out a year later, after which he fled to New York. Nobel Prize-winning writer **Elias Canetti** was another refugee from Nazi-occupied Europe, as was **Oskar Kokoschka** who, along with photomontage artist John Heartfield, was given assistance by the Hampstead-based Artists Refugee Committee, set up by local Surrealist artist, Roland Penrose. **General de Gaulle** lived on Frognal with his wife and two daughters and got some first-hand experience of Nazi air raids.

Ruth Ellis, the last woman to be hanged in Britain in 1955, shot her lover outside the *Magdala Tavern* by Hampstead Heath train station. **Sid Vicious** and **Johnny Rotten** lived in a squat on Hampstead High Street in 1976. **John le Carré** lived here in the 1980s and 1990s and set a murder in *Smiley's People* on Hampstead Heath. **Michael Foot**, the former Labour leader, lived in a house he bought with his redundancy cheque from Beaverbrook, until the age of 96. Actors Hugh Grant and Stephen Fry, writer Doris Lessing, and pop stars Robbie Williams and George Michael have homes here.

20

September 21, 1939, Freud's doctor fulfilled their secret pact and gave his patient a lethal dose of morphine.

The ground-floor study and library look exactly as they did when Freud lived here (they are modelled on his flat in Vienna); the large collection of antiquities and the psychiatrist's couch, sumptuously draped in opulent Persian carpets, were all brought here from Vienna in 1938. Upstairs, where the Freud archive now resides, there's some old footage of the family, while another room is dedicated to his favourite daughter, Anna, herself an influential child analyst, who lived in the house until her death in

1982. Sigmund's architect son, Ernst, designed a loggia at the back of the house so that Freud could sit out and enjoy the garden; it has since been enclosed and serves as the museum shop, which flogs Freudian merchandise such as a "Brainy Beanie" – Freud himself as a cuddly toy – and stocks a superb range of books.

Burgh House

New End Square • Wed–Sun noon–5pm; Sat art gallery only • Free • ☎ 020 7431 0144, ⓦ burghhouse.org.uk • ⊖ Hampstead

The Queen Anne mansion of **Burgh House** dates from Hampstead's halcyon days as a spa, known briefly as Hampstead Wells, and was at one time occupied by Dr Gibbons, the physician who discovered the spring's medicinal qualities. The house hosts art exhibitions and its attractive wood-panelled Music Room is a popular wedding venue. Upstairs, there's a modest museum, telling the history of Hampstead. The museum's most prized possessions are the modernist Isokon plywood stacking tables and a long chair by Marcel Breuer, found in a Hampstead skip by a local councillor. The *Buttery* café in the basement has outdoor seating in the summer on a lovely terrace.

2 Willow Road

March–Oct Wed–Sun 11am–5pm, Sat 11am–5pm (note that before 3pm, visits are by hourly guided tour) • NT • £5.80 • ☎ 020 7435 6166 • ⊖ Hampstead

Hampstead's most unusual sight is **2 Willow Road**, a modernist red-brick terrace, built in the 1930s by the Budapest-born architect **Ernö Goldfinger**, best known for his concrete brutalist high-rises, such as Trellick Tower (see p.278). Completed in 1939, this was a state-of-the-art house at the time, its open-plan rooms flooded with natural light and much of the furniture designed by Goldfinger himself. The family home for fifty years, the Goldfingers changed very little in the house, so what you see is a 1930s avant-garde dwelling preserved in aspic, a house at once both modern and old-fashioned. An added bonus is that the rooms are packed with Surrealist *objets trouvés* and works of art by the likes of Léger, Duchamp, Max Ernst, Henry Moore and Man Ray.

20

Keats' House

Keats Grove • May–Oct Tues–Sun 1–5pm; Nov–April Fri–Sun 1–5pm • £5 • ☎ 020 7332 3868; ⓦ keatshouse.cityoflondon.gov.uk • ⊖ Hampstead

Hampstead's most lustrous figure is celebrated at **Keats' House**, an elegant, whitewashed Regency double villa. The consumptive poet lodged here with his friend Charles Brown, in 1818, after his brother Tom had died of the same illness. Inspired by the peacefulness of Hampstead, and by his passion for girl-next-door Fanny Brawne (whose house is also part of the museum), Keats wrote some of his most famous works here before leaving for Rome, where he died in 1821 at the age of just 25.

In the pretty front garden, as you approach the house, a diminutive plum tree stands on the site of the much larger specimen in whose shade Keats is said to have sat for two or three hours before composing *Ode to a Nightingale*. The simple interior contains books and letters, an anatomical notebook from Keats' days as a medical student at Guy's Hospital, Fanny's engagement ring and the four-poster bed in which the poet first coughed up blood, and proclaimed "that drop of blood is my death warrant". There are regular events – poetry readings, performances and talks – so check out the website's events listings.

Hampstead Heath

ⓦ cityoflondon.gov.uk • ⊖ Hampstead or Hampstead Heath and Gospel Oak Overground

Hampstead Heath, north London's "green lung", is the city's most enjoyable public park. Little of the original heathland survives, but the Heath nevertheless packs in a wonderful variety of bucolic scenery, from the formal **Hill Garden** and rolling green pastures of **Parliament Hill** to the dense woodland of **West Heath** and the landscaped grounds of **Kenwood**. As it is, the Heath was lucky to survive the nineteenth century intact, for it endured more than forty years of campaigning by the Lord of the Manor, Thomas Maryon Wilson, who introduced no fewer than fifteen parliamentary bills in an attempt to build over it. It wasn't until after Wilson's death in 1871 that 220 acres of the Heath passed into public ownership. The Heath now covers over 800 acres, and is run by the Corporation of London (see p.155).

Parliament Hill

Parliament Hill, the Heath's southernmost ridge, is perhaps better known as Kite Hill, since this is north London's premier spot for **kite flying**, especially busy at weekends when some serious equipment takes to the air. The parliamentary connection is much disputed by historians, so take your pick: a Saxon parliament met here; Guy Fawkes' cronies gathered here (in vain) to watch the Houses of Parliament burn; the Parliamentarians placed cannon here during the Civil War to defend London against the Royalists; and the Middlesex parliamentary elections took place here in the seventeenth century. Whatever the reason for the name, the view over London is unrivalled.

Boudicca's Mound to Viaduct Pond

To the northwest of Parliament Hill is a fenced-off tumulus, known as **Boudicca's Mound**, where, according to tradition, Queen Boudicca was buried after she and 10,000 other Brits had been massacred at Battle Bridge; another legend says she's buried under Platform 10 in King's Cross Station. Due west lies the picturesque **Viaduct Pond**, named after its red-brick bridge, which is also known as Wilson's Folly. It was built as part of Thomas Maryon Wilson's abortive plans to drive an access road through the middle of the Heath to his projected estate of 28 villas.

Vale of Health

To the west, beyond the Viaduct Pond, an isolated network of streets nestles in the **Vale of Health**, an area that was, in fact, a malarial swamp until the late eighteenth century. Literary lion Leigh Hunt moved to this quiet backwater in 1816, after serving a two-year prison sentence for calling the Prince Regent "a fat Adonis of fifty", among other things; Hunt was instrumental in persuading Keats to give up medicine for poetry. Other artistic residents have included Nobel Prize-winner Rabindranath Tagore, who lived here in 1912, and painter Stanley Spencer, who stayed here with the Carline family and married their daughter Hilda in the 1920s. Author D.H. Lawrence spent a brief, unhappy period here in 1915: in September of that year his novel *The Rainbow* was banned for obscenity, and by December, Lawrence and his wife, Frieda von Richthofen, whose German origins were causing the couple immense problems with the authorities, had resolved to leave the country.

West Heath

Northwest of the Vale of Health is the busy road junction around **Whitestone Pond**, which marks the highest point in this part of north London (440ft), overlooked by the faux-ancient *Jack Straw's Castle* pub. To the west lies **West Heath**, a densely wooded, boggy area with a thick canopy of deciduous trees sloping down towards Childs Hill; it's a very peaceful place for a stroll and a popular gay cruising area.

POND DIPPING

The Heath is the source of several of London's lost rivers – the Tyburn, the Westbourne and the Fleet – and home to some 28 natural ponds, three of which are used as **Bathing Ponds**, all of which are very popular in good weather: the single-sex men's and ladies' ponds, on the Highgate side are open all year; mixed bathing on the Hampstead side in the summer only (see p.439).

A track leads northwest from *Jack Straw's Castle*, across West Heath, over to **The Hill Garden** (daily 8.30am to dusk), the Heath's most secretive and romantic little gem. Originally an extension to the grounds of nearby Hill House, built by Lord Leverhulme in 1906 (and now converted into flats), the garden's most startling feature is the 800ft-long zigzag **Pergola**, whose Doric columns support a host of climbers including a wonderfully gnarled wisteria. The pergola is elevated some 15ft above the ground in order to traverse a public footpath that Lord Leverhulme tried in vain to have removed.

Golders Hill Park

West Heath Ave • Daily 7.30am–dusk • Free • ⊖ Golders Green

Adjacent to the West Heath are the landscaped gardens of **Golders Hill Park**. Near the main entrance, is the park café, serving delicious Italian ice cream, courtesy of *Arte Gelato*, and close by, a beautifully kept walled garden and pond. The central section of the park is taken up by a **zoo** containing alpacas, red-legged seriemas, ring-tailed lemurs, and a series of impeccably maintained aviaries, home to white-naped cranes and other exotic birds.

Kenwood

Gardens Daily summer 8am–8pm; winter 8am–4pm • Free **House** Daily 11.30am–4pm • Free • ☎ 020 8348 1286 • Bus #210 from ⊖ Archway or Golders Green

The Heath's most celebrated sight is **Kenwood**, the former private estate, whose beautiful off-white Neoclassical mansion faces south to catch the sun. The house dates from the seventeenth century, but was later remodelled by Robert Adam for the Earl of Mansfield, the most powerful jurist in the country. Mansfield, who sent 102 people to the gallows and sentenced another 448 to transportation, was a deeply unpopular character and one of the prime targets of the 1780 Gordon Riots. Having ransacked his Bloomsbury house, a mob headed for Kenwood, but were waylaid by the canny landlord of the nearby *Spaniards Inn* (an ex-butler of Mansfield's), who plied them with free drink until soldiers arrived to disperse them.

Nowadays, with its free art collection and magnificently landscaped grounds, Kenwood is a deservedly popular spot. The gardens, to the west of the house, boast splendid azaleas and rhododendrons; to the south, a huge grassy amphitheatre slopes down to a lake. The whole area is something of a suntrap and a favourite picnic spot, while the provision-less can head for the excellent *Brew House Café* in the old coachhouse.

Kenwood House

The house is now home to a superb seventeenth- and eighteenth-century **art collection** from the English, Dutch and French schools. First off, head for the Dining Room, where a superb late self-portrait by **Rembrandt** shares space with marvellous portraits by Franz Hals, Van Dyck and Ferdinand Bols, and **Vermeer**'s delicate *Guitar Player*. Of the house's many wonderful period interiors, the most spectacular is Adam's sky-blue and gold **Library**, its book-filled apses separated from the central area by paired columns. The *pièce de résistance* is the tunnel-vaulted ceiling, decorated by Antonio Zucchi, who fell in love with and married Kenwood's other ceiling painter, Angelica Kauffmann.

Upstairs, you'll find more paintings, including William Larkin's full-length portraits, possibly of a Jacobean wedding party, the arrogant Richard Sackville, a dissolute aristocrat resplendent in pompom shoes, and his much nicer brother, Edward, sporting earrings festooned with ribbons. Don't miss the room of shoe buckles, jewellery and portrait miniatures donated by local collectors. Back downstairs in the Music Room, are more masterful portraits by **Gainsborough**, most strikingly the diaphanous *Countess Howe*, caught up in a bold, almost abstract landscape, plus several by **Reynolds**, including his whimsical *Venus Chiding Cupid for Learning to Cast Accounts*.

20

Highgate

Northeast of the Heath, and fractionally lower than Hampstead (appearances notwithstanding), **Highgate** lacks the literary cachet of Hampstead, but makes up for it with London's most famous **cemetery**, resting place of, among others, Karl Marx. It also retains more of its village origins, especially around **The Grove**, Highgate's finest row of houses, set back from the road in pairs overlooking the village green, and dating back to 1685. Their most famous one-time resident, the poet **Samuel Taylor Coleridge**, lived at no. 3 from 1816, with a certain Dr Gillman and his wife. With Gillman's help, Coleridge got his opium addiction under control and enjoyed the healthiest, if not necessarily the happiest, period of his life, until his death here in 1834.

Coleridge was initially buried in the local college chapel, but in 1961 his remains were reburied in **St Michael's Church**, in South Grove. Its spire is a landmark, but St Michael's is much less interesting architecturally than the grandiose, late seventeenth-century Old Hall next door, or the two tiny ramshackle cottages opposite, built for the servants of one of the luxurious mansions that once characterized Highgate. Arundel House, which stood on the site of the Old Hall, was where **Francis Bacon**, the Renaissance philosopher and statesman, is thought to have died, having caught a chill while trying to stuff a chicken full of ice for an early experiment in refrigeration.

Highgate High Street

Highgate gets its name from the tollgate – the highest in London and the oldest in the country – that stood where the *Gatehouse* pub now stands on **Highgate High Street**. The High Street itself, though architecturally pleasing, is packed out with franchises and estate agents, and marred by heavy traffic, as is its northern extension, North Road. If you persevere with North Road, however, you'll pass **Highgate School**, founded in 1565 for the local poor but long since established as an exclusive fee-paying public school, housed in suitably impressive Victorian buildings. T.S. Eliot was a master here for a while, and famous poetical alumni, known as Cholmeleians after the founder Sir Roger Cholmeley, include Gerard Manley Hopkins and John Betjeman.

Highpoint 1 and 2

Further up North Road, on the left, are the whitewashed high-rises of **Highpoint 1** and **2**, seminal early essays in modernist architecture designed by Berthold Lubetkin and his Tecton partnership from the late 1930s. Highpoint 1, the northernmost of the two blocks, was conceived as workers' housing, with communal roof terraces and a tearoom. The locals were outraged so Highpoint 2 ended up being luxury apartments, the caryatids at the entrance a joke at the expense of his anti-modernist critics. Lubetkin also designed himself a penthouse apartment on the roof in the style of a Georgian dacha, with views right across London, where he lived until 1955.

Waterlow Park

Daily dawn to dusk • Free • ⓦ waterlowpark.org.uk • ⊖ Archway

A short distance south down Highgate High Street is **Waterlow Park**, named after Sydney Waterlow, who donated it in 1889 as "a garden for the gardenless". Waterlow also bequeathed **Lauderdale House** (ⓦ lauderdalehouse.org.uk) a much-altered sixteenth-century building, which is thought to have been occupied at one time by Nell Gwynne and her infant son. The house stages live performances, puts on art exhibitions, and is also home to a decent **café** (Tues–Sun) that spills out into the terraced gardens. The park itself, occupying a dramatic sloping site, is an amalgamation of several house gardens, and is one of London's finest landscaped parks, providing a through route to Highgate Cemetery. Not far from the park, down Highgate Hill, you'll find the **Whittington Stone**, with cat, marking the spot where Dick Whittington miraculously heard the Bow Bells chime (see p.164).

Highgate Cemetery

Swain's Lane **East Cemetery** April–Oct Mon–Fri 10am–5pm, Sat & Sun 11am–5pm; Nov–March closes 4pm • £3 • Guided tour Sat 2pm; £7 **West Cemetery** Guided tours March–Nov Mon–Fri 2pm, Sat & Sun hourly 11am–4pm; Dec–Feb Sat & Sun hourly 11am–3pm; £7; No under-8s • ☎ 020 8340 1834, ⓦ highgate-cemetery.org • ⊖ Archway

Ranged on both sides of Swain's Lane and receiving far more visitors than Highgate itself, **Highgate Cemetery** is London's most famous graveyard. Opened in 1839, it quickly became the preferred resting place of wealthy Victorian families, who could rub shoulders with numerous intellectuals and artists. As long as prime plots were available, business was good and as many as 28 gardeners were employed to beautify the place.

But as the plots filled, funds dried up and the place fell prey to **vandalism**. The cemetery, which had provided inspiration for Bram Stoker's *Dracula*, found itself at the centre of a series of bizarre incidents in the early 1970s. Graves were smashed open, cadavers strewn about, and the High Priest of the British Occult Society, Allan Farrant, was arrested, armed with a stake and crucifix with which he hoped to destroy "the Highgate Vampire". He was eventually sentenced to four years' imprisonment, after being found guilty of damaging graves, interfering with corpses and sending death-spell dolls to two policemen.

In 1975, the old (west) cemetery was closed completely and was taken under the wing of the Friends of Highgate Cemetery. Nowadays, you have to take a guided tour to visit the West Cemetery, though you can still wander freely in the less dramatic east cemetery – both sections have entrance charges.

West Cemetery

The old, overgrown **West Cemetery** is the ultimate Hammer-horror graveyard, and one of London's most impressive sights. It may not have a celebrity corpse to compete with Karl Marx (in the East Cemetery), but wins hands down when it comes to atmosphere, with its huge vaults and eerie statuary. The most famous names here are Chubb (of the locks), Cruft (of the Dog Show) and scientist Michael Faraday, who, as a member of the Sandemanian sect, is buried along the unconsecrated north wall.

20

All tours are different, but you're quite likely to be shown the lion that snoozes above the tomb of menagerist George Wombwell, and the faithful dog (confusingly called Lion) that lies on bare-knuckle fighter Thomas Sayers' grave. Another popular sight is the **Rossetti family tomb**, resting place of Elizabeth Siddall, Pre-Raphaelite model and wife of Dante Gabriel Rossetti, who buried the only copy of his love poems along with her. Seven years later he changed his mind and had the poems exhumed and published. The poet Christina Rossetti, Dante's sister, is also buried in the vault.

The cemetery's spookiest section is around **Egyptian Avenue**, entered through an archway flanked by Egyptian half-pillars, known as the "Gateway to the City of the Dead". The avenue slopes gently upwards to the Circle of Lebanon, at the centre of which rises a giant cedar. The circular Egyptian-style sunken catacombs here include the tomb of the lesbian novelist Radclyffe Hall (her lover, Mabel Batten, is also buried here). Above are the **Terrace Catacombs**, and the cemetery's most ostentatious mausoleums, some of which hold up to fifteen coffins; the largest – based on the tomb of Mausolus at Halicarnassus – is that of Julius Beer, one-time owner of the *Observer* newspaper.

East Cemetery

What the **East Cemetery** lacks in atmosphere, it makes up for by the fact that you can wander at will through its maze of circuitous paths. The most publicized occupant is, of course, **Karl Marx**, who spent more than half his life in London, much of it in bourgeois Hampstead. Marx himself asked for a plain and simple grave topped by a headstone, but by 1954 the Communist movement decided to move his tomb to a more prominent position and erect the vulgar bronze bust that now surmounts a granite plinth bearing the words "Workers of all lands, unite", from *The Communist Manifesto*. He has been visited here by Khrushchev, Brezhnev and just about every postwar Communist leader in the world.

Buried along with Marx are his grandson, wife and housekeeper, Helene Delmuth, whom he got pregnant. Engels accepted paternity to avoid a bourgeois scandal and only told Marx's daughter, Eleanor, on his deathbed in 1895. Eleanor committed suicide a few years later after discovering her common-law husband had secretly married someone else. Her ashes were finally placed in the family vault in 1954, having been seized from the Communist Party headquarters in London by the police in 1921. Lesser-known Communists such as Yusef Mohamed Dadoo, chairman of the South African Communist Party until his death in 1983, cluster around Marx. Not far away is **George Eliot**'s grave and, behind it, that of her lover, George Henry Lewes.

Alexandra Palace

Alexandra Palace Way ☎ 020 8365 2121, ⓦ alexandrapalace.com • Bus #W3 from Alexandra Palace train station or walk from
⊖ Wood Green

Built in 1873 on North London's commanding heights of Muswell Hill, **Alexandra Palace** is now London's only surviving example of a Victorian "People's Palace", since its more famous rival, Crystal Palace, burnt down in 1936 (see p.313). However, the history of "Ally Pally" is almost as tragic as that of Crystal Palace. Sixteen days after the official opening, the place burnt down and, despite being rebuilt within two years and boasting a theatre, a reading room, an exhibition hall and a concert room with one of the largest organs in the world, it was a commercial failure. During World War I more than 17,000 German POWs passed through its gates, and in 1936 the world's first television transmission took place here. It was the venue for the "14 Hour Technicolour Dream" in 1967, organized by the *International Times* and featuring performances by, among others, Pink Floyd and Soft Machine. The palace was rebuilt again after another devastating fire in 1980, and continues to struggle to make itself commercially viable. In addition to the annual round of shows and gigs, there's a pub – appropriately named *Phoenix Bar* – with great views, an indoor ice rink, a boating lake, a pitch and putt course and a garden centre, as well as regular funfairs in the holidays.

Golders Green

If the East End is the spiritual home of working-class Jews, **Golders Green** and the suburbs to the northwest of Hampstead, are its middle-class equivalent. A hundred years ago this whole area was open countryside but, like much of suburbia, it was transformed overnight by the arrival of the tube in 1907. Before and after World War II, the area was heavily colonized by Jews moving out of the old East End ghetto around Spitalfields or fleeing as refugees from the Nazis. Nowadays, Golders Green, along with Stamford Hill, is one of the most distinctively Jewish areas in London. The Orthodox community has a particularly strong presence here and there's a profusion of kosher shops beyond the railway bridge on Golders Green Road, at their busiest on Sundays.

Hampstead Garden Suburb

ⓦ hgs.org.uk • ⊖ Golders Green

Much of Golders Green is architecturally bland, the one exception being **Hampstead Garden Suburb**, begun in 1907. This model housing development was the Utopian dream of **Henrietta Barnett**, who believed the key to social reform was to create a mixed social environment where "the poor shall teach the rich, and the rich, let us hope, shall help the poor to help themselves". Yet from the start the suburb was socially segregated, with artisan dwellings to the north, middle-class houses to the west and the wealthiest villas overlooking the Heath to the south. As a social engineering experiment it was a failure – the area has remained a thoroughly middle-class ghetto – but as a blueprint for suburban estates it has been enormously influential.

The suburb's formal entrance is the striking Arts and Crafts gateway of shops and flats on Finchley Road. From here, ivy-strewn houses, each with its own garden encased in privet, yew and beech hedges, fan out eastwards along tree-lined avenues towards **Central Square**, laid out by Edwin Lutyens in a neo-Georgian style he dubbed "Wren-aissance". (Pubs, shops, cinemas and all commercial buildings were, and still are, excluded from the suburb.) Lutyens also designed the square's twin churches: the Nonconformist Free Church, with an octagonal dome, and the Anglican St Jude's-on-the-Hill – the finer of the two – with its steeply pitched roof and spire, and unusual 1920s murals. East of Central Square is the Lutyens-designed **Institute**, with its clock tower, now occupied by an adult education centre and Henrietta Barnett Girls' School.

Golders Green Crematorium

Hoop Lane · Daily: summer 9am–6pm; winter 4pm · ⊖ Golders Green

The **Golders Green Crematorium** is where over 300,000 Londoners have been cremated since 1902. More famous names have been scattered over the unromantically named Dispersal Area than have been buried at any single London graveyard: Boris Anrep, Enid Blyton, Seán O'Casey, Charles Rennie Mackintosh, H.G. Wells, Kathleen Ferrier, Joe Orton, Don Revie, Peter Sellers, Peggy Ashcroft, Joyce Grenfell, Marc Bolan, Keith Moon, Bram Stoker and Prajadhipok, the former King of Thailand; Neville Chamberlain, Rudyard Kipling, Henry James and T.S. Eliot were cremated here, but their ashes lie elsewhere. Finding a particular memorial plaque among the serene red-brick chapels and arcades is no easy task, so it's best to enquire at the office in the main courtyard. The Ernst George Columbarium is where you'll find the ashes of Anna Pavlova; Freud and his wife Martha are contained within one of Freud's favourite Greek red-figure vases in an adjacent room, with their daughter Anna in her own urn close by.

Golders Green Jewish Cemetery

Hoop Lane · Daily except Sat 8.30am–5pm or dusk · ⊖ Golders Green

The **Jewish Cemetery** was founded in 1895 before the area was built up. The eastern section, to your right, is for Orthodox Sephardic Jews, whose tombs are traditionally laid flat with the deceased's feet pointing towards Jerusalem. To the left are the upright headstones of Reform Jews, including the great cellist Jacqueline du Pré, and Lord Hore-Belisha, Minister of Transport in the 1930s, who gave his name to "Belisha beacons" (the yellow flashing globes at zebra crossings for pedestrians).

Hendon: the RAF Museum

Grahame Park Way · Daily 10am–6pm; Grahame-White Factory closed for 1hr noon–2pm; Battle of Britain Hall daily noon–6pm · Free · ☎ 020 8205 2266, ⊛ rafmuseum.org.uk · ⊖ Colindale

One of the most impressive collections of historic military aircraft in the world is lodged at the **RAF Museum**, in the former Hendon Aerodrome beside the M1 motorway. The most obvious place to start is in the **Historic Hangars**, dominated by a vast 1920s Southampton reconnaissance flying boat. Be sure to check out the Hoverfly, the first really effective helicopter, and, of course, the most famous British plane of all time, the Spitfire. By the exit you'll find a Harrier jump jet, the world's first vertical takeoff and landing aircraft, labelled with a text extolling its role in the Falklands War. Those with children should head for the hands-on **Aeronauts** gallery, which teaches the basic principles of flight and airplane construction.

The most chilling section is the adjacent **Bomber Hall**, where you're greeted by a colossal Lancaster bomber, similar to those used in Operation Upkeep, the mission carried out by Squadron 617 (and immortalized in the film *The Dambusters*), about which there's a short documentary. To the museum's credit, the assessment of Bomber Command's wartime policy of blanket-bombing gives both sides of the argument. The video of the "precision bombing" conducted during the 1991 Gulf War is given rather less even-handed treatment. Two other exhibits deserve special mention: the crumbling carcass of a Halifax bomber, recovered from the bottom of a Norwegian fjord, and the clinically white Valiant, the first British aircraft to carry thermonuclear bombs.

The outbuildings

If you've still got time and energy, there are several more hangars across the courtyard. Closest to hand is **Milestones of Flight**, where there's a century's worth of aircraft from an early airship gondola to the state-of-the-art Eurofighter Typhoon. The **Grahame-White Factory** is the UK's first aircraft factory, purpose-built in Hendon in 1917, and now used to display the oldest aircraft including a Sopwith Triplane and a flimsy Hanriot fighter, both from World War I. Finally, there's the **Battle of Britain Hall**, which contains a huge Sunderland flying boat, a V-1 flying bomb and a V-2 rocket. The main event though, is *Our Finest Hour*, an unashamedly jingoistic fifteen-minute audiovisual on the aerial battle between the RAF and the Luftwaffe during the autumn of 1940.

Neasden: the Swaminarayan temple

The lotus blooms in splendour, but its roots lie in the dirt. Hindu proverb

105-119 Brentfield Rd • Daily 9am–6pm • Temple free; Understanding Hinduism £2 • ☎ 020 8965 2651, Ⓦ mandir.org • ⊖ Neasden

One of the most remarkable buildings in London lies just off the busy North Circular, in the glum suburb of Neasden. Rising majestically above the dismal interwar housing like a mirage, the **Shri Swaminarayan mandir** is a traditional Hindu temple topped with domes and *shikharas*, erected in 1995 in a style and scale unseen outside of India for over a millennium. The building's vital statistics are incredible: 3000 tons of Bulgarian limestone and 2000 tons of Carrara marble were shipped out to India, carved by over 1500 sculptors, and then shipped back to London and assembled in a matter of weeks. Even more surprising is the fact that **Lord Swaminarayan** (1781–1830), to whom the temple is dedicated, is a relatively obscure and very recent Hindu deity. There are no more than 10,000 followers in Britain, mostly from Gujarat, and no more than a million worldwide.

The mandir (temple)

To reach the temple, you must enter through the adjacent **haveli**, or cultural complex, with its carved wooden portico and balcony, and twin covered, carpeted courtyards. Shoes are the only thing that are sexually segregated inside the temple, so, having placed yours in the appropriate alcove, you can then proceed to the **mandir** itself. The temple is carved entirely out of Carrara marble, with every possible surface transformed into a honeycomb of arabesques, flowers and seated gods. The pillars are intricately decorated with figures of gods and goddesses, while on three sides are alcoves sheltering serene life-sized **murti** (idols), garish figures in resplendent clothes representing Rama, Sita, Ganesh the elephant god, Hanuman the monkey god, and, of course, Shri Swaminarayan himself. The murti are only periodically on display (9–11am, 11.45am–12.15pm & 4–6.30pm).

Understanding Hinduism

Beneath the mandir, an **exhibition** explains the basic tenets of Hinduism through dioramas, extols the virtues of vegetarianism and details the life of Lord Swaminarayan, who became a yogi at the age of 11, and stood naked on one leg for three months amid snowstorms and "torturing weather". At the end, there's a short video about the building's history.

OLD ROYAL NAVAL COLLEGE, GREENWICH

South London

Real and imagined, there's a big divide between North and South London,
certainly as far the residents are concerned. Put simply, North Londoners
generally don't go south, unless they can help it, and yet South London has a
lot of (albeit quite scattered) points of interest. One area, in particular, stands
head and shoulders above the rest: Greenwich, with its riverside setting,
nautical associations, Baroque architecture, and Royal Observatory. The rest
of this chapter is really just a hotchpotch of suburban sights, where, given
the distances and dire lack of tube lines, it pays to be selective. Stand outs
include Dulwich, whose public art gallery is even older than the National
Gallery, and, on the very edge of London, the Arts and Crafts Red House,
William Morris's former home, and Down House, home of Charles Darwin.

21

Brixton

Brixton is a classic Victorian suburb, transformed from open fields into bricks and mortar in a couple of decades following the arrival of the railways in the 1860s. The viaducts still dominate the landscape of central Brixton, with shops and arcades hidden under their arches, but it's the West Indian community, who arrived here in the 1950s and 1960s, who still define the character of the place – Notting Hill may have Carnival, but it's Brixton that has the most upfront African-Caribbean consciousness. Brixton also continues to suffer from a reputation for violence and gun crime, earned during the 1981, 1985 and 1995 riots when tensions between the police and the local youth came to a head.

Brixton's main axis is the junction of Brixton Road, Acre Lane and Coldharbour Lane, just to the south of the tube station and overlooked by the slender clock tower of the Edwardian **Lambeth Town Hall**; the dinky neo-Renaissance Tate Library built in 1892; the Ritzy cinema, which first opened in 1911 as the Electric Pavilion; and, on the triangular traffic island, the Neoclassical church of **St Matthew**, from 1824, with its grandiose Doric portico, its crypt now converted into a bar, restaurant and performance space.

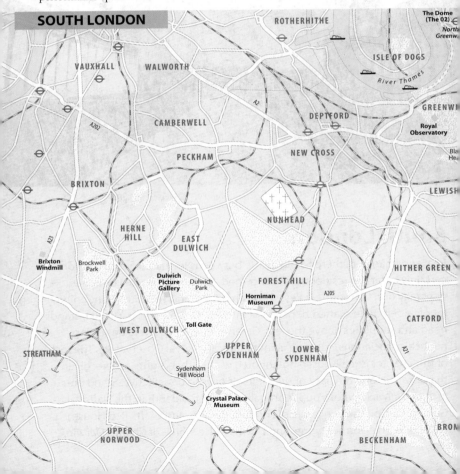

Brixton Market

Street stalls Mon–Sat 8am–6pm, Wed closes 3pm; Arcades Mon–Sat 8am–6pm, Thurs until 10pm, many of the cafés also open Fri & Sat until 10pm & Sun daytime; • Farmers' market Sun 10am–2pm • ⓦ brixtonmarket.net • ◉ Brixton

The commercial lifeblood of Brixton, however, pulses most strongly through **Brixton Market**, whose stalls spread out through the warren of streets and covered arcades east of Brixton Road. **Electric Avenue** – made famous by Eddy Grant's 1983 hit single – runs behind the tube station, and is so-called as it was one of the first London shopping streets to be lit by electricity in the 1880s. A network of interwar arcades, known as **Market Row**, runs parallel with the avenue, with another set called **Brixton Village**, originally the Granville Arcade, on the other side of Atlantic Road with main entrance past the bridge on Coldharbour Lane, where you can buy bold African and Asian fabrics, jewellery, West Indian fruit and meat, giant African snails, amazing wigs and much more besides. Recently a dozen or so new cafés have opened at the back of Brixton Village, serving everything from coffee and cakes to Thai food, while Market Row also has the famous *Franco Manca* (see p.385). On the far side of the railway tracks, the market veers eastwards along Brixton Station Road, with stalls selling everything from cheap secondhand clothes to reggae soundtracks.

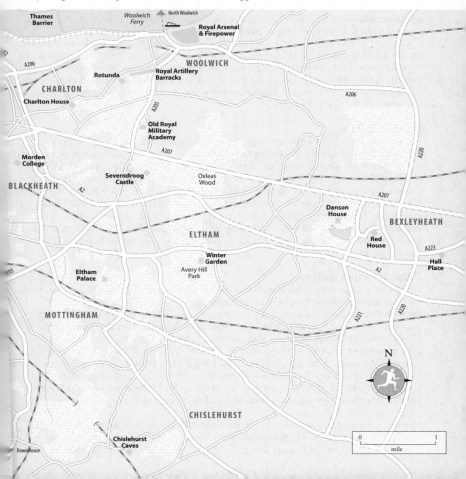

21

Brixton Windmill

Blenheim Gardens • April–Oct, second Sunday of the month, 2–4pm • ⓦ brixtonwindmill.org • ⊖ Brixton

Brixton is about the last place in London you'd expect to find a fully functioning **windmill**, but if you duck down Blenheim Gardens, off Brixton Hill, you'll see a tower mill nearly 40ft high, built in 1816, with its blades intact (but no sails) and a fetching weatherboarded "hood". Wind power drove the mill until 1862 when the area became too built-up, then steam and gas followed until the mill fell into disuse in the 1930s. Recently restored, it is currently open only on the second Sunday of the month. In the 1820s, the mill gained another source of power for its corn-grinding: the country's first **treadmill**, designed by William Cubitt and worked by inmates of Brixton Prison.

Dulwich and around

Dulwich is just two stops from Brixton on the railway, but light years away in every other respect. This affluent, middle-class enclave is one of southeast London's prettier patches – its leafy streets boast handsome Georgian houses and even a couple of weatherboarded cottages, while the Soane-designed **Dulwich Picture Gallery** is one of London's finest small museums. If Dulwich has a fault, it's the somewhat cloying self-consciousness about its "village" status, with its rather twee little shops, rural signposts and fully functioning tollgate – the only one remaining in London.

A day out in Dulwich can be combined with a visit to the nearby **Horniman Museum**, an enjoyable ethnographic collection, and, for the very curious, the remnants of the old **Crystal Palace**, further south. The green spaces between these sights are also worth exploring. **Dulwich Park**, opposite the Picture Gallery, is a pleasant enough public park, but for something a bit wilder, **Sydenham Hill Wood**, a nature reserve south of Dulwich Common, is the one to head for.

Dulwich College

Dulwich came to prominence in 1619 when its lord of the manor, actor-manager Edward Alleyn, founded the **College of God's Gift** as a school for twelve poor boys on the profits of his whorehouses and bear-baiting pits on Bankside. Dulwich College has long since outgrown its original buildings, which still stand to the north of the Picture Gallery, and is now housed in a fanciful Italianate complex designed by Charles Barry (son of the architect of the Houses of Parliament), south of Dulwich Common. The college is now a large, fee-paying, independent boys' school, with an impressive roll call of old boys, including Raymond Chandler, P.G. Wodehouse and Ernest Shackleton, although they tend to keep quiet about World War II traitor Lord Haw-Haw.

Dulwich Picture Gallery

Gallery Rd • Tues–Sun 10am–5pm • £5 • Guided tours Sat & Sun 3pm; free • ⓣ 020 8693 5254, ⓦ dulwichpicturegallery.org.uk • West Dulwich (from Victoria) or North Dulwich (from London Bridge) train station

Dulwich Picture Gallery, the nation's oldest public art gallery, was designed by John Soane in 1814, and houses, among other bequests, the collection assembled in the 1790s by the French dealer Noel Desenfans on behalf of King Stanislas of Poland, who planned to open a national gallery in Warsaw. In 1795, Poland disappeared from the map of Europe, Stanislas abdicated and Desenfans was left with the paintings. Neither the British nor Russians would buy the collection, so Desenfans proposed founding a national gallery. In the end it was left to his business partner, the landscape painter Francis Bourgeois, and Desenfans' widow, to complete the task and open the gallery in 1817.

Soane, who worked for no fee, created a beautifully spacious building, awash with natural light, and added a tiny **mausoleum** at the centre for the sarcophagi of the Desenfans family and of Francis Bourgeois. Based on an Alexandrian catacomb, it's suffused with golden-yellow light from the mausoleum's coloured glass – a characteristic Soane touch.

The paintings

The gallery itself is crammed with superb paintings – elegiac landscapes by **Cuyp**, one of the world's finest **Poussin** series and splendid works by Hogarth, Murillo and Rubens. There's an unusually cloudy **Canaletto** of Walton Bridge on the Thames, **Rembrandt**'s tiny *Portrait of a Young Man*, a top-class portrait of poet, playwright and Royalist, the future Earl of Bristol, by **Van Dyck**, and a moving one of his much lamented kinswoman by marriage, Venetia Stanley, on her deathbed. Among the gallery's fine array of **Gainsborough** portraits are his famous *Linley Sisters*, sittings for which were interrupted by the elopement of one of them with the playwright Sheridan, and a likeness of Samuel Linley that's said to have been painted in less than an hour. There are regular special exhibitions, for which there is an extra charge.

Horniman Museum

100 London Rd • Daily 10.30am–5.30pm • Museum free; Aquarium £6, free on the first Tues of the month 4–5.30pm • ☎ 020 8699 1872, ⓦ horniman.ac.uk • Forest Hill train station from Victoria or London Bridge

The wonderful **Horniman Museum** was purpose-built in 1901 by Frederick Horniman, a tea trader with a passion for collecting. The building itself is a striking edifice designed by Charles Harrison Townsend, architect of the Whitechapel Gallery. Its most arresting features are the massive clock tower, with its smoothly rounded bastions and circular cornice, and the polychrome mosaic of allegorical figures in classical dress on the facade.

Entry to the museum is from the **gardens** to the west, where you'll find turkeys, goats and hens, a sunken water garden and a graceful Victorian conservatory, brought here from the Horniman mansion in Croydon. Entry to the museum is free, except for the state-of-the-art **Aquarium** in the basement, featuring everything from British pond life to tropical jellyfish, sea horses and monkey frogs.

The collections

A ramp leads down from the foyer to the **Natural History** collection of stuffed animals and birds – everything from a half-dissected pigeon to an ostrich – and their skeletons, with pride of place going to the Horniman Walrus, lying flat out on a mocked-up iceberg. On the lower ground floor, head first for the dimly lit **Centenary Gallery**, which contains an eclectic ethnographic collection, much of it gathered by Horniman himself, from the precious butterflies that started his obsession at the age of 8 to a papier-mâché figure of Kali dancing on Siva. Equally arresting are the more recent acquisitions like the Nigerian puppets of Charles, Di and a British bobby, or the "ugly masks" used to chase the winter away in the Alps.

The **African Worlds** gallery contains a wide-ranging anthropological collection from African masks and voodoo altars to Egyptian sarcophagi and Sudanese dung bowls. In the **Music Gallery** you can see and hear more than 1500 instruments including Chinese gongs and electric guitars, or have a go at some of the instruments yourself in the hands-on room. Look out for the special sessions at the **Hands On Base**, which allow you to handle and learn more about a whole range of the museum's artefacts.

Crystal Palace

Museum Anerley Hill • Sat & Sun 11am–3.30pm • Free **Park** Daily 7.30am–dusk • Free • ☎ 020 8676 0700, ⓦ crystalpalacemuseum .org.uk • Crystal Palace train station

After the 1851 Great Exhibition (see p.244), the **Crystal Palace** was enlarged and re-erected on the commanding heights of Sydenham Hill, to the south of Dulwich, affording spectacular views over London, Kent and Surrey. A fantastic pleasure garden was laid out around this giant glasshouse, with a complex system of fountains, some of which reached a height of 250ft. Exhibitions, funfairs, ballooning, a pneumatic railway

21

and a whole range of events were staged here. Despite its initial success, though, the palace soon became a financial liability – then, in 1936, the entire structure burnt to the ground overnight.

All that remains now are the stone terraces, the triumphal staircase, a few sphinxes and a small **museum** on nearby Anerley Hill that tells the history of the place. Nowadays, the **park** is dominated by a TV transmitter, visible from all over London, and the **National Sports Centre**, whose tartan athletics track (Europe's first) was opened in the 1960s and where some 21 world records were set in the following two decades. The stadium stands on the site of the old Crystal Palace football ground, where the FA Cup Final was held from 1895 to 1914. There are further reminders of the park's Victorian heyday in and around **Lower Lake**, in the southeast corner of the park, whose islands feature around thirty life-sized **dinosaurs** lurking in the undergrowth, built out of brick and iron. Look out, too, for the circular hornbeam **Maze**, London's largest, originally established in 1872 and replanted in 1988.

Greenwich

Greenwich is the one area in southeast London that draws tourists out from the centre in considerable numbers. At its heart is the outstanding architectural set piece of the **Old Royal Naval College** and the **Queen's House**, courtesy of Christopher Wren and Inigo Jones respectively. Most visitors, however, come to see the **National Maritime Museum** and the **Royal Observatory** in Greenwich Park. With the added attractions of its riverside pubs and walks – plus startling views across to Canary Wharf and Docklands – it makes for one of the best weekend trips in the capital.

ARRIVAL AND INFORMATION

By DLR and train Greenwich can be reached by train from Charing Cross, Waterloo East or London Bridge (every 15–30min), or by Docklands Light Railway (DLR) from Bank or Tower Gateway direct to Cutty Sark DLR station. For the best view of the Wren buildings, get out at Island Gardens station to admire the view across the river, and then take the Greenwich Foot Tunnel under the Thames.

By boat The most scenic and leisurely way to reach Greenwich is to take a boat from one of the piers in central London (every 20–30min).

Information Greenwich tourist information centre (daily 10am–5pm; ☎ 0870 608 2000) is located in Pepys House in the Discover Greenwich centre.

Greenwich Market

Wed–Sun 10am–5.30pm • Ⓦ greenwich-market.co.uk • Cutty Sark DLR

Greenwich town centre was laid out in the 1820s, hence the Nash-style terraces of Nelson Road, College Approach and King William Walk, and is now a one-way system plagued with heavy traffic. However, at the centre of these busy streets, filled with nautical knick-knack shops and bookshops, stands **Greenwich Market** an old covered market where you can still see the wonderfully Victorian inscription on one of the archways: "A false balance is abomination to the Lord, but a just weight is his delight." Stalls differ on each day: food and homewares (Wed), antiques and crafts (Thurs & Fri), and food and crafts (Sat & Sun).

St Alfege's Church

Greenwich Church St • Mon, Tues, Thurs & Fri 9.30am–4pm, Sat 11.30am–4pm, Sun noon–4pm • ☎ 020 8853 0687, Ⓦ st-alfege.org • Cutty Sark DLR

Rising above the town centre is the Doric portico and broken pediment of Nicholas Hawksmoor's **St Alfege's Church**, built in 1712–18 to replace a twelfth-century structure in which Henry VIII was baptized and Thomas Tallis, the "father of English church music", was buried. The church was flattened in the Blitz, but its lovely wooden galleries and its trompe-l'oeil coffered apse, originally by Thornhill, have since been magnificently restored.

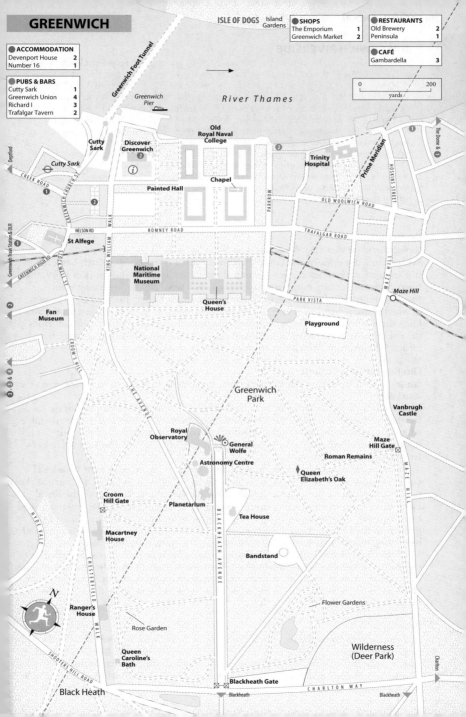

21

GREENWICH RIVERSIDE

A fine vantage point for viewing the Old Royal Naval College is the **Five-Foot Walk**, which squeezes between the college railings and the riverbank. It was here that George I, Elector of Hannover (and a Protestant), landed to take the throne on September 18, 1714, though it was estimated that over fifty other (Catholic) cousins had a better claim. If you're in need of riverside refreshment, drop into the Regency-style **Trafalgar Tavern** (see p.398), at the east end of the walk. Just beyond the pub down Crane Street is the **Trinity Hospital**, founded in 1613 by the Earl of Northampton for 21 pensioners; the entry requirements declared the hospital would admit "no common beggar, drunkard, whore-hunter, nor unclean person…nor any that is blind…nor any idiot". The cream-coloured mock-Gothic facade and chapel (which contains the earl's tomb) date from the nineteenth century, but the courtyard of almshouses remains much as it was at its foundation. Beyond the Trinity Hospital, the Thames Path continues along the river, past a few more pubs, and eventually all the way to the Dome (aka the O2).

Cutty Sark

Greenwich Church St • ☎ 020 8858 2698, ⓦ www.cuttysark.org.uk • Cutty Sark DLR

Wedged in a dry dock by the Greenwich Foot Tunnel is the majestic **Cutty Sark**, the world's last surviving tea clipper. Launched from the Clydeside shipyards in 1869, the *Cutty Sark* was actually more famous in its day as a wool clipper, returning from Australia in just 72 days. The vessel's name comes from Robert Burns' *Tam O'Shanter*, in which Tam, a drunken farmer, is chased by Nannie, an angry witch in a short Paisley linen dress, or "cutty sark"; the clipper's figurehead shows her clutching the hair from the tail of Tam's horse. The ship has been closed for over five years for restoration and repairs following a fire in 2007, but will reopen in 2012.

Old Royal Naval College

Cutty Sark Gardens • Grounds daily 8am–6pm; buildings daily 10am – 5pm • Free • ☎ 020 8269 4747, ⓦ oldroyalnavalcollege.org • Cutty Sark DLR

It's entirely appropriate that the one London building that makes the most of its riverbank location should be the **Old Royal Naval College**, a majestic Baroque ensemble which opens out onto the Thames. Despite the symmetry and grace of the four buildings, which perfectly frame the Queen's House beyond, the whole complex has a strange and piecemeal history.

The first of the four blocks was built in the 1660s as a **royal palace** for Charles II, but the money ran out. William and Mary preferred Hampton Court and turned the Greenwich building into a **Royal Hospital for Seamen**, along the lines of the Royal Hospital in Chelsea. Wren, working for nothing, then had his original designs vetoed by the queen, who insisted the new development must not obscure the view of the river from the Queen's House – what you see now is Wren's revised plan, augmented by, among others, Hawksmoor and Vanbrugh. The naval hospital moved out in 1869, to be replaced by the **Royal Naval College**, which, in turn, was supplanted by the current incumbents, the **University of Greenwich** and **Trinity College of Music**. The two grandest rooms, situated underneath Wren's twin domes, are open to the public and well worth visiting, and there's an exhibition on the history of the area called **Discover Greenwich.**

Painted Hall

The magnificent **Painted Hall**, in the west wing, is dominated by James Thornhill's gargantuan allegorical ceiling painting, which depicts William and Mary enthroned, with a vanquished Louis XIV clutching a broken sword. Equally remarkable are Thornhill's trompe-l'oeil fluted pilasters and decorative detailing, while on the far wall, behind the high table, Thornhill himself appears (bottom right) beside George I and family, with St Paul's in the background. Designed as the sailors' dining hall, it was later used for Nelson's lying-in-state in 1806 and then as a naval art gallery.

21

Chapel

The **Chapel** (service Sun 11am), in the east wing, was designed by James Stuart, after a fire in 1779 destroyed its predecessor. However, it is Stuart's assistant, William Newton, whom we have to thank for the chapel's exquisite pastel and sky-blue plasterwork and spectacular decorative detailing, among the finest in London. The altarpiece, by Benjamin West, depicts St Paul wrestling with the viper that leapt out of the fire after he was shipwrecked off Malta.

Discover Greenwich

If you're interested in Greenwich's rich history, you can get a good overview at **Discover Greenwich**, in the Pepys Building, which has a permanent exhibition on the area. Among the museum's prize possessions are *Beer* and *Gin*, two oak sculptures from the buttery screen of old Greenwich Palace. Adults can learn about scagliola and Coade stone, while junior Christopher Wrens can build their own version of Greenwich with building blocks. The building also contains a tourist information office and the Royal Hospital's old brewhouse, which used to supply a ration of three pints to each seaman, and has now been revived and turned into a micro-brewery (see p.398).

National Maritime Museum

Romney Rd • Daily 10am–5pm • Free • ☎ 020 8858 4422, ⓦ nmm.ac.uk • Cutty Sark DLR

The main building of the **National Maritime Museum** is centred on a glass-roofed courtyard and occupies the west wing of the former Naval Asylum. Ranged over three floors, the permanent **maritime galleries** and special exhibitions here are imaginatively designed to appeal to visitors of all ages, with plenty of hands-on stuff to keep children amused.

The museum also runs two other sights: the **Queen's House**, a beautiful Palladian villa used to display the cream of the museum's vast maritime art collection, located close by the main building (see p.318), and the **Royal Observatory**, perched on the hill in the adjacent park (see p.320).

Level G: Royal Barge and Explorers

With a gallery at its centre, used for special exhibitions, the museum has created several "streets" along the sides, which house some of the museum's largest artefacts, among them the splendid 63-foot-long **Royal Barge**, a gilded Rococo confection designed by William Kent for Prince Frederick, the much-unloved eldest son of George II.

The one permanent gallery, **Explorers**, takes you from the Vikings to Franklin's attempt to discover the Northwest Passage; on display are the relics recovered from the Arctic by John Rae in 1854, many of which had to be bought from the local Inuit.

Level 1: Nauticalia, Trade & Empire

The Upper Deck, on Level 1, houses the museum café, and is lined with cabinets filled with beautiful nauticalia from ship's badges and astrolabes to brass lamps and naval

---

ALL CHANGE AT THE NATIONAL MARITIME MUSEUM

The **National Maritime Museum** (NMM) seems to have been in a constant state of flux since the new millennium. As a national museum, the NMM remains free, but as of 2011 the Royal Observatory has been charging admission. Meanwhile the NMM's **Sammy Ofer Wing** has opened, with more space for special exhibitions, an archive research centre, a larger café-brasserie and a permanent gallery, **Voyagers**, focusing on Britain's relationship with the sea. And finally, in 2013, a new Nelson, the Navy and Nation gallery will open.

21

ROYAL GREENWICH

The history of Greenwich is replete with **royal connections**. Edward I appears to have been the first of the English kings to have stayed here, though there was nothing resembling a palace until Henry V's brother, the Duke of Gloucester, built **Bella Court** (later known as the Palace of Placentia) in 1447. Henry VI honeymooned here with his new wife, Margaret of Anjou, and eventually took over the place and rebuilt it in her honour. However, it was under the Tudors that the riverside palace enjoyed its royal heyday. **Henry VIII** was born there and made it his main base, pouring even more money into it than into Hampton Court. He added armouries, a banqueting hall and a huge tiltyard, hunted in the extensive grounds and kept a watchful eye over proceedings at the nearby **Royal Dockyards** in Deptford. His children, Mary and Elizabeth, were both born here.

Edward VI came to Greenwich in 1553 to try to restore his frail health, but died shortly afterwards. Mary came here rarely as queen, and on one of her few visits had the wall of her personal apartment blasted away by a cannonball fired in salute. For Elizabeth, Greenwich was the **chief summer residence**, and it was here in 1573 that she revived the Maundy Ceremony, washing the feet of 39 poor women (though only after three others had washed them first). The royal palace fell into disrepair during the 1650s Commonwealth, when it was turned into a biscuit factory, and was finally torn down by Charles II to make way for a new edifice, which eventually became the Royal Naval College.

---

swords. **Atlantic Worlds** focuses on the history of the trade links with the New World, from slavery to whaling. While you're here, don't miss the **stained glass** from the **Baltic Exchange**, a colourful 1920s memorial salvaged from the Baltic Exchange in the City, after it was blown up by the IRA in 1992.

Level 2: Hands-on galleries

Level 2 is the place to head if you've got children, as it boasts two excellent hands-on galleries. **The Bridge** is aimed at all ages, as it really does take some skill to navigate a catamaran, a paddle steamer and a rowing boat to shore. **All Hands** is aimed at a younger audience, and gives kids a taste of life on the seas, loading miniature cargo, firing a cannon, learning to use Morse code and so forth.

Also on this level is the **Oceans of Discovery** gallery, which concentrates on the voyages of Cook, Scott and Shackleton. Cook's K1 marine chronometer is here and there's a replica of the *James Caird*, in which Shackleton made the epic 700-mile journey from Elephant Island to South Georgia, plus lots of Scott memorabilia: his overshoes, his watch, his funky sledging goggles and a basic sketch of his planned route scrawled on some hotel notepaper. Finally, **Ship of War** displays the museum's collection of model sailing warships (1650–1815), most made by the Navy Board at the same time as the ships they represent.

Queen's House

Daily 10am–5pm • Free • ☎ 020 8858 4422, ⓦ nmm.ac.uk • Cutty Sark DLR

Inigo Jones's **Queen's House**, originally built on a cramped site amid the Tudor royal palace, is now the focal point of the Greenwich ensemble. As royal residences go, it's an unassuming little Palladian country house, "solid…masculine and unaffected" in Jones's own words. Its significance in terms of British architecture, however, is immense. Commissioned in 1616, it was the first Neoclassical building in the country, signifying a clear break with all that preceded it. The interior, exterior and setting of the Queen's House have all changed radically since Jones's day, making it difficult to imagine the impact the building must have had when it was built. The house is now linked to its neighbouring buildings by open colonnades, added in the early part of the nineteenth century along the course of the muddy road which the H-shaped block originally straddled.

Inside, very few features survive from Stuart times. The **Great Hall**, a perfect cube, remains, but Orazio Gentileschi's ceiling paintings were removed to Marlborough

House by the Duchess of Marlborough during the reign of Queen Anne. The southeastern corner of the hall leads to the beautiful **Tulip Staircase**, Britain's earliest cantilevered spiral staircase, whose name derives from the floral patterning in the wrought-iron balustrade. The only other significant interior decoration is upstairs, in the room intended as the bedchamber of Charles I and Henrietta Maria, which retains its ceiling decoration from the 1630s.

The art collection

The rooms of the Queen's House now provide a permanent home for the museum's vast **art collection**. Downstairs, there are paintings, portraits and models illustrating the history of royal Greenwich. Upstairs, in among the naval battles and portraits of admirals, there are works by the likes of Reynolds, Hogarth, Gainsborough, Lely, Kneller and Myrtens, as well as twentieth-century works by official war artists, plus one by Lowry and even an Alfred Wallis. Look out, too, for the oil paintings by the official artists on board Cook's last two voyages to the Pacific, Thornhill's portrait of an eldritch naval pensioner – the sort who would have inhabited the Royal Hospital for Seamen – and Zoffany's unfinished, nightmarish *Death of Captain Cook*. There's a typically infatuated portrait of Lady Hamilton as Aridane by Romney, a Canaletto of Greenwich, painted from Island Gardens, and the only major British portrait of (a wistful and dreamy) Napoleon, painted while he was a prisoner on board the *Bellerophon*. Back downstairs, one room is usually set aside for Turner's *Battle of Trafalgar, 21st October, 1805*, his largest work and only royal commission, which was intended for St James's Palace.

Greenwich Park

Daily 6am to dusk • ⓦ royalparks.gov.uk • Cutty Sark or Greenwich DLR

Greenwich Park is one of the city's oldest royal parks, having been enclosed in the fifteenth century by the Duke of Gloucester, who fancied it as a hunting ground. Henry VIII was particularly fond of the place, introducing deer in 1515, as well as archery and jousting tournaments, and sword-fighting contests. The park was opened to the public in the eighteenth century, but it was only after the arrival of the railway in 1838 that it began to attract Londoners in great numbers. In 1894, a young **French anarchist** called Martial Bourdin was killed in the park, outside the Royal Observatory, when the bomb he was carrying in a brown-paper bag exploded. Joseph Conrad used the unexplained incident as the inspiration for his novel *The Secret Agent*.

The descendants of Henry's deer are now safely enclosed within **The Wilderness**, a fenced area in the southeast corner where they laze around "tame as children", in Henry James's words. Don't miss **Vanbrugh Castle**, halfway down Maze Hill, on the east side of the park, England's first mock-medieval castle, designed by the architect John Vanbrugh as his private residence in 1726. Note, too, **Queen Caroline's Bath**, by the park's southern wall, which is all that remains of the house where the queen used to hold her famous orgies – the rest of the house was destroyed by her estranged husband George IV after she left the country in 1804. If you're heading for the Ranger's House, the best approach is via the semicircular **Rose Garden**, laid out in front of it, which is worth a visit itself from June to August.

General Wolfe

One of the park's chief delights is the view over to the Isle of Dogs from the steep hill crowned by a statue of **General James Wolfe** (1727–59), who spent part of his childhood in Greenwich, lived near the park, and is buried in St Alfege. Wolfe is famed for the audacious campaign in which he captured Quebec from the French in 1759, a battle in which he and his opposite number, General Montcalm, were both mortally wounded. Victory celebrations took place throughout England, but were forbidden in Greenwich out of respect for Wolfe's mother, who had also lost her husband only a few months previously.

21

GREENWICH MEAN TIME

Greenwich's greatest claim to fame is of course as the home of **Greenwich Mean Time (GMT)** and the **Prime Meridian** – a meridian being any north–south line used as a basis for astronomical observations, and therefore also for the calculation of longitude and time. In 1884, the International Meridian Conference in Washington DC agreed to make Greenwich the Prime Meridian of the World – in other words, **zero longitude**. As a result, the entire world sets its clocks in relation to GMT.

In many spheres of life and countries across the globe, GMT has been usurped by **Coordinated Universal Time (UTC)**, which is the same as GMT, except that it is more accurately calculated using atomic clocks and therefore better for sub-second precision. Even the meridian has moved slightly, since the global standard for air and sea navigation is now based on the **Global Positioning System (GPS)**, which makes its calculations from the centre of the earth, not the surface, and places the meridian approximately 336ft to the east of the observatory's red strip.

Royal Observatory

Blackheath Ave • **Astronomy Centre** Daily 10am–5pm • Free **Flamsteed House** Daily 10am–5pm • £10 **Planetarium** Mon–Fri 12.45–3.45pm; Sat & Sun & school holidays 11am–4pm • £6.50 • ☎ 020 8858 4422, ⓦ nmm.ac.uk • Greenwich DLR/train station

Established by Charles II in 1675, the **Royal Observatory** is the longest-established scientific institution in Britain. The chief task of John Flamsteed, the first Astronomer Royal, was to study the night sky in order to discover an astronomical method of finding the longitude of a ship at sea, the lack of which was causing enormous problems for the emerging British Empire. Astronomers continued to work here at Greenwich until the postwar smog and light pollution forced them to decamp to Herstmonceux Castle in Sussex; the observatory, meanwhile, is now a very popular museum.

Flamsteed House

The oldest part of the observatory is **Flamsteed House**, designed by Wren (himself a trained astronomer) "for the observator's habitation and a little for pompe". The northeastern turret sports a bright-red **Time Ball** that climbs the mast at 12.58pm and drops at 1pm GMT precisely; it was added in 1833 to allow ships on the Thames to set their clocks. The red strip in the observatory's main courtyard is the **Meridian Line**, and at night a green laser beam shines northwards along the meridian. On the house's balcony overlooking the Thames, you can take a look at a **Camera Obscura**, of the kind which Flamsteed used to make safe observations of the sun.

Inside, beyond the **Astronomer Royal's apartments** in which the cantankerous Flamsteed lived, you eventually reach the impressive **Octagon Room**, built so that the king could show off his astronomical toys to guests. The ceiling plasterwork is all that remains of the original decor, but there are replicas of the precision clocks installed behind the original walnut panelling in 1676.

Time Galleries

The **Time Galleries** focus on the search for longitude and display the first four marine chronometers built by **John Harrison**. Harrison eventually went on to win the £20,000 **Longitude Prize** in 1763 with his giant pocket watch, H4 – the only one that no longer functions – after much skulduggery against his claims, most notably by the Astronomer Royal at the time, Nevil Maskelyne (a story wonderfully told by Dava Sobel in her book *Longitude*). Downstairs you can learn about the story of GMT, UTC and even GPS, as well as viewing the electrical contacts that used to provide the hourly six pips for the BBC and listening to three generations of the speaking clock.

FROM TOP GREENWICH PARK AND THE ROYAL OBSERVATORY (P.320); PAINTED HALL, OLD ROYAL NAVAL COLLEGE (P.316) >

21

Meridian Building

Flamsteed carried out more than 30,000 observations – "nothing can exceed the tediousness and ennui of the life" was his dispirited description of the job – in the Quadrant House, which now forms part of the **Meridian Building**. Edmond Halley, who succeeded Flamsteed as Astronomer Royal, bought more sophisticated quadrants, sextants, spyglasses and telescopes, which are among those displayed in the **Quadrant Room**. With the aid of his 8ft iron quadrant he applied historical astronomy methods to predict the next appearance of the eponymous comet – though he never lived to see it. Next door, you'll find **Bradley's Meridian**, used for Ordnance Survey maps since 1801. Finally, you reach a room that's sliced in two by the present-day Greenwich Meridian, fixed by the cross hairs in "Airy's Transit Circle", the astronomical instrument that dominates the room.

Astronomy Centre and Planetarium

Housed in the fanciful, domed terracotta South Building, built in the 1890s, the **Astronomy Centre** houses hi-tech galleries giving a brief rundown of the Big Bang theory of the universe. You can conduct some hands-on experiments to explore concepts such as gravity and spectroscopy, and you're then invited to consider the big questions of astronomy today. You can also choose to watch one of the thirty-minute presentations in the state-of-the-art **Planetarium**, introduced by a Royal Observatory astronomer.

Ranger's House

By guided tour only April–Sept Mon–Wed & Sun 11.30am & 2.30pm (1hr 30min) • EH • £6.30 • ☎ 020 8853 0035 • Greenwich DLR or Blackheath train station

In the southern corner of Greenwich park is the **Ranger's House**, a red-brick Georgian villa which looks out over Blackheath. Built as a private residence, it became the official residence of the park ranger (hence its name), a sort of top-notch grace-and-favour home. The house currently displays the private collection of **Julius Wernher** (1850–1912), an Edwardian German-born millionaire who made his money by exploiting the

---

THE DOME

[A] yellow-spiked Teflon tent… a genetically modified mollusc… The Dome is a blob of correction fluid, a flick of Tipp-Ex to revise the mistakes of nineteenth-century industrialists… a poached egg designed by a committee of vegans.   Iain Sinclair, Sorry Meniscus

Clearly visible from Greenwich's riverside and park is the marquee-like former **Millennium Dome**: over half a mile in circumference and 160ft in height, it's the world's largest dome, held up by a dozen, 300ft, yellow steel masts. Built in 2000 at a cost of £800 million, it housed the Millennium Experience exhibition, which was panned by critics and dismantled after one year.

Since then entertainment giants AEG spent another £600 million turning it into **The O2** (ⓦ theo2.co.uk), a mall of restaurants and bars, a museum space (currently occupied by the British Music Experience (ⓦ britishmusicexperience.com), a nightclub, a multiplex cinema, and, occupying 40 percent of the Dome, the 23,000-seater **O2 Arena**, venue for the 2012 Olympic gymnastics and basketball. Meanwhile, the land to the southeast is being transformed into the Millennium Village, a conglomeration of riverside flats, plus the mini-wetlands of the **Greenwich Peninsula Ecology Park** (Wed–Sun 10am–5pm; free).

The easiest way to get to the Dome is to take the tube to **North Greenwich**, as the Dome has its very own Will Alsop-designed tube station (with a bus station by Norman Foster). It's also possible to walk or cycle the mile and a half along the riverside pathway from Greenwich or you can catch a boat to the **QEII Pier** by the Dome. From 2012, the most spectacular way to reach the dome will be by **cable car** across the Thames from the Royal Victoria Dock (Royal Victoria DLR), near ExCel London. The Dome itself is fenced off, but you can walk around the outside and admire the odd work of art: Anthony Gormley's very busy *Quantum Cloud* and Richard Wilson's *Slice of Reality*, the bridge of a boat cut away from its mother ship.

diamond deposits of South Africa, and at his death was one of the world's richest men. His taste in art is eclectic, ranging from medieval ivory miniatures to Iznik pottery, though he was definitely a man who placed technical virtuosity above artistic merit, and who, despite his Lutheran upbringing, amassed a vast array of Catholic bric-a-brac. Highlights on the top floor include Memlinc's *Virgin and Child*, the jewellery cabinet and the pair of sixteenth-century majolica dishes decorated with mythological scenes for Isabella d'Este, wife of the Marchese of Mantua and a great patron of the arts.

Downstairs, there's a sparkling Reynolds portrait of Lady Caroline Price, a top-notch de Hooch interior, and, in the splendid main gallery with its three bow windows and duck-egg-green coffered ceiling, a whole series of seventeenth-century French tapestries depicting life in the court of the Emperor of China. Finally, at the far end of the main gallery is Bergonzoli's striking *Love of Angels*, a highly charged sculpture that, despite weighing two tons, succeeds in appearing light and ethereal.

Fan Museum

12 Crooms Hill • Tues–Sat 11am–5pm, Sun noon–5pm • £4 • ☎ 020 8305 1441, ⓦ fan-museum.org • Greenwich DLR

At the bottom of Croom's Hill, you'll find the **Fan Museum.** It's a fascinating little place (and an extremely beautiful house), revealing the importance of the fan as a social and political document. The permanent exhibition on the ground floor traces the history of the fan and the materials employed, from peacock feathers to straw, while temporary exhibitions on the first floor explore conditions of production, the fan's link with the Empire and changing fashion. Outside, there's a tearoom, housed in the kitsch, hand-painted orangery, with afternoon tea served (Wed & Sun 3pm).

Blackheath

South of Greenwich lies the well-to-do former village of **Blackheath** (so-called because of the colour of the soil), whose bleak, windswept heath, crisscrossed with busy roads, couldn't be more different from the adjacent royal park. Nonetheless, with its pair of century-old pubs, the *Princess of Wales* and *Hare and Billet*, each set beside a pond, it can be pleasant on a summer afternoon. The odd fair takes place here on public holidays, and it's south London's chief kite-flying spot.

Lying on the main road to Dover, Blackheath was a convenient spot on which to pitch camp, as the Danes did in 1011, having kidnapped St Alfege. During the **1381 Peasants' Revolt** Wat Tyler's rebels were treated to a rousing revolutionary sermon by John Bull, which included the famous lines "When Adam delved and Eve span, who was then the gentleman?" **Henry V** was welcomed back from the Battle of Agincourt here in 1415, while Henry VII fought the Cornish rebels here in 1497. It was at Blackheath, also, that Henry VIII suffered disappointment on meeting his fourth wife, **Anne of Cleves**, in 1540; he famously referred to her as "the Flanders mare" and filed for divorce after just six months.

The heath's chief landmark is the rugged Kentish ragstone **All Saints' Church**, a Victorian church which nestles in a slight depression in the south corner. The most striking building on the heath, though, is **The Paragon**, to the east, a crescent of four-storey Georgian mansions linked by Doric colonnades. An even earlier ensemble, set in its own grounds further east, is **Morden College**, the aristocrat of almshouses, built in 1695 for "decayed Turkey merchants" who'd lost their fortunes. The quadrangular red-brick building, built by Wren's master mason, was designed to reflect the lost status of its original inhabitants.

Reminiscence Centre

11 Blackheath Village • Mon–Fri 10am–5pm, Sat 10am–4pm • Free • ☎ 020 8318 9105, ⓦ age-exchange.org.uk • Blackheath train station from London Bridge

It's worth venturing down the charmingly named Tranquil Vale into the village-like centre of Blackheath, if only to visit the **Reminiscence Centre**, situated opposite the train station. A favourite with the older folks of Blackheath, the centrepiece is an

21

DOWN IN DEPTFORD

Deptford, just west of Greenwich, is never going to be high up anyone's list of places to visit in London. However, it does have a rich history thanks to the **Royal Dockyards**, which existed here (and at Woolwich) from 1513 until 1869. It was at Deptford in 1581 that Francis Drake moored the *Golden Hinde* (see p.229) after circumnavigating the globe, had Elizabeth I on board for dinner, and was knighted for his efforts. And it was in Deptford that the playwright **Christopher Marlowe** was murdered (possibly) in the company of three men who had links with the criminal underworld and the Elizabethan intelligence service.

All that remains of the old dockyards today are a few officers' quarters hidden in the Pepys housing estate, and the **Master Shipwright's House** of 1708, at the bottom of Watergate Street – a little downstream, there's even a waterfront statue of Peter the Great (flanked by a dwarf and an empty chair), who came to Deptford in 1798 to learn about shipbuilding. You can get an idea of how prosperous the area once was just off the High Street at **St Paul's Church**, the local architectural gem, designed by Thomas Archer in 1720, whose interior Pevsner described as "closer to Borromini and the Roman Baroque than any other English church".

---

old-fashioned shop counter, whose drawers are filled with two-pin plugs, wooden clothes pegs, chalk powder and a whole host of everyday objects now rarely seen. Ask for a demonstration of the shop's rare surviving example of a rapid-wire cash system, via which banknotes could be whizzed from cashier to till worker. Out the back, you can get a cuppa from the museum's period tuck shop.

Woolwich

In 1847, a visitor to **Woolwich** commented that it was the "dirtiest, filthiest and most thoroughly mismanaged town of its size in the kingdom". With its docks and factories defunct, Woolwich remains one of the poorest parts of the old Docklands. However, if you have a fascination for military history, it's worth exploring the old dockyards and arsenal, for their architecture and the **Firepower** artillery museum. The other reason to come to Woolwich is to visit the **Thames Barrier**, an awesome piece of modern engineering and the largest movable flood barrier in the world.

ARRIVAL AND DEPARTURE

By DLR and train The easiest way to reach Woolwich is by DLR from Canning Town tube; you can also take a train from London Bridge to Woolwich Dockyard (for the Royal Artillery Barracks) or Woolwich Arsenal (for the Royal Arsenal).

By boat During the week, there's a limited commuter boat service to and from Woolwich Arsenal, and at the weekend a more regular service; there are also boat trips that cruise round the barrier (see ⓦ tfl.gov.uk for details).

Royal Arsenal

Close to Woolwich Arsenal DLR station, on the market square is **Beresford Gateway**, built in 1828 as the Arsenal's main entrance, but now separated from the rest of the complex to the north by busy Beresford Street/Plumstead Road.

Across the road, you enter **Dial Square**, overlooked by some of the most historic buildings, built by the likes of Vanbrugh, Wren and Hawksmoor: the Main Guard House, with its eighteenth-century Doric portico; Verbruggen's House, opposite, begun in 1772, and former residence of the Master Founder; and the Royal Brass Foundry, made of wood, but encased in brick, from 1717. To the north, the **Dial Arch Block** is distinguished by its central archway, sporting a sundial, pillars and a pile of cannonballs. A football on a plinth commemorates the fact that it was here in 1886 that a group of machinists formed Dial Square Football Club, later Woolwich Arsenal FC, and then just **Arsenal FC**, eventually moving to Highbury in north London. The team used to get changed in the toilets of the *Royal Oak* (now the *Pullman*), 27 Woolwich New Rd, right by Woolwich Arsenal train station.

Greenwich Heritage Centre

Tues–Sat 9am–5pm • Free • ☎ 020 8854 2452, ⓦ greenwichheritage.org • Woolwich Arsenal DLR

If you head down Number One Street, towards the river, you'll come to the **Greenwich Heritage Centre**, on the left, which houses a small permanent exhibition on the history of the Arsenal. Next door is the distinctive eighteenth-century brown-brick building that served as the Royal Military Academy, from 1741 until 1806, when new barracks were built.

Firepower: Royal Artillery Museum

April–Oct Wed–Sun 10.30am–5pm; Nov–March Fri–Sun 10.30am–5pm • £5.30; Camo Zone £1.50 • ☎ 020 8855 7755, ⓦ firepower .org.uk • Woolwich Arsenal DLR

Firepower, the Royal Artillery Museum, is housed, appropriately enough, in a former bomb factory. To enjoy the museum, you do have to be seriously into **guns** – lots of them. Inevitably, there's a propaganda video on today's Royal Artillery, along with a twenty-minute multimedia show, *Field of Fire*, concentrating on the chief conflicts of the twentieth century. The main **Gunnery Hall** features ancient World War I field guns, old and new howitzers, anti-tank guns, Thunderbird guided-missile launchers and Rapier surface-to-air missiles used in the Gulf War, and allows you to play various war games, fire simulator guns and watch lots of wartime film clips. Upstairs, the **History Gallery** takes you through the history of artillery and rocket science, features the gun carriage used in the funeral cortège for Georges V and VI, and includes the Medals Gallery. Finally, at the **Camo Zone**, you can have a go at the bungee run, test your marksmanship on the firing range and take part in a tank battle.

Royal Artillery Barracks

The **Royal Artillery Barracks,** half a mile to the south of the Royal Arsenal, are seen as the traditional home of the Royal Artillery, although the last artillery regiment moved out in 2007. Completed in 1802 by James Wyatt, the barracks' three-storey Georgian facade, interrupted by stucco pavilions and a central triumphal arch, runs for an amazing 1080ft, making it one of the longest in Europe. Appropriately enough, the barracks was chosen to host the shooting competition during the 2012 Olympics.

The barracks face south onto the grassy parade ground, to the east of which lies the abandoned **Garrison Church of St George**, built in neo-Romanesque style in 1863. Gutted in the last war, it's now an attractive husk, with fragments of its colourful interior decor still surviving. To the west of the Royal Artillery Barracks, off Repository Road, stands John Nash's bizarre Chinese-style **Rotunda** (closed to the public). Originally used as a marquee in the gardens of Carlton House during the celebrations at the end of the Napoleonic Wars, it was damaged by a gas explosion, repaired and re-erected on its present site.

MILITARY WOOLWICH

Woolwich, like Deptford, owes its existence to its **Royal Dockyards**, founded here in 1513 by Henry VIII. The men-of-war that established England as a world naval power were built in these dockyards: the *Great Harry*, the largest ship in the world, was launched from here in 1514; Walter Ralegh and Captain Cook set out from Woolwich on their voyages of discovery. The docks closed in 1869, and the area is better known for the **Royal Arsenal**, which reached its heyday during World War I, when it stretched for 3 miles along the Thames, employed nearly 100,000 workers (half of whom were women) and had its own internal railway system. The ordnance factories were closed altogether in 1967, and council housing built over much of the site. However, a fine collection of mostly eighteenth-century buildings survives and has been converted into flats, plus a couple of museums.

21

Royal Military Academy

On the south side of Woolwich Common stands James Wyatt's former **Royal Military Academy**, completed in 1806 in an imposing mock-Tudor style as a foil to his Royal Artillery Barracks (see above). The 720ft facade faces north onto a parade ground, with an imitation of the Tower of London's White Tower as its centrepiece. The academy, known as "The Shop" in the British Army – because its first building was a converted workshop in the Arsenal – closed in 1939, and merged with Sandhurst after the war.

Thames Barrier

Unity Way · Thurs–Sun: April–Sept 10.30am–5pm; Oct–March 11am–3.30pm · £3.50 · ☎ 020 8305 4188, ⓦ theenvironment-agency .gov.uk · Charlton or Woolwich Dockyard train station

London has been subject to flooding from surge tides since before 1236, when it was reported that in "the great Palace of Westminster men did row with wherries in the midst of the Hall". A flood barrier was advocated as far back as the 1850s, but it was only after the 1953 flood that serious consideration was given to defences. Opened in 1982, the **Thames Barrier** is a mind-blowing feat of engineering, with its gleaming fins and movable steel gates weighing 3300 tons. If you want to find out more, head for the **information centre**, on Unity Way, where glossy models and macho videos help explain the basic mechanism of the barrier (by no means obvious from above the water). If you want to see the barrier in action, phone ahead to find out the date of the monthly test.

Eltham Palace

Court Yard · Mon–Wed & Sun: April–Oct 10am–5pm; Nov–March 10am–4pm · EH · £9.30, gardens only £5.80 · ☎ 020 8294 2548, ⓦ elthampalace.org.uk · Eltham train station from Victoria, London Bridge or Charing Cross

Eltham Palace was one of the country's foremost medieval royal residences and even a venue for Parliament for some two hundred years from the reign of Edward II. All that remains now is the fifteenth-century bridge across what used to be the moat, and the **Great Hall**, built by Edward IV in 1479, with a fine hammerbeam roof hung with pendants, and two fan-vaulted stone oriels at the far end. The hall's two original fireplaces are now in Eltham's pubs; the best one, with its sixteenth-century Chinese tiles intact, can be seen in *The Greyhound* on the High Street.

The 1930s house

Somewhat incredibly, in the 1930s, millionaire **Stephen Courtauld** (of art-collecting fame) got permission to build his own "Wrenaissance"-style house onto the Great Hall, and convert the moat into landscaped gardens. He lavished a fortune on the place, creating a movie star's party palace for his glamorous half-Italian, half-Hungarian wife, Virginia (who sported a risqué tattoo of a snake above one ankle). The house was designed by **Seely and Paget**, furnished by the best Swedish and Italian designers, and kitted with the latest mod cons: underfloor heating, a centralized vacuum cleaner, a tannoy system and ten en-suite bedrooms. Then, shortly before the end of the war, the family left for Rhodesia, taking most of the furniture with them.

Inside, there are acres of exotic veneer, an onyx and gold-plated bathroom, and lots of quirky little **Art Deco** touches – check out the Alice in Wonderland relief above the door in the circular entrance hall, which is flooded with light from a spectacular glazed dome. The audiotours fill visitors in on the family's various eccentricities, which included keeping a pet ring-tailed lemur called **Mah-Jongg**, which had its own centrally heated bedroom approached by a bamboo ladder and was notorious for biting disliked male visitors.

Bexleyheath

Bexleyheath, three miles east of Eltham, is a pretty nondescript 1930s suburb, but it has three significant architectural attractions from the days when it was still mostly heath.

21

Danson House

April–Oct Wed, Thurs & Sun 11am–5pm • £6 • ☎ 020 8303 6699, ⓦ dansonhouse.org.uk • Bexleyheath train station from Victoria, Charing Cross or London Bridge

Danson House is a modest little Palladian villa, built in the 1760s as a country retreat for John Boyd, who'd made a fortune from the slave trade, and had a new 19-year-old bride to impress. The highlights of the *piano nobile* are the paintings telling the love story of Vertumnus and Pomona in the Dining Room, the Chinoiserie wallpaper in the octagonal Salon, and the built-in organ in the library, which is still used for recitals. It's also worth climbing up to inspect the trompe-l'oeil paintings of Jupiter's thunderbolts in the oval dome. There's a **tearoom** on the ground floor and a **pub-restaurant** in the old stables at the eastern edge of the park.

Red House

Red House Lane • March–Oct Wed–Sun 11am–5pm; Nov & Dec Fri–Sun 11am–5pm; pre-booked tours before 1.30pm • NT • £7.20; garden only 50p • ☎ 020 8304 9878, ⓦ nationaltrust.org.uk • Bexleyheath train station from Victoria, Charing Cross or London Bridge

Hidden among the surrounding suburbia lies **Red House**, a wonderful red-brick country house designed by Philip Webb in 1859 for his friend **William Morris**, following Morris's marriage to Pre-Raphaelite heart-throb Jane Burden. The mock-medieval exterior features pointed brick arches, steep gables, an oriel window and even a turreted well in the garden, and the whole enterprise stands as the embodiment of the Arts and Crafts movement. Sadly, after just five years, with "Janey" conducting an affair with Dante Gabriel Rossetti, the couple were forced to leave their dream home due to financial difficulties and move to Kelmscott in Oxfordshire. It has to be said the interior is a bit gloomy, half-finished even in Morris's time, still in need of restoration and not at all cosy, with only a few of the larger interior furnishings still in place. The tours are excellent at bringing the place to life, thanks to the various anecdotes about Morris and his entourage, about how they used to eat in the hallway, indulge in apple fights and wear medieval clothes at the weekend.

Hall Place

Bourne Rd • House: Mon–Sat 10am–4.30pm, Sun 11am–4.30pm; Nov–March closes 4pm. Gardens: daily 9am–dusk • Free • ☎ 01322 526574, ⓦ hallplace.org.uk • Bexley train station from Charing Cros or London Bridge

Hall Place is a mishmash of a place, but the Tudor half sports a wonderful chequerboard flintwork exterior and gardens full of top-class topiary, including an entire set of the Queen's Beasts wrought in yew. The house itself has a municipal feel (it's used by the local council), but there's an introductory gallery on the ground floor which gives you the background to the place. Downstairs, the wood-panelled Great Hall survives with its coved ceiling and carved bosses; upstairs, head for the principal bedroom which boasts an ornate Jacobean plasterwork ceiling featuring grotesques.

Down House

Luxted Rd, Downe • April–June, Sept & Oct Wed–Sun 11am–5pm; July & Aug daily 11am–5pm; March, Nov & Dec Wed–Sun 11am–4pm • EH • £9.90 • ☎ 01689 859119, ⓦ english-heriage.org.uk • Bus #146 from Bromley North or Bromley South train station

Down House was the home of the scientist **Charles Darwin** (1809–1882). Born in Shrewsbury, Darwin showed little academic promise at Cambridge. It was only after returning from his five-year tour of South America aboard HMS *Beagle* – when he visited the Galapagos Islands – that he began work on the theory he would publish in 1859 as *On the Origin of Species*. Darwin moved to Down House in 1842, shortly after marrying his cousin Emma Wedgwood, who nursed the valetudinarian scientist here until his death. The house itself is set in lovely grounds, and is stuffed with Darwin memorabilia, though there's no sign (or smell) of the barnacles which he spent eight years dissecting – he later moved on to the study of orchids (to the relief, no doubt, of his wife and children), several examples of which you can find in the glasshouse.

HAMPTON COURT PALACE

West London: Hammersmith to Hampton Court

Hammersmith to Hampton Court – a distance of some seven miles overland (more by the river) – takes you from the traffic-clogged western suburbs of London to the royal outpost of Hampton Court. In between, London seems to continue unabated, with only fleeting glimpses of the countryside, in particular the fabulous Kew Gardens and the two old royal hunting parks, Richmond and Bushy Park – though, as one nineteenth-century visitor observed, they are "no more like the real untrimmed genuine country than a garden is like a field". Running through the chapter, and linking many of the places described, is the River Thames, once known as the "Great Highway of London" and still the most pleasant way to travel in these parts during the summer.

Aside from the river and the parks, the chief attractions of West London are the royal palaces and lordly mansions that pepper the riverbanks: textbook Palladian style at **Chiswick House**, unspoilt Jacobean splendour at **Ham House**, and Tudor and Baroque excess (and the famous maze) at **Hampton Court**. We kick off this chapter at **Hammersmith** – London's gateway to the west, by road or tube – which, with neighbouring **Chiswick**, and **Kew**, **Richmond** and **Twickenham** beyond, has the additional appeal of its riverside walks and pubs.

ARRIVAL AND DEPARTURE

22

For the latest on boat services on the Thames, see ⓦ tfl.gov.uk.

From Westminster From April to October Westminster Passenger Services (☎ 020 7930 2062, ⓦ wpsa.co.uk) run a scheduled service from Westminster Pier to Kew, Richmond and Hampton Court. The full trip takes 3hrs one-way, and costs £15 single, £22.50 return.

Between Richmond and Hampton Court In addition, Turks (☎ 020 8546 2434, ⓦ turks.co.uk) runs a regular service from Richmond to Hampton Court (April to mid-Sept Tues–Sun; journey time 1hr 45min) which costs £6.80 single or £8.40 return.

Hammersmith

This chapter starts in the transport and traffic interchange hellhole of **Hammersmith**, for one simple reason: the tube station gives easy access to the Wetland Centre (see p.330) and to the riverside walk to Chiswick. The riverside walk begins a short way southwest of the tube, down Queen Caroline Street. First off, you pass underneath **Hammersmith Bridge**, a graceful green and gold suspension bridge from the 1880s that the IRA have tried to blow up three times: first in 1939, as part of their attempt to disrupt the British war effort, secondly by the Provisional IRA in 1996, and finally four years later by the Real IRA. From the bridge, you can walk all the way to Chiswick along the most picturesque stretch of riverbank in the whole of London, much of it closed to traffic.

The riverside

The first section of the riverside, just west of the bridge, known as **Lower Mall**, is a mixture of Victorian pubs, boathouses, Regency verandas and modern flats. An interesting array of boats huddles around the marina outside the *Dove*, an atmospheric seventeenth-century riverside pub (see p.398). This started out as a coffee house and has the smallest back bar in the country, copious literary associations – regulars have included Graham Greene, Ernest Hemingway and William Morris – and a canopied balcony overlooking the Thames.

Kelmscott House

26 Upper Mall • Thurs & Sat 2–5pm • Free • ☎ 020 8741 3735, ⓦ morrissociety.org • ⊖ Ravenscourt Park

It's strange to think that this genteel part of the Thames was once a hotbed of radicals, who used to congregate at **Kelmscott House**, where **William Morris** lived and worked from 1878 until his death in 1896. (Morris used to berate the locals from a soapbox on Hammersmith Bridge.) From 1885 onwards, the local socialists used to meet here on a Sunday evening, with Labour leader Keir Hardie, anarchist Prince Kropotkin, writer George Bernard Shaw and Fabian founders the Webbs among the speakers – their photos now line the walls.

7 Hammersmith Terrace

7 Hammersmith Terrace • April to mid-Sept pre-booked guided tours only Sat 11am, 12.30 & 2.30pm • £10 • ☎ 020 8741 4104, ⓦ emerywalker.org.uk • ⊖ Stamford Brook

Another socialist mate of Morris, the printer Emery Walker, lived just down the riverbank at **7 Hammersmith Terrace**, one of a line of tall Georgian houses built facing the river sometime before 1755. The house has a well-preserved Arts and Crafts interior and contains lots of Morris memorabilia as well as de Morgan ceramics and furniture by Philip Webb, architect of Morris's Red House in Bexleyheath (see p.327) – tours are very popular so book ahead online.

London Wetland Centre

Queen Elizabeth's Walk • Daily April–Oct 9.30am–6pm; Nov–March 9.30am–5pm • £9.59 • Guided tours daily 11am & 2pm, plus Sat & Sun noon; free • Duck feeding daily, 3pm • ☎ 020 8409 4400, ⓦ wwt.org.uk • Bus#283 from ⊖ Hammersmith

For anyone even remotely interested in wildlife, the **London Wetland Centre** in well-to-do Barnes is an absolute must. Lying on the site of four disused reservoirs, the Wildfowl & Wetlands Trust (WWT) has created a mosaic of wetland habitats. On arrival – unless it's raining – skip the introductory audiovisual, and head straight out to the ponds. If the weather's bad, head for the **Discovery Centre**, where kids can take part in a swan identification parade, or take a duck's-eye view of the world. You can also look out over the wetlands from the glass-walled **Observatory** next door, or from the tables of the *Water's Edge Café*. Visitors with children should make their way to **Explore**, a nature-themed adventure playground, while the **Pond Zone** gives younger children a chance to do some pond-dipping.

The centre basically serves a dual function: to attract native species of bird to its watery lagoons, and to assist in the WWT's programme of breeding rare wildfowl in captivity. The **World Wetlands** area harbours a variety of extremely rare wildfowl – from White-faced Whistling Ducks to the highly endangered Blue Duck – whose wetland habitats have been re-created in miniature (3pm is feeding time). In the **Wildside** are the reedbeds and pools that attract native species, such as lapwing, sand martins, water rail and, if you're lucky, even the odd wintering bittern, all of which you can view from a moss-roofed hide. At the far end is the **Peacock Tower**, the mother of all hides: a triple-decker octagonal one with a lift, allowing views over the whole of the reserve.

Chiswick

The old riverside village of **Chiswick** was centred on the Church of St Nicholas from medieval times until the Victorian period, when the action moved north to **Chiswick High Street**, near the tube. The most picturesque approach is to walk along the river from Hammersmith. If you do so, you'll soon come to **Chiswick Mall**, which continues for a mile or so along the river to the church. A riotous ensemble of seventeenth- and eighteenth-century mansions lines the north side of the Mall, which cuts them off from their modest riverside gardens. Halfway along, a particularly fine trio ends with **Walpole House**, once the home of Barbara Villiers, Duchess of Cleveland, Countess of Castlemaine and one of Charles II's many mistresses.

Church of St Nicholas

Church St • ☎ 020 8995 7876, ⓦ stnicholaschiswick.org • ⊖ Turnham Green

At the very western end of Chiswick Mall stands the church of **St Nicholas**, rebuilt in the 1880s, but still retaining its original fifteenth-century ragstone tower. Lord Burlington and his architect friends William Kent and Colen Campbell are all buried in the graveyard, as is the aforementioned Barbara Villiers, though only the painters William Hogarth and James Whistler are commemorated by gravestones, the former enclosed by wrought-iron railings.

Fuller's Griffin Brewery

Chiswick Lane South • Mon–Fri guided tours hourly 11am–3pm • £10 • ☎ 020 8996 2063, ⓦ fullers.co.uk • ⊖ Turnham Green

Church Lane was the medieval village high street, and its oldest building today is the Old Burlington, originally a sixteenth-century inn, and now a private residence.

Beyond, lies **Fuller's Griffin Brewery**, dating back to the seventeenth century and still going strong. You can book yourself onto one of the ninety-minute **guided tours**, which includes the inevitable tasting session, and also gives visitors the chance to see the country's oldest wisteria, which has clung to the brickwork for over 180 years.

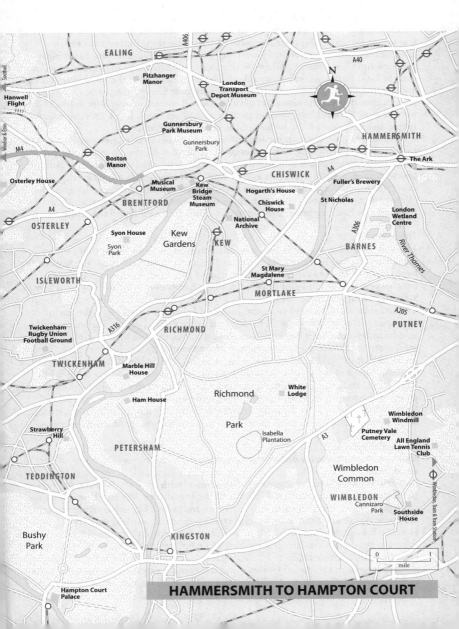

HAMMERSMITH TO HAMPTON COURT

22

Chiswick House

Great Chertsey Rd • **House** April–Oct Mon–Wed & Sun 10am–5pm • EH • £5.50 **Gardens** Daily 7am–dusk • Free **Conservatory** Mid-Feb to mid-March daily 10am–3pm; mid-March to Oct daily 10am–4pm • Mid-Feb to mid-March £5; mid-March to Oct free • ☎ 020 8995 0508, ⓦ chgt.org.uk • Chiswick train station from Waterloo or ⊖ Turnham Green

Chiswick House is a perfectly proportioned classical villa, designed by Richard Boyle, third Earl of Burlington, in the 1720s, and set in a beautifully landscaped garden. Like its prototype, Palladio's Villa Capra near Vicenza, the house was purpose-built as a "Temple to the Arts" – an extension to Burlington's adjacent Jacobean mansion (which was torn down in 1788). Here, amid his fine art collection, Burlington used to entertain such friends as Swift, Handel and Pope, who lived in nearby Twickenham.

Guests and visitors (who could view the property on payment of an admission fee even in Lord Burlington's day) would originally have ascended the quadruple staircase and entered the *piano nobile* through the magnificent Corinthian portico. The public entrance today is via the **lower floor**, where the earl had his own private rooms and kept his extensive library. Here, you can pick up an audioguide, watch a short video, and peruse an exhibition on the history of the house and grounds.

Entertaining took place on the **upper floor**, a series of cleverly interconnecting rooms, each enjoying a wonderful view out onto the gardens – all, that is, except the **Tribunal**, the domed octagonal hall at the centre of the villa, where the house's finest paintings and sculptures are displayed, just as they would have been in Burlington's day. The other rooms retain much of their rich decor, in particular the ceilings, designed by William Kent. The most sumptuous is the **Blue Velvet Room**, decorated in a deep Prussian blue, with eight pairs of heavy gilded brackets holding up the ceiling.

The gardens

Like the villa, the house's extensive **gardens** were influenced by descriptions of the gardens of classical Rome and, in their turn, became the inspiration for the **English landscape garden**. You can admire the northwest side of the house from the stone benches of the exedra, a set of yew-hedge niches harbouring lions and copies of **Roman statuary**, and overlooking a smooth carpet of grass, punctuated by urns and sphinxes, that sit under the shadow of two giant cedars of Lebanon. Other highlights include England's first **mock ruin** – the Kent-designed cascade – and the network of narrow yew-hedge avenues, each one ending at some diminutive building or statue. One of the most remarkable focal points is the grassy **amphitheatre**, by the side of the lake, centred on an obelisk in a pond and overlooked by an Ionic temple. To the north of the villa, beside a section of the gardens' old **ha-ha**, stands a grand stone gateway designed by Inigo Jones, and close by a **café**. Beyond lies a large **conservatory**, built to grow peaches, grapes and pineapples and now stuffed with camellias. It looks out onto the formal **Italian Garden**, laid out in the early nineteenth century by the sixth Duke of Devonshire, who also established a zoo (now gone) featuring an elephant, giraffe, elks and emus.

Hogarth's House

Hogarth's Lane, Great West Rd • Phone ☎ 020 8994 6757 for opening times • Free • Chiswick train station from Waterloo or ⊖ Turnham Green

Hogarth's House, where the artist spent each summer with his wife, sister and mother-in-law from 1749 until his death in 1764, sits by the thunderous A4 road. Nowadays it's difficult to believe Hogarth came here for "peace and quiet", but in the eighteenth century the house was almost entirely surrounded by countryside. Compared to nearby Chiswick House, whose pretentious Palladianism and excess epitomized everything Hogarth loathed the most, the domesticity here is something of a relief. Among the scores of Hogarth's engravings, you can see copies of his satirical series – *An Election*, *Marriage à la Mode*, *A Rake's Progress* and *A Harlot's Progress* – and compare the modern view from the parlour with the more idyllic scene in *Mr Ranby's House*. The house has been closed for renovation since 2008, but should be open again by the time you read this.

Brentford

Named after the River Brent, which empties into the Thames, just west of Chiswick, **Brentford** was the first point at which you could ford the tidal river in ancient times, and (very possibly) the place where Julius Caesar crossed in 54 BC. Nowadays, it's worth visiting, not for its humdrum high street, but for its various scattered historic landmarks, from the conspicuous campanile of **Kew Bridge Steam Museum** to the discreet charm of the aristocratic estate of **Syon**.

Gunnersbury Park

22

Park Daily 8am–dusk • Free **Museum** April–Oct daily 11am–5pm; Nov–March closes 4pm • Free • ☎ 020 8992 1612 • ⬌ Acton Town

Like Chiswick Park, **Gunnersbury Park** used to have a Palladian villa at its centre, in this case designed by Inigo Jones's son-in-law, John Webb, for George II's favourite daughter, Princess Amelia. Amelia used the place as a summer retreat and also erected the Neoclassical temple that overlooks the boating lake to this day. At one time, the temple was used as a private synagogue by the Rothschilds, the last owners of the estate, who sold it to the local council in the 1920s. The park has plenty of history – but it could do with some love and attention, too. Nevertheless, it's still worth popping into the **Gunnersbury Park Museum**, housed in the Rothschilds former double mansion. The highlights of the museum are a fully restored set of Victorian kitchens, and a permanent collection of historical vehicles, including a tandem tricycle and the Rothschilds' own Victorian "chariot".

Kensington Cemetery

143 Gunnersbury Ave • Daily 9am–dusk • Free • ⬌ Gunnersbury

When the local council bought neighbouring Gunnersbury Park in the 1920s, they put aside the southeast corner for a new cemetery, known as Gunnersbury or **Kensington Cemetery**. The nearby borough of Ealing has a large Polish community, and the cemetery contains a black marble obelisk erected in 1976 to the 14,500 **Polish POWs** who went missing in 1940, when the Nazi–Soviet Pact carved up Poland. A mass grave containing 4500 bodies was later discovered by the advancing Nazis at Katyn, near Smolensk, but responsibility for the massacre was denied by the Russians until fifty years later, as a plaque bitterly records. Fifty yards to the south is the grave of **General Komorowski**, leader of the Polish Home Army during the ill-fated 1944 Warsaw Uprising, who lived in exile in Britain until his death in 1966. Also buried here is the film director **Carol Reed**, best known for *The Third Man*. There's no direct access to the graveyard from the park, only from Gunnersbury Avenue.

Kew Bridge Steam Museum

Green Dragon Lane • **Museum** Tues–Sun 11am–4pm; **Railway** April–Oct Sun • £9.50 • ☎ 020 8568 4757, ⓦ kbsm.org • Bus #237 or #267 from ⬌ Gunnersbury or Kew Bridge train station from Waterloo

Difficult to miss thanks to its stylish, tapered, Italianate standpipe tower, **Kew Bridge Steam Museum** occupies an old pumping station, 100yd west of Kew Bridge. At the heart of the museum is the **Steam Hall**, which contains a green triple-expansion steam engine, similar to the one used by the *Titanic*, and four gigantic nineteenth-century Cornish beam engines, while two adjoining rooms house the pumping station's original beam engines, including the world's largest.

The steam engines may be things of great beauty, but they are primarily of interest to enthusiasts. Not so the museum's wonderfully imaginative and educational **Water for Life** gallery, situated in the basement and overlooked by a vast bank of ancient boilers, baths, sinks, taps and kettles. The exhibition tells the history of the capital's water supply: the section on rats and cockroaches goes down particularly well with kids, while the tales of the Victorian "toshers", who had to work the sewers in gangs of three to protect themselves from rat attacks, will make adults' stomachs turn. The best time to visit is at weekends, when each of the museum's industrial dinosaurs is put through its paces, and on Sundays in summer a narrow-gauge **steam railway** runs back and forth round the yard.

Musical Museum

399 Brentford High St • Tues–Sun 11am–5.30pm • £8 • ☎ 020 8560 8108, ⓦ musicalmuseum.co.uk • Bus #237 or #267 from ⊖ Gunnersbury or Kew Bridge train station from Waterloo

The **Musical Museum** is stuffed with the world's largest collection of self-playing instruments. The best time to come is on the weekend (or else phone ahead) when the enthusiastic staff will give noisy demonstrations of all the mechanical music-making machines from cleverly crafted music boxes, through badly tuned barrel organs, to the huge orchestrions that were once a feature of London cafés. The museum also boasts one of the world's finest collections of player-pianos, which can reproduce live performances of the great pianists. In addition, regular concerts, tea dances and silent films are put on to the accompaniment of the museum's enormous Art Deco Wurlitzer, which once graced the Regal cinema in Kingston upon Thames.

Boston Manor

Boston Manor Rd • Park daily 8am–dusk; house: April–Oct Sat & Sun 2.30–5pm • Free • ☎ 0845 456 2800 • ⊖ Boston Manor

Originally built by a wealthy widow who married into the Spencer family, the Jacobean **Boston Manor House** was bought by James Clitherow, a City merchant, in 1670 and remained in the family until taken over by the local council in the 1920s. With magnificent cedar trees and ornamental flowerbeds, the grounds are well worth a visit, despite the nearby presence of the M4. The highlight of the house is the Drawing Room on the first floor, which retains a sumptuous mantelpiece and an extraordinarily elaborate, original Jacobean plaster ceiling. In an unusual break with protocol, William IV and Queen Adelaide paid a visit to the Clitherows (mere commoners), and dined in the Dining Room, which also boasts a fine plaster ceiling, in 1834.

Syon Park

House Mid-March to Oct Wed, Thurs & Sun 11am–5pm • £10 **Gardens** March–Oct daily 10.30am–5pm or dusk; Nov–Feb Sat & Sun 10.30am–4pm • £5 • ☎ 020 8569 7497, ⓦ syonpark.co.uk • Bus #237 or #267 to Brent Lea bus stop from ⊖ Gunnersbury or Kew Bridge train station, or 15min walk from Syon Lane train station

Syon Park sits directly across the Thames from Kew Gardens, and is one of the few aristocratic estates left intact in London, with a fantastically lavish stately home, Syon House, at its heart. It has been in the hands of the Percy family since Elizabethan times, although these days it's more of a working commercial concern than a family retreat, with a garden centre, an indoor adventure playground and various other attractions on offer. The main reason to come here, though, is to view the magnificent house and its accompanying gardens. Syon started out as one of the richest monasteries in the country, established by Henry V after the Battle of Agincourt. Dissolved by Henry VIII, who incarcerated his fifth wife, Catherine Howard, here shortly before her execution in 1542, it was eventually granted to the Percys, earls (and later dukes) of Northumberland.

Syon House

From its rather plain castellated exterior, you'd never guess that **Syon House** contains the most opulent eighteenth-century interiors in London. The splendour of Robert Adam's refurbishment is immediately revealed, however, in the pristine **Great Hall**, where you can pick up the excellent audioguide. An apsed double cube with a screen of Doric columns at one end and classical statuary dotted around the edges, the hall has a chequered marble floor that cleverly mirrors the pattern of the coffered ceiling. It was in the hall's Tudor predecessor that Henry VIII's body lay in state en route to Windsor, and was discovered the next morning surrounded by a pack of hounds happily lapping the blood seeping from the coffin.

The state apartments

From the austerity of the Great Hall you enter the lavishly decorated **Ante Room**, with its florid scagliola floor (made from a mixture of marble-dust and resin) and its green-grey Ionic columns topped by brightly gilded classical statues. Here, guests could mingle before entering the **State Dining Room**, a compromise between the two preceding rooms, richly gilded with a double apse but otherwise calm in its overall effect. The remaining rooms are warmer and softer in tone, betraying their Elizabethan origins much more than the preceding ones. The **Red Drawing Room** retains its original red-silk wall hangings from Spitalfields, upon which are hung portraits of the Stuarts by Lely, Van Dyck and others, and features a splendid ceiling studded with over two hundred roundels set within gilded hexagons. Looking out to the Thames, the **Long Gallery** – 136ft by just 14ft – stretches the entire width of the house, decorated by Adam's busy pink and gold plasterwork and lined with 62 individually painted pilasters. It was in the Long Gallery that Lady Jane Grey was formally offered the crown by her father-in-law, John Dudley, the owner of Syon at the time; nine days later they were arrested and eventually beheaded.

The private apartments

The private apartments pale in comparison with the first five rooms. However, there are still one or two highlights to look out for: more works by Lely and Van Dyck, as well as Gainsborough and Reynolds in the **Print Room**; a superb Adam fireplace and ornate fan-patterned ceiling, plus portraits by Holbein and Reynolds, in the **Green Drawing Room** – still used by the family; and a monster golden Sèvres vase at the foot of the modest principal **staircase**. Upstairs, past the delicate thousand-piece Sèvres dinner service, there are several plush bedrooms, including two refurbished in 1832 for the future Queen Victoria and her mother, the Duchess of Kent, with magnificent canopied beds, blue silk outside and yellow within.

The gardens

While Adam beautified Syon House, Capability Brown laid out its **gardens** around an artificial lake, surrounding it with oaks, beeches, limes and cedars. Since then, the gardens have been further enhanced by still more exotic trees, ranging from an Indian bean tree to a pagoda tree. Beside the lake, there's a stretch of lawn overlooked by a Doric column topped by a fibreglass statue of Flora, but the gardens' real highlight is the crescent-shaped **Great Conservatory**, an early nineteenth-century addition which is said to have inspired Joseph Paxton, architect of the Crystal Palace.

Osterley Park

Jersey Rd · **Park** Daily 8am–6pm · Free **House** March Wed–Sun noon–3.30pm; April–Oct Wed–Sun noon–4.30pm; Nov & Dec Sat & Sun noon–3.30pm · NT · £8.25 · ☎ 020 8232 5050, ⓦ nationaltrust.org.uk · ⊖ Osterley

Robert Adam redesigned another colossal Elizabethan mansion three miles northwest of Syon at **Osterley Park** – one of London's largest surviving estate parks, which still gives the impression of being in the middle of the countryside, despite the M4 motorway to the north of the house. The main approach is along a splendid avenue of sweet chestnuts to the south, past the National Trust-sponsored **farmhouse** (whose produce you can buy all year round). The driveway curves past the southernmost of the park's three lakes, with a Chinese pagoda at one end. Cedars planted in the 1820s and oaks planted in Victorian times stand between the lake and the house, and to the north are the grandiose Tudor stables of first owner Thomas Gresham, now converted into a **café** (March–Dec Wed–Sun).

Osterley House

Unlike Syon, **Osterley House** was built with mercantile rather than aristocratic wealth: it was erected in 1576 by Thomas Gresham, the brains behind the City's Royal Exchange. Later it was bought by another City gent, the goldsmith and banker Francis Child, who used it merely as a kind of giant safe-deposit box – it was his grandsons who employed Robert Adam to create the house as it is today. From the outside, Osterley bears some similarity to Syon, the big difference being the grand entrance portico, with a broad flight of steps rising to a tall, Ionic colonnade, which gives access to the central courtyard.

The interior

From the central courtyard, you enter Adam's characteristically cool **Entrance Hall**, a double-apsed space decorated with grisaille paintings and classical statuary. The finest rooms are the State Rooms of the south wing, where the nouveaux riches Childs hoped, in vain, to entertain royalty as Gresham had once done. The **Drawing Room** is splendid, with Reynolds portraits on the damask walls and a coffered ceiling centred on a giant marigold, a theme continued in the lush carpet and elsewhere in the house. The **Tapestry Room** is hung with Boucher-designed Gobelins tapestries, while the silk-lined **State Bedchamber** features an outrageous domed bed designed by Adam. Lastly, there's the **Etruscan Dressing Room**, in which every surface is covered in delicate painted trelliswork, sphinxes and urns, dubbed "Etruscan" by Adam (and Wedgwood), though it is in fact derived from Greek vases found at Pompeii.

The **Long Gallery** is much broader, taller and plainer than the one at Syon and, like much of the house, features Adam-designed furniture, as well as some fine Chinoiserie. Sadly, the Childs' Rubens, Van Dyck and Claude pictures no longer hang here, having been transported to the family's home in the Channel Islands (where they were destroyed by fire), and replaced instead by B-list works from the V&A. In the north wing, the whitewashed Library is worth a quick peek as is the Neoclassical **Great Staircase**, with its replica Rubens ceiling painting.

PM Gallery & House

Mattock Lane · Tues–Fri & Sun 1–5pm, Sat 11am–5pm · Free · ☎ 020 8567 1227 · ⊖ Ealing Broadway

Now known as the **PM Gallery & House**, Pitzhanger Manor is the solitary jewel in the borough of Ealing, and is well worth a visit. Designed in 1770 by George Dance, but later bought and extensively remodelled by John Soane, the balustraded main facade, though small, is magnificent, its bays divided by Ionic pillars topped by terracotta statues. As soon as you enter the narrow vestibule, Soane stops you short with some spatial gymnastics by taking a section of the ceiling up through the first floor. To the right is the now book-less Library, which features a cross-vaulted ceiling, decorated with an unusual trelliswork pattern. Soane's masterpiece, though, is the **Breakfast Room**, with caryatids in the four corners and lush red porphyry and grey marbling on the walls.

An unexpected bonus is the **Martinware Gallery**, a display of the idiosyncratic stoneware pottery produced around 1900 by the four Martin brothers from the nearby Southall Pottery. Its centrepiece is their Moorish ceramic fireplace; the rest of the ware, including face mugs and bird jars, is more of an acquired taste. The manor's south wing is all that survives from Dance's original house (Soane's architectural teacher), the rest of which Soane demolished. The rooms here are on a much larger scale, providing an interesting contrast to Soane's intimate and highly wrought style, while the Monk's Dining Room in the basement is the precursor of Soane's Monk's Parlour (see p.145).

Kew

Kew is famous for its **Royal Botanic Gardens**, which manage the extremely difficult task of being both a world leader in botanic research and an extraordinarily beautiful and popular public park at the same time. Kew began life in the eighteenth century as the pleasure gardens of two royal estates, but it was Princess Augusta, the widow of Prince Frederick, eldest son of George II, who turned the estate into the first botanic gardens in the 1750s, with the help of her paramour, the Earl of Bute. Some of the earliest specimens were brought back from the voyages of Captain Cook, instantly establishing Kew as a leading botanical research centre. From its original eight acres the gardens have grown into a 300-acre site in which more than 33,000 species are grown in plantations and glasshouses, a display that attracts nearly two million visitors annually, most of them with no specialist interest at all. The only drawbacks with Kew are the hefty entry fee, and the fact that it's on the main flight path to Heathrow. That said, it's a wonderful place with something to see whatever the season. Outside of the gardens, there's not much reason to linger in Kew, although Kew Green, to the north of the gardens, is quite pretty, and the National Archives lurk in the backstreets.

22

Royal Botanic Gardens

Daily 9.30am–6.30pm or dusk; Queen Charlotte's Cottage April–Sept Sat & Sun 11am–4pm • £13.90 • ☎ 020 8332 5000, ⓦ kew.org • ⊖ Kew Gardens

Most folk arrive at **Kew Gardens** by tube and enter via the **Victoria Gate**, where you'll find the main shop and visitor centre, and the distinctive **campanile**, which originally served as the chimney for the furnaces below the glasshouses. Beyond lies the **Pond**, home to two ten-ton Ming lions, and the best vantage point from which to appreciate Kew's magnificent **Palm House**. This distinctive, curvaceous mound of glass and wrought iron, designed by Decimus Burton in the 1840s, nurtures most of the known palm species in its drippingly humid atmosphere, while in the basement there's a small, but excellent, tropical aquarium. From the Palm House, head north to the diminutive **Waterlily House**, where a canopy of plants and creepers overhangs a circular pond boasting spectacular, giant water lilies.

Further north still, is the rather less graceful **Princess of Wales Conservatory**, opened in 1987. However, the cacti collection here is awesome, as are the giant koi fish that swim stealthily beneath the pathways – look out, too, for the bizarre plants in the insectivorous section. Immediately east, set amid Kew's gargantuan Rock Garden, is the extraordinary **Alpine House**, a glasshouse shaped like the sail on the back of a dimetrodon.

The largest of the glasshouses is the **Temperate House**, another Decimus Burton structure, twice the size of the Palm House and almost forty years in the making. It contains plants from every continent, including one of the largest indoor palms in the world, the 60ft Chilean Wine Palm, first planted in 1846 and currently approaching the roof – and therefore the end of its life.

ARRIVAL AND INFORMATION

Arrival There are four entrances to Kew Gardens, but the majority of people arrive at Kew Gardens tube station, a short walk east of the Victoria Gate, at the end of Lichfield Road. On a summer weekend, it's worth getting here early to avoid the queues.

Kew for kids If you've kids with you, the good news is that they get in free. If it's raining, the aquarium beneath the Palm House usually goes down well, while under-10s will enjoy the indoor interactive play area, Climbers & Creepers. If the weather's good, head for the giant Badger Sett and the Beetle Loggery, home to stag beetles and the like.

The eighteenth-century gardens

His mosque, waxworks, observatory and House of Confucius may be gone, but several of the buildings William Chambers created in the 1760s for the amusement of Princess Augusta remain dotted about the gardens. The most famous is his 10-storey, 163ft-high **Pagoda**, Kew's most distinctive landmark, albeit minus the 80 enamelled dragons that used to adorn it. Standing nearby in a sort of miniature tea garden is the ornate

Japanese Gateway, a scaled-down version of the one in Kyoto and a legacy of the 1910 Japan–British Exhibition, built in cedar wood and topped by a copper roof.

North of the pagoda, you can walk through Chambers' **Ruined Arch**, purpose-built with sundry pieces of Roman masonry strewn about as if tossed there by barbarian hordes. Chambers is also responsible for the classical temples, the most picturesque being the **Temple of Aeolus**, situated on one of Kew's few hillocks near Cumberland Gate, surrounded in spring by a carpet of bluebells and daffodils.

Capability Brown's horticultural work has proved more durable than Chambers': his lake remains a focal point of the Syon vista from the Palm House, and the hidden **Rhododendron Dell** he devised survives to the south of it. More recent nearby additions include the **Bamboo Garden**, laid out in 1891, and the **Minka House**, a thatched wooden farmhouse built in the suburbs of Okazaki in Japan, and transferred here in 2001. Even more recent is the **Treetop Walkway**, in the centre of the gardens – not a thing of beauty in itself but the views are good and it's quite novel to be 60ft in the air among the tree canopy.

Queen Charlotte's Cottage

The thickly wooded, southwestern section of Kew Gardens is the bit to head for if you want to lose the crowds, few of whom ever make it to **Queen Charlotte's Cottage**, a fairly substantial thatched summerhouse built in brick and timber in the 1770s as a royal picnic spot for George III's wife. The cottage was adjacent to a mini royal menagerie, which featured England's first kangaroos and the now extinct, zebra-like, quagga. Today, there's very little to see inside, beyond a room of Hogarth prints and a trompe-l'oeil pergola (possibly painted by one of the Queen's daughters), but the surrounding native woodland is very peaceful and carpeted with bluebells in spring.

The museum and art galleries

Kew's Museum No. 1, designed by Decimus Burton across the Pond from the Palm House (and now called **Plants and People**), provides an excellent wet-weather retreat. Inside, an exhibition shows the myriad uses to which humans have put plants, from food and medicines to clothes and tools. Along with the usual static glass-case displays, there are also touch-screen computers to hand, a scent station and various hands-on exhibits which should keep younger visitors happy. There's also a great 1886 model of an Indian indigo factory, with over one hundred clay figures and one colonial overseer in a pith helmet.

Kew also boasts three art galleries. To the south of Victoria Gate is the **Shirley Sherwood Gallery of Botanical Art**, a modern space that displays the most exquisitely executed botanical art from the last three centuries. Next door stands the resolutely old-fashioned **Marianne North Gallery**, purpose-built in 1882 to house the prolific output of the self-trained artist Marianne North. Over 800 paintings, completed in 14 years of hectic world travel, are displayed end to end, filling every single space in the gallery. Finally, **Kew Gardens Gallery**, the largest of the lot, in the northeastern corner of the gardens, puts on temporary exhibitions often on more general botanical themes.

Kew Palace

April–Sept Mon 11am–5pm, Tues–Sun 10am–5pm • £5.30 • ☎ 0844 482 7777, ⊛ hrp.org.uk • ⊖ Kew Gardens

In the north of the gardens stands the country's smallest royal residence, **Kew Palace**, a three-storey red-brick mansion measuring a mere 70ft by 50ft, and commonly known as the "Dutch House", after its fancy Flemish-bond brickwork and its curly Dutch gables. It's the smallest (and sole survivor) of the three royal residences that once stood at Kew and was bought from a City merchant by George II as a nursery and schoolhouse for his umpteen children.

FROM TOP RICHMOND RIVERSIDE (P.342); KEW GARDENS (P.337) >

22

The only king to live here was **George III**, who was confined to the palace from 1801 onwards and subjected to the dubious attentions of doctors who attempted to find a cure for his "madness" by straitjacketing him and applying poultices of mustard and Spanish fly – only his strong constitution helped him to pull through. The ticket office and welcome centre, with an exhibition on the palace's history, stand apart.

Inside the palace, there are one or two bits and bobs belonging to the royals, like the much-loved doll's house, on the ground floor, which belonged to George III's daughters. Upstairs, you can view the chair in which Queen Charlotte passed away in 1818, while the top floor has been left pretty much untouched since those days. Take time, too, to explore the secluded **Queen's Garden**, behind the palace, set out in a formal late seventeenth-century style, with a pleached hornbeam avenue and a lovely sunken nosegay garden.

Kew Green

Kew's majestic **Main Gates**, designed by Decimus Burton, fulfilled their stated function until the arrival of the railway at Kew. Nowadays, you only get to see them if you're walking from Kew Bridge or exploring **Kew Green**, one of London's prettiest village greens. Lined with Georgian houses, the green is centred on the delightful church of **St Anne** (for opening times, visit ⓦsaintanne-kew.org.uk), an unusual building sporting a Victorian polygonal clock turret at one end and a peculiar Georgian octagonal cupola at the other; the painters Gainsborough and Zoffany lie in the churchyard. Inside, there's a royal Georgian gallery, held up by Tuscan columns, while at the east end is a rather fine late-Victorian chancel with scagliola columns and a top-lit dome. There are music recitals, tea and cakes on summer Sunday afternoons.

National Archives

Tues & Thurs 9am–7pm, Wed, Fri & Sat 9am–5pm • Free • ☎ 020 8876 3444, ⓦ nationalarchives.gov.uk • ⊖ Kew Gardens

Hidden in the residential backstreets of Kew is the Public Records Office, a rather nasty-looking beige and green premises housing the **National Archives**. Its research library is full of historians consulting primary source materials, while its exhibition gallery displays a changing rota of fascinating artefacts ranging from the likes of the Domesday Book and the trial record of Charles I, to Queen Victoria's 1851 census return and Elton John's Deed Poll certificate changing his name (wisely) from Reginald Kenneth Dwight.

Richmond

Richmond, upstream from Kew, basked for centuries in the glow of royal patronage, with Plantagenet kings and Tudor monarchs frequenting the riverside Palace of Shene, as Richmond Palace was then called. In the eighteenth century Richmond enjoyed a brief life as a spa, and its agreeable locale began to attract City merchants, as well as successful artists, actors and writers: Pope, Gainsborough, Garrick and Reynolds are just some of the plaque-worthy names associated with the place. Although most of the courtiers and aristocrats have gone, as has the Tudor palace on the green, Richmond is still a wealthy district, with two theatres and highbrow pretensions. To appreciate its attractions fully, you need to visit the old village green, take in the glorious view from **Richmond Hill** and pay a visit to the vast acreage of **Richmond Park**, the old royal hunting grounds, still wild and replete with deer, and walk along the riverside to the nearby Jacobean mansion of **Ham House**.

Richmond Green

George Street, Richmond's main street, is traffic-clogged and dominated by chain stores, but take one of the narrow pedestrianized alleyways, lined with arty shops and tearooms, and you'll emerge onto the wonderful open space of **Richmond**

Green, one of London's finest village greens, and one of the most peaceful, except for the planes using it as the main flight path into Heathrow. Handsome seventeenth- and eighteenth-century houses line the southwest and southeast sides of the green, with the most striking building of all, the flamboyant **Richmond Theatre**, designed by the great Frank Matcham in terracotta and brick in 1899, in the northeast corner.

Richmond Museum

Whittaker Ave • Tues–Sat 11am–5pm • Free • ☏ 020 8332 1141, ⓦ museumofrichmond.com • ⊖ Richmond

The old town hall, set slightly back from the riverside now houses the library and, on the top floor, the **Richmond Museum**. The museum contains a small permanent exhibition on the history of the town, plus the lowdown on (and a model of) the old royal palace; special exhibitions tend to focus on Richmond's past luminaries.

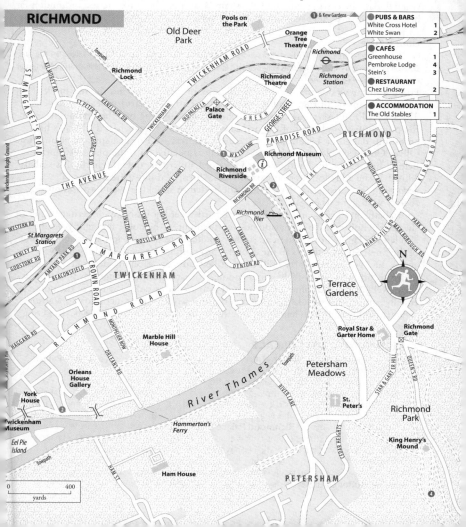

Richmond Riverside

To the untrained eye, the buildings that form the backdrop to the pedestrianized terraces of **Richmond Riverside** look Georgian, but closer inspection reveals the majority to be a sham: the cupolas conceal air vents, the chimneys are decorative and the facades hide offices and flats. Still, Quinlan Terry's pastiche from the late 1980s has proved very popular. One of the few originals is **Heron House**, a narrow three-storey building where Lady Hamilton and her daughter Horatia came to live shortly after Trafalgar, the battle in which the girl's father died.

To the south of the modern riverside development lies **Richmond Bridge**, an elegant span of five arches made from Purbeck stone in 1777, and cleverly widened in the 1930s, thus preserving London's oldest extant bridge. From April to September you can rent rowing boats from the nearby jetties, or take a boat trip to Hampton Court or Westminster (see p.329). If you continue along the towpath beyond Richmond Bridge, you will pass the cows grazing on **Petersham Meadows**, and leave the rest of London far behind, before eventually coming to Ham House.

Ham House

Ham St • **House** April–Oct daily except Fri noon–4pm • Guided tours only: Feb & March daily except Fri 11.30am–3.30pm; Nov Mon, Tues, Sat & Sun 11.30am–3pm • NT • £9.90 **Gardens** Mon–Wed, Sat & Sun 11am–6pm • NT • £3.30 • ☎ 020 8940 1950, ⓦ nationaltrust.org.uk • Bus #371 or #65 from ⊖ Richmond

Hidden in the woods that line the south bank of the Thames lies the red-brick Jacobean mansion of **Ham House**, home to the Earl of Dysart for nearly 300 years. The 1st Earl of Dysart was Charles I's childhood whipping boy (he literally received the punishment on behalf of the prince when the latter misbehaved), but it's his ambitious daughter, **Elizabeth**, the second Countess – a Royalist spy and at one time Oliver Cromwell's lover – who's most closely associated with the place. With the help of her second husband, the 1st Duke of Lauderdale, one of Charles II's Cabal Ministry, she added numerous extra rooms, "furnished like a great Prince's" according to diarist John Evelyn, and succeeded in shocking even **Restoration** society with her extravagance.

Elizabeth's profligacy, and a ruinous legal battle over her husband's inheritance, meant she died penniless in 1698, having not ventured out of the house for eight years. She also left the family heavily in debt, so they could afford to make few alterations to one of the finest **Stuart interiors** in the country, prompting Horace Walpole (who lived across the river at Strawberry Hill) to describe Ham as a "Sleeping Beauty". The Great Staircase, off the Central Hall, is stupendously ornate, featuring huge bowls of fruit at the newel posts and trophies of war carved into the balustrade. The rest of the house is equally sumptuous, with lavish plasterwork, silverwork and parquet flooring, **Verrio ceiling paintings** and rich hangings, tapestries, silk damasks and cut velvets. The Long

---

RICHMOND'S LOST PALACE

Richmond Palace was acquired by Henry I in 1125, when it was still known as **Shene Palace**. The first king to frequent the place was Edward III, who lay dying here in 1377 while his mistress urged the servants to prise the rings from his fingers. Seventeen years later a grief-stricken Richard II razed the place to the ground after his wife, Anne of Bohemia, died here of the plague. Henry V had it restored and Edward IV held jousting tournaments on the green, but it was Henry VII who, in an atypical burst of extravagance, constructed the largest complex of all, renaming it **Richmond Palace** after his Yorkshire earldom. Henry VIII granted the palace to his fourth wife, Anne of Cleves, as part of their divorce settlement. Queen Mary and Philip of Spain spent part of their honeymoon here and Elizabeth I came here to die in 1603. A lot of history is attached to the place, but very little of Richmond Palace survived the Commonwealth and even less is visible now. The most obvious relic is the unspectacular red-brick **Tudor Gateway**, in the southwest corner of Richmond Green.

Gallery, in the west wing, features a Van Dyck self-portrait, a portrait of Elizabeth Dysart, and six "Court Beauties" by **Peter Lely**.

The gardens

Ham House's formal seventeenth-century **gardens** have been beautifully restored to something like their former glory. To the east of the house lies the Cherry Garden, laid out with a pungent lavender parterre, and surrounded by yew hedges and pleached hornbeam arbours. On the south terrace, the Lauderdales would display their citrus trees, considered the height of luxury at the time, while across the lawn lies the "Wildernesse" of hornbeam hedges and maple trees. Finally, to the west, you'll find the partially resurrected kitchen garden, overlooked by the Orangery – the oldest in Britain – which serves as a tearoom.

22

Richmond Hill

If you're still wondering what's so special about Richmond, take a hike up **Richmond Hill**. To get there, head up Hill Rise from the top of Bridge Street, passing between the eighteenth-century antique shops and tearooms on your left, and the small sloping green on your right. Eventually you come to the **Terrace Gardens**, celebrated for the view up the thickly wooded Thames valley. Turner, Reynolds, Kokoschka and countless other artists have painted this view, which remains relatively unchanged and takes in six counties from Windsor to the North Downs. Richmond's wealthiest inhabitants have flocked to the hill's commanding heights over the centuries. The future George IV is alleged to have spent his secret honeymoon at **3 The Terrace**, after marrying Mrs Fitzherbert; twice divorced and a Catholic to boot, she was never likely to be Queen, though she bore the prince ten children.

Further along, on the opposite side of the street, William Chambers built **Wick House** in 1772 as a summer residence for the enormously successful Joshua Reynolds. The building currently houses the nurses who work at the nearby **Royal Star & Garter Home**, a rest home for war veterans built shortly after World War I, and now the dominant feature of the hillside. Disabled war veterans are also among the workforce at Richmond's **Poppy Factory** (Ⓦpoppyfactory.org), who produce the thousands of poppies, petals and wreaths used during the build-up to Remembrance Day in November; the factory welcomes visitors and conducts regular ninety-minute guided tours.

Richmond Park

Daily March–Sept 7am–dusk; Oct–Feb 7.30am–dusk • Free • ☎ 020 8948 3209, Ⓦroyalparks.gov.uk • Bus #371 from ⊖ Richmond to Richmond Gate or #65 from ⊖ Richmond to Petersham Gate

Richmond's greatest attraction is the enormous **Richmond Park**, at the top of Richmond Hill – 2500 acres of undulating grassland and bracken, dotted with coppiced woodland and as wild as anything in London. Royal hunting ground since the thirteenth century (when it was known as Shene Chase), this is Europe's largest city park – eight miles across at its widest point. It's famous for its red and fallow deer, which roam freely – and breed so successfully, they have to be culled twice a year – and for its ancient oaks. Though for the most part untamed, there are a couple of deliberately landscaped plantations which feature splendid springtime azaleas and rhododendrons.

From Richmond Gate, at the top of Richmond Hill, it's a short walk south along the crest of the hill to **Pembroke Lodge** (originally known as The Molecatcher's), the childhood home of the philosopher Bertrand Russell. Set in its own lovely garden, the house is now a tearoom with outdoor seating and more spectacular views up the Thames valley. Close by, to the north, is the highest point in the park, known as **King Henry VIII's Mount**, where tradition has it the king waited for the flare launched from the Tower of London, which signalled the execution of his second wife, Anne Boleyn, though historians believe he was in Wiltshire at the time.

22

Exploring the Park

For a longer stroll through the park, head east from Pembroke Lodge into **Sidmouth Wood**, whose sweet chestnuts, oaks and beeches were planted during the nineteenth century. Originally established as pheasant cover, the wood is now a bird sanctuary, and walkers must keep to the central path, known as the Driftway. A little further east lie the **Pen Ponds**, the largest stretches of water in the park and a good spot for birdwatching. To the south is the park's extremely popular **Isabella Plantation**, a carefully landscaped woodland park, with a little rivulet running through it, two small artificial ponds, and spectacular rhododendrons and azaleas in the spring. The round trip from Richmond Gate is about four miles.

The two most important historic buildings in the park are both closed to the public. Of the two, the **White Lodge**, to the east of the Pen Ponds, is the more attractive, a Palladian villa commissioned by George II, and frequented by his wife, Queen Caroline, and their daughter, Princess Amelia. Much altered over the years, it was also the birthplace of the ill-fated Edward VIII, and it was home to the Duke and Duchess of York (later George VI and the Queen Mother); it currently houses the Royal Ballet School. The **Thatched House Lodge**, in the southernmost corner of the park, was built in the 1670s for the park's rangers, and gets its name from the thatched gazebo that can be found in the garden. General Eisenhower hung out in the lodge during World War II, and it's now home to Princess Alexandra.

Twickenham

Twickenham, on the opposite side of the river from Richmond, is best known as the home of English rugby – there's a museum if you're really keen (see opposite) – but it also conceals a cluster of lesser-known sights close to the river, all of which repay a brief visit. Most sights are by the river, and, if you want to learn a bit more about the local area, pop into the **Twickenham Museum** (Tues & Sat 11am–3pm, Sun 2–4pm; free; ☎020 8408 0070, ⓦtwickenham-museum.org.uk), 25 The Embankment, which puts on changing historical exhibitions.

ARRIVAL AND DEPARTURE

By Ferry The most picturesque approach to Twickenham is to walk along the towpath from Richmond Riverside, until you get to Hammerton's Ferry, which will take people (and bicycles) over to the Twickenham side (March–Oct Mon–Fri 10am–6pm, Sat & Sun 10am–6.30pm; Oct–Jan Sat & Sun 10am–6.30pm; £1; ⓦhammertonsferry.co.uk).

Marble Hill House

Richmond Rd • Guided tours: April–Oct Sat 10.30am & noon, Sun 10.30am, noon, 2.15 & 3.30pm • EH • £5.30 • ☎020 8892 5115, ⓦenglish-heritage.org.uk • St Margarets train station from Waterloo

A stuccoed Palladian villa set in rolling green parkland, **Marble Hill House** was completed in 1729 for Henrietta Howard, Countess of Suffolk, mistress of George II for some twenty years and, conveniently, also a lady-in-waiting to his wife, Queen Caroline (apparently "they hated one another very civilly"). She was renowned not just for her "long chestnut tresses", but also for her wit and intelligence and she entertained the Twickenham Club of Alexander Pope, John Gay and Horace Walpole.

The few original furnishings in the house are enhanced with reproductions giving the place something of the feel of a fashionable Georgian villa. The Great Room, on the *piano nobile*, is a perfect cube whose coved ceiling carries on up into the top-floor apartments. Copies of Van Dycks decorate the walls as they did in Lady Suffolk's day, but the highlight is Lady Suffolk's Bedchamber, with its Ionic columned recess – a classic Palladian device – where she died in 1767 at the age of 79. In the grounds, there are open-air concerts on occasional summer evenings.

Orleans House Gallery

Riverside • April–Sept Tues–Sat 1–5.30pm, Sun 2–5.30pm; Oct–March closes 4.30pm • Free • ☎ 020 8831 6000 • St Margarets train station from Waterloo

Set in a small wood to the west of Marble Hill Park is the **Orleans House Gallery**, in what began life as a retirement villa built in 1710 for James Johnston, who had been Secretary of State for Scotland under William III. It was most famously occupied in 1815–17 by Louis-Philippe, the exiled Duke of Orléans (and future King of the French) who referred to it as "dear quiet Twick". In 1926, it was all but entirely demolished – all, that is, except for the **Octagon**, designed for Johnston by James Gibbs in 1720 in honour of a visit by Queen Caroline. The exhibitions staged in the old stables and the modern extension are interesting enough, but it's the Octagon that steals the limelight, an unusually exuberant Baroque confection celebrated for its masterly Italian stucco decoration.

22

York House

Sion Rd • Mon–Sat 7.30am to dusk, Sun 9am to dusk • Free • St Margaret's train station from Waterloo

Another Twickenham riverside residence, the early seventeenth-century **York House**, is owned by the local council. The house itself is used for weddings, but the **gardens**, laid out by the last private owner, the Indian businessman Ratan Tata, are open to the public. The bit to head for is the riverside section – a great picnic spot – that lies beyond the sunken garden, on the other side of the delicate arched bridge spanning the road. Here, in among the yew hedges, you'll find the gardens' celebrated "**naked ladies**", seven larger-than-life marble nymphs frolicking in the water lilies of an Italian fountain, above which Venus rises up at the head of two winged horses.

Twickenham World Rugby Museum

200 Whitton Rd • Tues–Sat 10am–5pm, Sun 11am–5pm • £6 • Stadium tours £14 • ☎ 020 8892 8877, ⓦ rfu.com • Twickenham train station from Waterloo

The English rugby fan's number-one pilgrimage site is the national stadium at Twickenham, and the pompously entitled **World Rugby Museum** in the East Stand. The exhibition is full of video footage and lots of memorabilia from the sport, which was famously invented in 1823, when W.W. Ellis picked up and ran with the ball during a game of football at Rugby School. There's not much here for the nonspecialist, however, save for the Calcutta Cup, an object of supreme beauty, having been made from 270 silver rupees, with great cobra handles and an elephant lid. You can also sign up for a **stadium tour**, which allows you to see the dressing rooms and walk onto the pitch itself, and includes a visit to the museum. Note that on match days the museum is only open to match ticket-holders.

ISLANDS IN THE THAMES

If you take the boat upriver (see p.329), or walk along the towpath, you'll pass a number of islands in the middle of the Thames. Several were used in the past to grow grass and willows for basketry, but most now act as formal or informal nature reserves, like **Brentford Ait** – "ait" or "eyot" is the word used on the Thames to denote an island – which supports a large heronry. There's even a makeshift raft floating mid-river, near Marble Hill House, where a local eccentric has live for over 25 years. The only inhabited island on the tidal Thames is **Eel Pie Island**, connected to the bank near York House by a pedestrian bridge. Tea dances began at the island's Eel Pie Hotel back in the 1920s; bawdy jazz nights were the staple diet in the 1950s; Pink Floyd, the Rolling Stones and the Who all played there in the 1960s. The hotel burned down in 1971 (ⓦ eelpie.org), and the island is now better known for its eccentric community of independent-spirited artisans, among them Trevor Baylis, inventor of the clockwork radio.

22

Strawberry Hill

268 Waldegrave Rd · Mon–Wed 2–6pm, Sat & Sun noon–6pm (last admission 4.20pm) · £8 · ☎ 020 8744 1241,
ⓦ strawberryhillhouse.org.uk · Strawberry Hill train station from Waterloo

One last oddity well worth making the effort to visit is **Strawberry Hill**. In 1747 writer, wit and fashion queen Horace Walpole, youngest son of former prime minister Robert Walpole, bought this "little play-thing house…the prettiest bauble you ever saw…set in enamelled meadows, with filigree hedges", renamed it Strawberry Hill and set about inventing the most influential building in the Gothic Revival. Walpole appointed a "Committee of Taste" to embellish his project with details from other Gothic buildings: screens from Old St Paul's and Rouen cathedrals, and fan vaulting from Henry VII's Chapel in Westminster Abbey.

The house quickly became the talk of London, a place of pilgrimage for royalty and foreign dignitaries alike. Walpole was forced to issue tickets in advance (never more than four and no children) to cut down the number of visitors. Those he wished to meet he greeted dressed in a lavender suit and silver-embroidered waistcoat, sporting a cravat carved in wood by Grinling Gibbons and an enormous pair of gloves that once belonged to James I. When he died in 1797, he left the house to his friend, the sculptor Anne Damer, who continued to entertain in the same spirit, giving lavish garden parties dressed in a man's coat, hat and shoes. Walpole wanted visits of Strawberry Hill to be a theatrical experience, and, with its eccentric Gothic décor, it remains so to this day.

Wimbledon

Wimbledon is a dreary, high, bleak, windy suburb, on the edge of a threadbare heath.   Virginia Woolf

Nowadays, of course, **Wimbledon** is best known for its tennis tournament, the Wimbledon Championships, held every year in the last week of June and the first week of July, on the grass courts of the All England Lawn Tennis and Croquet Club – to give the ground its grand title. For the rest of the year, Wimbledon's vast **common** is its most popular attraction, worth a visit for its **windmill**, and for the remarkable **Southside House**.

Wimbledon Lawn Tennis Museum

Church Rd · Daily 10am–5pm · £11 · Guided tours (1hr 30min) by appointment only; phone ☎ 020 8946 6131; £20 · ☎ 020 8946 2244,
ⓦ wimbledon.com · Bus #493 from ⊖ Southfields

If you've missed the tournament itself (see p.437), the next best thing for tennis fans is a quick spin around the state-of-the-art **Wimbledon Lawn Tennis Museum.** It traces the history of the game, which is descended from the *jeu de paume* played by the French clergy from the twelfth century onwards. The modern version, though, is considered to have been invented by a Victorian major, who called it "Sphairstike", a name that, not surprisingly, failed to stick. The new sport was initially seen as a genteel pastime, suitable for both gentlemen and ladies, and its early enthusiasts hailed almost exclusively from the aristocracy and the clergy – the museum's Edwardian dressing room is the epitome of upper-class masculinity. As well as the historical and fashion angles and the tennis-star memorabilia, there's also plenty of opportunity for watching vintage game footage.

Wimbledon Windmill

Wimbledon Rd · April–Oct Sat 2–5pm, Sun 11am–5pm · £2 · ☎ 020 8947 2825, ⓦ wimbledonwindmill.org.uk · Bus #93 from
⊖ Wimbledon

With none of the views of Richmond, **Wimbledon Common** can appear rather bleak: mostly rough grass and bracken punctuated by playing fields and golf courses, and cut through by the busy A3. The chief reason to come here is the **Wimbledon Windmill**, situated at the end of Windmill Road in the northern half of the common, with conveniently placed tearooms nearby. Built in 1817, the mill was closed down in 1864, and converted into cottages, one of which was home to Baden-Powell when he began writing his *Scouting for Boys* in 1908. Subsequently restored and turned into a museum, the windmill is the last remaining hollow-post flour mill in the country; you can also climb into the first section of the wooden cap and see the giant chain wheel.

Putney Vale Cemetery

Stag Lane • Mon–Sat 8am–dusk, Sun 10am–dusk • Free • Bus #85 or #265 from ⊖ Putney Bridge

Sandwiched between Wimbledon Common and Richmond Park, by the busy A3, is **Putney Vale Cemetery**, worth a visit for its wonderful array of Victorian angels and its peaceful Gardens of Remembrance, at their best in early summer. Once you enter, turn right, and head to the end of Richards Way, where you'll find the nautical grave of Bruce Ismay, *Titanic* survivor and chairman of the ill-fated White Star Line; close by lies Sandy Denny, lead singer of Fairport Convention. The cemetery's most illustrious incumbent is Alexander Kerensky, along Alexander Way, who died in New York, but was refused burial there by the Russian Orthodox Church. Kerensky was the leader of the Russian Revolution of February 1917, which overthrew the tsar, but was himself ousted by the Bolshevik Revolution of October 1917.

Cannizaro Park

West Side Common • Mon–Fri 8am to dusk, Sat & Sun 9am to dusk • Free • ☎ 020 8946 7349, ⓦ cannizaropark.com • Bus #93 from ⊖ Wimbledon

Cannizaro Park is a small, sheltered, wooded public park, made up of the grounds of Cannizaro House (now a hotel frequented by the tennis glitterati), and entered from Wimbledon Common. Within its walls are a grotesque teapot fountain, a lovely stretch of lawn for picnicking, a maze of paths, an aviary, an Italian garden and a wonderful array of rhododendrons, azaleas and magnolias. The park also stages occasional student art shows and has an open-air music and theatre festival every July.

Wat Buddhapadipa

14 Calonne Rd • Daily 9am–6pm • Free • ☎ 020 8946 1357, ⓦ buddhapadipa.org • Bus #93 from ⊖ Wimbledon

Probably the most unusual and intriguing sight in Wimbledon is the **Wat Buddhapadipa**, a startling, white-gabled Thai Buddhist temple, with a richly decorated red and gold roof, completed in 1982. You can visit the temple grounds any day of the week, and there are classes, courses and ceremonies throughout the year, but the temple itself is only accessible at the weekend.

Southside House

3–4 Woodhayes Rd • Easter–Sept Wed, Sat & Sun 2, 3 & 4pm • £6 • ☎ 020 8946 7643, ⓦ southsidehouse.com • Bus #93 from ⊖ Wimbledon

Hidden from the road behind high walls is the Dutch-Baroque mansion of **Southside House**, built in the late seventeenth century, and now hemmed in by Wimbledon's King's College School. Visiting the house is an unforgettable experience, not least because you may be guided round, and fed with anecdotes, by the eccentric descendants of the Pennington-Mellor-Munthe family who first built the house – several of whom still live here in a kind of time warp, using only candles for light and open fires for warmth, surrounded by the house's rich and slowly disintegrating decor, and the family's ancestral hangings, many of which are extremely valuable.

Inside, the place has a ramshackle feel, partly because at heart it's still an old Tudor farmhouse, onto which a Dutch facade has been added. Nevertheless, virtually every room is stuffed to the rafters with artworks and other sundry heirlooms. In the Dining Room alone, there are no fewer than 34, mostly full-length, portraits, including three by Van Dyck, one each by Hogarth and Goya, and a depiction of St George by

Burne-Jones. Other treasures on show include the sapphire worn by the last king of Serbia on the day of his assassination, and, in a cabinet of curiosities in the royal bedroom upstairs, you can see the pearl necklace worn by Marie Antoinette on the day of her execution. Finally, in the Music Room, there's a portrait of Angelica Kauffmann, a Reynolds self-portrait, a Fragonard and one of George Romney's famous portraits of Emma, Lady Hamilton, who used to strike her "attitudes" in that very room.

Hampton Court Palace

April–Oct daily 10am–6pm • Nov–March closes 4.30pm • £14.50 • ☎ 020 3166 6000, ⓦ hrp.org.uk • Hampton Court train station from Waterloo

Hampton Court Palace, a sprawling red-brick ensemble on the banks of the Thames, thirteen miles southwest of London, is the finest of England's royal abodes. And it's

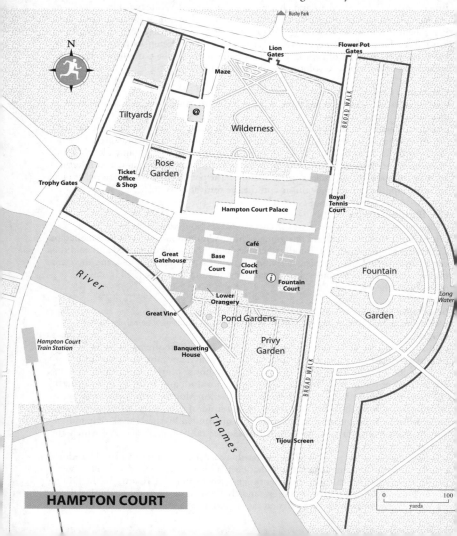

HAMPTON COURT

up there with the Tower of London when it comes to the variety of attractions on offer: not only does it boast Tudor halls and kitchens, it's got some fabulous Baroque interiors in the wings designed by Wren, superb works of art, a beautiful riverside setting, a yew hedge maze, a Real Tennis court, impressive formal gardens and a vast royal park. If your time is limited, the most rewarding sections are Henry VIII's Apartments, William III's Apartments and Henry VIII's Kitchens – and be sure to leave time for the Maze.

Brief history

The present building was begun in 1516 by the upwardly mobile **Cardinal Wolsey**, Henry VIII's high-powered, fast-living Lord Chancellor. Wolsey fell from favour when he failed to secure a papal annulment for Henry's marriage to Catherine of Aragon, and, in a vain attempt to ingratiate himself, gifted the place to the king in 1528.

Like Wolsey, **Henry VIII** spent enormous sums of money on the palace, enlarging the kitchens, rebuilding the chapel and altering the rooms to suit the tastes of the last five of his six wives. Under Elizabeth I and James I, Hampton Court became renowned for its masques, plays and balls; during the Civil War, it was a refuge and then a prison for Charles I. The palace was put up for sale during the Commonwealth, but, with no buyers forthcoming, Cromwell decided to move in and lived here on and off until his death in 1658. Charles II laid out the gardens, inspired by what he had seen at Versailles, but it was **William and Mary** who instigated the most radical alterations, hiring Christopher Wren to remodel the buildings. Wren intended to tear down the whole palace and build a new Versailles, but, in the end, had to content himself with rebuilding the east and south wings, adding the Banqueting House on the river and completing the chapel for Queen Anne.

George III eschewed the place, apparently because he associated it with the beatings he received here from his grandfather. Instead, he established grace-and-favour residences for indigent members of the royal household, which still exist today. The palace was opened to the public in 1838, and, along with the vast expanse of **Bushy Park**, it's now a major tourist attraction.

INFORMATION AND TOURS

Admission Tickets to the Royal Apartments cover entry to everything in the palace and grounds – to save money and avoid queuing, buy your tickets online. If you don't want to visit the apartments, you can buy a separate ticket for the gardens (April–Sept; £5.30) and the Maze (£3.85).

Tours The State Apartments are divided into six thematic walking tours, which are numbered and colour-coded. There's not a lot of information in the rooms, but guided tours, lasting half an hour or so, are available at no extra charge; all are led by period-costumed historians, who do a fine job of bringing the place to life. In addition, audioguides are available from the information centre on the east side of Clock Court.

Events The Hampton Court Palace Flower Show takes place in early July, rivals Chelsea for sheer snob factor, and is likewise organized by the Royal Horticultural Society (@rhs.org.uk). The Hampton Court Palace Festival (@hamptoncourtfestival.com) features stars from the classical and pop music worlds, and takes place each year in June.

The Palace

The Tudor west front may no longer be moated but it positively prickles with turrets, castellations, chimneypots and pinnacles. The **Great Gatehouse** looks suitably imposing, but it would have been five storeys high in Wolsey's day. The first and largest courtyard, **Base Court**, is reminiscent of an Oxbridge college and features another Tudor gateway known as Anne Boleyn's Gateway, though it too dates from the time of Wolsey. Beyond lies **Clock Court**, which has none of the uniformity of the other two quadrangles: to the north rises the Tudor Great Hall, to the south Wren's colonnade, announcing the new State Apartments, and to the east a fairly convincing mock-Tudor gateway by William Kent. Originally centred on a large fountain which was equipped by Elizabeth I with a nozzle that soaked innocent passers-by, the courtyard gets its current name from the

22

THE GHOST OF CATHERINE HOWARD

Henry VIII married his fifth wife, **Catherine Howard**, in July 1540, just weeks after having annulled his six-month marriage to Anne of Cleves. Unfortunately, despite being less than twenty, Catherine had already had sexual relations with her music tutor, **Henry Mannox**, was pre-contracted to marry her lover, another courtier named **Francis Dereham**, and began an affair with another courtier named **Thomas Culpeper**. Her ambitious family – who were out of favour since the execution of Anne Boleyn, Catherine's cousin – somewhat optimistically hoped to conceal these inconvenient truths from Henry, and to restore their influence at court.

It took until November 1541 for Henry to find out he'd been duped. Seated in the Royal Pew at Hampton Court, he was passed the note from Thomas Cranmer, the Archbishop of Canterbury, alleging that Catherine was not in fact a virgin when he married her. Catherine was arrested a few days later, but is alleged to have given her guards the slip and run down the **Haunted Gallery** in an attempt to make a final plea for mercy to the king, who was praying in the chapel. Henry refused to see her, and she was dragged kicking and screaming back to her chambers. To this day, a ghost can be heard re-enacting the scene – or so the story goes.

astronomical clock on the inside of the Anne Boleyn Gateway, made in 1540 for Henry VIII, which was used to calculate the high tide at London Bridge (and thus the estimated time of arrival of palace guests travelling by boat). The last and smallest of the three courtyards is Wren's **Fountain Court**, which crams in more windows than seems possible.

Henry VIII's Apartments

Henry VIII lavished more money on Hampton Court than on any other palace except Greenwich (which no longer exists). The only major survival from Tudor times, however, is his **Great Hall**, completed with remarkable speed in 1534, with Henry having made the builders work day and night – a highly dangerous exercise in candlelight. The ornate double hammerbeam roof would originally have been painted blue, red and gold and featured a louvre to allow the smoke to escape from the central hearth. Later, the hall served as the palace theatre, where theatrical troupes, among them Shakespeare's, entertained royalty. Even Cromwell had an organ installed here so he and his family could enjoy recitals by John Milton, an accomplished musician as well as a poet.

Passing through the Horn Room, you enter the **Great Watching Chamber**. The gilded oak-ribbed ceiling is studded with leather-mâché Tudor insignia, and hung with tapestries that were part of Wolsey's collection. Up to eighty yeomen would have been stationed here, guarding the principal entrance to the king's private chambers, which William and Mary found "old-fashioned and uncomfortable" and consequently demolished.

From here you reach the **Haunted Gallery**, built by Wolsey to connect his apartments to the chapel, and home to the ghost of Catherine Howard (see box above). The gallery gives access to the Royal Pew, from which you can look down on the **Chapel Royal**, and admire the colourful false-timber Tudor vaulting wrought in plaster, heavy with pendants of gilded music-making cherubs – one of the most memorable sights in the whole palace. It was here that Henry married the sixth of his wives (and the only one to outlive him), Catherine Parr.

Mary II's Apartments

The Queen's apartments remained unfinished at Queen Mary's death in 1694, and weren't fully furnished and decorated until the time of Queen Caroline, George II's wife. The main approach is via the grandiose **Queen's Staircase**, splendidly decorated with trompe-l'oeil reliefs and a coffered dome by William Kent.

One of the finest rooms here is the **Queen's Drawing Room**, decorated top to bottom with trompe-l'oeil paintings depicting Queen Anne's husband, George of

Denmark – in heroic naval guise, and also, on the south wall, riding naked and wigless on the back of a "dolphin". Queen Anne takes centre stage on the ceiling as Justice, somewhat inappropriately given her habit of not paying her craftsmen, including Verrio, the painter of this room. After Anne's death in 1714, the Prince and Princess of Wales (later George II and Queen Caroline) took over the Queen's Apartments, though they hated the trompe-l'oeil paintings and hung Mantegna's works over the top of them. In 1717, the couple fell out with the king and moved to Kew; the ceiling painting in the **Queen's Bedroom** by James Thornhill predates the quarrel, with four portraits of a seemingly happy Hanoverian family staring at one another from the coving.

The **Queen's Gallery** features one of the most ornate marble fireplaces in the palace – originally intended for the King's Bedchamber – with putti, doves and Venus frolicking above the mantelpiece; the walls, meanwhile, are hung with Gobelin tapestries depicting Alexander the Great's exploits and lined with Chinese vases and Delftware.

Georgian Private Apartments

The **Georgian Private Apartments** begin with the rooms of the **Cumberland Suite**, lived in by George II before his accession, then by his eldest son, Prince Frederick, and lastly by Frederick's brother, the Duke of Cumberland, better known as "Butcher Cumberland" for his ruthless suppression of the Jacobites in Scotland. The rooms were decorated by Kent, who added Gothic touches to the first two rooms and a grandiose Neoclassical alcove in the bedchamber.

Beyond here you'll find the tiny **Wolsey Closet**, which, although a Victorian invention, gives a tantalizing impression of the splendour of Wolsey's original palace. It's a jewel of a room – though at 12ft square it's easily missed – with brightly coloured early sixteenth-century paintings set above exquisite linenfold panelling and a fantastic gilded ceiling of interlaced octagons.

Next is the **Communication Gallery**, constructed to link the King's and Queen's apartments, now lined with Lely's "Windsor Beauties", flattering portraits of the best-looking women in the court of Charles II. The **Cartoon Gallery** was purpose-built by Wren to display the Raphael Cartoons – the originals are in the V&A, and what you see are late seventeenth-century copies. Tapestries made from the cartoons are scattered throughout William and Mary's apartments.

The next sequence of rooms is of minor interest, though they do include an excellent Gibbons overmantle in the Queen's Private Bedchamber. Last of all, you enter the **Queen's Private Oratory**, used by Queen Caroline for private worship – it's one of the few windowless rooms, hence the octagonal dome and skylight.

William III's Apartments

William III's Apartments are approached via the **King's Staircase**, the grandest of the lot thanks chiefly to Verrio's busy, militaristic trompe-l'oeil paintings glorifying the king, depicted here as Alexander the Great. The **King's Guard Chamber** is notable chiefly for its 3000-piece display of arms, arranged as they were laid out in the time of William III. William's rather modest throne still stands in the **King's Presence Chamber**, under a canopy of crimson damask. The sixteenth-century Brussels tapestries in the room were originally commissioned by Henry VIII for Whitehall Palace.

Further on, in the **King's Privy Chamber**, there's a much grander throne used by William, with a canopy that still retains its original ostrich feathers. The most impressive room here is the **Great Bed Chamber**, which boasts a superb vertical Gibbons frieze and ceiling paintings by Verrio – just as you're leaving this floor, you'll catch a glimpse of a splendidly throne-like velvet toilet. Ground-floor highlights include a semi-nude portrait by Van Dyck of his mistress Margaret Lemon, in the East Closet, the **Lower Orangery**, built to house the king's orange trees during the winter, and the only room in the palace lockable solely from the inside (a tryst room – highly unusual for the royals' very public life). Past here is the **King's Private Dining Room**, its table laden with pyramids of meringues and fruit and its walls hung with eight full-length portraits of Queen Mary's favourite ladies-in-waiting (known as the "Hampton Court Beauties"), for which the German-born painter Godfrey Kneller received a knighthood.

Young Henry VIII's Story

Several early Tudor rooms, with striking linenfold panelling and gilded strapwork ceilings, are now used to display **Young Henry VIII's Story**. This is a worthy attempt by the palace to portray Henry in his virile youth, during his happy, twenty-year marriage to his first wife, Catherine of Aragon. Interactive screens help tell the story of the Battle of the Spurs at Guinegate in 1613, when Henry led his troops from the front, and of the Field of the Cloth of Gold, Henry's famous meeting with the French king, François I, in 1620.

Henry VIII's Kitchens

After a surfeit of opulent interiors, the workaday **Tudor Kitchens** come as something of a relief. Henry VIII quadrupled the size of the kitchens, large sections of which have survived to this day and have been restored and embellished with historical reconstructions. Past the Boiling Room and Flesh Larder (not for squeamish vegetarians) you come to the **Great Kitchen**, where a fire is still lit in the main hearth every day. This kitchen is only one of three Henry built to cope with the prodigious consumption of the royal court – six oxen, forty sheep and a thousand or more larks, pheasants, pigeons and peacocks were an average daily total. The tour ends in Henry's vast **Wine Cellar**, where the palace's Rhineland wine was stored. At each main meal, the king and his special guests would be supplied with eight pints of wine; courtiers had to make do with three gallons of beer.

The Gardens

The gardens' magnificent **Broad Walk** runs for half a mile from the Thames past Wren's austere East Front to the putti-encrusted Flower Pot Gate and is lined with some of the country's finest herbaceous borders. Halfway along lies the indoor **Royal Tennis Court**, established here by Henry VIII (a keen player of Real Tennis himself), but extensively restored by Charles II. If you're lucky, you might even catch a game of this arcane precursor of modern tennis, though the rules are incredibly tricky.

Fanning out from the Broad Walk is William's **Fountain Garden**, a grand, semicircular parterre, which in William's day featured box hedges, thirteen fountains and dwarf yew trees pruned to look like obelisks. A fair number of these "black pyramids", as Virginia Woolf called them, have been reduced to chubby cone shapes, while a solitary pool stands in place of the fountains, and the box hedges have become plain lawns. A semicircular canal separates the Fountain Garden from the Home Park beyond, its waters feeding Charles II's **Long Water**, Hampton Court's most Versaillean feature, which slices the Home Park in two.

Privy Garden

Overlooked by Wren's magnificent South Front is the formal **Privy Garden**, laid out as it would have been under William III; the twelve magnificent wrought-iron panels at the river end of the garden are the work of Jean Tijou. To the west, you can peek into the **Pond Gardens**, which were originally constructed as ornamental fish ponds stocked with freshwater fish for the kitchens, and feature some of the gardens' most spectacularly colourful flowerbeds. Further along, protected by glass, is the palace's celebrated **Great Vine**, grown from a cutting in 1768 by Capability Brown and averaging about seven hundred pounds of Black Hamburg grapes per year (sold at the palace in September).

Close by stands the **Lower Orangery**, designed by Wren and used as a dimly lit gallery for *The Triumphs of Caesar* a series of heroic canvases by **Andrea Mantegna**, bought by Charles I in 1629 and kept here ever since. Painted around 1486 for the

Ducal Palace in Mantua, Mantegna's home town, these nine richly coloured paintings, depicting the general's victory parade, are among his best works, characterized by his obsessive interest in archeological and historical accuracy. Beyond the South Gardens, beside the river, is William III's dinky little red-brick **Banqueting House**, built for intimate riverside soirees, with castellations and mouldings by Gibbons and exuberant paintings by Verrio.

The Maze

To the north of the palace, Henry VIII laid out a **Tiltyard** with five towers for watching jousting tournaments, one of which survives near the garden restaurant. William III transformed the tiltyard into a **Wilderness** – an informal park of evergreens – which now contains the most famous feature of the palace gardens, the deceptively tricky trapezoidal **Maze**, laid out in 1714. Mazes, or labyrinths as they were called at the time, were used by pilgrims, who used to crawl along on hands and knees reciting prayers, as penance for not making a pilgrimage to the Holy Land. They were all the rage among the eighteenth-century nobility, who used them primarily for amusement, secret conversations and flirtation. The maze was originally planted with hornbeam, but, with the onset of the tourist boom in the 1960s, the hornbeam had to be replaced with yew.

Bushy Park

Beyond the Lion Gates, to the north of the Maze, across Hampton Court Road, lies **Bushy Park**, the palace's semi-wild enclosure of over a thousand acres, which sustains copious herds of fallow and red deer. Wren's mile-long royal road, Chestnut Avenue, cuts through the park, and is at its best in May when the trees are in blossom. The main architectural feature of the park is the **Diana Fountain**, situated a third of the way along the avenue to help break the monotony. The statue – which, in fact, depicts Arethusa – was commissioned by Charles II from Francesco Fanelli and originally graced the Privy Garden; stranded in the centre of this vast pond, she looks ill-proportioned and a bit forlorn.

Off to the west, a little further up the avenue, you'll come upon the **Waterhouse Woodland Gardens**, created in 1949, and at their most colourful each spring when the rhododendrons, azaleas and camellias are in bloom. The crowds are fairly thin even here, compared with the crush around the palace, but if you really want to seek out some of the park's abundant wildlife head for its wilder western section, where few visitors venture.

22

Accommodation

Accommodation in London is expensive. Compared with most European cities, you pay top dollar in every category from the cheapest hostel to the swankiest five-star. Add to that the fact that most B&Bs and many hotels are housed in former residential properties – so rooms tend to be small, and lifts are rare – and it's understandable that some unprepared visitors come away feeling shortchanged. With a little savvy, however, you can get some great deals – just don't expect a mansion for the price of a garret. Remember that rooms with shared facilities may be larger than en-suites, where showers and loos are often shoehorned into tiny corners. And in some of the newer breed of boutique guesthouses, small needn't mean inconvenient anyhow – bijou can be great fun when delivered with wit and style in a buzzy location.

Talking of **location**, bear in mind that travelling around London is not that difficult with an Oyster card and a tube map – while the central London hotels are the hippest and the most exciting, the prices reflect this, and it may suit you better to head out of zone 1, especially if you're not short of time.

Demand for beds is so great that the city doesn't really have a **low season**, though things do slacken off a little in the months just after Christmas.

ESSENTIALS

Costs London's hostels are among the most costly in the world, while an astonishing number of hotels charge guests the very top international prices – from £300 per luxurious night. Even the most basic B&Bs struggle to bring their tariffs below £60 for a double with shared facilities, which is why so many people head for the budget chain hotels (see p.356) for a cheap sleep. For a really decent hotel room, you shouldn't expect much change out of £100 a night. That said, even the basic places tend to have TVs, tea- and coffee-making facilities and telephones, and breakfast is very often included in the price. The way to get the best price is to look around online far enough in advance – with any luck, you should be able to shave £50–100 off room rates at some of the more upmarket hotels. The prices quoted here are for the cheapest double in high season.

British Hotel Reservation Centre (BHRC) 24hr helpline ☎ 020 7592 3055, ⓦ bhrc.co.uk. With desks at Heathrow, Gatwick and Stansted airports, and Paddington, St Pancras and Victoria train stations, BHRC offices are open daily from early till very late, and there's no booking fee – they can also get big discounts at the more upmarket hotels.

Useful websites You can book accommodation for free online at ⓦ londontown.com; payment is made directly to the hotel and they offer very good discounts. Other useful websites for last-minute offers include ⓦ laterooms.com and ⓦ lastminute.com. ⓦ londonbb.com sources classy B&B options, while ⓦ couchsurfing.com puts young travellers in touch with people to stay or hang out with for free. If you want a little more privacy, ⓦ crashpadder.com offers a similar service for people who want to rent a room in a private house for good, low rates. Going upmarket, ⓦ onefinestay.com offers luxurious "unhotels" – posh rooms in private residences with all manner of guest services thrown in.

Gay and lesbian accommodation For gay and lesbian accommodation see Chapter 27 (p.407).

23

HOTELS AND B&BS

The bulk of the recommendations here cost between £60 and £160 a double, though a few are considerably more expensive. Many hotels quote expensive walk-in or rack rates, but there are usually deals to be had online or at the weekend, which can bring down prices considerably. Prices given are for the **cheapest double room** – if not all the rooms are en suite, this will be for rooms with shared facilities. Trawling the net may produce further savings, and of course there may be additional low-season discounts.

WESTMINSTER

Sanctuary House 33 Tothill St, SW1 ☎ 020 7799 4044, ⓦ fullershotels.com; ⊖ St James's Park; map p.46. Fuller's pubs run three hotels in London; this one has a terrific location by St James's Park. Rooms, despite being above the drinking action, are quiet enough, decked out in comfortable and uncontroversial modern Victoriana. Breakfast is extra, and served in the pub. Rates depend on availability – ask about the weekend deals. Free wi-fi. __£120__

VICTORIA

B&B Belgravia 64–66 Ebury St, SW1 ☎ 020 7259 8570, ⓦ bb-belgravia.com; ⊖ Victoria; map p.36. A rarity in this neck of the woods – a light and well-designed B&B with flair, very close to the train and coach stations. The 17 slick rooms are boutique-hotel quality, with original features and modern touches; those on the ground floor can be noisy. They also offer nearby studios from £135. Free wi-fi and bike loan. __£129__

Cartref House 129 Ebury St, SW1 ☎ 020 7730 6176, ⓦ cartrefhouse.co.uk; ⊖ Victoria; map p.36. A family-run Georgian B&B with ten fresh, plain en-suite rooms, including a family room (£156) that sleeps four. Free wi-fi. __£98__

Cherry Court Hotel 23 Hugh St, SW1 ☎ 020 7828 2840, ⓦ cherrycourthotel.co.uk; ⊖ Victoria; map p.36. Bargain, mid-terrace Victorian B&B on a quiet street, with amiable staff and a small garden. The rooms are tiny, but all are en suite, there are several triples (£85) and the family room sleeps five (£120). Breakfast is minimal. __£60__

★ **Luna Simone Hotel** 47–49 Belgrave Rd, SW1 ☎ 020 7834 5897, ⓦ lunasimonehotel.com; ⊖ Victoria; map p.36. Very good-value family-run B&B with a bright foyer, friendly staff, colourful touches and spruce, well-maintained en-suite rooms, including triples (£130) and quads (£150). The full English breakfasts are large, and there's free wi-fi on the ground floor and in the lobby. __£95__

23

Morgan House 120 Ebury St, SW1 ☎020 7730 2384, ⓦmorganhouse.co.uk; ⊖ Victoria; map p.36. An above-average B&B in a comfortable Georgian building with a patio garden. Rooms are a good size, with character and mostly en suite; the family room (£148) crams in a double and a bunk bed. Full breakfasts, and free wi-fi in the lobby. **£78**

ST JAMES'S

Stafford London Kempinski 16–18 St James's Place, SW1 ☎020 7493 0111, ⓦthestaffordhotel.co.uk; ⊖ Green Park; map p.66. Tucked in a quiet backstreet off St James's St, the *Stafford* provides high-class boutique style in the main building, and even more indulgence in the Carriage House, a row of beautifully converted eighteenth-century stables. The hotel also has the quirky, memorabilia-stuffed *American Bar*, founded to provide cocktails for pioneering American visitors in the early 1930s, splendid breakfasts and a delightful courtyard. **£300**

MAYFAIR

Grosvenor House Park Lane, W1 ☎020 7499 6363, ⓦlondongrosvenorhouse.co.uk; ⊖ Marble Arch; map p.78. Now a Marriott property, this is one of the capital's *grandes dames*, open since 1929 – the Queen learnt to skate in the hotel's ice rink (now the gargantuan Great Hall). Rooms (nearly 500 of them) are nicely understated and although rack rates are high, online deals and Marriott promotions yield some five-star bargains. Breakfast not included. **£170**

MARYLEBONE

Lincoln House 33 Gloucester Place, W1 ☎020 7486 7630, ⓦlincoln-house-hotel.co.uk; ⊖ Marble Arch or Baker Street; map p.89. The location and the good prices are the main draw at this B&B, in one of Marylebone's lovely Georgian buildings: all rooms are en suite and well equipped, though walls can be thin. Rates vary according to the size of the bed and length of stay; there are some excellent online discounts. Breakfast costs extra. Free laundry facilities and wi-fi. **£75**

Minotel Wigmore Court Hotel 23 Gloucester Place, W1 ☎020 7935 0928, ⓦwigmore-hotel.co.uk; ⊖ Marble Arch or Baker Street; map p.89. The dated floral decor may not be to everyone's taste, but the eighteenth-century townhouse is handsome, and the en-suite rooms, including family rooms, are comfortable. Reliable standards and service have won this B&B a high tally of returning clients. Free wi-fi, but it's patchy. **£110**

Sumner Hotel 54 Upper Berkeley St, W1 ☎020 7723 2244, ⓦthesumner.com; ⊖ Marble Arch; map p.89. A spruce B&B – with the feel of a boutique hotel – in an elegant Georgian townhouse. Rooms vary in size and style – the best are light and modern; some have tiny balconies; those facing the street can be noisy – but all are tasteful and comfortable, with good bathrooms, and there's a tranquil sitting room for guests. Breakfast is a buffet. Free wi-fi. **£160**

SOHO AND FITZROVIA

Charlotte Street Hotel 15–17 Charlotte St, W1 ☎020 7806 2000, ⓦfirmdale.com; ⊖ Goodge Street or Tottenham Court Road; map p.97. Swanky Georgian townhouse hotel, part of the boutique hotel group Firmdale, in a restaurant-filled street just north of Oxford St. Public spaces are lined with Bloomsbury-set originals, while the quiet, English eccentric rooms – cool without being minimal

BUDGET CHAIN HOTELS

Chain hotels have pretty much got the **budget hotel** market sewn up. B&Bs may be able to offer a more personal touch and more character, but the franchises are often cheaper, in unbeatable central locations, and guarantee clean, no-surprises rooms.

Bumping along at the bottom are *easyHotel* (ⓦeasyhotel.com), whose prices start at just £29 for an en-suite double – the earlier you book the less you pay, and if you want a window, TV use or room cleaning, it's extra; there are branches in South Ken, Paddington, Victoria, Earl's Court and Heathrow, with more in the pipeline. Serious bargains can also be had at *Travelodge* (ⓦtravelodge.com), which has some handy locations in Covent Garden, King's Cross, Waterloo, Marylebone and Southwark; rooms are utilitarian, but if you book online well in advance, en-suite doubles can cost less than £50. *Premier Inn* (ⓦpremierinn.com) is the other top budget option. It's generally considered a cut above *Travelodge*, and also has good online bargains; locations are good, too, with branches by County Hall, near Tate Modern, by the Tower of London, in Hampstead and King's Cross, among others – and with one due to open in Leicester Square in 2012. Meanwhile, the Asian *Tune* chain offers one hotel in London (see p.360) and has plans for more.

If you want a quick nap at the airport – either Heathrow or Gatwick – the fast-growing international *Yotel* chain (ⓦyotel.com) is handy: rates start at £32 for 4hr, or £70 per night, which buys you a raised bed in a capsule, complete with tiny toilet and shower, foldout desk and TV.

The rest of the chain gang aren't worth considering – you can get better value elsewhere.

– have sumptuous fittings, Tivoli radios, DVD players and the like. There's a gym, a restaurant especially popular for afternoon tea, and a chic on-site cinema that hosts a popular Sunday movie club. Free wi-fi. **£240**

★ **Dean Street Townhouse** 69–71 Dean St, W1 ☎ 020 7434 1775, ⓦ deanstreettownhouse.com; ⊖ Tottenham Court Road or Leicester Square; map p.100. One of a chic set of hotels owned by the trendy Soho House members' club, this 1730s beauty sits next to its starry, stylishly bohemian dining room. There's a "broom cupboard" and a few "tiny" rooms (from £120) – manageable for solo travellers, or if you're just staying one night – but the "small" (from £160) rooms are ample, and once you get to "medium" and "bigger" (from £270) you have plenty of space. Each is different and all are luxurious, with gorgeous details including handpainted wallpaper, funky toiletries, fresh milk and cookies, and clawfoot tubs, some of them in the bedrooms themselves. Free wi-fi. **£120**

★ **Hazlitt's** 6 Frith St, W1 ☎ 020 7434 1771, ⓦ hazlittshotel.com; ⊖ Tottenham Court Road; map p.100. Off the south side of Soho Square, this early eighteenth-century building hides away a hotel of real character and charm. Creaky, crooked old stairs lead up to romantic en-suite rooms, exquisitely and quirkily decorated with period furniture and old books. Breakfast (served in the rooms) is not included. **£230**

St John Hotel 1 Leicester St, WC2 ☎ 020 3301 8069, ⓦ stjohnhotellondon.com; ⊖ Leicester Square; map p.100. A restaurant with rooms in the heart of Chinatown, providing diners at the newest *St John* dining room (see p.370) an opportunity to sleep off their pig's trotters and tripe feasts. Rooms continue the pared-down *St John* concept: fresh, modern, plain and clean, with a vaguely nautical feel, but they are pricey. The cheapest "table to bed" bunks are tiny. **£200**

Soho Hotel 4 Richmond Mews, W1 ☎ 020 7559 3000, ⓦ firmdale.com; ⊖ Tottenham Court Road; map p.100. Another Firmdale production, the *Soho* has a slightly more self-conscious swagger than its sister hotels (the *Charlotte Street* and the *Covent Garden*). The eclectic decor is bold and witty, from the Oriental lobby to the camp fuchsia boudoirs, while facilities are, as you'd expect, top-notch. They have two cinemas – one done out in fake fur and scarlet leather, and the other with a 3D screen – while the bar, *Refuel*, is one of London's coolest. Free wi-fi. **£295**

BLOOMSBURY

Arosfa Hotel 83 Gower St, WC1 ☎ 020 7636 2115, ⓦ arosfalondon.com; ⊖ Goodge Street or Euston Square; map p.120. Though the public spaces are impressively swish, the 15 en-suite rooms in this B&B are plain and bathrooms are tiny. But it's clean, with TVs, tea and coffee facilities, and a small garden space out back. Free wi-fi. **£97**

Arran House Hotel 77–79 Gower St, WC1 ☎ 020 7636 2186, ⓦ arranhotel-london.com; ⊖ Goodge Street; map p.120. Clean family-run B&B, with a variety of rooms from singles to quints and some hostel-style accommodation (£35–40). The cheaper rooms – which are best value – have shared bathrooms (larger than those in the en-suites) and there's a fridge for guests' use. Hearty breakfast included. Free wi-fi. **£97**

Celtic Hotel 61–63 Guilford St, WC1 ☎ 020 7837 6737; ⊖ Russell Square; map p.120. Simple, spotless and friendly family-run hotel just off Russell Square, with well-equipped rooms and two comfy lounges; the cheapest rooms have shared facilities. Rates include full English breakfast. **£70**

Jesmond Hotel 63 Gower St, WC1 ☎ 020 7636 3199, ⓦ jesmondhotel.org.uk; ⊖ Goodge Street; map p.120. Very good-value Bloomsbury hotel with a pretty, peaceful little garden at the back. Rooms are clean but can be on the small side; staff are unfailingly friendly and they'll do your laundry for £7.50. Six of the 15 rooms have shared facilities. Full breakfast included. **£80**

★ **Ridgemount Hotel** 65–67 Gower St, WC1 ☎ 020 7636 1141, ⓦ ridgemounthotel.co.uk; ⊖ Goodge Street; map p.120. Old-fashioned, cosy and justly popular B&B, with small rooms (15 of the 32 have shared facilities – which are spotless). A good, basic bargain for Bloomsbury. Full breakfast and free wi-fi. **£66**

KING'S CROSS

★ **Rough Luxe** 1 Birkenhead St, WC1 ☎ 020 7837 5338, ⓦ roughluxe.co.uk; ⊖ King's Cross St Pancras; map p.120. In an unlikely setting on the mean – but gentrifying – streets of King's Cross, this gorgeously quirky, and friendly, nine-room hotel offers warmth, comfort and shabby chic opulence. Each room is different, but the arty, nostalgic aesthetic – ripped wallpaper and peeling plaster, the odd vintage TV, original artworks, creaky old floorboards – runs throughout. They keep their own bees, and serve a lovely afternoon tea. Free wi-fi. **£200**

St Pancras Renaissance Euston Rd, NW1 ☎ 020 7841 3540, ⓦ marriott.co.uk/hotels/travel/lonpr-st-pancras; ⊖ King's Cross St Pancras; map p.120. Finally, in 2011, came the moment architecture buffs, trainspotters and nostalgia fans had all been waiting for – the reopening of George Gilbert Scott's Gothic Revival masterpiece (see p.128). Lying neglected for more than 75 years, and now a luxurious Marriott hotel, it is certainly a thrilling spectacle – the lofty public spaces and colossal, softly glowing lobby evoke the golden era of railway travel, and eccentric old-style glamour seeps from every surface. It's only worth staying in the main building, though – which has less than fifty of the total 245 rooms – these, with their arched windows and high ceilings, and slight rumblings from the station below, might justify the stratospheric prices. All the

23

others are in an annexe behind, and better value can be found elsewhere. There's an atmospheric bar, a restaurant in the old station ticket office, and a fancy spa in the basement. Online deals and Marriott promotions can halve the terrifying rack rates. **£385**

COVENT GARDEN AND THE STRAND

Covent Garden Hotel 10 Monmouth St, WC2 ☎ 020 7806 1000, ⓦ firmdale.com; ⊖ Covent Garden or Leicester Square; map p.132. Another gorgeous boutique hotel from the Firmdale group (see the *Soho* and *Charlotte Street* hotels), housed in a converted French hospital in a characterful location. This one feels clubbier and cosier than the others; the in-house cinema screens operas on Sunday, as well as hosting a Saturday evening movie club. Free wi-fi. **£250**

The Fielding 4 Broad Court, Bow St, WC2 ☎ 020 7836 8305, ⓦ thefieldinghotel.co.uk; ⊖ Covent Garden; map p.132. On a pedestrianized, gas-lit court, this hotel is delightfully quiet for central London. Its en-suite rooms – the refurbished ones are far more stylish than others – are a firm favourite with visiting performers, since it's just a few yards from the Royal Opera House. No lift and no breakfast. Free wi-fi. **£140**

One Aldwych 1 Aldwych, WC2 ☎ 020 7300 1000, ⓦ onealdwych.com; ⊖ Covent Garden or Temple; map p.132. This gorgeous Art Nouveau 1907 building, built for the *Morning Post*, houses one of London's most established designer hotels. Everything is sleek and contemporary, with a cool bar and two fashionable restaurants, underwater music in the pool, modern art everywhere and impeccable service. Free wi-fi. **£350**

The Savoy Strand, WC2 ☎ 020 7836 4343, ⓦ fairmont .com/savoy; ⊖ Covent Garden or Charing Cross; map p.132. The long-awaited reopening of London's iconic Art Deco hotel caused quite a buzz in 2010, and for good reason. Dripping with history, it's as glamorous as you'd expect, with amazing decor throughout, classic bars – who could resist the starry, bordello decadence of the *Beaufort* bar – a Gordon Ramsay restaurant and gorgeously comfortable rooms. And of course even if you can't afford to stay, it's still a splendid spot for a classic afternoon tea (a cool £36). **£370**

Seven Dials Hotel 7 Monmouth St, WC2 ☎ 020 7681 0791, ⓦ sevendialshotellondon.com; ⊖ Covent Garden;

map p.132. Pleasant family-run B&B brilliantly located on a lovely street in the heart of the West End. The staircase is narrow and steep (no lift) and the 18 en-suite rooms (from singles to quads) are small, but all are clean, well equipped and comfy. Free wi-fi. **£105**

CLERKENWELL

★ **The Rookery** 12 Peter's Lane, Cowcross St, EC1 ☎ 020 7336 0931, ⓦ rookeryhotel.com; ⊖ Farringdon; map p.150. Rambling Georgian townhouse, with a pretty walled garden, that makes a delightful little hideaway in trendy Clerkenwell. It's as charming as can be with its panelled walls, flagstoned floors and creaky timeworn floorboards; rooms offer faded Baroque glam, with antique fittings, lovely rugs and super bathrooms. There's even a friendly hotel cat. **£230**

The Zetter Hotel & Townhouse 86–88 Clerkenwell Rd, EC1 ☎ 020 7324 4444, ⓦ thezetter.com; ⊖ Farringdon; map p.150. The 60-room hotel, in a warehouse converted with style and a dash of 1960s glamour, is a fixture on Clerkenwell's laidback hipster scene. Rooms are simple but bold, with colourful panache and lots of eco touches (they even have their own well); because of its popular bar and bistro, and its lovely open atrium, some rooms suffer from noise at night. The Georgian *Townhouse*, across the square, is if anything even more whimsical, with thirteen colourful, boudoirish rooms, a fabulous, cosy cocktail bar and a table tennis room. Free wi-fi. **£220**

THE CITY

Andaz 40 Liverpool St, EC2 ☎ 020 7961 1234, ⓦ andaz .com; ⊖ Liverpool Street; map p.156. The venerable 1884 *Great Eastern Hotel* by Liverpool Street Station had a complete makeover in 2000 to become the first in Hyatt's hip *Andaz* hotel group (all the others, so far, are in the US), and is a consistent winner on the designer hotel scene. Rooms are cool and minimal, with free water and organic juices, but the public areas have retained some of the old-world clubby flavour. Service is so fashion-forward that there's not even a reception desk – you relax on a sofa while check-in staff come to you. The five restaurants and bars keep the place buzzing. **£250**

Apex City of London Hotel 1 Seething Lane, EC3 ☎ 020 7977 9593, ⓦ apexhotels.co.uk; ⊖ Tower Hill; map p.156. A swish hotel on a secluded City street near the Tower of London. It's geared towards a corporate clientele, but has a good variety of rooms – the cheapest have no windows, while the priciest have great views – and service is superb. Rates vary according to availability so book early. Free gym, sauna and steam room, and free wi-fi. There's another branch, nearby *Apex London Wall* (7–9 Copthall Ave, EC2; ⊖ Moorgate) which has more of a boutique feel but the same rates. **£120**

> **TOP 5 HIDEAWAYS**
> **The Fielding** Covent Garden. See above
> **Hazlitt's** Soho. See p.357
> **The King's Wardrobe** The City. See p.360
> **The Rookery** Clerkenwell. See above
> **Rough Luxe** King's Cross. See p.357

23

★ **The King's Wardrobe** 6 Wardrobe Place, Carter Lane, EC4 ☎020 7792 2222, ⊛bridgestreet.com; ⊖ St Paul's; map p.156. In a quiet courtyard just behind St Paul's Cathedral, this place is part of an international self-catering chain that proves exceptionally good value. It's a great favourite with business visitors – the luxury pads offer fully equipped kitchens and workstations, concierge service and housekeeping. Though housed in a fourteenth-century building that once contained Edward III's royal regalia, the interior is modern. **£133**

★ **Mint Hotel Tower of London** 7 Pepys St, EC3 ☎020 7709 1000, ⊛minthotel.com; ⊖ Tower Hill; map p.156. Though it's geared towards business travellers, this large, modern and bright hotel, sister property to the equally good but slightly less well-placed *Mint Westminster* near Pimlico, is a good option for all. Rooms – nearly 600 of them – are clean, airy and comfortable, all with iMacs, and some face an impressive, very leafy, living wall. The rooftop bar, *Sky Lounge*, offers amazing views. Lots of online promotions bring the already reasonable rack rates down. Free wi-fi. **£140**

THE EAST END

★ **40 Winks** 109 Mile End Rd, E1 ☎020 7790 0259, ⊛40winks.org; ⊖ Stepney Green; map p.190. To stay here – in the early eighteenth-century home of interior designer David Carter – is to enter a fairytale world. Witty, theatrical and achingly beautiful, it offers all the wow factor of a magazine lifestyle shoot, but with real creature comforts. The only problems may be snagging a room – there are just two, a single (£95) and a large double, sharing a jaw-droppingly glamorous bathroom – and living up to the stunning surroundings (it's a shoe-free house, so make sure your socks are clean). There's a kitchen for guests' use and free wi-fi. **£140**

★ **Hoxton Hotel** 81 Great Eastern St, EC2 ☎020 7550 1000, ⊛hoxtonhotels.com; ⊖ Old Street; map p.192. "The Hox" is a fittingly happening spot in this über-hip neighbourhood, with modern but warm public spaces – all exposed brick and burnished metal – and comfy boutique rooms. They've hit all the right notes with the extras – a light Pret à Manger breakfast is delivered to your room, wi-fi is free, and you get an hour's free local calls a day. Downstairs, the *Hoxton Grill* and the DJ bar are favourite hangouts for Shoreditch's bright young things. It can be very good value, but rates depend entirely on availability; you might pay as little as £80 or as much as £199, and every couple of months they hold an online competition selling off around fifty rooms for £1. **£80**

Shoreditch Rooms Shoreditch House, Ebor St, E1 ☎020 7739 5040, ⊛shoreditchrooms.com; Shoreditch High Street Overground; map p.192. From the same stable as the *Dean Street Townhouse*, this hip little place has the same no-nonsense room-naming policy, with 26 options from "Tiny" up to "Small-plus", some of which have minuscule balconies. Rooms may be small but they're beautifully designed, with lots of tongue-and-groove and fresh, sunbleached colours, old school desks and vintage tiled bathrooms. Refreshingly, no mobile phones are allowed in the public spaces. You can also hang out with the beautiful Hoxton types in the members' club next door. Free wi-fi. **£200**

DOCKLANDS

Four Seasons Hotel Canary Wharf 46 Westferry Circus, E14 ☎020 7510 1999, ⊛fourseasons.com /canarywharf; ⊖ Canary Wharf; map p.208. A spectacular riverfront setting, sleek modern interiors and good links to the City (including the option of taking a boat into town) have made this hotel very popular with business folk, but the low weekend rates make it an equally good base for sightseeing. All the five-star luxuries are spot-on, with a good pool, gym, spa and tennis courts. Several rooms have superb Thames views. **£190**

THE SOUTH BANK

★ **Captain Bligh House** 100 Lambeth Rd, SE1 ☎020 8928 2735, ⊛captainblighhouse; ⊖ Lambeth North; map p.216. Captain Bligh's former home can now be your home from home – it's a quirky, cosy Georgian guesthouse, opposite the Imperial War Museum and a short walk from the South Bank, run by a friendly couple. There are just two rooms and an apartment; all are comfortable and spacious, with self-catering facilities. Four-night minimum. **£85**

London Marriott Hotel County Hall County Hall, SE1 ☎020 7928 5200, ⊛marriott.co.uk; ⊖ Waterloo; map p.216. Historic County Hall, once home to London's government, stands in an unbeatable position on the river, opposite the Houses of Parliament. Many of its 200 rooms offer river views, and some have small balconies. It's all suitably splendid, with lots of old-fashioned dark wood and plush carpets, and there's a full-sized indoor pool and well-equipped gym. **£240**

Mad Hatter 3–7 Stamford St, SE1 ☎020 7401 9222, ⊛fullershotels.co.uk; ⊖ Southwark or Blackfriars; map p.216. Comfy, good-value Fuller's hotel, above a Fuller's pub, in an old hat factory. Breakfast is served in the pub, but this is a great location, a short walk from Tate Modern and the South Bank. Rates depend on availability – weekends are cheapest, and you pay less the longer you stay. **£110**

★ **Tune Westminster** 118–120 Westminster Bridge Rd, SE1 ⊛tunehotels.com; ⊖ Lambeth North or Waterloo; map p.216. The Southeast Asian cheapie chain has brought their down-to-earth pricing policy – "five-star beds at one-star prices" – to the UK. It's a welcome addition to the budget scene and a smart idea: by doing away with things like tables, chairs and closets, prices stay low and you simply opt to pay for extras, including towels, TV, hairdryers and wi-fi, on the easy-to-use booking site. Rooms are capsule-style, but well designed, with comfy beds and spotless showers. **£60**

SOUTHWARK

All Seasons London Southwark Rose 43–47 Southwark Bridge Rd, SE1 ☎020 7015 1480, ⓦall-seasons-hotels.com; ⊖ London Bridge; map p.226. The *Southwark Rose* has funky design touches that raise the rooms several notches above the bland chain hotels in the area. Giant aluminium lamps hover over the lobby, which is lined with colourful photographs, while the penthouse restaurant offers an all-you-can-eat breakfast with a rooftop view. Rates vary widely depending on availability. Free wi-fi. **£130**

London Bridge Hotel 8–18 London Bridge St, SE1 ☎020 7855 2200, ⓦlondonbridgehotel.com; ⊖ London Bridge; map p.226. Perfectly placed for Southwark and Bankside or the City, this is a plush, contemporary, independent hotel in a Victorian building in the heart of things right by the station. Free wi-fi. **£140**

HYDE PARK AND KENSINGTON GARDENS

Baglioni 60 Hyde Park Gate, SW7 ☎020 7368 5700, ⓦbaglionihotels.com; ⊖ High Street Kensington; map p.244. A dash of five-star Italian designer cool near the Albert Hall, overlooking Kensington Gardens. Decor is smoky grey and plush red, very much out to impress, and service is impeccable. They do a mean espresso, too. Free wi-fi. **£250**

Columbia Hotel 95–99 Lancaster Gate, W2 ☎020 7402 0021, ⓦcolumbiahotel.co.uk; ⊖ Lancaster Gate; map p.244. This large hotel, once five Victorian houses, offers en-suite singles, doubles, triples and quads, some with views over Hyde Park. It's all a bit dated, but comfortable and good value; the cocktail bar, and the spacious public lounge, with its vaguely Art Deco feel, have a certain faded charm. Free wi-fi in lobby and bar. **£99**

SOUTH KENSINGTON

Aster House 3 Sumner Place, SW7 ☎020 7581 5888, ⓦasterhouse.com; ⊖ South Kensington; map p.250. Fancy, award-winning B&B, wonderfully located in a luxurious South Ken white-stuccoed street; one of the thirteen rooms opens out onto the lovely garden, and there's a large conservatory, where the buffet breakfast is served. **£180**

The Halkin 5 Halkin St, SW1 ☎020 7333 1000, ⓦhalkin.como.bz; ⊖ Hyde Park Corner; map p.250. A luxury boutique hotel where elegant, East-meets-West minimalism prevails. Service is superb, and all the cons are super-mod – the sleek Zen theme is continued in *Nahm*, the Michelin-starred Thai restaurant, which overlooks a private garden. Free wi-fi. **£320**

EARL'S COURT AND FULHAM

Barclay House 21 Barclay Rd, SW6 ☎020 7384 3390, ⓦbarclayhouselondon.com; ⊖ Fulham Broadway; map p.250. Small Fulham B&B – just two rooms, with shared bath – in a quiet street very close to the tube. A friendly home from home, it's run by genuine music lovers, with a grand piano for the use of guests. A simple muffin and coffee breakfast is included from Sunday to Friday, served in the sunny breakfast room, but it's worth paying the little extra for a cooked one on Saturday. There's a roof terrace, too. Usually a three-night minimum stay. **£95**

★ **base2stay Kensington** 25 Courtfield Gardens, SW5 ☎020 7244 2255, ⓦbase2stay.com; ⊖ Earl's Court; map p.250. Excellent-value self-catering accommodation, with superb eco credentials and no fussy extras. Rooms range from "bijou singles" to "deluxe"; all are comfortable, clean and quiet, modern and attractive, with mini-kitchens and free wi-fi. **£111**

★ **The Garret** 267 Old Brompton Rd, SW5 ☎020 7370 1434 ⓦtroubadour.co.uk/the-garret.html; ⊖ Earl's Court; map p.250. Very stylish, comfortable attic apartment above the historic *Troubadour* café/music venue with gorgeous furnishings – quirky antiques, a huge Philippe Starck bed – and lots of space. A sofa bed means it can easily sleep four, and they are willing to provide a blow-up mattress for a larger group. Free wi-fi. **£165**

Twenty Nevern Square 20 Nevern Square, SW5 ☎020 7565 9555, ⓦ20nevernsquare.co.uk; ⊖ Earl's Court; map p.250. In an area of bog-standard B&Bs, this is a welcome and inexpensive alternative, a boutique hotel decked out in bold, warm colours and strewn with Oriental and European antiques. Rooms are en suite, comfortable and plush; some, however, are teensy. Buffet breakfast included. Free wi-fi. **£80**

HIGH STREET KENSINGTON

★ **Vicarage Hotel** 10 Vicarage Gate, W8 ☎020 7229 4030, ⓦlondonvicaragehotel.com; ⊖ Notting Hill Gate or High Street Kensington; map p.274. Laidback, quiet B&B on a residential street a step away from Kensington Gardens. The clean, smart rooms are traditionally decorated and good value; some have shared facilities, and quads are available. A full English breakfast

23

TOP 5 UNDER £100

Captain Bligh House The South Bank. See opposite

Hoxton Hotel Hoxton. See opposite

Luna Simone Victoria. See p.355

Ridgemount Hotel Bloomsbury. See p.357

Tune Westminster The South Bank. See opposite

23

included. Rates are around £15 lower in winter. Free wi-fi (in the lounge). **£102**

PADDINGTON

Caring Hotel 24 Craven Hill Gardens, W2 ☎020 7262 8708, ⓦcaringhotel.com; ⊖ Paddington, Bayswater or Lancaster Gate; map p.274. The decor isn't anything to shout about, but this is a popular, reliable budget B&B. Rooms are clean and quiet: some have shared facilities, some showers only, and others are full en-suites. Free wi-fi in public areas. **£76**

St David's Hotels 14–20 Norfolk Square, W2 ☎020 7706 2701, 020 723 3856 or 020 723 4963, ⓦstdavidshotels.com; ⊖ Paddington; map p.274. A friendly welcome is assured at this inexpensive, no-frills B&B, famed for its substantial English breakfast. Some single rooms, and good-value family rooms (£120); some are en suite. **£65**

BAYSWATER, WESTBOURNE GROVE AND NOTTING HILL

Garden Court Hotel 30–31 Kensington Gardens Square, W2 ☎020 7229 2553, ⓦgardencourthotel .co.uk; ⊖ Bayswater or Queensway; map p.274. No-fuss, friendly family-run B&B on a nice street close to Portobello Market; rooms are a little tired, but are clean and comfy, and the cheaper ones have shared facilities. There's a pretty little garden at the back. Buffet breakfast included. **£79**

Main House 6 Colville Rd, W11 ☎020 7221 9691, ⓦthemainhouse.co.uk; ⊖ Ladbroke Grove or Notting Hill Gate; map p.274. Quirky guesthouse that manages to be both homely – thanks to some lovely period furniture – and chic; the rooms are huge. Perfectly placed for Portobello Rd. Breakfast is not included, but you can have coffee brought to your room, and you are left to treat the place like home. **£120**

Portobello Gold 95–97 Portobello Rd, W1 ☎020 7460 4910, ⓦportobellogold.com; ⊖ Notting Hill Gate or Holland Park; map p.274. A fun and funky budget option above a scungy pub which serves good seafood. The rooms are basic and some tiny, with miniature en-suite bathrooms, but the hotel also has a homey apartment (sleeps 6 – at a pinch), with a roof terrace (and putting green). Breakfast not included. Free wi-fi. **£75**

Vancouver Studios 30 Prince's Square, W2 ☎020 7243 1270, ⓦvancouverstudios.co.uk; ⊖ Bayswater; map p.274. Comfortable, quiet self-catering suites in a grand old Victorian townhouse with maid service and a pretty walled garden. Decor is to a high standard, though the public spaces are a bit tired. They also have a good-value apartment that costs £250 per night for four people. Free wi-fi. **£130**

NORTH LONDON

Hampstead Village Guesthouse 2 Kemplay Rd, NW3 ☎020 7435 8679, ⓦhampsteadguesthouse .com; ⊖ Hampstead; map p.298. Prettily located on a quiet backstreet between Hampstead Village and the Heath, this is a bohemian guesthouse in a freestanding Victorian house. Rooms (most en suite) are tiny, but full of character, crammed with books, pictures, and handmade and antique furniture – you are definitely living in someone's home here. Breakfast costs £7. Free wi-fi. **£80**

New Inn 2 Allitsen Rd, NW8 ☎020 7722 0726, ⓦnewinnlondon.co.uk; ⊖ St John's Wood; map p.284. Landlady Jan runs a comfortable, clean B&B with just five en-suite rooms above a nice pub (with Thai food), in a swanky, quiet street a few minutes' walk from the north edge of Regent's Park. Breakfast adds another £6–9 to the cost. **£85**

Rose and Crown Guesthouse 199 Stoke Newington Church St, N16 ☎020 7923 3337, ⓦroseandcrownn16 .co.uk; ⊖ Manor House or Arsenal; map p.291. Boutique accommodation on lively Church Street with its quirky shops, restaurants and bars. Superbly placed above a splendid local pub and opposite Clissold Park, the six rooms are chic, large and luxurious, and although prices seem steep, the quality – including healthy breakfasts, and a roof terrace to chill out on in the evenings – make it worth it. **£110**

SOUTH LONDON

Devonport House King William Walk, SE10 ☎020 8269 5400, ⓦdeverevenues.co.uk; Greenwich train station from Charing Cross or DLR; map p.315. Right in the centre of Greenwich, in an imposing building with a lovely lawn, these conference-centre-style rooms are functional, but worth it if you can find an online bargain. Staff are friendly, and it is all clean and spruce. **£80**

WEST LONDON

The Old Stables 1 Bridle Lane, Twickenham ☎020 8892 4507, ⓦoldstables.com; St Margarets train station from Waterloo; map p.341. Three bedrooms and one studio apartment in an exceptionally pretty house in a quiet street right by the train station; walking distance to Richmond and the Thames. No on-site staff, but the friendly, efficient manager is a phone call away, and they provide a complimentary continental breakfast. **£85**

Villier's Lodge 1 Cranes Park, Surbiton ☎020 8399 6000, ⓦvillierslodgesurbiton.co.uk; Surbiton train station from Waterloo. This large, luxurious Victorian house – convenient for Hampton Court – has been converted to a spotless, sunny B&B with five stylish doubles and two singles – all en suite. Continental breakfast included. Free wi-fi. **£85**

HOSTELS

Hostels run the gamut from the efficient, but a little soulless, official YHA hostels, to much funkier and more relaxed independent hostels, some of which have a serious party vibe. Virtually all have dispensed with a curfew, all have internet/wi-fi access (usually for a fee), and most include breakfast in the price – we've noted the exceptions to these rules. A good website for booking hostels online is ⓦ hostellondon.com.

YHA HOSTELS

London's seven **Youth Hostel Association (YHA)** hostels are guaranteed to be clean and efficiently run. Their rates depend on availability: dorm prices start at around £19, doubles/twins at £50–60; breakfast is included, and wi-fi is available for around £5/24hr. Advance booking is recommended. You don't have to be a member of the YHA or an affiliated hostel association to stay, but nonmembers are charged a £3 surcharge per night (or you can join for £16). Note that you can book a bed in advance by phoning individual hostels or online at ⓦ yha.org.uk.

Central 104 Bolsover St, W1 ☎ 0845 371 9154, ⊜ londoncentral@yha.org.uk; ⊖ Great Portland Street; map p.97. YHA's newest hostel is in a quiet location, and yet walking distance from the West End. Free wi-fi, kitchen and a late-opening café-bar. No groups. Dorms only (4–8 beds).

Earls Court 38 Bolton Gardens, SW5 ☎ 0845 371 9114, ⊜ earlscourt@yha.org.uk; ⊖ Earl's Court; map p.250. Buzzy, busy 186-bed hostel with small kitchen, café and patio garden. Small groups. Single-sex dorms (4–10 beds), triples and doubles/twins.

Holland House Holland Walk, W8 ☎ 0845 371 9122, ⊜ hollandhouse@yha.org.uk; ⊖ Holland Park or High Street Kensington; map p.274. Idyllically situated in Holland Park and fairly convenient for the centre. Kitchen available and café. Popular with groups. Dorms (4–10+ beds), plus a single, a double and a triple.

Oxford Street 14 Noel St, W1 ☎ 0845 371 9133, ⊜ oxfordst@yha.org.uk; ⊖ Oxford Circus or Tottenham Court Road; map p.97. The Soho location and modest size (just 75 beds) mean this hostel tends to be full year-round, and the atmosphere is party central rather than family-friendly. No groups, no café, but a large kitchen, and everything is clean. Dorms (4 beds) and doubles/twins and triples.

St Pancras 79–81 Euston Rd, NW1 ☎ 0845 371 9344, ⊜ stpancras@yha.org.uk; ⊖ King's Cross St Pancras; map p.120. This eight-floor hostel on the busy Euston Road is popular with families. Rooms are clean, bright, double-glazed and have en-suite facilities. No kitchen, but there's a nice new café. No groups. Dorms (3–6 beds) and doubles/twins.

St Paul's 36 Carter Lane, EC4 ☎ 0845 371 9012, ⊜ stpauls@yha.org.uk; ⊖ St Paul's; map p.156. A 210-bed hostel in a superb location opposite St Paul's Cathedral. Breakfast included and a café for dinner, but no kitchen. Small groups only. Dorms (3–11 beds), singles and twins available.

Thameside 20 Salter Rd, SE16 ☎ 0845 371 9756, ⊜ thameside@yha.org.uk; ⊖ Rotherhithe; map p.224. London's largest purpose-built hostel, with 320 beds, is in a quiet spot near the river, fifteen minutes from the nearest tube. Can feel a bit out on a limb, but has space when more central places are full. No kitchen available, but there's a café-bar and restaurant. Dorms (4–10 beds) and doubles/twins – all en suite.

INDEPENDENT HOSTELS

23

Astor hostels ⓦ astorhostels.co.uk. Good hostel chain, with five central London locations – the fanciest is *Astor Quest* near Hyde Park (see map, p.244), with another, *Astor Hyde Park*, near the South Ken museums (see map, p.252), the *Astor Kensington* nearby (see map, p.250), the *Astor Victoria* near Pimlico (see map, p.36) and the *Astor Museum Inn*, in Bloomsbury (see map, p.120). They only take guests aged between 18 and 35, so there is quite a party atmosphere, but everything is clean, efficient and cheerful, with attractive, colourful decor and lots of comfortable details. All except the *Museum Inn* and *Victoria* hostels have en-suite facilities, and all have female dorms available, breakfast included and free wi-fi. Dorms (6–12 bed) £13, twins/doubles £50

Clink 261 Hostel 261–265 Gray's Inn Rd, WC1 ☎ 020 7833 9400, ⓦ ashleehouse.co.uk; ⊖ King's Cross; map p.120. "Boutique" hostel in a converted office block near King's Cross Station, with laundry, kitchen facilities and a very stylish lounge. Most dorms have 4–10 beds, with some budget 18-bed options and female-only rooms, and there are private rooms, sleeping up to three, with shared facilities. Breakfast included. Dorms £9, doubles £50

★ **Clink 78 Hostel** 78 King's Cross Rd, WC1 ☎ 020 7183 9400, ⓦ clinkhostel.com; ⊖ King's Cross; map p.120. This appealing place is run by the same folk as *Clink 261*, with funky decor, bargain pod beds, a hip bar, and plenty of period features from the days when it was a Victorian courthouse – you can even stay in one of the old prison cells. Dorms (4–16 beds) include special luxury "girls-only" options, and there are singles, doubles/twins and triples, some en suite. Breakfast included; kitchen facilities from 12.30pm–midnight. Groups welcome. Dorms £10, doubles £50

Generator 37 Tavistock Place, WC1 ☎ 020 7388 7666, ⓦ generatorhostels.com; ⊖ Russell Square or Euston; map p.120. One of a small European chain, this huge hostel, with over 870 beds, is tucked away in a converted police barracks on a cobbled street. The

23

STUDENT HALLS

Outside term-time, it's also possible to stay in **student halls of residence**. Prices are slightly higher than hostels because you usually get a room to yourself, and some locations are very central and attractive. The quality of the rooms varies enormously, but they tend to be small and basic and get booked up quickly. Some have shared kitchen facilities, some offer B&B – student and senior discounts are often available.

INTERNATIONAL STUDENTS HOUSE

International Students House 229 Great Portland St, W1 ☎020 7631 8300, ⓦish.org.uk; ⊖ Great Portland Street; map p.89. Hundreds of beds in a vast complex, with two sites near Regent's Park. Rooms are light and spacious. Rates include continental breakfast, but there is no kitchen. Open all year. Dorms (8–10 beds) from around £19; singles (from £39) and twins (from £62) with or without en suite; plus triples (around £80) and quads (around £100). Dorms £19, doubles £62

KING'S COLLEGE

Great Dover Street Apartments 165 Great Dover St, SE1 ☎020 7848 1700, ⓦkcl.ac.uk/kcvb ⊖ Borough; map p.224. Huge Victorian building not far from Bankside, with modern en-suite singles pus a few twins. July–Sept only. Singles £44, twins £65

Hampstead Residence Kidderpore Ave, NW3 ☎020 7848 1700, ⓦkcl.ac.uk/kcvb ⊖ Hampstead; map p.298. A nice Victorian building on a tree-lined avenue, off Finchley Road, within walking distance of the West Heath – the B&B rooms here have shared facilities (and no kitchen). July–Sept only. Singles £35, twins £58

King's College Hall Champion Hill, SE5 ☎020 7848 1700, ⓦkcl.ac.uk/kcvb. Rooms with shared facilities (and no kitchen) in Denmark Hill in suburban south London. B&B singles only £28

Stamford Street Apartments 127 Stamford St, SE1 ☎020 7848 1700, ⓦkcl.ac.uk/kcvb ⊖ Waterloo; map p.216. Modern, conveniently located purpose-built block close to the South Bank, with en-suite rooms. July–Sept only. Singles £44

LSE

LSE (London School of Economics) has a host of halls scattered across central London, all of which offer rooms in the vacations and sometimes beyond. For details of **self-catering apartments** (year-round; from around £110) at all the sites below – and at the **Anchorage** and **George IV Apartments**, on the main LSE campus – see ⓦlsetopfloor.co.uk. Most rooms available at Christmas and Easter and from July to September.

Bankside House 24 Sumner St, SE1 ☎020 7955 7676, ⓦlsevacations.co.uk ⊖ Southwark; map p.226. Rooms next to Tate Modern from July to the end of September. Everything from B&B singles with shared facilities, to en-suite quads. Singles £46, quads £115

Carr-Saunders Hall 18–24 Fitzroy St, W1 ☎020 7955 7676, ⓦlsevacations.co.uk ⊖ Warren Street; map p.97. In an office block north of Oxford Street, the B&B rooms have shared facilities, including a kitchen, and are available at Christmas, New Year, in spring and summer. The twins and doubles are a bargain. Singles £37, twins/doubles £53

Grosvenor House Studios 141–143 Drury Lane, WC2 ☎020 7955 7676, ⓦlsevacations.co.uk ⊖ Covent Garden; map p.132. Well situated in Covent Garden, offering self-catering en-suite rooms from mid-August to the end of September. Singles £63, twins/doubles £90

High Holborn Residence 178 High Holborn, WC1 ☎020 7955 7676, ⓦlsevacations.co.uk ⊖ Tottenhan Court Road; map p.132. A modern block on a busy street near Covent Garden. B&B rooms from the end of July to the end of September. Singles £50, twins £56, en-suite triples £86

Northumberland House 8a Northumberland Ave, WC2 ☎020 7955 7676, ⓦlsevacations.co.uk; map p.46. A grandiose building just off Trafalgar Square. Self-catering en-suite rooms from early July to the end of September. Singles £66, twins/doubles £86

Passfield Hall 1–7 Endsleigh Place, WC1 ☎020 7955 7676, ⓦlsevacations.co.uk ⊖ Euston; map p.120. In attractive, late Georgian buildings in Bloomsbury. Rooms, some en suite, available in spring and summer. Singles £40, twins £61, triple £76

Rosebery Hall 90 Rosebery Ave, EC1 ☎020 7955 7676, ⓦlsevacations.co.uk ⊖ Angel; map p.150. B&B rooms in trendy Clerkenwell available Christmas, New Year, spring and summer. Singles £33, twins £52, triples £69 postindustrial decor may not be to everyone's taste, but it is secure and clean, and good value. Dorms (some women-only) have 4–12 beds, and there are singles, twins, triples and quads – none en suite. There's a young, party atmosphere with themed nights in the late-night bar. Laundry, but no kitchen; breakfast included, plus cheap café. Free wi-fi. Groups welcome. Dorms £15, doubles £50

Meininger 65–67 Queen's Gate, SW7 ☎020 3051 8173, ⓦmeininger-hostels.com; ⊖ Gloucester Road or South Kensington; map p.252. Cheery modern hostel near the South Ken museums, run by a German chain. Dorms (4–12 beds), plus pricey singles and twins. Breakfast not included; there is a laundry. Dorms £14, doubles £120

Palmers Lodge Swiss Cottage 40 College Crescent, NW3 ☎020 7483 8470, ⓦpalmerslodge.co.uk; ⊖ Swiss Cottage. A decent backpackers' lodge in a vast Victorian mansion in south Hampstead with period features galore in the public rooms. Many of the dorms (mixed, male and female; 4–28 beds) have double beds with curtains and reading lights for added privacy; there are also en-suite doubles/twins. Breakfast is included, plus cheap meals in the scullery, and minimal kitchen facilities. Free wi-fi. Dorms £16, doubles £40

Piccadilly Backpackers 12 Sherwood St, W1 ☎020 7434 9009, ⓦpiccadillybackpackers.com; Piccadilly Circus; map p.97. Vast hostel with small rooms and funky, graffitiesque decor. Not the quietest place to crash out, nor perhaps the most spick and span, but it's incredibly cheap and central, on the Soho/Piccadilly border. Breakfast costs extra; laundry but no kitchen. Dorms £12, doubles £65

St Christopher's Inns ☎020 8600 7500, ⓦst -christophers.co.uk. St Christopher's run seven hostels across London, with three near London Bridge (see map, p.226), and branches in Camden, Greenwich, Shepherd's Bush and Hammersmith. The decor is upbeat and cheerful, and there's a party-animal ambience fuelled by the hostel bars. The London Bridge Village hostel also has a nightclub and comedy club, while the quieter London Bridge Oasis / Orient Espresso branch is women-only. Free breakfast and laundry facilities but no kitchens. Dorms £17, doubles £55

Smart Backpackers ☎020 7221 7773, ⓦsmart backpackers.com. Hard-partying mini-chain of hostels, with basic, functional furnishings, and cheap dorm beds around central London. Only some, including the Russell Square hostel (see map, p.120) and the Hyde Park Inn (see map, p.244) have kitchens; others, including Smart Hyde Park View also have en-suite doubles (which aren't good value). Rates include breakfast. Dorms £12, doubles £80

CAMPSITES

London has only a couple of **campsites** on the perimeter of the city. Pitches cost £6–10, plus a fee of around £6–8 per person per night, with reductions for children and during the winter months.

Abbey Wood Federation Rd, Abbey Wood, SE2 ☎020 8311 7708, ⓦcaravanclub.co.uk; Abbey Wood train station from Charing Cross or London Bridge. Spacious, woody, well-equipped Caravan Club site, ten miles southeast of central London. Open all year.

Crystal Palace Crystal Palace Parade, SE19 ☎020 8778 7155, ⓦcaravanclub.co.uk; Crystal Palace train station from Victoria or London Bridge. Another decent Caravan Club site on south London's most famous woody hill, best

suited for caravans and campervans. Station is five minutes' walk or bus #3 will take you all the way to Oxford St. Closed Jan & Feb.

Lee Valley Camping & Caravan Park Meridian Way, Edmonton N9 ☎020 8803 6900, ⓦleevalleypark.org.uk; Ponders End train station from Liverpool Street. Well-equipped site at Pickett's Lock on the River Lee, backing onto a vast reservoir. Multiplex cinema and 18-hole golf course on your doorstep. Open all year except Christmas.

23

STEIN'S, RICHMOND

Cafés and restaurants

London is an exciting place in which to eat out, and, compared to many cities in Europe, offers gratifyingly good value. As it's home to people from all over the globe, you can sample pretty much any kind of cuisine here. The city boasts some of the best Cantonese restaurants in the whole of Europe, and has plenty of places to eat Indian and Bangladeshi delicacies. As well as some excellent Italian, Japanese, French, Spanish and Thai restaurants, the capital also offers more unusual culinary options, from Polish and Peruvian to Korean and Brazilian. Fusion cuisine has finally seen the light here, having been honed in the Antipodes and USA, and of course, examples of wonderful British cooking can be found all over town, from eel and pie caffs to Michelin-starred "modern British" affairs.

This chapter covers the full range of eating places from unreconstructed cafés, known as "greasy spoons", which dish up traditional fried English breakfasts, fish and chips and other calorific treats, to London's smartest, most fashionable restaurants. Among the **cafés**, you'll find bakeries, brasseries, sandwich bars, coffee shops and several ethnic eating places where speedy service and low prices are the priority, whether you're grabbing a quick lunch or a late-night snack. In any of these, you should be able to fill up for under £10. Our **restaurant** listings, meanwhile, concentrate on places where you can get a sit-down meal, with full service and all the trimmings, usually in the evening but at lunchtime too.

We've also provided a rundown of the top **gastropubs**, where you can eat great, modern food in relaxed surroundings (see box, p.283), and there is a list of **delis** and specialist food stores for upmarket picnic supplies in our Shopping chapter (see p.430).

ESSENTIALS

Costs It is possible to pay an awful lot for a meal in London, but, compared with many major European cities, you can get considerable value in the mid-range places. Even in the most expensive restaurants, set menus (most often served at lunch) can be a great deal, and, as small "sharing plates" are currently all the rage it's possible to eat for a very reasonable price in some very smart venues. In the restaurant listings,

we've given price ranges for the main courses or dishes (though remember that side dishes are usually extra).

Tipping Tipping 12.5 to 15 percent for service is usually discretionary, but considered normal practice.

Opening hours We've provided the opening hours for every place we've reviewed, but it's always worth calling ahead to check.

WHITEHALL AND WESTMINSTER

CAFÉS

Café in the Crypt St Martin-in-the-Fields, Duncannon St, WC2 ☎ 020 7766 1158, ⓦ www.stmartin-in-the-fields.org; ⊖ Charing Cross; map p.46. The self-service buffet offers pretty standard British comfort food, but there are lots of veggie dishes, and the handy (and atmospheric) location – below the church in the eighteenth-century crypt – makes it a nice spot to fill up before hitting the West End. Weekly jazz nights (Wed 8pm). Mon & Tues 8am–8pm, Wed 8am–10.30pm (jazz ticket holders only after 7pm), Thurs–Sat 8am–9pm, Sun 11am–6pm.

RESTAURANTS

National Dining Rooms Sainsbury Wing, The National Gallery, Trafalgar Square, WC2 ☎ 020 7747 2525, ⓦ thenationaldiningrooms.co.uk; ⊖ Charing Cross; map p.46. British success story Peyton & Byrne's

café-restaurant features impeccably sourced artisan and rare breed British food, including salmon and oysters; round off your meal with violet custard or a sherry trifle. Each month they feature a special menu based on the food of one British county. Mains £14–18; two- or three-course set menus £24/£27. Mon–Thurs 10am–5.30pm, Fri 10am–8.30pm.

The Vincent Rooms 76 Vincent Square, SW1 ☎ 020 7802 8391, ⓦ thevincentrooms.com; ⊖ Victoria or St James's Park; map p.36. A daily changing menu of good, modern French food – duck confit, ravioli of spinach and dolcelatte, bouillabaisse – is cooked and served by the young student chefs of Westminster Kingsway College (where Jamie Oliver and Antony Worall Thompson, among others, learned their trade) in this good-value brasserie. Mains £6–10. Mon–Fri noon–2pm, plus some eves 6–9pm; closed Easter, July, Aug & Christmas.

ST JAMES'S

RESTAURANTS

Inn the Park St James's Park, SW1 ☎ 020 7451 9999, ⓦ innthepark.com; ⊖ St James's Park; map p.66. Another Peyton & Byrne hit (see above), serving the team's trademark delicious, pricey British food in a stylish

curving wooden building with panoramic windows, and decking, overlooking the park's lake. They do good afternoon teas (£6.50–26.50) and breakfasts. Mains £13.50–22.50. Daily 8–11am, noon–4.30pm & in summer 6–11pm.

MAYFAIR

CAFÉS

Mô 25 Heddon St, W1 ☎ 020 7434 4040, ⓦ momoresto.com; ⊖ Piccadilly Circus; map p.368. The café of the *Momo* restaurant (see p.78), *Mô* serves reasonably priced, tasty snacks, honey-soaked pastries and aromatic mint tea in a wonderful Arabic tearoom, stuffed with Moroccan

memorabila and spilling out onto a terrace. Everything, from the lanterns to the crockery, can be bought to take home. Daily noon–1am.

Tibits 12–14 Heddon St, W1 ☎ 020 7758 4110, ⓦ tibits.co.uk; ⊖ Piccadilly Circus; map p.78. Spacious, modernist Swiss-German veggie café offering a vast range of self-service salads and hot dishes from across the globe – and a kids' play area downstairs. Takeaway available. Mon–Sat 9am–midnight, Sun 11.30am–10.30pm.

★ **The Wolseley** 160 Piccadilly, W1 ☎020 7499 6996, ⓦ thewolseley.com; ⊖ Green Park; map p.78. The lofty and stylish 1920s interior (built as the showroom for Wolseley cars) is the big draw in this wonderfully grand old café-restaurant. The Viennese-inspired food is delicious, though pricey – come for a splendid breakfast or afternoon tea (£9.75–29.75). Mon–Fri 7am–midnight, Sat 8am–midnight, Sun 8am–11pm.

RESTAURANTS

Dehesa 25 Ganton St, W1 ☎020 7494 4170, ⓦ dehesa .co.uk; ⊖ Oxford Circus or Piccadilly Circus; map p.78. Spanish-Italian charcuterie and tapas bar that, unusually for places like this, does good brunches (Sat noon–3pm, Sun noon–5pm). The room is warm but modern, the rustic, robust tapas from the same stable as *Salt Yard* (see p.373) – try deep-fried courgette flowers with goat's cheese and honey, or salt cod croquettes, or just enjoy a plate of melt-in-the-mouth jamón Iberico and a glass of Albariño. Tapas £3–10. Mon–Fri noon–3pm & 5–11pm, Sat noon–11pm, Sun noon–5pm.

Kiku 17 Half Moon St, W1 ☎020 7499 4208, ⓦ kikurestaurant.co.uk; ⊖ Green Park; map p.78. An elegant, simple place serving up top-quality sushi and sashimi (£2–11) and more expensive "*hana*" tasting dinners for £50. Take a seat at the traditional sushi bar and wonder at the dexterity of the knife man. Set lunch £20. Mon–Sat noon–2.30pm & 6–10.15pm, Sun 5.30–9.45pm.

Momo 25 Heddon St, W1 ☎020 7434 4040, ⓦ momoresto.com; ⊖ Piccadilly Circus; map p.78. Fabulous Moroccan food – couscous and tagines – and creative North African/Mediterranean fusion in a glorious dining room that transports you straight to the Kasbah. Mains £13–24; two- and three-course set menus £15/£19. Mon–Sat noon–2.30pm & 6.30–11.30pm, Sun 6.30–11pm.

Patterson's 4 Mill St, W1 ☎020 7499 1308, ⓦ pattersonsrestaurant.com; ⊖ Oxford Circus; map p.78. A very smart family-run restaurant serving mostly local and organic produce – the seafood is sourced from the chef's home town of Eyemouth. The Modern European cooking looks and tastes superb. Mains (lunch) £12, (evening) £21. Mon–Fri noon–3pm & 6–11pm, Sat 5–11pm.

Truc Vert 42 North Audley St, W1 ☎020 7491 9988, ⓦ trucvert.co.uk; ⊖ Bond Street; map p.78. An upmarket but friendly restaurant, offering robust provincial southern French food in a comfortable, somewhat rustic setting. The menu changes daily and begins early with breakfast (£4–11); there's also a deli for takeaway. Mains from £16. Mon–Fri 7.30am–10pm, Sat 9am–10pm, Sun 9am–4pm.

Wild Honey 12 St George St, W1 ☎020 7758 9160, ⓦ wildhoneyrestaurant.co.uk; ⊖ Oxford Street or Bond Street; map p.78. Splendid slow-cooked, UK-sourced haute cuisine – bouillabaisse, smoked eel and spiced mango salad, wild honey ice cream – on regularly changing menus in a mellow, oak-panelled dining room. Mains from £18; Sun lunch menu £25.50. Mon–Sat noon–2.30pm & 6–11pm, Sun noon–3pm & 6–10.30pm.

MARYLEBONE

CAFÉS

Abu Ali 136–138 George St, W1 ☎020 7724 6338; ⊖ Marble Arch; map p.89. Lebanese equivalent of a working men's club, this basic caff serves honest Middle Eastern food – hummus, tabbouleh, wonderful grilled chicken – that's terrific value for money. Daily 9am–11pm.

★ **Comptoir Libanais** 65 Wigmore St, W1 ☎020 7935 1110, ⓦ lecomptoir.co.uk; ⊖ Marble Arch; map p.89. Bursting with atmosphere, with cheerful Lebanese kitsch splashed across everything from the cutlery cans to the ads on the wall, this is a cheap and cheerful Middle Eastern deli and diner; food is simple and honest, from crunchy falafels and herby Lavosh breads to steaming tagines and succulent rose-infused patisserie. It's BYOB, but you could do worse than stick with the delicious home-made lemonades. Main courses around £6. Mon–Fri 8am–10pm, Sat & Sun 10am–10pm.

Golden Hind 73 Marylebone Lane, W1 ☎020 7486 3644; ⊖ Bond Street; map p.89. Marylebone's heritage fish-and-chip restaurant, founded in 1914, serves classic cod and chips from around a fiver, as well as slightly fancier

food like steamed skate and even a deep-fried feta starter. BYOB. Mon–Fri noon–3pm & 6–10pm, Sat 6–10pm.

Patisserie Valerie at Sagne 105 Marylebone High St, W1 ☎020 7935 6240; ⊖ Bond Street; map p.89. Founded as Swiss-run *Maison Sagne* in the 1920s, and preserving its glorious decor from those days, the café is now run by Soho's fab patissiers (see p.370), and is without doubt Marylebone's finest. The light lunches and brunch dishes are great, but the plump, creamy cakes are the real deal. Mon–Fri 7.30am–7pm, Sat 8am–7pm, Sun 9am–6pm.

Paul Rothe & Son 35 Marylebone Lane, W1 ☎020 7935 6783; ⊖ Bond Street; map p.89. Wonderfully old-fashioned deli/corner shop established in 1900, selling "English & Foreign Provisions" and serving inexpensive soups, toasties and sandwiches at formica tables. Mon–Fri 8am–6pm, Sat 11.30am–5.30pm.

RESTAURANTS

Caffè Caldesi 118 Marylebone Lane, W1 ☎020 7487 0753, ⓦ caldesi.com; ⊖ Bond Street; map p.89. Eat in

24

the downstairs bar, rather than in the more formal dining room upstairs, and enjoy wonderfully executed Tuscan staples – fresh home-made pasta dressed with the simplest of sauces, colourful antipasti, herb-infused grills and fish. The two- or three-course set lunches are very good value. Mains £9–17, £11–22 upstairs; lunch menus £13.50/£16.50 (£19.50/£24.50 upstairs). Mon–Sat 9.30am–11pm, Sun 11.30am–10pm.

★ **The Providores and Tapa Room** 109 Marylebone High St, W1 ☎020 7935 6175, ⓦtheprovidores.co.uk; ⊖ Baker Street or Bond Street; map p.89. Outstanding fusion restaurant, run by the genius New Zealand chef Peter Gordon, with the more casual Tapa (not tapas!) Room downstairs. The food, which comes with all sorts of surprising combinations and Pacific Rim flavours, is original and wholly satisfying. Mains upstairs £17–25, set dinner menus £32–62, with smaller dishes in the Tapa Room from £5. Mon–Fri 9am–11pm, Sat 10am–11pm, Sun 10am–10pm.

> ## LONDON FOR VEGGIES
>
> Vegetarians will be able to eat well in most places in London. Below is a list of exclusively veggie cafés and restaurants.
> **Beatroot** Soho. See p.369.
> **Diwana Bhel Poori House** Bloomsbury. See p.373.
> **Food for Thought** Covent Garden. See p.373.
> **The Gate** Hammersmith. See p.385.
> **Manna** Camden. See p.383.
> **Mildred's** Soho. See p.370.
> **Poetry Café** Covent Garden. See p.374.
> **Rasa** Stoke Newington. See p.384.
> **Saf** Shoreditch. See p.378.
> **Tibits** Mayfair. See p.367.
> **World Food Café** Covent Garden. See p.374.

SOHO

CAFÉS

See also I. Camisa & Son, a deli, and Algerian Coffee Stores, a coffee shop, both of which are reviewed in our Shopping chapter (see p.431).

★ **Bar Italia** 22 Frith St, W1 ☎020 7437 4520, ⓦbaritaliasoho.co.uk; ⊖ Leicester Square; map p.100. Tiny, family-owned coffee bar that's been a Soho institution since the 50s, keeping many of its original features (including the Gaggia coffee machine) and its iconic neon sign. A happy crowd of clubbers, fans of Italian soccer, celebs and locals fill the place more or less around the clock for espressos, croissants, beers and sandwiches. A real slice of old Soho life. Nearly 24hr; closed Mon–Fri 4–6am.

Beatroot 92 Berwick St, W1 ☎020 7437 8591, ⓦbeatroot.org.uk; ⊖ Piccadilly Circus, Oxford Circus or Tottenham Court Road; map p.100. Established little veggie/vegan café by the market, doling out savoury bakes, stews and salads (plus great cakes and smoothies) in boxes priced from £4.50 to £6.50. Mon–Fri 9am–9pm, Sat 11am–9pm.

Breakfast Club 33 D'Arblay St, W1 ☎020 7434 2571, ⓦthebreakfastclubcafes.com; ⊖ Oxford Circus; map p.100. With its sunny yellow exterior and comfy, battered leather couches, this laidback place is an appealing spot to linger over substantial brunches (9am–5pm) – toasties, eggs Benedict, hash browns, fresh juices – and you can stop in for wraps, burgers and the like as the day progresses. Branches in Islington, Hoxton and Shoreditch. Mon–Fri 8am–9pm, Sat 9am–5pm, Sun 9am–5pm.

★ **Fernandez & Wells** 73 Beak St, W1 ☎020 287 8124, ⓦfernandezandwells.com; ⊖ Piccadilly Circus or Oxford Circus; map p.100. Superlative, freshly prepared

sandwiches for around £5, great coffee and amazing cakes for under £2 – most folk takeaway, but there are one or two tables. There are two branches nearby – a Spanish-style wine bar/deli around the corner at 43 Lexington St, which does small plates as well as sandwiches, and an espresso bar (closed Sun) on St Anne's Court off Dean St. Mon–Fri 7.30am–6pm, Sat 9am–6pm, Sun 9am–5pm.

Gaby's 30 Charing Cross Rd, WC2 ☎020 7836 4233; ⊖ Leicester Square; map p.97. This small, simple deli has long been beloved of Londoners for its home-cooked (non-kosher) Jewish specialities and its late hours. Good value and choice – the takeaway falafel is a bargain for these parts – and it's licensed, too. Mon–Sat 10am–midnight, Sun noon–10pm.

★ **Maison Bertaux** 28 Greek St, W1 ☎020 7437 6007, ⓦmaisonbertaux.com; ⊖ Leicester Square; map p.100. Venerable (established in 1871), gloriously old-fashioned and terribly French patisserie, with two floors and some outdoor seating. The decor is simple but the cakes are to die for, and a loyal clientele keeps the place busy all day long. Daily 8.30am–8pm.

★ **Mooli's** 50 Frith St, W1 ☎020 7494 9075, ⓦmoolis .com; ⊖ Leicester Square; map p.100. This bright, funky little place has made a fine art of its freshly made rotis filled with amazingly tasty, zingy mixtures – Punjabi goat, cumin potatoes and salsa; paneer, carrot and tomato chutney; Goan pork and pomegranate – for less than a fiver. If you're glucose intolerant they'll box it up for you without the bread. Mon–Wed noon–10pm, Thurs–Sat noon–11.30pm.

Nordic Bakery 14a Golden Square, W1 ☎020 3230 1077, ⓦnordicbakery.com; ⊖ Piccadilly Circus; map

24

p.97. Fill up on colossal cinnamon buns, rye-bread sandwiches and strong coffee at this super-sharp minimalist Scandinavian café. Mon–Fri 8am–8pm, Sat 9am–7pm, Sun 11am–6pm.

Patisserie Valerie 44 Old Compton St, W1 ☎020 7437 3466, ⓦpatisserie-valerie.co.uk; ⊖ Leicester Square; map p.100. This beloved old Soho patisserie dates back to the 1920s and is by far the nicest of the growing chain. It still sells croissants, mousses and gooey cakes to die for, as well as great brunches and sandwiches, with takeaway available. Many other branches. Mon & Tues 7.30am–9pm, Wed–Sat 7.30am–11pm, Sun 9am–9pm.

RESTAURANTS

Bar-shu 28 Frith St, W1 ☎020 7287 8822, ⓦbar-shu .co.uk; ⊖ Leicester Square or Tottenham Court Road; map p.100. *Bar-shu* was one of the first places to introduce fiery Szechuan cuisine to a city far more familiar with Cantonese food, offering speciality dishes – pepper-fragrant pigs' kidney on enoki mushrooms, for example, or fried sea bass in a mustard greens soup – in an atmospheric space decorated with wooden screens, masks and lanterns. Mains £9–30. Mon–Thurs & Sun noon–11pm, Fri & Sat noon–11.30pm.

Bocca di Lupo 12 Archer St, W1 ☎020 7734 2223, ⓦboccadilupo.com; ⊖ Piccadilly Circus; map p.100. Rustic specialities from all over Italy are served in this lively modern trattoria, where it's the done thing to share, tapas-style; ask for a seat at the bar, where you can see everything being prepared, and try the octopus braised with peas and basil or the nettle and borage pansotti with walnut sauce. Piling up the various dishes means costs can creep up – but it's worth it. Dishes from £5; lunch and pre-theatre one-dish meals from £12. Mon–Sat 12.30–3pm & 5.30pm–midnight, Sun noon–4pm.

Koya 49 Frith St, W1 ☎020 7434 4463, ⓦkoya.co.uk; ⊖ Leicester Square; map p.100. This low-key udon-ya dishes up some of the finest Sanuki udon noodles this side of Japan, freshly made each day and served three ways – hot in hot broth, cold in cold broth, or cold with a pouring/dipping sauce – with extra toppings (try the soft poached egg), donburi rice dishes and small plates. It's very moreish and hugely popular, so expect a wait before you get slurping. Bowls from £7.70; donburi from £9; small plates £2–10. Mon–Sat noon–2pm & 5.30–10.30pm.

Mildred's 45 Lexington St, W1 ☎020 7494 1634, ⓦmildreds.co.uk; ⊖ Oxford Circus or Piccadilly Circus; map p.97. *Mildred's* has a fresher and more contemporary feel than many veggie restaurants, and serves creative global cuisine. It's tiny, and can get very busy, but takes no bookings. Mains £8–10. Mon–Sat noon–11pm.

Polpetto 49 Dean St, W1 ☎020 7734 1969, ⓦpolpetto .co.uk; ⊖ Leicester Square; map p.100. Owner Russell Norman continues his winning formula in this offshoot of *Polpo* (see below), a cosy hideaway above the beloved Soho boozer *The French House* (see p.388). The style is much the same as at *Polpo* – shabby chic with rustic warmth and buzzy cachet – and the food, hearty Italian tapas, offers the same great value. Reservations for lunch only. *Cicheti* (Venetian-style bar snacks) from £3; small plates from £6. Mon–Sat noon–3pm & 5.30–11pm.

Polpo 41 Beak St, W1 ☎0207 734 4479, ⓦpolpo.co.uk; ⊖ Piccadilly Circus; map p.97. The dining room of this *bacaro* (a Venetian wine bar) is warm and welcoming, convivial and vibrant. Food is tapas-style, with *cicheti* (bar snacks) and small plates of Venetian specialities – try cuttlefish risotto and *polpette* (meatballs) – and the wines, served in jugs, are good. Reservations are taken for lunch only, which adds to the sense of triumph when you score an evening table. You'll spend about £20 for a filling meal. Mon–Sat noon–3pm & 5.30–11pm, Sun noon–4pm.

St John Hotel 1 Leicester St, WC2 ☎020 3301 8069, ⓦstjohnhotellondon.com; ⊖ Leicester Square; map p.100. Another bare-bones restaurant from the original *St John* (see p.376) team; this new venture may be slightly incongruous in its noisy, trashy Soho setting, but it offers the same superb modern British food, from pig's cheek croquettes to lamb sweetbreads. There's a simple hotel upstairs if you're too full to get yourself home (see p.357). Mains from £18. Daily 7–10.30am, noon–3pm & 5.30pm–2am.

★ **Spuntino** 61 Rupert St, W1 ⓦspuntino.co.uk; ⊖ Piccadilly Circus; map p.100. From the same team as *Polpo* and *Polpetto*, *Spuntino* presents a hip take on American regional and diner food – ambrosial mac cheese, sliders (mini burgers, or meatballs, in a brioche), cheesy grits – in an artfully distressed space that evokes a decaying Lower East Side warehouse. Other dishes reveal European and fusion influences – truffled egg on toast, deep-fried olives stuffed with anchovies – and all are served in small portions. No reservations, and it only seats around 30. About £25 a head with booze. Mon–Sat 11am–midnight, Sun noon–11pm.

Stockpot 18 Old Compton St, W1 ☎020 7287 1066; ⊖ Leicester Square or Tottenham Court Road; map p.100. (Very) cheap and cheerful old-fashioned comfort food at this spartan old Soho institution: large mounds of pasta, stews, omelettes and apple crumble keep hungry punters happy. Mains £4–6. Mon & Tues 11.30am–11.30pm, Wed–Sat 11.30am–midnight, Sun noon–11.30pm.

Yalla Yalla 1 Greens Court, W1 ☎020 70287 7663, ⓦyalla-yalla.co.uk; ⊖ Piccadilly Circus; map p.100. The name is Lebanese for "hurry, hurry!", and the ambience in this sleek hole-in-the-wall is buzzy and fast. Food, described as Beirut street food, includes good-value veggie

24

meze – baba ganoush, halloumi, spinach pies, tabbouleh and the like – and plenty of nicely spiced skewered meats to keep carnivores happy. Takeaway available. Meze from £3. Mon–Fri 10am–11.30pm, Sat11am–11pm.

Yauatcha 15 Broadwick St, W1 ☎020 7494 8888, ⓦyauatcha.com; ⊖ Piccadilly Circus; map p.100.

Popular, minimalist Chinese teahouse-restaurant serving up really good, contemporary dim sum and nice cakes. Come outside peak times to ensure a table and not be rushed. Dim sum £3.50–7. Mon–Sat noon–11.45pm, Sun noon–10.30pm.

CHINATOWN

RESTAURANTS

Four Seasons 12 Gerrard St, W1 ☎020 7494 0870, ⓦukfourseasons.com; ⊖ Leicester Square; map p.100. There's just one dish you need to order here – the roast duck, which even Heston Blumenthal raves about. All the barbecued and roast meats are good, as are the hotpots, but they are merely supporting players. The original branch is in Bayswater, but this place has the edge. Mains £8–32. Daily noon–midnight.

Leong's Legend 4 Macclesfield St, W1 ☎020 7287 0288; ⊖ Leicester Square; map p.100. The brusque service at this multistorey teahouse-style restaurant doesn't detract from the excellent Taiwanese cuisine – try the spicy noodle and dumpling soups – which makes a change in heavily Cantonese Chinatown. There's another branch nearby at 26 Lisle St. Dishes £4–11. Daily noon–11pm.

Misato 11 Wardour St, W1 ☎020 7734 0808; ⊖ Leicester Square; map p.100. Basic, canteen-style Japanese place serving filling rice and noodle dishes, plus hearty bento boxes and sushi, at rock-bottom prices. Mains £4–8. Daily noon–midnight.

★ **Mr Kong** 21 Lisle St, WC2 ☎020 7437 7341, ⓦmrkongrestaurant.com; ⊖ Leicester Square; map p.100. Chinatown stalwart, with a very long menu of Cantonese food – don't miss the wonderful mussels in black bean sauce – and a very good range of veggie dishes. Dishes £4–25. Mon–Sat noon–2.45am, Sun noon–1.45am.

Royal Dragon 30 Gerrard St, W1 ☎020 7734 1388; ⊖ Leicester Square; map p.100. A varied menu of Chinese and Hong Kong staples, but the delicious dim sum is a speciality, and after your meal you can repair to the karaoke room upstairs. Mains £8–23. Mon–Sat noon–3am, Sun 11am–3am.

Wong Kei 41–43 Wardour St, W1 ☎020 7437 8408; ⊖ Leicester Square; map p.100. Enormous (it seats around 500), beloved, Chinatown staple, with a glorious Art Nouveau exterior and four storeys of dining rooms. It's as notorious for brusque service – though this is largely for show nowadays – as for the huge portions of cheap, hearty (but not gourmet) food. Mains £5–10. Mon–Sat noon–11.30pm, Sun noon–10.30pm.

FITZROVIA

CAFÉS

Benito's Hat 56 Goodge St, W1 ☎020 7637 3732, ⓦbenitos-hat.com; ⊖ Goodge Street; map p.97. London isn't great for Mexican restaurants, but this popular, rush-em-through diner does a good job with its huge burritos stuffed with pulled pork, chicken or beef, along with tacos and salads. Also branches near Oxford Circus and in Covent Garden. Sun–Wed 11.30am–10pm, Thurs–Sat 11.30am–10pm.

Rasa Express W1 5 Rathbone St, W1 ☎020 7637 0222, ⓦrasarestaurants.com; ⊖ Goodge Street or Tottenham Court Road; map p.97. This takeaway, at the back of the very good, and pricey, Rasa Samudra Indian seafood restaurant (which is also well worth a visit) and one of the ever-growing Rasa family (see p.384), doles out sophisticated South Indian dishes for next to nothing. Mon–Fri noon–3pm.

Salumeria Dino 15 Charlotte Place, W1 ☎020 7580 3938; ⊖ Goodge Street; map p.97. Small, authentic Italian café-deli with a few outside tables on a pedestrian side street. Daily focaccia, hot dishes and pasta specials, served in generous quantities and with fine ingredients. Mon–Fri 9am–6pm.

RESTAURANTS

★ **Barrica** 62 Goodge St, W1 ☎020 7436 9448, ⓦbarrica.co.uk; ⊖ Goodge Street or Tottenham Court Road; map p.97. Be transported to Spain in this cosy tapas restaurant complete with hanging hams, dark wood furnishings, terracotta dishes and sunny yellow walls. Food is hearty and honest, with nuanced flavours, and drinks range through all the Iberian favourites from Asturian cider to oaky Riojas. Tapas £2–15 (for the finest lomo iberico ham); most prices hover around £3–7. Cold tapas only 3.30–5.30pm. Mon–Fri noon–11.30pm, Sat 1–11.30pm.

Hakkasan 8 Hanway Place, W1 ☎020 7927 7000, ⓦhakkasan.com; ⊖ Tottenham Court Road; map p.97. Impressive, atmospheric designer restaurant (complete with bouncers) serving novel Chinese dishes, with a long, fashionably crammed cocktail bar attached. It's expensive, so go at lunchtime for the dim sum. Mains £12–40. Mon–Fri noon–3pm & 6pm–midnight, Sat noon–5pm & 6pm–midnight, Sun 6–11pm.

Indian YMCA 41 Fitzroy Square, W1 ☎020 7387 0411; ⊖ Warren Street; map p.97. Ignore the signs saying the canteen is only for students – this basic place, which has a

24

cultish following, is open to all; just press the bell and pile in. The food (veg and non-veg) is great, and prices unbelievably low; simply collect what you want from plates on the counter and pay at the till. Dishes from £3. Mon–Fri 7.30–9.15am, noon–2pm & 7–8.30pm, Sat & Sun 8–9.30am, 12.30–1.30pm & 7–8.30pm.

Salt Yard 54 Goodge St, W1 ☎020 7637 0657, ⓦsaltyard.co.uk; ⊖ Goodge Street; map p.97. This sleek, stylish charcuterie/tapas bar brings a dash of Italy to the proceedings, too. Everything is top-notch, using the finest ingredients – the rarest hams, truffles – and menus change seasonally. The signature dish is the courgette flowers stuffed with goat's cheese (£7.55), which is phenomenal. Tapas £4–9. Mon–Fri noon–3pm & 6–11pm, Sat 5–11pm.

Sardo 45 Grafton Way, W1 ☎020 7387 2521, ⓦsardo -restaurant.com; ⊖ Warren Street; map p.97. Sardinian restaurant with a warm, unaffected interior and spectacular local cuisine, with lots of seafood and Mediterranean flavours. Mains £8–15. Mon–Fri noon–3pm & 6–10pm, Sat 6–10pm.

BLOOMSBURY

CAFÉS

Abeno 47 Museum St, WC1 ☎020 7405 3211, ⓦabeno .co.uk; ⊖ Tottenham Court Road or Holborn; map p.120. Small Japanese place that specializes in okonomiyaki (£7–12), a cabbage, egg and ginger pancake filled with pork, bacon, seafood, cheese, tofu – the sky's the limit – prepared before your eyes. There's another branch, *Abeno Too*, on Great Newport St. Mon–Sat noon–11pm, Sun noon–10.30pm.

★ **Hummus Bros** Victoria House, 37–63 Southampton Row, WC1 ☎020 7404 7079, ⓦhbros.co.uk; ⊖ Holborn; map p.120. Hummus and a choice of toppings – chicken, falafels, guacamole – with pitta bread, feta cheese, tabbouleh and salads on the side. Don't miss their refreshing mint and ginger lemonade. Also takeaway. Branches on Wardour St in Soho and on Cheapside in the City. Hummus plates from £5. Mon–Fri 11am–9pm.

Patisserie Deux Amis 63 Judd St, WC1 ☎020 7383 7029; ⊖ Russell Square or King's Cross; map p.120. Small, civilized French-style bakery specializing in pastries, filled baguettes and coffee, with a great cheese shop next door – a real find near King's Cross. Mon–Sat 9am–6pm, Sun 9am–2pm.

RESTAURANTS

Cigala 54 Lamb's Conduit St, WC1 ☎020 7405 1717, ⓦcigala.co.uk; ⊖ Russell Square; map p.120. Simple dishes, strong flavours, fresh ingredients and real passion at this sophisticated and established Iberian restaurant with seasonally changing menus. Mains £8–18; two- and three-course set lunch menus £16/£18; tapas £4–11. Mon–Fri noon–10.30pm, Sat 12.30–10.30pm, Sun noon–9.30pm.

★ **Diwana Bhel Poori House** 121–123 Drummond St, NW1 ☎020 7387 5556; ⊖ Euston; map p.120. On a street lined with good Indian restaurants, this South Indian veg diner wins out for its scrumptious all-you-can-eat lunchtime buffet (£7) and huge thalis (£8) brimming with freshly prepared, zingy dishes. Dishes from £4. Daily noon–11pm.

Hare & Tortoise 11–13 Brunswick Centre, WC1 ☎020 7278 9799, ⓦhareandtortoise.co.uk; ⊖ Russell Square; map p.120. Located in the Brunswick mall, this smart, budget café-restaurant serves very reasonably priced sashimi, nigiri, chow mein and ramen. Branches in Blackfriars, Kensington, Putney and Ealing. Sushi boxes from £8, noodles, ramen and rice dishes from £6. Daily noon–11pm.

La Porchetta 33 Boswell St, WC1 ☎020 7242 2434, ⓦlaporchetta.net; ⊖ Holborn or Russell Square; map p.120. Tiny, cramped, very loud, Italian place that dishes up huge, consistently good portions; the pizzas are great. Branches in Clerkenwell, Camden, Islington and Finsbury Park. Mains £6.50–14. Mon–Thurs noon–3pm & 6–11pm, Fri noon–3pm & 6pm–midnight, Sat 6–11pm.

COVENT GARDEN AND THE STRAND

CAFÉS

Canela 33 Earlham St, WC2 ☎020 7240 6926, ⓦcanelacafe.com; ⊖ Covent Garden or Leicester Square; map p.132. A little Brazilian/Portuguese café-bar that serves up authentic coffee, cakes and traditional dishes like cheese bread and *feijoada*, the pork and bean stew. The high-ceilinged, chandeliered interior makes it a nice place for a coffee, or you can sit outside and watch the action on Seven Dials. There's another branch in Soho. Mon–Wed 9.30am–10.30pm, Thurs & Fri 9.30am–11.30pm, Sat 10.30am–11.30pm, Sun 10.30am–8pm.

★ **Food for Thought** 31 Neal St, WC2 ☎020 7836 9072, ⓦfoodforthought-london.co.uk; ⊖ Covent Garden; map p.132. This minuscule veggie restaurant and takeaway is a very old friend in Covent Garden – dishing out its hearty veggie/vegan soups, salads, hot dishes and desserts for nearly forty years. The menu changes daily, but always features favourites like strawberry and banana "scrunch". Expect to queue and don't expect to linger at peak times. Mon–Sat noon–8.30pm, Sun noon–5pm.

★ **Kastner & Ovens** 52 Floral St, WC2 ☎020 7836 2700; ⊖ Covent Garden; map p.132. Minimalist lunch spot where the emphasis is on top-quality sandwiches and heart-warming savoury bakes, plus an amazing selection

24

of cakes, all made on the premises. A few tables inside. Mon–Fri 8am–5pm.

Monmouth Coffee Company 27 Monmouth St, WC2 Ⓦ monmouthcoffee.co.uk; ⊖ Covent Garden or Leicester Square; map p.132. The marvellous aroma is the first thing that greets you when you walk in to this tiny old coffee shop run by the quality Monmouth Coffee roasters. Pick and mix your coffee from a fine selection (or buy the beans to take home), grab a pastry and settle into one of the old-fashioned wooden booths. Branches in Borough Market and Bermondsey (where they roast on site). Mon–Sat 8am–6.30pm.

Poetry Café 22 Betterton St, WC2 Ⓣ 020 7420 9887, Ⓦ poetrysociety.org.uk; ⊖ Covent Garden or Holborn; map p.132. This simple veggie café is a pleasant place to relax and browse poetry magazines, with salads, quiche and cakes on offer; some fine poets have graced the stage here. Mon–Fri noon–11pm, Sat 7–11pm.

Rock & Sole Plaice 47 Endell St, WC2 Ⓣ 020 7836 3785; ⊖ Covent Garden; map p.132. No-nonsense fish-and-chip shop in central London, where they do all the staples just right; you can eat in or at one of the pavement tables, or takeaway. Mon–Sat 11.30am–11pm, Sat & Sun noon–10pm.

World Food Café 14 Neal's Yard, WC2 Ⓣ 020 7379 0298; ⊖ Covent Garden; map p.132. Upper-floor veggie café where the windows are flung open in summer and you can gaze down upon the pedestrianized square below while tucking into hearty dishes from all over the globe: tortillas, thalis, tagines or meze. Mon–Fri 11.30am–4.30pm, Sat 11.30am–5pm.

RESTAURANTS

★ **Dishoom** 12 Upper St Martin's Lane, WC2 Ⓣ 020 7420 9320, Ⓦ dishoom.com; ⊖ Leicester Square or Covent Garden; map p.132. Re-creating the atmosphere of the Persian cafés of Old Bombay, complete with arcane "rules of the house" signs, faded movie posters and

Thums-Up fizzy cola drinks, *Dishoom* is buzzy and witty but, most importantly, serves delicious food – don't miss the *pau bhaji*, a toasted bun filled with veggie curry and the really good, filling black dhal. Their breakfasts, with lassis and rotis with fruit and yoghurt, are a hit too. Mains from £6.50, small dishes for less. Mon–Thurs 8am–11pm, Friday 8am–midnight, Sat 10am–midnight, Sun 10am–10pm.

The Hawksmoor 11 Langley St, WC2 Ⓣ 020 7856 2154, Ⓦ thehawksmoor.co.uk; ⊖ Covent Garden; map p.132. This offshoot of the hot Spitalfields favourite (see p.379), in an atmospheric old brewery, offers the same best British meat cooked to perfection. The star dish here is the kimchi burger, succulent and complex, and, of course, the unmissable steaks. You could spend as much as £50, but there's a good-value lunch menu. Two-course lunch menu £20; burgers £15. Mon–Sat noon–3pm & 5–11.30pm, Sun noon–4.30pm.

J. Sheekey 28–32 St Martin's Court, WC2 Ⓣ 020 7240 2565, Ⓦ j-sheekey.co.uk; ⊖ Leicester Square; map p.132. A *grande dame* of the London dining scene – established in 1896 in the heart of theatreland, but elegantly refurbished since then – this splendid seafood restaurant is a glittering, special occasion kind of place. Price-wise, the weekend lunch three-course menu, at £26.50, is your best bet, and there's a good-value oyster bar. Mains from £15. Mon–Sat noon–3pm & 5.30pm–midnight, Sun noon–3.30pm & 6pm–11pm.

Kopapa 32–34 Monmouth St, WC2 Ⓣ 020 7240 6076, Ⓦ kopapa.co.uk; ⊖ Covent Garden; map p.132. Fusion food from the Kiwi chef behind *Providores* (see p.369), in a casual café where the plain setting belies the complex flavours of dishes like shichimi-crusted baked tofu with shiitake, carrot and miso mustard. Most dishes, as is currently the rage, are designed to share, though there are a handful of mains – the tempura spicy dahl-stuffed inari pocket on caramelised coconut with fried plantain and pickled green papaya is a hit. Mains from £11; tapas dishes

---

COFFEE AND LUNCH CHAINS

Although London's old-fashioned caffs of the 1950s and 60s have all but died out, London today has a number of reliable, if generally unexciting **chains** where you can grab a coffee and a sandwich. Three are particularly worthy of mention, offering healthy and well-priced food to grab and go.

Home-grown **sandwich** chains **Pret à Manger** (Ⓦ pret.com) and **EAT** (Ⓦ eat.co.uk) produce reliable lunchtime food, with good sandwiches, salads and cakes made on the premises daily. *Pret*, all chrome and zingy service, does its own healthy canned drinks, while *EAT* outlets have a more laidback, cosy feel and serve good hearty soups. *Pret* coffee uses organic, Fairtrade and Rainforest Alliance beans roasted in the UK; both *Pret* and *EAT* use only organic milk. ★ **Leon** (Ⓦ leonrestaurants.co.uk), meanwhile, is a far smaller, but gently expanding, family-owned chain that does delicious coffee, juices, breakfasts, wraps, soups and salads in sunny, bright premises whose artfully colourful decor evoke the sunny holidays of youth. Food is healthy and locally sourced, and the amazing cakes are made with almonds and fruit sugars.

24

cost less. Mon–Fri 8.30–11.30am & noon–10.45pm, Sat 10am–3pm & 3.30–10.45pm, Sun Sat 10am–3pm & 3.30–9.45pm.

Masala Zone 48 Floral St, W1 ☎020 7379 0101, ⓦmasalazone.com; ⊖ Covent Garden; map p.132. Smart, good-value restaurant, decorated with Rajasthani puppets, serving modern Indian food, including lots of veggie options. Start with little dishes of "street food", then move on to the well-balanced, richly flavoured curries or thalis. Branches in Soho, Camden, Islington, Earls Court, Fulham and Bayswater. Mains £5–15. Mon–Sat noon–11pm, Sun 12.30–10.30pm.

Mon Plaisir 21 Monmouth St, WC2 ☎020 7836 7243, ⓦmonplaisir.co.uk; ⊖ Covent Garden; map p.132. Claims to be the oldest French restaurant in London, and certainly has an authentic brasserie feel with its Deco posters and a glamorous mirrored bar. The classic French dishes are reliably good, with cheaper brasserie food being served out of peak times; and the pre- and post-theatre menu is a bargain at £16.95 for two courses, £18.95 for three. Mains £17–42; brasserie mains from £13. Mon–Fri noon–11.15pm (brasserie service only 2.30–5.45pm), Sat noon–2.30pm & 5.45–11.15pm.

Opera Tavern 23 Catherine St, WC2 ☎020 7836 3680, ⓦoperatavern.co.uk; ⊖ Covent Garden; map p.132. Another classy Spanish-Italian restaurant from the *Salt Yard* team (see p.373), with small sharing plates and fine wines by the glass. Star turns include a foie gras burger, the Iberico ham – which, unusually is cooked or served in a tartare, rather than cured and dried – and anything prepared on the charcoal grill. Sit in the bar rather than in the more formal upstairs dining room. Charcuterie and cheese from £4; bar snacks from £3; mains from £7. Mon–Fri noon–3pm & 5–11.30pm (bar snacks, charcuterie and cheese 3–5pm); Sat noon–11.30pm.

Terroirs 5 William IV St, WC2 ☎0207 036 0660, ⓦterroirswinebar.com; ⊖ Charing Cross; map p.132. Great wines – including "natural" wines with no additives – and carefully sourced Mediterranean/Modern British food at this light and airy, relaxed wine bar-restaurant. Dishes like *boudin noir* with broad beans, wild garlic and fried duck egg (£14) are full of hearty flavours, while the bar food – charcuterie, cheese and the like – is a cut above the norm. Mains from £9; bar food for less. Mon–Sat noon–11pm.

Wahaca 66 Chandos Place, WC2 ☎0207/240 1883, ⓦwahaca.co.uk; ⊖ Charing Cross, Leicester Square or Covent Garden; map p.132. No bookings are taken at this big, brash modern Mexican restaurant, so everyone ends up getting merry on Margaritas at the bar before being ushered to shared tables and tucking into hearty, inexpensive food. Burritos and tacos feature, of course, but it's worth going for more authentic choices, including a good queso fundido or *esquites*, a tangy sweetcorn broth. Dishes from £3. Mon–Sat noon–11pm, Sun noon–10.30pm.

CLERKENWELL

CAFÉS

See also the Shopping chapter for reviews of G. Gazzano & Son, a deli (see p.431), and Brill, a café/CD store (see p.432).

Caravan 11–13 Exmouth Market, EC1 ☎020 7833 8115, ⓦcaravanonexmouth.co.uk; ⊖ Farringdon; map p.150. True to its Kiwi roots, this funky Exmouth Market favourite, with a sunny vibe, is great for creative brunches (Sat & Sun 10am–4pm) – try the baked eggs with tomato, pepper and Greek yoghurt, buttery cornbread French toast, and avocado with chilli flakes on sourdough. At other times the modern fusion menu can feature anything from couscous to steamed mussels. Dishes £5–18. Mon–Fri 8am–10.30pm, Sat 10am–10.30pm, Sun 10am–4pm.

Clark & Sons 46 Exmouth Market, EC1 ☎020 7837 1974; ⊖ Angel or Farringdon; map p.150. A stalwart among Exmouth Market's rapid gentrification, this genuine pie-and-mash shop is still going strong – it's the most central spot in the capital to fill up on meat pies, mash with liquor (parsley sauce) and a side of eels. Mon–Thurs 10.30am–4pm, Fri & Sat 10.30am–5pm.

★ **Clerkenwell Kitchen** 27–31 Clerkenwell Close, EC1 ☎020 7101 9959, ⓦtheclerkenwellkitchen.co.uk; ⊖ Farringdon or Angel; map p.150. Bright, modern, airy place serving divine food from a *River Café* alumni. The menu is short and seasonal, using sustainably sourced ingredients, and the open-plan kitchen serves everything from breakfast through to tea and cakes, with deli sandwiches to takeaway and supper on Thursday. There's a nice courtyard for outdoor dining. Mains from £7. Mon–Fri 8am–5pm, till 10.30pm on Thurs.

★ **Kurz & Lang** 1 St John St, EC1 ☎020 7993 2923, ⓦkurzandlang.com; ⊖ Farringdon; map p.150. An *echt* German Bratwurst in a prominent corner site off Smithfield. Choose from a variety of fresh, authentic sausages, and help them down with bread, mustard and sauerkraut. Popular clubbers' pit stop. Mon–Wed 11am–11.30pm, Thurs 11am–1am, Fri 11am–6.30am, Sat noon–7am, Sun noon–7pm.

Pho 86 St John St, EC1 ☎020 7253 7624, ⓦphocafe .co.uk; ⊖ Farringdon or Barbican; map p.150. Small, bright café serving up very good, freshly made Vietnamese noodle soups, washed down with weasel coffee (don't ask). Larger branches in Oxford Circus, Soho and Shepherd's Bush, but this is the original. Dishes from £7. Mon–Thurs noon–3pm & 6–10pm, Fri noon–3pm & 6–10.30pm, Sat 6–10.30pm.

Prufrock Coffee 23–25 Leather Lane, EC1 ☎07852 243470, ⓦprufrockcoffee.com; ⊖ Chancery Lane or

24

Farringdon; map p.150. Having prepared London's finest coffee in a Shoreditch menswear store, world barista champion Gwilym Davies finally opened his own place, a vast and tranquil shrine to the coffee bean, in 2011. The coffee is exquisite – what with this and the also good *Department of Coffee & Social Affairs* opposite, Leather Lane has become quite the caffeine-fiend's haven. Mon–Fri 8am–6pm, Sat10am–4pm.

RESTAURANTS

Fish Central 149–155 Central St, EC1 ☎ 020 7253 4970, ⓦ fishcentral.co.uk; ⊖ Old Street; map p.150. Straddling the Barbican/City and Clerkenwell's council estates, this upmarket chippie attracts hungry diners from both. Great cod and chips, of course, but it's the availability of fresh scallops and oysters on the same menu that give this place the edge. Mains £7–20. Mon–Sat 11am–2.30pm & 5–10.30pm.

Medcalf 40 Exmouth Market, EC1 ☎ 020 7833 3533, ⓦ medcalfbar.co.uk; ⊖ Farringdon or Angel; map p.150. A turn-of-the-century butcher's shop opened in 1912 converted into an effortlessly stylish, appealing little restaurant. The atmosphere is relaxed, and the modern British cuisine fabulous, with fresh ingredients and excellent puds on daily changing menus. Mains £11–18. Mon–Thurs & Sat noon–11pm, Fri noon–1am, Sun noon–6pm.

The Modern Pantry 47–48 St John's Square, EC1 ☎ 020 7553 9210, ⓦ themodernpantry.co.uk; ⊖ Farringdon; map p.150. A brace of elegant Georgian townhouses make a lovely setting for this contemporary café with a smart dining room upstairs. Chef Anna Hansen, a Kiwi alumni of *Providores* (see p.369), brings Pacific Rim and fusion flavours to dishes from wok-fried spider crab to chorizo, date and feta fritters. The simpler café offers good value (breakfasts won't hit £20), and you can takeaway deli foods from the Pantry itself, on the ground floor. Mains £15–20, with a weekday two-course lunch menu for £19. Café: Mon 8am–11am & noon–10pm, Tues–Fri 8am–11am & noon–11pm, Sat 9am–4pm & 5.30–11pm, Sun 10am–4pm & 5.30–10pm. Restaurant: Tues–Fri noon–3pm & 6–10.30pm, Sat 11am–4pm & 6–10.30pm, Sun 11am–4pm.

Morito 32 Exmouth Market, EC1 ☎ 020 7278 7007;

⊖ Angel or Farringdon; map p.150. As an offshoot of *Moro* and right next door, this long, skinny tapas bar allows you to enjoy the same fabulous flavours and fine wines in a more casual, minimal atmosphere. Thinking of it as a cheap option, however, could be a mistake – though the most expensive dish (lamb chops grilled *a la plancha*) is just £6, everything is tiny and wickedly moreish, and what with all the great wines costs can really mount. Tapas from £4. Mon 5–11pm, Tues–Sun 12.30–11pm.

★ **Moro** 34–36 Exmouth Market, EC1 ☎ 020 7833 8336, ⓦ moro.co.uk; ⊖ Farringdon or Angel; map p.150. Attractive, warmly decorated restaurant that's a place of pilgrimage for disciples of Sam and Sam Clark's Moorish/Iberian cookbooks. Food on the daily changing menus is excellent, especially the lamb dishes and the lemon yoghurt cake, with lots of unusual ingredients, and service is friendly; it's best to book well in advance. Tapas (around £4) are served all day. Mains £16–19. Mon–Sat 12.30–10.30pm.

St John 26 St John St, EC1 ☎ 020 7251 0848, ⓦ stjohnrestaurant.com; ⊖ Farringdon; map p.150. Former smokehouse close to Smithfield meat market that's famous for its perfect execution of traditional British dishes – often involving unfashionable animal parts – on a menu that's as pared down as the space itself. Celebrated chef Fergus Henderson opened another branch in Soho in 2011 (see p.370), and there's also a less expensive sister restaurant in Spitalfields (see p.379). Mains £14–24. Mon–Fri noon–3pm & 6–11pm, Sat 6–11pm, Sun 1–4pm.

Smiths of Smithfield (SOS) 67–77 Charterhouse St, EC1 ☎ 020 7251 7950, ⓦ smithsofsmithfield.co.uk; ⊖ Farringdon; map p.150. A big, bustling warehouse-style place with dining rooms on four levels, all focusing on British ingredients, and of course, lots of meat. The ground-floor café-bar (open till 4.30pm) is the best bet, serving fine all-day breakfasts, bacon butties, salads, snacks, ice cream and sundaes. The first floor is a wine bar with British brasserie food, while on the second is a more sophisticated bistro-type place, and the top floor is very posh, but poor value. Café dishes from £5; 1st floor dishes from £6; 2nd floor mains from £13.50; top floor mains from £20. Mon 7am–11pm, Tues–Fri 7am–11.30pm, Sat 10am–11.30pm, Sun 9.30am–5pm.

THE CITY

CAFÉS

★ **Café Below** Church of St Mary-le-Bow, Cheapside, EC2 ☎ 020 7329 0789, ⓦ cafebelow.co.uk; ⊖ St Paul's or Bank; map p.170. A rare City gem: a cosy, good-value café-restaurant, set in a wonderful Norman church crypt, serving home-cooked modern Mediterranean food, with lots of veggie choices, and sticky breakfast pastries. Mains from £6.50 at lunch, £9.50 at dinner. Mon–Fri 7.30am–9pm.

Chilango 142 Fleet St, EC4 ☎ 020 7353 6761,

ⓦ chilango.co.uk; ⊖ Blackfriars; map p.156. If you're craving Mexican in a city notorious for not doing that cuisine justice, you could do worse than this busy, modern, colourful cantina chain, where the fast, fresh, soft tortilla burritos and tacos, salads and guacamole are all very tasty. Branches in Chancery Lane and Islington. Mon–Fri 11am–9pm.

De Gustibus 53–55 Carter Lane, EC4 ☎ 020 7236 0056, ⓦ degustibus.co.uk; ⊖ St Paul's or Blackfriars; map p.156. Award-winning artisan bakery that creates

AFTERNOON TEA

The classic English **afternoon tea** – sandwiches, scones and cream, cakes and tarts, and, of course, pots of tea – is available all over London. The most popular venues are the capital's top hotels and most fashionable department stores; a selection of the best is given below. To avoid disappointment, book – in the case of the *Ritz*, as far as twelve weeks ahead – and leave your jeans and trainers at home, as most hotels will expect at least "smart casual attire". Prices quoted here are for the standard teas; most places offer champagne teas for a little more.

TOP FIVE TEAS

★ **Claridge's** Brook St, W1 ☎020 7409 6307, ⓦ claridges.co.uk; ⊖ Bond Street; map p.78. Award-winning menu with more than thirty teas and exquisite cakes in stunning Art Deco surrounds. £35. Daily 3pm, 3.30pm, 5pm & 5.30pm.

★ **Fortnum & Mason** 181 Piccadilly, W1 ☎0845 602 5694, ⓦ fortnumandmason.com; ⊖ Green Park; map p.78. Take tea in this wonderful old store's *St James's* restaurant; menus change to reflect the seasons or cultural events, and they have vegetarian, vegan, egg-allergy, dairy-free, gluten-free and diabetic-friendly options for the same price. £34. Mon–Sat noon–6.30pm, Sun noon–4.30pm.

Lanesborough Hyde Park Corner, SW1 ☎020 7259 5599, ⓦ lanesborough.com; ⊖ Hyde Park Corner; map p.244. This one is so grand that a tea sommelier will discuss suitable tea and cake pairings with you. Gluten- and dairy-free choices available. £35. Daily 4pm, 4.30pm & 5pm.

The Ritz Piccadilly, W1 ☎020 7493 8181, ⓦ theritzlondon.com; ⊖ Green Park; map p.78. Seriously posh teas in the hotel's Palm Court – gents must wear a jacket and tie. £40. Daily 11.30am, 1.30pm, 3.30pm, 5.30pm & 7.30pm.

The Wolseley 160 Piccadilly, W1 ☎020 7499 6996, ⓦ thewolseley.com; ⊖ Green Park; map p.78. Sumptuous European pastries are the speciality at this grand Viennese-style café (see p.368). £21. Mon–Fri noon–3pm, Sat & Sun noon–3.30pm.

TEATIME TREATS

Inn the Park St James's Park, SW1 ☎020 7451 9999, ⓦ innthepark.com; ⊖ St James's Park; map p.66. The swish catering group Peyton & Byrne offer cream teas, including luxury and champagne options in a lovely, relaxed riverside setting (see p.367). From £5.50. Daily 3–4.30pm.

Prism 147 Leadenhall St, EC3 ☎020 7256 3888, ⓦ harveynichols.com/prism-london; ⊖ Bank; map p.156. A gorgeous setting (see p.378) and very good afternoon teas – the "gentleman's" version replaces finger sandwiches with a salt beef and mustard baguette and home-made scotch egg. £19.50. Mon–Fri 2–5.30pm.

Sotheby's 34–35 New Bond St, W1 ☎020 7293 5077, ⓦ sothebys.com; ⊖ Bond Street; map p.78. There's no dress code at this historic auction house (see p.82) restaurant, and the "small tea", with Welsh rarebit and hot buttered cheese scones, is a fraction of the cost of the top hotels nearby. £15. Mon–Fri 3–4.45pm.

24

sandwiches, bruschette, croques-monsieurs and quiche to eat in or takeaway. There's another branch in Borough Market. Mon–Fri 8am–5pm.

RESTAURANTS

Prism 147 Leadenhall St, EC3 ☎020 7256 3888, ⓦharveynichols.com/prism-london; ⊖ Bank; map p.156. In one of the City's great old banking halls, with the obligatory long bar, suave service and a menu comprising well-judged English favourites with modernist influences, *Prism* has a dash more style than many other business-account City restaurants – perhaps due to being owned by Harvey Nicks. The bar menu has scotch eggs (£6.50) and sausage and mash for around a tenner; and they do great afternoon teas (see p.377). Mains (bar) £5–15, (restaurant) £15–30. Mon–Fri 11.30am–5.30pm & 6–10pm.

SHOREDITCH

CAFÉS

Flavours 35 Charlotte Rd, EC2 ☎020 7739 5345, ⓦkitchenflavours.co.uk; ⊖ Old Street or Shoreditch High Street Overground; map p.192. Tiny café with just four stools, serving a range of tasty Mediterranean lunch options: big soups, grilled tuna, salads and great pastries, all of which are freshly prepared. Mon–Fri 8.30am–3.30pm.

Sông Quê 134 Kingsland Rd, E2 ☎020 7613 3222, ⓦsongque.co.uk; Hoxton Overground; map p.192. In a street heaving with a range of budget Vietnamese restaurants, this simple place consistently has the edge, with very good *phở* (£3.60–7) and lip-tinglingly spicy seafood dishes. Mon–Sat noon–3pm & 5.30–11pm, Sun noon–11pm.

RESTAURANTS

Eyre Brothers 70 Leonard St, EC2 ☎020 7613 5346, ⓦeyrebrothers.co.uk; ⊖ Old Street; map p.192. Very large, very swish. Strongly Iberian food, with Portuguese specialities, plus Italian dishes and some favourites from Mozambique. Mains £10–26; tapas and petiscos £4–7.50. Mon–Fri noon–3pm & 6.30–10.45pm, Sat 7–10.45pm.

★ **PINCHITOtapas** 32 Featherstone St, EC1 ☎020 7490 0121, ⓦpinchito.co.uk; ⊖ Old Street; map p.192. Whether you're after authentic chocolate con churros for breakfast, simple, perfectly executed tapas or elaborate Basque pintxos, this trendy, buzzy little place – all industrial steel and bare brick walls – does everything Spanish supremely well, and prices are astonishingly low. Takeaway available. Tapas £1.50–6.50; set menus £15 or £20 (for four or more, pre-ordered). Mon–Fri 10am–midnight, Sat 5pm–midnight.

★ **Saf** 152–154 Curtain Rd, E2 ☎020 7613 0007, ⓦsafrestaurant.co.uk; ⊖ Old Street; map p.192. Modern, shiny and (unique) botanical vegan restaurant specializing in exquisitely presented (mostly raw) and scrumptious fruit and veg dishes, most (including the dairy-free cheeses) prepared on site – *Saf* stands for "simply authentic food". Branch on High Street Kensington. Mains £12–15. Mon–Sat 11.30am–11pm, Sun noon–10.30pm.

SPITALFIELDS, BRICK LANE AND WHITECHAPEL

CAFÉS

See also A. Gold, a deli reviewed in our Shopping chapter (see p.431).

Brick Lane Beigel Bake 159 Brick Lane, E1 ☎020 7729 0616; Shoreditch High Street Overground; map p.192. Classic bagel takeaway in the heart of the East End – very cheap, even for your top-end filling, smoked salmon and cream cheese – and a particular hit late at night and in the early mornings. Daily 24hr.

Café 1001 1 Dray Walk, E1 ☎020 7247 9679, ⓦcafe1001.co.uk; ⊖ Shoreditch High Street Overground; map p.192. Just off Brick Lane, this café is archetypal Brick Lane hip, with a beaten-up studenty look, lots of outdoor seating, sofas to crash on, used books to read and simple snacks and cakes to sample. It's also a bar, with DJ sets and live music. Mon–Sat 6am–midnight, Sun 6am–11.30pm.

Leila's Shop 17 Calvert Ave, E2 ☎020 7729 9789; Shoreditch High Street Overground; map p.192. Relaxed deli-café serving great Mediterranean-tinged breakfasts, brunches and light hot lunches in an artfully shabby, nostalgic and very appealing little store. Mon–Sat 10am–6pm, Sun 10am–5pm.

★ **Sweet & Spicy** 40 Brick Lane, E1 ☎020 7247 1081; ⊖ Aldgate East; map p.192. Very basic self-service Bangladeshi café on a street renowned for its curry houses, decorated with ancient pictures of wrestlers, and serving up cheap hot curries with a minimum of fuss. Daily 8am–10.30pm.

★ **Verde and Co** 40 Brushfield St, E1 ☎020 7247 1924, ⓦjeanettewinterson.com/verdes.asp; ⊖ Liverpool Street; map p.192. Adorable Spitalfields deli/grocer's/café owned by author Jeanette Winterson, who has preserved the original eighteenth-century shopfront and bareboard interior. They sell all manner of classy and quirky deli goods, with seating for around six lucky people to enjoy superb

TOP 5 BRUNCH SPOTS

Breakfast Club Soho. See p.369
Caravan Clerkenwell. See p.374
Dehesa Mayfair. See p.368
Leila's Shop Shoreditch. See p.378
Towpath Café Hoxton/Dalston. See p.384

24

coffee, gourmet salads and fresh seasonal lunches. Mon–Fri 8am–8pm, Sat & Sun 11am–5pm.

RESTAURANTS

The Hawksmoor 157 Commercial St, E1 ☎020 7247 7392, ⓦthehawksmoor.co.uk; ⊖ Liverpool Street or Shoreditch High Street Overground; map p.192. Carnivores drool at the very mention of this steakhouse, where the charcoal-grilled cuts of meat, sourced from the famed Yorkshire suppliers Ginger Pig, are huge and succulent. The Sunday roasts are fantastic, or you could take on a huge breakfast (£35 for two) that includes dripping toast, black pudding and grilled bone marrow. A full meal could set you back around £40. Mon–Fri noon–3pm & 6–10.30pm, Sat 11am–4pm & 6–10.30pm, Sun 11am–5pm.

Lahore Kebab House 2–10 Umberston St, E1 ☎020 7481 9737, ⓦlahore-kebabhouse.com; ⊖ Aldgate East; map p.192. A legendary bargain Punjabi kebab house, just off Commercial Rd. Go for the lamb cutlets and roti, and go hungry. BYOB. Mains £7–11. Daily noon–midnight.

Needoo Grill 87 New Rd, E1 ☎020 7247 0648, ⓦneedoogrill.co.uk; ⊖ Whitechapel; map p.192. Run by a *Tayyabs* alumni (see below), this excellent, lively Pakistani restaurant maintains the standards, offers many of the same dishes, and has added some superb veggie specialities to boot. Mains from £6. Veggie mains from £4.50. Daily 11.30am–11.30pm.

St John Bread and Wine 94–96 Commercial St, E1 ☎020 3301 8069, ⓦstjohnbreadandwine.com; ⊖ Liverpool Street; map p.192. A simpler offshoot of *St John* (see p.376) with the same superlative British food – lots of offal, pig's cheek and the like. It's great for breakfasts (try the Old Spot bacon sandwich), puds and buns, while later on in the day the small sharing plates won't break the bank. Dishes £6–15. Mon–Fri 9–11am, noon–4pm & 6–10.30pm, Sat 10–11am, noon–4pm & 6–10.30pm, Sun 10–11am, noon–4pm & 6–9.30pm.

★ **Tayyabs** 83–89 Fieldgate St, E1 ☎020 7247 9543, ⓦtayyabs.co.uk; ⊖ Whitechapel; map p.192. Opened in 1974, *Tayyabs* still offers the same straightforward Pakistani food: good, freshly cooked and without pretension. Prices have remained low, booking is essential, and service is speedy and slick. BYOB. Mains from £6. Daily 5–11.30pm.

24

BETHNAL GREEN

CAFÉS

★ **E. Pellicci** 332 Bethnal Green Rd, E2 ☎020 7739 4873; ⊖ Bethnal Green; map p.192. London's old Italian-owned caffs are dropping like flies, and *Pellicci's* (operating since 1900) is a rare jewel: an iconic East End institution with its – stunning –1940s decor intact, serving great fry-ups and good Anglo-Italian grub at low prices. Don't miss the little family museum upstairs. Mon–Sat 6.30am–5pm.

★ **Frizzante@City Farm** 1a Goldsmith's Row, E2 ☎020 7739 2266, ⓦfrizzanteltd.co.uk; ⊖ Bethnal Green; map p.190. Hackney City Farm's rustic café serves great home-made family-friendly breakfasts, Italian-style lunches and Sunday roasts, all for less than a tenner. Don't miss the home-made ice cream. Tues–Sun 10am–4.30pm.

G. Kelly 414 Bethnal Green Rd, E2 ☎020 7739 3603; ⊖ Bethnal Green; map p.192. This old-school, no-frills (at all!) caff, lined with photos of local boxing heroes, is one of London's few remaining pie shops and a Cockney vanguard. Order meat pies with "liquor" (parsley sauce) and mash – and you'll pay less than a fiver. If you fancy a side of jellied eels, head to the other *G. Kelly* eel and pie shop (no relation), further into Bow at 526 Roman Rd, E3 (☎020 8980 3165; Mile End; map p.190). Mon–Thurs 10am–3pm, Fri 10am–6pm, Sat 9.30am–4pm.

Jones Dairy 23 Ezra St, E2 ☎020 7739 5372, ⓦjonesdairy.co.uk; ⊖ Bethnal Green; map p.192. Take a detour from Sunday's Columbia Road Market (see p.434) to this gorgeous, busy little place, which sells great breads, bagels and fine cheeses. Fri & Sat 9am–3pm, Sun 8am–2pm.

RESTAURANT

★ **Viajante** Patriot Square, E2 ☎020 7871 0461, ⓦviajante.co.uk; ⊖ Bethnal Green; map p.190. Exquisite global cuisine from cult chef Nuno Mendes, whose supper clubs were the talk of foodie Londoners in 2009. Food takes elements of molecular cuisine but is never pretentious – choose a number of courses and wait to see what turns up. Tiny plates offer amazing flavours – even the butter is flavoured with chicken skin, black pudding and jámon. Lunch £28 for 3 courses/£50 for 6/£70 for 9; dinner £65 for 6/£90 for 12. Mon & Tues 6–9.30pm, Wed–Sun noon–2pm & 6–9.30pm.

DOCKLANDS

CAFÉS

Hubbub 269 Westferry Rd, E14 ☎020 7515 5577, ⓦhubbubcafebar.com; Mudchute DLR; map p.208. A real oasis in the desert of Docklands, this café-bar is housed in a former Victorian church, now arts centre, and does decent fry-ups, sandwiches and tapas. Mon–Wed noon–11pm, Thurs & Fri noon–midnight, Sat 10am–midnight, Sun 10am–10.30pm.

Mudchute Kitchen Mudchute City Farm, Pier St, E14 ☎020 7515 5901, ⓦmudchute.org; Mudchute DLR;

map p.208. Run by the same team as *Frizzante* at the Hackney City Farm (see p.379), and serving the same satisfying, home-made food in a lovely green setting. Tues–Sun 9.30am–4.30pm.

RESTAURANTS

Mem Saheb on Thames 65–67 Amsterdam Rd, E14 ☎ 020 7538 3008, ⓦ memsaheb.net; Crossharbour DLR; map p.208. Very decent riverside Indian restaurant (Delia Smith is a fan!) in an area not known for its great places to eat, with a superb view over the river to the Dome. Mains £7–15. Mon–Fri noon–3pm & 6–11.30pm, Sat 6–11.30pm, Sun noon–4pm & 6–11.30pm.

Royal China 30 Westferry Circus, E14 ☎ 020 7719 0888, ⓦ royalchinagroup.biz; Canary Wharf; map p.208. You can eat well from the full menu, but it's the dim sum (£3–5; lunchtime only) that is most enticing here – the roast pork bun and spicy chicken feet are famous. Branches in Marylebone, Bayswater, Fulham and elsewhere. Mains £10–18. Mon–Thurs noon–11pm, Fri & Sat noon–11.30pm, Sun 11am–10pm.

SOUTH BANK

CAFÉS

★ **Ev** 97–99 Isabella St, SE1 ☎ 020 7620 6191, ⓦ tasrestaurant.com; Southwark or Waterloo; map p.216. A Middle Eastern organic deli-café and adjoining restaurant (which is also good) in a really pretty spot: tucked under a railway arch, it has a lofty barrel-vaulted ceiling, rustic wooden seating, lots of hanging plants and outside tables, shaded by ferns and bamboo, on a pedestrianized street. Great salads and bread, dried fruit and an array of Turkish delight. Mon–Sat noon–11.30pm, Sun noon–10.30pm.

Marsh Ruby 30 Lower Marsh, SE1 ☎ 020 7620 0593, ⓦ marshruby.com; Waterloo; map p.216. Terrific filling lunchtime curries for around a fiver: the food, on seasonally changing menus, is organic/free range and there's a basic but cheery communal dining area at the back. Mon–Fri 11.30am–3pm, Thurs & Fri 6.30–10.30pm.

RESTAURANTS

★ **Laughing Gravy** 154 Blackfriars Rd, SE1 ☎ 020 7998 1701, ⓦ thelaughinggravy.co.uk; Southwark; map p.216. Warm, welcoming brasserie serving robust modern English and Mediterranean food in a brick-lined dining room with a cosy, neighbourhood vibe. Mains £10–16. Mon–Fri 11am–11pm, Sat 5.30–11pm, Sun noon–6pm.

Masters Super Fish 191 Waterloo Rd, SE1 ☎ 020 7928 6924; Waterloo; map p.216. This old-fashioned, unpretentious fish-and-chip restaurant serves up huge portions with all the trimmings – gherkins, pickled onions, coleslaw and a few complimentary prawns – along with a few fancier seafood options. Mains £7.50–13. Mon 5.30–10.30pm, Tues–Thurs & Sat noon–3pm & 4.30–10.30pm, Fri noon–3pm & 4.30–11pm.

RSJ 33 Coin St, SE1 ☎ 020 7928 4554, ⓦ rsj.uk.com; Waterloo; map p.216. Good, solid Anglo-French cooking and relaxing ambience make this renovated old stable building a good spot for a meal before or after an evening at a South Bank theatre or concert hall. The two- and three-course set menus (£17/£19) are particularly good value. Mains £12–19. Mon–Fri noon–2.30pm & 5.30–11pm, Sat 5.30–11pm.

SOUTHWARK

CAFÉS

See also Brindisa, a deli reviewed in our Shopping chapter (see p.431).

El Vergel 132 Webber St, SE1 ☎ 020 7401 2308, ⓦ elvergel.co.uk; Borough; map p.224. Small, very busy Latin American/Mediterranean café that does great breakfast tacos, salads and gourmet sandwiches, along with Latin American specialities including empanadas, pasties filled with meat and spices or spinach and feta. Mon–Fri 8am–3pm, Sat 10am–10pm (bar service only 3–5pm).

RESTAURANTS

Roast The Floral Hall, Borough Market, Stoney St, SE1 ☎ 0845 034 7300, ⓦ roast-restaurant.com; London Bridge; map p.226. They pride themselves here on using sustainably sourced ingredients in everything from steak and ale pie to suckling pig; it's open for breakfast, too, when there are lots of healthy options (boiled egg and Marmite soldiers, anyone?) as well as a fabulous full English for £15. The glamorous contemporary dining room looks down on the bustle of Borough Market. Mains from £18. Mon & Tues 7–11am, noon–2.45pm & 5.30–10.30pm, Wed–Fri 7–11am, noon–3.45pm & 5.30–10.30pm, Sat 8am–3.45pm & 6–10.30pm, Sun 11.30am–6pm.

The Table 83 Southwark St, SE1 ☎ 020 7401 2760, ⓦ thetablecafe.com; Southwark or London Bridge; map p.226. Tucked behind the Tate, this friendly modern European café-restaurant has an excellent salad bar and chunky canteen tables. Owned and designed by neighbouring architects, with a nice industrial-style outdoor deck. Mains from £6 at lunch, £14 at dinner. Mon 7.30am–5pm, Tues–Thurs 7.30–5pm & 6–10pm, Fri & Sat 8.30am–3.30pm & 6–10.30pm, Sun 8.30am–3.30pm.

★ **Zucca** 184 Bermondsey St, SE1 ☎ 020 7378 6809, ⓦ zuccalondon.com; London Bridge; map p.224.

Prices for the exceptional modern Italian food here, made with the freshest, simplest ingredients, are far lower than you'd expect. Fresh pasta, risottos, grilled razor clams, lamb chop with potato and anchovy – all of it is seasonal, and portions are huge. Mains £9–15.Tues–Sat 12.30–3pm & 6.30–10pm, Sun 12.30–3pm.

SOUTH KENSINGTON & KNIGHTSBRIDGE

CAFÉS

Capote y Toros 157 Old Brompton Rd, SW5 ☎ 020 7373 0567, ⓦ cambiodetercio.co.uk; ⊖ Gloucester Rd or South Kensington; map p.250. The emphasis at this sunny bar is on Spain's wonderful sherries, with more than 40 available by the glass, and interesting tapas cooked with the stuff. The same people run another tapas bar, *Tendido Cero*, at 174 Old Brompton Rd, and a more formal restaurant, *Cambio de Tercio*, at 163, which are also great. Tapas £4.25–7. Tues–Sat 5–11.30pm.

The Troubadour 263–267 Old Brompton Rd, SW5 ☎ 020 7370 1434, ⓦ troubadour.co.uk; ⊖ Earl's Court; map p.250. A classic 1950s folk bar, this cluttered boho café-club once played host to Hendrix, Bob Dylan and Joni Mitchell. It still runs terrific folk and blues nights, and dishes up omelettes, steaks and burgers and great breakfasts. Daily 9am–midnight.

RESTAURANTS

★ **Dinner by Heston Blumenthal** Mandarin Oriental Hotel, 66 Knightsbridge, SW1 ☎ 020 7201 3833, ⓦ dinnerbyheston.com; ⊖ Knightsbridge; map p.250. You know what to expect from Heston – wildly imaginative, witty food that tastes amazing and gives you a once in a lifetime experience. Blumenthal doesn't actually cook here – the head chef worked with him at the *Fat Duck* – and there is less emphasis on flash and dazzle and molecular cuisine. Dishes are taken from British culinary history right through from medieval times, and some are marvellously odd – rice and flesh, "meat fruit", cockle ketchup, taffety tart. The sky's the limit as far as costs go, of course, though there's a three-course weekday lunch menu for £28 – that's if you get a reservation. Mains from £25. Daily noon–2.30pm & 6.30–10.30pm.

Gessler at Daquise 20 Thurloe St, SW7 ☎ 020 7589 6117, ⓦ gesslerlondon.com; ⊖ South Kensington; map p.252. This old-fashioned Polish café, a South Ken institution since 1947, has been taken over by a smart Polish restaurant group and while it keeps some of its old, rustic atmosphere, the Polish home cooking (much of it prepared, rather wonderfully, tableside) has gone rather upmarket – don't miss the cheese *pierogi*, and the amazing beetroot soup. Mains £12–23, three-course "tasting" menu £19.90 lunch/£30 dinner, two- or four-course lunch menu £9/14. Daily noon until "the last guests leave".

No.10 10 Hogarth Place, SW5 ☎ 020 7373 7000: ⊖ Earls Court; map p.250. Stick to the Szechuan food and you are onto a winner in this small, low-key restaurant. Many dishes offer the peppery kick you'd expect, but they also have a number of less fiery treats, like *Zhang ya zi* (smoked duck). Mains around £7; you won't spend more than £18 a head for a big meal. Daily noon–3pm & 6–11pm.

O Fado 50 Beauchamp Place, SW3 ☎ 020 7589 3002, ⓦ ofado.co.uk; ⊖ Knightsbridge; map p.250. Probably the oldest Portuguese restaurant in London, which speaks volumes for its authenticity. It can get rowdy at weekends what with the live fado (Fri & Sat) and the family parties, but that's half the fun. You'll need to reserve. Mains from £16. Mon–Sat noon–3pm & 6.30–11pm.

Racine 239 Brompton Rd, SW3 ☎ 020 7584 4477; ⊖ Knightsbridge or South Kensington; map p.252. The food here is French – rich, nostalgic dishes from the glory days of French cooking, perfectly executed. Booking is imperative. Mains from £16; two- or three-course menus £15.50/£17.75 Mon–Sat, £18/£20 Sun. Daily noon–3pm & 6–10.30pm.

24

CHELSEA

CAFÉS

Mona Lisa 417 King's Rd, SW10 ☎ 020 7376 5447; ⊖ Fulham Broadway; map p.265. This genuine old caff – very unusual in chichi Chelsea – dishes up cheap, good, old-fashioned food in plain, convivial surroundings. The mixed local crowd – from Sloanes to regulars from the adjoining council estate – enjoy anything from big fry-ups to great Italian comfort food – including good steaks and veal dishes. Mon–Sat 8am–6pm, Sun 9am–4pm.

★ **Poilâne** 46 Elizabeth St, SW1 ☎ 020 7808 4910; ⊖ Sloane Square; map p.250. Tiny London outlet of the legendary French boulangerie, which produces the city's best Parisian bread, croissants and sourdough. Mon–Fri 7.30am–7pm, Sat 7.30am–6pm.

RESTAURANTS

Chutney Mary 535 King's Rd, SW10 ☎ 020 7351 3113, ⓦ chutneymary.com; ⊖ Fulham Broadway; map p.250. Not your standard curry house, Chutney Mary turns out gourmet Indian food – complicated, subtle dishes with

---

TOP 5 BUDGET-BLOWERS

Dinner by Heston Knightsbridge.
  See above
The Ledbury Notting Hill. See p.382
The Providores Marylebone. See p.369
Viajante Bethnal Green. See p.379
The Wolseley Mayfair. See p.368

modern twists – and rather wonderful Anglo-Indian puds on changing menus. Mains £16–22. Mon–Fri 6.30–11pm, Sat 12.30–2.30pm & 6.30–11pm, Sun 12.30–2.30pm & 6.30–10pm.

Hunan 51 Pimlico Rd, SW1 ☎ 020 7730 5712, Ⓦ hunanlondon.com; ⊖ Sloane Square; map p.265. Don't go too much by its name – rather than Hunanese cuisine, this acclaimed restaurant serves delicious Taiwanese/Chinese fusion food. There's no menu: tell them how spicy you like things, and any other preferences, and they will bring you a vast array of small dishes to your table for a "leave-it-to-us feast". Reservations essential. Feasts from £45 per head, drinks included. Mon–Sat 12.30–2pm & 6.30–11pm.

HIGH STREET KENSINGTON TO NOTTING HILL

CAFÉS

★ **Books for Cooks** 4 Blenheim Crescent, W11 ☎ 020 7221 1992, Ⓦ booksforcooks.com; ⊖ Ladbroke Grove or Notting Hill Gate; map p.274. Tiny café within London's top cookery bookshop (see p.429). Conditions are cramped, but this is an experience not to be missed. Just wander in and have a coffee while browsing, or get there in time to grab a table for the set-menu lunch (noon–1.30pm). Tues–Sat 10am–6pm.

Hummingbird Bakery 133 Portobello Rd, W11 ☎ 020 7851 1795, Ⓦ hummingbirdbakery.com; ⊖ Notting Hill; map p.274. This cute little spot, halfway down Portobello Rd, was a major player in the mid-2000s cupcake revolution. Pick up sumptuous American-style goodies, from said cupcakes to sumptuous whoopee pies, many of which are gluten-free; wrought-iron chairs and tables outside make for great people-watching. Branches in South Kensington and Soho. Mon–Fri 10am–6pm, Sat 9am–6.30pm, Sun 11am–5pm.

★ **Lisboa Patisserie** 57 Golborne Rd, W10 ☎ 020 8968 5242; ⊖ Westbourne Park; map p.274. Authentic Portuguese pastelaria, with the best *pasteis de nata* (custard tarts) this side of Lisbon – also coffee, cakes and a friendly, crowded atmosphere. Café O'porto at 62a Golborne Rd is a good fall-back if this place is full. Daily 8am–7pm.

Tom's Deli 226 Westbourne Grove, W11 Notting Hill Gate ☎ 020 7221 8818; ⊖ Westbourne Park; map p.274. It's all very Notting Hill – retro, cluttered, boho-posh – at this cosy, crowded deli, which serves all-day breakfasts, soups, casseroles and gooey puds. Outdoor seating on a balcony in summer. Mon–Sat 8am–6.30pm, Sun 9am–6.30pm Sun.

RESTAURANTS

★ **Le Café Anglais** 8 Porchester Gardens, W2 ☎ 020 7221 1415, Ⓦ lecafeanglais.co.uk; ⊖ Bayswater; map p.274. Splendid modern British/European brasserie in an airy, vaguely Art Deco space set incongruously in the bland Whiteley's shopping mall. Food is stunning, from the pike boudin with beurre blanc to the signature parmesan custard with anchovy toast. Mains £14–28; set lunch menus (2/3 courses) £18.50/£23.50 Mon–Fri, £24.50/£28.50 Sun; daily changing two-course menu in the oyster bar £13.50. Mon–Thurs noon–3.30 pm & 6.30–10.30pm, Fri & Sat noon–3.30 pm & 6.30–11pm, Sun noon–3.30 pm & 6.30–10pm; oyster bar Mon–Sat noon–10.30 pm, Sun noon–5pm.

Hereford Road 3 Hereford Rd, W2 ☎ 020 7727 1144, Ⓦ herefordroad.org; ⊖ Queensway or Notting Hill Gate; map p.274. Robust English cooking from *St John* alumni Tom Pemberton, with the same concentration on simple, old-fashioned excellence – ham hock and pea shoots, stuffed lamb heart with nettles, and the like. The set meals are an astonishing bargain. Mains £10–33. Two- or three-course weekday lunch menu £13/£15.50, or an "express lunch" for £9.50. Daily noon–3pm & 6–10.30pm, till 10pm Sun.

★ **The Ledbury** 127 Ledbury Rd, W11 ☎ 020 7792 9090, Ⓦ theledbury.com; ⊖ Westbourne Park; map p.274. Australian wünderkind Brett Graham has won two Michelin stars for his fabulous French food – elegant, confident, a bit nouvelle, and packed with flavours. Mains £24–27.50, with set lunch menus at £27.50 for two courses or £33.50 for three. Mon 6.30–10.30pm, Tues–Sat noon–2pm & 6.30–10.30pm, Sun noon–2.30pm & 7–10pm.

★ **Mandalay** 444 Edgware Rd, W2 ☎ 020 7258 3696, Ⓦ mandalayway.com; ⊖ Edgware Road; map p.274. Authentic Burmese cuisine – a melange of Thai, Malaysian, a bit of Chinese and a lot of Indian. The portions are huge, the service friendly and the prices low. Booking essential in the evening. Mains £5–8. Mon–Sat noon–2.30pm & 6–10.30pm.

Pearl Liang 8 Sheldon Square, W2 ☎ 020 7289 700, Ⓦ pearlliang.co.uk; ⊖ Paddington; map p.274. The setting, in a modern development near Paddington railway station, is unpromising, but it's well worth the trek for superb dim sum (try the superb wasabi prawn dumplings) in an elegant, rather pink, dining room. Dim sum from £2.50, platters of nine dishes £9.80, takeaway lunch boxes from £5. Daily noon–11pm.

CAMDEN TOWN

CAFÉS

Garden Café Inner Circle, Regent's Park, NW1 ☎ 020 7935 5729, Ⓦ thegardencafe.co.uk; ⊖ Baker Street or Regent's Park; map p.284. A classic 1960s modernist building with a copper-domed roof. The excellent food is as retro as the decor, with mains such as fish pie and ribeye steak, and sticky toffee pud or rhubarb crumble for afters. Mains from £9. Daily noon–4pm; evenings in summer.

24

Marine Ices 8 Haverstock Hill, NW3 ☎ 020 7482 9003, ⓦ marineices.co.uk; ⊖ Chalk Farm; map p.284. Midway between Camden and Hampstead, this is a splendid and justly famous old-fashioned Italian ice-cream parlour established here in 1930; the ice cream is wonderful and they serve pizza and pasta in the adjacent kiddie-friendly restaurant (closed Tues–Fri 3–6pm). Tues–Sat noon–11pm, Sun noon–10pm.

RESTAURANTS

★ **El Parador** 245 Eversholt St, NW1 ☎ 020 7387 2789, ⓦ elparadorlondon.com; ⊖ Mornington Crescent; map p.284. Though there's little fuss here, the tapas, served in a small, simple dining room with a friendly neighbourhood buzz, are some of London's best. There's a splendid, creative veggie selection (try the roasted beet salad or the sweet potato cakes with caramelised leeks, thyme and goats

cheese). Tapas £4.60–7.20. Mon–Thurs noon–3pm & 6–11pm, Fri & Sat noon–3pm & 6–11.30pm, Sun 6.30–930pm.

Manna 4 Erskine Rd, NW3 ☎ 020 7722 8028, ⓦ manna-veg.com; ⊖ Chalk Farm; map p.284. Upscale veggie restaurant, full of gorgeous Primrose Hill yoga types, serving large portions of very good, mostly organic, food, much of it vegan, from around the world. Mains £11–14, less at lunch. Tues–Fri 6.30–10.30pm, Sat & Sun noon–3pm & 6.30–10.30pm.

Trojka 101 Regent's Park Rd, NW1 ☎ 020 7483 3765, ⓦ trojka.co.uk; ⊖ Chalk Farm; map p.284. The Eastern European food is inexpensive, filling and tasty: blinis and caviar, schnitzel and stroganoff, pierogi and pelmeni. Service can be a bit East European as well. Live Russian music on Friday and Saturday evenings. Mains £6–9; two-course lunch menu £7.95/£9.95.Daily 9am–10.30pm.

ISLINGTON

CAFÉS

Afghan Kitchen 35 Islington Green, N1 ☎ 020 7359 8019; ⊖ Angel; map p.284. Austere, two-floor café with bare bench seating, featuring a short menu of cheap, spicy stews with rice. Tues–Sat noon–3.30pm & 5.30–11pm.

Alpino 97 Chapel Market, N1 ☎ 020 7837 8330; ⊖ Angel; map p.284. A classic old Italian-British caff on Angel's noisy market street, with teak-veneer formica tables, wooden booths and glorious 1950s light fittings. The grub, of course, is cheap and filling. Tues–Fri 7am–3.30pm, Sat 7am–1pm.

Cà Phê! 149b Upper Street, N1 ☎ 07780 784696, ⓦ caphevn.co.uk; ⊖ Highbury & Islington; map p.284. Tiny Upper Street offshoot of a popular cart on Broadway Market, serving dark, rich Vietnamese drip coffee served with sweet condensed milk; order one of their pork *bánh mì* sandwiches for the real street food experience. Mon–Fri 11am–7pm, Sat & Sun 10am–7pm.

M. Manze 74 Chapel Market, N1 ☎ 020 7837 5270; ⊖ Angel; map p.284. With their gleaming tiled interiors and unchanging menus, London's old pie-and-mash shops are a unique experience, though the rewards are often more architectural and nostalgic than culinary. Tues–Sat 11am–4pm.

RESTAURANTS

Elk in the Woods 39 Camden Passage, N1 ☎ 020 7226 3535, ⓦ the-elk-in-the-woods.co.uk; ⊖ Angel; map p.284. A rather hip, bare-brick-and-wood bar-café-restaurant cross, with a stuffed elk looking down on the shabby chic proceedings. Food is modern European, with Scandinavian influences – mains can include frikadeller, lamb stew and rabbit and prawn paella, but they do breakfasts, sandwiches and small plates (from £4) too. Mains £11–17. Mon–Sat 8.30am–11pm, Sun 10.30am–11pm.

★ **Gem** 265 Upper St, N1 ☎ 020 7359 0405, ⓦ gemrestaurant.org.uk; ⊖ Highbury and Islington; map p.284. This airy Turkish and Kurdish restaurant specializes in charcoal-grilled dishes and smoky pide (a kind of Turkish pizza) – you can see the bread being freshly prepared at the front of the restaurant. Mains from £7. Mon–Thurs noon–11pm, Fri & Sat noon–midnight, Sun noon–10.30pm.

Ottolenghi 287 Upper St, N1 ☎ 020 7288 1454, ⓦ ottolenghi.co.uk; ⊖ Angel; map p.284. An elegant, if crammed café-restaurant with long white communal tables. The robust Mediterranean food is great, with imaginative salads and fantastic desserts (check out those meringues!). They do breakfast, too, with at-table toasters and piles of newspapers. It's not, in any way, cheap. Takeaway available. Branches in Notting Hill, Kensington, Belgravia and Soho. Mains from £11. Mon–Sat 8am–11pm, Sun 9am–7pm.

24

GREAT GASTROPUBS

Gone are the days when eating in a pub meant settling for a Ploughman's and a packet of pork scratchings – the following places, reviewed in our Pubs and bars chapter, offer gourmet food to rival some of the city's best restaurants, in laidback, friendly surroundings.

The Dove Hackney. See p.397
The Duke of Cambridge Islington. See p.396
The Eagle Clerkenwell. See p.390
The Greenwich Union Greenwich. See p.398
The Lansdowne Camden/Primrose Hill. See p.396
The Westbourne Notting Hill. See p.395

STOKE NEWINGTON AND DALSTON

CAFÉS

Blue Legume 101 Stoke Newington Church St, N16 ☎020 7923 1303, ⓦthebluelegume.co.uk; Stoke Newington train station; map p.291. Buzzy atmosphere, arty decor, mosaic tables and wholesome fresh lunches – big salads, pies, stuffed veggies – make this a fabulous stalwart on Stoke Newington's liveliest street. Good all-day breakfasts too – eggs Benedict, wild mushrooms on toast and the like – and great cakes and fresh juices. Branch in Islington. Mon–Sat 9.30am–11pm, Sun 9.30am–6.30pm.

F.Cooke 9 Broadway Market, E8 ☎020 7254 6458; London Fields train station; map p.291. "Eat more eels!" announces an old sign at this friendly, traditional eel and pie shop that's been in the family for generations and on this spot since 1900. Order pie, mash, liquor (parsley gravy) and a side of jellied eels and enjoy a slice of old East End history on the increasingly gentrifying Broadway Market. Mon–Thurs 10am–7pm, Fri & Sat: 10.30am–8pm.

★ **Towpath Café** Whitmore Bridge, 42 de Beauvoir Crescent, N1 ☎020 7254 7606, ⓦtowpathcafe .wordpress.com; Haggerston Overground; map p.291. With outdoor benches by the Regent's canal near Dalston, Hoxton and Broadway Market, this is a lovely, sunny find; food is simple and seasonal, with a dash of Mediterranean flair – great for brunch, with truffle and parmesan buns, organic sausages and toasted cheese on sourdough, or something a bit more complex, like a paella, later on. Good soups, coffees and fresh home-made juices, too. Dishes from £4; no credit cards. Tues–Fri 8am–dusk, Sat 9am–dusk, Sun 10am–dusk.

RESTAURANTS

Mangal Ocakbasi 10 Arcola St, E8 ☎020 7275 8981, ⓦmangal1.com; Dalston Junction Overground; map p.291. Generally agreed to be the best of the excellent Turkish diners around here, *Mangal* is renowned for its grills and skewered meats, many of them served with yoghurt sauce; the veggie mezes and fresh breads are good, too. At its sister restaurant, *Mangal II*, around the corner on Stoke Newington High Street, you will join artists Gilbert and George, who eat here every night, for similarly simple food and friendly service. Dishes from £5. Daily noon–midnight.

★ **Rasa** 55 Stoke Newington Church St, N16 ☎020 7249 0344, ⓦrasarestaurants.com; Stoke Newington train station; map p.291. Cosy Keralan restaurant, the first in the expanding *Rasa* dynasty, with amazingly good, very inexpensive South Indian vegetarian specialities. The equally fine Rasa Travancore across the road specializes in Syrian Christian cooking, serving some meat and fish. Mains £4–6. Mon–Thurs 6–10.45pm, Fri 6–11.30pm, Sat noon–3pm & 6–11.30pm, Sun noon–3pm, & 6–10.45pm.

HAMPSTEAD AND HIGHGATE

CAFÉS

★ **Brew House** Kenwood House, Hampstead Lane, NW3 ☎020 8341 5384; ⊖ Highgate; map p.298. Splendid café serving everything from full English breakfasts to gourmet sandwiches, cakes and teas, either in the house's old servants' wing or in the huge, sunny garden courtyard. Daily 9am–6pm.

Kalendar 15 Swains Lane, N6 ☎020 8348 8300; Gospel Oak train station; map p.298. In a nice road on the southeast side of Hampstead Heath, this café pulls in a happy mix of locals for long, lazy breakfasts, deli lunches and Konditor & Cook (see p.430) cakes. Mon–Thurs 9am–10pm, Sat & Sun 9am–10pm.

Lauderdale House Waterlow Park, Highgate Hill, N6 ☎020 8341 4807; ⊖ Archway; map p.298. Fill up on comforting, home-made food in this friendly arts centre café, and make sure to try their strawberry-and-cream scones on summer weekends, when you can sit out on the terrace overlooking the park. Tues–Sun 9am–5pm.

★ **Louis Patisserie** 32 Heath St, NW3 ☎020 7435 9908; ⊖ Hampstead; map p.298. For some fifty years now this tiny, understated and gloriously old-fashioned Hungarian tearoom/patisserie has been serving sticky cakes, tea and coffee to a mixed local crowd. Daily 9am–6pm.

RESTAURANTS

Czechoslovak Restaurant 74 West End Lane, NW6 ☎020 7372 1193, ⓦczechoslovak-restaurant.co.uk; ⊖ West Hampstead; map p.298. Classic, unreconstructed Czech & Slovak meat and dumplings washed down with Czech beer. Set in an attractive house with a garden out back, and very popular with Czech expats – book ahead if you want to come for Sunday lunch. Mains £8–13. Tues–Fri 5–10pm, Sat & Sun noon–10pm.

Jin Kichi 73 Heath St, NW3 ☎020 7794 6158, ⓦjinkichi.com; ⊖ Hampstead; map p.298. *Jin Kichi* is a cramped, homely and very busy (book ahead) neighbourhood Japanese place that specializes in charcoal-grilled skewers of meat. Mains £8–12. Tues–Sat 12.30–2pm & 6–10.45pm, Sun 12.30–2pm & 6–10.45pm.

BRIXTON

CAFÉS

Rosie's 14e Market Row, SW9 ☎07807 505397, ⓦrosiesdelicafe.com; ⊖ Brixton. The deli sells artisan cheese, handmade pasta and charcuterie, with a cute, friendly café serving freshly made sandwiches, tarts and hot dishes in a comfy retro setting. Mon–Sat 8am–5.30pm.

24

RESTAURANTS

⭐ **Franco Manca** 4 Market Row, SW9 ☎020 7738 3021, Ⓦfrancomanca.co.uk; ⊖ Brixton. Very popular, tiny gourmet pizza joint in Brixton Market that offers surprisingly inexpensive sourdough pizzas – there are just six options, all wood-fired and made with the finest ingredients – washed down with organic wine or lemonade. Mon–Sat noon–5pm, and variable later opening Thurs–Sat – phone to check.

Upstairs Bar and Restaurant 89b Acre Lane, SW2 ☎020 7733 8855, Ⓦupstairslondon.com; ⊖ Brixton. A small, cool fixture on the Brixton scene, with white leather seats and real fires. Food is modern British, creative and seasonal with unusual dishes like brawn and porchetta or cauliflower and truffle custard. Two-, three- and four-course menus £26/£32/£37. Tues–Thurs 6.30–9.30pm, Fri & Sat 6.30–10.30pm.

GREENWICH

CAFÉS

Gambardella 48 Vanbrugh Park, SE3 ☎020 8858 0327; Maze Hill or Blackheath train station from Charing Cross; map p.315. Historic old Italian caff to the southeast of Greenwich Park, serving filling comfort food in a beautiful Art Deco interior with lots of chrome and formica. Mon–Fri 8am–5pm, Sat 8am–2.30pm.

RESTAURANTS

⭐ **Old Brewery** Pepys Building, The Old Royal Naval College, SE10 ☎0203 327 1280, Ⓦwww.oldbrewery greenwich.com; Cutty Sark DLR; map p.315. Until 5pm, this warm, historic dining room serves full English breakfasts

(just £3), creative wraps and light deli lunches to tourists, before transforming with aplomb into a relaxed neighbourhood brasserie at night. Food is modern British, bursting with fresh, seasonal, ingredients, and the artisan beer is brewed on the premises. Mains £10.50–22.50, or from £7 at lunch. Daily 10am–11pm (10.30pm on Sun).

Peninsula Holiday Inn, Bugsbys Way, SE10 ☎020 8269 1638, Ⓦmychinesefood.co.uk; ⊖ North Greenwich; map p.315. The hotel setting near the 02 Dome may lack atmosphere, but aficionados come from far and wide for the authentic dim sum, hotpots and fabulous array of fresh seafood. Dim sum from £2. Mon–Fri 2–11.30pm, Sat 11am–11.30pm, Sun 11am–11pm.

HAMMERSMITH AND CHISWICK

RESTAURANTS

⭐ **Azou** 35 King St, W6 ☎020 8563 7266, Ⓦazou.co.uk; ⊖ Stamford Brook. Small, informal and atmospheric North African restaurant where you can enter into the spirit and end up sitting on a cushion on the floor. A warm welcome is assured and the classics – tagines and couscous – are presented with panache. Mains £10–19. Mon–Fri 6–11.30pm, Sat & Sun 12.30–2pm & 6–11.30pm.

The Gate 51 Queen Caroline St, W6 ☎020 8748 6932, Ⓦthegate.tv; ⊖ Hammersmith. In a converted church with an appealing outside courtyard, *The Gate* serves excellent and original vegetarian and vegan dishes – Arabic/Jewish with Mediterranean influences – with intense and satisfying tastes. Mains £10–14. Mon–Fri noon–2.30pm & 6–10.30pm, Sat 6–11pm.

KEW AND RICHMOND

CAFÉS

Greenhouse 1 Station Parade, Richmond, TW9 ☎020 8940 0183; ⊖ Kew Gardens; map p.344. A delightfully old-fashioned and pretty place near Kew Gardens, with light lunches, cream teas and home-made tarts. Daily 8am–dusk.

Pembroke Lodge Richmond Park, Richmond, TW10 ☎020 8940 8207; ⊖ Richmond; map p.344. This park café, in a gorgeous Georgian mansion in Richmond Park, has one of the best views in London, looking west over the Thames valley, and nice outdoor seating – food doesn't stretch much further than sandwiches and cakes. Daily 10am–5.30pm or dusk.

⭐ **Stein's** Richmond Towpath, Richmond, TW10 ☎020 8948 8189, Ⓦstein-s.com; ⊖ Richmond; map

p.344. An authentic Bavarian beer garden, serving up wurst and sauerkraut washed down with *echt* beers and finished off with strudel. Outdoor seating only, so it's closed in wet weather. May to mid-Oct Mon–Fri noon–10pm, Sat & Sun 10am–10pm; mid-Oct to April Fri–Sun noon–10pm.

RESTAURANTS

Chez Lindsay 11 Hill Rise, Richmond, TW10 ☎020 8948 7473, Ⓦchezlindsay.co.uk; ⊖ Richmond; map p.344. Small, bright, riverside Breton restaurant, with a loyal local following. There's a wide choice of galettes, crêpes and more formal French main courses, including lots of fresh fish and shellfish. Galettes from £5, mains £10–19. Mon–Sat noon–11pm, Sun noon–10pm.

24

ROYAL OAK, BOROUGH

Pubs and bars

The range and quality of the pubs and bars in London is extraordinary, and the drinking scene today is more vibrant and diverse than it's ever been. Whether you're looking for a classic Victorian drinking palace or the latest in twenty-first-century bar culture, the problem isn't finding it but making a choice. Charming, historic pubs can be found all over the city, often in unlikely spots in the backstreets, while many of the capital's bars – serving everything from fine wine and designer beers to cutting-edge cocktails – are clustered around areas like Soho and Shoreditch. Not only are there great places to drink in every part of the city, but the range of drinks available in most places has improved in recent years and decent pub food has become the rule. With a bit of planning, it's also still possible to drink on a budget.

25

The **pub** remains one of the country's most enduring social institutions, and is still the place where folk of all ages choose to meet up of an evening. Most decent pubs serve at least two or three **real ales** (see p.389) of varying strength, as well as the usual array of drinks. The emergence of **gastropubs**, where the food is as important as the drink, has had a knock-on effect on all pubs; it's meant all pubs can now charge (and make) a lot more money out of food, but also that the overall standard of cooking has improved enormously. Alongside pubs, we've also listed a selection of the capital's **bars**, which go in and out of fashion with incredible speed. These are very different places to your average pub, but attract an equally wide range of drinkers.

Note that this chapter covers pubs and bars that are good for drinking – and, sometimes, eating – in. It doesn't include club-bars or pubs and bars that are primarily live-music venues, which you'll find in Chapter 26, or gay and lesbian pubs and bars, which are covered in Chapter 27.

ESSENTIALS

Costs Prices in London's pubs and bars can be pretty steep, with the £4 pint now a frequent experience. Sam Smith's pubs remain a great exception, as not only are the excellent drinks a lot cheaper, but many of the pubs are very attractive, too. Pubs are also very happy to let you try something first. This isn't usually done with lagers, but it's perfectly acceptable to try English ales and bitters, or anything at all unusual (such as a Belgian beer) – you'll probably feel obliged to buy something afterwards, but no pub will be offended if you decide not to have whatever you've sampled. Many of the city's bars also run happy hours during the week, usually 5–7pm, when drinks are either half-price or significantly discounted.

Opening hours Due to a relaxation of licensing laws, opening hours are now increasingly varied, and although most pubs still close at 11pm (10.30pm on Sundays) many places are open later. Note that many bars in and around the City are only open during the week.

WHITEHALL AND WESTMINSTER

The Chandos 29 St Martin's Lane, WC2 ☎020 7836 1401; ⊖ Charing Cross; map, p.46. If you can get one of the booths downstairs, or the leather sofas upstairs in the more relaxed Opera Room Bar, then you'll find it difficult to leave this Sam Smith's pub. Mon–Sat 11am–11pm, Sun noon–10.30pm.

St Stephen's Tavern 10 Bridge St, SW1 ☎020 7925 2286 ⊖ Westminster; map.46. A beautifully restored, opulent Victorian pub, built in 1867, wall to wall with civil servants and MPs (there's a division bell), and serving good real ales. Mon–Fri 11am–11pm, Sat 11am–8pm, Sun noon–6pm.

ST JAMES'S

ICA Bar The Mall, SW1 ☎020 7930 3647, ⓦica.org.uk; ⊖ Piccadilly Circus or Charing Cross; map p.66. Cool late-opening drinking venue, with a noir dress code observed by the arty crowd and staff. Wed noon–11pm, Thurs–Sat noon–1am, Sun noon–9pm.

Red Lion 23 Crown Passage, SW1 ☎020 7930 4141; ⊖ Green Park; map p.66. Hidden away in a passageway off Pall Mall, this is a genuinely warm and cosy local, with super friendly bar staff, well-kept beer and excellent sandwiches. Mon–Sat 11.30am–11pm.

Red Lion 2 Duke of York St, SW1 ☎020 7321 0782; ⊖ Piccadilly Circus; map p.66. Genuine old Victorian gin palace with elegant etched mirrors, lots of polished wood and a great ceiling. Mon–Sat 11.30am–11pm.

MAYFAIR

Audley 41 Mount St, W1 ☎020 7499 1843; ⊖ Hyde Park Corner or Bond Street; map p.78. A grand Mayfair pub, with original Victorian burgundy lincrusta ceiling, beautiful wood-panelled walls, chandeliers and clocks. Mon–Sat 11am–11pm, Sun noon–10.30pm.

Guinea 30 Bruton Place, W1 ☎020 7409 1728, ⓦtheguinea.co.uk; ⊖ Bond Street or Oxford Circus; map p.78. Pretty, old-fashioned, flower-strewn mews pub, serving good Young's bitter. Invariably packed to its tiny rafters. Mon–Fri 11am–11pm, Sat 6–11pm.

The Windmill 6–8 Mill St, W1 ☎020 7491 8050; ⊖ Oxford Circus; map p.78. Convivial, well-regarded pub just off Regent St, and a perfect retreat for exhausted shoppers. The Young's beers are top-notch, as are the steak-and-kidney pies, for which the pub has won numerous awards. Mon–Fri 11am–midnight, Sat noon–4pm.

Ye Grapes 16 Shepherd Market, W1 ☎020 74934216, ⓦye-grapes.co.uk; ⊖ Green Park or Hyde Park Corner; map p.78. Very popular pub in Shepherd Market, a charming corner of Mayfair hidden away to the north of Piccadilly. If the *Grapes* is too busy, try the *King's Arms*, also in Shepherd Market. Mon–Sat 11pm, Sun noon–10pm.

25

WHERE TO GO

Clerkenwell A great place to head to for a wide range of traditional pubs in a small area, all of an extremely high standard, together with a good selection of fashionable bars. The newest places are concentrated on Exmouth Market and around Smithfield Market. Most of the pubs do good or extremely good food as well – *The Eagle* on Farringdon Road was a pioneer of the Gastropub scene (see p.390).

Notting Hill The pick of West London's neighbourhoods for drinking, with a great mix of old favourites and newer places striving to make a name for themselves. The area around Portobello Road and Westbourne Grove is the best place to start exploring.

The riverside A drink by the river is one of the best ways to enjoy the city, but the centre is notoriously thin on riverside pubs – you have to travel out a little bit to find anywhere that's worth visiting. The best areas to head for are Hammersmith to the west and Wapping and Bermondsey to the east, on the north and south sides of the river respectively.

Shoreditch Although it's no longer the new discovery that it was in the 1990s, nowhere else in London has quite such an eclectic mix of historic pubs, rough-and-ready boozers, established bars and trendy new arrivals.

Soho Soho has been experiencing something of a renaissance recently, with lots of new places opening in the last few years. It's always crowded, but boasts an unrivalled range of watering holes within a small area, and an undiminished feeling of being at the very heart of the action.

Southwark The area around Borough Market has many enjoyable places to drink, from historic gems like *The George* (see p.394) to the newer bars around the market itself. There's a great concentration of top-notch places in a small area here, but it can be extremely busy so be prepared to wander around a bit in search of the perfect spot.

MARYLEBONE

Dover Castle 43 Weymouth Mews, W1 ☎020 7580 4412; ⊖ Regent's Park or Great Portland Street; map p.89. A traditional, quiet, cheap Sam Smith's boozer hidden away down a picturesque Marylebone mews. Green upholstery, dark wood and a nicotine-stained lincrusta ceiling add to the atmosphere. Mon–Sat 11.30am–11pm, Sun noon–10.30pm.

Golden Eagle 59 Marylebone Lane, W1 ☎020 7935 3228; ⊖ Bond Street; map p.89. Proper old one-room, neighbourhood pub, with a good range of real ales, and singalongs on the old "Joanna" (Tues, Thurs & Fri). Mon–Sat 11am–11pm, Sun noon–7pm.

Gunmakers 33 Aybrook Street, W1 ☎020 7487 4937; ⊖ Bond Street; map p.89. One of Marylebone's best pubs, tucked away to the west of the high street, with attractive wood panelling and Churchill memorabilia – you can even get the same seat where the great man is sat in the large photograph behind the bar. Can be very busy on Saturdays, and avoid if you're bothered by sport on the TV. Mon–Sat 11am–12pm, Sun 11am–10.30pm.

SOHO

Academy 12 Old Compton St, W1 ☎020 7437 7820, ⊛labbaruk.com; ⊖ Leicester Square; map p.100. Cocktail-school graduates serve up classics and new concoctions in this two-floor retro cocktail bar that's considered one of the best in London. DJs on various nights – check their website for details. Mon–Sat 4pm–midnight, Sun 4pm–10.30pm.

Argyll Arms 18 Argyll St, W1 ☎020 7734 6117; ⊖ Oxford Circus; map p.97. Mobbed by shoppers and tourists alike, this Victorian pub has preserved many features of its traditional interior and offers a good range of real ales. Mon–Sat 11am–11.30pm, Sun noon–10.30pm.

De Hems 11 Macclesfield St, W1 ☎020 7437 2494; ⊖ Leicester Square; map p.100. London's official Dutch pub since 1890, the frequently jam-packed downstairs bar is a simple wood-panelled affair, while the contemporary upstairs space is good for more relaxed drinking. Good selection of mainly Belgian and Dutch beers and food. Mon–Sat noon–midnight, Sun noon–10.30pm.

★ **Dog & Duck** 18 Bateman St, W1 ☎020 7494 0697; ⊖ Tottenham Court Road; map p.100. Tiny Soho pub that retains much of its old character, beautiful Victorian tiling and mosaics, a good range of real ales and a loyal clientele. If it gets too busy downstairs, head upstairs to the George Orwell Bar (he used to drink here). Mon–Sat 11am–11pm, Sun noon–10.30pm.

French House 49 Dean St, W1 ☎020 7437 2799; ⊖ Leicester Square; map p.100. This tiny French pub has been a Soho institution since Belgian Victor Berlemont bought the place shortly before World War I. Free French and literary associations galore, and half-pints only at the bar (no real ale). Mon–Fri noon–11pm, Sat & Sun noon–10.30pm.

FITZROVIA

Bradley's Spanish Bar 42–44 Hanway St, W1 ☎020 7636 0359; ⊖ Tottenham Court Road; map p.97. Appealingly unpretentious backstreet bar, set over two very small floors, with a mixed but faithful clientele and an excellent vinyl jukebox full of old favourites. Mon–Sat noon–11pm, Sun 3–10.30pm.

The Green Man 36 Riding House St, W1 ☎020 7580 9087, ⓦthegreenmanw1.co.uk; ⊖ Oxford Circus; map p.97. With more of a bohemian and offbeat flavour than most pubs this close to Oxford and Regent streets, *The Green Man* is a real find, with an excellent range of ciders and beers and (except on Fridays) a decent chance of getting a table. Mon–Sat noon–11pm, Sun noon–10.30pm.

Newman Arms 23 Rathbone St, W1 ☎020 7636 1127, ⓦnewmanarms.co.uk; ⊖ Tottenham Court Road or Goodge Street; map p.97. Intimate, extremely friendly, family-run local, popular with a mixed and loyal crowd. Upstairs you can sample one of the pub's fabulous pies, from lamb-and-rosemary to steak-and-kidney. Mon–Fri noon–12am.

★ **The Social** 5 Little Portland St, W1 ☎020 7636 4992, ⓦthesocial.com; ⊖ Oxford Circus; map p.97. Industrial club-bar and diner, with great DJs playing everything from indie to hip-hop for a truly hedonistic-cum-alcoholic crowd. Mon 5pm–midnight, Tues & Wed noon–midnight, Thurs & Fri noon–1am, Sat 5pm–1am, Sun 5pm–midnight.

The Yorkshire Grey 46 Langham St, W1 ☎020 7636 4788; ⊖ Oxford Circus; map p.97. Very cosy and appealing pub with great value Sam Smith's beer, a snug corner beside the fire (something you'll need to compete for) and extra seating upstairs. For a contrasting experience the *Crown and Sceptre* – big, noisy, popular and fun – is just across Great Titchfield Street. Mon–Sat noon–11pm, Sun 6pm–10.30pm.

BLOOMSBURY

Booking Office ☎020 7841 3540; ⊖ King's Cross St Pancras; map p.120. Smart, expensive bar belonging to the *St Pancras Renaissance hotel*. You can chose between tables set out on the upper level of St Pancras station or in the impressive, historic interior. Mon–Sun noon–late.

★ **The Duke** 7 Roger St, WC1 ☎020 7242 7230, ⓦdukepub.co.uk; ⊖ Russell Square; map p.120. Lovely little neighbourhood gastropub, without the pretensions often associated with the breed, and an unusual Art Deco bent to the decor. Its discreet location keeps the crowd in the small bar manageable. Mon–Sat noon–11pm, Sun noon–10.30pm.

King Charles I 55–57 Northdown St, N1 ☎020 7837 7758; ⊖ King's Cross; map p.120. In a quiet street just off the Caledonian Road, near King's Cross, this pub has a ragged charm and a convivial atmosphere – the kind of place where you can easily find yourself playing a game on the traditional bar billiards table with people you've met five minutes earlier. Mon–Thurs noon–11pm, Fri to 1am, Sat 5–11pm, Sun 5–10.30pm.

The Lamb 94 Lamb's Conduit St, WC1 ☎020 7405 0713; ⊖ Russell Square; map p.120. Marvellously well-preserved Victorian pub, with mirrors, polished wood and etched glass "snob" screens. Deep green leather banquettes and small circular tables with dinky brass balustrades round things off splendidly. Excellent Young's beers. Mon–Sat 11am–midnight, Sun noon–10.30pm.

Museum Tavern 49 Great Russell St, WC1 ☎020 7242 8987; ⊖ Tottenham Court Road or Russell Square; map p.120. The erstwhile drinking hole of Karl Marx is a handsome old pub right opposite the main entrance to the British Museum. A choice range of ales available. Mon–Sat 11am–11pm, Sun noon–10.30pm.

The Somers Town Coffee House 60 Chalton St, NW1 ☎020 7691 9136; ⊖ King's Cross or Euston; map p.120. Very pleasant place, with the kind of civilized atmosphere its name suggests, despite its proximity to Euston, King's Cross and St Pancras Stations. Mon–Sat noon–11pm, Sun noon–10.30pm.

ENGLISH BEER

Although lager has now overtaken bitter in popularity, the classic pub drink is **real ale**. It was CAMRA (Campaign for Real Ale; ⓦcamra.org.uk) that first coined the term, to differentiate traditional ale from processed keg beer. Real ale is an uncarbonated and dark beverage that matures in barrels or casks and is pumped by hand fresh from the cellar. Most real ales are also referred to as **bitter**; terms like Mild, Best and Special merely refer to the strength; the acronym IPA (India Pale Ale) refers to bitter's colonial precursor. Real ales are brewed all over the country, and in one or two brew-pubs within the capital, but the only large-scale London brewery of distinction left is Fuller's, producer of London Pride.

25

COVENT GARDEN AND THE STRAND

Coal Hole 91 Strand, WC2 ☎020 7379 9883; ⊖ Charing Cross or Embankment; map p.132. Popular Edwardian pub next to *The Savoy*. Take a look up at the high wooden beams and stone friezes as you sip one of the fine ales on offer, or head to the cellar bar for wine. Mon–Sat 11am–midnight, Sun noon–10.30pm.

Cross Keys 31 Endell St, WC2 ☎020 7836 5185; ⊖ Covent Garden; map p.132. Stuffed with copper pots, brass instruments, paintings and memorabilia, this most welcoming of West End pubs attracts an appealing blend of older Covent Garden residents, young workers and tourists – you'll do well to find a seat. Mon–Sat 11am–11pm, Sun noon–10.30pm.

Gordon's 47 Villiers St, WC2 ☎020 7930 1408, ⓦgordons winebar.com; ⊖ Charing Cross or Embankment; map p.132. Cavernous, shabby, atmospheric wine bar specializing in ports, sherries and Madeiras. The genial atmosphere makes this a favourite with local office workers, who spill outdoors in the summer. Mon–Sat 11am–11pm, Sun noon–10pm.

Lamb & Flag 33 Rose St, WC2 ☎020 7497 9504; ⊖ Leicester Square; map p.132. Over 300 years old, this agreeably tatty pub, tucked away down an alley between Garrick and Floral streets, was where John Dryden was attacked in 1679 (see p.134). This is the one pub in Covent Garden that everyone returns to. Mon–Sat 11am–11pm, Sun noon–10.30pm.

★ **Princess Louise** 208 High Holborn, WC1 ☎020 7405 8816; ⊖ Holborn; map p.132. Architecturally, this is one of London's most impressive Victorian pubs, featuring gold-trimmed mirrors, gorgeous mosaics and a fine moulded ceiling. Even the toilets are listed for their historic features! Get here at the right time and you might get one of the tiny bars all to yourself. The Sam Smith's beer is very reasonably priced and there's always a lively crowd. Mon–Fri 11am–11pm, Sat noon–11pm.

The Salisbury 90 St Martin's Lane, WC2 ☎020 7836 5863; ⊖ Leicester Square; map p.132. One of the capital's most beautifully preserved Victorian pubs, with etched and engraved windows, bronze figures and Art Nouveau light fittings. A wide and unusual range of ales and unusually attentive staff add to the general joy of the place. Mon–Fri 11am–11pm, Sat noon–midnight, Sun noon–10.30pm.

HOLBORN & THE INNS OF COURT

Bar Polski 11 Little Turnstile, WC1 ☎020 7831 9679; ⊖ Holborn; map p.144. Modern Polish bar hidden in an alleyway behind Holborn tube, with a wicked selection of flavoured vodkas and beers, and good, cheap Polish food. Mon 4–11pm, Tues–Thurs 12.30pm–11pm, Fri 12.30–11.30pm, Sat 6–11pm, Sun closed.

Cittie of Yorke 22 High Holborn, WC1 ☎020 7242 7670; ⊖ Chancery Lane; map p.144. A venerable London lawyers' pub now run by Sam Smith's. Head for the vaulted cellar bar or the grand, quasi-medieval wine hall at the back with its rows of cosy cubicles. Mon–Fri 11.30am–11pm, Sat noon–11pm.

Old Bank of England 194 Fleet St, EC4 ☎020 7430 2255; ⊖ Temple or Chancery Lane; map p.144. Not the actual Bank of England, but the former Law Courts' branch, this imposing High Victorian banking hall is now a magnificently opulent Fuller's ale-and-pie pub. Mon–Fri 11am–11pm.

Seven Stars 53–54 Carey St, WC1 ☎020 7242 8521; ⊖ Holborn; map p.144. This diminutive boozer dates from 1602, and despite the legal crowd, it oozes charm, and attracts a surprisingly mixed clientele. Mon–Fri 11am–11pm, Sat noon–11pm, Sun noon–10.30pm.

★ **Ye Olde Mitre** 1 Ely Court, EC1 ☎020 7405 4751; ⊖ Farringdon; map p.144. Hidden down a tiny alleyway between Ely Place and Hatton Garden, this wonderfully atmospheric pub dates back to 1546, although it was actually rebuilt in the eighteenth century. The low-ceilinged, wood-panelled rooms are packed with history and the real ales are excellent. Mon–Fri 11am–11pm.

CLERKENWELL

Café Kick 43 Exmouth Market, EC1 ☎020 7837 8077, ⓦcafekick.co.uk; ⊖ Farringdon or Angel; map p.150. This chaotic, very popular French-style café-bar is great fun, enlivened by three busy table-football games. Branch (*Bar Kick*) at 127 Shoreditch High St, E1. Mon–Thurs noon–11pm, Fri & Sat noon–12am, Sun 1.30pm–10.30pm.

Dovetail 9 Jerusalem Passage, EC1 ☎020 7490 7321; ⊖ Farringdon; map p.150. Marvellous, understated Belgian bar offering an enormous variety of beers (including a dozen or so on tap). The curious decor comprises pew-style seating, green-tiled tables and kitchen-style wall tiling. First-rate Belgian food, too. Mon–Sat noon–11pm.

The Eagle 159 Farringdon Rd, EC1 ☎020 7837 1353; ⊖ Farringdon; map p.150. The first (and still one of the best) of London's gastropubs, this place is often heaving for lunch and dinner, but you should be able to find a seat at other times. Mon–Sat noon–11pm, Sun noon–5pm.

★ **Jerusalem Tavern** 55 Britton St, EC1 ☎020 7490 4281; ⊖ Farringdon; map p.150. Converted Georgian coffee house – the frontage dates from 1810 – that has retained much of its original character. Better still, the excellent draught beers are from St Peter's Brewery in Suffolk. Mon–Fri 11am–11pm.

The Peasant 240 St John St, EC1 ☎020 7336 7726, ⓦthepeasant.co.uk; ⊖ Farringdon or Angel; map p.150. Large, handsome, spacious pub – smart but relaxed

– towards the upper end of St John Street, with a superb restaurant upstairs. Can get very busy, but it's large enough never to be oppressive. Mon–Sat noon–11pm, Sun noon–10.30pm.

Slaughtered Lamb 34–35 Great Sutton St, EC1 ☎ 020 7253 1516, ⓦ theslaughteredlambpub.co.uk; ⊖ Barbican or Farringdon; map p.150. Self-consciously trendy former art gallery, filled with sofas and old furniture. Lots of live music and events – moustaches must be worn on Saturday evenings. They also serve ironically old-fashioned pub grub. Mon–Thurs noon–midnight, Fri & Sat noon–1am, Sun noon–10.30pm.

★ **The Three Kings** 7 Clerkenwell Close, EC1 ☎ 020 7253 0483; ⊖ Farringdon; map p.150. Unimprovable Clerkenwell favourite tucked away just north of Clerkenwell

TOP 5 HISTORIC PUBS

Ye Olde Cheshire Cheese Fleet Street. See below

George Inn Southwark. See p.394

The Jerusalem Tavern Clerkenwell. See opposite

The Mayflower Rotherhithe. See 394

Princess Louise Holborn. See opposite

Green, with a delightfully eclectic interior and two small rooms upstairs perfect for long occupation. It's right next to *The Crown*, on Clerkenwell Green itself, which is also well worth a trip, particularly on summer evenings. Mon–Sat noon–11pm, Sun closed.

THE CITY

The Bell 95 Fleet St, EC4 ☎ 020 7583 0216; ⊖ Blackfriars or St Paul's; map p.156. Excellent Fleet Street pub – second only to *The Cheshire Cheese* as a place to go out of your way for in this corner of town. The atmosphere combines the bustle of Fleet Street with the quiet calm of St Bride's, which the pub opens out to at its rear. Mon–Fri 10am–11.30pm, Sat noon–6pm, closed Sundays.

The Black Friar 174 Queen Victoria St, EC4 ☎ 020 7236 5474; ⊖ Blackfriars; map p.156. Utterly original place with Art Nouveau marble friezes of boozy monks and a highly decorated alcove – all original, dating from 1905. A lovely fireplace, and an unhurried atmosphere make this a relaxing place to drink. Mon–Fri 11am–11pm, Sat 11am–11.30pm, Sun noon–10.30pm.

Jamaica Wine House St Michael's Alley, EC3 ☎ 020 7929 6972; ⊖ Bank; map p.156. Located down a narrow alleyway, on the site of London's first coffee house (1652), this old City institution is known locally as the "Jam Pot". Despite the name, it is really just a pub, divided into four large "snugs" by original, high wood-

panelled partitions. Mon–Fri 11am–11pm.

The Lamb Tavern 10–12 Leadenhall Market, EC3 ☎ 020 7626 2454; ⊖ Monument; map p.156. Situated in the middle of beautiful Leadenhall Market, it's almost exclusively standing room only (both inside and out) at this super Young's pub. Excellent roast beef, pork and sausage sandwiches at lunchtime. Mon–Fri 11am–11pm.

Viaduct Tavern 126 Newgate St, EC1 ☎ 020 7600 1863; ⊖ St Paul's; map p.156. Fuller's pub situated across from the Old Bailey, with a glorious Victorian interior from 1869. The red ceiling and walls are adorned with oils of faded ladies representing Commerce, Agriculture and the Arts. Mon–Fri 11am–11pm.

★ **Ye Olde Cheshire Cheese** Wine Office Court, 145 Fleet St, EC4 ☎ 020 7353 6170; ⊖ Temple or Blackfriars; map p.156. A famous seventeenth-century watering hole – chiefly because of patrons such as Dickens and Dr Johnson – with several snug, dark-panelled bars and real fires. Popular with tourists and locals alike. Mon–Fri 11am–11pm, Sat noon–11pm, Sun noon–5pm.

WHITECHAPEL AND SPITALFIELDS

★ **The Carpenter's Arms** 73 Cheshire St, E2 ☎ 020 7739 6342; Shoreditch High Street Overground; map p.192. Superb pub, slightly off the beaten track to the east of Brick Lane, with an excellent range of beers (including London's own Meantime Pale Ale brewed in Greenwich) and a tiny courtyard for warm evenings. A very relaxed place that avoids the hectic feel of some of the other pubs and bars nearby, but is just as cool. Mon 4pm–11.30pm, Tues–Thurs and Sun 12pm–11.30pm, Fri & Sat 12pm–12.30am.

★ **Indo** 133 Whitechapel Road, E1 ☎ 020 7247 4926; ⊖ Aldgate East or Whitechapel; map p.192. Small and dark bar, with an ever-changing display of art, good pizzas and a decent range of beers. Despite its small size and popularity, you can often find a comfortable spot. Mon–Sun 12pm–1am (to 3am Fri and Sat).

Ten Bells 84 Commercial St, E1 ☎ 020 7366 1721; ⊖ Shoreditch High Street Overground; map, p.192. Stripped-down, pleasantly ramshackle pub (with Jack the Ripper associations), with some great Victorian tiling. Attracts a relentlessly hip and young crowd these days. Mon–Thurs & Sun noon–midnight, Fri & Sat noon–1am.

Vibe Bar Old Truman Brewery, 91–95 Brick Lane, E1 ☎ 020 7377 2899, ⓦ vibe-bar.co.uk; ⊖ Shoreditch High Street Overground; map, p.192. Trendy bar in an old brewery with good sofas and DJs and live bands in the evenings. The great beer garden is used for summer barbecues at weekends, and occasionally as a festival venue. Mon–Thurs & Sun 11am–11.30pm, Fri & Sat 11am–1am.

25

SHOREDITCH

The Barley Mow 127 Curtain Rd, EC2 ☎ 020 7729 3910; ⊖ Old Street; map p.192. There are lots of fashionably down-at-heel pubs in Shoreditch (the *Bricklayer's Arms* next door is a real stalwart) but this is one of the best. Mon–Sat 11am–11pm, Sun 12pm–10.30pm.

Cantaloupe 35 Charlotte Rd, EC2 ☎ 020 7729 5566, ⓦ cantaloupe.co.uk; ⊖ Old Street; map p.192. A pioneer of the Hoxton transformation, this place still pulls in the crowds, with its cocktails, tapas and bottled beers. Mon–Fri 11am–12am, Sat 12pm–12am, Sun 12pm–11.30pm.

Casita 5 Ravey St, EC2 ☎ 020 7729 7230; ⊖ Old Street; map p.192. Tiny South American-style bar with very friendly staff, well concealed in the little streets just south of the main Hoxton scene. Mon–Sat 5pm–1am.

Loungelover 1 Whitby St, E1 ☎ 020 7012 1234, ⓦ loungelover.co.uk; Shoreditch High Street Overground; map, p.192. Behind the unprepossessing facade of this former meat-packing factory lies a bizarre array of opulently camp bric-a-brac, expertly slung together to create an extraordinary-looking cocktail bar. Mon–Thurs & Sun 6pm–midnight, Fri 5.30pm–1am, Sat 6pm–1am.

Mason & Taylor 51–55 Bethnal Green Road, E2 ☎ 020 7749 9670, ⓦ masonandtaylor.co.uk; Shoreditch High Street Overground; map p.192. Fashionably minimalist bar with a great location and wonderfully big windows for people watching. There's a great range of beers to try and a good choice of small, sharing plates if you're hungry. DJs in the basement till late. Mon–Wed 5pm–12am, Thurs 5pm–1am, Fri & Sat noon–2am, Sun noon–12am.

The Owl and Pussycat 34 Redchurch St, E2 ☎ 020 3487 0088, ⓦ owlandpussycatshoreditch.com; Shoreditch High Street Overground; map p.192. One of many old boozers in the area to have been turned into a hipster hangout, this backstreet pub has a decent range of beers and a courtyard out back. On Fri and Sat you'll hardly be able to move for wispy moustaches and pre-club excitement. If it's too hectic, try the American-themed *Redchurch* bar which serves excellent Sierra Nevada beer. Mon–Sun 12pm–late.

BETHNAL GREEN

★ **The Approach** 47 Approach Rd, E2 ☎ 020 8983 3878; ⊖ Bethnal Green; map p.192. One of the best pubs in an area becoming increasingly well stocked. *The Approach* is both cosy and spacious, and offers good food and a fine range of beers, including the Fullers family, Litovel and Palm. Mon–Sat noon–11pm, Sun noon–10.30pm.

Bistrotheque 23–27 Wadeson St, E2 ☎ 020 8983 7900, ⓦ bistrotheque.com; Cambridge Heath station; map p.192. Great little bar belonging to the restaurant and arts venue of the same name. This area of Hackney has now been conquered by artists' studios, galleries and performance spaces, and like many of these, *Bistrotheque* is hidden behind an anonymous warehouse frontage. Tues–Sat 6pm–12am, Sun 6pm–11pm. Closed Mon.

AROUND THE OLYMPIC PARK

Edward VII 47 Broadway, E15 ☎ 020 8534 2313, ⓦ kingeddie.co.uk; ⊖ Stratford; map p.190. The only notable pub in Stratford itself, the *Edward VII* has a wonderfully atmospheric, low-ceilinged front bar, spacious rooms behind and a decent range of food. Mon–Wed noon–11pm, Thurs–Sat noon–12am, Sun noon–11.30pm.

Morgan Arms 43 Morgan St, E3 ☎ 020 8980 6389; ⊖ Mile End or Bow Road; map p.190. The *Morgan Arms* is one of the best places to drink close to the Olympic Park. It's won the *Evening Standard* pub-of-the-year award and has excellent food. Mon–Thurs noon–11pm, Fri & Sat noon–11.30pm, Sun noon–10.30pm.

DOCKLANDS

The Grapes 76 Narrow St, E14 ☎ 020 7987 4396; Westferry DLR; map p.208. A lovely, narrow little pub on a quiet street, with lots of seafaring paraphernalia and a great riverside balcony. The ales are good and there's an expensive fish restaurant upstairs. Mon–Fri noon–3.30pm & 5.30–11pm, Sat noon–11pm, Sun noon–10.30pm.

★ **The Gun** 27 Coldharbour, E14 ☎ 020 7515 5222, ⓦ thegundocklands.com; ⊖ Canary Wharf, South Quay or Blackwall DLR; map p.208. Legendary dockers' pub, once the haunt of Lord Nelson, *The Gun* is now a classy gastropub, with a cosy back bar and an outside deck offering unrivalled views. Out on a limb on the eastern side of the Isle of Dogs, but well worth the excursion. Mon–Sat 11am–midnight, Sun 11am–11pm.

Prospect of Whitby 57 Wapping Wall, E1 ☎ 020 7481 1095; ⊖ Wapping; map p.208. Steeped in history, this is London's most famous riverside pub, with a pewter bar, flagstone floor, ancient timber beams and stacks of maritime memorabilia. Decent beers and terrific views out across the Thames. Mon–Sat noon–11pm, Sun noon–10.30pm.

Town of Ramsgate 62 Wapping High St, E1 ☎ 020 7264 0001; ⊖ Wapping; map p.208. Dark, narrow, medieval pub located by Wapping Old Stairs – in the beautiful part of Wapping – which once led down to Execution Dock. Captain Blood was discovered here with the Crown Jewels under his cloak, and Admiral Bligh and Fletcher Christian were regular drinking partners in pre-mutiny days. Mon–Sat noon–midnight, Sun noon–10.30pm.

CLOCKWISE FROM TOP LEF THE RED LION, DUKE OF YORK ST (P.387); ACADEMY (P.388); THE LAMB (P.389); THE SOCIAL (P.389)>

25

SOUTH BANK

Anchor & Hope 36 The Cut, SE1 ☎020 7928 9898; ⊖ Southwark; map p.216. *The Anchor* is a gastropub that dishes up truly excellent, yet simple grub: soups, salads and mains such as slow-cooked pork with choucroute, as well as mouthwatering puds. You can't book a table, so the bar is basically the waiting room. Mon 5–11pm, Tues–Sat 11am–11pm, Sun 12.30–5pm.

★ **Kings Arms** 25 Roupell St, SE1 ☎020 7207 0784; ⊖ Waterloo; map p.216. Situated on a quiet Victorian terraced street, this terrific local is divided into two parts; the front part is a traditional drinking area, while the rear is a tastefully cluttered, glass and wood conservatory-style space adorned with bric-a-brac and featuring a large open fire and long wooden table. There's Thai food on offer, too. Mon–Sat 11am–11pm, Sun noon–10.30pm.

The Young Vic Bar 66 The Cut, SE1 ☎020 7928 4400 ⓦthecutbar.com; ⊖ Waterloo or Southwark; map p.216. Very lively theatre bar spread over two floors plus an outside terrace – it's big enough to find a corner even when it's packed with theatregoers. Mon–Fri 9am–late, Sat 10am–late, closed Sundays.

SOUTHWARK

The Anchor 34 Park St, SE1 ☎020 7407 1577; ⊖ London Bridge. See map, p.226. First built in 1770, this sprawling pub retains only a few vestiges of the past, but it does have one of the few riverside terraces towards the centre of town – inevitably it's often mobbed by tourists. Mon–Sat 11am–11pm, Sun noon–10.30pm.

George Inn 77 Borough High St, SE1 ☎020 7407 2056; ⊖ Borough or London Bridge. See map p.226. London's only surviving galleried coaching inn (see p.230), dating from the seventeenth century and now owned by the National Trust; mobbed by tourists, but it does serve a good range of real ales. Mon–Thurs 11am–11pm, Fri & Sat 11am–midnight, Sun noon–10.30pm.

Market Porter 9 Stoney St, SE1 ☎020 7407 2495; ⊖ London Bridge; map p.226. Handsome semicircular pub by Borough Market, with an interesting range of real ales and decent food. Outrageously popular, as evidenced by the masses that spill out onto the surrounding pavements. Mon–Fri 6–8.30am & 11am–11pm, Sat noon–11pm, Sun noon–10.30pm.

The Rake 14 Winchester Walk, SE1 ☎020 7407 0557; ⊖ London Bridge; map p.226. Sleek, bright, little bar whose enthusiastic staff are happy to advise on half a dozen (very strong and very expensive) draught beers from Germany, America, Belgium and Holland, as well as over a hundred bottled beers from around the globe. There's also a pleasant decked terrace. Tues–Fri noon–11pm, Sat 9am–11pm, Sun noon–10.30pm.

Royal Oak 44 Tabard St, SE1 ☎020 7357 7173; ⊖ Borough; map p.224. Beautiful, lovingly restored Victorian pub that eschews jukeboxes and one-armed bandits and opts simply for serving a superb stock of real ales (mild, pale and old) from Harvey's brewery in Sussex and some good pub grub. Mon–Fri 11am–11pm, Sat 6–11pm, Sun noon–6pm.

The Southwark Tavern 22 Southwark St, SE1 ☎020 7403 0257; ⓦthesouthwarktavern.co.uk; ⊖ London Bridge; map p.226. All the pubs and bars in this area can get extremely busy, but *The Southwark Tavern* is big enough to soak up the crowds and remain pleasant. There are some small booths downstairs and a very good range of beers. Mon–Wed 11am–12am, Thurs & Fri 11am–1am, Sat 10am–1am, Sun 12pm–12am.

ROTHERHITHE

The Angel 101 Bermondsey Wall East, SE16 ☎020 7394 3214; ⊖ Rotherhithe; map p.224. Comprehensively refurbished, historic pub that stands on its own in the middle of nowhere on the path between Butler's Wharf and Rotherhithe. Mon–Sat noon–11pm, Sun noon–10.30pm.

The Mayflower 117 Rotherhithe St, SE16 ☎020 7237 4088; ⊖ Rotherhithe; map p.224. This eighteenth-century pub, in the heart of old Rotherhithe – a very quiet and attractive spot – is steeped in history. The blackened brick walls, wonky timber frames and creaky floorboards give it genuine character, while the wooden terrace offers splendid views out across the Thames. Decent real ales and pub food. Mon–Sat noon–11pm, Sun noon–10.30pm.

SOUTH KENSINGTON

Anglesea Arms 15 Selwood Terrace, SW7 ☎020 7373 7960; ⊖ South Kensington; map p.265. Charming little local, with hanging flower baskets on the outside and dark wooden tables and green leather benches inside. In addition, there's an elegant dining area to the rear of the bar and a very pleasant courtyard area. There are half a dozen first-class ales on offer. Mon–Sat 11am–11pm, Sun noon–10.30pm.

TOP 5 RIVERSIDE DRINKS

Dove Hammersmith. See p.398
The Grapes Docklands. See p.392
The Gun Docklands. See p.392
The Mayflower Rotherhithe. See above
Trafalgar Tavern Greenwich. See p.398

KNIGHTSBRIDGE

Grenadier 18 Wilton Row, SW1 ☎020 7235 3074; ⊖ Hyde Park Corner or Knightsbridge; map p.250. Located in a private mews, this quaint little pub was Wellington's local (his horse block survives outside) and his officers' mess; the original pewter bar survives, while there's plenty of military paraphernalia to gawp at. Classy but pricey bar food. Very charming if you can find a space. Mon–Sat noon–11pm, Sun noon–10.30pm.

★ **The Nag's Head** 53 Kinnerton St, SW1 ☎020 7235 1135; ⊖ Hyde Park Corner or Knightsbridge; map p.250. A convivial, quirky and down-to-earth little pub in a posh cobbled mews, with dark wood panelling, china handpumps and old prints on hunting, shooting and fishing. The unusual sunken back room has a flagstone floor and fires in winter. The pub grub's good. The landlord doesn't like mobiles and insists that all coats are hung up on pegs. Mon–Sat 11am–11pm, Sun noon–10.30pm.

Star Tavern 6 Belgrave Mews West, SW1 ☎020 7235 3019; ⊖ Hyde Park Corner or Knightsbridge; map p.250. Quiet two-storey mews pub with a large open sitting room and a murky past: allegedly, it was from here that the Great Train Robbery was planned. Fine Fuller's beer and traditional pub grub. Mon–Sat 11am–11pm, Sun noon–10.30pm.

CHELSEA

Cooper's Arms Bar 87 Flood St, SW3 ☎020 7376 3120; ⊖ Sloane Square; map p.265. Decent, spacious neighbourhood pub, which may not be quite the sum of its parts – reasonable food, a good range of beers, plenty of spots to choose from – but is still a good find so close to the King's Road. Mon–Sat 11am–11pm, Sun noon–10pm.

Fox and Hounds 29 Passmore St, SW1 ☎020 7730 6367; ⊖ Sloane Square; map p.265. With an open fire, faux books, oil paintings and a flagstone floor, plus plenty of hunting memorabilia, it feels as if you've stumbled into a country squire's living room. Mon–Sat 11am–11pm, Sun noon–10.30pm.

The Pig's Ear 35 Old Church St, SW3 ☎020 7352 2908, ⓦthepigsear.info; ⊖ Sloane Square; map p.265. Genuinely charming despite its moneyed milieu, *The Pig's Ear* has a busy and beguiling interior, classy pub grub and the feeling of somewhere treasured by those fortunate enough to call it their local. Mon–Sat noon–11pm, Sun noon–10.30pm.

PADDINGTON

★ **Victoria** 10a Strathearn Place, W2 ☎020 7724 1191; ⊖ Lancaster Gate or Paddington; map p.274. Beautiful interior, with green and gold wallpapered walls enclosing a long bar with fine mirrors and wooden carvings. This is an especially valuable find in this area, just within sight of Paddington station. Excellent Fuller's beer. Mon–Sat 11am–11pm, Sun noon–10.30pm.

NOTTING HILL

Churchill Arms 119 Kensington Church St, W8 ☎020 7229 4242; ⊖ Notting Hill Gate; map p.274. Justifiably popular, flower-festooned pub serving Fuller's beers, superb Guinness and good Thai food. Mon–Wed 11am–11pm, Thurs–Sat 11am–midnight, Sun noon–10.30pm.

Cock & Bottle 17 Needham Rd, W11 ☎020 7229 1550; ⊖ Westbourne Park or Notting Hill Gate; map p.274. Remarkably unpretentious two-room corner pub – given the area – with a warm and friendly staff, smart Victorian fittings and good ales. Mon–Sat noon–11pm, Sun noon–10.30pm.

The Cow 89 Westbourne Park Rd, W2 ☎020 7221 0021, ⓦthecowlondon.co.uk; ⊖ Westbourne Park or Royal Oak; map p.274. This pub pulls in the beautiful W11 types, thanks to its spectacular food, including a daily supply of fresh oysters. Mon–Thurs noon–11pm, Fri & Sat noon–midnight, Sun noon–10.30pm.

The Elgin 96 Ladbroke Grove, W11 ☎020 7229 5663; ⊖ Ladbroke Grove; map p.274. Enormous pub on Ladbroke Grove with a riot of original features as well as new decorative schemes. The atmosphere echoes that of the buzzy streets close to Portobello Road. Mon–Sat 11am–11pm, Sun noon–10.30pm.

Paradise by Way of Kensal Green 19 Kilburn Lane, W10 ☎020 8969 0098, ⓦtheparadise.co.uk; Kensal Green; map p.274. Giant gastropub near the Kensal Green Cemetery, with an artfully and theatrically dishevelled interior. Mon–Wed 4pm–midnight, Thurs 4pm–1am, Fri & Sat 12.30pm–2am, Sun noon–11.30pm.

The Westbourne 101 Westbourne Park Villas, W2 ☎020 7221 1332, ⓦthewestbourne.com; ⊖ Westbourne Park or Royal Oak; map p.274. Extremely popular, appealing place with a ramshackle interior and a lot of space outside at the front. Notable food. Mon 5pm–11pm, Tues–Sat noon–11pm, Sun noon–10.30pm.

★ **Windsor Castle** 114 Campden Hill Rd, W8 ☎020 7243 9551; ⊖ Notting Hill; map p.274. Pretty, popular, early Victorian wood-panelled English pub with a great courtyard, more like something you might find in the country than tucked away in the backstreets of one of London's poshest residential neighbourhoods. Mon–Sat noon–11pm, Sun noon–10.30pm.

25

ST JOHN'S WOOD

Bridge House 13 Westbourne Terrace Rd, NW8 ☎020 7432 1361, ⓦthebridgehouselittlevenice.co.uk; ⊖ Warwick Avenue; map p.284. Theatre pub right by the canal in Little Venice, a positively bohemian hangout for the area. Excellent real ales and good food. Mon–Thurs noon–11pm, Fri & Sat noon–11.30pm, Sun noon–10.30pm.

Prince Alfred 5a Formosa St, W9 ☎020 7286 3027; ⊖ Warwick Avenue; map p.284. A period-piece Victorian pub with all its original 1862 fittings intact, right down to the glazed "snob" screens that divide the bar into a series of snugs.

Along with the heritage, the pub also runs a pricey Modern European restaurant at the back. A stylish and relaxing place. Mon–Sat noon–11pm, Sun noon– 10.30pm.

Warrington Hotel 93 Warrington Crescent, W9 ☎020 7286 2929, ⓦgordonramsay.com; ⊖ Warwick Avenue or Maida Vale; map p.284. Grandiose Gordon Ramsay-owned pub (in a former hotel) with a flamboyant Edwardian Art Nouveau interior. Worth it for the architecture alone. Mon–Thurs noon–11pm, Fri and Sat noon–12pm, Sun noon–10.30pm.

PRIMROSE HILL, CAMDEN TOWN AND AROUND

The Albert 11 Princess Road, NW1 ☎020 7722 1886; ⊖ Camden Town; map p.284. Unpretentious, relaxed Primrose Hill watering hole, which can offer a safe retreat if the area's other pubs are very crowded. Mon–Sat 11am–11pm, Sun 12pm–10.30pm.

Edinboro Castle 57 Mornington Terrace, NW1 ☎020 7255 9651, ⓦedinborocastlepub.co.uk; ⊖ Camden Town; map p.284. A large, high-ceilinged pub with an attractively glammed-up interior. The main draw, though, is the large, leafy beer garden which hosts summer weekend barbecues. Above-average selection of draught continental lagers and a couple of real-ale options. Mon–Sat noon–11pm, Sun noon–10.30pm.

The Engineer 65 Gloucester Avenue, NW1 ☎020 7722 0950 ⓦthe-engineer.com; ⊖ Chalk Farm; map p.284. Very classy Primrose Hill pub known for its food. Mon–Sat 9am–11pm, Sun 9am–10.30pm.

The Enterprise 2 Haverstock Hill, NW3 ☎020 7485 2659 ⓦcamdenenterprise.com; ⊖ Chalk Farm; map p.284. Chalk Farm institution, right next to the tube, with an unmatched atmosphere in an area that can

sometimes be very quiet. Sun–Thurs 11am–11pm, Fri & Sat 11am–1am.

★ **The Lansdowne** 90 Gloucester Avenue, NW1 ☎020 7483 0409, ⓦthelansdownepub.co.uk; ⊖ Chalk Farm; map p.284. Primrose Hill's liveliest and coolest pub, with a diverse crowd and a reliable buzz about it. One of those places where everyone seems delighted to be there. Mon–Fri noon–11pm, Sat 10am–11pm, Sun 10am–10.30pm.

Lock Tavern 35 Chalk Farm Rd, NW1 ☎020 7482 7163, ⓦlock-tavern.co.uk; ⊖ Chalk Farm; map p.284. Rambling pub with large, battered wooden tables, comfy sofas, a leafy upstairs terrace and beer garden down below, as well as posh pub grub and DJs playing anything from punk funk and electro to rock. Effortlessly cool. Mon–Thurs noon–midnight, Fri & Sat noon–1am, Sun noon–11pm.

Sir Richard Steele 97 Haverstock Hill, NW3 ☎020 7483 1261; ⊖ Belsize Park or Chalk Farm; map p.284. The cluttered and oddball decor and clientele here make for a fun, laidback atmosphere; Thai food, occasional live music and small beer garden. Mon–Sat 11am–midnight, Sun noon–11.30pm.

ISLINGTON

Camden Head 2 Camden Walk, N1 ☎020 7359 0851; ⊖ Angel; map p.284. In the midst of Islington's antique market on a dainty street, the *Camden Head* is a fabulous-looking Victorian boozer, with engraved glass fittings and frosted mirrors. Cracking atmosphere, enlivened by regular comedy nights upstairs. Mon & Tues 11am–11pm, Wed & Thurs 11am–midnight, Fri & Sat noon–1am, Sun noon–11pm.

The Charles Lamb 16 Elia St, N1 ☎020 7837 5040, ⓦthecharleslambpub.com; ⊖ Angel; map p.284. Justifiably popular Islington local, with good food and a very pleasant interior. The ambience is somewhere between that of a café and a traditional pub. Mon & Tues 4pm–late, Wed–Sun 12pm–late.

The Crown 116 Cloudesley Road, N1 ☎020 7837 7107; ⊖ Angel; map p.284. Refined neighbourhood pub on beautiful Cloudesley Road, which is usually calmer than the other pubs and bars closer to Upper Street. Mon–Sat 11am–11pm, Sun 12pm–10.30pm.

Duke of Cambridge 30 St Peter's St, N1 ☎020 7359 3066, ⓦsloeberry.co.uk; ⊖ Angel; map p.284. The focus at this bright and hip corner pub is most definitely organic, with an award-winning organic food menu, as well as half a dozen organic beers (including real ales), wines and soft drinks. Unsurprisingly, none of it comes cheap. Mon–Sat noon–11pm, Sun noon–10.30pm.

★ **Island Queen** 87 Noel Rd, N1 ☎020 7704 7631; ⊖ Angel; map p.284. Beautiful, weathered, wood-panelled Victorian pub in the backstreets of Islington, with lovely etched glass and high ceilings. Good range of beers and decent pub food. Mon & Sun noon–11pm, Tues & Wed noon–11.30pm, Thurs–Sat noon–midnight.

King's Head 115 Upper St, N1 ☎020 7226 0364; ⊖ Angel; map p.284. The original pub theatre in the heart of Islington, with two real fires, large spotlights, big curtains and lots of theatrical posters and photos. Mon–Thurs 11am–1am, Fri & Sat 11am–2am, Sun noon–12.30am.

25

HACKNEY

★ **Dove Freehouse** 24–28 Broadway Market ☎020 7275 7617; London Fields or Cambridge Heath train stations from Liverpool Street; map p.291. Cosy, low-lit and plant-filled, this characterful pub offers a stupendous selection of draught and bottled Belgian beers, plus a few real ales; also does specially made sausages and burgers, as well as moules frites. Mon–Thurs noon–11pm, Fri & Sat noon–midnight, Sun noon–10.30pm.

The Empress 130 Lauriston Road, E9 ☎020 8533 5123 ⓦtheempressofindia.com; ⊖ Bethnal Green; map p.291. Very smart Victoria Park gastropub at the heart of the South Hackney boom. Mon–Sun 9am–11pm.

Off Broadway 63–65 Broadway Market, E8 ☎020 7241 2786 ⓦoffbroadway.org.uk; ⊖ Bethnal Green or and Cambridge Heath or London Fields stations; map

p.291. Stylish, friendly, popular American bar on Broadway Market. Some great American beers on tap. Mon–Fri 4pm–midnight, Sat & Sun 10am–midnight.

The Prince George 40 Parkholme Rd, E8 ☎0871 258 5259; Dalston Junction or Hackney Central Overground; map p.291. One of a cluster of good pubs just to the west of Hackney Central, *The George* is the pick for its reliably buzzy atmosphere and air of faded grandeur. Mon–Fri 5pm–12am, Sat 2pm–1am, Sun 2pm–11.30pm.

Royal Inn on the Park 111 Lauriston Rd, E9 ☎020 8985 3321; ⊖ Bethnal Green or Mile End; map p.291. Big, grand Victorian pub with laidback tunes, real ale, beer garden and, as the name suggests, a location right on the edge of Victoria Park. Mon–Sat noon–11pm, Sun noon–10.30pm.

HAMPSTEAD AND HIGHGATE

The Flask 77 Highgate West Hill, N6 ☎020 8348 7346; Bus #210 from ⊖ Archway; map p.298. Ideally situated at the heart of Highgate village green – with a rambling, low-ceilinged interior and a summer terrace – and, as a result, very, very popular at the weekend. Mon–Sat noon–11pm, Sun noon–10.30pm.

The Holly Bush 22 Holly Mount, off Holly Hill, NW3 ☎020 7435 2892; ⊖ Hampstead; map p.298. A lovely old pub, with a real fire in winter, tucked away in the steep backstreets of Hampstead village. Some fine real ales on offer, as well as decent food (particularly the sausages and pies), though it can get pretty mobbed at weekends. Mon–Sat noon–11pm, Sun noon–10.30pm.

Prince of Wales 53 Highgate High St, N6 ☎020 8340 0445; Bus #210 from ⊖ Archway; map p.298. If *The Flask* is mobbed, this is a great alternative: a cosy, tiny local with good real ales, Thai food and a nice terrace out the back. Quiz night (Tues) is crazily popular. Mon–Thurs noon–11pm, Fri & Sat noon–midnight, Sun noon–10.30pm.

The Spaniards Inn Spaniards Rd, NW3 ☎020 8731 6571; ⊖ Hampstead or bus #210 from Golders Green; map p.298. Big, atmospheric sixteenth-century coaching inn near Kenwood and the Heath, frequented by everyone from Dick Turpin to John Keats. Extremely busy on Sunday afternoons. Mon–Thurs 11am–11pm, Fri & Sat 11am–midnight, Sun 11am–11pm.

BRIXTON AND CLAPHAM

Bread & Roses 68 Clapham Manor St, SW4 ☎020 7498 1779; ⓦbreadandrosespub.com; ⊖ Clapham North or Clapham Common. One good reason for venturing into Clapham, this Workers' Beer Company pub serves fine ales, has comedy and cabaret evenings, political events and occasional live music. It's also very welcoming to those with kids. Mon–Thurs 4–11pm, Fri 4pm–12.30am, Sat noon–11.30pm, Sun noon–11pm.

Ritzy Bar and Cafe 1 Brixton Oval, SW2 ☎020 7326 2617; ⊖ Brixton. Right in the centre of Brixton, with a

relaxed vibe and a café-style interior extending out onto a paved area. Later-opening bar upstairs. Mon–Thurs 9am–11pm, Fri 9am–midnight, Sat 10am–midnight, Sun 10am–11pm.

Trinity Arms 45 Trinity Gardens, SW2 ☎020 7274 4544; ⊖ Brixton. Charming situation in a quiet square just off Acre Lane, with a very traditional interior and an eclectic crowd. Mon–Thurs 11am–11pm, Fri & Sat 11am–midnight, Sun noon–11pm.

DULWICH

Crown & Greyhound 73 Dulwich Village, SE21 ☎020 8299 4976; North Dulwich station from London Bridge. Grandiose Victorian pub, convenient for the Picture Gallery, with an ornate plasterwork ceiling and lots of polished

wood and stained glass. The two-tiered beer garden is perfect for the summer barbecues that take place here. Mon–Wed 11am–11pm, Thurs–Sat 11am–midnight, Sun noon–10.30pm.

GREENWICH

Cutty Sark Ballast Quay, off Lassell St, SE10 ☎020 8858 3146; Cutty Sark DLR or Maze Hill station from Charing Cross; map p.315. This Georgian pub is a good

place for a riverside pint and much less touristy than the *Trafalgar Tavern* (see p.398). Mon–Sat 11am–11pm, Sun noon–10.30pm.

25

★ **Greenwich Union** 56 Royal Hill, SE10 ☎ 020 8692 6258; Greenwich DLR & station; map p.315. A modern, laidback place with a youthful, unpretentious feel, fine gastro grub and a nice garden. Go for free samples of blonde ale, raspberry beer, chocolate stout or the house Union, before committing yourself to a pint. Mon–Fri 11am–11pm, Sat 10am–11pm, Sun noon–6pm.

Richard I 52–54 Royal Hill, SE10 ☎ 020 8692 2996; Greenwich DLR & station; map p.315. Popular and very traditional Greenwich local tucked away on an attractive street. Good Young's beers and a lovely, spacious garden make it an ideal post-market/museum retreat. Mon–Sat 11am–11pm, Sun noon–10.30pm.

Trafalgar Tavern 5 Park Row, SE10 ☎ 020 8858 2437; Cutty Sark DLR or Maze Hill station from Charing Cross; map p.315. Great riverside position and a mention in Dickens' *Our Mutual Friend* have made this Regency-style inn a firm tourist favourite. Good whitebait and other snacks. Mon–Thurs noon–11pm, Fri & Sat noon–midnight, Sun noon–10.30pm.

BLACKHEATH

Hare & Billet 1a Eliot Cottages, SE3 ☎ 020 8852 2352; Blackheath station from Charing Cross. A ten-minute walk from the village up on the heath, this pleasantly refurbished, comfortable, rustic Greene King pub is the place to visit for a slow, quiet drink. Mon–Wed 11am–11pm, Thurs–Sat 11am–midnight, Sun noon–11pm.

Zerodegrees 29–31 Montpelier Vale, SE3 ☎ 020 8852 5619; Blackheath train station from Charing Cross. The somewhat hollow atmosphere at this popular microbrewery is more than compensated for by the beer – Black, Pale, Pilsner and Wheat are the four main varieties, in addition to some speciality offerings. Appealing wood-fired pizzas in the adjoining dining area. Mon–Sat noon–midnight, Sun noon–11pm.

BEXLEYHEATH

Robin Hood & Little John 78 Lion Rd, Bexleyheath ☎ 020 8303 1128; Bexleyheath station from Charing Cross. This small pub, in the residential side streets of Bexleyheath, has an impressive range of very well-kept ales, and is the perfect place for a post-Red House pint. Mon–Sat 11am–3pm & 7–11pm, Sun noon–3pm & 7–10.30pm.

HAMMERSMITH AND CHISWICK

Blue Anchor 13 Lower Mall, W6 ☎ 020 8748 5774; ⊖ Hammersmith or Ravenscourt Park. First of Hammersmith's riverside pubs, with a boaty theme and a beautiful pewter bar; the upstairs room offers good views of Hammersmith Bridge, though most people sit outside and enjoy the river. Mon–Sat 11am–11pm, Sun noon–10.30pm.

★ **Dove** 19 Upper Mall, W6 ☎ 020 8748 5405; ⊖ Ravenscourt Park. Wonderful low-beamed, old riverside pub with literary associations – Ernest Hemingway and Graham Greene used to drink here – the smallest bar in the UK (4ft by 7ft), and very popular Sunday roast dinners. Continue along Upper Mall for other riverside pubs (all the way to the Fuller's Brewery where much of London's beer originates). Mon–Sat 11am–11pm, Sun noon–10.30pm.

ACTON AND EALING

George & Dragon 183 High St, W3 ☎ 020 8992 3712; ⊖ Acton Central. Dark wood-panelled interior, with real fires and – in the back room – high ceilings and Art Nouveau statues. Fuller's beers and good pub food. Mon–Sat 11am–11pm, Sun noon–10.30pm.

Red Lion 13 St Mary's Rd, W5 ☎ 020 8567 2541; ⊖ South Ealing or Ealing Broadway. A good mixed crowd frequents this grand Fuller's pub, decorated with mementoes from the days when the Ealing Studios stood opposite. Mon–Sat 11am–11pm, Sun noon–10.30pm.

KEW, RICHMOND, TWICKENHAM AND WIMBLEDON

Fox & Grapes 9 Camp Rd, SW19 ☎ 020 8946 5599; ⊖ Wimbledon. Right on the edge of Wimbledon Common, with good real ales and upmarket food, this place is great in the summer, when you can sit outside on the grass. Mon–Thurs 11am–11pm, Fri & Sat 11am–midnight, Sun noon–10.30pm.

The Railway Kew Gardens Station Parade, Kew ☎ 020 8332 1162; ⊖ Kew Gardens. Convenient pub in Kew Gardens station's former ticket office. Real ales, good pub grub and very convenient for the botanic gardens. Mon–Sat 11am–midnight, Sun noon–10.30pm.

White Cross Hotel Water Lane, Richmond ☎ 020 8940 6844; ⊖ Richmond; map p.344. With a longer pedigree and more character than its rivals, the *White Cross* has a very popular, large garden overlooking the river. In winter, you can decamp to the lovely upstairs lounge with its big bay windows and open fire. Mon–Sat 11am–midnight, Sun noon–10.30pm.

White Swan Riverside, Twickenham ☎ 020 8892 2166; Twickenham station from Waterloo; map p.344. Filling pub food, draught beer and a quiet riverside location – except on rugby match days – make this a good halt on any towpath ramble. The excellent summer Sunday barbecues are a big draw. Mon–Sat 11am–11pm, Sun noon–10.30pm.

FABRIC

Live music and clubs

Genres, venues, fashions and intoxicants come and go, but London's nightlife – sprawling, chaotic and impossibly varied – carries on regardless. Clubs play everything from pop to house, techno to punk, and drum'n'bass to r'n'b on virtually any night of the week. Gigs are equally wide ranging, encompassing rock, roots, hip-hop and world music, while London's jazz clubs host a highly individual scene of home-based artists supplemented by top-name visiting players. Dividing these scenes into categories makes them easier to navigate, but shouldn't obscure the crossover: club nights take over music venues, DJ sets are lifted by live percussion, gay venues host mixed nights and jazz acts play at rock venues. Almost all the venues listed have events' calendars on their websites – keep your eyes peeled and your dancing shoes ready.

There are clubs and venues all over town but, with the City pretty dead after pub closing time and the West End dominated by tacky, overpriced joints, the most vibrant **scenes** tend to be on the edge of the centre, with **Camden** (fairly rocky) and **Shoreditch** (anything that fancies itself as a bit hip) two of the key spots. Don't ignore London's **fringes** either: Brixton or Stoke Newington can be as cutting edge as Clerkenwell or Hoxton.

LIVE MUSIC

26

Few cities in the world can match London for **live music**. Quite apart from its array of fine venues and impressive home-grown talent, the city's media spotlight makes it pretty much *the* place for young **bands** to break into the global mainstream. Those acts who've already made it head for the bright lights and vast seating plans of Wembley Arena (Ⓦ livenation.co.uk/wembley), Wembley Stadium (Ⓦ wembleystadium.com), Earls Court (Ⓦ eco.co.uk) and the 02 (Ⓦ theo2.co.uk). The Royal Albert Hall (Ⓦ royalalberthall.com) – traditionally a classical music venue – and the beautiful courtyard at Somerset House (Ⓦ somerset-house.org.uk) are smaller, more atmospheric alternatives. London's small and medium-sized venues may be pub backrooms, converted warehouses or old cinemas; you might get in free to see an unknown band or pay £80 for a visiting legend, but most acts will set you back £10–30, not counting drinks.

Booking tickets You may get cheaper tickets if you book online, although booking fees can nullify any saving – the real advantage is that you can be sure of getting in. Try sites such as Ⓦ seetickets.com, Ⓦ gigsandtours.com, Ⓦ ticketmaster.co.uk or Ⓦ musicglue.com. Magazines *NME* (Ⓦ nme.com) and *Time Out* (Ⓦ timeout.com/london/music) and website Drowned in Sound (Ⓦ drownedinsound.com) deliver news and listings; London Gigs (Ⓦ londongigs.net) goes large on the latter.

GENERAL VENUES

★ **Academy Brixton** 211 Stockwell Rd, SW9 ☎ 020 7771 3000, Ⓦ o2academybrixton.co.uk; ⊖ Brixton. The Academy has seen them all, from mods and rockers to Chase and Status. The 4000-capacity Victorian hall doesn't always deliver perfect sound quality, but remains a cracking place to see mid-level bands. Upstairs has seats, downstairs has a sloping floor for standing and bags of atmosphere.

Academy Islington N1 Centre, N1 ☎ 020 7288 4400, Ⓦ o2academyislington.co.uk; ⊖ Angel; map p.284. Despite its shopping-centre location, the Academy has some good up-and-coming bands, as well as tribute acts and club nights in *Bar Academy* (same building). Good views from the main venue's mezzanine level, which opens for well-attended gigs.

★ **Cargo** 83 Rivington St, EC2 ☎ 020 7749 7840, Ⓦ cargo-london.com; ⊖ Old Street or Shoreditch High Street Overground; map p.192. Small and groovy venue in what was once a railway arch, with an attached restaurant and chillsome garden area. Hosts a variety of live acts, including jazz, hip-hop, indie and folk, and an excellent line-up of club nights (see p.403).

Coronet 28 New Kent Rd, SE1 ☎ 020 7701 1500, Ⓦ coronettheatre.co.uk; ⊖ Elephant and Castle; map p.224. Theatre-turned-cinema-turned-music venue, with a gorgeous Art Deco interior, regular clubnights and gigs and an often heroically long cloakroom queue.

Forum 9–17 Highgate Rd, NW5 ☎ 020 7428 4099, Ⓦ meanfiddler.com; ⊖ Kentish Town; map p.284.

Mid-sized venue, with wide stage hosting a mix of successful new acts and groups inching their way onto the nostalgia circuit.

Hammersmith Apollo 45 Queen Caroline St, W6 ☎ 020 8563 3800, Ⓦ hammersmithapollo.net; ⊖ Hammersmith; map p.250. The former Hammersmith Odeon is a cavernous, theatre-style space (downstairs can be seating or standing), featuring everyone from Lou Reed to Olly Murs, plus stand-up and popular theatre.

Roundhouse Chalk Farm Rd, NW1 ☎ 0844 482 8008, Ⓦ roundhouse.org.uk; ⊖ Chalk Farm; map p.284. Originally dating from 1846, this magnificent Grade II listed building is one of London's premier performing arts centres; alongside community work and theatres, its programme includes regular appearances by artier rock acts and world music stars.

★ **Shepherd's Bush Empire** Shepherd's Bush Green, W12 ☎ 0844 477 2000, Ⓦ shepherds-bush-empire. co.uk; ⊖ Shepherd's Bush. Another grand old theatre, the Empire now plays host to a fine cross-section of mid-league UK and US bands. There's often a superb atmosphere downstairs, while the vertigo-inducing upstairs balconies provide great stage views.

★ **Union Chapel** Compton Terrace, N1 ☎ 020 7226 1686, Ⓦ unionchapel.org.uk; ⊖ Highbury & Islington; map p.284. Wonderful, intimate venue that doubles as a church, hence the pew-style seating; the array of artists ranges from contemporary stars to world-music legends, and there are regular Saturday-lunchtime sessions.

ROCK, BLUES AND INDIE

★ **12 Bar Club** Denmark St, WC2 ☎ 020 7240 2622, Ⓦ 12barclub.com; ⊖ Tottenham Court Road; map p.100. Tiny, atmospheric bar and venue offering up-and-coming, cheap and often pleasantly eccentric indie gigs as well as blues and folk.

Barfly 49 Chalk Farm Rd, NW1 ☎ 020 7688 8994, Ⓦ barflyclub.com; ⊖ Chalk Farm; map p.284. Barfly offers a relentless roster of gigs (three nightly), typically indie, rock, punk and metal, in its simple upstairs space.

Borderline Orange Yd, Manette St, W1 ☎020 7734 5547, ⓦmeanfiddler.com; ⊖ Tottenham Court Road; map p.100. Small and slightly ramshackle basement joint with awkward pillars but good sound and diverse music policy.

Bull & Gate 389 Kentish Town Rd, NW5 ☎020 7093 4820, ⓦbullandgate.co.uk; ⊖ Kentish Town; map p.284. Decent-enough pub that has one of London's key venues for unsigned indie bands out back. Gigs nightly for about £5.

Cafe OTO 18–22 Ashwin st, E8 ⓦcafeoto.co.uk; Dalston Kingsland Overground; map p.291. Right-on little café and bar with a big reputation for its music. You'll hear folk, classical, electronica, world music and more – it might be mad and it might be mellow, but micro-brewery beer and organic fruit juice is guaranteed.

Dingwalls Middle Yard, Camden Lock, NW1 ☎020 7428 5829, ⓦdingwalls.com; ⊖ Camden Town; map p.284. This split-level music/club venue is a good place to catch new indie and rock, though views aren't always great.

Hope & Anchor 207 Upper St, N1 ☎020 7354 1312, ⓦbugbearbookings.com; ⊖ Angel; map p.284. This cramped venue is popular with punkish indie acts, many playing their first gigs here.

Hoxton Square Bar & Kitchen 2–4 Hoxton Square, N1 ☎020 7613 0709, ⓦ hoxtonsquarebar.com; ⊖ Old Street; map p.192. The bar is self-conscious and unexceptional, but it gets some fine rock and electronic talent through its doors, and the occasional groovy secret gig.

KOKO 1a Camden High St, NW1 ☎0870 432 5527, ⓦkoko.uk.com; ⊖ Mornington Crescent; map p.284. An institution since its days as the Camden Palace, the grand interior hosts clubs (Fri & Sat) and gigs (the rest of the time), with a cracking assortment of indie-pop types dominating proceedings.

Lexington 96–98 Pentonville Road, N2 ☎020 7837 5371, ⓦthelexington.co.uk; ⊖ Angel; map p.284. Above the bourbon-packed downstairs lounge bar is a 200-capacity venue with good sound, a hip but relaxed vibe and a solid, indie-dominated roster.

Underworld 174 Camden High St, NW1 ☎020 7482 1932, ⓦtheunderworldcamden.co.uk; ⊖ Camden Town; map p.284. Shouty, scruffy, tattoo-packed warren under the *World's End* pub that's a great place to check out metal, hardcore and heavy-rock bands.

Windmill 22 Blenheim Gardens, SW2 ☎020 8671 0700, ⓦwindmillbrixton.co.uk; ⊖ Brixton. A fine, leftfield mix of bands play at this poky pub halfway up Brixton Hill. Entry for everything from swirly electronica to throbbing post-rock is rarely much over £5.

XOYO 42–37 Cowper Street, EC2 ☎0207 729 595, ⓦxoyo.co.uk; ⊖ Old Street; map p.192. This big (it can hold 900) 2010-opened Shoreditch venue and club has an annoying layout (the main corridors get packed) but its well-connected team bring in some tasty rock and hip-hop talent.

JAZZ

100 Club 100 Oxford St, W1 ☎020 7636 0933, ⓦthe100club.co.uk; ⊖ Tottenham Court Road; map p.97. Saved from closure in 2011 thanks to shoe sponsorship, this fun jazz venue's history stretches back to 1942 and takes in Louis Armstrong, Glen Miller and the Sex Pistols. Now mixes mostly trad bands with DJ-led nights.

606 Club 90 Lots Rd, SW10 ☎020 7352 5953, ⓦ606club .co.uk; ⊖ Fulham Broadway; map p.250. Just off the King's Rd, this basement jazz venue and restaurant has a particular focus on home-bred talent. It's open to all, but alcohol is only served to non members with a meal.

Bull's Head Barnes Barnes Bridge, SW13 ☎020 8876 5241, ⓦthebullshead.com; bus #209 from

26

LONDON'S FESTIVALS

Noisy, densely populated and about as bucolic as a tube door in the face, London might not seem an obvious place to hold a **music festival**. But recent years have seen a number of events draw on the capital's pulling power. Perhaps the most entertaining of the bunch is Groove Armada's **Lovebox** (ⓦlovebox.net), held in East London's Victoria Park, which mixes dance, pop and rock – Duran Duran, Sly and the Family Stone and Snoop Dogg have all played in recent years. **Field Day** (Aug; ⓦfielddayfestivals.com), an indier-than-thou freakout that uses the same patch of grass, has hosted everyone from The Fall to Wild Beasts. Down South, Clapham Common houses **Get Loaded in the Park**, a fairly poppy and party-focused one-dayer (June; ⓦgetloadedinthepark.com). Hyde Park, fittingly enough, is the venue for more mainstream events that make up in headliner clout what they lose in underground cred: **Hard Rock Calling** (June; ⓦhardrockcalling.co.uk) featured Bruce Springsteen in 2009 and Rod Stewart in 2011, while the slightly groovier **Wireless** (July; ⓦwirelessfestival.co.uk) grabbed Pulp and the Chemical brothers in 2011.

The sunshine is never guaranteed, sadly, but various events use London's plethora of clubs and halls to great effect. The **Camden Crawl** (April; ⓦthecamdencrawl.com), a chaotic mass of gigs and DJs spilling through London's indie-rock capital in the spring, is the highest profile of an ear-bursting bunch.

26

↔ Hammersmith or Barnes Bridge train station from Waterloo. This relaxed riverside alehouse has been attracting Britain's finest jazz musicians for almost fifty years – these days performers tend to be at the traditional end of the spectrum. Live music nightly and Sunday lunchtimes. Good Thai restaurant here too.

Cafe OTO 18–22 Ashwin street, E8 ⓦ cafeoto.co.uk; Dalston Kingsland Overground; map p.294. There's plenty of jazz, often of a pretty out-there variety, among the mixed-up delights that this favourite of the East-End chattering classes brings to town.

Charlie Wright's 45 Pitfield St, N1 ☎ 020 7490 8345, ⓦ charliewrights.com; ↔ Old Street; map p.192. Likeable no-nonsense Hoxton boozer with decent jazz most nights of the week, most starting late (around 10pm). The eclectic line-up takes in jam sessions, fusion and more straightforward acts.

Jazz Cafe 5 Parkway, NW1 ☎ 020 7485 6834, ⓦ jazzcafelive.com; ↔ Camden Town; map p.284. There's the odd cheesy pop night here, but a combination of big names (at big prices) and clubbier jazz acts keep the dancefloor and balcony buzzing. There's dining if you book in advance – though the service gets mixed reports.

★ **King's Place** 90 York Way, N1 ☎ 020 7520 1490, ⓦ kingsplace.co.uk; ↔ King's Cross; map p.120. Two halls host classical and jazz gigs at this rather swish development beneath *The Guardian*'s offices – the acoustics are excellent and the acts class.

Pizza Express 10 Dean St, W1 ☎ 0845 602 7017, ⓦ pizzaexpresslive.com; ↔ Tottenham Court Road; map p.100. Also known as *Jazz Club Soho*, the small basement of this branch of the pizza chain hosts consistent quality, with both established and new jazz artists.

Ronnie Scott's 47 Frith St, W1 ☎ 020 7439 0747, ⓦ ronniescotts.co.uk; ↔ Leicester Square; map p.100. The most famous jazz club in London, this small and atmospheric place has smartened up in recent years but, after a flirtation with pop, is firmly back in the jazz fold. Many people opt for the dinner package, but you don't have to.

★ **The Vortex** 11 Gillett Square, N16 ☎ 020 7254 4097, ⓦ vortexjazz.co.uk; Dalston Kingsland Overground; map p.291. Sat in snazzy Dalston Cultural House, this small venue

GETTING THE LOWDOWN

Plenty of **websites** offer listings of upcoming club nights, and **magazines** are useful if you want a bit more of a breakdown. **Bars** and **record shops** are good places to pick up the latest club flyers, especially around hotspots like Shoreditch – there are also plenty of the latter on Berwick Street in Soho.

MAGAZINES AND WEBSITES
DJ Magazine ⓦ djmag.com
Mixmag ⓦ mixmag.net
Resident Advisor ⓦ residentadvisor.net
Time Out ⓦ timeout.com/london/clubs

is a serious player on the live jazz scene, managing to combine a touch of urban style with a cosy, friendly atmosphere.

WORLD MUSIC, FOLK AND ROOTS

Barbican Silk St, EC2 ☎ 020 7638 8891, ⓦ barbican.org .uk; ↔ Barbican; map p.156. It's easy to lose yourself in the expansive Barbican, the largest arts centre in Europe and a focal point for the best world-music bands and orchestras. It also hosts one-off contemporary music events and festivals, and there's often free music in the foyer.

Bush Hall 310 Uxbridge Rd, W12 ☎ 020 8222 6955, ⓦ bushhallmusic.co.uk; ↔ Sherpherd's Bush. Acoustic performers, folkies and blues artists play beneath the cool chandeliers of this appealing former dancehall – it gets the odd rock band too.

Cecil Sharp House 2 Regent's Park Rd, NW1 ☎ 020 7485 2206, ⓦ efdss.org; ↔ Camden Town; map p.284. Headquarters of the English Folk Dance and Song Society, with singing and dancing performances as well as workshops and classes.

Southbank Centre South Bank, SE1 ☎ 0844 875 0073, ⓦ southbankcentre.co.uk; ↔ Waterloo; map p.216. The all-seater Royal Festival Hall, Queen Elizabeth Hall and Purcell Room host imaginative programmes of world music, jazz and folk, as well as classical concerts and the odd pop event.

CLUBS

Twenty-five years after acid house irreversibly shook up British **clubs**, London remains the place to come if you want to party after dark. The superclubs may be dying out, with *Matter* the most recent of a slew of casualties, but there's more variety than ever, both in terms of music being played and the small to mid-sized venues available. Secret events and one-off warehouse nights are also popular – you may have to text or email for the venue address. And as well as the clubs we've highlighted below, lots of the venues above offer boogying of some sort or other.

Countless places pump out **pop**, **r'n'b** and general good-times tuneage – we've flagged up some fun nights if you want to shake your stuff in (see box, p.404). Of the more serious genres, **house** music still dominates, although dubstep and its various permutations have an important influence. **Drum'n'bass**, **reggae** and **hip-hop** still command a loyal following, and **Latin** and **world music** fans have their own clubs too, although none are as visible as the capital's alternative **rock** and **punk** scene, which remains centred on Camden.

Opening time for most clubs is between 10pm and midnight, with most favouring 11pm. Some keep irregular days, others just open at the weekend and many have their hours determined almost entirely by the club night. We've summed up hours in the listings below, but treat them as a rough guide – check online and on the door. Some venues stop serving alcohol as much as an hour before they shut.

Admission prices vary enormously, with midweek nights often charging a few quid or less and some big events charging as much as £30; £10–15 is the average at the weekend, but bear in mind that profit margins at the bar can be even more outrageous than at live-music venues. London's scene is fairly dressed down – West End clubs may want you to wear smart shoes, and a few venues discourage baseball caps, but trainers are generally fine – although in some Shoreditch clubs you may feel underdressed if you haven't made at least some effort to wear some vintage or grow a bad moustache.

SOHO

Madame JoJo's 8–10 Brewer St, W1 ☎020 7734 3040, ⓦ madamejojos.com; ⊖ Piccadilly Circus; map p.100. Louche, enjoyable and ever-so-slightly battered Soho institution. Alongside burlesque and magic shows, you'll find electronica, disco, rock and funk – the big nights here include funky groovefest The Good Foot (Fri), and indie White Heat (Tues). Usually Tues–Sun 10pm–3am, with shows earlier in the evening.

CLERKENWELL

★ **Fabric** 77a Charterhouse St, EC1 ☎020 7336 8898, ⓦ fabriclondon.com; ⊖ Farringdon; map p.150. Despite big queues (arrive early or late or buy tickets online) and a confusing layout that means you may take hours to find friends, jackets and some of its numerous rooms, this 1600-capacity club remains one of the world's finest. Genres booming from the devastating soundsystem include drum'n'bass and dubstep (most Fri) and techno and house (most Sat & Sun), but live bands and lengthy DJ line-ups means you can hear a huge variety of acts, including the biggest names in underground dance music. Some Thurs 9pm–4am, all Fri & Sun 10pm–6am, Sat 11pm–8am.

SHOREDITCH

93 Feet East 150 Brick Lane, E2 ☎020 770 6006, ⓦ 93feeteast.co.uk; ⊖ Old Street; map p.192. Perched cheerfully in Brick Lane's buzzing epicentre, this engaging small venue hosts indie, soul, electro and funk nights alongside its gigs – there are often daytime sessions at the weekends too. Usually daily 7–11pm, occasionally till 4am.

Aquarium 256–264 Old St, EC1 ☎020 7253 3558, ⓦ clubaquarium.co.uk; ⊖ Old Street; map p.192. Big, fairly mainstream (disco, house and pop – you may need smart shoes to get in) venue with a splendid selling point – a good-sized pool and jacuzzi. The hardcore after-hours

events are dominated by electro-house and minimal techno. Thurs–Sun usually 11pm–6am, sometimes 8pm–midnight & 2.30am–9am.

Bethnal Green Working Men's Club 44–46 Pollard Row, E2 ☎020 7739 7170, ⓦ workersplaytime.net; ⊖ Bethnal Green; map p.192. As old school as they come, this working men's club caught the mid-noughties trend for burlesque and is still riding it with style. Expect disco, rock'n'roll, party games, stand-up comedy and merrily kitsch decor, plus a whole lot of dressing up. Usually Tues–Thurs 8pm–midnight, Fri & Sun 9pm–2am.

★ **Cargo** 83 Rivington St, EC2 ☎020 7739 3440, ⓦ cargo-london.com; ⊖ Old Street or Shoreditch High Street Overground; map p.192. Plays host to a variety of fine club nights, from deep house to jazz, and often features live bands alongside the DJs. Mon–Thurs 6pm–1am, Fri–Sat 6pm–3am, Sun 6pm–1am.

East Village 89 Great Eastern Street, EC2A ☎020 7739 5173, ⓦ eastvillageclub.co.uk; ⊖ Old Street; map p.192. House music, often of the old school variety, rules at this slick and comfortable (well, for Shoreditch) basement-and-lounge. Solid, but don't expect to be blown away. Bar daily, clubs usually Fri–Sat 9.30pm–2.30am, Sun 5pm–midnight.

★ **Plastic People** 147–149 Curtain Rd, EC2 ☎020 7739 6471, ⓦ plasticpeople.co.uk; ⊖ Old Street; map p.192. Thumping basement club whose cheeringly broad booking policy stretches through techno, rock'n'roll, Afro-pop and splendid dubstep night FWD>>. Usually Thurs 10pm–2am; Fri & Sat 10pm–4am.

Rhythm Factory 16–18 Whitechapel Rd, E1 ☎020 7375 3774, ⓦ rhythmfactory.co.uk; ⊖ Aldgate East or Whitechapel; map p.192. This textile-factory-turned-cutting-edge club houses a bar and separate, often fairly packed, dancefloor. Live bands fairly regularly during the week; drum'n'bass and techno dominate the weekends. Weeknight usually 7pm–11pm when open; Fri–Sat 10pm–6am.

KENSINGTON TO NOTTING HILL

★ **Notting Hill Arts Club** 21 Notting Hill Gate, W11 ☎020 7460 4459, ⓦ nottinghillartsclub.com; ⊖ Notting Hill Gate; map p.274. Groovy, arty, dressed-down basement club-bar that's popular for everything from Latin-inspired funk, jazz and hip-hop through to soul, house and indie; Saturday afternoon has free gigs courtesy of Rough Trade records. Usually Wed–Sun 7pm–2am.

NORTH LONDON

Dalston Superstore 177 Kinglsand High Street, E8 ☎020 7254 2273, ⓦ www.facebook.com/dalston superstore; Dalston Kingsland Overgound; map p.291. Hip little venues have been colonizing Dalston's main drag for several years now; with its arty murals, picky door staff,

26

largely gay clientele and hedonistic mix of disco, house and party tunes, this is one of the hottest of the moment. Food and drink in the day, clubs usually Fri–Sun 9pm–2am.

EGG 200 York Way, N7 ☎ 020 7609 8364, ⓦ egglondon .net; ⊖ King's Cross; map p.284. Two exposed-brick, medium-sized rooms, a smart loft-style bar and a decent outdoor space host a mixed crowd and house and rave tunes. You may need smart shoes. Usually Fri–Sun 10pm–6am.

Electric Ballroom 184 Camden High St, NW1 ☎ 020 7485 9006, ⓦ electricballroom.co.uk; ⊖ Camden Town; map p.284. Historic club and rock venue that hosts party-tastic rock and metal (Fri) and indie and pop nights (Sat), plus several gigs a week. Fri–Sat 10.30pm–3am.

The Nest 36 Stoke Newington Rd, N16 ☎ 0020 7354 9993, ⓦ ilovethenest.com; Dalston Kingsland Overground; map p.291. The former *Bardens Boudoir* got a makeover and now looks slightly smarter, but is still packed with hip young things, bands and DJs playing electro-house, disco and more. Fri–Sat 9pm–4am, various other nights.

Proud Camden Stables Market, NW1 ☎ 0207 482 3867, ⓦ proudcamden.com; ⊖ Camden Town; map p.284. Indie, rave, live acts, costume parties, exhibitions and more – Proud Camden is as mixed up as you'd expect a former horse hospital to be, with decent food early on and an outdoor terrace in summer. Hours vary – clubs usually till 2.30am.

Scala 275 Pentonville Rd, N1 ☎ 020 7833 2022, ⓦ scala-london.co.uk; ⊖ King's Cross map p.120. Once a cinema (it was forced to shut down after illegally showing Kubrick's *A Clockwork Orange*), the Scala stages some fine gigs, while the mixed-up weekend club nights take in hardcore rock, dubstep, tech-house, soca and the ripest cheese. Clubs usually Fri–Sun 10pm–6am.

SOUTH LONDON

Cable Bermondsey St Tunnel, SE1 ☎ 020 7403 7730, ⓦ cable-london.com; ⊖ London Bridge; map p.224. Big, bold recent entrant to the scene, with a classic railway-arch-and-piping interior, heavy sounds (drum 'n' bass, breaks, techno and a bit of house) and lots of gloomy corners. Fri–Sat 10pm–6am, occasional weekday opening.

Corsica Studios 5 Elephant Rd, SE17 ☎ 020 7703 4760, ⓦ corsicastudios.com; ⊖ Elephant & Castle; map p.224. Faintly scuzzy and very cool mid-sized venue that pretty much worships the bass, with breaks, dubstep, electro and techno dominating the speakers, frequent live sessions and artistic/community projects. Usually Fri–Sun 10pm–6am.

Ministry of Sound 103 Gaunt St, SE1 ☎ 020 7378 6528, ⓦ ministryofsound.com; ⊖ Elephant & Castle; map p.224. The vast headquarters of this clubbing brand may sometimes seem peopled largely by corporate clubbers and gawping visitors, but the soundsystem is exceptional and it gets the pick of visiting house and trance DJs. Usually Thurs 10pm–4am, Fri–Sat 11pm–6am.

Plan B 418 Brixton Rd, SW9 ☎ 08701 165421, ⓦ plan -brixton.co.uk; ⊖ Brixton. Small, laidback Brixton club, with a good soundsystem, friendly staff, a great bar and a house- and hip-hop-oriented music policy. Usually Fri–Sun 10pm–4am.

BARGAIN BASEMENTS

Our selection focuses on quality nights – which often means forward planning and paying on the door. If you just want to shake your stuff, here's five cheap and occasionally cheesy options.

Big Chill House 257–259 Pentonville Road, N1 ☎ 020 7427 2540; ⊖ King's Cross; map p.284. Has decent visiting DJs, but more importantly there's almost never a door charge. Go early and bag some space among the swaying punters – queues can get large. Mon–Wed & Sun noon–midnight, Thurs noon–1am, Fri & Sat noon–2am/4am – only clubby around the weekend.

Da Vinci's 6 Baylis Road, SE1 ☎ 020 7928 8099; ⊖ Waterloo; map p.216. This titchy café-club boasts pop, r'n'b, pints in plastic glasses and a strangely luxuriant carpet – and it's free and lively when most folk are long in bed. Mon–Thurs & Sun usually 5pm–3am, Fri & Sat 9.30pm–4am.

Mother 333 Old St, EC1 ☎ 020 7739 5949, ⓦ 333mother.com; ⊖ Old Street; map p.192. Upstairs from the *333* (which you'll generally have to pay for), this Hoxton old-timer is a decent spot for a grimy end-of-night twist and shout. Usually daily 8pm–3am (333 Fri & Sat 10pm–3/5am).

The Old Blue Last 38 Great Eastern St, EC2 ☎ 020 7739 7033, ⓦ theoldbluelast.com; ⊖ Old Street or Shoreditch High Street Overground; map p.192. Definitive Shoreditch pub and venue, with hip gigs and semi-ironic dancefloor cheese upstairs, a decent bar downstairs and energetic hipsters everywhere, many complaining that it isn't as cool as it was last year. Occasional charges for bands, otherwise free. Daily 8pm–midnight, until 2am Fri–Sat.

The Roxy 3–5 Rathbone Place, W1 ☎ 020 255 1098, ⓦ theroxy.co.uk; ⊖ Tottenham Court Road; map p.97. Consistently raucous, very studenty and broadly indie club (they play a fair bit of pop too) that's a decent enough West End bet and is usually free if you get there early (before 10.30pm during the week and before 8.30pm on Fri – Sat, sadly, starts from £5 students, £7 non-students). Frequent happy hours. Mon–Thurs 5pm–3am, Fri 5pm–3.30am, Sat 9.30pm–3.30am.

KITSCH CABARET, MADAME JOJO'S

Lesbian and gay London

London's lesbian and gay scene today is so huge, diverse and well established that it's easy to forget just how much – and just how fast – it has grown and moved into the mainstream over the last couple of decades. Political progress has been accompanied by a certain amount of depoliticization of the scene, so that pink power has given way to the pink pound, gay liberation to gay lifestyle, and the central lesbian and gay "village" of Soho is vibrant, self-assured and unashamedly commercial. As a result of this high-profile activity, straight Londoners tend to be a fairly homo-savvy bunch and, on the whole, happy to embrace and even dip into the city's large range of queer offerings.

The last few years have seen the London gay and lesbian scene expand to a more evenly spread array of locations, but central London's **Soho** remains its spiritual heart. Soho's **Old Compton Street** (see p.99) is, so to speak, its main drag; traditional gay pubs rub alongside cafés and bars selling expensive designer beers and lattes, while hairdressers, letting agencies, sex boutiques and spiritual health centres offer a vast range of gay-run services. Lesbian bars complete the diverse mix in Soho.

The biggest and best **clubs** are now found just south of the river in **Vauxhall**, catering for every musical, sartorial and sexual taste, but there are well-established venues all over the city.

East and northeast London is fast becoming something of a third leg to the gay scene in London, with Shoreditch and Dalston catering for a younger, cooler and often more mixed crowd, and, especially for lesbians, Stoke Newington and Hackney in the northeast. **Clapham** hosts a smaller gay contingent for the south.

Anti-gay **hostility** is rare in London, but there have been some recent high-profile homophobic attacks so it's probably wise not to hold hands or smooch too obviously in areas you don't know well.

27

ESSENTIALS

LESBIAN AND GAY MEDIA

PRINT

Though they carry entertainment listings, most lesbian- and gay-oriented **magazines** these days tend towards the glossy and consumerist, with celebrity features, fashion, lifestyle and the inevitable eye candy. Many titles have gone online-only in recent years, but some paid-for magazines, including **Attitude** (ⓦ attitude.co.uk) and rival **Gay Times** (ⓦ gaytimes.co.uk), are still going strong, with **Diva** (ⓦ divamag.co.uk) aimed squarely at the lesbian market. In the place of paid-for titles, free magazines have made inroads, led by glossies like **Out In The City** (ⓦ outmag .co.uk) and **G3** (ⓦ g3mag.co.uk) for girls. Listings-based freesheets like **Boyz** (ⓦ boyz.co.uk) and **qx** (ⓦ qxmagazine.com) abound in clubs and bars and are also available in full on their websites.

ONLINE

While print media has wilted, online resources have gone from strength to strength.

ⓦ **pinknews.co.uk** Award-winning website putting an LGBT slant on news from the UK and abroad.

ⓦ **pinkpaper.com** The online home of the old print publication, addressing lesbian and gay issues.

ⓦ **gayuknews.com** Up-to-date news digest, with entertainment, scene and Pride sections.

ⓦ **gaytoz.com** Directory of gay, lesbian, bisexual and TV/TS-friendly organizations and businesses.

ⓦ **gingerbeer.co.uk** Regularly updated website for London lesbians, offering listings and reviews of bars, clubs and events.

ⓦ **gaydargirls.com** Online dating for queer girls nationwide.

ⓦ **grindr.com** London's favourite iPhone, Android and Blackberry hook-up app.

ⓦ **gaydar.co.uk** The capital's pre-eminent dating and hook-up site.

HELPLINES

The following services provide information, advice and counselling, and can point you in the direction of specific organizations and community or support groups.

Antidote ☎ 020 7437 3523, ⓦ thehungerford.org /antidote.asp. Despite their illegality, drugs are a part of London's queer clubbing scene. Antidote provides a lesbian, gay, bi and transgender-specific drugs counselling and support service, including a weekly drop-in at 32a Wardour St, W1 (Thurs 6.30–8.30pm).

London Lesbian & Gay Switchboard ☎ 020 7837 7324, ⓦ llgs.org.uk. Huge database on everything you might ever want to know, plus legal advice and counselling. Lines are open 24hr: keep trying if you can't get through, or try their instant messaging or email services through the website.

THT Direct ☎ 0845 1221 200, ⓦ tht.org.uk. Helpline for anyone worried about HIV, as well as other STIs and problems, from the Terrence Higgins Trust.

TOURS

A good introduction to Soho's lesbian and gay history is offered by the walking tour (2–4pm) organized by Kairos on the third Sunday of every month (☎ 020 7437 6063; ⓦ kairosinsoho.org.uk; £5) – meet outside the *Admiral Duncan* pub (see opposite).

TAXIS

When it's throwing-out time and you need a guaranteed harassment-free **cab service**, Liberty Cars, 297 Old St, EC1 (☎ 020 7739 9080), offer a cheap way to get a gay-friendly ride home.

HOTELS

London's best-known gay accommodation options cater mostly for men, though all are lesbian friendly, and a full breakfast is almost always included. Self-catering **apartments** are available through the gay-run Outlet Gay Accommodation, 32 Old Compton St, W1 (☎ 020 7287 4244; ⊛ outlet4holidays.com).

Fitzbb 15 Colville Place, W1 ☎ 07834 372866; ⊛ fitzbb .me.uk; ⊖ Goodge St; map p.97. This 18th-century townhouse only has two rooms so book ahead, but it's a great price in stumbling distance from Soho. There's a minimum booking of three nights. Or try its younger sibling via ⊛ sohobb.me.uk, from £55. **£65**

Griffin House Holiday Apartments 22 Stockwell Green, SW9 ☎ 020 7096 3332, ⊛ griffinhouse.info; ⊖ Stockwell. Highly rated self-catering accommodation

with an emphasis on providing a home from home. Convenient for the Vauxhall and Clapham scenes. Apartments from **£90**

Number 16 16 St Alfege Passage, SE10 ☎ 020 8853 4337, ⊛ st-alfeges.co.uk. Cutty Sark DLR; map p.315. Charming, tiny gay-run B&B in a peaceful location in historic Greenwich, with tasteful yet quirky Victorian decor. A good hideaway. **£125**

CAFÉS, BARS AND PUBS

27

There are loads of lesbian and gay eating and watering holes in London, many of them operating as cafés by day and transforming into drinking dens by night. Lots have cabaret or disco nights and are open until the early hours, making them a fine (and affordable) alternative to the big clubs. Most of these cafés and bars have free admission, though a few levy a charge after 10.30pm (expect to pay about £5) if there's music, cabaret or a disco.

The places below represent a selective list of the best and most accessible, from self-consciously minimalist eateries to shabby old pubs. We use "mixed" to mean places for both gays and lesbians, though many "mixed" places are mostly frequented by men.

MIXED CAFÉS, BARS AND PUBS
SOHO

The Admiral Duncan 54 Old Compton St, W1 ☎ 020 7437 5300; ⊖ Leicester Square; map p.100. Unpretentious, traditional-style gay bar in the heart of Soho, popular and busy with the post-work crowd. Expect cocktails and camp classics on the jukebox. Mon–Thurs noon –11pm, Fri & Sat noon–midnight, Sun noon–10.30pm.

Balans 34 Old Compton St, W1 ☎ 020 7439 3309; 60 Old Compton St, W1 ☎ 020 7439 2183; ⊛ balans.co.uk; ⊖ Leicester Square; map p.100. Balans has spawned several branches across the city but these two remain a Soho institution, serving a menu that includes a lengthy hangover-busting breakfast and brunch section. 34 Old Compton St open 24 hours; 60 Old Compton St Sun– Thurs 8am–5am, Fri & Sat 8am–6am.

Duke of Wellington 77 Wardour St, W1 ☎ 020 7439 1274; ⊖ Piccadilly Circus; map p.100. Traditional pub on two floors in the heart of Soho, with cheap lager and real ale on pump and a down-to-earth, male-dominated crowd, keen on chatting and socializing. Mon–Thurs noon–11pm, Fri & Sat noon–midnight, Sun noon–10.30pm.

Escape 10a Brewer St, W1 ☎ 020 7734 3040, ⊛ escape soho.com; ⊖ Piccadilly Circus; map, p.100. If you're heading to *Madame Jojo's*, then head to *Escape* first, the club's trendy sister DJ bar. Right at the heart of Soho, it attracts a mixed crowd. Tues–Sun 5pm–3am, call for times on Mon.

Freedom 66 Wardour St, W1 ☎ 020 7734 0071, ⊛ freedombarsoho.com; ⊖ Piccadilly Circus; map p.100.

Hip metrosexual place, popular with a straight/gay Soho crowd. The basement becomes an intimate club at night, complete with pink banquettes and glitter balls, that plays home to cabaret and comedy. Mon–Thurs 4pm–3am, Fri & Sat 2pm–3am, Sun 2pm–10.30pm.

G-A-Y Bar 30 Old Compton St, W1 ☎ 020 7494 2756, ⊛ g-a-y.co.uk; ⊖ Tottenham Court Road or Leicester Square; map p.100. Vast, pinky-purple video bar that attracts a young, fashionable, pre-G-A-Y crowd. The basement bar is for women and guests only in the evening. Daily noon–midnight.

★ **Ku Bar** 30 Lisle St, WC2, ☎ 020 7437 4303; 25 Frith St, W1, ☎ 020 7287 7986, ⊛ ku-bar.co.uk; ⊖ Leicester Square; map p.100. The Lisle St original, with a downstairs club open til 3am, is one of Soho's largest and best-loved gay bars, serving a scene-conscious yet low-on-attitude clientele. It's now joined by a stylish sibling bar on Frith St. Lisle St Mon–Sat noon–3am, Sun noon–10.30pm; Frith St Mon–Thurs noon–11pm, Fri & Sat noon– midnight, Sun noon–10.30pm.

Rupert Street 50 Rupert St, W1; ⊖ Piccadilly Circus; map p.100. Smart, mainstream bar attracting a mixed after-work crowd, but with a more pre-club vibe at weekends when they remove the furniture and it's frequently packed to the rafters. Mon-Fri noon to 11pm, Sat noon–midnight, Sun noon–10.30pm.

Village Soho 81 Wardour St, W1 ☎ 020 7478 0530, ⊛ village-soho.co.uk; ⊖ Piccadilly Circus; map p.100. Elegant café-bar attracting pretty boyz: clean and modern on the ground floor, with a stylish basement and a plush, comfortable upstairs boudoir. Mon–Sat 4pm–1am, Sun 4pm–11.30pm.

The Yard 57 Rupert St, W1 ☎020 7437 2652, ⓦyardbar .co.uk; ⊖ Piccadilly Circus; map p.100. Ignore the recent tacky makeover: the bar, courtyard and loft areas have retained their laidback, sociable atmosphere. *The Yard* often heaves with a varied post-work crowd and in fine weather it's one of the best spots in the village for alfresco drinking. Sun–Thurs noon–11.30pm, Fri & Sat noon–midnight.

COVENT GARDEN

First Out 52 St Giles High St, WC2 ☎020 7240 8042, ⓦfirstoutcafebar.com; ⊖ Tottenham Court Road; map p.132. The West End's first gay café-bar, serving good veggie food. Upstairs is airy, the downstairs bar is dark. Girl Friday is a pre-club session for grrrls; gay men allowed as guests. Daily 9am–11pm.

Halfway 2 Heaven 7 Duncannon St, WC2 ☎0207 484 0746; ⊖ Charing Cross; map p.132. Friendly, traditional pub off Trafalgar Square, featuring pub quizzes, karaoke and occasional cabaret. Attracts a largely male crowd slightly older than that in Soho. Daily noon–midnight.

Retro Bar 2 George Court (off Strand), WC2 ☎020 7839 8760; ⊖ Charing Cross; map p.132. Tucked down a quiet alleyway off the Strand, this friendly, indie/retro bar plays 1970s, 80s, rock, pop, goth and alternative sounds, and features regular DIY DJ nights. Mon–Fri noon–11pm, Sat 2–11pm, Sun 2–10.30pm.

SHOREDITCH

George & Dragon 2–4 Hackney Rd, E2 ☎020 7012 1100; ⊖ Old Street; map p.192. Dandies, fashionistas and locals meet in this lively, often rammed east London hangout. The interior set-up is traditional, but the attitudes are not. A perfect place to start a night in the east – it's only stumbling distance from the *Joiners Arms*. Daily 6pm–midnight.

Joiners Arms 116–118 Hackney Rd, E2 ☎07976 892541; ⊖ Old Street; map p.192. Atmospheric bar with regular DJs and funky dancefloor. Open late at weekends, it attracts a diverse and mixed crowd, with everything from East End stalwarts to pre-clubbing, loft-living trendies. Mon–Wed 5pm–2am, Thurs 5pm–3am, Fri & Sat 5pm–4am, Sun 2pm–2am.

NORTH LONDON

The Black Cap 171 Camden High St, NW1 ☎020 7485 0538, ⓦtheblackcap.com; ⊖ Camden Town; map p.284. Venerable north London establishment offering cabaret and dancing almost every night, check the website for what's on. The upstairs Shufflewick bar is in a quieter pub style, and opens onto the Fong Terrace in the summer. Sun noon–1am, Mon–Thurs noon–2am, Fri noon–3am.

Central Station 37 Wharfdale Rd, N1 ☎020 7278 3294, ⓦcentralstation.co.uk; ⊖ King's Cross; map p.120. Award-winning, late-opening community pub offering cabaret, cruisey club nights and the UK's only gay sports bar. Sun–Wed noon–1am, Thurs noon–2am, Fri & Sat noon–4am.

★ **Dalston Superstore** 117 Kingsland High St, E8 ☎020 7254 2273, ⓦfacebook.com/dalstonsuperstore; Dalston Junction Overground; map p.291. *Dalston Superstore* came out of nowhere to become the hottest late-night destination in east London, catering for a fashionably mixed but often gay crowd, and with many dedicated gay nights. Daytimes bring music, art and food. Sun–Thurs 10am–2am, Fri & Sat 10am–3am.

The Green 74 Upper St, N1 ☎020 7226 8895, ⓦthegreenislington.co.uk; ⊖ Angel; map p.284. Relaxed, stylish Soho-style bar-restaurant fronting Islington Green, with interesting food, wine, beers and cocktails, attracting a thoroughly mixed crowd. Mon–Wed 5pm–midnight, Thurs 5pm–1am, Fri 5pm–2am, Sat noon–2am, Sun noon–midnight.

SOUTH LONDON

Kazbar 50 Clapham High St, SW4 ☎020 7622 0070, ⓦkazbarclapham.com; ⊖ Clapham Common or

27

EVENTS AND FESTIVALS

The main **outdoor even**t of the year is **Pride London** in late June or early July, encompassing a rally in Trafalgar Square, a colourful, whistle-blowing march through the city streets, live cabaret in Leicester Square and a women's stage in Soho. 2012 will also see **WorldPride** come to London ahead of the Olympics, bolstering the **Pride Festival Fortnight**, a mix of theatre, concerts, sports and films in the run-up to Pride itself. Full details on what should be the gay party of the century are at the website ⓦpridelondon.org.

In March and April, the British Film Institute hosts the annual **Lesbian and Gay Film Festival** (ⓦllgff.org.uk), which celebrates new cinema from around the world. Elsewhere, queer theatre and arts events take place all year round in the city's many fringe theatres, arts centres, galleries and clubs. If none of this appeals, there are also a huge number of **gay groups and organizations** which offer everything from ballroom dancing to spanking seminars – check the local gay press for details.

Clapham North. Modern, mostly boyz, split-level bar, with a video screen playing happy, poppy hits. Upstairs is a lounge area, and there is seating out front on the street. A good place to start a night out in south London. Mon & Tues 5–11pm, Wed & Thurs 5pm–midnight, Fri & Sat 4pm–1.30am, Sun 1pm–12.30am.

The Royal Vauxhall Tavern 372 Kennington Lane, SE11 ☎ 020 7820 1222, ⓦ rvt.org.uk; ⊖ Vauxhall. This huge, disreputable, divey drag and cabaret pub is home to legendary alternative night Duckie on Saturdays. The rest of the week brings bingo, comedy and a changing calendar of performance that attracts a varied but often older crowd. Mon–Thurs 7pm–midnight, Fri 7pm–2am, Sat 9pm–2am, Sun 2pm–midnight.

Two Brewers 114 Clapham High St, SW4 ☎ 020 7819 9539, ⓦ the2brewers.com; ⊖ Clapham Common or Clapham North. Big, long-established and popular south London pub, with nightly cabaret in the front bar and a more cruisey dancefloor in the back that stays open late. Sun–Thurs 5pm–2am, Fri & Sat 5pm–4am.

LESBIAN CAFÉS, BARS AND PUBS
SOHO

Candy Bar 4 Carlisle St, WC2 ☎ 020 7287 5041, ⓦ candybarsoho.com; ⊖ Tottenham Court Road; map p.100. Now part of the Ku group of gay bars, this Sapphic magnet has been in operation since 1996 and still has the same crucial, cruisey vibe that makes it the hottest girl bar in central London. Mon, Wed & Thurs 5pm–3am, Tues 7pm–3am, Fri & Sat 4pm–3am, Sun 5pm–12.30am.

Lounge Penthouse, 1 Leicester Sq, WC2 ☎ 020 734 0900, ⓦ lounge.uk.net; ⊖ Leicester Sq. Bar, restaurant and club, *Lounge* is a monthly night of classy drinks and dressier vibes than you'll find elsewhere in town. From 9pm on every third Thurs.

Star at Night 22 Great Chapel St, W1 ☎ 020 7494 2488, ⓦ thestaratnight.com; ⊖ Tottenham Court Rd; map p.100. Comfortable mixed but female-led venue, popular with a slightly older crowd who want somewhere to sit, a decent glass of wine and good conversation. Tues–Sat 6–11.30pm.

NORTH LONDON

★ **Blush** 8 Cazenove Rd, Stoke Newington, N16 ☎ 020 7923 9202; bus #73 from ⊖ King's Cross or Angel; map p.291. Two floors of fun with quizzes, games nights and lazy Sundays with roast dinners and the newspapers make this local popular among lesbians. Mon–Thurs & Sat 5pm–12.30am, Fri 5pm–1am, Sun 1pm–12.30am.

The Oak Bar 79 Green Lanes, N16 ☎ 020 7354 2791, ⓦ oak-bar.co.uk; Dalston Kingsland Overground; map p.291. Friendly, spacious local pub with a dancefloor and pool table, mixed but a female favourite, and hosting a range of club nights and events. Sun–Thurs 5pm–midnight, Fri & Sat 5pm–3am.

GAY MEN'S CAFÉS, BARS AND PUBS
SOHO

BarCode Soho 3–4 Archer St, W1 ☎ 020 7734 3342, ⓦ bar-code.co.uk; ⊖ Piccadilly Circus; map p.100. Busy, stylish cruise and dance bar, attracting a buff, masculine crowd. The older clientele make it a great destination if you're in Soho and aren't after a boyz bar to finish up the night. Mon–Sat 4pm–1am, Sun 4–11pm.

Comptons of Soho 51–53 Old Compton St, W1; ⊖ Leicester Square or Piccadilly Circus; map p.100. This large, traditional-style pub attracts a butch, cruising yet relaxed 25-plus crowd. Upstairs is more chilled and draws younger folks. Mon–Fri noon–11pm, Sat 11am–11pm, Sun noon–10.30pm.

The King's Arms 23 Poland St, W1 ☎ 020 7734 5907; ⊖ Oxford Circus; map p.97. London's best-known and perennially popular bear bar, with a traditional London pub atmosphere. Head down on Sundays for the raucous karaoke night. Mon & Tues noon–11pm, Wed & Thurs noon–11.30pm, Fri & Sat noon–midnight, Sun 1pm–10.30pm.

SOUTH LONDON

★ **BarCode Vauxhall** Arch 69, Albert Embankment, SE11 ☎ 020 7582 4180, ⓦ bar-code.co.uk; ⊖ Vauxhall. Slick, spacious outpost of the cruisey gay men's bar in the heart of Vauxhall's clubbing quarter, convenient for *Area* and *Fire*. Mon–Wed 4pm–1am, Thurs 4pm–2am, Fri 4pm–5am, Sat 4pm–7am, Sun 5pm–1am.

CLUBS

London's club nights tend to open up and shut down with surreal frequency, so do check listings magazines and individual websites for up-to-date times and prices before you plan your night out. Places are listed by club name if this is well known and long lived, and by venue where there's a variety of changing theme nights.

Prices Entry prices start at around £3–5, but are more often between £8 and £15 for all-nighters, rising to around £35 or even £50 for special events like New Year's Eve extravaganzas. A few places offer concessions for students and those on benefits, and some extend discounts if you've managed to pick up the right flyer from a bar earlier in the evening or printed a flyer for the night from their websites.

Opening hours Most clubs open at around 11pm (although some don't get going until the small hours) and close between 3am and 5am, while after-hours clubs provide somewhere to dance the next morning.

27

27

SAUNAS

London's burgeoning male sauna scene runs from small, intimate affairs with just a steam room and jacuzzi, to labyrinthine venues with swimming pools and gyms. They all charge around £10–14.

Chariots 1 Fairchild St, EC2 ☎ 020 7247 5333, ⊖ Old Street; 63–64 Albert Embankment, SE1 ☎ 020 7735 6709, ⊖ Vauxhall; 101 Lower Marsh, SE1 ☎ 020 7401 8484, ⊖ Waterloo; 574 Commercial Rd, E14, ☎ 020 7 791 2808, ⊖ Limehouse; 292 Streatham High Rd, SW16, ☎ 020 8 696 0929, ⊖ Waterloo; ⓦ gaysauna.co.uk. London's Roman sauna chain has five locations: the Waterloo branch never closes, while the other four are open daily. Expect steam, sweat and saucy videos, plus private rest rooms to retire to with your man of choice. The recently refurbished Shoreditch branch on Old Street is the largest and has a heated pool.

Pleasuredrome Sauna Arch 124, Alaska St, SE1 ☎ 020 7633 9194 ⓦ pleasuredrome.com; ⊖ Waterloo. Facilities here include two saunas, two steam rooms, dark areas and private rooms, plus café-bar and spa. Mixed ages, fast turnover, highly rated. Open 24/7.

The Sauna Bar 29 Endell St, WC2 ☎ 020 7836 2236, ⓦ thesaunabar.co.uk; ⊖ Covent Garden. Very central, this friendly place offers the usual facilities, along with masseurs, a bar and video entertainment. Sun–Thurs noon–midnight, Fri & Sat noon–7am.

MIXED CLUBS

SOHO

79CXR 79 Charing Cross Rd, WC2 ☎ 020 7734 0769, ⓦ 79cxr.co.uk/home.htm; ⊖ Leicester Square; map p.100. Big, busy, cruisey older men den on two floors, with industrial decor, late licence and a no-messing atmosphere.

Madame Jojo's 8–10 Brewer St, W1 ☎ 020 7734 3040, ⓦ madamejojos.com; ⊖ Piccadilly Circus; map p.100. Lush, louche club offering cabaret and drag shows for office girls, gay boys and those in between, plus a variety of dance nights. Surrender your gender at Trannyshack on Wednesdays. Opening hours vary every day so call ahead.

COVENT GARDEN

Heaven Villiers St, WC2 ☎ 020 7930 2020, ⓦ heaven-london.com; ⊖ Charing Cross or Embankment; map p.132. Said to be the UK's most popular gay club, this 2000-capacity venue is now home to G-A-Y from Thursrsdays to Saturdays, the queen of London's scene nights, with big-name DJs, PAs and shows. More Muscle Mary than Diesel Doris.

Popstarz The Den, 18a West Central St, WC1, ⓦ popstarz.org; ⊖ Tottenham Court Rd. The original Friday-night indie club's still-winning formula of alternative tunes, 1970s and 80s trash, cheap beer and no attitude attracts a mixed, studenty crowd til 6am.

THE CITY

WayOut Club Charlie's 9 Crosswall, off Minories, EC3; ☎ 07778 157 290, ⓦ thewayoutclub.com; ⊖ Tower Hill or Aldgate. Long-established Saturday night for gays, straights, cross-dressers, drag queens, TVs, TSs and friends offers a warm welcome, changing rooms, video screen and cabaret.

THE EAST END

East Bloc 217 City Road, EC1, ☎ 020 7253 0367, ⓦ eastbloc.co.uk; ⊖ Old Street; map p.192. The nights vary from electro disco to the latest Shoreditch beats, but the relentlessly cool crowd remains the consistent selling point.

★ **Sink the Pink** Bethnal Green Working Men's Club, 42-46 Pollard Row, E2, ⓦ sinkthepink.blogspot.com; ⊖ Bethnal Green. Silly, young and stupidly fun – attracting a handsome, mixed and inclusive crowd. Also keep an eye out for Sink the Pink events elsewhere, including *Dalston Superstore*.

Unskinny Bop The Star of Bethnal Green, 359 Bethnal Green Rd, E2 ⓦ unskinnybop.co.uk; ⊖ Bethnal Green. Monthly alternative night that strays out of standard indie to bring the best of everything from pop to hip-hop. Born out of female festival Ladyfest, it's particularly welcoming for girls. Every third Sat.

NORTH LONDON

Club Kali The Dome, 178 Junction Park, N19 ⓦ clubkali .com; ⊖ Tufnell Park. Held on the third Friday of every month, Kali is the world's biggest Asian music LGBT night, offering bhangra, Bollywood, Arabic, r'n'b and dance flavours for an attitude-free crowd.

Dirty Converse Kings Cross Social Club, 2 Britannia St, WC1 ⓦ dirtyconverse.com; ⊖ King's Cross. The music is an anything-goes mix of indie, pop and party, serving a fashionable crowd with a strong grrrl contingent. East London vibes in a north London location, open the second Saturday of every month.

SOUTH LONDON

Area 67–68 Albert Embankment, SE1 ☎ 020 3242 0040, ⓦ areaclublondon.com; ⊖ Vauxhall. With two dancefloors, chic decor and impressive laser and light displays, it offers a London venue for big-name international DJs, as well as hosting the after-hours club *Beyond* on Sunday mornings.

Bootylicious Club Colosseum, 1 Nine Elms Lane, SW8 ⓦbootylicious-club.co.uk; ⊖ Vauxhall. Despite London's large black community, this is the capital's only dedicated gay and lesbian urban music night, held every third Saturday of the month and featuring r'n'b, hip-hop, dancehall, house and classic vibes.

★ **Duckie** Royal Vauxhall Tavern, 372 Kennington Lane, SE11 ☎020 7737 4043, ⓦduckie.co.uk; ⊖ Vauxhall. Duckie's mix of regular live art performances and theme nights, as well as cult DJs The Readers Wifes playing everything from Kim Wilde to the Velvet Underground, has kept the night going strong for 15 years.

Exilio Latino Guy's Bar, St Thomas St, SE1 ☎07956 983230, ⓦexilio.co.uk; ⊖ London Bridge. Every Saturday night, Exilio erupts in a lesbian and gay Latin frenzy, spinning salsa, reggaeton and merengue.

Fire South Lambeth Rd, SW8 ☎020 7582 9890, ⓦfireclub.co.uk; ⊖ Vauxhall. Fire is London's superclub of choice for a mixed though mostly male crowd of disco bunnies and hardboyz. The party runs from Saturday night to Sunday morning, then on Sunday afternoon, and from Sunday night to Monday morning.

Hard-On Hidden, 65 Goding St, SE11 ☎07533 402 985, ⓦhardonclub.co.uk; ⊖ Vauxhall. Suzie Krueger's celebrated raunchy fetish/dance club has recently relocated but it has kept the strict dress code and members-only status: you can apply online.

LESBIAN CLUBS
SOHO
100% Babe The Roxy, 3 Rathbone Place, W1, ☎07956 514574, ⓦmyspace.comhundredpercentbabe; ⊖ Tottenham Court Road; map p.97. Babelicious dance parties held several times a year on bank holiday Sundays in this plush, central London venue.

THE CITY
Rumours Minories, 64–73 Minories, EC3 ☎07949 477 804, ⓦgirl-rumours.co.uk; ⊖ Tower Hill or Aldgate. There's room for 500 grrrls at this monthly, women-only Saturday-nighter. The popular and cheap club night offers two bars, quiet lounges and a dancefloor until 3am.

NORTH LONDON
Chicks Rock!! Zenith Bar, 125 Packington St, N1 ☎07817 989 368; ⊖ Angel. Party every third Saturday,

bringing together girls who like getting up and giving it a go. The formula involves an open mike and a melange of music, comedy and dancing.

★ **Twat Boutique** *Dalston Superstore*, 117 Kingsland High St, E8, ⓦtwatboutique.com; Dalston Junction Overground. The first Thursday of every month, east London's most fashionable girls (and indie celebs) come out to play. Dress up and arrive early to be sure you get in.

Waltzing with Hilda Jacksons Lane Arts Centre, 269a Archway Rd, N6 ☎07939 072958, ⓦhildas.org.uk; ⊖ Highgate. Women-only Latin and ballroom dancing club with classes for beginners and the more experienced. Held on the second Sat of every month (7.30–11.30pm) but closed in Aug.

GAY MEN'S CLUBS
SOHO
Room Service Diu London, 12–13 Greek St, W1; ⊖ Tottenham Court Road. Created by legendary party maker Jodie Harsh in late 2010, this is the latest attempt to re-create 1970s New York in old London town. Probably only worth it if you're feeling confident in your abs...and you can get on the guest list.

SOUTH LONDON
★ **The Eagle** 349 Kennington Lane, SE11 ☎020 7793 0903, ⓦeaglelondon.com; ⊖ Vauxhall. Home to the excellent disco Sunday-nighter Horse Meat Disco, the vibe here is a loose, friendly re-creation of late 1970s New York, complete with facial hair, checked shirts and a pool table.

The Fort 131 Grange Rd, SE1 ☎020 8691 0089, ⓦthefortlondon.com; ⊖ London Bridge. Sleazy, sexy cruise bar. Check the free press or phone for details about special themed nights, which include frequent boots-only or underwear parties.

The Hoist Railway Arches, 47b–47c South Lambeth Rd, SW8 ☎020 7735 9972, ⓦthehoist.co.uk; ⊖ Vauxhall. London's biggest and best-known leather/dress code bar for men with few inhibitions. *The Hoist* also hosts regular nights for rubber and other fetishes.

Union 66 Albert Embankment, SE1 ☎07970 193236, ⓦclubunion.co.uk; ⊖ Vauxhall. With semi-clothed, arousing nights such as Bodyshakers and Fitladz, this venue appeals to the unabashedly cruisey. Also offers after-hours Crunch on Sunday mornings.

XXL The Arches, 51/53 Southwark St, SE1, ⓦxxl -london.com; ⊖ London Bridge. Massively popular Wednesday and Saturday dance club for big, burly men and their fans, attracting a diverse crowd with its two dance floors, two bars and a chillout area.

27

Classical music, opera and dance

With the Southbank Centre, the Barbican and Wigmore Hall offering year-round appearances by first-rate musicians, and numerous smaller venues providing a stage for less-established or more specialized performers, the capital should satisfy most devotees of classical music. What's more, in the annual Proms (see opposite), London has one of the world's greatest, most democratic music festivals. Despite its elitist image, opera has an enthusiastic following, too, with live screenings and a new small venue making it increasingly accessible to those who can't afford full-price tickets. Meanwhile, the more modest economic demands of dance mean that you'll find a broad spectrum of ambitious work on offer in a range of excellent venues to suit all pockets.

While the **Royal Opera House** (ROH) can attract top international stars, the downside is the prohibitive price (and availability) of most of the tickets. The nearby **English National Opera** (ENO) is better value, and can be more adventurous in its repertoire and productions. Apart from the two major companies, the exciting new Little Opera House, with patrons including Jonathan Miller, Joanna Lumley and Tom Stoppard, has brought opera to the masses, while outfits like the Almeida Theatre, Soho Theatre and Battersea Arts Centre extend the boundaries of contemporary music theatre in lively and adventurous ways.

As for dance, your first stop should be **Sadler's Wells**, where some of the world's outstanding companies regularly appear. Meanwhile, fans of classicism can revel in the **Royal Ballet**, a company with some of the most accomplished dancers in Europe.

CLASSICAL MUSIC

London is spoilt for choice when it comes to **orchestras**. On most days you should be able to catch a concert by one of the five major orchestras based in the capital or one of the more specialized ensembles. Unless a glamorous guest conductor is wielding the baton, or one of the world's high-profile orchestras is giving a performance, full houses are a rarity, so even at the biggest concert halls you should be able to pick up a ticket for around £15 (the usual range is about £12–50).

Free concerts During the week there are numerous free concerts by students or professionals, often at lunchtimes (usually around 1pm), in London's churches (ⓦ cityevents. co.uk), the best of which are listed here (see p.414). London's two leading conservatoires, the Royal College of Music (ⓦ rcm.ac.uk) and Royal Academy of Music (ⓦ ram.ac.uk), also give regular concerts of an amazingly high standard, some of them free, with programming that is often more varied and adventurous than in commercial venues.

Festivals The Proms provide a feast of music at bargain-basement prices (see below), and there are several other regular music festivals throughout the year. The most prestigious is probably the City of London Festival (ⓦ colf .org), which takes place in the City's churches and livery halls from late June to mid-July. St Leonard's Church, Spitalfields, is at the centre of several music events, the largest of which is Spitalfields' summer festival in June (ⓦ spitalfieldsfestival .org.uk). Other annual musicfests to look out for include the Festival of Baroque Music (ⓦ lufthansafestival.org.uk), held in May in St John's Smith Square, St Gabriel's Warwick

Square and Westminster Abbey, and the Early Music Festival (ⓦ earlymusicfestival.com), held in Greenwich's beautiful Old Royal Naval College.

CONCERT VENUES

Barbican Centre Silk St, EC2 ☎ 020 7638 8891, ⓦ barbican.org.uk; ⊖ Barbican or Moorgate. With the outstanding resident London Symphony Orchestra (ⓦ lso .co.uk), the BBC Symphony Orchestra (ⓦ bbc.co.uk /orchestras) as associate orchestra, and top foreign orchestras and big-name soloists in regular attendance, the Barbican is one of the outstanding arenas for classical music. The free music in the foyer is often very good, too.

Cadogan Hall Sloane Terrace, SW1 ☎ 020 7730 4500, ⓦ cadoganhall.com; ⊖ Sloane Square. This handsome neo-Byzantine building, built in 1901 as a Christian Science church, now serves as a 900-seat concert hall with outstanding acoustics. The Royal Philharmonic (ⓦ rpo .co.uk) is its resident orchestra and it's the venue for the Proms chamber concerts (see below).

28

THE PROMS

The **BBC Henry Wood Promenade Concerts** (Royal Albert Hall ☎ 0845 401 5045, ⓦ bbc .co.uk/proms; ⊖ South Kensington), or the Proms, tend to be associated with the raucous "Last Night", when the flag-waving audience sings its patriotic heart out to *Land of Hope and Glory*. In truth, however, this jingoistic knees-up is untypical of the season (mid-July to mid-Sept), which features around seventy concerts with an exhilarating mix of favourites and new and recondite works. The unique aspect of the Proms is that seats in the stalls, and the upper gallery, are removed to create more than five hundred **standing places** – these cost £5, even on the last night, and must be bought on the door, on the day. Seated **tickets** cost £7.50–90; those for the last night are allocated by ballot, and start at £55. The acoustics aren't the world's best – OK for orchestral blockbusters, less so for small-scale works – but the performers are usually outstanding, the atmosphere is great, and the hall is so vast that the likelihood of being turned away if you turn up on the night is slim. A handful of lunchtime chamber music concerts are also held in Cadogan Hall, just off Sloane Square.

28

Kings Place 90 York Way, N1 ☎020 7520 1490, ⓦkingsplace.co.uk; ⊖ King's Cross. Home of the London Sinfonietta (ⓦlondonsinfonietta.org.uk), one of the world's finest contemporary music groups, and the Orchestra of the Age of Enlightenment (ⓦoae.co.uk), who play on period instruments, this impressive, purpose-built venue, by the canal behind King's Cross, has two performance spaces. The London Chamber Music Society (ⓦlondonchambermusic.org.uk) holds excellent Sunday evening concerts. Online "saver" tickets for all performances go for less than £10.

LSO St Luke's 161 Old St, EC1 ☎020 7588 1116, ⓦlso .co.uk/lsostlukes; ⊖ Old Street. This Hawksmoor church has been beautifully converted into a 400-seat performance space for the London Symphony Orchestra, but is also used for a wide variety of concerts from classical world music to free jazz. Thursday lunchtimes see popular chamber recitals for a tenner.

St John's Smith Square, SW1 ☎020 7222 1061, ⓦsjss .org.uk; ⊖ Westminster. Built in 1728 and firebombed in 1941, this striking Baroque church is home to an exceptional concert hall, with fine acoustics and a great organ. Its varied musical menu includes orchestral and choral concerts, chamber music and solo recitals, mostly in the evenings but also on some Thursday lunchtimes. There's a good restaurant in the crypt.

Southbank Centre Belvedere Rd, South Bank, SE1 ☎0844 875 0073, ⓦsouthbankcentre.co.uk; ⊖ Waterloo or Embankment. The SBC has three concert venues, none of which is exclusively used for classical music. The 3000-seat Royal Festival Hall (RFH) is a gargantuan space, tailor-made for large-scale choral and orchestral works, and home to the Philharmonia (ⓦphilharmonia .co.uk) and the London Philharmonic (ⓦlpo.co.uk). The lugubrious Queen Elizabeth Hall (QEH) is the prime location for chamber concerts, solo recitals, opera and choirs; while the Purcell Room, in the QEH building, is the most intimate venue, excellent for chamber music and recitals by up-and-coming instrumentalists and singers.

Wigmore Hall 36 Wigmore St, W1 ☎020 7935 2141, ⓦwigmore-hall.org.uk; ⊖ Bond Street or Oxford Circus. With its near-perfect acoustics, the intimate Wigmore Hall – built in 1901 as a hall for the adjacent Bechstein piano showroom – is a favourite with artists and audiences alike, so book well in advance. It's brilliant for piano recitals and chamber music, but best known for its song recitals by some of the world's greatest singers. Tickets for the Monday lunchtime concerts and Sunday mid-morning concerts cost around £12.

Wilton Music Hall Grace's Alley, off Cable St, E1 ☎020 7702 2789, ⓦwiltons.org.uk; ⊖ Tower Hill. This Victorian music hall, built in 1858, seeps history and atmosphere with its barley-sugar wrought-iron columns and peeling plaster walls. As well as theatre and comedy,

they host an intriguing programme of classical concerts, often with an avant-garde edge, and the occasional opera.

FREE CONCERTS

BBC SO Studio Concerts Delaware Rd, W9 ⓦbbc .co.uk/orchestras; ⊖ Warwick Avenue or Maida Vale. The BBC Symphony Orchestra hosts free concerts, performed by various BBC ensembles and artists, at the Maida Vale Studios. All concerts are later broadcast.

Royal Academy of Music Marylebone Rd, NW1 ☎020 7873 7373, ⓦram.ac.uk; ⊖ Regent's Park or Baker Street. During term time, there are masterclasses, free concerts and recitals either at the RAM itself or at venues around town.

Royal College of Music Prince Consort Rd, SW7 ☎020 7591 4314, ⓦrcm.ac.uk; ⊖ South Kensington. Free and fee-paying concerts and events during term time, either in the RCM or in external venues.

St Anne and St Agnes Gresham St, EC2 ☎020 7606 4986, ⓦstanneslutheranchurch.org; ⊖ St Paul's. As well as free lunchtime recitals (Mon & Fri), this Wren-designed Lutheran church has guest musicians for various services, and occasional Bach vespers.

St Giles-in-the-Fields 60 St Giles High St, WC2 ☎020 7240 2532, ⓦstgilesonline.org; ⊖ Tottenham Court Road. Free lunchtime organ recitals or chamber music (Fri) in the spring and autumn, plus evening concerts, some of which are also free.

St James Piccadilly 197 Piccadilly, W1 ☎020 7734 4511, ⓦst-james-piccadilly.org; ⊖ Piccadilly Circus. One of Sir Christopher Wren's churches, with free lunchtime piano and chamber recitals (Mon, Wed & Fri), plus fee-paying evening concerts.

St Lawrence Jewry Next Guildhall, Gresham St, EC2 ☎020 7600 9478, ⓦstlawrencejewry.org.uk; ⊖ Bank or St Paul's. There's a full schedule of free concerts in this Wren church, from piano concerts – on an instrument owned by Benjamin Britten (Mon), organ recitals (Tues) – including a series showcasing the best international young organists – and a special summer season.

St Martin-in-the-Fields Trafalgar Square, WC2 ☎020 7839 8362, ⓦstmartin-in-the-fields.org; ⊖ Charing Cross or Leicester Square. St Martin's has a fine musical pedigree, having hosted musicians including Handel and Mozart. Free lunchtime recitals (Mon, Tues & Fri) feature new talent, while fee-charging evening concerts feature acclaimed musicians, including the top-notch orchestra or chamber ensemble of the Academy of St Martin-in-the-Fields.

St Olave 8 Hart St, EC3 ☎020 7488 4318, ⓦsanctuaryinthecity.net; ⊖ Tower Hill. St Olave's is an atmospheric medieval setting – Samuel Pepys is buried here, too – for superb chamber pieces or solo recitals (Wed & Thurs lunchtimes), except in August, plus fee-paying evening concerts.

St Sepulchre-without-Newgate Holborn Viaduct and Giltspur St junction, EC1 ☎020 7248 3826, ⊕st-sepulchre.org.uk; ⊖ St Paul's. With a strong, long-held association with musicians, this "National Musicians' Church" holds regular free piano recitals, chamber and organ concerts (Wed lunchtimes and some Thurs evenings) and the occasional fee-paying evening performance.

St Stephen Walbrook 39 Walbrook, EC4 ☎020 7626 9000, ⊕ststephenwalbrook.net; ⊖ Bank. Organ recitals (Fri, 12.30pm), lunchtime concerts (Tues) and regular sung Eucharist from the professional choir (Thurs lunchtime) in one of the finest of all Wren's churches.

Temple Church Fleet St, EC4 ☎020 7353 8559, ⊕templechurch.com; ⊖ Temple. Lunchtime organ recitals (Wed), usually by leading organists, and fee-paying choral and chamber evening concerts – but not in August and September.

OPERA

Of the two main companies, the **Royal Opera House** is the place to go to see the top international stars, while **English National Opera** continues to show what can be achieved with largely home-grown talent and lively, radical productions. Other, smaller venues, continue to provide more intimate and less expensive alternatives.

OPERA COMPANIES AND VENUES

Barbican Centre Silk St, EC2 ☎020 7638 8891, ⊕barbican.org.uk; ⊖ Barbican or Moorgate. The Barbican's excellent opera rep seasons, usually employing top soloists and companies, and often supported by the resident London Symphony Orchestra, throw up interesting and offbeat works.

English National Opera Coliseum, St Martin's Lane, WC2 ☎0871 911 0200, ⊕eno.org; ⊖ Leicester Square or Charing Cross. The ENO is committed to keeping opera accessible, with operas sung in English, an adventurous repertoire (they even occasionally include musicals), modern productions and non-prohibitive pricing (£26–99). Day seats (£10–15), in the balcony, are also available to personal callers after 10am on the day of the performance; any remaining at 12.30pm are then sold on a special phone line (☎0871/472 0800). Standbys performance for students, senior citizens, under-16s and the unemployed (£15–35) go on sale three hours before the performance.

London's Little Opera House King's Head, 115 Upper St, N1 ☎020 7478 0160, ⊕kingsheadtheatre.com; ⊖ Angel or Highbury and Islington. Previously acclaimed as a pub theatre, in 2010 the *King's Head* reinvented itself as London's first new opera house in forty years. The intimate space – just 100 bench seats – now hosts an exciting fringe rep programme of new writing, experimental pieces and old favourites with a modern twist from resident company Opera Up Close. The intimate space makes a welcome change, and most tickets go for £17.50.

Opera Holland Park Holland Park, Kensington High St, W8 ☎0300 999 1000, ⊕ohp.rbkc.gov.uk; ⊖ High Street Kensington or Holland Park. Opera takes to the great outdoors in green and pleasant Holland Park (June–Aug). Standard repertoire is the order of the day, and productions range unpredictably from the inspired to the workaday. There's a canopy to cover you in case of rain. Tickets £12–63.50.

Royal Opera House Bow St, WC2 ☎020 7304 4000, ⊕roh.org.uk; ⊖ Covent Garden. The ROH is one of the world's leading opera houses and puts on lavish, high-quality operas, with slightly more experimental productions staged in the Linbury Studio Theatre. All are performed in the original language with surtitles. Most tickets are expensive (reaching as high as £900), though there is limited restricted-view seating (or standing room) from around £15, and some of the Linley Studio shows are less expensive than those in the main hall. Just 67 day seats (at various prices) go on sale from 10am on the day of a performance (not from visiting companies); these are restricted to one per person, and you need to get there before 9am for popular shows. Student standby tickets (subject to availability) can be bought for £10 online. In summer, some performances are relayed live to screens in Trafalgar Square and Canary Wharf, for free.

28

COMING TO A SCREEN NEAR YOU...

If you are hungry for high culture, but have very low funds, simply head to the pictures. An increasing number of **cinemas** throughout the capital screen live performances of the finest ballets, operas and theatrical performances – beamed from gilded venues including the Royal Opera House, the National Theatre and the Globe – for little more than the price of a movie ticket. It's an odd feeling, giving a rousing round of applause to performers who can't see or hear you, but the acoustics and HD visuals tend to be superb, and the cost can't be argued with. Check the websites of the venues (see p.420) themselves to see schedules.

DANCE

For classical ballet lovers, the **Royal Ballet** possesses a number of truly outstanding soloists, while those interested in more cutting-edge work can choose between the intimacy of **The Place** or the larger **Sadler's Wells**, both venues for the best contemporary work. London also has a good reputation for international dance festivals showcasing the work of a wide range of companies. The biggest of the annual events is the **Dance Umbrella** (ⓦ danceumbrella.co.uk), a season (Oct–Nov) of often groundbreaking new work at various venues across town. For an excellent **round-up** of all the major dance events in town, check ⓦ londondance.com.

DANCE COMPANIES AND VENUES

Barbican Centre Silk St, EC2 ☎ 020 7638 8891, ⓦ barbican.org.uk; ⊖ Barbican or Moorgate. As part of its mixed programming the Barbican regularly stages contemporary dance by top international companies. It's also used as a venue for Dance Umbrella events.

English National Ballet ☎ 020 7581 1245, ⓦ ballet .org.uk. The English National Ballet tours nationally, but also regularly performs seasons at the Coliseum, home of the ENO (see p.415), with occasional appearances at the Royal Festival Hall and the Royal Albert Hall.

Laban Creekside, SE8 ☎ 020 8691 8600, ⓦ laban .org; Cutty Sark DLR or Deptford or Greenwich train stations from Charing Cross. This funky Herzog & de Meuron building in deepest Deptford includes a 300-seat theatre. The venue showcases many leading names in contemporary dance as well as staging work by students at the Trinity Laban Conservatoire of Music and Dance.

The Place 17 Duke's Rd, WC1 ☎ 020 7121 1100, ⓦ theplace.org.uk; ⊖ Euston. The Place has a small theatre that presents the work of contemporary choreographers and student performers.

Rich Mix 35–47 Bethnal Green Rd, E1 ☎ 020 7613 7498, ⓦ richmix.org.uk; Shoreditch High Street Overground. Excellent physical theatre and dance, with an emphasis on black companies and choreographers, from this cutting-edge cultural centre in the East End.

Royal Opera House Bow St, WC2 ☎ 020 7304 4000, ⓦ roh.org.uk; ⊖ Covent Garden. Based at the Opera House, the Royal Ballet is a world-renowned classical company, whose outstanding principals include Carlos Acosta, Alina Cojocaru and Zenaida Yanowsky. Tickets for the main house are cheaper than for opera (£7–400), and there are two small performing spaces, the Linbury Studio Theatre (£8–20) and the Clore Studio (£10–15), where more experimental work can be seen. In 2011, some performances were also held at the O2 (£10–60), which may become a regular addition to the programme. Sell-outs are frequent so book early.

Sadler's Wells Theatre Rosebery Ave, EC1 ☎ 0844 412 4300, ⓦ sadlerswells.com; ⊖ Angel. Sadler's Wells hosts Britain's best contemporary dance companies, including the Rambert, and many of the finest international companies are regular visitors. The Lillian Baylis Theatre, tucked around the back, puts on smaller-scale shows, while the Peacock Theatre near Covent Garden in the West End adds some populist shows, including street dance, to the mix.

Southbank Centre Belvedere Rd, South Bank, SE1 ☎ 0844 875 0073, ⓦ southbankcentre.co.uk; ⊖ Waterloo or Embankment. The Southbank Centre's three venues all stage dance performances; the Dance Umbrella festival visits every year in the autumn and it's also the main centre for large-scale Asian dance in the capital.

28

Theatre, comedy and cinema

London has enjoyed a reputation for quality theatre since the time of Shakespeare and still provides platforms for innovation and new writing. The West End is the heart of London's "Theatreland", with Shaftesbury Avenue its most congested drag; the less mainstream, "off-West End" theatres, and the smaller, edgier places on the fringe are often more interesting. The capital's comedy scene is lively, too, from intimate neighbourhood pub nights to high-profile shows with huge audiences. As for film, London has plenty of multiscreen cinemas, along with trendy chains where you can sip wine and snuggle up on velvet sofas while watching world movies and indie classics, and an increasing number of offbeat little clubs beyond central London provide obscure and B-movie fun.

29

THEATRE

On any given night in the West End there are more people watching musicals than all other forms of theatre put together, and the trend shows no sign of abating, despite the fact that only half the shows actually make money. *Les Misérables* is the longest-running musical at the moment, on the go since 1985, closely followed by *The Phantom of the Opera*, which opened in 1986. Both are mere babies, though, compared with *The Mousetrap* by Agatha Christie, which began its West End run in 1952. For details (and tickets) for all the West End's long runners, see ⓦ albemarle-london.com. The **Royal Shakespeare Company** (ⓦ rsc.org.uk), who tour in London each year, and the **National Theatre** (ⓦ nationaltheatre. uk) often put on extremely original performances of mainstream masterpieces, while some of the most exciting work is found in what have become known as the **Off-West End** theatres, which consistently stage challenging productions. At the **Fringe** theatres, more often than not pub venues, ticket prices are lower and quality more variable.

Prices Tickets for £10 are restricted to the Fringe; the box-office average is closer to £20–30, with £50–70 the usual top price. The cheapest way to buy your ticket is to go to the box office in person; if you book over the phone or online, you will probably be charged a booking fee. It's worth looking out for special deals: cheap Monday tickets or standby tickets are often very good value, and although tickets for the durable musicals and well-reviewed plays are like gold dust, some major theatres do keep some tickets to sell on the door on the day; check the website of the venue. Students, senior citizens and the unemployed can get concessionary rates on tickets for most shows, and many theatres offer reductions on standby tickets to these groups.
Discount tickets The Society of London Theatre (ⓦ officiallondontheatre.co.uk) runs a very useful booth called "tkts" (Mon–Sat 10am–7pm, Sun 11am–4pm; ⓦ tkts.co.uk), in Leicester Square, which sells on-the-day tickets for all the West End shows at discounts of up to fifty percent, though they tend to be in the top end of the price range, are limited to four per person, and carry a service charge of £3 per ticket. Tkts also sells some advance tickets, with no booking fee, for a smaller selection of shows. Whatever you do, avoid the touts and the ticket agencies that abound in the West End – there's no guarantee that the tickets are genuine. Ticket agencies such as Ticketmaster (ⓦ ticketmaster.co.uk) can get seats for most West End shows well in advance, but can add hefty booking fees.
Festivals Look out for London's two main theatre festivals: the Mimefest (ⓦ mimefest.co.uk), a feast of puppetry, mime and physical theatre which takes place over a fortnight in January, and LIFT (ⓦ liftfestival.com), an international theatrical jamboree held in July and August.
Cinema screenings For details of live cinema screenings, when you can watch performances from the NT and other prestigious companies as they happen, for a fraction of the cost of the real thing (see p.420).

THE VENUES

What follows is a select list of West End theatres that offer a changing roster of good plays, along with the most consistent of the off-West End and fringe venues. This by no means represents the full tally of London's stages – there are plenty more West End theatres showing long-running

musicals and family-friendly mainstream entertainment, plus scores of fringe places that present work intermittently. *Time Out* provides the most comprehensive and detailed up-to-the-minute survey.

WEST END

Barbican Centre Silk St, EC2 ☎020 7638 8891, ⓦ barbican.org.uk; ⊖ Barbican or Moorgate. The Barbican's two venues – the excellently designed Barbican Theatre and the much smaller Pit – put on a wide variety of spectacles from puppetry and musicals to new drama works.
National Theatre Southbank Centre, South Bank, SE1 ☎020 7452 3000, ⓦ nationaltheatre.org.uk; ⊖ Waterloo. The NT consists of three separate theatres: the raked, 1150-seat Olivier, the proscenium Lyttelton and the experimental Cottesloe. Standards set by the late Laurence Olivier, founding artistic director, are maintained by the country's top actors and directors in a programme ranging from Greek tragedies to Broadway musicals. Tickets needn't break the bank – and on special "Travelex" performances, half the seats go for £12. Some productions sell out months in advance, but day tickets, available for the lowest-priced seats available, go on sale at 9.30am on the morning of each performance – get there by 8am for the popular shows (two tickets per person only).
Old Vic The Cut, SE1 ☎0844 871 7628, ⓦ oldvictheatre .com; ⊖ Waterloo. The venerable Old Vic, established in 1811, is a producing house under the stewardship of Oscar-winning American actor Kevin Spacey, who occasionally treads the boards himself.
Royal Court Sloane Square, SW1 ☎020 7565 5000, ⓦ royalcourttheatre.com; ⊖ Sloane Square. The Royal Court is one of the best places in London to catch radical new writing, either in the proscenium arch Theatre Downstairs, or the smaller-scale Theatre Upstairs. All tickets £10 on Monday.
Shakespeare's Globe New Globe Walk, SE1 ☎020 7401 9919, ⓦ shakespeares-globe.com; ⊖ London Bridge, Blackfriars or Southwark. This open-roofed replica Elizabethan theatre uses only natural light and the minimum of scenery, and puts on fun Shakespearean shows – along with works from the Bard's contemporaries, including Christopher Marlowe, and even some modern

works on Elizabethan themes – from April to mid-September, with seats from £15 and "Yard" tickets (standing-room only) for around a fiver.

OFF-WEST END

Almeida Almeida St, N1 ☎020 7359 4404, ⓦalmeida .co.uk; ⊖ Angel. Popular little Islington venue that premieres excellent new plays and excitingly reworked classics, and has attracted some big Hollywood names.

Battersea Arts Centre 176 Lavender Hill, SW11 ☎020 7223 2223, ⓦbac.org.uk; Clapham Junction train station from Victoria or Waterloo. The BAC is a multi-stage building, housed in an old town hall in south London, and is known for excellent cutting-edge productions, from contemporary drama and physical theatre to comedy and cabaret.

Bush Shepherd's Bush Green, W12 ☎020 8743 5050, ⓦbushtheatre.co.uk; ⊖ Shepherd's Bush. This minuscule above-pub theatre is London's most reliable venue for new writing after the Royal Court.

Donmar Warehouse 41 Earlham St, WC2 ☎0844 871 7624, ⓦdonmarwarehouse.com; ⊖ Covent Garden. A small, central performance space, noted for new writing and top-quality reappraisals of the classics.

The Gate The Prince Albert, 11 Pembridge Rd, W11 ☎020 7229 0706, ⓦgatetheatre.co.uk; ⊖ Notting Hill Gate. Seating just seventy, this small producing pub-theatre has a huge reputation for its excellent, innovative revivals of neglected international classics.

Hampstead Theatre Eton Ave, NW3 ☎020 7722 9301, ⓦhampsteadtheatre.com; ⊖ Swiss Cottage. A prestigious, modern zinc-and-glass-fronted theatre in Swiss Cottage (not in Hampstead proper) whose productions often move on to the West End. The RSC regularly perform here.

Menier Chocolate Factory 51–53 Southwark St, SE1 ☎020 7378 1713, ⓦmenierchocolatefactory.com; ⊖ London Bridge. Great name, great venue in a former Victorian factory, with a decent bar and restaurant attached; the shows are consistently good.

Open Air Theatre Regent's Park, Inner Circle, NW1 ☎0844 826 4242, ⓦopenairtheatre.org; ⊖ Baker Street. If the weather's good, there's nothing like a dose of alfresco drama. This beautiful space in Regent's Park hosts a tourist-friendly summer programme of Shakespeare, musicals, plays and concerts.

Riverside Studios Crisp Rd, W6 ☎020 8237 1111, ⓦriversidestudios.co.uk; ⊖ Hammersmith. Edgy performance and physical theatre in a converted film studio in West London.

Soho Theatre 21 Dean St, W1 ☎020 7478 0100, ⓦsohotheatre.com; ⊖ Tottenham Court Road. Great, very central theatre that specializes in new writing from around the globe, as well as regular comedy and cabaret.

Theatre Royal Stratford East Gerry Raffles Square, E15

☎020 8534 0310, ⓦstratfordeast.com; ⊖ Stratford. Beautiful Victorian theatre in the East End, where the community-pleasing shows include excellent Christmas panto.

Tricycle Theatre 269 Kilburn High Rd, NW6 ☎020 7328 1000, ⓦtricycle.co.uk; ⊖ Kilburn. One of London's most dynamic venues, showcasing a mixed bag of new plays, often aimed at the theatre's multicultural neighbourhood, and often with a sharp political focus.

Young Vic 66 The Cut, SE1 ☎020 7922 2922, ⓦyoungvic.org; ⊖ Waterloo. The Young Vic opened in 1970 as a temporary structure with a five-year lifespan – more than forty years later, it has been rebuilt from scratch and has a consistently strong contemporary programme, concentrating on the work of young directors.

FRINGE AND OCCASIONAL VENUES

Arcola Theatre 24 Ashwin St, E8 ☎020 7503 1646, ⓦarcolatheatre.com; Dalston Junction Overground. Exciting fringe theatre in an old factory opposite Dalston Junction station. They have a strong reputation for their challenging plays – classics and modern works – with shows from young, international companies. Some nights have a "Pay what you can" policy.

New End Theatre 27 New End, NW3 ☎0870 033 2733, ⓦnewendtheatre.co.uk; ⊖ Hampstead. Cosy neighbourhood venue in literary-minded Hampstead. The resident Pluto Productions company offers a reliable programme of classics and new writing.

Rich Mix 35–47 Bethnal Green Rd, E1 ☎020 7613 7498, ⓦrichmix.org.uk; Shoreditch High Street Overground. A vibrant mix of new theatre, spoken word, comedy and dance, with a strong emphasis on black and minority works from the local area and around the world.

Roundhouse Chalk Farm Rd, NW1 ☎0844 482 8008, ⓦroundhouse.org.uk; ⊖ Chalk Farm. Camden's exciting cultural venue in an old – round – engine repairs shed, puts on cutting-edge theatre, performance art, circus and cabaret, with regular shows from the RSC and Hampstead Theatre company.

Southwark Playhouse Corner of Tooley and Bermondsey Sts, SE1 ☎020 7407 0234, ⓦsouthwarkplayhouse.co.uk; ⊖ London Bridge. With two vaulted theatre spaces beneath the London Bridge railway station, this atmospheric theatre concentrates on new and young writers, reinterpreting old classics and contemporary plays.

Wilton Music Hall Grace's Alley, off Cable St, E1 ☎020 7702 2789, ⓦwiltons.org.uk; ⊖ Tower Hill. The world's oldest surviving music hall, built in 1858, is a crumbling, very atmospheric space, with barley-sugar wrought-iron columns holding up the gallery, peeling walls and a hip little bar. It's a wonderful venue for innovative theatre and comedy, as well as magic shows, cinema nights and even ping pong tournaments.

29

COMEDY

From the big-name, big-theatre, big-ticket shows, to old favourites like the Comedy Store – at the heart of the alternative comedy movement of the 1980s – or even shabby neighbourhood pubs hosting new young hopefuls, you're never too far away from a chuckle, and Soho and Camden Town in particular both have a very healthy crop of clubs and comedy nights. Full listings appear on ⓦ chortle.co.uk and in *Time Out*. Note that many venues only have gigs on Friday and Saturday nights, and that August can be a lean month, as much of London's talent heads north for the Edinburgh Fringe.

Amused Moose Soho 17 Greek St, W1 ☎ 020 7287 3727, ⓦ amusedmoose.com; ⊖ Tottenham Court Road. Top-notch stand-up in Soho, and comedy courses too. Every Sat, plus other occasional nights, and Edinburgh previews in July. Branches in Covent Garden and Chalk Farm.

Boat Show Comedy Club Tattershall Castle, Victoria Embankment, SW1 ☎ 07932 658 895, ⓦ boatshow comedy.co.uk; ⊖ Embankment. It's certainly a novel venue – on a paddlesteamer, bobbing on the Thames opposite the London Eye – and the comedy nights (Fri & Sat, and 1st Mon of the month) frequently feature big names trying out their TV material.

Camden Head 100 Camden High St, NW1 ☎ 020 7485 4019, ⓦ camdenhead.com; ⊖ Camden Town. Consistently good open mic, fringe sessions and the best headliners on the circuit, in this friendly Camden boozer.

Canal Café Theatre The Bridge House, Delamere Terrace, W2 ☎ 020 7289 6054, ⓦ canalcafetheatre .com; ⊖ Warwick Ave. Perched on the water's edge in Little Venice, this venue is good for improvisation acts and

is home to the NewsRevue team of topical gagsters.

Comedy Store 1a Oxendon St, SW1 ☎ 0844 871 7699, ⓦ thecomedystore.co.uk; ⊖ Piccadilly Circus. Widely regarded as the birthplace of alternative comedy, the Comedy Store has catapulted many a stand-up onto primetime TV. Improvisation by in-house comics on Wednesdays and Sundays, in addition to a stand-up bill; Friday and Saturday are the busiest nights, with two shows, at 7.30pm and 11pm – book ahead.

The Funny Side The George, 213 The Strand, WC2 ☎ 0844 478 0404, ⓦ thefunnyside.info; ⊖ Temple. Creative, well-run comedy club offering a reliably good roster of stand-ups (Fri & Sat), with additional clubs in Leicester Square (Wed) and the City (Thurs).

Rich Mix 35–47 Bethnal Green Rd, E1 ☎ 020 7613 7498, ⓦ richmix.org.uk; ⊖ Shoreditch High Street Overground. Cutting-edge urban comedy shows at this exciting East End arts centre, including Edinburgh hits and gigs from international artists.

CINEMA

There are an awful lot of cinemas in London, especially the **West End**. The biggest are on and around Leicester Square, including the **Empire Leicester Square** (ⓦ empirecinemas.co.uk), a former Victorian variety theatre whose 2000-seat main auditorium is one of London's largest, and the 1700-seat **Odeon Leicester Square** (ⓦ odeon.co.uk), a favourite for celeb-packed premieres. These concentrate on Hollywood crowdpleasers and new releases, but there are a few classy indie chains that show more offbeat screenings – check out the **Picturehouse** (ⓦ picturehouses.co.uk), **Curzon** (ⓦ curzoncinemas.com) and **Everyman** (ⓦ everymancinema.com) websites for locations – and a number of one-off arthouse cinemas. Many of London's more cultish **arthouse** cinemas – showing obscure and B-movies to a keen crowd of cinephiles – may have gone, but the gap has been filled somewhat in recent years by a rash of **indie film clubs**, which, usually for one night a month, colonize pub basements and back rooms all over the city. Organized by enthusiasts and often free, these offer a splendid night out with their witty double bills and themed nights, usually adding music, quizzes and all sorts of extras to the mix.

Tickets at the major West End screens cost at least £11, although afternoon shows are usually discounted. The less central multiplexes (see *Time Out* for full listings) tend to be a couple of pounds cheaper, as do independent cinemas. Concessionary rates are offered for some shows at virtually all cinemas, usually all day Monday or at other off-peak times on weekdays, and anyone with an Orange phone can make use of the half-price "Orange Wednesday" tickets.

ARTHOUSE CINEMAS

Barbican Silk St, EC2 ☎ 020 7638 8891, ⓦ barbican .org.uk; ⊖ Barbican or Moorgate. Comfy seats, three screens and a superb rota of obscure classics, silent

movies and world cinema, with excellent festivals and seasons.

BFI Southbank Belvedere Rd, South Bank, SE1 ☎ 020 7928 3232, ⓦ bfi.org.uk; ⊖ Waterloo. Exhaustive, eclectic programmes based around themed seasons, showing between seven and fourteen films daily on four screens. The BFI also runs the IMAX (☎ 020 7199 6000, ⓦ bfi.org.uk/imax), a huge glazed drum in the middle of Waterloo roundabout where the colossal screen (20m high by 26m wide) is not recommended for anyone with vertigo.

Electric 191 Portobello Rd, W11 ☎ 020 7908 9696, ⓦ the-electric.co.uk; ⊖ Notting Hill Gate or Ladbroke Grove. One of the oldest cinemas in the country (opened

MOVIES ALFRESCO

A new wave of moviewatching has swept the capital recently, taking the cinema-going experience out of dark, popcorn-scattered screening rooms and into the fresh air. Whether it's at a hip Hoxton bar or a leafy royal park, if you're willing to brave the elements (and you can always take a blanket) there's nothing like watching a movie classic with hundreds of other wide-eyed fans beneath the stars. Each year sees different events and pop-up screenings in a variety of venues – and summer is, naturally, the most popular time; the following is a list of the more established events.

Film4 Summer Screen Somerset House, Strand, WC2 ⓦsomersethouse.org.uk/film; ⊖ Covent Garden, Charing Cross or Holborn. This is the big one: for ten days or so in late July and early August, this magnificent setting (see p.138), home to the Courtauld gallery and an ice rink in winter, is a venue for classic, indie and mainstream movies, with "behind the screen" talks and events; bring your own cushion. Tickets sell out fast. From £14.50.

More London Free Festival Near Tower Bridge, SE1 ⓦmorelondon.com; ⊖ London Bridge or Tower Hill. The location – a modern mixed-use development that includes City Hall – may sound unpromising, but More London's vibrant annual festival in mid-September screens family-friendly free films – mainstream hits, guilty pleasures and a few golden oldies – in the "Scoop", a splendid, 800-seat, riverside amphitheatre.

Nomad Cinema ⓦwhereisthenomad.com. Showing classics, arthouse movies and fond old favourites, this peripatetic screen doesn't confine itself to a summer season. Year round, it might turn up anywhere – a circus tent in Mile End, under the trees in a royal park, in the elevated surrounds of the Old Royal Naval College – always offering intriguing movie "happenings". Around £12.50.

Rooftop Film Club Queen of Hoxton 1, Curtain Rd, EC2 ⓦrooftopfilmclub.com; ⊖ Liverpool Street or Old Street or Shoreditch High Street Overground. Settle down in a comfy seat, grab a cocktail and hook up to your own wireless headphones at these trendy summertime screenings – cultish blockbusters and 80s classics, mostly – in the rooftop garden of a hip pub/club/arts venue. Five nights a week June–Sept; £9.

1910), the Electric keeps much of its lovely old interior, but has added trendy leather armchairs, footstools and two-seater sofas. The programme concentrates on mainstream hits, with more offbeat offerings on Sundays.

ICA Cinema Nash House, The Mall, SW1 ☎020 7930 3647, ⓦica.org.uk; ⊖ Piccadilly Circus or Charing Cross. One of the capital's most cutting-edge programmes – offering vintage, world, documentary and underground movies on two tiny screens (no armchairs here!) in the avant-garde HQ of the Institute of Contemporary Arts.

Phoenix 52 East Finchley High Rd, N2 ☎020 8444 6789, ⓦphoenixcinema.co.uk; ⊖ East Finchley. Run by a charitable trust, this glorious Art Deco cinema, open since 1910, shows a good mix of indies and classics, with regular events including Q&A sessions and live ballet, opera and theatre screenings.

Prince Charles 7 Leicester Place, WC2 ☎020 7494 3654, ⓦprincecharlescinema.com; ⊖ Leicester Square or Piccadilly Circus. Two screens in the heart of the West End, with good prices (rep tickets start at just £5.50, new releases at £8) and a daily changing programme of newish movies, classics and cult favourites, plus participatory "singalong" romps.

Riverside Studios Crisp Rd, W6 ☎020 8237 1111, ⓦriversidestudios.co.uk; ⊖ Hammersmith. In addition to its splendid fringe theatre (see p.419), this space is worth checking out for its mini film festivals and innovative programming – including themed double bills and art movies.

Roxy 128 Borough High St, SE1 ☎020 7407 4057, ⓦroxybarandscreen.com; ⊖ Borough. Excellent, imaginative output – midnight screenings, recent indie releases, cult offerings, shorts – in a swish space with sofas, a big screen, and surroundsound. Sun–Wed only; members (£30, with various perks) can reserve a sofa or a table, otherwise it's first come-first served.

FILM CLUBS

Duke Mitchell Film Club King's Cross Social Club, 2 Britannia St, WC1 ☎020 7278 4252, ⓦfacebook.com/thedukemitchell; ⊖ King's Cross St Pancras. Quirky and obscure movies with great themed evenings – heist night, lost films night and New York night, for example – all for free. Last Wed of the month.

Filmbar Roxy Bar and Screen, 128 Borough High St, SE1 ☎020 7407 4057, ⓦfilmbar70.com; ⊖ Borough. Monthly screenings of rare grimehouse and exploitation movies, with retro ads and trailers, at the indie Roxy cinema (see above). £3.

Jameson Cult Film Club ⓦjamesoncultfilmclub.com. It's location, location, location when it comes to these cult

29

FILM FESTIVALS

Birds Eye View Film Festival ⓦ birds-eye-view .co.uk. Splendid ten-day film festival, held at various venues in March, celebrating the work of women directors – and pioneers in all areas of moviemaking – from around the world. Programming is creative – celebrating women in horror, for example, or screening silent movies with accompaniment from cutting-edge female musicians.

East End Film Festival ⓦ eastendfilmfestival .com. The end of April sees a packed six days of features and shorts from around the world, some of them free, peaking with a "Movie May Day" which uses a host of quirky East End venues for exciting, immersive screenings.

London Film Festival ⓦ lff.org.uk. One of the major players on the world movie festival circuit, the LFF is held over a fortnight in late October, with films shown across half a dozen West End cinemas. Many sell out soon after publication of the programme in early Sept.

London International Animation Festival ⓦ liaf.org.uk. Over 250 animated shorts, features, documentaries and retrospectives from all over the world are shown during this ten-day festival, held at various venues in late summer.

Portobello Film Festival ⓦ portobellofilmfestival .com. Fortnight-long free film festival, in September, showing innovative works by British filmmakers in cinemas, clubs and bars in West London.

Raindance Festival ⓦ raindance.co.uk. Major independent film festival, held over two weeks in late September/early October, showing new work by first-time directors from all over the globe.

movie screenings, held in atmospheric and unusual venues – throughout the UK, but most often in London – including underground car parks and churches. All are free, but you need to be a member (sign up for free online).

Sun and Doves Film Nights 61 Coldharbour Lane, SE5 ☏ 020 7733 1525, ⓦ sunanddoves.co.uk/film; ⊖ Brixton. Classic and cult movies are screened for free every Tuesday at this hip, friendly community-minded pub.

Shops and markets

From the *folie de grandeur* that is Harrods to the scruffy street markets of the
East End, London is a shopper's playground – whether you want to spend
enormous amounts of money, loading yourself up with posh bags of designer
gear, or to rifle around vintage markets seeking out quirky treasures for a few
quid. As befits a city of villages, London's shopping districts all have their own
flavour, and many of them are known for their specialities – Oxford Street's
the place to head for chains and department stores; Jermyn Street for posh
gentlemen's outfitters; Charing Cross Road for used books; Brick Lane for
vintage, for example. In the sections that follow, we've listed shops according
to what they sell, rather than by area, and have erred away from chain stores
unless they display some distinctive – and distinctively British – style.

ESSENTIALS

Sales The cheapest time to shop in London is during one of the two big annual sale seasons, centred on January and July, when prices are routinely slashed by anything between twenty and seventy percent. The best place to find details of other discount events is in *Time Out* magazine (ⓦ timeout.com).

Cash and cards Some stores, notably Selfridges and Harrods, will take payment in euros, although this is still quite rare. Market stalls tend to take cash only. Always keep receipts: whatever the shop may tell you, the law allows a full refund or replacement on purchases which turn out to be faulty. There's no such legal protection if you just decide you don't like something, but most retailers will offer a credit note.

Tax Finally, overseas (non-EU) visitors can sometimes claim back the value-added tax (VAT) that applies to most goods sold in British shops, although you will need to spend well over £100 for this to be worthwhile. Check ⓦ hmrc.gov.uk/vat/sectors/consumers/overseas-visitors .htm for the latest details.

Opening hours We've given the days and hours for each shop reviewed below, but as a rough rule of thumb central London shops open from Monday to Saturday from 10am to 6pm. Some of the bigger stores stay open later, and extend their hours on Thursdays and in the weeks leading up to Christmas, and many also open on Sunday, from around noon to 5pm or 6pm.

CLOTHES AND SHOES

The listings below concentrate on the home-grown and local rather than the ubiquitous international names, but if it's global **designer wear** you're after, bear in mind that nearly all the department stores stock lines from major and up-and-coming names. For designer-style fashion at lower prices, try the more upmarket high-street **chains** such as Jigsaw and Whistles. Mango, Zara, Monsoon, H&M, Warehouse and Topshop are a good bet for cheaper versions of the same, while Primark is able to offer bargain-basement prices. For street, club, secondhand and vintage gear, also try London's **markets** (see p.433).

WHERE TO GO

In the centre of town, **Oxford Street** is the city's hectic chain-store heartland and, together with **Regent Street**, offers pretty much every mainstream clothing label you could wish for. Just off Oxford Street expensive designer outlets clutter **St Christopher's Place** and **South Molton Street**, with even pricier designers and jewellers lining chic **Bond Street**. To the north, **Marylebone High Street** offers a pretty village oasis in the middle of town – a laidback place to get all your labels, treats and gifts away from the bustle.

Tottenham Court Road is the place for electrical goods, sportswear and, in its northern section, furniture and design shops, while **New Oxford Street** has a few new and used camera equipment shops. **Charing Cross Road** is the centre of London's book trade, both new and secondhand. At its northern end, particularly on **Denmark Street** (once the heart of Britain's music industry), music shops sell everything from instruments to sound equipment and sheet music. On the other side of Charing Cross Road, stretching down to Piccadilly, **Soho** offers an offbeat mix of sex shops, specialist record stores and fabric retailers, while the streets surrounding **Covent Garden** yield art and design, mainstream fashion, designer wear and camping gear; **Neal Street** is the place to go to indulge a shoe-shopping habit.

Just off Piccadilly, **St James's** is the domain of the quintessential English gentleman, with the shops of **Jermyn Street** in particular dedicated to his grooming. Stultifyingly swanky **Knightsbridge**, further west, is home to Harrods and the big-name fashion stores of **Sloane Street** and **Brompton Road**. On the South Bank, east of the National Theatre, you'll find the appealing arts and crafts stores of **Gabriel's Wharf**. Less well known, and just a stone's throw from the bustle of Waterloo, **Lower Marsh** harbours one-off shops and studios on either side of the daily local street market.

Hampstead, in a luxurious and leafy world of its own to the north of the centre, is a great place to spend an afternoon browsing upmarket fashion stores, posh delis and patisseries, antiquarian booksellers and tasteful arts and crafts. **Greenwich**, south of the river, has an eclectic range of shops and markets, while **Richmond**, out to the west, has the mainstream staples and one-off boutiques in a swanky riverside setting. For an edgier experience, head for the east, where independent stores and markets in **Brick Lane**, **Shoreditch** and **Spitalfields** specialize in quirky one-offs for hip young things. Other popular market areas, like **Camden**, **Greenwich** and **Portobello Road**, are good for small independent stores selling offbeat gear.

DESIGNER FASHION

b Store 24A Savile Row, W1 ☎020 7734 6846, ⓦbstorelondon.com; ⊖ Oxford Circus; map, p.78. London label whose classic English basics-with-an-edge, for men and women, have, over the last decade, become fashionista must-haves. Mon–Fri 10am–6pm.

Browns 24–27 South Molton St, W1 ☎020 7514 0016, ⓦbrownsfashion.com; ⊖ Bond Street; map p.78. London's biggest range of designer wear, handpicked with impeccable taste from all the major labels, including international names and hip young things. This is the main store, but they have spread all along South Molton Street: Browns Focus (38–39 South Molton St, W1 ☎020 7514 0063) has a slightly more avant-garde bent, Browns Menswear is for the gents (23 South Molton St, W1 ☎020 7514 0038) and Browns Labels for Less (50 South Molton St, W1 ☎020 7514 0052) offers discounts. All Mon–Sat 10am–6.30pm, Thurs 10am–7pm.

Dover Street Market 17–18 Dover St, W1 ☎020 7518 0680, ⓦdoverstreetmarket.com; ⊖ Green Park; map p.78. Uber-fierce six-floor megastore, showcasing directional designers such as Comme des Garçons, Hussein Chalayan and Azzedine Alaïa. Mon–Wed 11am–6.30pm, Thurs–Sat 11am–7pm.

Kokon to Zai 86 Golborne Rd, W10 ☎020 8960 3736, ⓦkokontozai.co.uk; ⊖ Ladbroke Grove or Westbourne Park; map p.274. Fashion forward pieces, many of them from graduates from the nearby Saint Martin's Art School. You'll find anything from Marjan Pejoski's wild jeux d'esprits to the in-house line of clubwear, KTZ, beloved by London's funkier young celebs and musos. There's a second branch at 57 Greek St, W1 (☎020 7434 1316). Mon–Sat 10am–6pm.

Paul Smith Westbourne House, 122 Kensington Park Rd, W11 ☎020 7727 3553; ⓦpaulsmith.co.uk; ⊖ Notting Hill Gate or Ladbroke Grove; map p.274. With branches throughout London, Paul Smith's Notting Hill shop-in-a-house, and his cosily contemporary Covent Garden store (40–44 Floral St, ☎020 7379 7133; ⊖ Covent Garden; map p.132) are particularly worth a visit: they're ever so English in Smith's quirky way, and sell the range of his well-tailored and whimsical clothes and accessories for men, women and children. The Paul Smith Sale Shop (23 Avery Row, W1 ☎020 7493 1287; ⊖ Bond Street; map p.78) offers good discounts (minimum 50 percent) on the menswear line. Notting Hill: Mon–Fri 10am–6pm, Sat 10am–6.30pm. Floral St: Mon–Wed 10.30am–6.30pm, Thurs & Fri 10.30am–7pm, Sat 10am–7pm, Sun 12.30–5.30pm. Sale shop: Mon–Wed, Fri & Sat 10.30am–6.30pm, Thurs 10.30am–7pm, Sun 1–5.30pm.

Precious 16 Artillery Passage, E1 ☎020 7377 6668, ⓦprecious-london.com; ⊖ Liverpool Street; map p.192. An elegant little store tucked away in a narrow street near Spitalfields. Luxury designer gear – from giants like Diane Von Furstenberg and McQueen, as well as newer names – including accessories. Mon–Fri 11am–6.30pm, Sat 11am–5pm.

Vivienne Westwood 44 Conduit St, W1 ☎020 7439 1109, ⓦviviennewestwood.co.uk; ⊖ Oxford Circus; map p.78. Revered by the international fashion pack, this quintessentially English maverick is going strong. Punks-at-heart with money to burn should make for the historic World's End shop (430 King's Rd, SW10 ☎020 7352 6551, ⓦworldendshop.co.uk; ⊖ Sloane Square; map p.265). Mon–Wed, Fri & Sat 10am–6pm, Thurs 10am–7pm, Sun noon–5pm.

BUDGET AND MID-RANGE FASHION

Anthropologie 158 Regent St, W1 ☎020 7529 9800, ⓦanthropologie.co.uk; ⊖ Piccadilly Circus; map p.78. Dreamy women's clothes and accessories, with some fabulous, witty homeware – it's rather like shopping in a magazine lifestyle shoot, and they promise to make women feel "beautiful, hopeful and connected". Also at 131–141 King's Rd, SW3 (☎020 7349 3110; map p.265). Regent Street: Mon–Wed, Fri & Sat 10am–7pm, Thurs 10am–8pm, Sun noon–6pm. King's Road: Mon–Sat 10am–7pm, Sun noon–6pm.

The Laden Showroom 103 Brick Lane, E1 ☎020 7247 2431, ⓦladen.co.uk; ⊖ Aldgate East or Shoreditch High Street Overground; map p.192. Beloved of the hipper London celebs, the showroom showcases loads of independent designers, and is great for exuberant dressers on a budget. Mon–Fri 11am–6.30pm, Sat 11am–7pm, Sun 10.30am–6pm.

New Look 203–207 Oxford St, W1 ☎020 7851 7360, ⓦnewlook.com; ⊖ Oxford Circus; map p.78. One of the West End's most reliable go-tos for cheap-and-cheerful, pile 'em high catwalk-inspired garments. This is the flagship branch; there are dozens more all over the city (and country). Mon–Fri 8am–9pm, Sat 9am–9pm, Sun noon–6pm.

Oliver Bonas 23 Kensington Park Rd, W11 ☎020 7727 4932, ⓦoliverbonas.com; ⊖ Ladbroke Grove; map p.274. Notting Hill branch of this very pretty store, which has branches in most of the more villagey London neighbourhoods, all selling vibrant, feminine clothing at reasonable prices, along with bright homewares and offbeat accessories. Mon–Fri 10am–6.30pm, Sat 10am–6pm, Sun 11am–5pm.

Topshop 214 Oxford St, W1 ☎0844 848 7487, ⓦtopshop.co.uk or topman.co.uk; ⊖ Oxford Circus; map p.78. A big hit with both celebs and mere mortals, Topshop's flagship store is the place to go for this season's must-haves – with a limited edition section and maternity gear – at a snip of the designer prices. Mon–Wed, Fri & Sat 9am–9pm, Thurs 9am–10pm, Sun 11.30am–6pm.

30

DEPARTMENT STORES

Although all London's **department stores** offer a huge range of high-quality goods under one roof, most specialize in fashion and food. Many are worth visiting just to admire the scale, architecture and interior design, and the majority have cafés or restaurants.

Fortnum & Mason 181 Piccadilly, W1 ✆ 020 7734 8040, ⓦ fortnumandmason.com; ⊖ Green Park or Piccadilly Circus; map p.78. A beautiful and eccentric 300-year-old store with heavenly murals, cherubs, chandeliers and fountains as a backdrop to its perfectly English offerings. Justly famous for its fabulous, pricey food, it also specializes in the best and most upmarket designer clothes, furniture, luggage and stationery. Mon–Sat 10am–8pm, Sun noon–6pm.

Harrods 87–135 Brompton Rd, Knightsbridge, SW1 ✆ 020 7730 1234, ⓦ harrods.com; ⊖ Knightsbridge; map p.250. An enduring landmark of quirks and pretensions – don't wear shorts, a sleeveless T-shirt or a backpack, or you may fall foul of the draconian dress code. Harrods has everything, but is most notable for its Art Nouveau tiled food hall, the huge toy department and its range of designer labels. Mon–Sat 10am–8pm, Sun noon–6pm.

Harvey Nichols 109–125 Knightsbridge, SW1 ✆ 020 7235 5000, ⓦ harveynichols.com; ⊖ Knightsbridge; map p.250. Absolutely fabulous, sweetie, "Harvey Nicks" has all the latest designer collections and shop assistants who look like models. The gorgeous cosmetics department is frequented by A- and Z-listers alike, while the fifth-floor food hall offers frivolous goodies at high prices. Mon–Sat 10am–8pm, Sun noon–6pm.

John Lewis 300 Oxford St, W1 ✆ 020 7629 7711, ⓦ johnlewis.co.uk; ⊖ Oxford Circus; map p.78. Famous for being "never knowingly undersold", this

reliable, much loved and trusted institution can't be beaten for basics. Every kind of button, stocking, pen and rug can be found here, along with reasonably priced and well-made clothes, furniture and household goods. Mon–Sat 9.30am–8pm, Sun noon–6pm.

★ **Liberty** 210–220 Regent St, W1 ✆ 020 7734 1234, ⓦ liberty.co.uk; ⊖ Oxford Circus; map p.78. A fabulous emporium of luxury, this exquisite store, with its mock-Tudor exterior, is most famous for its fabrics, design and accessories, but also has an excellent reputation for both mainstream and high fashion. The perfume, cosmetics, gift and household departments are recommended, too. Mon–Sat 10am–9pm, Sun noon–6pm.

Marks & Spencer 458 Oxford St, W1 ✆ 020 7935 7954, ⓦ marksandspencer.com; ⊖ Marble Arch; map p.78. London's largest branch of this British institution offers a huge range of own-brand clothes, food, homeware and furnishings. The underwear is essential, the ready-meals good value, and the clothes well made and reliable. Mon–Fri 9am–9pm, Sat 9am–8pm, Sun noon–6pm.

★ **Selfridges** 400 Oxford St, W1 ✆ 0800 123 400 ⓦ selfridges.com; ⊖ Bond Street; map p.78. This huge, airy palace of clothes, food and furnishings was London's first great department store and remains its best. The vast mens- and womenswear departments offer mainstream designers and casual lines alongside hipper, younger names and labels. The food hall is superb, too. Mon–Sat 9.30am–9pm, Sun noon–6pm.

VINTAGE, RETRO AND SECONDHAND

Absolute Vintage 15 Hanbury St, E1 ✆ 020 7247 3883, ⓦ absolutevintage.co.uk; ⊖ Liverpool Street or Aldgate East; map p.100. A Spitalfields treasure trove of 1920s to 1980s clobber, with one of the biggest collections of vintage shoes and bags in the UK. There's a branch in Soho (79 Berwick St, W1; map p.192). Spitalfields: daily 11am–7pm. Soho: Mon–Sat 10am–7pm, Sun noon–6pm.

★ **Annie's Vintage Costume & Textiles** 12 Camden Passage, N1 ✆ 020 7359 0796, ⓦ anniesvintageclothing .co.uk; ⊖ Angel; map p.284. This well-stocked, pricey shop, draped in shimmering fabrics and specializing in fabulous 1920s and 1930s glamour – from sequinned party dresses and embroidered Chinese jackets to vintage petticoats and nighties – is a firm favourite with stylists and movie production artists. Daily 11am–6pm.

★ **Beyond Retro** 110–112 Cheshire St, E2 ✆ 020 7613 3636, ⓦ beyondretro.com; ⊖ Liverpool St or Shoreditch High Street Overground; map p.192. Cavernous warehouse of twentieth-century classics, with thousands of well-priced goodies including vintage jeans, 1950s frocks, battered cowboy boots, punk gear and 1920s evening gowns. Sister store Beyond Retro Soho, 58 Great Marlborough St, glams it up a bit with a boudoir vibe (✆ 020 7434 1406; ⊖ Oxford Circus; map p.97). Cheshire St: Mon–Wed & Fri 10am–7pm, Thurs 10am–8pm, Sun 10am–6pm. Soho: Mon–Wed 10.30am–7.30pm, Thurs & Fri 10.30am–8.30pm, Sat 10.30an –7.30pm, Sun noon–6pm.

Blondie 114–118 Commercial St, E1 ✆ 020 7247 0050, ⓦ absolutevintage.co.uk; ⊖ Liverpool Street; map p.192. Sister store to Absolutely Vintage (see opposite), and just around the corner, this is a slightly more glamorous

CLOCKWISE FROM TOP HARRODS FOODHALL (P.426); AGENT PROVOCATEUR (P.428); PORTOBELLO ROAD (P.434) >

30

outfit filled with pre-loved designer gear. Daily 11am–7pm.

The Emporium 330–332 Creek Rd, SE10 ☎020 8305 1670; Cutty Sark DLR or Greenwich train station from Charing Cross; map p.315. Swanky retro store specializing in 1940s to 1960s clothes for men and women, and featuring kitsch and well-preserved bras, stockings, compacts and cigarette-holders. Wed–Sun 10.30am–6pm.

The Loft 35 Monmouth St, WC2 ☎020 7240 3807, ⓦthe-loft.co.uk; ⊖ Covent Garden; map p.132. A huge array of used designer clothes for men and women. Many are sourced from film shoots or the catwalk, so are in good nick. Labels include Jimmy Choo, Chanel and Alexander McQueen. Mon–Sat 11am–6pm, Sun 12.30–4.30pm.

Modern Age Vintage Clothing 65 Chalk Farm Rd, NW1 ☎020 7482 3787, ⓦmodern-age.co.uk; ⊖ Chalk Farm; map p.284. Splendid clobber (particularly strong on menswear) for lovers of 1940s and 1950s American-style gear, along with some good pieces from the 1960s, and their own-line reproductions of classic styles. Daily 11am–6pm.

Rokit 101 & 107 Brick Lane, E1 ☎020 7375 3864 & 020 7247 3777, ⓦrokit.co.uk; ⊖ Aldgate East or Shoreditch High Street Overground; map p.192. Quintessential Brick Lane retro, nicely presented – you'll find sparkly knits, cocktail dresses, petticoat skirts and funky rollerskates, plus a host of goodies for the boys. Also at 225 Camden High St, NW1 (☎020 7267 3046; ⊖ Camden Town) and 42 Shelton St, WC2 (☎020 7836 6547; ⊖ Covent Garden). Mon–Fri 11am–7pm, Sat & Sun 10am–7pm.

LINGERIE

Agent Provocateur 6 Broadwick St, W1 ☎020 7439 0229, ⓦagentprovocateur.com; ⊖ Oxford Circus or Tottenham Court Road; map p.100. Agent Provocateur led the way when it came to playful, glamorous undies in a shamelessly sexy setting. And they've branched out – from fringed bikinis and satin eyemasks to fluffy mules with marabou trim, there's something to appeal to the diva in every girl. Other branches throughout London. Mon–Wed, Fri & Sat 11am–7pm, Thurs 11am–8pm, Sun noon–5pm.

Coco de Mer 23 Monmouth St, WC2 ☎020 7836 8882, ⓦcoco-de-mer.co.uk; ⊖ Covent Garden; map p.132. Upmarket and stylish, this sex shop for women has an inviting boudoir feel, and Ann Summers it most certainly isn't. The lingerie ranges from floaty to filthy minded, but is always in the best possible taste. Pick up a feather tickler while you're here. Another branch at 108 Draycott Ave, SW3 (☎020 7584 7615, ⊖ South Kensington; map p.250; Mon–Sat 11am–7pm, Sun noon–6pm). Mon–Wed, Fri & Sat 11am–7pm, Thurs 11am–8pm, Sun noon–6pm.

Rigby & Peller 13 Kings Rd, SW3 ☎0845 076 5545, ⓦrigbyandpeller.com; ⊖ Sloane Square; map p.265. Corsetières to HM the Queen, if that can be counted as a recommendation, this old-fashioned store stocks a wide range of beautiful lingerie and swimwear, including designer names and its own range, for all shapes and sizes. The personal fitting service is deemed to be London's best. This is the flagship; there are branches throughout London. Mon, Tues & Thurs–Sat 10am–7pm, Wed 10am–8pm, Sun noon–6pm.

SHOES

Camper 39 Floral St, WC2 ☎020 7379 8678, ⓦcamper.es; ⊖ Covent Garden; map p.132. A Spanish store selling well-made, colourful and quirky shoes, many of which have different designs for the left and right feet. Mon–Wed, Fri & Sat 11am–7pm, Thurs 11am–8pm, Sun noon–6pm.

Georgina Goodman 44 Old Bond St, W1 ☎020 7493 7673, ⓦgeorginagoodman.com; ⊖ Green Park; map p.78. Racy and eccentric women's shoes in a splash of colours, materials and styles – all trend-setting and covetable. Mon–Sat 10am–6pm, Thurs 10am–7pm.

Manolo Blahnik 49–51 Old Church St, SW3 ☎020 7352 8622, ⓦmanoloblahnik.com; ⊖ Sloane Square; map p.265. This secluded, exclusive store on a leafy street off the King's Rd is perfect for fantasy window-shopping, with the slender footwear worshipped by *Sex and the City*'s Carrie dramatically lit and theatrically framed. Mon–Fri 10am–5.30pm, Sat 10.30am–5pm.

Natural Shoe Store 13 Neal St, WC2 ☎020 7836 5254, ⓦthenaturalshoestore.com; ⊖ Covent Garden; map p.132. Worthy, socially responsible and ecologically sound shoes – stylish, comfortable and sometimes strange, with a great selection of Birkenstocks. Good value, but not cheap. Other branches in London. Mon–Wed & Sat 10am–7pm, Thurs & Fri 10am–8pm, Sun noon–6pm.

★**Terra Plana** 64 Neal St, WC2 ☎020 7379 5959, ⓦterraplana.com; ⊖ Covent Garden; map p.132. A brilliant option for ecofriendly shoe fetishists, Terra Plana make exuberant use of recycled materials and hi-tech invention in their bright, funky styles. Each shoe comes with its own eco-matrix rating its environmentally friendly components. Also 124 Bermondsey St, SE1 ☎020 7407 3758; map p.224 (Thurs–Sat 10.30am–6.30pm), plus other branches in Kensington and Spitalfields. Mon–Sat 10.30am–7pm, Sun noon–6pm.

★ **Tracey Neuls** 29 Marylebone Lane, W1 ☎020 7935 0039, ⓦtn29.com; ⊖ Bond Street; map p.89. Quirkily presented and lovingly crafted, Tracey Neuls' sculptural shoes are playful, comfortable and quite inspired, with genius innovations (heels that look higher than they are) and witty details that make you smile. Mon–Fri 11am–6.30pm, Sat & Sun noon–5pm.

BOOKS

While the remaining big-name chain bookstores struggle to stay afloat, London is blessed with a good number of local, independent and specialist bookshops. Charing Cross Road and Bloomsbury are the two main centres for used bookstores.

GENERAL INTEREST AND CHAINS

Blackwell's 100 Charing Cross Rd, WC2 ☎020 7292 5100, ⊛bookshop.blackwell.co.uk; ⊖ Tottenham Court Road or Leicester Square; map p.100. The London flagship of Oxford's best academic bookshop is bigger than it looks and has a much wider range than you might expect. Its academic stock is, unsurprisingly, excellent, but so too is its range of travel and fiction titles. If you can't find what you want, check their Espresso Book Machine, which takes just minutes to print and bind a book on demand from a list of hundreds of thousands of titles. Mon–Sat 9.30am–8pm, Sun noon–6pm.

Foyles 113–119 Charing Cross Rd, WC2 ☎020 7437 5660, ⊛foyles.co.uk; ⊖ Tottenham Court Road; map p.100. Long-established, huge and famous London bookshop with a big antiquarian section and Ray's Jazz Shop selling CDs. Other branches include a riverside store outside the Royal Festival Hall on the South Bank (☎020 7440 3212; ⊖ Waterloo; map p.216). Charing Cross: Mon–Sat 9.30am–9pm, Sun noon–6pm. South Bank: daily 10am–10pm.

Hatchards 187 Piccadilly, W1 ☎020 7439 9921, ⊛hatchards.co.uk; ⊖ Piccadilly Circus; map p.78. A little overshadowed by the colossal Waterstone's down the road, and actually part of the Waterstone's group, the venerable Hatchards holds its own when it comes to quality fiction, biography, history and travel. The regal interiors are all you'd expect of a bookseller by appointment to HM the Queen. Mon–Sat 9.30am–7pm, Sun noon–6pm.

Waterstone's 203–206 Piccadilly, W1 ☎020 7851 2400, ⊛waterstones.co.uk; ⊖ Piccadilly Circus; map p.78. This flagship bookstore – Europe's largest – occupies the former Simpson's department store building and boasts a café, bar, gallery and events rooms as well five floors of books. Mon–Sat 9am–10pm, Sun 11.30am–6pm.

INDEPENDENT AND SPECIALIST

Arthur Probsthain 41 Great Russell St, WC1 ☎020 7636 1096, ⊛apandtea.co.uk; ⊖ Tottenham Court Road; map p.120. With another branch in the nearby School of Oriental and African Studies, this impressive old store specializes in books on the arts and cultures of Africa and The Middle East, with a small art gallery and a sweet tearoom downstairs. Mon–Fri 9.30am–5.30pm, Sat noon–4pm.

Bookmarks 1 Bloomsbury St, WC1 ☎020 7637 1848, ⊛bookmarks.uk.com; ⊖ Tottenham Court Road; map p.120. Leftist and radical fare in the heart of Bloomsbury, with a wide range of political biography, history, theory and assorted political ephemera. Mon noon–7pm, Tues–Fri 10am–7pm, Sat 11am–7pm.

Books for Cooks 4 Blenheim Crescent, W11 ☎020 7221 1992, ⊛booksforcooks.com; ⊖ Ladbroke Grove; map p.274. Anything and everything to do with food at this wonderful new and used bookshop, which also has a tiny café and cookery classes. Tues–Sat 10am–6pm.

★ **Daunt Books** 83 Marylebone High St, W1 ☎020 7224 2295, ⊛dauntbooks.co.uk; ⊖ Bond Street or Baker Street; map p.89. Wide and inspirational range of travel literature as well as the usual guidebooks, presented by expert staff in the beautiful, galleried interior of this famous Edwardian shop. Other branches. Mon–Sat 9am–7.30pm, Sun 11am–6pm.

Gay's the Word 66 Marchmont St, WC1 ☎020 7278 7654, ⊛freespace.virgin.net/gays.theword; ⊖ Russell Square; map p.120. Venerable community bookshop, famed for the weekly lesbian discussion groups and readings, and offering an extensive collection of lesbian and gay classics, pulps, contemporary fiction and nonfiction, plus cards and calendars. Mon–Sat 10am–6.30pm, Sun 2–6pm.

Gosh! 39 Great Russell St, WC1 ☎020 7636 1011, ⊛goshlondon.com; ⊖ Tottenham Court Rd; map p.120. All kinds of comics for the casually curious to the serious collector, with gorgeous vintage items, Manga, small-press oddities and superhero standards. Mon–Wed, Sat & Sun 10am–6pm, Thurs & Fri 10am–7pm.

Housmans 5 Caledonian Rd, N1 ☎020 7837 4473, ⊛housmans.com; King's Cross; map p.120. Dilapidated and friendly radical book store established in 1945, with a wide variety of titles on socialism, anarchism and peace studies, gender studies, black interest and human rights. Mon–Fri 10am–6.30pm, Sun noon–6pm.

ICA Bookshop The Mall, SW1 ☎020 7766 1452, ⊛ica .org.uk; ⊖ Piccadilly Circus or Charing Cross; map p.66. Tiny, artsy store, with a strong style bent and lots of funky magazines, postcards and book imports. Wed–Fri noon–9.30pm, Sat noon–10pm, Sun noon–8.30pm.

John Sandoe 10 Blacklands Terrace, SW3 ☎020 7589 9473, ⊛johnsandoe.com; ⊖ Sloane Square; map p.265. One of London's finest literary bookshops, with a personally selected range of titles spread across three floors of an eighteenth-century building; whether you're after classic genre fiction or obscure tomes on psychology, this is the place to come. Mon–Sat 9.30am–5.30pm, Wed 9.30am–7.30pm, Sun noon–6pm.

★ **London Review Bookshop** 14 Bury Place, WC1 ☎020 7269 9030, ⊛lrbshop.co.uk; ⊖ Tottenham Court Rd; map p.120. All the books reviewed in the august literary journal and many, many more in this superb, tranquil Bloomsbury bookstore. Particularly strong on literary fiction,

30

poetry, history, politics and current affairs, it hosts regular readings and events and has a nice little coffee and cake shop. Mon–Sat 10am–6.30pm, Sun noon–6pm.

★ **Persephone Books** 59 Lamb's Conduit St, WC1 ☎020 7242 9292, ⓦpersephonebooks.co.uk; ⊖ Russell Square or Holborn; map p.120. Lovely bookshop offspring of a publishing house that specializes in neglected twentieth-century writing by women. The books are beautifully produced, all with endpapers in a textile design from the relevant period. Mon–Fri 10am–6pm, Sat noon–5pm.

School of Life 70 Marchmont St, WC1 ☎020 7833 1010, ⓦtheschooloflife.com; ⊖ Russell Square; map p.120. A bijou little store, part of the ingenious School of Life concept, which aims to offer "good ideas for everyday living" – relationships, work, play, politics, philosophy – with its books, short courses, meals, "sermons" and weekends. The shop sells notebooks and gifts as well as books, while its "bibliotherapy" service can design you a bespoke reading list on any subject or theme. Mon–Fri noon–6pm.

Stanford's Map and Travel Bookshop 12–14 Long Acre, WC2 ☎020 7836 1321, ⓦstanfords.co.uk; ⊖ Covent Garden; map p.132. The world's largest specialist travel bookshop, selling pretty much any map of anywhere, plus a huge range of books, guides, literature, travel accessories and gifts. There's a branch of the outdoor outfitters Craghoppers on site, plus a café. Mon, Wed & Thurs 9am–8pm, Tues 9.30am–8pm, Fri 9am–7.30pm, Sat 10am–8pm, Sun noon–6pm.

FOOD AND DRINK

As you'd expect of a city that has some of the best restaurants in the world, London offers great shopping for even the most discerning of food buffs. In the centre of town, **Soho** and **Covent Garden**, in particular, are a gourmand's delight: the former good for Chinese supermarkets and Italian delicatessens, the latter harbouring health-conscious **Neal's Yard**. Numerous **supermarkets** line the high streets of nearly every residential area with the two biggest, Tesco and Sainsbury's, also making forays into the city centre; with late (and even 24hr) opening hours, all offer a good range of groceries and fresh foods and inexpensive lunch-on-the-go options. **Marks & Spencer** is excellent for fresh foods and quality ready-meals, as are the major department-store food halls (see box, p.426), while **specialist stores** and the many local **food markets** – Borough Market is currently the best in town, if expensive – offer a more atmospheric shopping experience.

The specialist **beer, wine and spirits** outlets listed are the pick of central London's numerous retailers, but you'll also find ever-improving ranges in the main supermarkets. Though **licensing laws** don't specify that outlets have to close between 3pm and 7pm on Sundays, some – usually local, family-run places – do.

BAKERIES, PATISSERIES AND CONFECTIONERY

Charbonnel et Walker 1 Royal Arcade, W1 ☎020 7491 0939, ⓦcharbonnel.co.uk; ⊖ Green Park; map p.78. It might sound French, but this is a very English affair from 1875, offering beautifully presented chocolates, truffles and peppermint creams, with jars of indulgent chocolate sauce, pretty gift boxes and hampers. Mon–Sat 10am–6pm.

Konditor & Cook 22 Cornwall Rd, SE1 ☎020 7261 0456, ⓦkonditorandcook.com; ⊖ Waterloo; map p.216. A cut above your average bakery, Konditor & Cook (with six branches) make the most wonderful cakes, cupcakes, meringues and biscuits. Mon–Fri 7.30am–6.30pm, Sat 8.30am–3pm.

Treacle 110 Columbia Rd, E2 ☎020 7729 0538, ⓦtreacleworld.com; ⊖ Bethnal Green; map p.192. Avoiding the supermodel smugness that came with much of the cupcake craze, this cute little tearoom in the heart of the flower market keeps things real, celebrating British baking with scrumptious fairy cakes, Victoria sponges and fruit loaves, with racks of nostalgic crockery and cake stands to boot. Sun 9.30am–3.30pm.

TOP 5 ENGLISH CLASSICS
Berry Bros & Rudd See p.432
Hatchards See p.429
Liberty See p.426
Paxton & Whitfield See opposite
Vivienne Westwood See p.425

SECONDHAND AND ANTIQUARIAN

Any Amount of Books 56 Charing Cross Rd, WC2 ☎020 7836 3697, ⓦanyamountofbooks.com; ⊖ Leicester Square; map p.100. Wonderful, sprawling secondhand bookshop stocking everything from obscure fifty-pence bargains to rare and expensive first editions. Especially strong on fiction, the arts and literary biography. Daily 10.30am–9.30pm.

Quinto 72 Charing Cross Rd, WC2 ☎0207/379 7669, ⓦquintobookshop.co.uk; ⊖ Leicester Square; map p.100. Another Charing Cross Rd treasure, this secondhand bookshop has a huge choice from battered paperbacks to precious first editions, and regularly refreshes its stock. Mon–Sat 9am–9pm, Sun noon–8pm.

South Bank Book Market Under Waterloo Bridge on the South Bank, SE1; ⊖ Waterloo or Embankment; map p.216. A book market by the Thames, opposite the BFI Southbank, offering everything from current and pulp fiction to obscure textbooks and modern European poetry – most of it reasonably priced, although rarely a complete bargain. Daily early morning till late, rain or shine.

DELI DELIGHTS AND CAKES TO GO

A number of places in our Cafés and restaurants chapter offer takeaway deli food for posh picnics. Among them, the following are also well worth a look if you want to buy foodie gifts or souvenirs – whether you want to take home cakes, jams, coffees or pickles, or even a tin of old-fashioned English humbugs. From Thursday to Saturday, Borough Market (see p.433) is also an excellent source of artisan deli food.

DELIS

De Gustibus The City. See p.378
Ev South Bank. See p.380
Jones Dairy Hoxton. See p.379
The Modern Pantry Shoreditch. See p.376
Monmouth Coffee Company Covent Garden and many other branches. See p.373.
Paul Rothe & Son Marylebone. See p.368
Rosie's Brixton. See p.384

Truc Vert Mayfair. See p.368
Verde and Co Spitalfields. See p.378

PATISSERIES

Hummingbird Bakery Notting Hill. See p.382
Louis Patisserie Hampstead. See p.384
Maison Bertaux Soho. See p.369
Patisserie Valerie Soho, Marylebone and many other branches. See p.369

30

CHEESE

⭐ **Neal's Yard Dairy** 17 Shorts Gardens, WC2 ☎020 7240 5700, ⓦnealsyarddairy.co.uk; ⊖ Covent Garden; map p.132. Pungent store packed to the rafters with quality cheeses from around the British Isles, with a few exceptionally good choices from further afield. You can taste before you buy. Also 6 Park St, Borough Market, SE1 ☎020 7367 0799, ⊖ Borough; map p.226. Covent Garden: Mon–Sat 10am–7pm. Borough: Mon–Fri 9am–9pm, Sat 8am–5pm.

Paxton & Whitfield 93 Jermyn St, SW1 ☎020 7930 0259, ⓦpaxtonandwhitfield.co.uk; ⊖ Green Park or Piccadilly Circus; map p.66. Quintessentially English, 200-year-old cheese shop offering a very traditional range of English and European varieties, plus fine wines and ports. Mon–Sat 9.30am–6pm.

COFFEE AND TEA

Algerian Coffee Stores 52 Old Compton St, W1 ☎020 7437 2480, ⓦalgcoffee.co.uk; ⊖ Leicester Square; map p.100. With its original dark wood fittings and glass display cases, and its rich, dark fragrance, this unassuming old store, here since 1887, looks and feels much as it must have done 120 years ago. Choose from hundreds of coffees – from house blends to rare beans – and grab a quick espresso to go for just £1. Mon–Wed 9am–7pm, Thurs & Fri 9am–9pm, Sat 9am–8pm.

R. Twining & Co 216 Strand, WC2 ☎020 7583 1359, ⓦshop.twinings.co.uk/shop/strand; ⊖ Temple; map p.132. The oldest established tea company in Britain has traded from these premises since the early eighteenth century. It stocks the full Twinings range and also hosts a small museum on the history of the company. Mon–Fri 9am–5pm, Sat 10am–4pm.

The Tea House 15a Neal St, WC2 ☎020 7240 7539; ⊖ Covent Garden; map p.132. The distinctive red-tiled facade conceals two fragrant floors of teas – black, green, white and caffeine-free – with a wealth of accessories including infusers, teapots and cosies. Mon–Sat 10am–7pm, Sun noon–6pm.

WORLD FOOD

A. Gold 42 Brushfield St, E1 ☎020 7247 2487, ⓦagoldshop.com; ⊖ Liverpool Street; map p.192. Next door to Jeanette Winterson's *Verde's* (see p.378), *A. Gold* is a similarly classy old establishment selling peculiarly British foodstuffs: spiced ginger wine, sugar mice, home-made Scotch eggs and humbugs. They do good take away hot sandwiches, too. Mon–Fri 10am–4pm, Sat & Sun 11am–5pm.

⭐ **Brindisa** Floral Hall, Stoney St, Borough Market, SE1 ☎020 7407 1036, ⓦbrindisa.com; ⊖ Borough; map p.226. If you're craving pimientos, manchego and habas fritas, this superb and stylish Spanish deli is the place for you; they also do a mean takeaway chorizo barbecue. Tues–Thurs 10am–5.30pm, Fri 10am–6pm, Sat 8.30am–5pm.

G. Gazzano & Son 167 Farringdon Rd, EC1 ☎020 7837 1586; ⊖ Farringdon; map p.150. This popular Clerkenwell establishment has been keeping the area in honest Italian food for a century, and the old wooden cabinets are still holding up under the weight of all that quality produce. Tues–Fri 7.30am–5.30pm, Sat 8am–5pm, Sun 10am–2pm.

I. Camisa & Son 61 Old Compton St, W1 ☎020 7437 7610, ⓦcamisa.co.uk; ⊖ Leicester Square; map p.100. The whole classic Italian deli range packed into one small Soho space. Excellent cheeses, salamis, pastas and dried foods, plus Italian wines and spirits, and very cheap, tasty takeaway sandwiches. Mon–Sat 9.30am–6pm.

Loon Fung Supermarket 42–44 Gerrard St, W1 ☎020 7437 7332, ⓦloonfung.com; ⊖ Leicester Square; map p.100. This warren of a supermarket in the heart of

30

Chinatown offers every kind of Chinese food item you can imagine, and probably some you can't. There's also a huge range of foods and groceries in the shops of neighbouring Newport St, Newport Place and Lisle St. Daily 10am–8pm.

Taj Stores 112 Brick Lane, E1 ☎020 7377 0061; ⊖ Aldgate East; map p.192. Big Bangladeshi supermarket established in 1936, offering everything from halal meats, herbs and spices to fish, fruit and vegetables. Daily 9am–9pm.

WINE, BEER AND SPIRITS

Berry Bros & Rudd 3 St James's St, SW1 ☎0800 280 2440, ⓦbbr.com; ⊖ Green Park; map p.66. This glorious 300-year-old wine merchant houses a huge range of fine wines – from £5 to £5000 – in a ravishing seventeenth-century building. Mon–Fri 10am–6pm, Sat 10am–5pm.

Gerry's 74 Old Compton St, W1 ☎020 7734 4215, ⓦgerrys.uk.com; ⊖ Leicester Square; map p.100. Characterful old Soho store, crammed with the best, most eclectic and sometimes downright weird range of spirits you'll find anywhere in London; vodka is a speciality. Mon–Thurs & Sat 9am–6.30pm, Fri 9am–7.30pm, Sun noon–6pm.

Royal Mile Whiskies 3 Bloomsbury St, WC1 ☎020 7436 4763, ⓦroyalmilewhiskies.com; ⊖ Tottenham Court Rd; map p.120. Wide range of whiskies – Scotch, Irish, bourbon, grain, blends – brandies, gins and other spirits. Mon–Sat 10am–6pm, Sun noon–5pm.

Vintage House 42 Old Compton St, W1 ☎020 7437 2592, ⓦvintagehouse.co.uk; ⊖ Leicester Square; map p.100. Fine wines, brandies and more than 1350 malt whiskies line the shelves of this old, family-run drinker's paradise in the heart of Soho. Mon–Fri 9am–11pm, Sat 10am–11pm, Sun noon–10pm.

MUSIC

While the **megastores** collapse under the might of the MP3, plenty of mainstream, independent and specialist **music shops** in London cater for the CD bulk-buyer and the obsessive rare-vinyl collector. Berwick Street in Soho, and London's markets, especially Camden, are good sources of vinyl (see opposite).

INDEPENDENT, SPECIALIST AND SECONDHAND

Brill 27 Exmouth Market, EC1 ☎020 7833 9757; ⊖ Farringdon or Angel; map p.150. Tiny CD store/coffee bar with a small but well-chosen selection of rock, pop, dance, country, soul and reggae. Good coffee and bagels, too. Mon–Fri 7.30am–6pm, Sun 9am–6pm.

Dub Vendor 274 Lavender Hill, SW11 ☎020 7223 3757, ⓦdubvendor.co.uk; Clapham Junction train station from Victoria or Waterloo. Essential reggae outlet, with up-to-the-minute imports and good advice. Mon–Sat 10am–7pm.

★ **Gramex** 25 Lower Marsh, SE1 ☎020 7401 3830; ⊖ Waterloo or Lambeth North; map p.216. A splendid find for classical-music and jazz lovers, this eccentric new and secondhand record store features CDs and vinyl, and comfy leather armchairs to sample or discuss your finds at leisure. Mon–Sat 11am–7pm.

Harold Moores Records 2 Great Marlborough St, W1 ☎020 7437 1576, ⓦhmrecords.co.uk; ⊖ Oxford Circus or Tottenham Court Road; map p.97. Two welcoming floors of CDs and vinyl, mostly classical and jazz, with rare releases and lots of contemporary, avant-garde selections. Mon–Sat 10am–6.30pm.

★ **Honest Jon's** 278 Portobello Rd, W10 ☎020 8969 9822, ⓦhonestjons.com; ⊖ Ladbroke Grove or Westbourne Park; map p.274. A fine selection of jazz, soul, funk, r'n'b, rare groove, reggae, world music and more in this West London stalwart, with current releases, secondhand finds and reissues. Mon–Sat 10am–6pm, Sun 11am–5pm.

Revival Records 30 Berwick St, W1 ☎020 7437 4271, ⓦrevivalrecords.uk.com; ⊖ Oxford Circus or Tottenham Court Road; map p.100. This relatively new arrival on the Soho scene sells new, used and rare vinyl and CDs, specializing in rock, soul, jazz, dance, punk and reggae. Mon–Sat 10am–7pm.

Rough Trade 130 Talbot Rd, W11 ☎020 7229 8541, ⓦroughtrade.com; ⊖ Ladbroke Grove; map p.274. The musos' favourite, this historic indie specialist has knowledgeable, friendly staff and a dizzying array from electronica to hardcore and beyond. Regular in-store performances. Newer branch in the Old Truman Brewery, 91 Brick Lane, E1 ☎020 7392 7788; ⊖ Aldgate East or Shoreditch High Street Overground; map p.192. Ladbroke Grove: Mon–Sat 10am–6.30pm, Sun 11am–5pm. Brick Lane: Mon–Thurs 8am–9pm, Fri 8am–8pm, Sat 10am–8pm, Sun 11am–7pm.

GIFTS AND ODDITIES

You don't have to settle for Beefeater teddy bears or tacky T-shirts to take home from London. In addition to the city's many fabulous museum stores (the V&A shop and the Southbank Centre Shop, by the Royal Festival Hall, yield particularly rich pickings when it comes to arts, crafts and jewellery), and its department stores (see box, p.426) – Liberty and Selfridges are the best for gifts – London has plenty of quirky places that are perfect for out-of-the-ordinary souvenirs and presents.

Caravan 3 Redchurch St, E2 ☎020 7033 3532, ⓦcaravanstyle.com; Shoreditch High Street Overground; map p.192. Everything in this pretty shop – books, gifts and homeware – is kooky with a retro edge, from the knitted dogs to the vintage-style hot water bottles and classy hand-printed wallpaper. Tues–Fri 11am–6.30pm, Sat & Sun noon–6pm.

Duke of Uke 22 Hanbury St, London, E1 ☎020 7247 7924, ⓦdukeofuke.co.uk; ➋ Aldgate East or Liverpool Street or Shoreditch High Street Overground; map p.192. Lively little uke-nuts' hub, stuffed to the rafters with ukuleles, banjos and harmonicas, with a friendly, welcoming vibe. Check the website for details of live jams and singalongs. Tues–Fri noon–7pm, Sat & Sun 11am–6pm.

Hamleys 188–196 Regent St, W1 ☎0871 704 1977, ⓦhamleys.com; ➋ Oxford Circus; map p.78. You may well hear this grand old toy store – a London landmark, standing on this spot for 250 years – before you see it. Just listen out for the clamour of shrieking kids on the rampage – Hamleys has no less than seven floors of fun, from wooden rocking horses to Wii games, to entice them. Mon–Wed & Sat 10am–8pm, Thurs & Fri 10am–9pm, Sun noon–6pm.

J. M. Pennifeather 4 Flask Walk, NW3 ☎020 7794 0488, ⓦjmpennifeather.co.uk; ➋ Hampstead; map p.298. If you're going to drag your fingers from your keyboard to write a letter, it may as well be with one of the beautifully crafted pens sold at this historic little Hampstead store. All the big names are here – Waterman, Lamy and Parker among them – along with some more workaday models, a few luscious inks and even perfumes to dab on your *billets doux*. Mon–Sat 10am–6pm, Sun 11am–5pm.

Le Labo 28A Devonshire St, W1 ☎020 3441 1535, ⓦlelabofragrances.com; ➋ Baker Street or Regent's Park; map p.89. Cult, hip perfumier where the fragrances – the simple names, things like Rose 31 or Bergamot 22, include just their essence and the number of ingredients – are mixed for you on the spot in plain, no-nonsense bottles. Prices aren't over the top for this level of individual quality. Mon–Wed, Fri & Sat 10am–6.30pm, Thurs 10am–7pm, Sun noon–5pm.

Lomography Gallery Store 3 Newburgh St, W1 ☎020 7434 1466, ⓦlomography.com; ➋ Oxford Circus; map p.97. For anyone who thinks photography lost its soul when it went digital, or for hipsters who just want the latest cool toy, this superstylish store sells all the cult analogue cameras including the Lomo LC-As, the Diana and the Holga, with lots of cheapies too. There's another branch in Spitalfields at 117 Commercial St (☎020 7426 0999; map p.192). Newburgh St: Mon–Wed 10am–7pm, Thurs 10am–9pm, Fri & Sat 10am–7pm, Sun 11am–5pm. Commercial St: daily 10am–7pm.

30

MARKETS

London's markets are more than just a cheap alternative to high-street shopping: the best of them are significant holdouts for communities endangered by the heedless expansion of the city. You haven't really got to grips with London unless you've rummaged through the junk at Brick Lane on a Sunday morning, or haggled over a leather jacket at Camden. Do keep an eye out for **pickpockets**, however.

Bermondsey (New Caledonian) Bermondsey St and Long Lane, SE1 ⓦbermondseysquare.co.uk/antiques.html; ➋ London Bridge; map p.224. Huge antique market offering everything from obscure nautical instruments to pricey furniture. The real collectors arrive at dawn to pick up the bargains. Fri 4am–1pm.

Berwick Street Berwick and Rupert streets, W1; ➋ Piccadilly Circus; map p.100. This famous and chaotic fruit and veg market is a piece of living Soho history, with ferociously fast vendors working the crowds like showmen. There's bread, fish, cheese and herbs, too, all very cheap after 4pm. You'll also find cheap clothes, music and DVDs aplenty along Berwick Street's southerly extension, Rupert St. Mon–Sat 9am–6pm.

★ **Borough Market** 8 Southwark St, SE1 ☎020 7407 1002, ⓦboroughmarket.org.uk; ➋ London Bridge or Borough; map p.226. Fine-food heaven – suppliers from all over the UK converge here to sell piles of organic veg, venison, fish, wines and home-baked goodies. The Victorian structure itself, with its slender grass-green wrought-iron columns, is lovely. Saturdays can be a crush. Thurs 11am–5pm, Fri noon–6pm, Sat 8am–5pm.

Brick Lane Brick Lane, Cygnet and Sclater streets, E1; Bacon, Cheshire and Chilton streets, E2; ➋ Aldgate East or Liverpool Street; map p.192. Huge, sprawling, cheap and frenzied, this famous East End market has become a fixture on the hipster circuit. Fruit and veg, household goods, clothes, antique furniture, scratched records, new young designers and broken spectacles – it's hard to say what you can't find here, most of it going for a song. Sun 9am–5pm.

Brixton Electric Ave, Pope's, Brixton Station and Atlantic rds, SW9 ⓦbrixtonmarket.net; ➋ Brixton. Based in the arcades just off Atlantic Rd, but spilling out along nearly all of the neighbouring streets, this huge, energetic market is the centre of Brixton life, offering a vast range of African and Caribbean foods, beauty products, records, clothes, fabrics and even triple-fast-action spiritual-cleanser-cum-floor-wash. Sunday is farmers' market day on Brixton Station Road. Mon, Tues &

30

Thurs–Sat 8am–6pm, Wed 8am–3pm; arcades till 10pm Thurs. Farmers' market Sun 10am–2pm.

★ **Broadway Market** Broadway Market, E8 ⓦ broadwaymarket.co.uk; ⊖ Bethnal Green; map p.291. Running from the Regent's Canal down to London Fields, this is a "farmers' style" foodies' market, so beware the distinction – you're not buying straight from the growers, as prices suggest. But the organic produce is terrific, and you can pick up plenty of good clothes, crafts and accessories, too, in this increasingly hip destination for trendy Hackneyites. Sat 9am–5pm.

Camden Camden High St to Chalk Farm Rd, NW1 ⓦ camdenlock.net; ⊖ Camden Town; map p.284. This legendary market – once beloved of hippies, punks and Goths, and now a firm favourite with European tourists – is actually a gaggle of markets, segueing into each other and supplemented by lively stores and restaurants in the surrounding streets, creating one enormous shopping district. Nearest Camden tube, **Camden Market** (Camden High St at Buck St; daily 9.30am–6.30pm, but most action Thurs–Sun) has around 200 stalls selling new, used, retro and young designer clothes, as well as jewellery, records and ephemera. **Camden Lock** (Camden Lock Place, off Chalk Farm Rd; daily 10am–6pm; most outdoor stalls Sat & Sun 10am–6pm) offers mainly arts, crafts and clothes, with the shops adding a few hip designers, antique dealers and booksellers to the mix. **Stables Yard** (leading off from Camden Lock or from Chalk Farm Rd; daily 9.30am–5.30pm, but most stalls Sat & Sun 10.30am–6pm) is a sprawling adventure of clubwear, more young designers, furniture, retro design, trinkets and antiques. There are also more stalls running alongside the Regents Canal towpath, northeast of the road bridge on Chalk Farm Road; given the name **Camden Lock village**, this area is good for independent stalls selling crafts and antiques (daily 10am–6pm).

★ **Columbia Road** Columbia Rd, E2 ⓦ columbiaroad .info; Shoreditch High Street or Hoxton Overground; map p.192. Fabulous, funky flower market in the heart of the East End, with bargains galore, especially late in the day, for the serious plant-lover. Get here early, have breakfast in one of the many cafés or coffee stalls, and check out the area's increasingly hip shops while you're at it. Sun 8am–2pm.

Greenwich Greenwich High Rd, Stockwell St and College Approach, SE10 ⓦ shopgreenwich.co.uk /market/ and ⓦ clocktowermarket.co.uk; Greenwich train station from Charing Cross or Cutty Sark DLR; map p.315. Sprawling set of flea markets with some 150 stalls crafts, modern antiques, vintage clothes, bric-a-brac and furniture in a rather more scenic setting than Camden. Wednesday is mainly food; antiques are the speciality on Thursday and Friday, with Thursday the best for unusual and distinctive collectibles. The surrounding streets, and the shops inside the covered market, offer more treasures,

with lots of secondhand books and retro clothes, while the Clocktower market around the corner at 166 Greenwich High Rd has around fifty stalls selling quirky vintage treasures. Stalls Wed–Sun 10am–5.30pm; shops daily or Tues–Sun. Clocktower Market Sat & Sun 10am–5pm.

Petticoat Lane Middlesex St and around, E1; Liverpool Street; map p.192. Cheap, cheerful and heaving, this famous clothes and bric-a-brac market (there's a lot of tat) is like any other local offering – but much, much bigger. Famously, it's where Lord Alan Sugar, of *The Apprentice* fame, started out as a young market stall trader. Mon–Fri (Wentworth Street only) 9am–3pm, Sun 9am–2pm.

Portobello Road Portobello and Golborne rds, W10 and W11 ⓦ portobelloroad.co.uk; ⊖ Ladbroke Grove or Notting Hill Gate; map p.274. Probably the best way to approach this enormous market is from the Notting Hill end, working your way through the antiques and bric-a-brac down to the fruit and veg stalls, and then under the Westway to hip new and secondhand clothes stalls and shops. Friday is better than Saturday to pick up a bargain here. Still further up again, beyond Portobello Green, the secondhand becomes pure boot-sale material, laid out on rugs on the road. The Golborne Rd market is cheaper and less crowded, with some very attractive antique and retro furniture. Antique market Sat 4am–6pm; surrounding shops daily.

Ridley Road Ridley Rd, E8; Dalston Kingsland Overground; map p.291. A very cheap food and clothes market in the heart of Hackney, Ridley Rd, like Brixton Market, is worth travelling to for the sheer diversity of goods on display. African and Caribbean fruit, veg and fish predominate, but there are also Turkish and Asian staples and a long line of shops offering fabrics, hair and beauty products, old gospel albums, cheap shoes, and much else. Mon–Thurs 6am–6pm, Fri & Sat 6am–7pm.

Spitalfields Commercial St, between Brushfield and Lamb streets, E1 ⓦ visitspitalfields.com; ⊖ Liverpool St; map p.192. The East End's historic Victorian fruit and veg hall now houses a rather fashionable organic food, crafts and secondhand goods market. Lots of tasty food stalls and fabulous gifts – but prices aren't particularly low. There are no market stalls from Monday to Wednesday and on Saturday, but the surrounding shops sell lots of good stuff. Thurs (antiques & vintage stalls) & Fri (fashion & art stalls) 10am–4pm; Sun (all stalls) 9am–5pm.

Sunday Upmarket/Backyard Market Old Truman Brewery, Brick Lane/Hanbury St, E1 ⓦ sundayupmarket .co.uk; ⊖ Aldgate East or Liverpool Street or Shoreditch High Street Overground; map p.192. Supercool fashion and accessories for East End hipsters – vintage jewellery, limited edition T-shirts, handmade handbags – plus contemporary lighting, art and homewares, and some great food stalls. The Backyard Market, across the road, offers much of the same. Upmarket: Sun 10am–5pm. Backyard: Sat 11am–6pm, Sun 10am–5pm.

WIMBLEDON

Activities and sports

Many of the crucial international fixtures of football, rugby and cricket take place in the capital, and London also hosts one of the world's top tennis tournaments, Wimbledon. As well as using existing venues, the 2012 Olympics is supplying a number of new world-class arenas in the Olympic Park (see p.202). Domestically, football (soccer) remains the most popular sport, with London clubs Chelsea and Arsenal among Europe's top teams. The rest of the sporting calendar is chock-full of quality events, from the sedate pleasures of county cricket to the idiosyncrasies of greyhound racing. For those who'd rather compete than spectate, there's a wide range of facilities, including inexpensive access to swimming pools, gyms, tennis courts, while even golf enthusiasts can find a course within the city limits.

SPECTATOR SPORTS

For the top international events, it can be almost impossible to track down a ticket without paying over the odds through a ticket agency. Should you be thwarted in your attempts to gain admission, you can often fall back on **TV or radio coverage**. BBC Radio 5 live (909 & 693 Mhz) has live commentaries on almost all major sporting events, while one of the free-to-view TV channels nearly always carries live transmission of international rugby and soccer. To watch some sports (including live Premiership football), you'll need to find a TV that has the Sky stations – many pubs show Sky games (sometimes on big screens) to draw in custom.

FOOTBALL

The English **football** (soccer) season runs from mid-August to early May, when the **FA Cup Final** at Wembley finishes off the season. There are four professional leagues: at the top is the twenty-club Premiership, followed by the Championship and leagues one and two. There are London clubs in every single division, with around five or six in the Premiership at any one time. Over the decades, London's most successful club by far has been **Arsenal**. However, since the arrival of Russian oil tycoon Roman Abramovich, fellow London club **Chelsea** have had a resurgence, winning the league for the first time in fifty years in 2005, and twice more since then.

Tickets Tickets for most Premiership games start at £40–50 and are virtually impossible to get hold of on a casual basis, though you may be able to see one of the Cup fixtures. It's a lot easier and cheaper to see a game in the Championship or one of the lower leagues, or to go on a stadium tour (see club websites for details).

Fixtures Most Premiership fixtures kick off at 3pm on Saturday, though there's also an early and late kick-off on Saturday, plus a couple on Sunday and the occasional midweek match; all matches, apart from the Saturday 3pm kick-offs, are broadcast live on Sky TV.

NATIONAL STADIUM

Wembley Stadium Wembley Way (90,000 capacity) ☎0844 800 2755, ⓦ wembleystadium.com; ⊖ Wembley Park or Wembley Central. The new stadium, designed by Norman Foster and featuring a massive steel arch, is the world's most expensive football ground, but it'll never reach the iconic status of the old stadium, constructed for the 1924 British Empire Exhibition, and the main focus for the 1948 Olympic Games. The stadium's most famous features were its "twin towers", forever associated with England's victory here in the 1966 World Cup Final. Erected as a mute reference to the old Raj, they were, in fact, only added in 1963, to celebrate the hundredth anniversary of the Football League. Guided tours are available (daily 10am–4pm; £15).

FOOTBALL CLUBS

Arsenal (Premiership) Emirates Stadium, Ashburton Grove, N7 (60,000 capacity) ☎020 7619 5003, ⓦ arsenal .com; ⊖ Arsenal.

Barnet (League Two) Underhill Stadium, Barnet Lane, Barnet (6000 capacity) ☎020 8441 6932, ⓦ barnetfc .com; ⊖ High Barnet.

Brentford (League One) Griffin Park, Braemar Rd (12,700 capacity) ☎0845 345 6442, ⓦ brentfordfc .co.uk; Brentford train station from Waterloo.

Charlton Athletic (League One) The Valley, Floyd Rd, SE7 (27,000 capacity) ☎0871 226 1905, ⓦ cafc.co.uk; Charlton train station from Charing Cross.

Chelsea (Premiership) Stamford Bridge, Fulham Rd, SW6 (41,800 capacity) ☎020 7835 6000, ⓦ chelseafc .com; ⊖ Fulham Broadway.

Crystal Palace (Championship) Selhurst Park, Whitehorse Lane, SE25 (26,000 capacity) ☎0871 200 0071, ⓦ cpfc.co.uk; Selhurst train station from Victoria.

Dagenham & Redbridge (League Two) Victoria Rd, Dagenham (6000 capacity) ☎020 8592 1549, ⓦ daggers .co.uk; ⊖ Dagenham.

Fulham (Premiership) Craven Cottage, Stevenage Rd, SW6 (25,000 capacity) ☎0843 208 1222, ⓦ fulhamfc .com; ⊖ Putney Bridge.

Leyton Orient (League One) Brisbane Rd, E10 (9200 capacity) ☎0871 310 1883, ⓦ leytonorient.co.uk; ⊖ Leyton.

Millwall (Championship) The Den, Zampa Rd, SE16 (20,000 capacity) ☎020 7231 9999, ⓦ millwallfc.co.uk; South Bermondsey train station from London Bridge.

Queens Park Rangers (Premiership) Loftus Road Stadium, South Africa Rd, W12 (18,300 capacity) ☎0844 477 7007, ⓦ qpr.co.uk; ⊖ White City.

Tottenham Hotspur (Premiership) White Hart Lane Stadium, Tottenham High Rd, N17 (36,000 capacity) ☎0844 499 5000, ⓦ tottenhamhotspur.com; White Hart Lane train station from Liverpool Street.

West Ham United (Championship) Upton Park, Green St, E13 (35,500 capacity) ☎0871 222 2700, ⓦ whufc .com; ⊖ Upton Park.

Wimbledon (League Two) Kingsmeadow, Kingston-upon-Thames (5200 capacity) ☎020 8547 3528, ⓦ afcwimbledon.co.uk; Norbiton train station from Waterloo.

CRICKET

The cricket season runs from April to September. If you're new to the sport, the best introduction is to go to an inter-county **Twenty20** knock-out match, which lasts three to four hours and represents the game at its most frenetic. The other option is to attend a match, either in one of the fast and furious **one-day competitions** or in the old-fashioned

county championship. Games in the latter take place over the course of four days and are never sold out. Two county teams are based in London: **Middlesex**, who play at Lord's, and **Surrey**, who play at The Oval.

Two international sides visit each summer and play a series of **Test matches** against England, which last up to five days. In tandem with the full-blown five-day Tests, there's also a series of **one-day internationals**, two of which are usually held in London.

Tickets Test match tickets can be difficult unless you book months in advance, and cost £30 and upwards. However, not all matches last the full five days, so tickets for the fifth day are usually sold on the day and can cost as little as £10. Tickets for Twenty20 matches, one-day competitions and county championship matches cost in the region of £15–20.

CRICKET GROUNDS

Lord's St John's Wood, NW8 (28,000 capacity) ☏020 7432 1000, ⊛lords.org; ⊖ St John's Wood.
The Oval Kennington Oval, SE11 (23,500 capacity) ☏020 7820 5700, ⊛kiaoval.com; ⊖ Oval.

RUGBY

There are two types of rugby played in England. Thirteen-a-side **Rugby League** is played almost exclusively in the north of England. However, the Super League does feature one London club, **Harlequins**, who play at the Stoop Memorial Ground in Twickenham. The season runs from February to September, and games traditionally take place on Sundays at 3pm, but there are now as many matches on Friday and Saturday. The final of the knock-out Challenge Cup is traditionally held at Wembley Stadium (see opposite). In London, however, virtually all rugby clubs play fifteen-a-side **Rugby Union**, which has upper-class associations and only went professional in 1995. **Harlequins**, who play at the same stadium as their Rugby League namesake, are the only Premiership team to actually play in London. Despite their names, **London Wasps** and **London Irish** play outside the city. Matches are traditionally on Saturdays at 3pm and the season runs from September until May, finishing off with the two knock-out finals for the European Rugby Cup (better known as the Heineken Cup) and the European Challenge Cup.

Tickets International matches are played at Twickenham Stadium, but unless you're affiliated to a rugby club, it's tough (and expensive) to get a ticket. A better bet is to go and see a Premiership game, where there's bound to be an international player or two on display – you usually get in for £20–40.

MAJOR RUGBY STADIUMS AND CLUBS

Harlequins Twickenham Stoop Stadium, Langhorn Drive, Twickenham (12,700 capacity) ☏0871 527 1315, ⊛quins.co.uk; Twickenham train station from Waterloo.
Twickenham Stadium Whitton Rd, Twickenham (82,000 capacity) ☏0871 222 2120, ⊛rfu.com; Twickenham train station from Waterloo.

TENNIS

Tennis in England is synonymous with **Wimbledon**, the only Grand Slam tournament still played on grass. The Wimbledon championships last a fortnight, in the last week of June and the first week of July. An easier opportunity to see big-name players is the Men's Championship at **Queen's** Club in Hammersmith, which finishes a week before Wimbledon. Many of the male tennis stars use this tournament to acclimatize themselves to English grass-court conditions.

Tickets Getting hold of a ticket for Wimbledon is a bit of a palaver. You really need to camp overnight if you want to get one of the 500 day tickets for the show courts (prices from around £35–90); otherwise, if you get there by 9am, you should get admission to the outside courts (where you'll catch some top players in the first week of the tournament), which costs £15–20. Avoid the middle Saturday, when thousands of people camp overnight and don't bother queuing for show court tickets on the last five days as all seats are pre-sold. For advance tickets, you have to enter a public ballot: a stamped, addressed envelope to the club for an application form (available from the August preceding the championship) and return it by December 31. As with Wimbledon, you have to apply for Queen's tickets in advance, although there are ground tickets (£20) and a limited number of show court returns on sale at 10am each day (£35–100). For priority booking, you need to put your name on the Mailing List and you will be sent an application form in January.

TENNIS CLUBS

All England Lawn Tennis and Croquet Club Church Rd, Wimbledon, SW19 ☏020 8971 2473, ⊛wimbledon.org; ⊖ Southfields or Wimbledon Park.
Queen's Club Palliser Rd, Hammersmith, W14; ☏020 7386 3400, ⊛queensclub.co.uk; ⊖ Barons Court.

GREYHOUND RACING AND MOTORSPORT

Wimbledon Plough Lane ☏0870 840 8905, ⊛lovethedogs.co.uk; ⊖ Wimbledon Park or Earlsfield train station from Waterloo. The most central London venue for watching greyhound racing (Fri & Sat evenings). Trackside admission costs £6. Evening meetings usually start around 7.30pm and finish at 10.30pm, and generally include around a dozen races. The stadium also hosts stock-car and banger races, every Sunday from October to April (⊛spedeworth.co.uk), with tickets from £12.

31

PARTICIPATING SPORTS

The following section lists most of the **sporting activities** possible in the capital. As a rule, the most reasonably priced facilities are provided by community leisure and sports centres, where you can simply turn up and pay to use the facilities. Most boroughs also have membership schemes that allow you to use the facilities for free or give discounts to regular users.

31

GOLF

At most places, you don't need to be a member – a pay-and-play round usually costs in the region of £15 – but it's often advisable to book ahead at the weekend. There are also a few (often quite transitory) places closer to the city centre, where you can hone your driving and putting for considerably less. Below is a selection of the city's golf courses; for more information visit w londongolf.info.

Central London Golf Centre Burntwood Lane, SW17 ☎ 020 8871 2468, w clgc.co.uk; Earlsfield train station from Vauxhall. "Central" might be stretching it, but still a decent 9-hole pay-and-play course and a floodlit driving range. Daily 7am to 1hr before sunset.

Lee Valley Golf Course Picketts Lock Lane, N9 ☎ 020 8803 3611, w leevalleypark.org.uk; Ponders End train station from Liverpool Street. Public 18-hole course set in the watery landscape along the River Lee. Mon–Fri 8am to dusk, Sat & Sun 7am to dusk.

Richmond Park Golf Club Roehampton Gate, Priory Lane, SW15 ☎ 020 8876 3205, w richmondparkgolfclub .org.uk; Barnes train station from Waterloo or bus #371 or #65 from ⊖ Richmond. Two long-established 18-hole courses and a driving range. Mon–Fri 7am to 30min before sunset, Sat & Sun 6am to 30min before sunset.

HORSERIDING

Strange though it might seem, there are places in the metropolis where you can **saddle up**, though at a price – £25 per hour is the average. It's usually possible to borrow a hard hat, but you must wear shoes or boots with a heel.

Hyde Park Stables 63 Bathurst Mews, W2 ☎ 020 7823 2813, w hydeparkstables.com; ⊖ Lancaster Gate. The only stables in central London, situated on the north side of Hyde Park. An hour's ride or lesson in a group costs £59–69, or £69–99 for a private lesson. Mon–Fri 7.15am–5pm, Sat & Sun 9am–5pm.

Lee Valley Riding Centre 71 Lee Bridge Rd, E10 ☎ 020 8556 2629, w leevalleypark.org.uk; Clapton train station from Liverpool St. Stables over in northeast London by the River Lee. A one-hour class will cost £25, whereas private lessons cost upwards of £30 for half an hour. Mon–Thurs 7.15am–9pm, Fri–Sun 8am–7pm.

Wimbledon Village Stables 24 High St, SW19 ☎ 020 8946 8579, w wvstables.com; ⊖ Wimbledon. Hack over the wilds of Wimbledon Common and Richmond Park for £55–60 per hour. Private lessons available from British Horse Society-approved instructors at £75–80 per hour – if you're not a member, you'll be lucky to get a ride at the weekend. Tues–Sun 9am–5pm.

TENNIS

There are loads of reasonably priced outdoor **courts** in council-run parks, costing £5–10 an hour; the downside is that they're rarely perfectly maintained. If you want to book in advance, you might have to join the local borough's scheme (£10–20 per year); we've given phone numbers for courts in the main central London parks or visit w londontennis.co.uk. However, during the day it's generally possible to turn up and play within half an hour or so, except in July and August, when Wimbledon (and decent weather) spurs a mass of couch potatoes into activity.

Battersea Park SW11 (19 courts) ☎ 020 8871 7542, w batterseapark.org; Battersea Park train station from Victoria.

Highbury Fields Baalbec Rd, N1 (11 courts) ☎ 020 7226 2334; ⊖ Highbury & Islington.

CLIMBING WALLS

Indoor climbing centres are run by serious climbers, and you must be a registered climber to climb unsupervised. Registration is a fairly straightforward process, however, and you can rent helmet, harness and footwear when they get there; total novices should book themselves on a course.

The Castle Green Lanes, N4 ☎ 020 8211 7000, w castle-climbing.co.uk; ⊖ Manor House. London's hippest climbing centre is housed in an old Victorian water pumping station that looks like a Hammer Horror Gothic castle. Mon–Fri 2–10pm, Sat & Sun 10am–7pm.

Mile End Climbing Wall Haverfield Rd, E3 ☎ 020 8980 0289, w mileendwall.org.uk; ⊖ Mile End. Smaller climbing centre housed in an old pipe-bending factory in the East End's Mile End Park. Mon–Thurs noon–9.30pm, Fri noon–9pm, Sat & Sun 10am–6pm.

Westway Climbing Centre Crowthorne Rd, W10 ☎ 020 8969 0992, w westwaysportscentre.org.uk; ⊖ Latimer Road. Large-scale climbing centre in a leisure centre that's tucked under the Westway flyover. Mon–Wed & Fri 9.30am–10pm, Thurs 8am–10pm, Sat & Sun 10am–8pm.

OPEN-AIR SWIMS

If you fancy an alfresco dip, a swim will cost you £5 or less at the places listed below:

Brockwell Lido Brockwell Park, SE24 ☎ 020 7274 3088, ⓦfusion-lifestyle.com; Herne Hill train station from Victoria or St Pancras. Laidback lido at the heart of Brixton's Brockwell Park. May & Sept Mon–Fri 6.30–10am & 4–8pm, Sat & Sun 8am–6pm; Oct Mon–Fri 7–11am & 4–7pm, Sat & Sun 8am–6pm.

Hampstead Ponds Hampstead Heath, NW3 ☎ 020 7485 5757, ⓦcityoflondon.gov.uk; ⊖ Hampstead. The Heath has three natural ponds: the Women's and Men's ponds are on the Highgate side (bus #214 from ⊖ Kentish Town), while the Mixed Bathing pond is nearer Hampstead. Daily 7 or 8am to 9pm or dusk.

Hampton Pool Hampton High St, Hampton ☎ 020 8255 1116, ⓦhamptonpool.co.uk; Hampton train station from Waterloo. Heated outdoor pool on the western edge of Bushy Park, about a mile's walk from Hampton Court Palace. Open all year; phone for hours.

London Fields Lido London Fields, E8 ☎ 020 7254 9038, ⓦgll.org; London Fields train station from Liverpool Street. Refurbished interwar lido with a 164ft heated outdoor pool. Open daily all year round, but hours vary (Tues women only).

Oasis 32 Endell St, WC2 ☎ 020 7831 1804, ⓦgll.org; ⊖ Covent Garden. The outdoor pool is small, but the water is a bath-like temperature and it's open all year. Other facilities include a gym, a health suite with sauna and sunbed, massage and squash courts. Mon–Fri 6.30am–10pm, Sat & Sun 9.30am–6pm.

Parliament Hill Lido Gordon House Road, NW5 ☎ 020 7485 3873; Gospel Oak Overground. Beautiful 200ft by 90ft open-air pool with Art Deco touches and notoriously chilly water. Daily: May to mid-Sept 7am–8.30pm; mid-Sept to April 7am–noon.

Pools on the Park Old Deer Park, Richmond ☎ 020 8940 0561; ⊖ Richmond. Not in Richmond Park, but in the Old Deer Park near the Thames, adjacent to modern leisure centre. Easter to Sept Mon 6.30am–7.45pm, Tues–Fri 6.30am–8pm, Sat & Sun 7am–5.45pm.

Serpentine Lido Hyde Park, W2 ☎ 020 7706 3422, ⓦserpentinelido.com; ⊖ Knightsbridge. Offers 110yd of swimming in Hyde Park's lake, plus a paddling pool; deck chairs and sun loungers for rent. May Sat & Sun only; June to mid-Sept daily 10am–6pm.

Tooting Bec Lido Tooting Bec Rd, SW16 ☎ 020 8871 7198; bus #249 from ⊖ Tooting Bec. At 300ft by 100ft, this is England's (and one of Europe's) largest freshwater, open-air swimming pools. June–Aug daily 6am–7.30pm, Sept 6am–4.30pm.

31

Holland Park W8 (6 courts) ☎ 020 7602 2226; ⊖ High Street Kensington.

Hyde Park Sporting Club South Carriage Drive, W2 (6 courts) ☎ 020 7262 3474, ⓦroyalparks.gov.uk; ⊖ South Kensington or Knightsbridge.

Islington Tennis Centre Market Rd, N7 (2 floodlit outdoor and 6 indoor courts) ☎ 020 7700 1370, ⓦaquaterra.org; ⊖ Caledonian Road.

Paddington Recreation Ground Randolph Ave, W9 (15 courts) ☎ 020 7625 4303; ⊖ Maida Vale.

Regent's Park South Lower Circle, NW1 (12 courts) ☎ 020 7486 4216, ⓦroyalparks.gov.uk; ⊖ Baker Street.

SPAS, GYMS AND LEISURE CENTRES

Below is a selection of the best-equipped and most central multipurpose **leisure centres**: almost all have gyms, fitness classes and pools; for local addresses visit ⓦyell.com.

Ironmonger Row Baths Ironmonger Row, EC1 ☎ 020 7253 4011, ⓦaquaterra.org; ⊖ Old Street. An old-fashioned kind of place that attracts all shapes and sizes, with a steam room, sauna, small plunge pool, masseurs, a lounge area with beds, and a large pool. Phone for times and prices.

Porchester Spa 225 Queensway, W2 ☎ 020 7792 3980, ⓦcourtneys.co.uk; ⊖ Bayswater or Queensway. Built in the 1920s, the Porchester's baths are well worth a visit for the Art Deco tiling alone. Admission is around £22 for a three-hour session, and entitles you to use the saunas, steam rooms, plunge pool, jacuzzi and swimming pool. Men: Mon, Wed & Sat 10am–10pm; women: Tues, Thurs & Fri 10am–10pm; couples Sun 4–10pm.

The Sanctuary 12 Floral St, WC2 ☎ 0844 875 8443, ⓦthesanctuary.co.uk; ⊖ Covent Garden. For a day of serious self-indulgence, this women-only club is the place to go: the interior is filled with lush tropical plants and you can swim naked in the pool. It's a major investment at £50–85 for day/eve membership, but your money gets you unlimited use of the pool, jacuzzi, sauna and steam room, plus one sunbed session. Mon & Tues 9.30am–6pm, Wed–Fri 9.30am–10pm, Sat & Sun 9.30am–8pm.

WHITE WATER SPORTS

Lee Valley White Water Centre Station Rd, Waltham Cross ☎ 0845 677 0606, ⓦgowhitewater.co.uk; Waltham Cross train station from Liverpool Street. Thanks to the 2012 Olympics, London has a whitewater rafting centre on the edge of the city, where you can shoot the rapids in a raft, canoe or kayak. Rafting starts at around £50; canoe/kayak paddling from £25. Wed–Sun 10am–6pm; longer hours in summer.

DIANA MEMORIAL PLAYGROUND

Kids' London

London is a great place for children and it needn't overly strain the parental pocket. Buskers and jugglers provide free entertainment at Covent Garden (see p.130) and the South Bank (see p.214), where a traffic-free riverside walk stretches from the London Eye to Tower Bridge. And if you don't fancy the walk, plenty of boats stop off at piers along the way (see p.22). The spread of children's shows is at its best during school holidays, and at Christmas there's a glut of traditional British pantomimes, stage shows based on folk stories or fairy tales, invariably featuring a showbiz star, and often with an undercurrent of innuendo for the adults. If that's too passive, there are plenty of indoor play centres where kids can burn off excess energy. And of course, London Zoo (p.286) and the Aquarium (see p.219) are sure-fire winners.

THEATRE, PUPPETRY AND CIRCUSES

Shows that appeal to children play in the West End all the time. What follows is a pretty selective rundown of theatre, puppetry and circuses that are consistently aimed at kids. For the latest listings, check out the "Around Town" section of *Time Out*.

Half Moon Young People's Theatre 43 Whitehorse Rd, E1 ☎020 7709 8900, ⓦhalfmoon.org.uk; Limehouse DLR or ⊖ Stepney Green. Well-established theatre that hosts touring youth shows, puts on its own productions, and runs a programme of workshops and theatre sessions for over-5s. Oct–April Sat 11.30am & 2pm; all tickets £6.

Little Angel Puppet Theatre 14 Dagmar Passage, off Cross St, N1 ☎020 7226 1787, ⓦlittleangeltheatre.com; ⊖ Angel. Puppet theatre, which specializes in table-top, rod and glove puppetry, with shows usually on Saturdays and Sundays at 11am and 2pm. Extra performances during holidays. No babies are admitted. Adults £10, children £5–8.

Polka Theatre 240 The Broadway, SW19 ☎020 8543 4888, ⓦpolkatheatre.com; ⊖ Wimbledon or South Wimbledon. Aimed at kids aged up to 12, this is a specially designed junior arts centre, with two theatres, a playground, a café and a toyshop. Storytellers, puppeteers and mime artists make regular appearances. Tickets £10–16.

Puppet Theatre Barge Little Venice, W2 ☎020 7249 6876 or 07836 202745, ⓦpuppetbarge.com; ⊖ Warwick Avenue. Wonderfully imaginative string marionette shows on a unique fifty-seat barge moored in Little Venice from October to July, and at Richmond in August and September. Shows start at 3pm at weekends and in the holidays. Adults £10, children £8.50.

Tricycle Theatre 269 Kilburn High Rd, NW6 ☎020 7328 1000, ⓦtricycle.co.uk; ⊖ Kilburn. High-quality children's shows Sept–June Saturdays at 11.30am & 2pm. Budding thespians can also attend drama and dance workshops after school and during the holidays; for toddlers, a performance workshop/playgroup. Tickets £6.

Unicorn Theatre 147 Tooley St, SE1 ☎020 7645 0560, ⓦunicorntheatre.com; ⊖ London Bridge. The oldest professional children's theatre in London now lives in purpose-built premises near City Hall in Southwark. Shows run the gamut from story-telling sessions and traditional plays to creative-writing workshops and mime and puppetry. Tickets £9–11.

Zippo's Circus ☎0871 210 2100, ⓦzipposcircus.co.uk. Zippo's Circus performs in and around London for much of the year. It's a totally traditional, big-top circus offering a variety of standard acts from clowning and tightrope walking to acrobatic budgies and equine tricks, compered by an old-fashioned ringmaster. Adults £8–20, children £6–14.

32

PARKS

Right in the centre of the city, there are plentiful green spaces, such as **St James's Park** (see p.67) and **Regent's Park** (see p.283), providing playgrounds and ample room for general mayhem, as well as a diverting array of city wildlife. If you want something more unusual than ducks and squirrels, head for one of London's several **city farms** (see p.442), which provide urbanites with a free taste of country life. Below is a list of the best parks and playgrounds.

Battersea Park Albert Bridge Rd, SW11 ☎020 8871 7539 (playground), ⓦbatterseapark.org; Battersea Park or Queenstown Road train station from Victoria. The park has an excellent free adventure playground, a boating lake and a children's zoo (see p.271). Zoo: adults £7.95, children 3–12 £6.50. Playground: term time weekdays 3.30–7pm, Sat & Sun 11am–6pm; holidays daily 11am–6pm. Zoo: daily 10am–5pm.

Camley Street Natural Park 12 Camley St, NW1 ☎020 7833 2311, ⓦwildlondon.org.uk; ⊖ King's

MUSEUMS

Museums are an obvious diversion and many of the big museums are free of charge. The **Science Museum** (see p.257), the **Natural History Museum** (see p.260) and the **National Maritime Museum** (see p.317), in particular, have hi-tech, hands-on sections that will keep young kids busy for hours, and they might even learn something while they're at it. At the other end of the scale, the **London Dungeon** (see p.232) and **Madame Tussauds**, with its infamous Chamber of Horrors (see p.93), remain very popular with teenagers, but are among the most expensive sights in the entire city.

Smaller museums specifically designed with children in mind include the **Horniman Museum** (see p.313), which houses an aquarium, and the **Kew Bridge Steam Museum**, which runs a miniature steam train on Sundays throughout the summer (see p.333). There are also museums devoted to childhood and toys, from the atmospheric **Pollock's Toy Museum** (see p.104) to the much larger V&A outpost, the **Museum of Childhood** (see p.202).

MUSIC

There are plenty of **free music** options worth looking out for: the Barbican (see p.413) puts on excellent weekend foyer concerts; the Royal Festival Hall (see p.414) and the National Theatre (see p.418) run regular seasonal festivals where you can catch some world-class music. In addition, most of the established orchestras run special **children's concerts**: look out for the London Philharmonic Orchestra (W lpo.co.uk), London Symphony Orchestra (W lso.co.uk) and National Children's Orchestra (W nco.org.uk).

Cross St Pancras. Canalside wildlife haven, run by the London Wildlife Trust, with pond dipping and a good info centre. Free. See p.129. **Daily 10am–5pm.**

Coram's Fields 93 Guilford St, WC1 ☎ 020 7837 6138, W coramsfields.org; ⊖ Russell Square. Very useful, centrally located playground with lots of water and sand play plus mini-farm with hens, rabbits, sheep, goats and ducks. Adults admitted only if accompanied by a child. Veggie café (March–Nov). Free. See p.123. **Daily 9am to dusk.**

Hampstead Heath NW3 ☎ 020 7485 4491, W cityoflondon.gov.uk; ⊖ Hampstead, Gospel Oak or Hampstead Heath train station. Nine hundred acres of grassland and woodland, with superb views of the city. Excellent kite-flying potential, too, and plenty of playgrounds, sports facilities, music events and fun days throughout the summer. See p.301. **Open daily 24hr.**

Hyde Park/Kensington Gardens W8 ☎ 020 7298 2100, W royalparks.gov.uk; ⊖ Hyde Park Corner, Knightsbridge, Lancaster Gate or Queensway. Hyde Park is central London's

main open space and features the Diana Fountain in which the kids can dip their feet; in Kensington Gardens (daily 6am to dusk), adjoining its western side, you can find the famous Peter Pan statue and a groovy playground also dedicated to Princess Diana. See p.244. **Daily 5am–midnight.**

Kew Gardens Richmond, Surrey ☎ 020 8332 5000, W kew.org; ⊖ Kew Gardens. Come here for the edifying open spaces, though the glasshouses usually go down well too, and there's a small aquarium in the basement of the Palm House. Adults £14, children under 17 free. See p.337. **Daily 9.30am–5.30pm or dusk.**

Richmond Park Richmond, Surrey ☎ 020 8948 3209, W royalparks.gov.uk; ⊖ Richmond or Richmond train station from Waterloo. A fabulous stretch of countryside, with opportunities for duck-feeding, deer-spotting, mushroom-hunting and cycling. Playground situated near Petersham Gate or toddlers' play area near Kingston Gate. See p.343. **Daily: March–Sept 7am–dusk; Oct–Feb 7.30am–dusk.**

CITY FARMS

Free fun is available at the city's various working farms, the majority of them located in London's East End. The website W farmgarden.org.uk is also worth a visit for details of other, smaller gardens and wildlife havens in London.

Brooks Farm Skelton's Lane Park, Leyton, E10 ☎ 020 8539 4278, W walthamforest.gov.uk; ⊖ Leyton. Very much a community resource, this farm has pigs, goats, Shetland ponies, llamas and more, as well as its own allotments and an adventure playground. Tues–Sun: April–Oct 10.30am–12.30pm & 1.30–5.30pm; Nov–March 9.30am–12.30pm & 1.30–4.30pm.

Freightliners Farm Sheringham Road, N7 ☎ 020 7609 0467, W freightlinersfarm.org.uk; ⊖ Highbury & Islington or Holloway Road. Small farm (with a shop and café) with cows, pigs, goats, hens, ducks, turkeys, geese, sheep and giant rabbits. Tues–Sun 10am–4.45pm; winter closes 4pm.

Hackney City Farm 1a Goldsmith's Row, E2 ☎ 020 7729 6381, W hackneycityfarm.co.uk; ⊖ Hoxton Overground. Converted brewery that's now a small city farm (with an excellent café), housing cows, sheep, pigs, hens, chinchillas, degus, rabbits and a donkey; also has an organic garden. Weekend kids' activities. Tues–Sun 10am–4.30pm.

Kentish Town City Farm 1 Cressfield Close, Grafton Rd, NW5 ☎ 020 7916 5421, W ktcityfarm.org.uk; ⊖ Chalk

Farm or Kentish Town. Five acres of farmland with cows, horses, pigs, goats, sheep and chickens. Daily 9am–5pm.

Mudchute City Farm Pier St, E14 ☎ 020 7515 5901, W mudchute.org; ⊖ Mudchute, Crossharbour or Island Gardens DLR. London's largest city farm, with farmyard animals, llamas, pets' corner, aviary and equestrian centre. Fantastic location with great views of Canary Wharf. Tues–Sun 9am–5pm.

Spitalfields City Farm Buxton St, E1 ☎ 020 7247 8762, W spitalfieldscityfarm.org; ⊖ Shoreditch High Street Overground. Another tiny East End farm (with a shop and café) housing sheep, donkeys, goats, pigs, ducks, geese, rabbits and guinea pigs. Also runs a propagation scheme and organic vegetable garden. Tues–Sun: April–Sept 10am–4.30pm; Oct–March 10am–4pm.

Stepney City Farm Stepney Way, E1 ☎ 020 7790 8204, W stepneycityfarm.org; ⊖ Stepney Green. A rural haven in the East End, with cows, pigs, goats, sheep, donkeys, rabbits, ferrets and guinea pigs. Also has a coffee shop, nature trail and toddlers' play area. Tues–Sun 10am–5pm.

Surrey Docks Farm Rotherhithe Street, SE16 ☎ 020

KIDS GO FREE

Don't underestimate the value of London's **public transport** as a source of fun – and remember kids travel free (see p.22). **The Underground** is a buzz for a lot of kids, and you can get your bearings while entertaining your offspring by installing them in the front seats on the top deck of a red **double-decker bus**. The driverless **Docklands Light Railway** (see p.22) is another source of amusement, too – grab a seat at the front of the train and pretend to be the driver.

7231 1010, ⓦ surreydocksfarm.org.uk; Surrey Quays Overground. A corner of southeast London set aside for goats, sheep, donkeys, chickens, pigs, ducks and bees in hives, with a smithy, a dairy and a great café (Wed–Sun). Tues–Sun 10am–5pm.

Vauxhall City Farm 165 Tyers St, SE11; ☎ 020 7582 4204, ⓦ vauxhallcityfarm.org; ⊖ Vauxhall. Little city farm with sheep, pigs, ducks, ponies and donkeys. Activities at weekends and on holidays. Wed–Sun 10.30am–4pm.

INDOOR ADVENTURE PLAY CENTRES AND SWIMMING POOLS

Most local leisure centres offer "soft play" sessions for pre-school toddlers during the week. Listed below are some of the bigger operations which also cater for older children.

Bramley's Big Adventure 136 Bramley Rd, W10 ☎ 020 8960 1515, ⓦ bramleysbig.co.uk; ⊖ Latimer Road or Ladbroke Grove. Indoor play centre with sophisticated equipment suitable for children up to 11 and magazines for bored adults. £4–6 for 2hr or more. Mon–Fri 10am–6pm, Sat & Sun 10am–6.30pm.

Discover 385–387 High St, E15 ☎ 020 8536 5555, ⓦ discover.org.uk; ⊖ Stratford. A hands-on interactive creative learning centre with a great outdoor play garden,

aimed at story-building for under-11s. £4.50. Mon–Fri 10am–5pm, Sat & Sun 11am–5pm.

Waterfront Leisure Centre High St, Woolwich, SE18 ☎ 020 8317 5000, ⓦ gll.org; Woolwich Arsenal DLR. Massive Wild and Wet adventure swimming pool with 100ft-plus slide, wave machine, waterfall and all the usual aquatic high-jinks. Under-3s free; 3–15s from £4; adults £5.60. Mon–Fri 7am–11pm, Sat & Sun 8am–9.30pm.

32

THE GREAT FIRE OF LONDON

Contexts

History

The citizens of London are universally held up for admiration and renown for the elegance of their manners and dress, and the delights of their tables...The only plagues of London are the immoderate drinking of fools and the frequency of fires.   William Fitzstephen, companion of Thomas Becket

Conflagrations and drunkenness certainly feature strongly in London's complex two-thousand-year history. What follows is a highly compressed account featuring riots and revolutions, plagues, fires, slum clearances, lashings of gin, Boris Johnson and the London people. For more detailed histories, see our book recommendations (see p.462).

Roman Londinium

Although there is evidence of scattered Celtic settlements along the Thames, no firm proof exists to show that central London was permanently settled before the arrival of the Romans. **Julius Caesar** led two small cross-Channel incursions in 55 and 54 BC, but it wasn't until nearly a century later, in **43 AD**, that a full-scale invasion force of some 40,000 Roman troops landed in Kent. Britain's rumoured mineral wealth was certainly one motive behind the Roman invasion, but the immediate spur was the need of Emperor Claudius, who owed his power to the army, for an easy military triumph. The Romans, under Aulus Plautius, defeated the main Celtic tribe of southern Britain, the Catuvellauni, on the Medway, southeast of London, crossed the Thames and then set up camp to await the triumphant arrival of Claudius, his elephants and the Praetorian Guard.

It's now thought that the site of this first Roman camp was, in fact, in Westminster – the lowest fordable point on the Thames – and not in what is now the City. However, around 50 AD, when the Romans decided to establish the permanent military camp of **Londinium** here, they chose a point further downstream, building a bridge some 50 yards east of today's London Bridge. London became the hub of the Roman road system, but it was not the Romans' principal colonial settlement, which remained at **Camulodunum** (modern Colchester) to the northeast.

In 60 AD, the East Anglian people, known as the Iceni, rose up against the invaders under their queen **Boudicca** (or Boadicea) and sacked Camulodunum, slaughtering most of the legion sent from Lindum (Lincoln) and making their way to the ill-defended town of Londinium. According to archeological evidence, Londinium was burnt to the ground and, according to the Roman historian, Tacitus, whose father-in-law was in Britain at the time (and later served as its governor), the inhabitants were "massacred, hanged, burned and crucified". The Iceni were eventually defeated, and Boudicca committed suicide (62 AD).

In the aftermath, Londinium emerged as the new commercial and administrative (though not military) **capital of Britannia**, and was endowed with a military fort for around a thousand troops, an imposing basilica and forum, a governor's palace, temples, bathhouses and an amphitheatre (see p.171). Archeological evidence suggests

122	200	293	312
Emperor Hadrian visits Londinium	The Romans build a defensive wall around the city	Emperor Carausius declares himself Emperor of Britain and northern Gaul	Christianity becomes the state religion throughout the Roman Empire

LEGENDS

Until Elizabethan times, most Londoners believed that London had been founded around 1000 BC as New Troy or *Troia Nova* (later corrupted to Trinovantum), capital of Albion (aka Britain), by the Trojan prince **Brutus**. At the time, according to medieval chronicler Geoffrey of Monmouth, Britain was "uninhabited except for a few giants", several of whom the Trojans subsequently killed. They even captured one called Goemagog (more commonly referred to as Gogmagog), who was believed to be the son of Poseidon, Greek god of the sea, and whom one of the Trojans, called Corineus, challenged to unarmed combat and defeated.

For some reason, by late medieval times, Gogmagog had become better known as two giants, **Gog and Magog**, whose statues can still be seen in the Guildhall (see p.169) and on the clock outside St Dunstan-in-the-West (see p.158). According to Geoffrey of Monmouth's elaborate genealogical tree, Brutus is related to Leir (of Shakespeare's *King Lear*), Arthur (of the Round Table) and eventually to **King Lud**. Around 70 BC, Lud is credited with fortifying New Troy and renaming it *Caer Ludd* (Lud's Town), which was later corrupted to Caerlundein and finally London.

that Londinium was at its most prosperous and populous from around 80 AD to 120 AD, during which time it is thought to have evolved into the empire's fifth largest city north of the Alps.

Between 150 AD and 400 AD, however, London appears to have sheltered less than half the former population, probably due to economic decline. Nevertheless, it remained strategically and politically important and, as an imperial outpost, actually appears to have benefited from the chaos that engulfed the rest of the empire during much of the third century. In those uncertain times, **fortifications** were built, three miles long, 20ft high and 9ft thick, whose Kentish ragstone walls can still be seen near today's Museum of London (see p.169), home to many of the city's most significant Roman finds.

In 406 AD, the Roman army in Britain mutinied for the last time and invaded Gaul under the self-proclaimed Emperor Constantine III. The empire was on its last legs, and the Romans were never in a position to return, officially abandoning the city in **410 AD** (when Rome was sacked by the Visigoths), and leaving the country and its chief city at the mercy of the marauding Saxon pirates, who had been making increasingly persistent raids on the coast since the middle of the previous century.

Saxon Lundenwic and the Danes

Roman London appears to have been more or less abandoned from the first couple of decades of the fifth century until the ninth century. Instead, the **Anglo-Saxon** invaders, who controlled most of southern England by the sixth century, appear to have settled, initially at least, to the west of the Roman city. When Augustine was sent to reconvert Britain to Christianity, the Saxon city of **Lundenwic** was considered important enough to be granted a bishopric in 604, though it was Canterbury, not London, that was chosen as the seat of the Primate of England. Nevertheless, trade flourished once more during this period, as attested by the Venerable Bede, who wrote of London in 730 as "the mart of many nations resorting to it by land and sea".

410	604	878	1066
The Romans withdraw from Britain	Mellitus, the first Bishop of London, begins the first St Paul's Cathedral	King Alfred defeats the Vikings and England is divided between Danelaw and Wessex	William the Conqueror defeats King Harold at the Battle of Hastings

EDWARD THE CONFESSOR

When Edward came to the throne in 1042, he moved the court and church upstream to Thorney Island (or the Isle of Brambles), where he built a splendid new palace so that he could oversee construction of his "West Minster" (later to become Westminster Abbey). Edward was too weak to attend the official consecration and died just ten days later: he is buried in the great church he founded, where his shrine became a place of pilgrimage for centuries. Of greater political and social significance, however, was his geographical separation of power, with royal government based in the **City of Westminster**, while the **City of London** remained the commercial centre.

In 841 and 851 London suffered Danish Viking attacks, and it may have been in response to these raids that the Saxons decided to reoccupy the walled Roman city. By 871 the **Danes** were confident enough to attack and established London as their winter base, but in 886 Alfred the Great, King of Wessex, recaptured the city, rebuilt the walls and formally re-established London as a fortified town and a trading port. After a lull, the Vikings returned once more during the reign of Ethelred the Unready (978–1016), attacking unsuccessfully in 994, 1009 and 1013. The following year, the Danes, under Swein Forkbeard, finally recaptured London, only for Ethelred to reclaim it later that year, with help from King Olaf of Norway.

In 1016, following the death of Ethelred, and his son, Edmund Ironside, the Danish leader Cnut (or Canute), son of Swein, became King of All England, and made London the **national capital** (in preference to the Wessex base of Winchester), a position it has held ever since. Danish rule lasted only 26 years, however, and with the death of Cnut's two sons, the English throne returned to the House of Wessex, and to Ethelred's exiled son, **Edward the Confessor** (1042–66).

1066 and all that

On his deathbed, in the new year of 1066, the celibate Edward made **Harold**, Earl of Wessex, his appointed successor. Having crowned himself in the new abbey – establishing a tradition that continues to this day – Harold went on to defeat his brother Tostig (who was in cahoots with the Norwegians), but was himself defeated by **William of Normandy** (aka William the Conqueror) and his invading Norman army at the Battle of Hastings. On Christmas Day of 1066, William crowned himself king in Westminster Abbey. Elsewhere in England, the Normans ruthlessly suppressed all opposition, but in London, William granted the City a charter guaranteeing to preserve the privileges it had enjoyed under Edward. However, as an insurance policy, he also built three forts in the city, of which the sole remnant is the White Tower, now the nucleus of the **Tower of London**.

Over the next few centuries, the City waged a continuous struggle with the monarchy for a degree of self-government and independence. After all, when there was a fight over the throne, the support of London's wealth and manpower could be decisive, as **King Stephen** (1135–54) discovered, when Londoners attacked his cousin and rival for the throne, Mathilda, daughter of Henry I, preventing her from being crowned at Westminster. Again, in 1191, when the future **King John** (1199–1216) was tussling with

1089	1189	1209	1215
Cluniac Monastery established in Bermondsey	Henry Fitz-Ailwin becomes the first Mayor of London	Old London Bridge completed	Magna Carta signed – Mayor of London is one of the signatories

William Longchamp over the kingdom during the absence of Richard the Lionheart (1189–99), it was the Londoners who made sure Longchamp remained cooped up in the Tower. For this particular favour, London was granted the right to elect its own sheriff, or lord mayor, an office that was officially acknowledged in the Magna Carta of 1215.

Occasionally, of course, Londoners backed the wrong side, as they did when they turned up at Old St Paul's to accept **Prince Louis of France** (the future Louis VIII) as ruler of England during the barons' rebellion against King John in 1216, and again with Simon de Montfort, when he was engaged in civil war with **Henry III** (1216–72) during the 1260s. As a result, the City found itself temporarily stripped of its privileges. In any case, London was chiefly of importance to the medieval kings as a source of wealth, and traditionally it was to the Jewish community, which arrived in 1066 with William the Conqueror, that the sovereign turned for a loan. By the second half of the thirteenth century, however, the Jews had been squeezed dry, and in 1290, after a series of increasingly bloody attacks, **London's Jews** were expelled by Edward I (1272–1307), who turned instead to the City's Italian merchants for financial assistance.

From the Black Death to the Wars of the Roses

London backed the right side in the struggle between Edward II (1307–27) and his queen, Isabella, who, along with her lover Mortimer, succeeded in deposing the king. The couple's son Edward III (1327–77) was duly crowned, and London enjoyed a period of relative peace and prosperity, thanks to the wealth generated by the wool trade. All this was cut short, however, by the arrival of the Europe-wide bubonic plague outbreak, known as the **Black Death**, in 1348. This disease, carried by black rats and transmitted to humans by flea bites, wiped out something like two-thirds of the capital's 75,000 population in the space of two years. Other epidemics followed in 1361, 1369 and 1375, creating a volatile economic situation that was worsened by the financial strains imposed on the capital by having to bankroll the country's involvement in the Hundred Years' War with France.

Matters came to a head with the introduction of the poll tax, a head tax imposed in the 1370s on all men regardless of means. During the ensuing **Peasants' Revolt** of 1381, London's citizens opened the City gates to Wat Tyler's Kentish rebels and joined in the lynching of the archbishop, plus countless rich merchants and clerics. Tyler was then lured to meet the boy-king Richard II at Smithfield, just outside the City, where he was murdered by Lord Mayor Walworth, who was subsequently knighted for his treachery. Tyler's supporters were fobbed off with promises of political changes that never came, as Richard unleashed a wave of repression and retribution.

After the Peasants' Revolt, the next serious disturbance was **Jack Cade's Revolt**, which took place in 1450. An army of 25,000 Kentish rebels – including gentry, clergy and craftsmen – defeated King Henry VI's forces at Sevenoaks, marched to Blackheath, withdrew temporarily and then eventually reached Southwark in early July. Having threatened to burn down London Bridge, the insurgents entered the City and spent three days wreaking vengeance on their enemies before being ejected. A subsequent attempt to enter the City via London Bridge was repulsed, and the army was dispersed with yet more false promises. The reprisals, which became known as the "harvest of

1290	1305	1337–1453	1380	1415
Jews expelled from London	William Wallace executed at Smithfield	Hundred Years' War	Chaucer's Canterbury Tales published	Henry V wins the Battle of Agincourt

JOHN WYCLIFFE AND THE LOLLARDS

Parallel with the social unrest of the 1370s were the demands for clerical reforms made by the scholar and heretic **John Wycliffe**, whose ideas were keenly taken up by Londoners. A fierce critic of the papacy and the monastic orders, Wycliffe produced the first translation of the Bible into English in 1380. He was tried for heresy at Lambeth Palace, and his followers, known as **Lollards**, were harshly persecuted. In 1415, the Council of Constance, which burned the Czech heretic Jan Hus at the stake, also ordered Wycliffe's body to be exhumed and burnt.

heads", were as harsh as before – Cade himself was captured, killed and brought to the capital for dismemberment.

A decade later, the country was plunged into more widespread conflict during the so-called **Wars of the Roses**, the name now given to the strife between the rival noble houses of Lancaster and York. Londoners wisely tended to sit on the fence throughout the conflict, only committing themselves in 1461, when they opened the gates to the Yorkist king Edward IV (1461–70 and 1471–83), thus helping him to depose the mad Henry VI (1422–61 and 1470–71). In 1470, Henry, who had spent five years in the Tower, was proclaimed king once more, only to be deposed again a year later, following Lancastrian defeats at the battles of Barnet and Tewkesbury.

Tudor London

The **Tudor** family, which with the coronation of **Henry VII** (1485–1509) emerged triumphant from the mayhem of the Wars of the Roses, reinforced London's pre-eminence during the sixteenth century, when the Tower of London and the royal palaces of Whitehall, St James's, Richmond, Greenwich, Hampton Court and Windsor provided the backdrop for the most momentous events of the period. At the same time, the city's population, which had remained constant at around fifty thousand since the Black Death, increased dramatically, trebling in size during the course of the century.

One of the crucial developments of the century was the English **Reformation**, the separation of the English Church from Rome, a split initially prompted not by doctrinal issues, but by the failure of Catherine of Aragon, first wife of **Henry VIII** (1509–47), to produce a male heir. In fact, prior to his desire to divorce Catherine, Henry, along with his lord chancellor, Cardinal Wolsey, had been zealously persecuting Protestants. However, when the Pope refused to annul Henry's marriage, Henry knew he could rely on a large amount of popular support, as anti-clerical feelings were running high. By contrast, Henry's new chancellor, Thomas More, wouldn't countenance divorce, and resigned in 1532. Henry then broke with Rome, appointed himself head of the English Church and demanded both citizens and clergy swear allegiance to him. Very few refused, though More was among them, becoming the country's first Catholic martyr with his execution in 1535.

Henry may have been the one who kickstarted the English Reformation, but he was, in fact, a religious conservative, and in the last ten years of his reign he succeeded in executing as many Protestants as he did Catholics. Religious turmoil only intensified in the decade following Henry's death. First, Henry's sickly son, **Edward VI** (1547–53), pursued a staunchly anti-Catholic policy. By the end of his short reign, London's

1422	1455–85	1476	1483
Riot ensues after victory of City of London over the City of Westminster in a wrestling match	Wars of the Roses	William Caxton sets up the first printing press in the precincts of Westminster Abbey	Death of the Princes in the Tower, Edward V and his brother the Duke of York

> ## DISSOLUTION OF THE MONASTERIES
>
> Henry's VIII's most far-reaching act was his **Dissolution of the Monasteries**, a programme to close down the country's monasteries and appropriate their assets, commenced in 1536 in order to bump up the royal coffers. Medieval London boasted over 100 places of worship and some 20 religious houses, with two-thirds of the land in the City belonging to the Church. The Dissolution changed the entire fabric of both the city and the country: London's property market was suddenly flooded with confiscated estates, which were quickly snapped up and redeveloped by the Tudor nobility.

churches had lost their altars, their paintings, their relics and virtually all their statuary. After an abortive attempt to secure the succession of Edward's Protestant cousin, Lady Jane Grey, the religious pendulum swung the other way for the next five years with the accession of "**Bloody Mary**" (1553–58). This time, it was Protestants who were martyred with abandon at Tyburn and Smithfield.

Despite all the religious strife, the Tudor economy remained in good health for the most part, reaching its height in the reign of **Elizabeth I** (1558–1603), when the piratical exploits of seafarers Walter Raleigh, Francis Drake, Martin Frobisher and John Hawkins helped to map out the world for English commerce. London's commercial success was epitomized by the millionaire merchant Thomas Gresham, who erected the **Royal Exchange** in 1571, establishing London as the premier world trade market.

The 45 years of Elizabeth's reign also witnessed the efflorescence of a specifically **English Renaissance**, especially in the field of literature, which reached its apogee in the brilliant careers of **Christopher Marlowe**, **Ben Jonson** and **William Shakespeare**. The presses of **Fleet Street**, established a century earlier by William Caxton's apprentice Wynkyn de Worde, ensured London's position as a centre for the printed word. Beyond the jurisdiction of the City censors, in the entertainment district of Southwark, whorehouses, animal-baiting pits and theatres flourished. The carpenter-cum-actor James Burbage designed the first purpose-built playhouse in 1576, eventually rebuilding it south of the river as the **Globe Theatre**, where Shakespeare premiered many of his works. The theatre has since been reconstructed (see p.228).

From Gunpowder Plot to Civil War

On Elizabeth's death in 1603, James VI of Scotland became **James I** (1603–25) of England, thereby uniting the two crowns and marking the beginning of the **Stuart dynasty**. His intention of exercising religious tolerance after the anti-Catholicism of Elizabeth's reign was thwarted by the public outrage that followed the **Gunpowder Plot** of 1605, when Guy Fawkes and a group of Catholic conspirators were discovered attempting to blow up the king at the state opening of Parliament. James, who clung to the medieval notion of the divine right of kings, inevitably clashed with the landed gentry who dominated Parliament, and tensions between Crown and Parliament were worsened by his persecution of the Puritans, an extreme but increasingly powerful Protestant group.

Under James's successor, **Charles I** (1625–49), the animosity between Crown and Parliament came to a head. From 1629 to 1640 Charles ruled without the services of Parliament, but was forced to recall it when he ran into problems in Scotland, where he

1512	1534	1553–58	1561	1571
Royal Dockyards established in Woolwich	Henry VIII breaks with the Roman Catholic Church	Queen Mary reinstates Catholicism	Lightning strikes Old St Paul's and the spire falls to the ground	The opening of the Royal Exchange in the City

LONDON IN THE CIVIL WAR

London was the key to victory for both sides in the Civil War, and as a **Parliamentarian stronghold** it came under attack almost immediately from Royalist forces. Having defeated the Parliamentary troops to the west of London at **Brentford** in November 1642, the way was open for Charles to take the capital. Londoners turned out in numbers to defend their city, some 24,000 assembling at **Turnham Green**. A stand-off ensued, Charles hesitated and in the end withdrew to Reading, thus missing his greatest chance of victory. A complex system of fortifications was thrown up around London, but was never put to the test. In the end, the capital remained intact throughout the war, which culminated in the execution of the king outside Whitehall's Banqueting House in January 1649.

was attempting to subdue the Presbyterians. Faced with extremely antagonistic MPs, Charles attempted unsuccessfully to arrest several of their number at Westminster. Acting on a tip-off, the MPs fled by river to the City, which sided with Parliament. Charles withdrew to Nottingham, where he raised his standard, the opening military act of the **Civil War**.

For the next eleven years, after the execution of Charles I, England was a **Commonwealth** – at first a true republic, then, after 1653, a Protectorate under **Oliver Cromwell**, who was ultimately as impatient of Parliament and as arbitrary as Charles had been. London found itself in the grip of the Puritans' zealous laws, which closed down all theatres, enforced observance of the Sabbath and banned the celebration of Christmas, which was considered a papist superstition.

Plague and fire

Just as London proved Charles I's undoing, so the ecstatic reception given to **Charles II** (1660–85) helped ease the **Restoration** of the monarchy in 1660. The "Merry Monarch" immediately caught the mood of the public by opening up the theatres, and he encouraged the sciences by helping the establishment of the **Royal Society** for Improving Natural Knowledge, whose founder members included **Christopher Wren**, **John Evelyn** and **Isaac Newton**.

The good times that rolled in the early period of Charles's reign came to an abrupt end with the onset of the **Great Plague** of 1665. Epidemics of bubonic plague were nothing new to London – there had been major outbreaks in 1593, 1603, 1625, 1636 and 1647 – but the combination of a warm summer and the chronic overcrowding of the city proved calamitous in this instance. Those with money left the city (the court moved to Oxford), while the poorer districts outside the City were the hardest hit. The extermination of the city's dog and cat population – believed to be the source of the epidemic – only exacerbated the situation by allowing the flea-carrying rat population to explode. In September, the death toll peaked at twelve thousand a week, and in total an estimated hundred thousand lost their lives.

A cold snap in November extinguished the plague, but the following year London had to contend with yet another disaster, the **Great Fire** of 1666. As with the plague, outbreaks of fire were fairly commonplace in London, whose buildings were predominantly timber-framed, and whose streets were narrow, allowing fires to spread

1588	1599	1605	1642–1651	1642	1643
Defeat of the Spanish Armada	Globe Theatre opens on Bankside	Gunpowder Plot foiled	Civil War	London theatres closed down	Cheapside Cross torn down by iconoclasts

THE GREAT FIRE

In the early hours of September 2, 1666, the **Great Fire** broke out at Farriner's, the king's bakery in Pudding Lane. The Lord Mayor refused to lose any sleep over it, dismissing it with the line "Pish! A woman might piss it out." Pepys was also roused from his bed, but saw no cause for alarm. Four days and four nights later, the Lord Mayor was found crying "like a fainting woman", and Pepys had fled, having famously buried his Parmesan cheese in the garden: the Fire had destroyed some four-fifths of the City of London, including 87 churches, 44 livery halls and 13,200 houses. The medieval city was no more.

Miraculously, there were only eight recorded fatalities, but 100,000 people were made homeless. "The hand of God upon us, a great wind and the season so very dry", was the verdict of the parliamentary report on the Fire, but Londoners preferred to blame Catholics and foreigners. The poor baker eventually "confessed" to being an agent of the pope and was executed, after which the following words, "but Popish frenzy, which wrought such horrors, is not yet quenched", were added to the Latin inscription on the Monument (see p.178), and only erased in 1830.

rapidly. However, this particular fire raged for five days and destroyed some four-fifths of the City of London (see box above).

Within five years, nine thousand houses had been rebuilt with bricks and mortar (timber was banned), and fifty years later **Christopher Wren** had almost single-handedly rebuilt all the City churches and completed the world's first purpose-built Protestant cathedral, **St Paul's**. Medieval London was no more, though the grandiose masterplans of Wren and other architects had to be rejected due to the legal intricacies of property rights within the City. The **Great Rebuilding**, as it was known, was one of London's most remarkable achievements – and all achieved in spite of a chronic lack of funds, a series of very severe winters and continuing wars against the Dutch.

Religious differences once again came to the fore with the accession of Charles's Catholic brother, **James II** (1685–88), who successfully put down the Monmouth Rebellion of 1685, but failed to halt the "Glorious Revolution" of 1688, which brought the Dutch king William of Orange to the throne, much to most people's relief. **William** (1689–1702) and his wife **Mary** (1689–95), daughter of James II, were made joint sovereigns, having agreed to a Bill of Rights defining the limitations of the monarch's power and the rights of his or her subjects. This, together with the Act of Settlement of 1701 – which among other things barred Catholics, or anyone married to one, from succession to the throne – made Britain the first country in the world to be governed by a **constitutional monarchy**, in which the roles of legislature and executive were separate and interdependent. A further development during the reign of **Anne** (1702–14), second daughter of James II, was the Act of Union of 1707, which united the English and Scottish parliaments.

Georgian London

When Queen Anne died childless in 1714 (despite having given birth seventeen times), the Stuart line ended, though pro-Stuart or Jacobite rebellions continued on and off until 1745. In accordance with the Act of Settlement, the succession passed to a non-English-speaking German, the Duke of Hanover, who became **George I** (1714–27)

1645	1649	1649–1660	1652
Archbishop of Canterbury, William Laud, executed on Tower Hill	King Charles I executed in Whitehall	The Commonwealth of England	Pasqua Rosée opens the first coffee house in London

THE GIN CRAZE

It's difficult to exaggerate the effects of the gin-drinking orgy which took place among the poorer sections of London's population between 1720 and 1751. At its height, **gin consumption** was averaging two pints a week for every man, woman and child, and the burial rate exceeded the baptism rate by more than 2:1. The origins of this lay in the country's enormous surplus of corn, which had to be sold in some form or another to keep the landowners happy. Deregulation of the distilling trade was Parliament's answer, thereby flooding the urban market with cheap, intoxicating liquor, which resulted in an enormous increase in crime, prostitution, **child mortality** and general misery among the poor. Papers in the Old Bailey archives relate a typical story of the period: a mother who "fetched her child from the workhouse, where it had just been 'new-clothed', for the afternoon. She strangled it and left it in a ditch in Bethnal Green in order to sell its clothes. The money was spent on gin." Eventually, in the face of huge vested interests, the government was forced to pass an Act in 1751 that restricted gin retailing and brought the epidemic to a halt.

of England. As power leaked from the monarchy, the king ceased to attend cabinet meetings (which he couldn't understand anyway), his place being taken by his chief minister. Most prominent among these chief ministers or "prime ministers", as they became known, was **Robert Walpole**, the first politician to live at **10 Downing Street**, and effective ruler of the country from 1721 to 1742.

Meanwhile, London's expansion continued unabated. The shops of the newly developed **West End** stocked the most fashionable goods in the country, the volume of trade more than tripled, and London's growing population – it was by now the largest city in the world, with a population rapidly approaching one million – created a huge market for food and other produce, as well as fuelling a building boom. In the City, the **Bank of England** – founded in 1694 to raise funds to conduct war against France – was providing a sound foundation for the economy. It could not, however, prevent the mania for financial speculation that resulted in the fiasco of the **South Sea Company**, which in 1720 sold shares in its monopoly of trade in the Pacific and along the east coast of South America. The "bubble" burst when the shareholders took fright at the extent of their own investments, and the value of the shares dropped to nothing, reducing many to penury and almost wrecking the government, which was saved only by the astute intervention of Walpole.

Wealthy though London was, it was also experiencing the worst mortality rates since records began in the reign of Henry VIII. Disease was rife in the overcrowded immigrant quarter of the East End and other slum districts, but the real killer during this period was **gin** (see box above).

Policing the metropolis was an increasing preoccupation for the government. It was proving a task far beyond the city's three thousand beadles, constables and nightwatchmen, who were, in any case, "old men chosen from the dregs of the people who have no other arms but a lantern and a pole", according to one French visitor. As a result, **crime** continued unabated throughout the eighteenth century, so that, in the words of Horace Walpole, one was "forced to travel even at noon as if one was going into battle". The government imposed draconian measures, introducing **capital punishment** for the most minor misdemeanours. The prison population swelled,

1665	1666	1694	1702	1710
The Great Plague kills 100,000 people	The Great Fire of London	Bank of England established	*The Daily Courant*, the world's first daily newspaper, published on Fleet Street	Completion of St Paul's Cathedral, designed by Christopher Wren

transportations began, and 1200 Londoners were hanged at Tyburn's gallows.

Despite such measures, and the passing of the Riot Act in 1715, rioting remained a popular pastime among the poorer classes in London. Anti-Irish riots had taken place in 1736; in 1743 there were further riots in defence of cheap liquor; and in the 1760s there were more organized mobilizations by supporters of the great agitator **John Wilkes**, calling for political reform. The most serious insurrection of the lot, however, were the **Gordon Riots** of 1780, when up to fifty thousand Londoners went on a five-day rampage through the city. Although anti-Catholicism was the spark that lit the fire, the majority of the rioters' targets were chosen not for their religion but for their wealth. The most dramatic incidents took place at Newgate Prison, where thousands of inmates were freed, and at the Bank of England, which was saved only by the intervention of the military – and John Wilkes, of all people. The death toll was in excess of three hundred, 25 rioters were subsequently hanged, and further calls were made in Parliament for the establishment of a proper police force.

Nineteenth-century London

The **nineteenth century** witnessed the emergence of London as the capital of an empire that stretched across the globe. The world's largest enclosed **dock system** was built in the marshes to the east of the City, Tory reformer **Robert Peel** established the world's first civilian **police force**, and the world's first public-transport network was created, with horse-buses, trains, trams and an underground railway.

The city's population grew dramatically from just over one million in 1801 (the first official census) to nearly seven million by 1901. **Industrialization** brought pollution and overcrowding, especially in the slums of the East End. Smallpox, measles, whooping cough and scarlet fever killed thousands of working-class families, as did the cholera outbreaks of 1832 and 1848–49. The **Poor Law** of 1834 formalized **workhouses** for the destitute, but these failed to alleviate the problem, in the end becoming little more than prison hospitals for the penniless. It is this era of slum life and huge social divides that Dickens evoked in his novels.

Architecturally, London was changing rapidly. **George IV** (1820–30), who became Prince Regent in 1811 during the declining years of his father, George III, instigated several grandiose projects that survive to this day. With the architect **John Nash**, he laid out London's first planned processional route, Regent Street, and a prototype garden city around **Regent's Park**. The Regent's Canal was driven through the northern fringe of the city, and Trafalgar Square began to take shape. The city already boasted the first secular public museum in the world, the **British Museum**, and in 1814 London's first public art gallery opened in the suburb of Dulwich, followed shortly afterwards by the National Gallery, founded in 1824. London finally got its own university, too, in 1826.

The accession of **Queen Victoria** (1837–1901) coincided with a period in which the country's international standing reached unprecedented heights, and as a result Victoria became as much a national icon as Elizabeth I had been. Though the intellectual achievements of Victoria's reign were immense – typified by the publication of Darwin's *The Origin of Species* in 1859 – the country saw itself above all as an imperial power founded on industrial and commercial prowess. Its spirit was perhaps best embodied by

1720	1750	1751	1759	1760
The South Sea Bubble causes financial ruin for many	Westminster Bridge opens	The Gin Act brings the decades of London's Gin Craze to an end	British Museum opens	City of London gates demolished

THE CHARTIST MOVEMENT IN LONDON

The **Chartist movement**, which campaigned for universal male suffrage (among other things), was much stronger in the industrialized north than in the capital, at least until the 1840s. Support for the movement reached its height in the revolutionary year of 1848. In March, some 10,000 Chartists occupied Trafalgar Square and held out against the police for two days. Then, on April 10, the Chartists organized a mass demonstration on Kennington Common. The government panicked and drafted in 80,000 "special constables" to boost the capital's 4000 police officers, and troops were garrisoned around all public buildings. In the end, London was a long way off experiencing a revolution: the demo took place, but the planned march on Parliament was called off.

the great engineering feats of **Isambard Kingdom Brunel** and by the **Great Exhibition** of 1851, a display of manufacturing achievements from all over the world, which took place in the Crystal Palace, erected in Hyde Park.

Despite being more than twice the size of Paris, London did not experience the political upheavals of the French capital – the terrorists who planned to wipe out the cabinet in the **1820 Cato Street Conspiracy** were the exception (see p.86). Mass demonstrations and the occasional minor fracas preceded the passing of the **1832 Reform Act**, which acknowledged the principle of popular representation (though few men and no women had the vote), but there was no real threat of revolution. London doubled its number of MPs in the new parliament, but its own administration remained dominated by the City oligarchy.

The birth of local government

The first tentative steps towards a cohesive form of metropolitan government were taken in 1855 with the establishment of the **Metropolitan Board of Works** (**MBW**). Its initial remit only covered sewerage, lighting and street maintenance, but it was soon extended to include gas, fire services, public parks and slum clearance. The achievements of the MBW – and in particular those of its chief engineer, **Joseph Bazalgette** – were immense, creating an underground sewer system (much of it still in use), improving transport routes and wiping out some of the city's more notorious slums. However, vested interests and resistance to reform from the City hampered the efforts of the MBW, which was also found to be involved in widespread malpractice.

In 1888 the **London County Council** (**LCC**) was established. It was the first directly elected London-wide government, though as ever the City held on jealously to its independence (and in 1899, the municipal boroughs were set up deliberately to undermine the power of the LCC). The arrival of the LCC coincided with an increase in working-class militancy within the capital. In 1884, 120,000 gathered in Hyde Park to support the ultimately unsuccessful London Government Bill, while a demonstration held in 1886 in Trafalgar Square in protest against unemployment ended in a riot through St James's. The following year the government banned any further demos, and the resultant protest brought even larger numbers to Trafalgar Square. The brutality of the police in breaking up this last demonstration led to its becoming known as "Bloody Sunday".

1780	1811	1812	1814	1826
Gordon Riots	London's population exceeds one million	Prime Minister Spencer Perceval becomes the first (and so far) last PM to be assassinated	The last Frost Fair takes place on the frozen River Thames	London University opens

In 1888 the Bryant & May matchgirls won their landmark **strike action** over working conditions, a victory followed up the next year by further successful strikes by the gasworkers and dockers. Charles Booth published his seventeen-volume *Life and Labour of the People of London* in 1890, providing the first clear picture of the social fabric of the city and shaming the council into action. In the face of powerful vested interests – landlords, factory owners and private utility companies – the LCC's Liberal leadership attempted to tackle the enormous problems, partly by taking gas, water, electricity and transport into municipal ownership, a process that took several more decades to achieve. The LCC's ambitious housing programme was beset with problems, too. Slum clearances only exacerbated overcrowding, and the new dwellings were too expensive for those in greatest need. Rehousing the poor in the suburbs also proved unpopular, since there was a policy of excluding pubs, traditionally the social centre of working-class communities, from these developments.

While half of London struggled to make ends meet, the other half enjoyed the fruits of the richest nation in the world. Luxury establishments such as *The Ritz* and Harrods belong to this period, which was personified by the dissolute and complacent Prince of Wales, later **Edward VII** (1901–10). For the masses, too, there were new entertainments to be enjoyed: music halls boomed, public houses prospered, and the circulation of populist newspapers such as the *Daily Mirror* topped one million. The first "Test" cricket match between England and Australia took place in 1880 at the Kennington Oval in front of 20,000 spectators, and during the following 25 years nearly all of London's professional football clubs were founded.

From World War I to World War II

Public patriotism peaked at the outbreak of **World War I** (1914–18), with crowds cheering the troops off from Victoria and Waterloo stations, convinced the fighting would all be over by Christmas. In the course of the next four years London experienced its first aerial attacks, with Zeppelin raids leaving some 650 dead, but these were minor casualties in the context of a war that destroyed millions of lives and eradicated whatever remained of the majority's respect for the ruling classes.

At the war's end in 1918, the country's social fabric was changed drastically as the voting franchise was extended to all men aged 21 and over and to women of 30 or over. The tardy liberalization of women's rights – largely due to the radical **Suffragette** movement led by Emmeline Pankhurst and her daughters – was not completed until 1928, the year of Emmeline's death, when women were at last granted the vote on equal terms with men.

Between the wars, London's population increased dramatically, reaching close to nine million by 1939, and representing one-fifth of the country's population. In contrast to the nineteenth century, however, there was a marked shift in population out into the **suburbs**. Some took advantage of the new "model dwellings" of LCC estates in places such as Dagenham in the east, though far more settled in "Metroland", the sprawling new suburban districts that followed the extension of the Underground out into northwest London.

In 1924 the **British Empire Exhibition** was held, with the intention of emulating the success of the Great Exhibition. Some 27 million people visited the show, but its success

1836	1851	1858	1863
The first railway is built in London between London Bridge and Greenwich	Great Exhibition held in Hyde Park	The Great Stink when the smell of untreated waste in the Thames reached an unprecedented level	The first section of the Underground opens between Paddington and Farringdon

THE BLITZ

The Luftwaffe bombing of London in World War II – commonly known as the **Blitz** – began on September 7, 1940, when in one night alone some 430 Londoners lost their lives, and over 1600 were seriously injured. It continued for 57 consecutive nights, then intermittently until the final and most devastating attack on the night of May 10, 1941, when 550 planes dropped over 100,000 incendiaries and hundreds of explosive bombs in a matter of hours. The death toll that night was over 1400, bringing the total killed during the Blitz to between 20,000 and 30,000, with some 230,000 homes wrecked. Along with the East End, the City was particularly badly hit: in a single raid on December 29 (dubbed the "Second Fire of London"), 1400 fires broke out across the Square Mile. Some say the Luftwaffe left St Paul's standing as a navigation aid, but it came close to destruction when a bomb landed near the southwest tower; luckily the bomb didn't go off, and it was successfully removed to the Hackney marshes where the 100ft-wide crater left by its detonation is still visible.

The authorities were ready to build mass graves for potential victims, but were unable to provide adequate air-raid shelters to prevent widespread carnage. The corrugated steel **Anderson shelters** issued by the government were of use to only one in four London households – those with gardens in which to bury them. Around 180,000 made use of the tube, despite initial government reluctance, by simply buying a ticket and staying below ground. The cheery photos of singing and dancing in the Underground which the censors allowed to be published tell nothing of the stale air, rats and lice that folk had to contend with. And even the tube stations couldn't withstand a direct hit, as occurred at Bank in January 1941, when over a hundred died. The vast majority of Londoners – some sixty percent – simply hid under the sheets and prayed.

couldn't hide the tensions that had been simmering since the end of the war. In 1926, a wage dispute between the miners' unions and their bosses developed into the **General Strike**. For nine days, more than half a million workers stayed away from work, until the government called in the army and thousands of volunteers to break the strike.

The economic situation deteriorated even further after the crash of the New York Stock Exchange in 1929, with unemployment in Britain reaching over three million in 1931. The Jarrow Marchers, the most famous protesters of the **Depression** years, shocked London on their arrival in 1936. In the same year thousands of British fascists tried to march through the predominantly Jewish East End, only to be stopped in the so-called **Battle of Cable Street** (see p.196). The end of the year brought a crisis within the Royal Family, too, when Edward VIII abdicated following his decision to marry Wallis Simpson, a twice-divorced American. His brother, **George VI** (1936–52), took over.

There were few public displays of patriotism with the outbreak of **World War II** (1939–45), and even fewer preparations were made against the likelihood of aerial bombardment. The most significant step was the evacuation of six hundred thousand of London's most vulnerable citizens (mostly children), but around half that number had drifted back to the capital by the Christmas of 1939, the midpoint of the "phoney war". The Luftwaffe's bombing campaign, known as the **Blitz** (see box above), lasted from September 1940 to May 1941. Further carnage was caused towards the end of the war by the pilotless V-1 "doodlebugs" and V-2 rockets, which caused another twenty thousand casualties.

1908	1911	1926	1936
London hosts the Olympic Games and wins the most medals	London population exceeds seven million	The General Strike lasts for nine days	Police, fascists and anti-fascist protesters clash in the Battle of Cable Street in the East End

Postwar London

The end of the war in 1945 was followed by a general election, which brought a landslide victory for the Labour Party under **Clement Attlee**. The Attlee government created the **welfare state**, and initiated a radical programme of **nationalization**, which brought the gas, electricity, coal, steel and iron industries under state control, along with the inland transport services. London itself was left with a severe accommodation crisis, with some eighty percent of the housing stock damaged to some degree. In response, prefabricated houses were erected all over the city, some of which were to remain occupied for well over forty years. The LCC also began building huge housing estates on many of the city's numerous bombsites, an often misconceived strategy which ran in tandem with the equally disastrous New Towns policy of central government.

To lift the country out of its gloom, the **Festival of Britain** was staged in 1951 on derelict land on the south bank of the Thames, a site that was eventually transformed into the Southbank Arts Centre. Londoners turned up at this technological funfair in their thousands, but at the same time many were abandoning the city for good, starting a slow process of population decline that has continued ever since. The consequent labour shortage was made good by mass **immigration** from the former colonies, in particular the Indian subcontinent and the West Indies. The first large group to arrive was the 492 West Indians aboard the SS *Empire Windrush*, which docked at Tilbury in June 1948. The newcomers, a large percentage of whom settled in London, were given small welcome, and within ten years were subjected to **race riots**, which broke out in Notting Hill in 1958.

The riots are thought to have been carried out, for the most part, by "Teddy Boys", working-class lads from London's slum areas and new housing estates, who formed the city's first postwar youth cult. Subsequent cults, and their accompanying music, helped turn London into the epicentre of the so-called **Swinging Sixties**, the Teddy Boys being usurped in the early 1960s by the "Mods", whose sharp suits came from London's Carnaby Street. Fashion hit the capital in a big way, and, thanks to the likes of The Beatles, The Rolling Stones and Twiggy, London was proclaimed hippest city on the planet on the front pages of *Time* magazine.

Life for most Londoners, however, was rather less groovy. In the middle of the decade London's local government was reorganized, the LCC being supplanted by the **Greater London Council (GLC)**, whose jurisdiction covered a much wider area, including many Tory-dominated suburbs. As a result, the Conservatives gained power in the capital for the first time since 1934, and one of their first acts was to support a huge urban motorway scheme that would have displaced as many people as did the railway boom of the Victorian period. Luckily for London, Labour won control of the GLC in 1973 and halted the plans. The Labour victory also ensured that the Covent Garden Market building was saved for posterity, but this ran against the grain. Elsewhere, whole areas of the city were pulled down and redeveloped, and many of London's worst tower blocks were built.

Thatcherite London

In 1979 **Margaret Thatcher** won the general election for the Conservatives, and the country and the capital would never be quite the same again. Thatcher went on to win

1948	1951	1952	1953
London hosts the Olympic Games	Festival of Britain held on the South Bank	London's tram system is abandoned	Coronation of Queen Elizabeth II

THE BIG BANG

In 1986, at the same time as homelessness and unemployment were on the increase, the so-called "**Big Bang**", which abolished a whole range of restrictive practices on the Stock Exchange, took place. The immediate effect of this deregulation was that foreign banks began to take over brokers and form new, competitive conglomerates. The side effect, however, was to send stocks and shares into the stratosphere, shortly after which they inevitably crashed, ushering in a recession that dragged on for the best part of the next ten years. The one great physical legacy of the Thatcherite experiment in the capital is the **Docklands** development (see p.206), a new business quarter in the derelict docks of the East End, which came about as a direct result of the Big Bang.

three general elections, steering Britain into a period of ever greater social polarization. While taxation policies and easy credit fuelled a consumer boom for the professional classes (the yuppies of the 1980s), the erosion of the manufacturing industry and weakening of the welfare state created a calamitous number of people trapped in long-term unemployment, which topped three million in the early 1980s. The Brixton riots of 1981 and 1985 and the Tottenham riot of 1985 were reminders of the price of such divisive policies, and of the long-standing resentment and feeling of social exclusion rife among the city's black youth.

Nationally, the Labour Party went into sharp decline, but in London the party won a narrow victory in the GLC elections on a radical manifesto that was implemented by its youthful new leader **Ken Livingstone**, or "Red Ken" as the tabloids dubbed him. Under Livingstone, the GLC poured money into projects among London's ethnic minorities, into the arts and, most famously, into a subsidized fares policy which saw thousands abandon their cars in favour of inexpensive public transport. Such schemes endeared Livingstone to the hearts of many Londoners, but his popular brand of socialism was too much for the Thatcher government, who, in 1986, abolished the GLC, leaving London as the only European capital without a directly elected body to represent it.

Abolition exacerbated tensions between the poorer and richer boroughs of the city. Rich Tory councils like Westminster proceeded to slash public services and sell off council houses to boost Tory support in marginal wards. Meanwhile in impoverished Labour-held Lambeth and Hackney, millions were being squandered by corrupt council employees. **Homelessness** returned to London in a big way for the first time since Victorian times, and the underside of Waterloo Bridge was transformed into a "Cardboard City", sheltering up to two thousand vagrants on any one night. Great efforts were made by nongovernmental organizations to alleviate homelessness, not least the establishment of a weekly magazine, the *Big Issue*, which continues to be sold by the homeless right across London, earning them a small wage.

Thatcher's greatest folly, however, was the introduction of the **Poll Tax**, a head tax levied regardless of means, which hit the poorest sections of the community hardest. The tax also highlighted the disparity between the city's boroughs. In wealthy, Tory-controlled Wandsworth, Poll Tax bills were zero, while those in poorer, neighbouring, Labour-run Lambeth were the highest in the country. In 1990, the Poll Tax provoked the first full-blooded riot in central London for a long time, and played a significant role in Thatcher's downfall later that year.

1956	1966	1971	1973
Clean Air Act	England win the World Cup at Wembley	Decimal currency introduced	Britain joins the EEC

LONDON IN FILM THROUGH THE DECADES

As early as 1889 Wordsworth Donisthorpe made a primitive motion picture of Trafalgar Square, and since then London has been featured in countless films. Below is a snapshot selection of films culled from each decade since the 1920s.

Blackmail (Alfred Hitchcock, 1929). The first British talkie feature film, this thriller stars the Czech actress Anny Ondra and has its dramatic finale on the dome of the British Museum.

The Adventures of Sherlock Holmes (Alfred Werker, 1939). The Baker Street detective has made countless screen appearances, but Basil Rathbone remains the most convincing incarnation. Here Holmes and Watson (Nigel Bruce) are pitted against Moriarty (George Zucco), out to steal the Crown Jewels.

Passport to Pimlico (Henry Cornelius, 1948). The quintessential Ealing Comedy, in which the inhabitants of Pimlico, discovering that they are actually part of Burgundy, abolish rationing and closing time. Full of all the usual eccentrics, among them Margaret Rutherford in particularly fine form as an excitable history don.

The Ladykillers (Alexander Mackendrick, 1955). Delightfully black comedy set somewhere at the back of King's Cross (a favourite location for filmmakers). Katie Johnson plays the nice old lady getting the better of Alec Guinness, Peter Sellers and assorted other crooks.

Blow-Up (Michelangelo Antonioni, 1966). Swinging London and some less obvious backgrounds (notably Maryon Wilson Park, Charlton) feature in this metaphysical mystery about a photographer (David Hemmings) who may unwittingly have recorded evidence of a murder.

Jubilee (Derek Jarman, 1978). Jarman's angry punk collage, in which Elizabeth I finds herself transported to the urban decay of late twentieth-century Deptford.

My Beautiful Laundrette (Stephen Frears, 1985). A surreal comedy of Thatcher's London, offering the unlikely combination of an entrepreneurial Asian (Gordon Warnecke), his ex-National Front boyfriend (Daniel Day-Lewis) and a laundrette called Powders.

Naked (Mike Leigh, 1993). David Thewlis is brilliant as the disaffected and garrulous misogynist who goes on a tour through the underside of what he calls "the big shitty" – life is anything but sweet in Leigh's darkest but most substantial film.

Dirty Pretty Things (Stephen Frears, 2002). Entertaining romantic thriller set in London's asylum-seeking, multicultural underbelly, shot through with plenty of humour and lots of pace.

The King's Speech (Tom Hooper, 2011). Moving, funny account of King George VI's battle to overcome his stammer, after finding himself catapulted onto the throne following the abdication of Edward VIII.

Twenty-first-century London

On the surface at least, **twenty-first-century London** has come a long way since the bleak Thatcher years. Funded by money from the National Lottery and the Millennium Commission, the face of the city has certainly changed for the better: the city's national museums have been totally transformed into state-of-the-art visitor attractions, and all of them are free; there are new pedestrian bridges over the Thames; and Tate Modern towers like a beacon of optimism over the South Bank.

The most significant political development for London has been the creation of the **Greater London Assembly** (**GLA**), along with an American-style Mayor of London, both

1986	1991	2000	2005
GLC abolished leaving London without a central government	The first buildings at Canary Wharf completed	Establishment of the Greater London Authority (GLA)	July 7 a series of terrorist bombs across the London transport network leaves 56 dead

elected by popular mandate. The Labour government, which came to power on a wave of enthusiasm in 1997, did everything it could to prevent the election of the former GLC leader **Ken Livingstone** as the first mayor, but, despite being forced to leave the Labour Party and run as an independent, he won a resounding victory in the 2000 mayoral elections.

Livingstone was eventually succeeded by Boris Johnson in 2008, but his lasting legacy has been in **transport**. As well as creating more bus routes and introducing more buses, he successfully introduced a **congestion charge** for every vehicle entering central London (see p.23). As a result, traffic levels in central London have been reduced, and, although the congestion charge hasn't solved all the city's problems, at least it showed that, with a little vision and perseverance, something concrete can be achieved.

Livingstone was also instrumental in helping London win the **2012 Olympics** (see p.202). The bid emphasized its regenerative potential for a deprived, multicultural area of London's East End and, against all the odds, beat Paris in the final head-to-head vote. For a moment, London celebrated wildly. Unfortunately, the euphoria was all too brief. A day after hearing the news about the Olympics, on **July 7, 2005**, London was hit by four **suicide bombers** who killed themselves and over fifty innocent commuters in four separate explosions: on tube trains at Aldgate, Edgware Road and King's Cross and one on a bus in Tavistock Square. Two weeks later a similar attack was unsuccessful after the bombers' detonators failed. Despite everyone's worst fears, however, these two attacks proved to be isolated incidents and not the beginning of a concerted campaign.

The 2010 election produced no overall winner and resulted in a hung parliament for only the second time since World War II. The Conservatives formed a coalition with the Liberal Democrats and began the harshest series of spending cuts since 1945. In August 2011, against a background of deepening economic hardship, London suffered the worst **riots** since the 1980s, not just in areas such as Tottenham (where the riots began) and Brixton, but across the capital from Bromley to Waltham Forest. The Conservatives responded with talk of arming the police with plastic bullets and water cannon, and handing out long sentences to those involved, but it remains to be seen whether they will also tackle the underlying social divisions within the city.

2008	2010	2011	2012
Boris Johnson becomes Mayor of London	Boris Bikes free cycle hire scheme introduced	August riots in London	London hosts the Olympic Games

Books

Given the enormous number of books on London, the list below is necessarily a selective one, with books marked ★ being particularly recommended. London's bookshops are covered in detail in the Shopping chapter (see p.423). The best known online bookshop is ⊛amazon.com, but if you're looking for a particular book in the UK, ⊛bookbrain.co.uk will tell you which online bookshop is selling it for the cheapest price. Most of the books recommended are in paperback, but the more expensive books can often be bought secondhand online these days.

TRAVEL, JOURNALS AND MEMOIRS

Paul Bailey (ed) *The Oxford Book of London*. Large anthology of musings on London, arranged in chronological order from twelfth-century monks via Dostoevsky and Van Gogh to Hanif Kureishi and Angela Carter.

John Betjeman *Betjeman's London*. A selection of writings and poems by the then Poet Laureate, who spearheaded the campaign to save London's architectural heritage in the 1960s.

★ **James Boswell** *London Journal*. Boswell's diary, written in 1792–93 when he was lodging in Downing Street, is remarkably candid about his frequent dealings with the city's prostitutes, and is a fascinating insight into eighteenth-century life.

John Evelyn *The Diary of John Evelyn*. In contrast to his contemporary, Pepys, Evelyn gives away very little of his personal life, but his diaries cover a much greater period of English history and a much wider range of topics.

Ford Madox Ford *The Soul of London*. Experimental, impressionist portrait of London published in 1905.

Tarquin Hall *Salaam Brick Lane: A Year in the New East End*. The lively and impassioned account of living above a Bangladeshi sweatshop in modern-day Brick Lane.

Doris Lessing *Walking in the Shade 1949–62*. The second volume of Lessing's autobiography, set in London in the 1950s, deals with the writing and theatre scenes and party politics, including her association with the Communist Party, with which she eventually became disenchanted.

George Orwell *Down and Out in Paris and London*. Orwell's tramp's-eye view of the 1930s, written from first-hand experience. The London section is particularly harrowing.

★ **Samuel Pepys** *The Shorter Pepys*; *The Illustrated Pepys*. Pepys kept a voluminous diary while he was living in London from 1660 until 1669, recording the fall of the Commonwealth, the Restoration, the Great Plague and the Great Fire, as well as describing the daily life of the nation's capital. Penguin's *The Shorter Pepys*, although abridged from eleven volumes, is still massive; *The Illustrated Pepys* is made up of the choicest extracts accompanied by contemporary illustrations.

Christopher Ross *Tunnel Visions*. Witty and perceptive musings of popular philosopher Ross as he spends a year working as a station assistant on the Tube at Oxford Circus.

Iain Sinclair *Hackney, That Rose-Red Empire: a Confidential Report*; *Liquid City*; and *London Orbital*. Sinclair is one of the most original (and virtually unreadable) London writers of his generation. *Hackney* is an absorbing biography of the author's favourite borough. *Liquid City* contains beautiful photos and entertaining text about London's hidden rivers and canals; and *London Orbital* is an account of his walk round the M25, delving into obscure parts of the city's periphery.

HISTORY, SOCIETY AND POLITICS

Peter Ackroyd *Dickens*; *Blake*; *Sir Thomas More*; *Thames: Sacred River* and *London: The Biography*. Few writers know quite as much about London as Ackroyd does, and London is central to all three of his biographical subjects – the result is scholarly, enthusiastic and eminently readable. *London: The Biography* is the massive culmination of a lifetime's love affair with a living city and its intimate history.

★ **Paul Begg** *Jack the Ripper: The Definitive History*. This book, whose author has given talks to the FBI on the subject, sets the murders in their Victorian context and aims to debunk the myths.

Piers Dudgeon *Our East End: Memoirs of Life in Disappearing Britain*. Packed with extracts from written accounts and diaries as well as literary sources, this is a patchwork of the East End with its legendary community spirit and a dash of realism.

Markman Ellis *The Coffee House*. Tracing the unlikely connection between the strange bitter drink from Turkey, which reached London in the seventeenth century, and today's ubiquitous Starbucks and the like.

Clive Emsley *The Newgate Calendar*. Grim and gory account of the most famous London criminals of the day – Captain Kidd, Jack Sheppard, Dick Turpin – with potted biographies of each victim, ending with an account of his execution. Starting out as a collection of papers and booklets, *The Newgate Calendar* was first published in 1828 and was second in popularity only to the Bible at the time of publication, but is now difficult to get hold of.

Juliet Gardiner *The Blitz: the British Under Attack*. A far-reaching account of the Blitz which dispels some of the myths, combining first-hand accounts with some surprising statistics.

★ **Jonathan Glancey** *London Bread and Circuses*. In this small, illustrated book, the *Guardian*'s architecture critic extols the virtues of the old LCC and visionaries like Frank Pick, who transformed London's transport in the 1930s, discusses the millennium projects (the "circuses" of the title), and bemoans the city's creaking infrastructure.

★ **Ed Glinert** *The London Compendium*. Glinert dissects every street, every park, every house and every tube station and produces juicy anecdotes every time. The same author's *East End Chronicles: 300 Years of Mystery and Mayhem* is a readable revelation of all the nefarious doings of the East End, sorting myth from fact, and hoping the spirit will somehow survive in spite of Docklands.

Rahila Gupta *From Homebreakers to Jailbreakers: Southall Black Sisters*. The story of a radical Asian women's group which, against all the odds, was founded in London in 1979 and became internationally famous for campaigning for all disempowered black women.

Sarah Hartley *Mrs P's Journey: The Remarkable Story of the Woman Who Created the A–Z Map*. The tale of Phyllis Pearsall, the indomitable woman who survived a horrific childhood and went on to found London's most famous mapmaking company – you won't feel the same about the A–Z again.

Rachel Lichtenstein and Iain Sinclair *Rodinsky's Room*. A fascinating search into the Jewish past of the East End, centred on the nebulous figure of David Rodinsky.

Peter Linebaugh *The London Hanged*. Superb, Marxist analysis of crime and punishment in the eighteenth century, drawing on the history of those hanged at Tyburn.

Jack London *The People of the Abyss*. The author went undercover in 1902 to uncover East End poverty.

Henry Mayhew *London Labour and the London Poor*. Mayhew's pioneering study of Victorian London, based on research carried out in the 1840s and 1850s.

Roy Porter *London: A Social History*. This immensely readable history is one of the best books on London published since the war, particularly strong on the saga of the capital's local government.

Stephen Porter *London's Plague Years: Lord Have Mercy Upon Us*. Drawing on various contemporary sources, Porter paints a vivid picture of what it was like to live with a horror which killed 70,000 Londoners.

Maude Pember Reeves *Round About a Pound a Week*. From 1909 to 1913, the Fabian Women's Group, part of the British Labour Party, recorded the daily budget of thirty families in Lambeth living in extreme poverty. This is the accompanying comment, which is both enlightening and enlightened.

John Stow *A Survey of London*. Stow, a retired tailor, set himself the unenviable task of writing the first-ever account of the city in 1598, for which he is now revered, though at the time the task forced him into penury.

Judith R. Walkowitz *City of Dreadful Delight: Narratives of Sexual Danger in Late-Victorian London*. Weighty feminist tract on issues such as child prostitution and the Ripper murders, giving a powerful overview of the image of women in the fiction and media of the day.

Maureen Waller *1700: Scenes from London Life*. Fascinating minutiae of the crazy, everyday life of eighteenth-century London. Equally enthralling is *London 1945: Life in the Debris of War* which explores a very different era.

★ **Ben Weinreb & Christopher Hibbert** *The London Encyclopaedia*. More than a thousand pages of concisely presented information on London past and present, accompanied by the odd illustration. The most fascinating book on the capital.

Jerry White *London in the Nineteenth Century; London in the Twentieth Century*. Comprehensive history of the most momentous centuries in the city's history.

Sarah Wise *The Blackest Streets: The Life and Death of a Victorian Slum*. A meticulously researched work which reveals the depths of poverty in the area north of Bethnal Green Road.

ART, ARCHITECTURE AND ARCHEOLOGY

Felix Barker & Peter Jackson *The History of London in Maps*. A beautiful volume of maps, from the earliest surviving chart of 1558 to the new Docklands, with accompanying text explaining the history of the city and its cartography.

Bill Brandt *London in the Thirties*. Brandt's superb black-and-white photos bear witness to a London lost in the Blitz.

Elaine Harwood & Andrew Saint *London*. Part of the excellent Exploring England's Heritage series, sponsored by English Heritage. It's highly selective, though each building is discussed at some length and is well illustrated.

Leo Hollis *The Stones of London*. An illuminating social history of London illustrated by studying twelve of the city's buildings ranging from the iconic (Westminster Abbey) to the obscure (a tower block in the East End).

Derek Kendall *The City of London Churches*. A beautifully illustrated book, comprised mostly of colour photos, covering the remarkable City churches, many of them designed by Wren after the Great Fire.

Andrew Richard Kershman *London's Monuments*. A stroll around some of the well-known and the more obscure monuments of the city.

Nikolaus Pevsner and others *The Buildings of England*. Magisterial series, started by Pevsner, to which others have added, inserting newer buildings but generally respecting the founder's personal tone. London comes in six volumes, plus a special volume on the City churches.

Arnold Schwartzman *London Art Deco: A Celebration of the Architectural Style of the Metropolis During the Twenties and Thirties*. Generously illustrated, this book bears witness to the British version of Art Deco in the likes of the Savoy and the Hoover building.

Anthony Sutcliffe *Architectural History of London*. A weighty tome, extensively illustrated, which traces the history of building in London from the Romans to the twenty-first century.

Richard Trench & Ellis Hillman *London under London*. Fascinating book revealing the secrets of every aspect of the capital's subterranean history, from the lost rivers of the underground to the gas and water systems.

David Whitehead & Henning Klattenhof *London – the Architectural Guide*. A chronological study from the Romans to the present day with excellent colour photographs and information about architects and styles as well as buildings.

LONDON IN FICTION

Peter Ackroyd *English Music; Hawksmoor; The House of Doctor Dee; The Great Fire of London;* and *Dan Leno and the Limehouse Golem*. Ackroyd's novels are all based on arcane aspects of London, wrapped into thriller-like narratives, and conjuring up kaleidoscopic visions of various ages of English culture. *Hawksmoor*, about the great church architect, is the most popular and enjoyable.

★ **Monica Ali** *Brick Lane*. Acute, involving, and slyly humorous, novel about a young Bengali woman who comes over with her husband to live in London's East End.

Hanan Al-Shaykh *Only in London*. An amusing and sympathetic tale of four people from different parts of the Arab world who arrive in London on the same flight.

Martin Amis *London Fields; Yellow Dog*. Short sentences and cartoon characters, Amis's novels tend to provoke extreme reactions in readers. Love 'em or hate 'em, these two are set in London.

J.G. Ballard *The Drowned World; Concrete Island; The Millennium People; High Rise*. Wild stuff. *The Drowned World*, Ballard's first novel, is set in a futuristic, flooded and tropical London. In *Concrete Island*, a car crashes on the Westway, leaving its driver stranded on the central reservation, unable to flag down passing cars. In *The Millennium People* the middle classes turn urban terrorist. In *High Rise*, the residents of a high-rise block of flats in East London go slowly mad.

Samuel Beckett *Murphy*. Nihilistic, dark-humoured vision of the city, written in 1938, and told through the eyes of anti-hero Murphy.

Elizabeth Bowen *The Heat of the Day*. Bowen worked for the Ministry of Information during World War II, and witnessed the Blitz first-hand from her Marylebone flat; this novel perfectly captures the dislocation and rootlessness of wartime London.

Anthony Burgess *A Dead Man in Deptford*. Playwright Christopher Marlowe's unexplained murder in a tavern in Deptford provides the background for this historical novel, which brims over with Elizabethan life and language.

Angela Carter *The Magic Toyshop; Wise Children*. The *Magic Toyshop* was Carter's celebrated 1967 novel, about a provincial woman moving to London, while *Wise Children*, published a year before her untimely death, is set in a carnivalesque London.

G.K. Chesterton *The Napoleon of Notting Hill*. Written in 1904, but set eighty years in the future, in a London divided into squabbling independent boroughs – something prophetic there – and ruled by royalty selected on a rotational basis.

Clare Clark *The Great Stink; The Nature of Monsters*. You need a very strong stomach for either of these historical novels, the first set in Victorian sewers and the second in the eighteenth century.

J.M. Coetzee *Youth*. Claustrophobic, semi-autobiographical novel by South African Booker Prize-winner, centred on a self-obsessed colonial, struggling to find the meaning of life and become a writer in London in the 1960s.

★ **Arthur Conan Doyle** *The Complete Sherlock Holmes*. Deerstalkered sleuth Sherlock Holmes and dependable sidekick Dr Watson penetrate all levels of Victorian London, from Limehouse opium dens to millionaires' pads. *A Study in Scarlet* and *The Sign of Four* are based entirely in London.

Joseph Conrad *The Secret Agent*. Conrad's wonderful spy story is based on the botched anarchist bombing of Greenwich Observatory in 1894, and exposes the hypocrisies of both the police and the anarchists.

Daniel Defoe *Journal of the Plague Year*. An account of the Great Plague seen through the eyes of an East End saddler, written some sixty years after the event.

Charles Dickens *Bleak House; A Christmas Tale; Little Dorrit; Oliver Twist*. The descriptions in Dickens' London-based novels have become the clichés of the Victorian city:

the fog, the slums and the stinking river. *Little Dorrit* is set mostly in Borough and contains some of his most trenchant pieces of social analysis. Much of *Bleak House* is set around the Inns of Court that Dickens knew so well.

Maureen Duffy *Capital*. First published in 1975, the novel is like a many-layered sandwich full of startling flavours, as the focus shifts from the central character, an unbalanced squatter with an obsession with London's past and future, to vivid slices of history.

Nell Dunn *Up the Junction; Poor Cow*. Perceptive and unsentimental account of the downside of south London life in the 1950s after the hype of the Festival of Britain.

George Gissing *New Grub Street*. Classic 1891 story of intrigue and jealousy among London's Fleet Street hacks.

Graham Greene *The Human Factor; It's a Battlefield; The Ministry of Fear; The End of the Affair*. Greene's London novels are all fairly bleak, ranging from *The Human Factor*, which probes the underworld of the city's spies, to *The Ministry of Fear*, which is set during the Blitz.

Patrick Hamilton *Hangover Square; Twenty Thousand Streets Under the Sky*. The first is a story of unrequited love and violence in Earls Court in the 1940s, while the latter is a trilogy of stories set in seedy 1930s London.

Neil Hanson *The Dreadful Judgement*. A docu-fiction account in which modern scientific methods and historical knowledge are applied to the Fire of London so vividly you can almost feel the heat.

Aldous Huxley *Point Counter Point*. Sharp satire of London's high-society wastrels and dilettantes of the Roaring Twenties.

Henry James *The Awkward Age*. Light, ironic portrayal of London high society at the turn of the twentieth century.

Hanif Kureishi *The Buddha of Suburbia; Love in a Blue Time; My Ear at His Heart*. The Buddha of Suburbia is a raunchy account of life as an Anglo-Asian in late-1960s suburbia, and the art scene of the 1970s; *Love in a Blue Time* is a collection of short stories set in 1990s London; *My Ear at His Heart* is a biography of Kureishi's father from his privileged childhood in Mumbai to a life in Bromley.

Andrea Levy *Small Island*. A warm-hearted novel in which postwar London struggles to adapt to the influx of Jamaicans who in turn find that the land of their dreams is full of prejudice.

Colin MacInnes *Absolute Beginners; Omnibus*. Absolute Beginners, a story of life in Soho and Notting Hill in the 1950s – much influenced by Selvon (see below) – is infinitely better than the film of the same name. *Omnibus* is set in 1957, in a Victoria Station packed with hopeful black immigrants; white welfare officer meets black man from Lagos with surprising results.

Somerset Maugham *Liza of Lambeth*. Maugham considered himself a "second-rater", but this early novel, written in 1897, about Cockney lowlife, is packed with vivid local colour.

★ **Ian McEwan** *Saturday*. Set on the day of a protest march against the war in Iraq, this book captures the mood of London post-9/11, as the main character is forced to consider his attitude to this and many other issues.

Timothy Mo *Sour Sweet*. Very funny and very sad story of a newly arrived Chinese family struggling to understand the English way of life in the 1970s, written with great insight by Mo, who is himself of mixed parentage.

Michael Moorcock *Mother London*. A magnificent, rambling, kaleidoscopic portrait of London from the Blitz to Thatcher by a once-fashionable, but now very much underrated, writer.

Iris Murdoch *Under the Net; The Black Prince; An Accidental Man; Bruno's Dream. Under the Net* was Murdoch's first, funniest and arguably her best novel, published in 1954, starring a hack writer living in London. Many of her subsequent works are set in various parts of middle-class London and span several decades of the second half of the twentieth century.

George Orwell *Keep the Aspidistra Flying*. Orwell's 1930s critique of Mammon is equally critical of its chief protagonist, whose attempt to rebel against the system only condemns him to poverty, working in a London bookshop and freezing his evenings away in a miserable rented room.

Jonathan Raban *Soft City*. An early work from 1974 that's both a portrait of, and paean to, metropolitan life.

★ **Derek Raymond** *Not till the Red Fog Rises*. A book which "reeks with the pervasive stench of excrement" as Iain Sinclair (see below) put it, this is a lowlife spectacular set in the seediest sections of the capital.

Barnaby Rogerson (ed) *London: Poetry of Place*. A delightful pocket-sized book complete with potted biographies of the poets.

Edward Rutherford *London*. A big, big novel (perhaps too big) that stretches from Roman times to the present and deals with the most dramatic moments of London's history. Masses of historical detail woven in with the story of several families.

Samuel Selvon *The Lonely Londoners*. "Gives us the smell and feel of this rather horrifying life. Not for the squeamish", ran the quote from the *Evening Standard* on the original cover. This is, in fact, a wry and witty account of the Afro-Caribbean experience in London in the 1950s.

★ **Iain Sinclair** *White Chappell, Scarlet Tracings; Downriver; Radon Daughters*. Sinclair's idiosyncratic and richly textured novels are a strange mix of Hogarthian caricature, New Age mysticism and conspiracy-theory rant. Deeply offensive and highly recommended.

Stevie Smith *Novel on Yellow Paper*. Poet Stevie Smith's first novel takes place in the publishing world of the London of 1930s.

Zadie Smith *White Teeth*. Highly acclaimed and funny first novel about race, gender and class in the ethnic melting pot of North London.

John Sommerfield *May Day*. Set in the revolutionary fervour of the 1930s, this novel is "as if Mrs Dalloway was written by a Communist Party bus driver", in the words of one reviewer.

Muriel Spark *The Bachelors*; *The Ballad of Peckham Rye*. Two London-based novels written one after the other by the Scots-born author, best known for *The Prime of Miss Jean Brodie*.

Graham Swift *Last Orders*. Four friends recall the East End as it was during the war, in an unsentimental view of Cockney life.

Edith Templeton *Gordon*. A tale of sex and humiliation in postwar London, banned in the 1960s when it was published under a pseudonym (Louisa Walbrook).

Rose Tremain *The Road Home*. The moving story of Lev, an Eastern European economic migrant, who heads for London and finds the streets are not paved with gold in the late twentieth century.

Sarah Waters *Affinity*, *Fingersmith*, and *Tipping the Velvet*. Racy modern novels set in Victorian London: *Affinity* is set in the spiritualist milieu, *Fingersmith* focuses on an orphan girl, while *Tipping the Velvet* is about lesbian love in the music hall. *The Night Watch* is a tale of London during World War II.

Evelyn Waugh *Vile Bodies*. Waugh's target, the "vile bodies" of the title, are the flippant rich kids of the Roaring Twenties, as in Huxley's *Point Counter Point* (see p.465).

Patrick White *The Living and the Dead*. Australian Nobel Prize-winner's second novel is a sombre portrait of family life in London at the time of the Spanish Civil War.

Angus Wilson *The Wrong Set*. A collection of short stories written in 1949 satirizing contemporary upper-middle-class characters in Knightsbridge and Kensington.

P.G. Wodehouse *Jeeves Omnibus*. Bertie Wooster and his stalwart butler, Jeeves, were based in Mayfair, and many of their exploits take place with London showgirls and in the Drones gentlemen's club.

★ **Virginia Woolf** *Mrs Dalloway*. Woolf's novel relates the thoughts of a London society hostess and a shell-shocked war veteran, with her "stream-of-consciousness" style in full flow. *The London Scene* consists of six musings on Woolf's favourite London walks, originally written for *Good Housekeeping* in 1932.

SPECIALIST GUIDES

Jill Billington *London's Parks and Gardens*. An expensive coffee-table item, but the photos are beautiful.

Judi Culbertson & Tom Randall *Permanent Londoners*. An illustrated guide to the finest of London's cemeteries, from Westminster Abbey and St Paul's to the Victorian splendours of Highgate and Kensal Green. Very good on biographical histories of the deceased, too.

Andrew Duncan *Secret London*. With boundless enthusiasm, Duncan takes you along the lost rivers, unmasks the property tycoons, exposes dead tube stations and uncovers just about every undiscovered nook and cranny in the city.

Paul Goldsack *River Thames: In the Footsteps of the Famous*. Written in conjunction with English Heritage this is a racy romp up the river, spotting connections with the famous and the infamous.

David Long *Hidden City: The Secret Alleys, Courts and Yards of London's Square Mile*. This book will send you scurrying through narrow alleyways in search of historical relics.

Jean Moorcroft Wilson *Virginia Woolf's London*. A book of place, tracing Woolf's connections with Kensington, Bloomsbury and Richmond, and the footsteps of some of her characters.

Christian Wolmar *The Subterranean Railway*. A fascinating history of the Tube, the world's first underground railway and product of the vision of Victorian pioneers.

Glossary of architectural terms

Aisle Clear space parallel to the nave of a church, usually with lower ceiling than the nave.

Altar Table at which the Eucharist is celebrated, at the east end of a church. (When the church is not aligned to the geographical east, the altar end is still referred to as the "east" end.)

Ambulatory Passage behind and around the chancel.

Apse The curved or polygonal east end of a church.

Arcade Row of arches on top of columns or piers, supporting a wall.

Baldachin Canopy over an altar.

Barbican Defensive structure built in front of main gate fortress.

Barrel vault Continuous rounded vault, like a semi-cylinder.

Blue plaque English Heritage plaques placed on a building associated with a prominent figure (who must have been dead for at least 25 years).

Boss A decorative carving at the meeting point of the lines of a vault.

Buttress Stone support for a wall; some buttresses are wholly attached to the wall, others, known as "flying buttresses", take the form of a tower with a connecting arch.

Capital Upper section of a column or pier, usually carved.

Chancel Section of a church where the altar is located.

Choir Area in which the church service is conducted; next to or same as chancel.

Clerestory Upper storey of nave, containing a line of windows.

Coffering Regular recessed spaces set into a ceiling.

Corbel Jutting stone support, often carved.

Crenellations Battlements with square indentations.

Fan vault Late Gothic form of vaulting, in which the area between walls and ceiling is covered with stone ribs in the shape of an open fan.

Finial Any decorated tip of an architectural feature.

Gallery A raised passageway.

Hammerbeam Type of internal roofing in which horizontal beams support vertical timbers that connect to and support the roof.

Lady Chapel Chapel dedicated to the Virgin, often found at the east end of major churches.

Lantern Structure on top of a dome or tower, often glazed to let in light.

Listed building A building which has been put on English Heritage's protected list; buildings are classed (in descending order of importance) Grade I, Grade II* and Grade II.

Misericord Carved ledge below a tip-up seat, usually in choir stalls.

Nave The main part of a church on the other (usually western) side of the crossing from the chancel.

Oriel Projecting window.

Palladian Eighteenth-century classical style adhering to the principles of Andrea Palladio.

Pediment Triangular space above a window or doorway.

Perpendicular Late Gothic style, about 1380–1550.

Piano nobile Principal floor of a large house usually located above the ground floor.

Pilaster Flat column set against a wall.

Reredos Painted or carved panel at the back of an altar.

Rood screen Wooden screen supporting a crucifix (or rood), separating the choir from the nave; few survived the Reformation.

Rose window Large, circular window, divided into vaguely petal-shaped sections.

Stalls Seating for clergy in the choir area of a church.

Tracery Pattern formed by narrow bands of stone in a window or on a wall surface.

Transept Sections of the main body of a church at right angles to the choir and nave.

Tympanum Panel over a doorway, often carved in medieval churches.

Vault Arched ceiling.

Glossary of British terms

Bill	Restaurant check	**Lift**	Elevator
Biscuit	Cookie or cracker	**Lorry**	Truck
Bonnet	Car hood	**Motorway**	Highway
Boot	Car trunk	**NHS**	National Health Service
British Rail	State railways (1945–1997)	**Off-licence**	Liquor store
Caravan	Trailer	**Pants**	Underwear
Car park	Parking lot	**Petrol**	Gasoline
Cheap	Inexpensive	**Pudding**	Dessert
Chemist	Pharmacist	**Queue**	Line
Chips	French fries	**Quid**	Pound (money)
Coach	Bus	**Return ticket**	Round-trip ticket
Crisps	Potato chips	**Roundabout**	Rotary interchange
Dodgy	Suspect or unreliable	**Single ticket**	One-way ticket
Dustbin	Trash can	**Stalls**	Orchestra seats
First floor	Second floor	**Stone**	Fourteen pounds (weight)
Fiver	Five-pound note	**Subway**	Pedestrian passageway
Flat	Apartment	**Sweets**	Candy
Fortnight	Two weeks	**Tap**	Faucet
Ground floor	First floor	**Tenner**	Ten-pound note
High Street	Main Street	**Tights**	Pantyhose
Hire	Rent	**Tory**	Conservative (politics)
Jam	Jelly	**Trainers**	Sneakers
Jelly	Jell-O	**Trousers**	Pants
Jumper	Sweater	**Tube/Underground**	Subway (train)
Leaflet	Pamphlet	**Whig**	Liberal (politics)

COCKNEY RHYMING SLANG

The term **Cockney** originally meant cock's egg or misshapen egg such as a young hen might lay, in other words, a lily-livered townie as opposed to a strong countryman. From the seventeenth century, it was used as a pejorative term for any Londoner, but was later appropriated by Londoners to describe themselves (and their accent). Traditionally, to be a true Cockney, you had to be born within earshot of the **Bow Bells** (see p.164), an area estimated to be roughly a five-mile radius around the City. However, with increased traffic noise, and no maternity ward in the near vicinity, this traditional definition is of little use nowadays. As for **Cockney rhyming slang**, it's basically a coded language, where a word is replaced by two or more words, the last one of which rhymes with the original. For example, instead of the word "stairs" you have "apples and pears"; a piano (pronounced "pianner") is a "Joanna"; and pinch becomes "half-inch".

The general theory is that it evolved in the criminal underworld of the **East End** as a secret means of communication, and many folk nowadays think of Cockney rhyming slang as a bit of a joke. In actual fact, it's alive and well, you just need to know a few basic rules. For a start, Londoners often don't use the part of the phrase which rhymes with the original at all. In other words, rather than say "butcher's hook" (for "look"), they say "Have a butcher's at that"; instead of "loaf of bread" (for "head"), you hear "Use your loaf!", and when it's cold, it's "'tat'ers" not "potatoes in the mould". Rhyming slang is constantly evolving, too, with public figures providing rich pickings: Brad Pitt (shit), Posh & Becks (specs) and Gordon Brown (clown). For the latest rhyming slang, and all the old favourites, visit ⓦ www.cockneyrhymingslang.co.uk.

Index and small print

A ROUGH GUIDE TO ROUGH GUIDES

Published in 1982, the first Rough Guide – to Greece – was a student scheme that became a publishing phenomenon. Mark Ellingham, a recent graduate in English from Bristol University, had been travelling in Greece the previous summer and couldn't find the right guidebook. With a small group of friends he wrote his own guide, combining a highly contemporary, journalistic style with a thoroughly practical approach to travellers' needs.

The immediate success of the book spawned a series that rapidly covered dozens of destinations. And, in addition to impecunious backpackers, Rough Guides soon acquired a much broader readership that relished the guides' wit and inquisitiveness as much as their enthusiastic, critical approach and value-for-money ethos.

These days, Rough Guides include recommendations from budget to luxury and cover more than 200 destinations around the globe, as well as producing an ever-growing range of ebooks and apps.

Visit **roughguides.com** to see our latest publications.

Rough Guide credits

Editors: Eleanor Aldridge, Andy Turner
Layout: Umesh Aggarwal
Cartography: Deshpal Dabas
Picture editor: Mark Thomas
Proofreader: Amanda Jones
Managing editor: Mani Ramaswamy
Executive Editor: Alice Park
Assistant editor: Dipika Dasgupta
Production: Rebecca Short
Cover design: Nicole Newman, Umesh Aggarwal
Photographers: Roger Norum, Natascha Sturny, Mark Thomas

Editorial assistant: Lorna North
Senior pre-press designer: Dan May
Design director: Scott Stickland
Travel publisher: Joanna Kirby
Digital travel publisher: Peter Buckley
Reference director: Andrew Lockett
Operations coordinator: Becky Doyle
Operations assistant: Johanna Wurm
Publishing director (Travel): Clare Currie
Commercial manager: Gino Magnotta
Managing director: John Duhigg

Publishing information

This ninth edition published January 2012 by
Rough Guides Ltd,
80 Strand, London WC2R 0RL
11, Community Centre, Panchsheel Park,
New Delhi 110017, India

Distributed by the Penguin Group
Penguin Books Ltd,
80 Strand, London WC2R 0RL

Penguin Group (USA)
375 Hudson Street, NY 10014, USA

Penguin Group (Australia)
250 Camberwell Road, Camberwell,
Victoria 3124, Australia

Penguin Group (NZ)
67 Apollo Drive, Mairangi Bay, Auckland 1310, New
Zealand

Rough Guides is represented in Canada by Tourmaline
Editions Inc. 662 King Street West, Suite 304, Toronto,
Ontario M5V 1M7

Printed in Singapore

© Rob Humphreys 2012

Maps © Rough Guides
Contains Ordnance Survey data © Crown copyright and
database rights 2012
No part of this book may be reproduced in any form
without permission from the publisher except for the
quotation of brief passages in reviews.
496pp includes index
A catalogue record for this book is available from the
British Library
ISBN: 978-1-40538-698-2
The publishers and authors have done their best to ensure
the accuracy and currency of all the information in
The Rough Guide to London, however, they can accept
no responsibility for any loss, injury, or inconvenience
sustained by any traveller as a result of information or
advice contained in the guide.
1 3 5 7 9 8 6 4 2

MIX
Paper from
responsible sources
FSC www.fsc.org **FSC™ C018179**

Help us update

We've gone to a lot of effort to ensure that the ninth
edition of **The Rough Guide to London** is accurate
and up-to-date. However, things change – places get
"discovered", opening hours are notoriously fickle,
restaurants and rooms raise prices or lower standards. If
you feel we've got it wrong or left something out, we'd like
to know, and if you can remember the address, the price,
the hours, the phone number, so much the better.

Please send your comments with the subject line
"Rough Guide London Update" to ✉ mail
@uk.roughguides.com. We'll credit all contributions and
send a copy of the next edition (or any other Rough Guide
if you prefer) for the very best emails.
Find more travel information, connect with fellow
travellers and book your trip on ⓦ roughguides.com.

ABOUT THE AUTHOR

Rob Humphreys has lived in London for over 20 years. He has travelled extensively in Scotland and central Europe writing books for Rough Guides. He recently qualified as a City of London Tour Guide and spends his spare time directing shows on the Puppet Theatre Barge.

Acknowledgements

The author would like to thank to Kate as always and Val for some last minute research and the biblio. Thanks, too, to all the contributors, many of whom won't be on the call. And special thanks to Ellie for making the transition to the new design so painless.

Readers' letters

Thanks to all the readers who have taken the time to write in with comments and suggestions (and apologies if we've inadvertently omitted or misspelt anyone's name):

Adam Csatadi, Michael Gilmartin, Jonas Ludvigsson, Yevgeniy Segal and J. T. Johnson.

Photo credits

All photos © Rough Guides except the following:
(Key: a-above; b-below/bottom; c-centre; f-far; l-left; r-right; t-top)

p.1 John Callen
p.2 Getty Images/Laurie Noble
p.4 Getty Images/Alan Copson
p.6 Getty Images/Justin Guariglia
p.7 Alamy/Nigel Dickinson (t)
p.9 Getty Images/Robin MacDougall (t), Getty Images/ Frank Whitney (c), AWL Images/ Travel Pix Collection (b)
p.11 Alamy/David Pearson
p.12 Alamy/John Kellerman
p.13 Getty Images/Robert Harding (tl), Alamy/M Son People (c), Alamy/Alex Segre (br)
p.14 Getty Images/Terry Williams (t), Axiom/ Marc Jackson (b)
p.15 Getty Images/Fraser Hall (t), Getty Images/ Latitudestock (c), National Gallery (b)
p.16 Alamy/Ian Shaw (t), Getty Images/Jason Hawkes (cl), Alamy/Directphoto.org (b)
p.17 Alamy/John Kellerman (t), 4Corners/Colin Dutton (c)
p.19 Getty Images/Jeremy Walker
p.34 Getty Images/Peter Adams
p.43 The National Gallery (b)
p.57 Axiom/James Morris (bl)
p.65 Getty Images/Peter Adams
p.69 Alamy/David Jones (b)
p.78 Getty Images/Travelpix
p.87 Alamy/Alex Segre
p.93 Getty Images/Ludovic Maisant
p.106 Alamy/Brian Harris
p.110 Getty Images/Travel Ink (t), Alamy/Imagepast (br), Alamy/Interfoto (bl)
p.118 Axiom/Ian Cumming
p.132 Getty/Travelpix Ltd

p.142 Getty Images/Ed Pritchard
p.148 Alamy/M Sobreira
p.154 Getty Images/Dominic Burke
p.160 St Paul's Cathedral (tr & bl), Alamy/Paul Carstairs (tl)
p.177 Getty Images/Rudi Sebastian
p.180 Getty Images/Travelpix Ltd
p.189 Alamy/Iain Chambers
p.195 Alamy/Alistair Laming (br) Alamy/Gregory Wrona (tl)
p.215 Getty Images/Pawel Libera
p.232 Globe Image Library
p.248 Getty Images/Eric Nathan
p.259 Alamy/Peter D Noyce (tr)
p.280 Alamy/Ilpo Musto
p.293 Alamy/Robert Harding (br), Alamy/Pat Tuson (tl)
p.320 Axiom/Charles Bowman (t)
p.354 St Pancras International
p.358 The Savoy (tr), Zetter Townhouse (bl), 40 Winks (tl)
p.366 Steins
p.399 Fabric/Tom Stapley
p.403 Madame Jojo's
p.412 Getty Images/Ian Gavan
p.417 Getty Images/Andrea Pistolesi
p.422 Alamy/ Lifestyle
p.426 Axiom/Anthony Webb
p.434 Getty Images/Clive Brunskill
p.440 Diana Memorial Playground
p.444 Getty Images/Imagno

Front cover: Big Ben, Pictures Colour Library/A1 Images
Back cover: Old Royal Naval College, Getty Images/ John Miller; guards at Buckingham Palace, Rough Guides; St James's Park, Rough Guides

Index

Maps are marked in grey

Y

Z

Maps

Index

Listings key

● Accommodation
● Restaurant/café
● Bar/pub/club
● Shop

City plan

The **city plan** on the pages that follow is divided as shown:

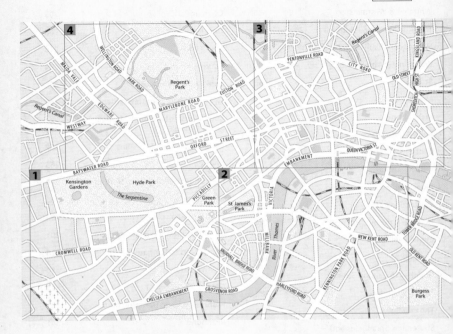

Map symbols

🚻	Toilets	♦	Place of interest	▲	Mountain peak	▭	Building
✉	Post office	@	Internet café	🚤	Boat	⊡	Church
ⓘ	Tourist information	⊤	Gardens/fountain	○	Train station	◯	Stadium
✚	Hospital	⊙	Statue	⊖	Underground station	▱	Park
☪	Mosque	‿	Bridge	⊖	Overground station	⊞	Christian cemetery
✡	Synagogue	⊠	Gate	⊖	DLR station	●-●	Cable car

Key bus routes in central London

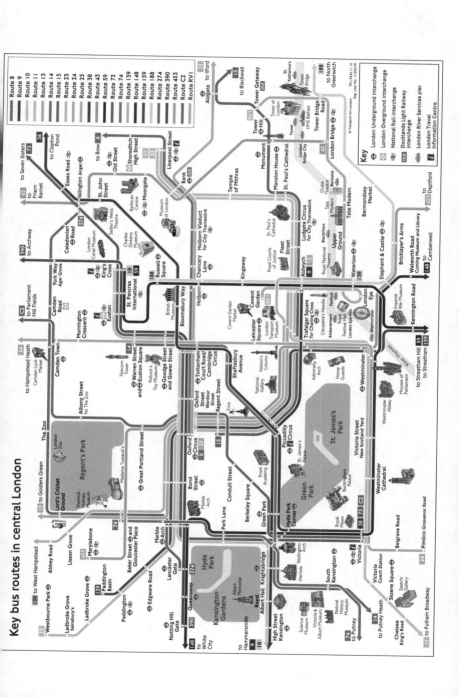

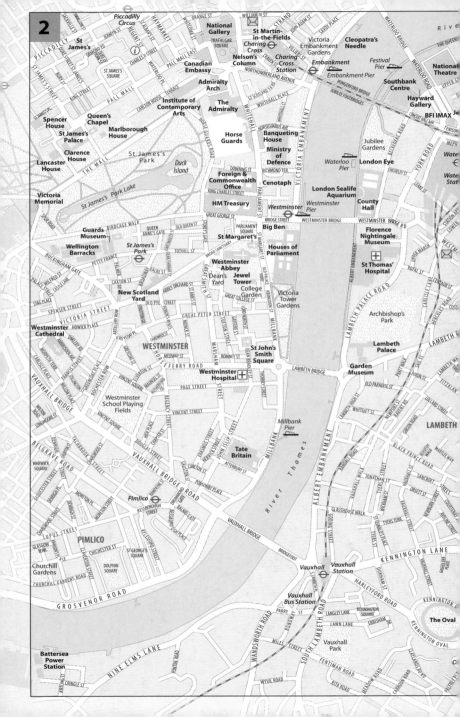

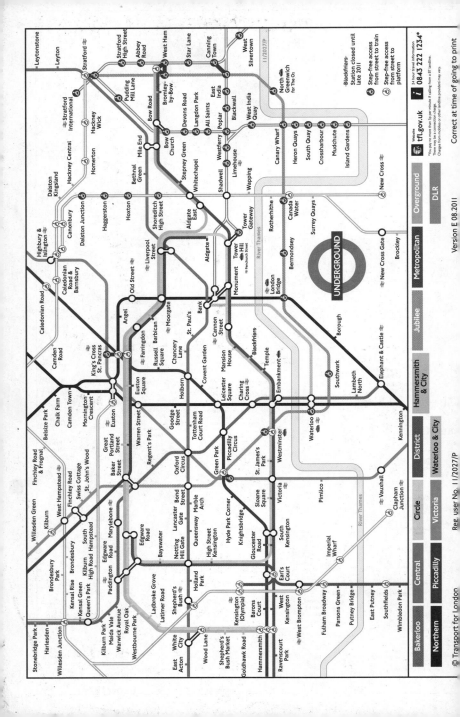